W9-ASO-198

THE MAKING OF
MODERN DRAMA
SERIES

C'est beau, n'est-ce pas, la fin du monde?
Sodome et Gomorrhe II, 2

THE END
OF THE WORLD

An Introduction to Contemporary Drama

MAURICE VALENCY

SCHOCKEN BOOKS · NEW YORK

First published by Schocken Books 1983
10 9 8 7 6 5 4 3 2 1   83 84 85 86
Copyright © 1980 by Oxford University Press, Inc.
Preface copyright © 1983 by Maurice Valency
All rights reserved
Published by agreement with Oxford University Press

Library of Congress Cataloging in Publication Data
Valency, Maurice Jacques, 1903–
The end of the world.
(The Making of modern drama series; v. 4)
Reprint. Originally published: New York: Oxford
University Press, 1980. With new introd.
Includes bibliographical references and index.
1. European drama—20th century—History and
criticism. 2. Symbolism in literature. I. Title.
II. Series: Valency, Maurice Jacques, 1903–
Making of modern drama series; v. 4.
PN1861.V26   1983   809.2′915   83–42706

Manufactured in the United States of America
ISBN 0-8052-0751-1

CONTENTS

PREFACE TO THE SCHOCKEN EDITION

When this book was first published, several years ago, I was under the impression that the remarkable development of nineteenth-century symbolism was most readily understood as a symptom of that *mal de siècle* which still afflicts us. For the symbolists of that time the idea of God was inextricably bound up with the idea of nature: the loss of faith in the one was necessarily attended by a loss of faith in the other. I have no reason to alter this opinion; but it seems to me now that one might do well to adjust the emphasis. At the heart of the aesthetic revolution which so profoundly influenced the art of our time there was something more than a doubt as to the reality of nature. What was called in question was, in fact, the nature of reality.

The problem of reality touches the drama rather more closely than it does the related arts, for the dramatist is peculiarly engaged in the manipulation of the unreal. Nevertheless, until the full significance of the symbolist movement became apparent there was no need to complicate a critical discussion with considerations of metaphysical character. But with the rise of existentialism the problem of being became virtually inescapable in any serious study of current literature, and it became evident that for the better part of a century artists of every stripe had joined in an earnest effort to pull down the pillars of the sky.

The break with tradition that the symbolists brought about was indeed so sudden and so complete that in some remote future those who study our times may well conclude that in this age the world somehow came to an end. So far it has not. The heavens are still intact, as seductive and as impalpable as ever. The ground is still tolerably firm under our feet. It was the symbolists who came to an end.

Their heirs and next of kin, however, are everywhere among us, and there are unmistakable signs of disaster. Around the modern poet nature lies in ruins like the remains of an ancient temple, and the chief business of the artist of our time is to root about in the rubble for whatever bits of reality may be stuck together in a frame or assembled with propriety on a stage. We have regressed, one might say, to the stage of hunters and gatherers.

From Eliot to Beckett the artisans of our age speak to us in elegiacal tones, as the dazed survivors of a seismic upheaval, the magnitude of which can only be surmised. Doubtless the epicenter of the shock will be located somewhere near the moral crisis precipitated by Darwin and his followers toward the turn of the century, though study may reveal an earlier point. What is certain is that in the 1880's there was an urgent need to rediscover God, and this time God proved to be more than ordinarily elusive.

The idealistic movement that ultimately deified the Symbol originated in an effort, under mystic auspices, to explore a plane of being which is not apparent to the senses, and which is inaccessible also to the reason. But, in the end, the ascent to this Absolute defied the labors of the most resolute alpinist. The effort to see into the life of things was pretty well exhausted in the interval between the wars. When the vogue of existentialism began, there were some who had experienced a sudden access of grace, but in the main the result was a progressive disenchantment both with the outerworld and the world beyond. What remained was the cult of the Word.

The world had been on the verge of dissolution many times before, or so it seemed; but in former ages there had been God and his angels to preside over the final obsequies. Now there was nothing; only the eternal absence, the void, a vast uncharted wilderness, attractive to prospective developers, but stubbornly resistant to the plough.

The quest for enlightenment thus ended in an aimless errand that soon lost itself in the dim labyrinths of the soul. The alternatives to despair were either a blind renewal of faith in the God of our fathers, in the manner of Kierkegaard, or some more esoteric method of accommodating the psyche to life in the eternal emptiness that had once made Pascal shudder. In these circumstances, a miracle occurred. Suddenly the void was seen to be no longer void. Its infinite recesses brimmed over with the Unconscious.

For the nineteenth century the Unconscious was another name for God. For some this God was a mindless demiurge; for others a vital energy in majestic evolution; and even when Freud cut the Unconscious down to size, it retained some vestige of divinity as the creative aspect of the human psyche.

It was upon this divinity that the surrealists founded their church.

Surrealism renewed the symbolist program; but in declaring their independence of the rational faculty, the surrealists submitted themselves to the dictatorship of a muse that long antedated Homer, a primitive power that would tolerate no sort of discipline. This gave unusual sparkle to their utterance, while at the same time it closed the ordinary channels of communication, so that the surrealist poet, though remarkably voluble, was for all practical purposes incommunicado. Surrealism spoke everywhere. It manifested itself urgently in all the arts. It spoke with Orphic resonance, but chiefly in tongues. The consequence is the tantalizing opacity of twentieth-century art, and the touching humility of the multitude that presses its nose against the glass.

At the core of this art is a gnawing doubt as to the validity of its metaphors, which can in no way be assuaged, since its images have no counterpart in the outerworld. This doubt calls in question, inevitably, even the occult sources of its inspiration, and this in some sense accounts for the equivocal character of the modern masterpiece. Classic art was, at bottom, the celebration of a sensual image in its perfection, expressed in terms of clarity and proportion. Such ideals could be defined and suggested, and even depicted. The artist had no need to abstract them. He could safely leave that task to the philosopher. His art, nevertheless, purported to give some foretaste of heaven; and this heaven, as a sublimation of the sensual world, could be enjoyed, even in anticipation, without prejudice to the beauty of nature.

In our time we have managed to dispense with heaven, and even with the beauty that was once the subject of art, and perhaps our lives are the poorer for it. But to dispense with nature is a more serious matter. Nature is our mother, and to reject her authority is to be thrust back into the narrow crawl space that lies under our consciousness, and that opens up as frightening a prospect as the vast emptiness that awed Pascal.

It is probably inevitable that under such conditions the artist will produce works that border on madness. The results are in fact evident in the type of art that fills our galleries and our anthologies with incomprehensible symbols. It cannot be denied that there is something engaging in these excursions into the meaningless and the enigmatic. They provide, at the very least, a refreshing alternative to the solemn stereotypes of the past, and awaken apprehension only when they crowd the vision with stereotypes of their own. But madness, unlike sanity, has no limits, and in the end its fruits are disquieting.

There are, doubtless, those who in these troubled times still quaintly feel, as did Wordsworth,

> A presence that disturbs me with the joy
> Of elevated thoughts, a sense sublime
> Of something far more deeply interfused
> Whose dwelling is the light of setting suns . . .

Those are the lucky ones, the collectors of picture postcards, the fortunate heirs of a madness more comfortable than ours, and it is possible that to these favored few we shall owe whatever in our time may prove of enduring value. For in the main the break with the past which the symbolists initiated has not perceptibly enriched our lives. The azure remains as far above our reach as ever, and the unconscious speaks more cogently to the analyst than to the poet.

In the theatre, particularly, the poet has always fancied himself in the role of iconoclast, and this role is most appropriate to the drama; but everything indicates that here too it is far easier to wreck than to build. The symbolist theatre has provided us with a handful of exceptional plays, but it is unlikely that the period which is closing will be counted among the great ages of dramatic history. The symbolist movement was nourished on the assumption that the world we live in is a fantasy created not by God but by man. It is nevertheless not a fantasy with which we can readily dispense; and in the absence of a better myth, one might urge the advantage of clinging with some tenacity to the dream-world we have made. For, in spite of all evidence to the contrary, the fact remains that the earth is flat, is at the center of the universe, and was created for our special benefit, that the sun revolves about it punctually once a day, that God is enthroned in majesty above the sky, is busily engaged in the reward of virtue and the punishment of sin, and that his just wrath is appeased only by an uninterrupted flow of prayer from below and the melodious song of the angels above.

In all likelihood it is on these premises that the great drama of the future will be based, even as it was in the past.

1983   M.J.V.

PREFACE

This is a book mainly about Symbolism.

In the various phases of its development, from Cubism to Surrealism, Symbolism has been at the core of everything that is specifically modern in modern art. The result has been in the nature of a revolution —nothing less, in fact, than the rejection of the doctrine of mimesis, and with it the dissection of the myth of the ordered cosmos. The ultimate consequence is the end of that reality that has been, from the time of the ancients, the subject of representation—that is to say, the end of the world. If this has as yet not come about in fact, at least the way has been thoroughly prepared in fancy.

The conflict of Realism and Symbolism has, of course, been evident from the earliest times; but the issues were never so explicitly drawn as in the period following the decline of romanticism at the end of the nineteenth century. For the Symbolists of that time the reality of the sensible world was an illusion that must be dispelled. When it was at length dispelled, art came face to face with the void. The drama, from Maeterlinck to Beckett, has centered on the collapse of the moral universe. Concomitantly, representation—the imitation of reality which Aristotle considered the essence of artistic activity—has turned from the outward to the inner landscape, and the drama has progressively become a transcript of the unconscious life.

In the pages that follow I have attempted to describe the principal stages of the development of Symbolism in the theatre of our time, without losing sight of the other arts that have come under its influence. Such an account might well begin with Baudelaire; but it was Mallarmé who effectively shaped the history of contemporary Symbolism, and this study properly begins with a consideration of the ideas associated with his circle. It ends with some comment on the plays of Samuel Beckett, in which these ideas, in some sense, find their consummation. Between the two is comprised, I believe, whatever of importance has taken place in the theatre of the twentieth century. In the course of this discussion I have, no doubt, omitted much that is of interest. I am sorry for that; but this is already a very long book, much longer than I intended, and I must beg the reader's forgiveness both for its length and for its brevity.

I have tried to bring to this study, so far as is possible, a fresh mind, and therefore have concerned the reader mainly with primary materials. A wealth of brilliant criticism has grown up in this field, from which I have greatly benefited; but since the relevant works are readily available, I have not often quoted from them. The translations—unless there is a specific attribution—are my own. Those who may find it amusing to compare the translations in this book with the versions I have from time to time made for the stage will not need to be reminded of the exigencies of stage-adaptation. The stage-versions were made for the use of English-speaking actors, and were adapted to the normal cadences of English speech, and the listening habits of English-speaking audiences. The present versions are meant to represent as accurately as possible what appears in the original text. There is naturally some difference in the result, and this may lead to reflections on the perfidious nature of translation.

Parts of the concluding chapter are drawn, with the kind permission of the publisher, from an essay published in *Essays on Drama and Theatre, Liber amicorum Benjamin Hunningher*, Amsterdam (Moussault), 1973. I might add that the present volume will be the fourth in the series of studies in modern drama of which the first, entitled *The Flower and the Castle: An Introduction to Modern Drama*, was published by Macmillan in 1963. It may well be the last.

It remains only to say a word of thanks to my friends and colleagues whose interest and encouragement have added greatly to the pleasure I have had in putting these chapters together. I am especially indebted in this respect to Dr. Carl Woodring of Columbia University, and to Dr. Toby Lelyveld and Mrs. Virginia Heady, both of The Juilliard School, who have read the manuscript critically and made valuable suggestions. I am grateful also to Mr. Sheldon Meyer and most particularly to Vicky Bijur of the Oxford University Press whose expert guidance and support have saved me much tribulation.

New York   September 1979   M.J.V.

REALISM AND SYMBOLISM

The erosion of the cosmic fantasy which for some twenty centuries shaped the culture of the West was attended by social cataclysms which left no part of its structure untouched. A consequence was the mood of despair which characterized the thought and art of the later nineteenth century and motivated its frantic efforts at renovation. The art of the present is rooted, no doubt, in the rubble of the past; but its roots are shallow. Compared with the art and letters of the sixteenth century, contemporary art and contemporary literature seem provisional in substance and ephemeral in workmanship, as if the artist were in each case aware of the impermanence of his efforts and the futility of trying to assure their preservation. In our day not even the most blatant self-advertiser dares speak of the imperishable character of his works. "Nous sommes," Barbey d'Aurevilly wrote, a century ago, "une race à sa dernière heure." It was an apt slogan for the *Décadence* of the 1880's. It will serve the mood of the 1980's equally well.

In the early years of the nineteenth century the Renaissance came to an end. The eighteenth century had been proud of its heritage, and romanticism also had been inclined to unseemly shows of grandeur, but sometime before the midpoint of the century, romanticism had become an affliction, and the idea gained ground that the springs of Helicon were drying up, and this time perhaps forever.

Such things had been said before, and would be said again. Romanticism had a fatalistic strain which long survived it. The wave of pessimism which marked the end of the Great Revolution was briefly stemmed in the first years of the Empire only to surge up with renewed intensity following the upheavals of 1830 and 1848. In the 1870's Ed-

3

mond de Goncourt spoke of "the obliteration of a civilization" in his day, and in the 1880's Paul Bourget wrote of "cette reprise inattendue de ce qu'on appelait en 1830 le mal du siècle."[1] The recurring attacks of chills and fever which afflicted this period were clearly symptomatic of a deepset ill. The age was in fact moribund. At the close of the eighteenth century reason and faith were already at loggerheads; after Darwin the cosmic myth was doomed. For many centuries God had guaranteed the stability of the world-order, and given meaning to such invigorating words as eternity, infinity, right, and justice. In the absence of God existence hardly justified itself. The consequent waves of hysteria and depression account in large part for the character of the arts and letters of the following years.

The search for a principle of order—that is to say, for a more durable myth—produced violently opposed attitudes emotionally charged in proportion to the urgency of the issue. Very likely the polarity of realism and idealism in these years had profound psychological connotations which no one was yet in a position to fathom. The intensity of partisanship in those who concerned themselves with the problem was extraordinary. In perspective the controversy looks rather like a tempest in a teapot, diminished as it is in the light of more recent exigencies. At the time it had all the asperity of a religious war. The result was the development of two sharply contrasted theories of art and, in the theatre, two quite different dramatic genres.

In the closing decades of the nineteenth century Paris was the cultural center of the world. The cafés of Montmartre, Montparnasse, and St. Germain teemed with artists and writers of every stripe and nationality, and art and politics were inextricably intertwined. In this respect, at least, nothing had changed very much since the days of the Second Empire.

At that time the artist's lot in Paris had been miserable. In the *Journal* of the Goncourt brothers we read:

> It must be said that this government with its indifference, its inability to recognize talent or anything that is productive, forces wretches like us to join the papers of the opposition, the only ones that will give us enough to eat! It is true, there is no alternative! And I have so many enemies! It is so hard to make oneself known![2]

According to Jules de Goncourt these were the words of Émile Zola, who was at that time clawing his way up the ladder of success as a journalist. This was written in 1868. In 1880 there was a severe economic depression, and the situation in artistic circles became truly desperate. In the following years it was all but impossible for a writer, even a novelist, to earn an honest living, and for poets the financial outlook was hopeless. The successful Impressionists of the 1870's, Pissarro, Monet, and Renoir, who had been enjoying a steady sale, suddenly found no market for their canvases. The theatre was better supported. Seats were cheap, expenses were high, and actors were wretchedly underpaid, but a dramatic author might occasionally expect a windfall. Under the influence of Dumas *fils*, Augier, and Sardou, the Scribean plot-formulas were endlessly rehashed in the guise of a drama of ideas, while the boulevard managers continued to amuse their public with the sentimental trash to which it was accustomed.

Under these unlikely conditions there developed a surprising upsurge of creative activity in France. The initial wave did not survive the century; but the First World War, and the strong emotional currents it unleashed, brought about so significant a renewal of vitality that the results of the aesthetic revolution of 1885 are clearly manifest to the present day.

The history of the drama after 1870 may be summed up in terms of the interplay of the intellectual cross-currents designated by the terms Symbolism and Realism. What is meant by these terms goes well beyond aesthetic considerations. They identify a philosophic issue with its basis in religion, and this perhaps accounts for the vehemence of its partisans. The opposition is ancient. It goes back as far as it is possible to trace our cultural tradition, at least as far as the eleventh century. In the middle ages we may find its traces everywhere—in the contrast of realism and nominalism, in discussions of the active and contemplative life, in the two strains of the troubadour poetry, and later in the religious drama and the popular farce. What was involved in all this was, at bottom, two psychic attitudes—for want of better terms we might call the one materialistic and the other spiritual.

In the 1880's, for a variety of reasons, the issue was sharply drawn, and there was a wide divergence in the philosophic and literary attitudes of the time. Those who had no reason to distrust the validity of the objective world called themselves Realists, looked about assiduously, and produced works of art and scientific theories which stressed common sense, precision, and accuracy of observation. Ranged against them were those who had no faith in the outerworld, and who looked beyond the world of the senses to transcendental realities that eluded the eye. These were called Idealists. These terms served their purpose for some little time. They were soon found confusing, and were replaced with terms that were even more confusing. Realism became Naturalism. Idealism became Symbolism. Symbolism died, and was reborn as Surrealism. Of the many other terms that the issue generated, and the nuances they served to identify, it is perhaps not necessary at the moment to speak. However confusing the terminology, the issue—at least on a superficial level—was clear. As an aesthetic principle, Naturalism was a quest for facts. Symbolism was a search for the Ideal.

These opposed attitudes seemed to find clear reflections in the art and literature of the age, in poetry, painting, sculpture, and music, and in the drama. But, in truth, the distinction, for all its apparent clarity, was never entirely clear. In spite of their positivistic convictions, the Naturalists found it impossible to relinquish all vestiges of Idealism. The Idealists, for their part, were by no means averse to scientific inquiry. If the Idea could have been isolated in the laboratory, and grown in a suitable broth, the Idealists would have gladly joined hands with their enemies in a common cause. Unhappily the Idea was beyond the reach of science. In consequence they became mystics, and began speaking in tongues.

Drama in the 1880's was not a vital art. Its prevailing attitudes were materialistic; its moral standards, bourgeois. Its subject-matter was principally domestic relations, and its interest was focused predominantly on problems of sex, money, marriage, legitimacy, and adultery. The subsidized theatres, the Théâtre-Français and the Odéon, continued to exploit the classic repertory, occasionally enlivened with a carefully chosen novelty. The boulevard theatres were strictly professional enterprises that had no interest in innovation. It was in these circumstances that the theatre was subjected to simultaneous attacks from the Right and the Left of the avant garde, in the name of Realism on the one hand, of Idealism on the other.

The Realism of the 1880's was neither the realism of Diderot, nor the realism of Balzac, nor yet the realism of Restif de la Bretonne. It was inspired by science and smacked of the laboratory. It was a movement designed to purge the contemporary novel and the drama of their shams and pretenses, to sweep aside the sentimentality and cheap eloquence associated with the romantic excesses of the first half of the century, and to direct serious attention to the facts of "life as it is." In the last decades of the century this movement was called Naturalism, a term invented by Zola.

Zola began his journalistic career in 1866 on the staff of Villemessant's *L'Événement*. He was at this time, according to the Goncourt, "a vigorous-looking young man, but with the delicate quality of a fine piece of porcelain on his features . . . All in all, a difficult creature to grasp, profound, confused, distressed, full of anxiety, disturbed, ambiguous."[3] At this time he was a close friend of Cézanne, and a staunch supporter of the Impressionists, of Édouard Manet, in particular, and of Renoir, both of whom he considered to be realists. His early views of the burgeoning controversy were both accommodating and romantic:

> I don't give a hang for realism; this term has no precise meaning for me. If you mean by realism the duty of all painters to study and to depict nature, it cannot be disputed that all painters should be realists. Painting dreams is a game for women and children; men are charged with painting realities. They take nature and they give it, they transmit it to us through their particular temperaments. Thus each artist will give us a different world, and I willingly accept them all, providing each is the living expression of a heart. . . . Science is in the air, in spite of ourselves we are pushed towards the close study of objects and events. . . . The movement of the age is certainly toward realism, or rather positivism. . . . But every school displeases me; a school is in essence the negation of the freedom to create. . . . Therefore no more Realism than anything else. Let us have truth, if you will, life; but, above all, many hearts and hands, giving different interpretations of nature. The definition of a work of art cannot be other than this: a work of art is a corner of nature seen through a temperament.[4]

A dozen years later positivism was so firmly entrenched in literature, and science had made such inroads on the imagination that no one could doubt that reason held the key which would in time unlock all the mysteries of the universe. In 1869 Jules de Goncourt reported a conversation at one of the literary dinners at the Restaurant Magny:

> They were saying that Berthelot predicts that in a hundred years of science man will know the secret of the atom and will be able at will to put out or turn on the sun; that, for his part, Claude Bernard asserts that after a hundred years of physiological research we shall have learnt the laws of organic life, of human creation. . . .[5]

By this time, indeed, the researches of Claude Bernard at the Sorbonne, and later at the Jardin des Plantes, had attracted a great deal of attention. Many artists and writers attended his lectures, Zola among them. He was deeply impressed not only by the results of Bernard's experiments but even more by his literary style, and he concluded that the methods of the physiologist in the laboratory were admirably suited to the purposes of the serious novelist. Art was, as he now conceived it, the study of nature. It depended on the exact observation of natural phenomena, and works of this order should properly be called Naturalistic. Balzac had filled his novels with realistic detail; but Balzac's work was marred by improbable plots and bizarre coincidences. Naturalism would have no room for the story-teller's contrivances. It would deal with reality, and depend on the fertile imagination of nature for its surprises. These would be rigidly determined by the play of cause and consequence. By the end of the 1870's Zola was the acknowledged apostle of Naturalism, and in 1880 he set forth his views in a vigorous essay entitled *Le Roman expérimental*, which was supplemented the following year by *Le Naturalisme au théâtre*.

In both these books the basis of his discussion was Claude Bernard's *Introduction à l'étude de la médecine expérimentale* (1865). Zola's text was larded with copious extracts from this fascinating work. The new and more rigorous realism which would result from the application of scientific method to artistic creation had already been widely publicized, but Zola's books brought the new techniques very sharply to the attention of his public, and it became evident that there were as yet no masterpieces in this genre, and certainly nothing of the sort in the theatre.

The term Naturalism, when Zola first used it in this context, was new, but Zola claimed an ancient lineage for it. He might indeed have referred it to the pre-Socratic philosophers, but philosophy was not his strong point, and for his purposes it was enough to trace its ancestry to the *philosophes* of the preceding century, specifically to Diderot and Rousseau. It was they, in his opinion, who had developed the Naturalistic concept of the universe. So great a leap in human understanding, he argued, could not have failed to bring about a corresponding social upheaval. This was, of course, the French Revolution, the "tempest which was to wipe out the old world and make place for the new." The prospect for art and letters was inspiring:

> We are at the beginning of this new world; in all things we are the direct children of Naturalism, in politics, in philosophy, in science, as well as in literature and art. I extend the bounds of this word Naturalism because in reality it includes the entire century, the movement of

contemporary intelligence, the force which is sweeping us onward, and which is working toward the molding of future centuries. . . .

Naturalism, that is, a return to nature—it is this operation which the savants performed on that day when they decided to initiate the study of bodies and visible phenomena, to build on experiment, and to proceed by analysis. Naturalism in letters is also a return to nature and to man, to direct observation, exact anatomy, the acceptance and representation of what is. For the artist and the scientist the task is the same. Therefore no more abstract characters in books, no more lying fictions, no more talk of the Absolute; but real people, the true history of each individual; the story of daily life.

From Zola's viewpoint the arch enemy of Naturalism was romanticism, "that singular outburst" of irrationality on the very threshold of the scientific age. Fortunately romanticism had no longer any future:

Romanticism, which corresponded to nothing durable, which expressed a restless nostalgia for the old world and was its bugle call to battle, gave way readily before Naturalism, which rose up stronger and more powerful to lead the century of which it is, in reality, the vital breath. . . .[6]

In reality the battle was far from over; it had hardly begun. Gautier was dead, but Hugo was alive and still enjoyed enormous prestige. It was only after his death in 1885 that it became clear that the romantic stereotypes of the past generation would not survive, and that something new would have to be invented to take their place. As Naturalism came into fashion the characters of fiction were progressively stripped of their magnificence and subjected to such scrutiny as had heretofore been the lot of mice and monkeys. For a time novelists and, a while later, dramatists devoted themselves to the pursuit of scientific truth. It was an exciting prospect, at least at the start. The Goncourt, always a step ahead of the fashion, noted in their *Journal:*

There is only one consuming passion left in our life, the passion for the study of living reality. Apart from that there is nothing but ennui and emptiness. Admittedly, we have galvanized history into reality, and with greater truthfulness than other historians. But now the truth that is dead holds no more interest for us. We are like one accustomed to drawing from a wax figure who has suddenly been presented with a living model, or rather with life itself, with its entrails warm and quivering.

The transition was apparently not entirely effortless. Edmond de Goncourt evidently felt some weariness in the course of his researches:

> Today I went in search of *human documents* in the vicinity of the École Militaire. Nobody will ever know how much the low and ugly documents cost us from which we make our books, in view of our natural shyness, our uneasiness among common people, our horror of vulgarity. This role of conscientious detective ferretting out materials for the novel of the people is the most abominable part that a man of artistocratic taste can play.
>
> But the attraction of this new world is that it has something of the glamor of a region never before explored by any traveller. . . .[7]

The Goncourt considered Zola their disciple in the new genre; but they were fastidious, and for them the Naturalistic novel was in the nature of a slumming expedition justified largely by its romantic aspects. It was, indeed, difficult to avoid some color of romanticism in the study of "life as it is." The tendency to follow Hugo and Eugène Sue, or even Dickens was irresistible in these safaris into the lower depths where life, presumably, was more clearly visible in its nudity than on the more polite levels of society. Earlier in the nineteenth century, realism in literature had been stimulated by humanitarian ideas, but the results were seen to be unduly condescending and sentimental. As late as 1864, in England, George Eliot had felt it necessary to write in defence of the truth that is not beautiful:

> I am content to tell my simple story, without trying to make things better than they are; dreading nothing, indeed, but falsity, which in spite of our best efforts there is reason to dread. Falsehood is so easy, Truth so difficult.[8]

In theory the Naturalists were, as George Eliot felt herself to be, stoic and objective observers of life. In practice they were as sentimental as the realists of the preceding age, but as their doctrine committed them to an attitude of strict unemotional detachment they compensated for their romantic upbringing by operating behind a façade of granite. They did not preach. In their novels and plays the facts were left to speak for themselves; but the facts they selected were naturally eloquent, and the writers invariably indicated their sympathies by stressing with particular care the sordidness of the reality they depicted. From the beginning, Naturalism had an inherently sermonic tendency. Its protest was implicit in its candor, and its proponents, even in the days of the Empire, did not trouble to conceal their aggressiveness.

Some twenty years before the publication of *Le Roman expérimental* the painter Gustave Courbet had defined realism in terms which fully anticipated Zola's manifesto:

> The basis of realism is the negation of the ideal, a negation towards which my studies have led me for fifteen years and which no artist has dared to affirm categorically until now. . . . Through my affirmation of the negation of the ideal and all that springs from the ideal, I have arrived at the emancipation of the individual and finally at democracy. Realism is essentially the democratic art.[9]

Courbet was a professed socialist, but his realism stemmed, at least in part, from the need to extend the subject-matter of the painter's art. In the 1850's the Salons were firmly dedicated to the doctrine that the function of art was the depiction of the beautiful, and that the artist's goal was the propagation of the ideal. In advocating the pursuit of truth rather than beauty, Courbet was opening up a whole new area of representation, in much the same way that Ibsen was endeavoring to extend the domain of the drama. Unlike Ibsen, Courbet was a reformer; but he was first of all an artist, and not, like Champfleury his supporter, primarily a social critic. *La Baigneuse* was essentially no more a sermon than was *L'Assommoir*, though both works could be made to serve the purposes of oratory. Zola, a naturally noisy man, insisted in his books that "the bitter science of life, the high lesson of the real" would necessarily motivate social change. Courbet very likely had the same idea. The exponents of realism in this period—Proudhon, Taine, Renan, Sainte-Beuve, Flaubert, Maupassant, the Goncourt—were all more or less inclined, like Zola, toward social reform. Those, however, who advocated Naturalism on purely aesthetic grounds, devotees of *l'art pour l'art*, had greater difficulty in justifying their tastes. There was, undeniably, something unhealthy in the cult of the disagreeable, something reminiscent of Sade, a perverse pleasure in playing in the dirt which aroused resistance, if not repugnance, among the dainty. There was also resistance to the bohemians' incessant efforts to attract attention by scandalizing the bourgeois. The more vociferous Naturalists, accordingly, encountered hostility from several quarters, including the police, and notably from the well-established bureaucracy of art which based its preferences, and its subsidies, on the assumption that beauty and truth are synonymous—an assumption that implies that only the beautiful is true—and that on earth that is all one knows or needs to know.

Naturalism was positivistic. Its aesthetic was grounded on the assumption that art was primarily mimetic, that its subject was nature, and its function the representation of nature. Courbet, for example, was categorical on this point:

> Painting is a CONCRETE art, and can consist only in the representation of REAL and EXISTING objects. It is a completely physical language all the words of which are visible objects, so that an AB-STRACT object, invisible and non-existent, is not part of the domain of painting. Imagination in art consists in knowing how to find the most complete expression of an existent object, but never in imagining or in creating the object itself.[10]

From this standpoint, basically Aristotelian, the artist's business is representational, not creative. He is not required to interpret, only to reveal; least of all is he required to invent. Nature invents, not art. The novelists of the school of Médan, and the Naturalistic playwrights—Zola, Daudet, Brieux, Mirbeau, Jullien, Curel—and the poets of the Parnasse, like the early Impressionists, considered that they were working in the classic tradition, observing and recording facts with calm Homeric detachment.

But a concrete art implies a concrete subject. The intense scrutiny to which the Impressionists subjected nature could not fail to make them aware of its changing face. In time it became apparent that nature was no less mutable than the artist, and the relations of subject and object became hopelessly confused. The Impressionists had been working assiduously on the assumption that they were faithfully recording the facts of life as they saw them. The implications of this idea took some years to become clear. It was a question of the relation of nature to temperament. When it was at last understood that the art of landscape was a kind of self-portraiture, the realization radically changed the course of art. The Naturalists became Expressionists. It seems a long way from Monet's "Old Gare Saint-Lazare" to van Gogh's "Café at Arles"; but it took very little time to make the transition—a dozen years sufficed. Less than twenty years later Picasso was showing his friends "Les Demoiselles d'Avignon." The date was 1906. Strindberg had already written *To Damascus* and *The Dream Play*.

Meanwhile the Naturalists declined to question the facts. For them nature was a solid and incontrovertible datum, the reality of which no man could doubt and preserve his sanity. Since human nature was, in their view, subject to the inexorable laws of cause and consequence that were observable everywhere else, their psychology was rigorously mechanistic. "An identical determinism," Zola wrote, "rules the stone in the road and the mind of man." Accordingly, the Naturalistic work of art would have "the exactness, the solidity and the practical application of a work of science." Forty years before, in the preface to the *Comédie humaine* (1842), Balzac had also assimilated his narrative to a work of science; but he had expressly repudiated the charges of materialism which might be leveled against it and—referring to *Louis Lambert* and to Swedenborg—he had emphatically declared his orthodoxy in matters of religion.

In 1880 it was no longer necessary to take such precautions. Zola's religious views are not entirely clear. He was possibly a pantheist. But in *Le Roman expérimental* he was playing the savant, and therefore felt free to express his contempt for the mystical leanings of his idealistic contemporaries:

> We naturalistic writers submit each fact to the test of observation and experiment, while the idealists admit mysterious elements which elude analysis and therefore remain outside the influence of the laws that govern nature. . . . What constitutes the Ideal is everything that we do not know, all that escapes us, and the aim of our human nature is each day to reduce the Ideal, to wrest the truth from the unknown.[11]

All this did not, however, prevent Zola from writing novels and plays with carefully constructed plots and freely invented coincidences. His *Thérèse Raquin* (1873) is one of the few masterpieces of the Naturalistic drama, but its method can hardly be considered scientific.

Zola's formula for the new drama, "faire grand, faire simple, faire vrai," was based on what he decided was the essence of classic tragedy, "an event unfolding in its reality and arousing in its characters passions and feelings of which the exact analysis would be the sole interest of the play."[12] This was doubtless what Zola had in mind when *Thérèse Raquin* was first conceived, but in adapting his novel for the stage he evidently found it necessary to make important concessions to the system of the theatre.

In the preface to his play Zola recalled how in his youth he had studied the *système du théâtre*, the *numérotage* of scenes, the symmetrical arrangement of entrances, the importance of the sympathetic role, the disposition of climaxes, and the rest of the intricate methodology of the drama. The time had come, he added, to make a new departure. "The well-known recipes for knotting and unknotting a plot have served their turn; now we must have a simple, broad picture of men and things. . . . Outside of certain scenic necessities, what we call the science of the theatre is only a pile of clever tricks."[13]

Some of these tricks, nevertheless, were evidently found indispensable in the arrangement of his play. "I have simply done on two living bodies the work which surgeons do on cadavers," Zola had noted in the preface to the novel; but, in fact, the pathological procedures of the play were entirely subordinated to the story of crime and punishment which shapes the action, and when the play was put on the stage it was distinguishable from other examples of domestic melodrama chiefly by the excellence of the characterization, and the novelty of the lower-class milieu in which it was set. Just as physiology was at this time restricted to experiments on the lower animals, Naturalism limited its studies to the life of the lower classes. It took some time before the brutal passions of the slums were permitted to intrude on the polite atmosphere of the Salon drama.

The truth is that on fundamental questions Zola did not differ essentially from his Idealist contemporaries. Like Idealism, Naturalism proceeded on the assumption that there was an ideal world-order toward which one might aspire, and that all things were subject to natural justice. The study of facts was thus intended to contrast the sorry conditions of our earthly existence with the ideal order of the transcendent world. But while the Idealists thought to penetrate the mystery of the universe through revelation and intuition, the Naturalists relied on the gradual accumulation of data, and the inferences to which these data led. The Idealists were, in the main, Platonists; not scientists, but poets whose works were professions of faith in the essential harmony of the universe. The empiricists, on the contrary, were becoming progressively aware of the tremendous disorder of nature, and for them the idea of the ordered creation on which Augustine had founded his church bit by bit slipped away into the realm of fantasy. The idea of evolution put order at the end of the creative process of nature, not at its beginning; and, for the Naturalists, it was science, not faith, that would bring order out of chaos. Nevertheless they were at no time willing to relinquish the idea of natural justice and the existence of the moral order. Thus in the end right and justice operate inexorably in *Thérèse Raquin*, and the moral law is vindicated. It was only when faith in the eternal verities was at last relinquished that the stage was ready for the theatre of Ionesco and Beckett, and perhaps not even then.

Although Zola relied heavily on Claude Bernard for his theory of the novel, it was Taine who provided the groundwork for the Naturalist doctrine. In the introduction to his *Histoire de la littérature anglaise* (1864) Taine established the basis for a wholly rationalistic approach to art. In his view the artist, his work, and his moral outlook are conditioned in precisely the same way as any other natural phenomena, and are therefore equally subject to scientific investigation. The result of this positivistic approach to the psychology of art was to reduce the workings of the artist's soul to an entirely intelligible play of natural forces. Given the necessary data, presumably, the art historian could analyze an attitude, a passion, a mood, or a technique very much as a chemist analyzes the elements of an unknown solution.

Taine thought of art as the imitation of nature, but in his view what art imitates is not the detail of natural objects, but the relations of their parts, their essential character. Thus it is the business of the artist to reveal what nature sometimes conceals or obscures, namely, the dominant character, the archetype of the subject of representation. "The work of art has as its aim the manifestation of some essential or outstanding character; it must communicate some important idea more clearly and more completely than real objects do." Such, in Taine's opinion, was the justification of the work of art, and the measure of its worth.[14]

This was an Aristotelian idea. It had furnished Theophrastus, and afterwards La Bruyère with a useful theory of characterization. In his *Salon de 1846* Baudelaire, also, had noted that even in the type of portraiture he calls historical, the artist must go beyond the accurate depiction of the subject's features. He must idealize. In order to do this one must know how to give

> to each important detail a reasonable exaggeration, to bring to light everything that is naturally salient, accentuated and principal, and to neglect, or to merge in the ensemble, whatever is insignificant or that is the result of an accidental degradation.[15]

As the chiefs of the historic school he named David and Ingres. Thus, for Baudelaire, as for Taine, the artist's faithful interpretation of nature was in every case an idealization, and much more so in the type of portraiture he calls romantic. "If art is to be profound," Baudelaire wrote, "it must aim at constant idealization," and idealization, he explained, was the restoration of the individual subject to "the dazzling truth of its original harmony." For Taine, similarly, characterization involved the identification of the individual with its archetype, and the work of art was in essence a conceptualization. In portraiture, as in the characterization of dramatic personages, the artist must first seize upon the subject's dominant characteristic, the *faculté maîtresse*, and upon this, as on an armature, construct the rest of the figure. In this manner, according to Taine, art renders nature intelligible, and every work of art is aesthetically valuable in proportion to its lack of ambiguity, that is to say, the clarity with which it reveals the ideal which its subject embodies.[16]

The positivist aesthetic which Taine developed in his literary studies, along with Comte, Littré, and Renan, was thus essentially classic. It reflected not only the love of clarity which characterized French thought long before the time of Descartes, but also its Platonic basis. This aesthetic was not in accord with the empirical methods which Zola desired to emulate and, insofar as Zola found it acceptable, it involved him in some confusion. It was, nevertheless, in accordance with such notions that Balzac had painted his magnificent gallery of portraits, and it was difficult to diverge from such an example. In the drama, as in the novel, a clear characterization was essential, and this would depend on some exaggeration of the *caractère essentiel* of the subject. The result was that both in the novel and in the drama the price of clarity was caricature, and a consequence of the positivistic approach to art—which in this case was indistinguishable from idealism—was to remove it even further from reality than romanticism had done.

The views of the opposition were summed up in an article by Albert Aurier published in *La Revue Encyclopédique* in April 1892:

> After having proclaimed the omnipotence of scientific observation and deduction for eighty years with childlike enthusiasm, and after asserting that no mystery was proof against its lenses and scalpels, the nineteenth century at last seems to perceive that its efforts have been in vain, and its boasts childish. Man is still groping among the same enigmas, in the same formidable unknown, which has become even darker and more disconcerting because of his habitual neglect. Today many scientists and scholars have come to a standstill in discouragement. They realize that this experimental science of which they were so proud is a thousand times less certain than the most bizarre

theogony, the maddest metaphysical revery, the least acceptable poet's dream, and they have a presentiment that this haughty science which they proudly used to call "positive" may perhaps be only the science of what is relative, of appearances, of shadows. . . .[17]

The forces opposed to Naturalism had been mobilized long before the publication of Zola's Naturalist manifestoes. The positivists had declared all ultimate questions insoluble and therefore irrelevant to the practical business of life. But in the 1870's there were many young artists to whom positivism said nothing, and it was among these that the reaction took shape. A new movement developed. Essentially it was a search for symbols.

Nobody was quite sure of what these symbols were, or what it was that they symbolized, but the idea rapidly gained ground that nature had a calligraphy of its own which wisdom could decipher. It was hardly a new idea, and had not been new in the middle ages; but in the 1880's it seemed new and full of promise. Both Taine and Baudelaire, very contrary spirits, had felt that art involved a search for the ideal, and that the ideal was somehow inherent in the relation of things rather than in the things themselves. Relation was an abstraction. Obviously it could not be directly represented, nor could it be revealed by a dissection of the object, nor brought to the eye by the telescope and scale. In reviewing the work of Paul Gauguin, Albert Aurier condemned the Naturalists to the darkness of the Cave:

> Let us leave them to contemplate the shadows they take for reality, and let us go back to those who, their chains broken and free of the cruel native dungeon, ecstatically contemplate the radiant heaven of ideas. The normal and final end of painting, as well as the other arts, can never be the direct representation of objects. Its purpose is to express Ideas by translating them into its special language.[18]

The special language of painting is paint. Maurice Denis noted: "It is well to remember that a picture, before being a war horse, a nude woman, or some anecdote, is essentially a plane surface covered with colors arranged in a certain order."[19] The calligraphy of painting was a transcription of the calligraphy of nature. It could be read, and it provided meaning often without reference to the objects the painting represented. Thus the painter's symbols went further in the deciphering of nature, and the ideas immanent in nature, than anything the Naturalist's inspection of objects could afford. The difference lay in the eye of the painter, the discerning eye of the artist, which no photographic lens, no matter how sharp, could rival.

It is impossible to say at what point in the nineteenth century Symbolism began to exert an important influence in France. Baudelaire is usually credited with bringing about its literary revival, and he furnishes a useful date. At any rate, by 1885 the vogue of Naturalism was over, at least for the time; Symbolism was in the ascendant, and Edmond de Goncourt hastened to assume control of the new movement, as he had endeavored to do with the old. He noted in his *Journal:*

> In my interview with Huret I could have said: I provided the complete formula for Naturalism in *Germinie Lacerteux;* and *L'Assommoir* was written from beginning to end along the lines laid down in that book. Later I was the first to abandon Naturalism—not, like Zola, for such a sordid reason as the success of *L'Abbé Constantin,* which made him write *Le Rêve*—but because I considered that the genre in its original form was worn out. . . . Yes, when I wrote *Les Frères Zemganno* and *La Faustin,* I was the first to abandon Naturalism for what the young writers are now using to fill its place—dreams, symbolism, Satanism, etc., etc.—for in these books I, the inventor of Naturalism, tried to dematerialize it long before anyone else thought of doing so.[20]

In fact, Naturalism seemed barely to have survived its own success. It had come under fire soon after the publication of *Le Naturalisme au théâtre* in 1881, and Brunetière launched a full scale attack against it in 1883. Five years later the *Manifeste des Cinq* violently protested the publication of Zola's *La Terre* (1888). In 1889 Paul Bourget, who had not long ago been an ardent Positivist, attacked the whole Realist position in *Le Disciple.* And by 1891 Jules Huret, after pondering over the replies to his *Enquête* for *L'Écho de Paris,* reached the conclusion that Naturalism was dead. Jean Moréas, indeed, had sounded its knell as early as 1886. These obsequies, however, were premature. Naturalism was no longer in vogue; but it was by no means dead. The year after Huret published the results of his questionnaire, André Antoine announced the opening of the Théâtre-libre.

Nineteenth-century Idealism was of German origin; but its roots could be traced to the remotest antiquity. In France the young poets of the 1860's who were no longer entirely Christian were hardly versed in philosophy, but out of the scraps of philosophy that came their way from the German transcendentalists, from Fichte, Schelling, Hegel, and Schopenhauer, they managed to fashion a doctrine which passed for a system of philosophy. The word they used to describe it, Idealism, was already practically devoid of meaning, but it served to distinguish their notions from those of the Positivists. What it implied was a belief in the existence of a transcendental world, the sphere of ideas immanent in, but distinct from the objective world that mirrored them—as the constant stars are mirrored in the ever-changing sea. The image was both striking and poetic. It recurred many times in the poetry and the prose of Baudelaire; Mallarmé found it most congenial, and in time it became a cliché.

The ideal world had glamor. It was perfectly beautiful. It was immutable. It was the world of the intellect, the only real abode of truth and certainty, and obviously the place of choice for a poet to spend his time. But the way to it was by no means sure. In the *Symposium* it is suggested that it may be reached by a process of intellectual escalation corresponding to the hierarchy of abstractions, a learning process motivated by the love of beauty. In that way the lover ascends from the beauty of earthly things to the beauty of immaterial forms step by step "until from fair notions he arrives at the notion of absolute beauty, and at last knows what the essence of beauty is." At that point a poet is enabled "to bring forth, not images of beauty, but realities; for he has hold not of an image but of a reality."[21] It was not an easy climb, obviously. The ascent was a wholly intellectual process through a series of progressive abstractions. But the Wise Woman of Mantineia conceded that the last step was beyond the power of reason and would necessitate an intuitive leap, and thus suggested a less arduous way to the Absolute for the mystical spirit.

The Symbolist movement was initiated by a group of young artists and men of letters who professed their dissatisfaction with Positivism. They were not logicians. They were, in the main, vague souls, inclined to mysticism, and they welcomed the suggestion that a revelation would come spontaneously to the properly oriented receptive mind. In its origins, nineteenth-century symbolism was closely allied with the occult. It was, at bottom, an effort to by-pass the processes of the rational mind and to revert to the primary faculty which, it was thought, primitive peoples possess, and which civilization suppresses. From the first Symbolism was a search for a lost Eden and a lost innocence, a time when man was at one with the infinite, and thus had no need for reason, the condition of the ideal Adam.

Symbolism came of age on the terraces of Paris cafés in an atmosphere of heated discussion and thick tobacco smoke. The elm-shaded Brasserie Gambrinus, a few steps from the Odéon, avenue de Médicis, was a favorite meeting place of a group of radical painters whose work did not often pass the juries of the Paris Salon, and who therefore had no way of exhibiting their work to the public. In 1884 the Ministry of Fine Arts was prevailed upon to authorize an exhibition of the *refusés* in the barracks of the Tuileries. It was called *Le Salon des artistes indépendants*. The Impressionist movement was by this time well on its way to acceptance, and the established Impressionists, Renoir, Monet, and Pissarro, declined to exhibit their canvases in this radical environment. Among those who showed their work were Paul Signac and Du Bois Pillet.

Associated with these dissidents was a group of aspiring writers also unable to reach a public. Most of these were recent graduates of the lycées, young men in their teens or early twenties. Among them were Gustave Kahn, Jean Moréas, Félix Fénéon, Théodor de Wyzéwa, Charles Morice, the musician Edouard Dujardin, the poet Jules Laforgue, and the physicist Charles Henry—all precocious young men of great ambition. In the spring of 1884 Wyzéwa conceived the idea of organizing a review which would promote the advanced views they seemed to share. He called it *La Revue indépendante*. Its offices were in the avenue de Médicis. Among its contributors were Edmond de Goncourt, Émile Zola, Joris-Karl Huysmans, and Paul Verlaine. The oldest of these was Goncourt, then in his sixties. The other editors were mostly in their middle years. Almost at once they were joined by Stéphane Mallarmé. He was at this time forty-two, a professor of English literature at a lycée in Paris. He had spent half his life teaching in the provinces, and had published, mostly in periodicals of limited circulation, a small body of difficult poetry, mainly sonnets. It is questionable if anyone knew at this time how important a part he was to play in the new movement that he was helping to organize.

MALLARMÉ

Like all young poets of his day
Mallarmé grew up in the radiance of Victor Hugo. In 1861 *Les Fleurs du
mal* was reprinted in its second edition. Mallarmé came at once under the
spell of Baudelaire. He was at that time nineteen, employed as a clerk in
the Imperial Registry at Sens. Through a friend who was teaching at the
local lycée he came to know a group of young writers in nearby Paris
who dreamed of launching a new poetry which would react against the
influence of romanticism. This was to be a classic style, cool and formal,
impersonal, and of meticulous workmanship. Under the energetic leadership of Leconte de Lisle and Théodore de Banville, these young men
organized a coterie which came to be known as Le Parnasse. The group
included Catulle Mendès, a lively youth who at eighteen had already
edited a periodical called *La Revue fantaisiste*, and also François Coppée,
Xavier de Ricart, Louis Bouilhet, and Villiers de l'Isle Adam. Among
those who frequented this group was Henri Cazalis. He became Mallarmé's close friend and principal correspondent.

In 1866 Mendès and Ricart published the first fascicules of *Le Parnasse
contemporain*. Mallarmé contributed ten poems. He was at that time a
professor of English at the lycée of Besançon. He had come to know the
poetry of Poe through the translations of Baudelaire, and had been so
deeply impressed that at twenty he undertook to learn English in order
to read Poe in the original and perhaps to translate him for himself. His
interest in Poe led to a career in education. In 1863, after a stay in
London, he took the necessary examinations, and was assigned to a
probationary post at the Imperial college at Tournon in the Ardèche.
From Tournon he was posted to Besançon, thence to Avignon. After the
debacle of 1870, he came to Sens, and after another stay in London, dur-

ing which he became friendly with John Payne, he came to live in Paris with his wife, his seven-year-old daughter, and his infant son. He was penniless; but before the end of the year he managed to secure an appointment at the Lycée Fontanes. He continued teaching at various schools in Paris for the next twenty-three years, until his retirement in 1894. He took little pleasure in this work. He was a man of letters, a poet, and for him teaching was a burden. He bore it a long time, conscientiously, as the martyrdom that is the special lot of poets.

He had brought with him to Paris a sheaf of unpublished poetry of very dense texture, composed in a style which to many seemed impenetrable. He himself had no reason to doubt its value. As early as 1866, at the time of the first *Parnasse*, Cazalis—himself a prolific poet—had written to him, evidently with complete sincerity:

> You are the greatest poet of our time, Stéphane, know it. And, exhausted as you may be, may this homage, my poor friend, whose life has been so painful, so holy, so sad, may this homage console what human feelings are left in you. Next to you we are all nothing. We are children who can hardly stammer. . . .

The year he settled in Paris, the second anthology of the *Parnasse contemporain* published his *Scène d'Hérodiade;* but he was no longer in favor with the Parnasse, and the third *Parnasse* rejected *L'Après-midi d'un faune.* In 1876 Derenne published the poem for him in a deluxe edition decorated by Édouard Manet, on hand-made paper with a Japanese cover and silk tie-cords in pink and black. Only three or four copies were put on sale. The rest were presented to friends; but in 1877 *La Revue indépendante* issued a popular edition and this excited some attention. There followed a period in which Mallarmé published nothing but school books. Meanwhile the various avant-garde groups that had formed in the cafés of the Latin Quarter were becoming increasingly vociferous, and several were on the point of bursting into print with reviews of their own. In 1880 Mallarmé began holding literary evenings for his friends in his apartment at number 87, rue de Rome. Among those who attended his *mardis* were some of the most fervent of the avant garde; but Mallarmé steadfastly refused all invitations to take part in the manifestations they organized, and he did not contribute to any of the new reviews.

In 1883, however, he was thrust quite unexpectedly into the limelight. That year Verlaine published *Les Poètes maudits.* It included an essay on Mallarmé and some examples of his work, together with essays on Corbière, Rimbaud, and, of course, on Verlaine himself. That year Huysmans's *À rebours* fell "like a meteor into the literary marketplace." Mallarmé had furnished Huysmans with some detail while he was composing this novel, and in it Floressas des Esseintes—who was supposedly modeled on Robert de Montesquiou-Fesenzac—was said to be a devotee of Mallarmé's poetry, a superb example of "the decadence of a literature, irreparably stricken in its soul, and in haste to express everything in its decline."

The attendant publicity put Mallarmé at the head of the *Décadents*, an ephemeral group hastily assembled to fill what was in fact a cultural vacuum. The *Décadents* claimed some spiritual relation to the writers of the decadence of Rome. They had until now considered Verlaine their leader. When they transferred their allegiance to Mallarmé, Fénéon invited him to contribute to the newly organized *La Revue indépendante*. Mallarmé offered him a strange poem. It was entitled "Prose pour des Esseintes." The allusion was, to be sure, marvellously witty. But the poem was disconcerting.

In May 1885 the new poetry was the subject of a hilarious satire called *Les Déliquescences: Poèmes décadents d'Adoré Floupette*. This squib included a poem entitled "Idylle symbolique," an obvious parody of Mallarmé's "Prose pour des Esseintes." This work was attributed to the Decadent poet Arsénal, who, together with his friend Bleucoton—an unmistakable allusion to Verlaine—was said to be "one of the two great initiators of the poetry of the future." It was a delicious prank, and when the laughter had subsided Mallarmé was famous. Thus "Prose pour des Esseintes" became a landmark in the history of literature in somewhat the same way that, twenty years later, "Les Demoiselles d'Avignon" became a turning point in the history of art.

The result of this outburst of publicity was to put Mallarmé at the head of a movement which he had done nothing to organize, but with which he was in complete sympathy. It had not yet much shape, and he did what he could to define it, and to give it coherence and direction. The Tuesday evenings in his dining-room were now thronged with disciples, so that "the little house of Socrates" scarcely sufficed to seat them all. The apostles-in-chief—Gustave Kahn, Jean Moréas, Louis Le Cardonnel—vied with one another in spreading the master's gospel, which, indeed, nobody entirely understood, and which therefore gave its evangelists the widest scope of operation. There was a vigorous contingent of Wagnerites—Dujardin, Wyzéwa, Fénéon. There was a splinter group of

"Instrumentalists," headed by René Ghil, who inclined to the methods of Poe and Verlaine. Relations were established with musicians and painters, and the movement took on unexpected proportions. Many hastened to associate themselves—Henri Régnier, Francis Viélé-Griffin, Pierre Quillard, Saint-Pol-Roux, André Fontainas, Laurent Tailhade, Claude Debussy. There was a strong foreign contingent: the Belgians, Albert Mockel and Emile Verhaeren; Arthur Symons and Oscar Wilde from England; Stefan George from Germany. By this time the movement had acquired the name it was destined to bear for the next fifty years. It was called Symbolism.

The word seems to have appeared first in December 1884 in an article on Mallarmé, in *Les Taches d'encre*, in which Maurice Barrès spoke of Mallarmé's work as symbolic poetry. The following year the activity in the avant-garde periodicals began to attract the attention of the bourgeois press. In August 1885 *Le Temps* published an article by Paul Bourde in which the new movement was described in terms that recalled the tone of an indulgent schoolmaster reporting the antics of a parcel of talented schoolboys. Moréas replied with a boisterous piece on the Decadent poets. "In their art," he wrote, "the so-called Decadents seek above all the pure Concept and the Eternal Symbol." And since, he added, the pursuit of the symbol was their principal aim, these poets should properly be called Symbolists.

The year before, in fact, Moréas had organized a literary *cénacle* that called itself *Les Symboliques*. The name rapidly gained currency. It was hardly clear to anyone—least of all, judging by their writings, to the Symbolists—what, precisely, Symbolism was; but it was quite clear what it was not. It was not in any sense realism. And it was not for the vulgar profane. The Symbolist poetry was not intended to be accessible to anyone who took the trouble to read it. It was poetry for the initiate, the adept, the elite.

If the term Symbolism was not clear, however, it was not for lack of explanation. In these years little reviews sprang up like mushrooms in the night, all dedicated to the task of elucidating the new movement. Among the earliest of these was *La Nouvelle Rive Gauche*, a periodical later called *Lutèce*. It lasted three years, from 1883 to 1886. It was followed by *Les Taches d'encre*, a one-man enterprise which endured for a year. *La Revue wagnérienne*, edited by Édouard Dujardin, was subsidized by various wealthy music lovers. It lasted from 1885 to 1888. There were also *Le Décadent*, *La Revue indépendante*, *La Vogue*, *La Revue blanche*, *Entre-*

tiens politiques et littéraires, and fully a dozen others. Only *Le Mercure de France* outlived the century. These publications assumed no particular political posture. Most of their contributors were inclined toward some variety of socialism. Some, like Pissarro, were anarchists. But in the main their editors followed Baudelaire in rejecting any connection of art with social utility. The Symbolists were dedicated to the cause of pure art, but not to art for art's sake. Symbolist art was a religion. Its aim was not pleasure, but truth. Poetry, like music, was a revelation of the transcendental, that is to say, the supernatural. The poet was a *voyant,* a seer, and also, in the highest sense, an alchemist.

In *Le Figaro littéraire* of 18 September 1886 Moréas published what purported to be a Symbolist manifesto. Romanticism, he wrote, was dead. The Parnasse had shot its bolt. The Naturalists were spent. The time had come for a new departure. The Symbolist movement favored neither romantic subjectivity, nor Parnassian description, nor the declamatory technique of Hugo. Its aim was to give concrete expression to the Ideal, to "attire the Idea in a perceptible form." Baudelaire, he wrote, was the true ancestor of this movement. Mallarmé and Verlaine were its principal living exponents.

Baudelaire had died nineteen years before, in 1867. He was perhaps a true ancestor of the Symbolist movement, but it was stretching a point to call him the father of Symbolism. The theory of signatures and correspondences was at the core of Renaissance art and letters. It had a full development in the literature of the seventeenth century. Through the influence of Swedenborg, Lavater, and Fourier it brought about a revival of mysticism in the following period, and through Blake, Wordsworth, Coleridge, Shelley, Carlyle, and Emerson it immensely broadened the horizons of romanticism.

For such gifted mystics as Giordano Bruno or Emanuel Swedenborg the order of the ascent to the Absolute was indicated by the correspondence of forms with their counterparts on the next higher level of being; but to less enlightened enthusiasts the analogies were not always altogether obvious. Baudelaire and the young Rimbaud had manifested in dramatic—one might say, theatrical—fashion their effort to ascend the scale of being through the development of their imaginative powers under various kinds of stimulation. Rimbaud called himself a *voyant;* Baudelaire, an *imaginatif.* In his *Salon de 1859* Baudelaire wrote: "The whole universe is but a storehouse of signs and symbols to which imagination will assign a relative place and value."[22] Plato had described the ascent of the soul as essentially a progress in comprehension, an intellectual adventure. But for Baudelaire the imagination was the prime perceptive faculty. In this belief he felt he had the support of two of the poets he most admired: Hugo and Gautier were both highly gifted in this regard. Gautier was one who possessed, he wrote, together with his infallible sense of the order of things, "an immense innate intelligence of the correspondence and symbolism of the universe."[23] Hugo's imagination knew no bounds. Baudelaire was aware, moreover, at a comparatively early date, of the aesthetic implications of German transcendental philosophy, and principally of the doctrines of Schopenhauer.

Die Welt als Wille und Vorstellung was first published in 1818 and made no great stir. Twenty-six years later, in 1844, the two volumes of the second edition appeared in a run of 500 copies. They were sold with the greatest difficulty. The collection of essays entitled *Parerga und Paralipomena* was issued in 1851, nine years before the author's death. By this time Schopenhauer was beginning to be read in France, and in 1874 Ribot's excellent translation made his works widely available to French scholars. But even then it was not apparent to anyone that Schopenhauer's doctrine was to become influential in the development of French literature.

What captured the imagination in French avant-garde circles was not the metaphysical groundwork of Schopenhauer's system. Save for the writings of Laforgue, who was evidently more deeply impressed by von Hartmann's *Philosophy of the Unconscious* than by anything he found in Schopenhauer, there is little mention in the early literature of Symbolism of the primacy of the Will. What interested them was Schopenhauer's theory of representation.

According to Schopenhauer the essential reality of the universe is grounded in an aimless and unconscious energy which realizes itself eternally in matter. This force he called the Will To Live. But the living forms in which this energy is manifested are not of its own devising. They are shaped in accordance with the ideal forms of the transcendental world, the archetypes. These are perfect, immutable, absolutely determined and, of course, lifeless. Evidently Schopenhauer had in mind here the Ideas of Plato. In time the Will, in its effort to survive, developed consciousness and mind, but the mind can reason only on the basis of what is presented to it by the senses. We have no other evidence as to the nature of reality:

> For whatever other kind of existence or reality should we attribute to
> the rest of the material world? Whence should we take the elements out
> of which we construct such a world? Besides Will and Representation
> nothing is known to us or thinkable. If we wish to attribute the greatest
> known reality to the natural world, which exists immediately only in
> our representation, we give it the reality which our own body has for
> each of us, that is the realest thing for everyone.[24]

Thus the ideal forms, not being accessible through the senses, are
completely beyond the reach of the logical faculty. They can, however,
be apprehended intuitively by the artist through an exceptional effort of
the imagination. To be capable of such an effort the artist must have
freed himself completely of the illusions of material being, for the ideal is
knowable only when the mind, having divested itself of all consciousness
of self and individuation, can rise to the plane of universality. Art is the
expression of the ideal. But the world of the ideal is open only to the exceptional mind, the mind of genius.

In 1867 Mallarmé wrote to Cazalis:

> I have just spent a horrible year: my Thought has thought itself out and
> has arrived at a Divine Concept. What my being suffered as a result in
> the course of that long agony cannot be told; fortunately, I am perfectly
> dead, and the most impure region in which my mind can wander is
> Eternity; my mind, that solitary denizen of its own Purity, which even
> the reflection of time no longer obscures. . . .
>
> This is to tell you that I am now impersonal and no longer Stéphane
> that you once knew—but an aptitude of the spiritual universe for seeing
> and developing itself through what was once I. . . .[25]

It seems likely that Schopenhauer's notions had a powerful influence
on the twenty-four-year-old poet; but Hegel too had written that the
negation of self was a necessary step in the purification of the mind to
the point where it could unite with the Idea. It is equally possible that
Mallarmé founded his theory of poetry on Hegel, and it is known that
his friends Lefébure and Villiers were both admirers of Hegel. In any
case the doctrine of the negation of self was common to many systems of
thought. The Buddhist and Taoist writings which influenced the German transcendentalists stressed the necessity of attaining the blessed
state of emptiness which follows the release from the illusions of being,
and it was doubtless to such sources that Cazalis humorously attributed
Mallarmé's conversion:

> If you become a Buddhist, you understand that all is lost. Whither are
> we bound? Lefébure a Hegelian, Mallarmé a Buddhist, Cazalis in Lour-
> cine, Catulle married—what a mess! It foreshadows the Apocalypse.[26]

This was written in 1868. Ten years later Schopenhauer's phrase,
"Die Welt ist meine Vorstellung," evidently burst like a bombshell on
the literary circles of Paris. Remy de Gourmont wrote:

> A new truth has recently entered the sphere of art and literature. This
> truth . . . is the principle of the ideality of the world. In relation to
> man, a thinking subject, the world, and everything in it that is external
> to the self, exists only according to the idea that one has of it. . . . We
> know nothing but phenomena. We reason solely on the basis of appear-
> ances; whatever is true in itself escapes us; the essence is beyond our
> reach. That is what Schopenhauer has popularized with this very clear
> and simple formulation: the world is my representation. I do not see
> what it is; what it is, is what I see. There are as many different worlds
> as there are thinking men.[27]

This was not exactly Schopenhauer's notion, and the fact that his own
interpretation involved the inconvenience of solipsism does not appear to
have troubled Gourmont. Mallarmé, however, had been troubled by
doubt to the point of a mental collapse. He had struggled with God in
his twenties. For him the divine denizen of the sky was dead. His "terrible struggle with that old and evil plumage—brought down, fortunately,
God!" was over. In a similar situation Strindberg had acknowledged
defeat. Mallarmé claimed a victory; but his triumph had brought him to
the edge of despair. Where formerly there had been angels, now he saw
only the void, *le néant*. In March 1866 he had written to Cazalis apropos
of *Hérodiade:*

> Unhappily in digging so deeply into poetry, I have come upon two
> abysses that reduce me to despair. One is the void which I have reached
> without knowing Buddhism, and I am still too wretched to be able to
> believe even in my poetry, and to get myself back to the work that this
> crushing thought has made me abandon.[28]

But for Mallarmé it was not at this point that the poetic adventure left
off. Here it began. If there was, in truth, nothing, then the poetic challenge was clear. It was the poet's task, through the power of imagination,
to create a world:

> Yes, *I know it*, we are only empty forms of matter—nonetheless sub-
> lime for having invented God and our soul. So truly sublime, my

friend! that I wish to experience the spectacle of matter, knowing itself to be, and nevertheless launching itself by force into this Dream which it knows is unreal, celebrating the Soul and all such other divine impressions which have accumulated in us from the earliest times, and proclaiming, in the face of the Nothing which is the truth, these glorious lies! Such is the plan of my book of poems, and such perhaps will be its title, *The Glory of the Lie* or *The Glorious Lie*. I shall sing as one in despair.[29]

The song of despair was also a song of hope. For Mallarmé the old world was gone, and the myth of the universe dispelled. But now, in the absence of God, the poet could take on divinity, at least he could undertake a god-like task, and through the magic of the imagination a new world might take shape as a significant reality in accordance with the ideal.

From this conviction, which in the 1880's many shared, sprang what has since been called—not always with complete admiration—modern art.

"We saw," Schopenhauer wrote,

that the inner being of unconscious nature is a constant striving without end and without rest. And this appears to us much more distinctly when we consider the nature of man and the beasts. Willing and striving is its whole being, which may very well be compared to an unquenchable thirst. But the basis of all willing is need, deficiency, and thus, pain. Consequently the nature of man and the beasts is subject to pain originally and through its very being. If, on the other hand, it lacks objects of desire, because it is at once deprived of them by a too easy satisfaction, a terrible void and ennui comes over it, i.e., its being and existence itself becomes an unbearable burden to it. Thus its life swings like a pendulum backwards and forwards between pain and ennui.[30]

Out of this predicament Schopenhauer saw only two ways of escape. One was reliable, but inhumanly difficult—by renouncing life through ascetism and enlightenment, the exceptional individual might achieve the condition of Nirvana. For mankind this process, were it generally followed, would lead ultimately to the extinction of conscious being. The alternative was to escape into the world of art. This was the way that Mallarmé, at great personal cost, had chosen, and in this direction his admirers did their best to follow.

The quest for the ideal world through art was, however, no simple matter, for the imagination knows no rules and is not subject to correction; moreover, the indispensable negation of self presents problems which few can solve. In any case, from the Schopenhauerian standpoint the traditional aesthetic made no sense. If nature was the work of the human mind, there was no point in the type of art that imitated natural objects, nor could a work of art be valued in terms of its likeness to something in the external world. The only possible function of art was the depiction of Ideas, since these alone could be said to exist. But Ideas were not perceptible to the senses. They could only be suggested through appropriate symbols. It followed that the business of art was the search for symbols.

In a study called *Modern Naturalism and Artistic Truth* (1881) the German art critic Conrad Fiedler launched a vigorous attack on Naturalism based on philosophic considerations, possibly Hegelian. In the introduction to his posthumously published treatise *Art and Reality* he argued that nature was not a system of incontrovertible data imposed on the senses, but an evolving concept:

> Even though the great majority of men, in using language, remain unaware of its restrictive character, its limitations have long been recognized. This is not true of the visual forms by which men become conscious of the world. . . .
>
> A productive process creates visual images when sensory stimuli, reaching the brain, are built up gradually into objective forms . . . The object exists only in the image; what we call a true mental image is only what corresponds to the established images of others. Such is the formalism, the convention, to which man is subject from the moment he begins to see and to think . . . an arbitrary agreement based on deception. . . .
>
> To him who understands that the content of being can consist only of perception and images, this reality, which for the naive mind is the model and cause of perception and imagery, becomes simply an unconscious convention, in which the mental formative process of a perceptual world has come to a seeming standstill. What does it mean when an individual is referred to nature as to a final tribunal that judges all opinion and all errors? Where does this nature exist other than in human perception? [31]

Fiedler carried his thought a step further: "The meaning of all artistic expression is none other than the effort to develop the existent into still other forms of existence. As a result of this insight the great gulf which divides scientific investigation from formative activity is closed."

In this manner, as it seemed, the portals of the mind were flung open for a spectacular flight of the artistic imagination. If reality as we know it were considered to be a work of art created not by God but by man, there would be no reason other than convenience why reality should retain its traditional character. If man is an evolving being, then reality is subject to change in accordance with his changing insights. The function of art was thus considerably clarified. It was by no means an imitation of nature. Its aim was nothing less than the re-creation of the world, a continuing task. From the Idealistic point of view this would be a spiritual process, the result of which would be the progressive realization of the world in its essential structure, and ultimately the revelation of the Absolute.

In the absence of anything definite in the way of a revelation, Mallarmé consciously set about the construction of an imaginary reality based on intuitions in which he had no great faith, but which yet seemed promising for the future. The work of creation—*L'Oeuvre*—was to be a vast undertaking. It would be, of course, a poem, a work in five, perhaps in twenty, volumes which would take twenty years to write. Mallarmé described it in response to a request by Verlaine:

> What is it? It is difficult to say: a book, in short, in many volumes, a book which will be book, architectural and premeditated, and not a collection of chance inspirations, however marvellous. . . . I will go further, I will say: The Book, convinced that at bottom there is but one, unconsciously attempted by everyone who has ever written, even the Geniuses: the Orphic explication of the World, which is the poet's sole duty and the supreme literary game.[32]

Since the Great Work—Mallarmé was entirely aware of its alchemical connotations—was aimed at nothing less than a solution of the mystery of the universe, he felt that he had attained the necessary state of purity, and had now become a speculum in which the essential reality would be reflected. Thus the Book he was projecting, *Le Livre*, was a sorcerer's manual, a *grimoire*, a grammar, embodying incantations by virtue of which out of nothing something might come. The enterprise itself was a voyage in uncharted seas, hazardous for the voyager, and subject to shipwreck. It was also, one might say, a gamble, a desperate game played with words of price, any one of which might, by chance, return a treasure.

Such metaphors were, perhaps, unduly stimulating, but they served to indicate the excitement and the fervor of the quest. It is possible that all this is reducible, as Michaud has argued, to a purely Hegelian concept; if so, the concept underwent considerable transformation in the poet's hands. More likely the source of Mallarmé's magic is traceable to Baudelaire. In the *Salon de 1859* Baudelaire had written:

> It is the imagination that taught man the moral sense of color, shape, sound and odor. In the beginning of the world it created analogy and metaphor. It decomposes all creation, and with the materials thus accumulated and disposed in accordance with rules, the origin of which can be found only in the deepest reaches of the soul, it creates a new world, it produces the sensation of the new. As it created the world (one may well say this, I think, even in a religious sense) it is right that it should govern it.[33]

For his idea of the creative imagination Baudelaire was, in his turn, indebted to Coleridge and to Poe, but he did not develop his ideas any more systematically than they. It was left to the Symbolists to arrange these notions into something like a system. Baudelaire was content to be a poet and a critic. Mallarmé was touched by a Messianic impulse. He believed—no doubt as sincerely as Shaw—that he was singled out to perform the Great Work of elucidation which had been neglected since the creation of light.

In the latter half of the nineteenth century many intelligent men had occupied themselves with alchemical operations, and there was much talk of the Elixir and the Philosopher's Stone. Mallarmé did not, like Strindberg, concern himself with crucibles and alembics. His was a purely spiritual undertaking, nevertheless an architectural enterprise of some magnitude. He was inspired to construct with words—the symbols of reality—a cosmic structure in accordance with the image of the Absolute that was taking form in his mind. The resulting work of art would be nothing less than reality itself, a new and authentic reality, consciously fashioned in all the beauty of its truth. Now, through the poet, the vital Will would at last become aware of what it had been about from the beginning of time, and would realize the archetypal pattern which from the first had guided it in shaping its material forms. It would, at last, know itself. As for the poet, he was no more than the temporary embodiment of the Will. He was, indeed, the Will but, as an individual, subject to the transitory nature of material forms.

When he came to these conclusions, Mallarmé was twenty-five. He wrote to Cazalis:

> So fragile is my terrestrial apparition that I can endure only those de-
> velopments which are absolutely necessary in order for the Universe to
> recover its identity through the self which is I. Thus I have just now, at
> the hour of Synthesis, delimited the Work which will be the image of
> this development. Three poems in verse, of which *Hérodiade* is the
> Overture, but of a purity which man has not attained—and will per-
> haps never attain—for it may be that I am nothing but the toy of an
> illusion, and that the human machine is not sufficiently perfect to arrive
> at such results. And four poems in prose on the spiritual concept of the
> Void . . . I will need ten years. Will I have them? [34]

The idea that the poet's insights represent the efforts of the universe to
know itself became in time a basic tenet of Symbolist theory. For twenty
years Mallarmé's disciples waited patiently for the master to bring the
Great Work to light, and everything that Mallarmé published in the
meantime was considered in some sense preparatory to its completion. In
the end, unhappily, there was nothing. His last words were an admonition to his family to destroy his notes:

> There is no literary legacy there, my poor children. Do not even sub-
> mit them to the appreciation of anyone; and refuse any curious or
> friendly meddling. Say that nothing can be made of it, indeed, it is
> true, and you, my poor downcast darlings, the only beings in the world
> capable of respecting properly a whole sincere artist's life, believe that it
> would have been very beautiful. [35]

Some years later others took up the task, among them Yeats and Shaw,
but the Orphic explication of the universe has yet to be accomplished.
What was accomplished, however, quite changed the character of art in
our time.

The effort to probe the mystery of the universe sent the disciples of
Mallarmé off in many directions, including Catholicism, but most of all
it inclined them toward the occult sciences. The type of sustained meditation out of which the Symbolist poem developed already had in it some
esoteric flavor. It was, indeed, not long before the Symbolists and Spiri-
tists joined hands in the effort to explore the supernatural.

Between 1885 and 1900 Paris was a center of Spiritist activity. In
these years the pursuit of the occult burgeoned into an industry. Esoteric
works were published by the score. Spiritist journals such as Papus's *Ini-
tiation* were widely supported. In Edmond Bailly's bookshop in the

Chaussée d'Antin the initiates held daily meetings at which the *illumi-nati*—Guaita, Papus, Ernest Hello, Maurice Barrès, Paul Adam, and Charles Morice—held forth, and adepts of the type of Eliphas Lévi and Sâr Péladan instructed large audiences on arcane topics. Such books as George Vahors's *L'Art symboliste*, Morice's *La Littérature de tout à l'heure*, and Péladan's *L'Art idéaliste* made it clear that art was a spiritual commu-nion. "Art," Péladan wrote, "is the relation of man to the Absolute." Mauclair elaborated on this idea: "Line and color are abstract elements imposed on matter, but distinct from it . . . they are the traces of the divine in the world. The poet and the artist are therefore in some sense priests. They teach men to see God in his symbols. . . . Poetry is consequently a song that expresses musically and symbolically a religious idea."[36]

Mallarmé had done with God; but for him also the poet was one who was charged with the duty and the power *de voir divinement*. Baudelaire had been of the same persuasion. But quite apart from orthodox belief, Symbolism was an attempt to recover for poetry the exalted position it had abdicated after the time of Milton, and which Blake and Coleridge had tried, in their time, to regain for the lyric. From first to last Mallar-mé maintained the dignity of the poet's calling. In his opinion, poetry was the highest art. It bordered on sorcery, on magic, in its power to create images. It involved the manipulation of words of power. Such things were dangerous. Accordingly, Mallarmé labored to make his ut-terance obscure. His traffic, in any case, was not with ordinary things, but with entities far removed from ordinary experience, with intimations of another sphere of being, not necessarily related to recollections of childhood, though they might have something to do with the primitive mind.

Upon the vision of an ideal world, beautiful and true beyond human experience, all Symbolist art was centered. Rimbaud had tried to capture this vision by a voluntary distortion of his normal faculties: "The poet makes himself a seer by a long, immense and calculated derangement of all his senses." But the paradise he briefly experienced in the feverish fantasies of *Le Bateau ivre* (1871) seems far removed from the calm and lifeless sphere of the ideal that Schopenhauer had envisaged. In *À rebours* des Esseintes came closer to the Symbolist paradise. He felt, we are told, "des transports, des élans vers un idéal, vers un univers inconnu, vers une béatitude lointaine, désirable comme celle que nous promettent les Écritures."[37]

In order to gain this paradise the Symbolists gladly relinquished—at least, in theory—the Positivist world of material things. "Seule vit notre âme," Édouard Dujardin declared: "only our soul exists." His phrase was widely echoed. "At this hour," Remy de Gourmont noted, "the idealist theory is no longer contested save by a few old ducks who enjoy living in the ancient marshes."[38] To the reality of the objective world, the Symbolists opposed the superior reality of the world of dreams, in which might be found a more congenial climate of existence than anything the material world afforded. The dreamworld, in Baudelaire's opinion, represented the supernatural aspect of life, in which "the artificial distinction between the true and the false is nullified, and the dreamer communes with a superior power." This "hieroglyphic" world was the special domain of the *voyant— l'homme chargé de voir divinement*. On this point, according to Mallarmé, all the various schools of Symbolism were in accord,

> Decadent, mystical, the schools thus declaring themselves, or so labelled in haste by our press of information, adopt as their meeting place an Idealism which (as with fugues and sonatas) refuses the materials of nature and the brutal intrusion of an organizing thought; it retains only the suggestion of organization and aims at finding a relation between images, exact, so that there should arise a third aspect, fusible and clear, which is present in divination.

Mallarmé's prose is seldom transparent; but his meaning in this passage is not in doubt. The third aspect which arises when the relation between two images is properly revealed is the Idea that relates them, the *notion pure* which it is the sole object of poetry to realize.[39]

The Idea, indeed, is not the relation between images as such, but the conceptualized image which results from the perception of the relationship: this is the symbol. When the necessary connections are made, this "third aspect" will arise spontaneously in the mind. The process of abstraction will not be syllogistic. It will be, in Mallarmé's term, musical:

> Of what use is the marvel of transposing a fact of nature in its almost vibratory evanescence in accordance, nevertheless, with the play of words, if not, in order that there should emanate from it, without the embarrassment of a peremptory or concrete summons, the pure notion?
>
> I say, a flower! And out of the limbo to which my voice relegates any shape, as something other than any known bloom, there arises musi-

cally the idea, real and suave, the flower that is absent from all
bouquets.

The verse which out of several words refashions a word that is total,
new, a stranger to the language and, one might say, incantatory,
achieves this distinction from ordinary speech: it rejects by a sovereign
act the chance element residual in words in spite of the artifice of their
retempering alternately in sense and sound, and causes you the surprise
of never having heard before this ordinary fragment of elocution, at the
same time that the reminiscence of the object named bathes in a new atmosphere.[40]

Since, in general, the relation of "the pure notion," the Idea, and its
objective manifestation is indicated by words, it was evident from the
beginning of the Symbolist movement that language is the primary concern of the poet. But there are other ways, obviously, of indicating relations. There are such things as musical, visual, and dramatic metaphors.
The metaphor expresses relations and reveals analogies. It also creates
them. It was possible, accordingly, to argue that in reality there are no
analogies, no relations, and no Ideas—but only the random association of
words, leading nowhere. This doubt was at the core of Symbolism from
the first, and Mallarmé never escaped its torment. In the end it turned
Symbolism from the exploration of the universe to the exploration of the
self, so that the infinite was thought of as a surface entirely blank and
empty in which the poet might see, if he was fortunate, the reflections of
his mind. Thus Symbolism became associated early with the myth of
Narcissus which, in time, Valéry was to develop in all its complexity. It
became an introspective genre in which the self was so closely identified
with the universe that the Symbolist could by turns contemplate it in
himself, and himself in it. In these embarrassing psychic oscillations the
only firm anchor was the Idea, the far-off reality which came to the mind
like the scintillation of the seven stars reflected in the mirror in the
empty room of Mallarmé's sonnet, "Ses purs ongles." The Symbolist
clung to the Idea with desperate tenacity. When that faith was gone,
Symbolism went with it.

It was the quest of the Idea that gave Symbolism its special fervor,
and also its sadness. For Mallarmé, as years later for Beckett, art was a
tragic quest. In a letter to Odilon Redon, in praise of a portfolio of his li-
thographs, Mallarmé wrote:

But all my admiration to the great Mage, inconsolable and stubborn
searcher after a mystery which he knows does not exist, and which he

will therefore pursue forever, in the clear sorrow of his despair, for it
should have been the truth.

The sentence describes the poet, obviously, more accurately than the
artist to whom it was addressed. It provides, at least, a useful insight not
only into Mallarmé's obsession, but into the ambiguity that is at the
heart of so much of the art of our day.

Between their skepticism with regard to material reality and their
doubts as to the reality of the ideal world the Symbolists found a narrow
space in which it was possible to live without too much discomfort. The
world of fantasy had perhaps no existence outside the human mind; nevertheless it had a very full and demonstrable existence within it. There
was reason to believe that in the interplay between the psyche and the
external world there was a reality of sorts, which was solid enough for
the purposes of art. "Ich bin zu Hause zwischen Tag und Traum," Rilke
wrote. It was indeed in this habitable no-man's land between dream and
day that the Symbolist felt most at home, and in this nebulous area—
later called Surreality—the Symbolist drama had its fullest development.

This development, like the analogous development of Symbolist poetry, proceeded along two lines, seemingly parallel, but in fact con-
vergent. The one, laid down by Baudelaire in the essays of *L'Art roman-
tique*, and celebrated in his famous sonnet "Correspondances," involved
the metaphysical concept of the Idea, and it became central in Symbolist
theory. The other, associated with Poe, Laforgue, and Verlaine, was
primarily linguistic. It was an exploration of the properties of verbal
sonority and visual image not as a means of probing the mystery of existence, but as a way of realizing through poetic expression the elusive sensations of the inner life. The possibility that these psychic states might
have special validity as reflections of a truer reality than the more definite elements of consciousness afforded gave a mystical tinge also to this
aspect of Symbolism.

The theory of signatures which Symbolism adapted from the mystical
writings of Swedenborg and Boehme involved the assumption that the
creative Word of God was operative simultaneously on all levels of being
from the lowliest creature to the celestial intelligences. Thus each creature in the chain of being had its analogues in the hierarchy both above
and below. The world of transcendental forms to which Baudelaire
aspired was evidently none other than the Christian paradise more or less

as Dante had described it. The ascesis through beauty led to God. For Baudelaire, as for Swedenborg, the visible world was God's allegory, which could be read by anyone who had the key. The nineteenth-century Symbolists, however, objected to allegory on the ground that it was redundant, an intellectual game which translated into concrete images what was already known in the abstract. Symbolism, on the other hand, was the exploration of a mystery, the nature of which would be discovered only when its visible symbols were decoded. Camille Mauclair summed up the necessary assumptions:

> Every object is the fleeting symbol of its essential idea. The world is none other than a system of symbols subordinated to a system of pure ideas governed by cosmic laws, and the sum-total of these laws constitutes divinity. The universe, so to speak, is a vast writing in which each object is a letter and the whole reveals the divine.[41]

The theory of signatures had interesting implications. Since the signs that constituted the perceptible world were perceived by the various sense-organs according to their special receptivity, sensations of sight, sound, taste, and smell might all be considered evidences of the same Idea—one saw with the eye what one heard with the ear. It would therefore be possible for the mind to arrange its perceptions so that sound had color, and color was audible. Those who actually experienced synaesthesia of this sort could testify to the web of correspondence which gave unity and significance to the universe. Baudelaire wrote:

> Swedenborg has taught us that everything, form, movement, number, color, scent, in the spiritual as in the natural order, is significant, reciprocal, related, correspondent. . . .
>
>   Thus what is a poet (I take the word in its widest sense) if not a translator, a decipherer?[42]

For Baudelaire poetry in its widest sense meant creation. It included all artistic expression. All the arts were counterparts. Each was a language. All expressed the same truth. From the Symbolist viewpoint, accordingly, the visual signs which the painter composes on canvas, the characters the dramatist assembles and moves on the stage, may be read in the same way as the words the poet sets down on paper. The signs themselves had no special interest. It was what they signified that was valuable.

The movement and direction of line, the psychological connotations of color, and the arrangement of planes, spaces, and shapes had in the last

decades of the century been studied with some care. The result was
something like a science of art. On the basis of the optical researches of
Helmholtz, Charles Henry among others developed a system of optical
psychology which was widely influential in the early 1900's. It was considered that through a skilful disposition of line and color it was possible
to evoke mood and emotion directly without recourse to representation.
A painting therefore would not need a subject; it might affect the feelings without conveying any meaning to the intellect. Obviously the same
thing might be said of a poem or a play.

The art of the poet and the painter in this period thus went hand in
hand as they once had—though under a different dispensation—in the
days of Botticelli and Poliziano; and once again the arts were united in a
common faith. *Ut pictura poesis.* In the circumstances this faith could not
be long sustained. Another decade would bring about the spiritual upheavals consequent on the Great War, and the corrosive influences of
Expressionism and Dada were destined to eat into the texture of nineteenth-century Idealism. The unriddling of the divine poem depended,
obviously, upon the existence of the divine Poet.

In the seventeenth century it was normal for Newton to think of natural science as a study of the ways of God, just as 300 years before it had
been possible for Boccaccio to speak of poetry as theology. In the nineteenth century it was possible to dissociate Symbolism from religion, but
the mystical tendency was strong. Camille Mauclair constituted himself
Mallarmé's principal spokesman. In *L'Art en silence* Mauclair wrote that
he saw everywhere the reflection of divinity in nature. In *Sartor Resartus,*
Carlyle had written to much the same effect:

> In the Symbol proper, what we call call a Symbol, there is ever, more
> or less distinctly and directly, some embodiment and revelation of the
> Infinite; the Infinite is made to blend itself with the Finite, to stand visi-
> ble, and as it were, attainable there. By Symbols, accordingly, is man
> guided and commanded, made happy, made wretched. He everywhere
> finds himself encompassed with Symbols, recognized as such or not
> recognized: the Universe is but one vast Symbol of God; nay if thou
> wilt have it, what is man himself but a Symbol of God; is not all that he
> does symbolical; a revelation to Sense of the mystic god-given force that
> is in him . . . ?[43]

In Gauguin's portrait of Meyer de Hahn the two books displayed
prominently on the table are *Sartor Resartus* and *Paradise Lost,* masterpieces which must have seemed childishly transparent to those who were

trying to fathom the works of Mallarmé. To Albert Aurier the symbolism of Gauguin seemed marvellously effective; but Gauguin was too
deeply involved with objective reality to suit the taste of the next generation of artists. The Dadaists of the Cabaret Voltaire saw nothing worth
saving in the objective world that was reducing itself to rubbish all
around them. They rejected both realism and idealism. Richard Huelsenbeck wrote in 1920:

> Archipenko, whom we honored as an exemplary model in the field of
> plastic art, insisted that art must be neither realistic nor idealistic; it
> must be true. He meant above all that any imitation of nature, however
> well concealed, is a lie.[44]

When Dada formally destroyed itself in 1921, it left the Surrealists as
its heirs. André Breton, who staged the last great Dada soirée in 1920 at
the Théâtre de l'oeuvre, issued the first Surrealist manifesto in 1924. It
expressed with some asperity the artist's revulsion against the absurdities
of the material world, and proposed a systematic exploration of the unconscious in search of the Ideal. But the Ideal proved to be as elusive
here as elsewhere, and the Surrealists, in their turn, were accused of
being unduly romantic. In 1937 Piet Mondrian wrote:

> As for surrealism we must recognize that it deepened thought and feel-
> ing, but since this deepening is limited by individualism it cannot reach
> the foundation, the universal. So long as it remains in the realm of
> dreams, which are only a rearrangement of the events of life, it cannot
> touch reality.[45]

The way to reach the true reality was evidently to destroy the world
of appearances. Since in practice such wholesale destruction might safely
be left to the military, the artist was forced to vent his aggressions by
imagining a world stripped down to its barest essentials. Pure art would
then consist in the depiction of fundamental relations of line and color. It
took a long time to translate these ideas into such terms as might be
useful in the theatre; but in time the attempt was made.

Under such influences, art—now under the influence of Freud and
Jung—moved its base further and further into the darkness of the unconscious, metaphor took on new connotations, and the symbols which had
served to evoke the divinity of the creative spirit now worked increasingly to reveal its humanity. The age of Mallarmé made way quite
smoothly for the age of Apollinaire and Breton, but the transition was

more apparent than real. The public which had accepted the mysteries of Symbolism was equally willing to accept the mysteries of Surrealism. Those who did not comprehend Mallarmé had no difficulty in not comprehending Eluard.

The Symbolists had been much concerned with psychic states—*états d'âme*—but Mallarmé never relinquished the intellectual aspects of poetry. He intended his writings to be difficult, but intelligible "to those who can read," and he insisted that his poems had meaning which study would reveal. Later Symbolists were content to dispense with meaning. Mauclair wrote: "There are two things: to make one see and to make one feel . . . to make one feel! Words cannot do that, only song; it is the great power!"[46]

The failure of Symbolism to furnish information regarding the transcendental thus led to a quest for enlightenment on a lower plane of communication, where symbols conveyed something other than meaning. What cannot be understood may perhaps be felt: it is possible to know without comprehending. We listen to music as intently as if we were receiving instruction, and perhaps with more profit. In advocating a type of art that dispenses with meaning the Symbolists moved some steps further from science, and distinguished their work even more sharply from Realism. It was no great distance from the mysticism of the early Symbolists to the primitivistic tendencies that ushered in the age of Cubism and Surrealism, and the theatre of Jarry and Artaud.

As his work matured, Mallarmé gradually abandoned normal linguistic practice, and his expression became increasingly private and correspondingly obscure. In the circumstances the question of meaning became embarrassing, and while Mallarmé himself continued to use words meaningfully, their significance became increasingly doubtful even to his most fervent admirers. In these circumstances the temptation to curtail discussion was difficult to resist, and questions of meaning were turned aside with statements such as "a poem should not mean, but be." This saved trouble; but the consequence was that poems took on the quality of objects and, insofar as they were considered to be symbols, they became virtually indistinguishable from paintings, and were arranged on the page as typographical designs. Mallarmé's last composition, "Un Coup de dés," was, in fact, arranged as a verbal landscape in patterns more accessible to the eye than to the mind, and it is not impossible that the poet dreamed of something of the sort when he described in an early letter to Cazalis the "très nouvelle poétique" that *Hérodiade* was to exemplify:

> The verse, there, will not be composed of words, but of intentions,
> and all the words will vanish in sensations.[47]

Such poetry, like the later canvases of Gauguin and van Gogh, was aimed at the realization of an inner experience less tangible than anything the current modes of art could manage. The obscurity of such works was not felt to be an inconvenience; on the contrary, it helped to convey some of the mystery with which such experiences were colored. Since normal speech was not able to reach the affective centers that are accessible, for example, to music and drama, the language of Symbolism was framed so as to communicate feeling on a level below the plane of the intellect, and therefore surrendered denotation in favor of more primitive methods of communication—association, suggestion, the language of revery, and even the language of pictures, insects, and birds. And since Symbolist art was not intended to make statements but to arouse sensibility, poets avoided "the brutal intrusion of an organizing thought," the more readily as the inflexible forms of logical structure were felt to deform expression by forcing it into conventional social forms that stifled the individuality of the artist. Thus Mallarmé believed that it was necessary to preserve the exact order and relation of the images that arose in his mind, and he was scrupulous to manipulate his ever-lengthening sentences so as not to damage the patterns in which "the demon of analogy" presented its symbols to the consciousness. The resulting expression cost him great effort, and frequently it was absolutely opaque to the understanding. Apparently he had no alternative as an artist but to express himself in sibylline terms. Mauclair quoted him as saying:

> Many times I have resolved to write the books I am carrying in my
> head, contenting myself with a normal French style, more or less ele-
> gant and expressive, using the customary rhythms and syntax, swearing
> that I would shake off the yoke; but then, the moment I began, I knew
> I could not, that no one has the right to misuse the written form that
> way. . . .[48]

The written forms to which he was addicted, and which his disciples aped, were, in truth, strangely contorted in ways so startling as to approximate a foreign tongue. Mallarmé was above all intent on distinguishing his prose from the prose of everyday speech. Huysmans evidently thought that this style was distinguished chiefly by its density and concision. In À rebours he describes it in terms which might more aptly apply to the style of Flaubert. By finding a precise and rare similitude, he wrote, des Esseintes spared the reader "from dissipating his attention on each of the qualities which might have been presented one by one by adjectives strung out single file, and concentrated it on a single word, on a whole, producing, as if for a picture, for example, a unique and complete impression, an ensemble."[49]

In fact the Symbolist effect was achieved through a rather painterly use of language, in which words were applied to the page not in the orderly hypotactic sequences of normal prose, but in the manner of the *tachiste*, like touches of the brush on canvas, so that the eye, at first bewildered by a seeming muddle of impressions, is gratified when at a certain distance this chaos springs into order. "To name an object," Mallarmé wrote, "is to suppress three-quarters of the enjoyment of a poem, which is derived from the happiness of guessing little by little; to suggest it, that is the dream. It is the perfect management of this mystery which constitutes Symbolism, little by little to evoke an object in order to reveal a psychic state."[50] It was a style, undoubtedly, that owed much to the graphic arts as they were then developing, and which in turn inspired a later school of painting. But it was not a style that recommended itself to the ordinary reader; nor was it intended for him.

Symbolist poetry was born and nourished in mystery; mystery was its soul and its reason for being. "Nous ne nous grandissons," Maeterlinck wrote, "qu'en grandissant les mystères qui nous accablent."[51] But mystery was the special province of the mystic, and even those poets who declined to join the Rosicrucians felt that they were somehow in communion with the supernatural. Under the influence mainly of Poe, poets gracefully assumed the prophetic mantle and the verbal eccentricities appropriate to prophets. In 1886 Mallarmé defined poetry in very summary fashion:

> Poetry is the expression in the language of humanity, brought back to
> its essential rhythm, of the mysterious sense of being. It thus endows
> our life with authenticity and constitutes the only spiritual task.[52]

By virtue of their special sensitivity as artists the Symbolists avowedly undertook to penetrate the mystery of being in a spirit similar to that in which the explorers of the period undertook to explore the sources of the Nile. In fact they did what they could to enhance their subject-matter. In their view what was clear was not poetic. The comprehensible lay outside their domain. Once it was assumed that the truth is incomprehensible, whatever was clear was suspect. To understand a work of art was, accordingly, to misapprehend it; for whatever in it was truly art could not be touched by reason. The critic's task was, in consequence, enormously simplified. To explain was to kill.

Clarity was a Renaissance virtue which mannerism corrupted. The Renaissance poet, in general, felt secure in his certainties. But the emphasis on individual style which the sixteenth century fostered progressively developed the subjective element in the representation of nature until at last in the nineteenth century, manner and matter became synonymous. At this point clarity was no longer an artistic criterion. There was, in any case, little left to be clear about. In the 1880's the skeptical outlook was such that many felt that the universe, which Dante had once rummaged gloriously from cellar to attic, would forever elude rational analysis. For the artist the task of elucidation would necessarily be a solitary enterprise, and without the guidance of the sovereign Idea, probably hopeless. In Villiers's *Axël* the hero is told:

> Know once and for all that there is no other universe for you than the conception of it which is mirrored in the depths of your thought, for you cannot see it clearly, nor can you know it, or distinguish even a single point as this mysterious point must be true in its reality. . . . If you are capable of possessing the truth, create it! Like all the others! You will not bear away, you will not be, anything but your own creation. . . . The world's appearance, however it may seem, is at bottom no more than a fiction, changeable, illusory, beyond reach.[53]

Faced with a task of this character, the Symbolist avoided committing himself. The Symbol—unlike its counterpart in allegory—was, above all, equivocal. It was intended to awaken an echo wherever it found resonance, but it forebore definition. Thus, long before the time of Beckett or Pinter, Émile Hennequin wrote:

> One may say in sum that any spectacle, any scene, passionate or spiritual, which can be, or is, exactly described or analyzed in detail, will cease to be poetic; and, on the contrary, any spectacle that remains obscure and diffused, far-off and strange, which is represented generally and by way of suggestion, but yet coherently, leaving the field open for the emotions associated with it, and even those that result from its idealization, will be poetic.[54]

In this passage Hennequin had in mind not *La Princesse Maleine*—it was not produced until 1890, two years after his article—but plays like *Peer*

Gynt, The Wild Duck, and *Rosmersholm,* which in 1888 were considered obscurely symbolic. Compared with dramatic compositions such as *Hérodiade* or *L'Après-midi d'un faune,* Ibsen's plays were as transparent as gossamers, but Ibsen was moving toward mystery quite as rapidly as everyone else in this period. *The Master Builder* (1892) is set in that indeterminate zone *zwischen Tag und Traum* which was the Symbolist's preferred habitat, and its mystery is indeed the source of its poetic effect. Symbolist drama, as it developed, had much in common with Symbolist poetry. It was both mystical and mysterious. In *The Master Builder* the symbol, bridging the abyss between the world of the imagination and the real world, was dangerously charged with emotion, and had overtones that might be thought of as religious. In Ibsen's play Solness speaks with God on the steeples of churches, and his fall is attended by celestial music. In *When We Dead Awaken,* as in *Brand,* the avalanche that engulfs the hero is providential.

Such events, obviously, must be shadowy, since they partake of the supernatural. Similarly, the poetry with which Mallarmé foreshadowed the great *Oeuvre* was made consciously obscure, partly out of snobbery, but largely because of the awe-inspiring nature of the material. The order of difficulty which Mallarmé imposed on his utterance both in poetry and prose was doubtless in some respects an affectation; but it was a sincere one. In a very early work entitled *Hérésie artistique: l'Art pour tous,* published in *L'Artiste* in 1862 when he was twenty, Mallarmé noted in terms that recall the pronouncements of Pico, that "everything sacred which desires to remain sacred is enveloped in mystery. Since art partakes of the sanctity of religion, it should be preserved from the vulgar profane. Access to it is not for everyone. Like the medieval missals, poetry should be closed with golden clasps."

There is every indication that in making his expression inaccessible to the ordinary reader Mallarmé was following hermetic practices traditional in France from the time of the closed poetry of the troubadours, whose work his friends, the "Félibriques" of Avignon, occasionally imitated. It is even more clear that he imitated the poets of the *trobar ric* in the choice of rare and difficult rhymes, and doubtless, like them, he found rhyme useful in directing the association of images along unexpected lines. But the singular opacity of his utterance, which so profoundly influenced the poetry and the drama of the following age, was very likely founded on deeper motives. Obscurity is, after all, a form of silence. In the case of Mallarmé, and later of Valéry, everything points to the supposition that these poets had exhibitionistic difficulties of more than usual complexity. The artist's need to exhibit himself to the world without actually appearing before it in person troubled neither Baudelaire nor Verlaine, nor Rimbaud, nor Strindberg. These were essentially dramatic artists, actors who were able to devise an appropriate *persona* to speak their lines. Rimbaud disclaimed all personal responsibility for his art: "Je est un autre." But Mallarmé had no dramatic gift. He was a lyricist. His finest poems concern himself, and his attempts at drama are painfully autobiographical.

Obscurity is a form of silence that enables one to shout without being heard. Mallarmé was highly successful in concealing what he was at pains to publish to the world. In its thirty pages of tumultuous verse, "Un Coup de dés" gives us absolutely no information. It is a truly astonishing feat of virtuosity. This poem tells us nothing, of course, in an extraordinarily impressive fashion which dazzles the eye and leaves the mind shaken; but it is clear that at this stage of its development poetry has reached the point of intense silence, its ultimate perfection. In the type of drama which Symbolism inspired, nobody so far has achieved this miracle, but several have tried to achieve it.

The Symbolists insisted often and emphatically that it is not necessary to understand in order to know; but this is not the sort of comment that is apposite to compositions of the type of "Un Coup de dés." In any case, it has little to do with Mallarmé. He wished very much to be understood, but not by everybody, and perhaps by nobody, an extremely shadowy presence. "All writings," he wrote, "should present an external meaning, even an indifferent meaning, if only to turn away the dabbler, charmed that, at first reading, there is nothing in it that concerns him." But they should have, he added, under the visible text, "an air or chant which might guide the imagination through the work and suggest what is really meant." Evidently he did not have in mind in this connection the *sovrasenso* of Renaissance poetry, which results in a kind of allegorical polyphony. What Mallarmé apparently intended was something that was implied by nothing in the text save the music of the words, an odor of significance which emanates from the poem without the possibility of localization.

There are as many interpretations of "Prose pour des Esseintes" as there are interpreters, and no one has so far managed to secure a hold on "Un Coup de dés." To attempt an interpretation of these works is doubtless to do them a disservice. The same may be said of much of the drama of Ionesco, Beckett, Pinter, and Arrabal. Ambiguity is an essential element of this genre. A great part of the pleasure of this art, when it is pleasurable, is its elusiveness. It is coy. Whatever it does is done, not to limit the apprehension, but to open all possible avenues of approach. The result, often enough, is an insoluble riddle, and this is the vital secret of much of this work, for a riddle once solved no longer exists, and many of these plays, if we knew what they meant, would disappear. It is entirely possible that the riddling element in language is essential to its use in poetry. In comparing language with other methods of communication, Lewis Thomas writes, in clearer terms than Mallarmé, but to somewhat the same effect:

> If it were not for the capacity for ambiguity, for the sensing of strangeness that words in all languages provide, we would have no way of recognizing the layers of counterpoint in meaning, and we might be spending all our time sitting on stone fences, staring into the sun. To be sure, we would always have had some everyday use to make of the alphabet, and we might have reached the same capacity for small talk, but it is unlikely that we would have been able to evolve from words to Bach. The great thing about human language is that it prevents us from sticking to the matter in hand.[55]

In his effort to interpret the imagery of "Prose pour des Esseintes," Mallarmé's young disciple Théodor de Wyzéwa routinely noted that the poem was an attempt to pierce the veil of appearance and to see, through the contingencies of the material world, the reality that lies beyond it. With respect to Mallarmé, he added:

> He admits the reality of the world, but he admits it as a reality of fiction. Nature, with its intriguing fairyland, its changing spectacle, rapid and colored with clouds, and the bustle of human societies, these are the dreams of the Soul: but dreams, are they not real?[56]

Most likely, for Mallarmé, as for Strindberg, the dreamworld was quite as convincing as any other. He seems to have willingly relinquished what Freud calls the reality principle, and he even called—perhaps seriously—for the foundation of an association of dreamers, with an official publication for the reporting of newsworthy dream-events, since the dreamworld needed only a social consensus to become as real as the reality of those who are awake.[57]

Dreams are obviously sensual experiences; but their sensations have no material correlatives: they are wholly abstract. From the Symbolist viewpoint these experiences, with their extraordinary vividness and spontaneity, and their strange logic, came closer to the ultimate reality than anything in the world of matter, and the syntax of revery seemed closer to the primal language of humanity than the artificial constructions of the grammarian. It was, therefore, to revery and dream, and not to the stereotyped perceptions of waking life, that the Symbolist looked for a glimpse of reality. In the works of Symbolism the free association of images was cherished as the true basis of artistic design. Since the reality of material forms was considered to be the result of a collective fantasy—that is to say, a stereotype—it was considered that the individual imagination was a surer guide to truth. Consequently it was by the free exercise of this faculty that the visible world might in time be brought into a closer approximation of the ideal. It was through such reasoning that the ground was laid for the Surrealism of the time of Apollinaire and Breton.

The imagination, however, had as yet no proper language. There as yet existed, in Mallarmé's opinion, only the conventional forms of speech which centuries of mishandling had coarsened or defaced to the point where they were useful only for the exchange of stereotypes. Fantasy expressed itself in images. In translating these images into words Mallarmé took pains to mobilize, as he said, "the diverse lights of the mind around an idea." This involved not only a pictorial arrangement of words, but also a skilful disposition of verbal sonorities so that the words resonated both musically and chromatically. As early as 1866 Mallarmé told Coppée:

> What we must aim at particularly is that the words in the poem which are already enough in themselves so as not to receive any further external impression should reflect upon one another until they seem no longer to have their own color but to be only notes in a scale.

Symbolism, from the first, was deeply involved with music. The search for a new language in which to transcribe the life of the soul was initiated under Wagnerian influence. Mallarmé did not believe that the inner life was beyond the poet's reach; but many agreed that no single art could encompass its complexities. Wagner had suggested that what no single art could do, a synthesis of all the arts might accomplish, and to him it seemed that the music-drama provided the basis for just such a synthesis. Of all the arts, obviously, music comes closest to the condition of revery and it alone, in Wagner's opinion, moved in the sphere of Ideas. Walter Pater's felicitous phrase, "All art aspires to the condition of music" had special reference to painting—it occurs in his essay on Giorgione—but it was found most congenial by the Wagnerites, and it precipitated a polemic in Symbolist circles. Mallarmé was not especially interested in music; but Catulle Mendès and Villiers de l'Isle Adam had visited Wagner in Triebschen, and Dujardin had spent some time in Bayreuth shortly after Wagner's death in 1883. He was at the time twenty-three. His enthusiasm knew no bounds, and on his return to Paris he lost no time in founding *La Revue wagnérienne*. Through its influence Symbolism and Wagnerism somehow became synonymous.

Mendès had tried to initiate Mallarmé in the cult of Wagner as early as 1869, but Mallarmé heard Wagner's music for the first time when he was forty-five. On Good Friday in 1885 Dujardin and Huysmans took him to one of the Lamoureux concerts. He was deeply impressed. Six months later he wrote, "Richard Wagner: Rêverie d'un poète français." It was a most equivocal piece of appreciation.

In spite of their enthusiasm, none of Mallarmé's friends, with the exception of Dujardin, knew very much about Wagner or Wagner's theories. After the disastrous reception of *Tannhäuser* in Paris in 1861, Wagner's work was kept off the French stage until the 1890's. His theoretical writings, *Kunst und Revolution, Der Kunstwerk der Zukunft*, and *Oper und Drama*, were not yet available in French. In these years *La Revue wagnérienne* was the principal vehicle for the propagation of Wagnerian ideas in France; but since the ardent Wagnerites, Wyzéwa and Dujardin, were not quite sure of what these ideas were, they had no difficulty in adjusting the master's theories in accordance with their own views.

Whatever else he was, Wagner was a sincere revolutionist. The purpose of art, in his opinion, was the regeneration of mankind. It is through great works of art, he thought, that the eyes of men are opened and their hearts moved to bring about the changes on which the future of the race depends. It is, accordingly, the sacred task of the artist to evolve a new world-order in which the individual will be free of slavery and injustice. Thus art, at the present stage of evolution, must address itself primarily to the mind. It must "actualize all feeling in thought." The drama of the future, perhaps, will find it unnecessary to address itself to the intellect, and will turn once again from understanding to feeling, but for the present art must serve another purpose. In the 1860's and 1870's such ideas were taken seriously. They were the subject of the early correspondence of Ibsen and Brandes; two generations later they were echoed by Malevich, Mondrian, Kandinsky, and Breton. As for Mallarmé, he dreamed all his life of the *Oeuvre* through which all mankind would be united in the realization of its true identity.[58]

The Symbolists joined gladly in the artistic movement that was to transform the world. No one was quite sure how this was to happen; but obviously the goal was enlightenment. The Naturalists had also declared themselves on the side of revolution; they were largely socialists. But it seemed clear to the followers of Mallarmé that a far different approach to the world's problems was indicated from the snail-like advances of science or the painstaking imitations of representative art. "This honest and mediocre business of copying, all one's life, farms, geese and cabbage plants," Camille Mauclair wrote, "is it to arrive at this that the masters existed?"[59]

What was needed, evidently, was something world-shaking, a revelation of truth that would transform the souls of men like an act of grace. The only key to such a miracle, in the opinion of the Symbolists, was poetry, and particularly the poetry of the theatre.

Such ideas aroused extraordinary enthusiasm among the young men who attended Mallarmé's *mardis*, and they cheerfully dedicated themselves to the task of reforming the world through art. Mallarmé fully shared their ardor. He declared himself a Wagnerite and contributed generously to Dujardin's review. He was not, however, willing to accept Wagner's subordination of poetry to music in the *Gesamtkunstwerk* of the future. In his view music and poetry were inextricably allied; they were twin aspects of the same mental faculty, and, Janus-like, they looked two ways: "Music and letters are alternate faces, the one welcoming darkness, the other sparkling with certitude of the one, the only Phenomenon: I call it the Idea."[60]

In his essay on *Tannhäuser* Baudelaire had tried to demonstrate that the language of music is universally meaningful. But for Mallarmé the superiority of sound over speech in the communication of ideas was hardly demonstrable. It was arguable, of course, that music by reason of its abstract quality was capable of revealing relations that words could not reveal; but Ideas suggested in this manner seemed elusive. Music, in Mallarmé's view, was immanent in language. It was unnecessary to reduce poetry to the condition of musical sound. What was necessary was to elevate music to the plane of precise poetic utterance. This result could be achieved by retrieving those musical elements which poetry had lost. When this was done poetry would be music in its highest sense. In an essay called "Crise de vers" Mallarmé wrote that poetry "is the art of achieving the transposition of the symphony to the Book . . . For undeniably it is not from the elementary sonorities of brasses, strings and woodwinds, but from the intellectual word at its apogee that music results, amply and clearly, as the sum of the relationships that exist among all things."[61]

It was conceded, nevertheless, that words have sonorous qualities which through rhyme, assonance, alliteration, and other such devices might be organized and orchestrated in ways similar to those of the composer. Mallarmé thought of himself, it would seem, sometimes as a painter, sometimes as a composer, occasionally as a setter of precious stones, a jeweler. In his opinion words had tangible qualities. They were jewels, each with its special hue and brilliance. The fact that words also implied sound and had tonality made it necessary, of course, to take account of the melodic connotations of a line of verse; but this was not, as he saw it, the primary element of the poet's craft. The suggestion of Idea through tonal symbols was the special function of the composer, not the poet. The musical value of poetry was in proportion to the clarity with which it suggested the essential harmony of the universe. In this respect poetry had the advantage of music. *L'Après-midi d'un faune* might have been a revery played on a flute; in fact it was a flute-melody made into words so as to render wholly articulate what would be only partly intelligible as melody.

In *The Philosophy of Composition* Poe had sketched out a wholly scientific approach to this type of artifice, and both Verlaine and Swinburne developed the tonal properties of language with impressive virtuosity. But none of these had attempted to suggest through sound anything beyond mood and atmosphere. Baudelaire, on the other hand, had fashioned in his *Petits poèmes en prose* a poetic language "musical, but without measure and without rhyme, which was supple enough and sufficiently responsive to adapt itself to the lyric movements of the soul, the undulations of revery, and the levels of consciousness."[62] The success of Verlaine's *Romances sans paroles*, with their remarkable management of verbal sonority, led directly to the "instrumentalist school" of Symbolism. Its methods were carried to absurd lengths by René Ghil in *Le Traité du verbe*. In that curious work the theory of synaesthesia was applied systematically to language, sounds were assigned special hues and tints, and poetry was subjected to the same sort of technical criticism as painting.

Mallarmé's idea of the musical aspect of poetry was quite different from this. In his view it was through the proper use of symbols that the subject of poetry must be materialized *musicalement*, that is to say, by incantation, in the manner in which Coleridge suggested that the pleasure dome of Kubla Khan might be built in air. There was, for Mallarmé, no need of instrumentation to achieve this magic. Words would suffice. In speaking of the plays of Maeterlinck, in which the playwright attempted analogous feats of symbolic thaumaturgy, Mallarmé noted that the effect was achieved "to such a point that in this art where all becomes music in the real sense of the word, the intervention of an instrument, even so pensive an instrument as a violin, would annoy through its uselessness." [63]

The Wagnerian influence on Symbolism, nevertheless, was very strong, the more so in the light of recently elaborated theories of synaesthesia and the *Esthétique scientifique* of Charles Henry. As Symbolist drama developed it tended to make much use of music and spectacle, and the idea rapidly gained ground that the ultimate art would be synthetic, a dramatic presentation that combined all the arts in a harmonious unity that would constitute a new art. In an essay entitled "The Symbolism of Poetry," Yeats noted

> All sounds, all colours, all forms, either because of their pre-ordained
> energies or because of long association, evoke indefinable and yet pre-
> cise emotions. . . . When sound and colour and form are in a musical
> relation to one another they become, as it were, one sound, one colour,
> one form, and evoke an emotion that is made out of their distinct evoca-
> tions and yet is one emotion. [64]

The writing of "literature" necessarily entailed a reformation of the language, but Mallarmé did not advocate anything like a complete break with tradition. It was his aim, rather, to return poetry, as well as the other arts, to its origins, that is to say, to the native sources of the cultural tradition. It was a program in some ways analogous to that proposed by Wordsworth almost a century earlier in the preface of 1800 to the *Lyrical Ballads*, but Mallarmé made no effort to return to the natural simplicity which Wordsworth had admired in the speech of the English peasantry. What he had in mind, apparently, was an attempt to reproduce in words the order of thought as it came to mind before the learned disciplines of the schools distorted it into the forms of grammar. It was, indeed, a step toward what came to be called Surrealism.

To his more enthusiastic adherents, however, his program suggested more draconian methods of reform. They felt it necessary to destroy all traditional aesthetic concepts. "The essence of art," Remy de Gourmont declared, "is liberty. Art can admit of no code, nor can it submit itself to the obligatory expression of the Beautiful." Such views, violently romantic, were hardly consonant with the ideas of Mallarmé for whom art was essentially formal, and the Ideal indistinguishable from the beautiful. Laforgue, too, had written in terms which came closer to Naturalism than to Idealism: "The Beautiful Ideal, and the beautiful works in literature, philosophy (systems), poetry, painting, sculpture and the hierarchy of Genres, all that is a legend of mediocre minds, perpetuated by the authority of mediocre people."[65]

Laforgue was destined to exert a considerable influence on the development of twentieth-century literature, more particularly on its more extreme manifestations, but the Symbolists did not know his theoretical writings until after his death in 1887. In spite of its revolutionary vigor, the art of the 1880's broke very reluctantly with tradition. It was innovative, beyond doubt, but it clung to its cultural inheritance with the tenacity of a French *rentier*. When in 1890 Albert Aurier wrote in the *Mercure de France* that van Gogh, whose work he had seen at the Galérie Goupil, "regards colors primarily as a fantastic language, a means of interpreting and visualizing ideas," he drew an indignant denial from the painter. He would prefer, van Gogh replied, "to be a cobbler rather than a musician of colors," and, apropos of an article reviewing the avant-garde exhibition of *Les XX* in Brussels, he wrote Aurier that he considered his work to be in the tradition of Delacroix, Millet, and Meissonier, and totally rejected any connection with Symbolism.[66]

The break with tradition was nevertheless taking place. In poetry it was clearly perceptible in the elaboration of new verse forms. Baudelaire had written poems in prose; Verlaine violated the sanctity of the Alexandrine; and after Verlaine, Laforgue, Régnier, and others began writing verse in irregular lines. Finally, free verse was introduced, perhaps by Gustave Kahn. These developments made Mallarmé uneasy. He feared that with the breakdown of form, and the loss of meaning, poetry might become simply a suggestive art.

Similar ferments were at work in the other arts. In painting, hyperbole, reduction, distortion, and grimace were rapidly transforming the representation of nature into an art of caricature. Portrait painters, increasingly aware of the encroachments of photography, gave up likeness as a criterion of success, and concentrated instead on individual reflections of a psychological nature. The Impressionists had been concerned mainly with light. Those who followed them emphasized design, volumes, forms, and structures modeled in color, which bore only a theoretical resemblance to the traditional forms of nature.

Secure in the reflection that the world was his representation, the artist set about valiantly to create reality in his own image, and, free of external restraint, composed and recomposed his impressions with the spontaneity of a dreamer. The way was now open for every type of aesthetic vagary and, as all artistic forms were judged to be of equal validity, reality became—at least in theory—an expression of the artist's sensibility. The Cubists depicted the outerworld as a kaleidoscope of jagged patterns which represented, presumably, the elements of its essential structure. The Futurists stressed motion as the essence of being. The Expressionists practised a systematic deformation of the forms of nature in accordance with the *état d'âme* of the artist. There were dozens of other styles and genres, some of which barely survived identification. Meanwhile the outerworld, as an artistic concept, disintegrated into myriad parts, the sum of which did not make a whole.

In 1864, when he was twenty-two, Mallarmé had written Cazalis of the new poetic he was developing, a poetic which he could define "in these two words: *Peindre non la chose, mais l'effet qu'elle produit.*" The phrase was in fact prophetic of the art of the following generation. But those who followed went beyond Mallarmé. Mallarmé did not deny the outerworld. On the contrary, he was firmly convinced of its existence, though he had no faith in the validity of the impressions it made upon him. The following generation of artists, however, defined form in wholly subjective terms. Thus Vassily Kandinsky, at that time an Expressionist, wrote: "The form is the outer expression of the inner content. . . . Thus the spirit of the individual artist is mirrored in the form. The form bears the stamp of the personality." Such a statement seems, at first sight, not much different from Zola's "Art is a corner of nature seen through a temperament," or from Taine's idea that the artist's psychology is an essential element of the work of art. The difference is in the degree of autonomy which the artist arrogates to himself with relation to the outerworld. For Zola and for Taine art, however qualified, was an imitation of nature. For the Expressionists it was nature that imitated art.[67] Formulated in these terms the outerworld virtually ceased to exist for the artist, and wherever he looked he saw himself. The result, for many, was frightening. In the drama, particularly, from Maeterlinck to Ionesco the dominant emotion was fear.

The major tendency in the period following the death of Mallarmé in 1898 was the effort to reduce art to its first principles. It was, indeed, in just such terms that the *Décadents* had defined the task of the artist. In 1889 Erneste Raynaud wrote:

> We must restore to our impressions their originality, their primitive value; we must repudiate preconceived ideas and formulas. . . . We must learn to see, to judge for ourselves, and to express sincerely what we sincerely feel.
>
> The literature that is called "decadent" is above all a true and conscientious literature.[68]

A true and conscientious literature was also the aim of the contemporary Realists. But the two schools of art differed mainly in their conception of reality. From the common-sense viewpoint of the Realists, reality was everywhere save in dreams and madness. For the Idealists and Decadents it was nowhere else. Reality was the creation of the imagination. The two viewpoints seemed very far apart, but anything might be imagined, even common sense, and the two attitudes came in time to an accommodation. The solipsistic position of the early Symbolists soon proved to be untenable. It gave place quickly to the deification of the Idea. But the quest of the Idea led nowhere and when it was given up, there was nothing left but the material world to justify existence. Thus, sooner or later, most of the Symbolists came to terms in some fashion with external reality. Some arrived at an acceptable duality of attitude reminiscent of scholasticism; others at more banal positions. Aurier, for example, wrote that since objects had a material as well as an ideal aspect, there are two worlds—the phenomenal world of the senses, and the intuitive world created by the soul—and that since the latter borrows the forms of matter in order to translate itself, Realism and Idealism are compatible as two aspects of life. Remy de Gourmont revised his early views in similar fashion. In his view Idealism and Realism blended into one another. Wyzéwa, who had been among the most zealous of the young Idealists, eventually came to lament the baneful influence of German transcendentalism on the order and clarity of the French spirit.[69]

A literary genre was thus developed in which it was possible to combine Realism and Symbolism in a manner acceptable to a wider public than the Symbolists had so far been able to reach. But the relatively calm period that fostered the art of Gide, Proust, and Thomas Mann was interrupted by the turbulence of the war years and the political changes consequent upon them. In the new totalitarian states art was considered a cultural resource at the service of the government. In Germany, under National Socialism, the museums were given a thorough housecleaning and all "degenerate" art from van Gogh to Kandinsky was consigned to the cellars. In 1937 *Das Haus des Deutschen Kunst* was opened, and the avant garde became an object of interest to the Ministry of the Interior. It was instructed to examine whether further inheritance of such gruesome malfunctioning of the eye could not at least be checked.

In the Soviet Union these procedures had been anticipated by the slowly evolving doctrine of "socialist realism." In 1924 Leon Trotsky published *Literature and Revolution*. It put art and technology on an equal footing as utilitarian activities in the service of the socialist state and made them subject, therefore, to government regulation. Experiments in pure form by such artists as Tatlin and Lipchitz, as well as the literary symbolism of writers like Blok, were considered useless aberrations in the march of progress toward the point where the whole world would be an artistic masterpiece. In France, under Trotsky's influence, the Surrealists formally dedicated themselves to the service of the social revolution. They were, however, not wholly acceptable to the Marxist program. In an official manifesto entitled "Aspects of Two Cultures" (1947) Vladimir Kemenov attacked "formalistic" art and letters, especially the "wretched, pathological and deformed" art of Picasso, and defined the type of artistic activity which was worthy of the great Stalin epoch:

> As opposed to decadent bourgeois art with its falseness, its rejection of a realistic truthful reflection of life as it is, Soviet artists present the wholesome and integral art of socialist realism, expressed in profound artistic images reflecting true life, showing the struggle between the old and the new and the inevitable triumph of the new and progressive, an art mobilizing Soviet people for further victories.
>
> As opposed to decadent bourgeois art, divorced from the people, hostile to the interests of the democratic masses, permeated with biological individualism and mysticism, reactionary and anti-popular, Soviet artists present an art created for the people inspired by the thoughts, feelings and achievements of the people, and which in turn enriches the people with its lofty ideas and noble images.[70]

Socialist realism brought up sharply once again the question of the relation of form and substance in literature and in the graphic and plastic arts. Zola had written in 1880: "If you desire my true opinion upon this subject, it is this: that today an exaggerated importance is given to form . . . We are actually rotten with lyricism; we are very much mistaken when we think that the characteristic of a good style is a sublime confusion with just an added touch of madness; in reality, the excellence of a style depends on its logic and clarity."[71]

In the tussle between Realism and Symbolism in the free countries it was, strangely enough, the Realists who gave way. Instead of being coldly scientific and practical minded in its bourgeois environment, art became more and more deeply involved with the inner life of the artist. In poetry this brought about a revaluation of language; in painting a reconsideration of visual symbols; in the theatre a reappraisal of form and function. In the theatre of the 1950's the line that divided Brecht from Ionesco was charged with fire, but both writers were, at bottom, Symbolists.

The obsession with form which had so deeply troubled Mallarmé had also brought the "realist" Flaubert to the verge of madness, and his painstaking pursuit of the word led him to a negation of everything but form. Like Mallarmé, Flaubert was driven by "the demon of analogy," so that he arrived more than once at a position much like Mallarmé's, a position far removed, indeed, from the doctrine of *Le Roman expérimental*. In 1857 he wrote to Mlle. de Chantepie:

> Art must rise above personal emotions and nervous susceptibilities. The time has come to endow it with pitiless method, with the exactness of the physical sciences. Yet for me the great difficulty remains style, form, that indefinable beauty resident in the concept, which represents, as Plato wrote, the splendor of truth. . . .

Five years before, in 1852, he had written to Louise Colet:

> The most beautiful works are those in which there is the least matter; the more closely the expression approximates thought, the more completely the word merges with the idea and disappears in it, the more beautiful the result. I believe the future of art lies in this direction. . . . Form, as it evolves, becomes progressively attenuated; it abandons all liturgy, all rules, all measure; it deserts the epic for the novel, and verse for prose; it no longer recognizes any orthodoxy, and becomes as free as the individual will that shapes it. This liberation from matter may be

seen everywhere, for instance in the evolution of governments, from the despotisms of the Orient to the socialist states of the future.

That is why there are neither beautiful nor ugly subjects, and why one might lay down as an axiom, from the standpoint of pure art that there is no such thing as subject, style being itself an absolute way of seeing things.[72]

The emphasis on style at the expense of substance implied that the shape of things is ultimately dependent on the subjectivity of the observer, an individualistic attitude which would hardly recommend itself to a society which stressed above all the interests of the collective. The issue boiled down to the age-long conflict of the individual and society; but underlying this conflict was the fundamental question of the nature of reality. The formalism that results from the quest for the exact word and the precise analogy has for its purpose not the exact representation of an external nature which is the same for all, but the exhibition of the artist's private reality, in terms of which he constructs the world around him. In this work, obviously, style is everything. Two generations after Flaubert, Giraudoux took for his own the slogan: "Tout est dans le style."

The construction of an acceptable reality was, indeed, the chief preoccupation of art in the decades around the turn of the century, a period during which the nations of Europe busily prepared themselves for mutual destruction. From the time of Baudelaire both Realists and Idealists had treated nature as if it were a recalcitrant informant undergoing interrogation. But as neither approach succeeded in eliciting anything convincing by way of an answer, it became progressively evident that perhaps there was nothing to be gained by prolonging the examination. Nature, as a subject, was relinquished to the scientists, and as the outerworld ceased to sit for its portrait, the speculum of art increasingly became a portrait of the artist, his moods, his dreams, and even his convictions. The mirror was wide. It accommodated everything from "Guernica" to *Krapp's Last Tape*.

In these circumstances, myth and primitive art achieved unusual interest as a means of acquiring insight into the workings of the primary faculty which civilization presumably obscured. Following the example of Mallarmé, poets began to treat language as a material substance of more or less plastic consistency, that could be molded like glass, or modeled like clay, spread on a surface like pigment, or even thrown on the wheel into useful shapes. It became commonplace to think of a poem as an artifact as, indeed, the troubadours had thought of it long ago. Meanwhile,

in the time of the Great War the absurdity of the artistic enterprise became painfully evident to those who had already reconciled themselves
to the absurdity of everything else. The result was Dada.

The justification of *l'art pour l'art* involved, on the one hand, the liberation of art from its servitude to practical ends and, on the other, the extension of artistic activity as a means of self-knowledge. Pure art was justified on the same basis as pure science, as an important human activity,
self-justified, but which might one day come in handy. The attack on the
utilitarian basis of art had not begun with Baudelaire; but Baudelaire had
made it explicit for his time. In 1861 he had written, in terms which
would infuriate the Soviet theoreticians of a later age:

> Most people assume that the object of poetry is some sort of instruc-
> tion, that it must either fortify the conscience or perfect manners, or, in
> sum, demonstrate something useful. . . . Poetry, however little one de-
> scends into the self, or interrogates the soul, or recalls memories of
> one's enthusiasm, has no object but itself. It can have no other object,
> and no poem will be so great, so noble, so truly worthy of the name of
> poetry, as that which was written solely for the pleasure of creating a
> poem.[73]

Oscar Wilde, a generation later, added some resonant phrases: "No
artist desires to prove anything. . . . All art is quite useless."[74] Such
ideas found little support in the troubled times to come, and least of all
in the theatre. For Artaud art was not a game, but a form of social therapy. For Ionesco, as for Beckett, it was the result of an irresistible inner
need commensurate with the need to breathe, that is to say, a means of
survival in a world that did not otherwise justify existence. In the absence of such peremptory needs, the conception of the artist as a manu-
facturer of expensive bibelots inevitably brought up the question of the
desirability of adding to the clutter of objects in a world that was already
at a loss for storage space. The result was a progressive disparagement of
the idea of art, so that the painter gave less thought to the permanence of
his materials, and writers rarely labored over matters of form, since
nothing they made would escape obsolescence in a world that was perhaps drawing to an end. In fiddling a little while the world went up in
flames it was praiseworthy no doubt to play well; but it was not essential.

Symbolism began as a quest for meaning in a world that, in the last
years of the nineteenth century, no longer seemed to have any. The

quest, obviously, ended in failure; but the effort was far from fruitless. In France, Valéry, Proust, Gide, and Giraudoux, and, in England, Yeats, Joyce, and Eliot, brought about something like a renaissance of letters, and there were important repercussions in Italy and in Spain, and even some reflections in America. But even before the Second World War it was apparent that the movement that Mallarmé had fostered was undergoing a radical transition.

The most enduring aspect of the Symbolist program was the desire to recover for art and for language the emotional potential of their origins. By the turn of the century primitivism was the order of the day. In the Salon d'Automne of 1905 the work of the worthy douanier Rousseau was proudly exhibited alongside the canvases of Matisse, Derain, Vlaminck, and Rouault. In an effort to renew the language of painting the art of the remote past and of aboriginal cultures was ransacked for inspiration and for models. The result was a new romanticism, together with a bewildering confusion of styles and modes. In the period between wars much attention was centered upon the Unconscious, not the metaphysical Unconscious of Schopenhauer and von Hartmann, but the Unconscious of Freud and Jung. With this came a resurgence of faith in the value of free association, and of accident and chance as artistic resources—ideas that Mallarmé had already enunciated with some emphasis. Accordingly, artists manifested a widespread desire to do away with calculation, contrivance, preconceived design, and the rational control of thought and expression. The end-product of these tendencies was the unfolding of a type of art that was seldom far from madness. It was an art which, having plumbed, as far as it could, the depths of the psyche, came up with tidings that occasionally inspired terror, but more often pity, and was in this sense tragic.

In the early days of Symbolism Saint-Pol-Roux had written:

> I say that the temples of the future will be theatres: theatres having nothing in common, it is necessary to add, with these "conventicles of stupidity" which the greater part of our playhouses represent, where craft counts for much and art for nothing. I consider, therefore, the Theatre of tomorrow as the most powerful, perhaps the only means of social renewal.
>
> The art of the theatre is the art through which man dares to rival God. God creates. The dramatic work which brings no dowry, and does not affirm itself a creation, must be classed as a miscarriage. It

belongs to the dramatic poet to be the total poet, in the Greek sense of the word, the creator.[75]

The drama was, in fact, among the first of the arts to feel the influence of Symbolism. By 1900 all the major dramatists of Europe were in one way or another Symbolists—Ibsen, Strindberg, Chekhov, Hauptmann, Yeats, Synge, even Shaw. But not all of these writers would have accepted the designation and, with the exception of Yeats, none had any direct relation with Mallarmé or with his immediate circle. The first of the French Symbolists to reach the stage was Maeterlinck. He was a Belgian.

MAETERLINCK

In the spring of 1887 André An-
toine opened the doors of his tiny theatre in the Impasse de l'Elysée des
Beaux Arts on the Butte Montmartre, and Naturalism made its debut on
the French stage. From the first the fortunes of the Théâtre-libre were
precarious. When Antoine inaugurated his second season across the river
in the little playhouse in Montparnasse, he began with a list of thirty-five
subscribers, most of them personally solicited on street corners or in
cafés. But Antoine was both dedicated and persistent. In the six years of
its existence his theatre established the Naturalist drama in France. In
addition it extended its hospitality to a number of distinguished for-
eigners whose plays the commercial managers would not touch, among
them Ibsen, Turgenev, Björnson, Hauptmann, Strindberg. In 1884,
when Antoine closed his theatre and went on to greener pastures at the
Odéon, the phrase, *ce n'est pas du théâtre*, which had served so long as a
term of condemnation, had acquired new significance as a term of praise.

Symbolism came to the stage with greater difficulty, but with more
grandiose expectations. "The drama is an inferior art," Charles Morice
wrote in 1905, "unless it is the supreme art. . . . I believe that the logical development of the modern spirit will give us back the theatre *soon*,
under the conditions which are properly its own, of a social art."[1] These
ambitious hopes came to nothing. The theatre of the boulevard remained
staunchly commercial, and the state-supported theatres resisted the
temptation to become the temples of the future. There was, indeed,
something faintly absurd in the efforts of these little bands of bohemians
to break down the formidable barriers of the professional theatre.

In his youth Mallarmé had dreamed of writing a play which would
transform the theatre of his time into a sacred precinct. In his opinion

the essence of drama was the confrontation of man and nature. The definition was perfectly general, but it is likely that Mallarmé understood the essential dramatic conflict in terms of the spiritual struggle that he had himself undergone in the course of his love affair with Marie Gerhard whom, after considerable soul-searching, he married. *Hérodiade* has to do with the plight of a beautiful girl whose absorption in the ideal causes her to reject life and love. *Le Monologue d'un faune* (1865), the first version of his masterpiece, was intended to stage the revery of a faun who had vainly attempted to ravish a pair of elusive nymphs.[2] Théodore de Banville had liked the idea of the *Faune* and had undertaken, somewhat hastily, to present it at the Comédie-Française; but when the composition was submitted Coquelin thought it lacked dramatic action, and Banville changed his mind. Mallarmé turned once again to poetry: "I am relegating my subject to a drawer for several months," he wrote Cazalis, "to be fully rewritten later . . . and I am beginning *Hérodiade*, no longer a tragedy but a poem . . . especially as in this way I acquire the whole attitude, the costumes, the settings, and the furniture, to say nothing of the mystery."[3]

The play of the future, he concluded, would be in the nature of an ode, a dramatic monologue with a single character. This accorded with his idea of Hamlet, a character he greatly admired, whose inability to act he associated with his own inability to write. *Hamlet*, as he understood the play, was essentially a dream-play:

> The play, a culminating point in the history of the drama, marks in the work of Shakespeare a transition between the old multiple action and the Monologue, or drama with the Self, of the future. The hero, comprising everything in himself, walks about, no more, reading in the book of himself, a high and living sign, denying with his glance the existence of others. He is not content to express, among the others, the solitude of the thinker; he kills with indifference, or, at least, people die because of him. . . .[4]

Mallarmé's idea of theatre, however, was less eccentric than this passage suggests. He admired Villiers's *Axël*, was deeply impressed by Maeterlinck's *Pelléas et Mélisande*, and praised Jarry's *Ubu roi*. The Symbolist drama, it developed, would have much to do with dreams, but these dreams would involve considerably more stage business than Mallarmé had originally thought necessary. It was not, indeed, until the time of Beckett that the play of the future took the form of a monologue.

Villiers de l'Isle Adam had written several plays along Symbolist lines before he wrote *Axël*—there were *Elën* (1865), *Morgane* (1866), and, later, *La Révolte* (1870). *Axël* was published, in part, in 1872. It could not have been seriously intended for the stage, and was only partly playable. When Lugné produced it in 1894 its difficulties were painfully evident. It is a sort of Gothic novel, complete with the traditional accoutrements—an ancient castle, a siege, a duel, buried treasure, and the rest—but it centers, like *Hérodiade*, on the relation of the ideal to the real, with prejudice to the latter, and in some sense it heralds the plays of Maeterlinck.

Mallarmé had defined the drama as "the confrontation of the human being, endowed with consciousness, and nature"—an entity presumably free of this embarrassment. The conception, however poetically expressed, was familiar. It involved the incompatibility of the two aspects of man, the physical and the spiritual, the body and the soul. Mallarmé saw this as an inner struggle, best expressed in poetry, as a monologue or, at the most, as dialogue. In the theatre, however, an idea of this sort would normally be dramatized in terms of a conflict of characters, or of groups of characters, as a conflict of nations, or even of worlds. It was, in fact, along just such lines that the new drama developed. The confrontation of man and nature provided the theme of most of Maeterlinck's plays, and nearly all of Giraudoux's; indeed, it became the characteristic theme of Symbolist drama up to the time of Ionesco.

In 1886 Mallarmé undertook the post of drama critic on *La Revue indépendante*, at that time under the editorship of Dujardin. Mallarmé had come by this time under the spell of Wagner. He readily adopted the official position that before Wagner the theatre was moribund.

It was the ritualistic aspect of the Wagnerian music-drama, its ceremonial grandeur, as well as its ability to arouse emotion on a grand scale, that captured the imagination of the Symbolists. Wagner, Dujardin wrote in a retrospective article in *La Revue musicale* of October 1923, had rediscovered the antique mode; he had succeeded in transforming the theatre once again into the temple of Dionysos. But the Wagnerian mode, as we have seen, did not entirely please Mallarmé. He objected to the use of myth in the drama because it was not essentially French; to the use of actors because they intruded their presence between the poet and the auditor; and to the use of spectacle because it distracted the mind from the revery which it was the function of the dramatic poem to induce. In his view the ideal drama would be a recital by a single actor in which the music of the word would replace the sound of instruments in the pit. The ballet, in his opinion, would have greater dramatic possibilities than the synthetic work, since it involved a kind of writing in space, "capable of carrying the fleeting and the sudden as far as the Idea."

Unfortunately his own efforts to demonstrate these theories in the theatre were unsuccessful. *L'Après-midi d'un faune* reached the stage, but only in the form of a ballet choreographed by Nijinsky to the music of Debussy; and neither *Hérodiade* nor *Igitur* was developed into forms even remotely suitable for stage presentation. Much the same might be said of those of his disciples who tried at this time to write for the theatre. The drama of the 1880's was primarily a narrative medium. The Symbolist mode was lyric. Racine, in his time, had very effectively combined the two modes, but the Symbolists were striking out in another direction. Villiers, Dujardin, Péladan, Saint-Pol-Roux, Édouard Schuré, all tried their hand at the new drama. But before Maeterlinck nobody managed to fuse these elements effectively on the stage.

For a time, nevertheless, the Symbolist position with regard to the theatre remained ambitious. It was never clear; and what was written to clarify it did little to dispel its uncertainty. In 1886 Gustave Kahn issued what amounted to a Symbolist manifesto for the drama.

> We wish to substitute for the conflict of individuals the conflict of feelings and ideas; and for the environment of the action, instead of a décor abstracted from streets and crossroads, the mind itself in whole or in part. The essential goal of an art is to objectify the subjective (the externalization of the Idea) instead of subjectifying the objective (nature seen through a temperament). Analogous reflections have created the multitonic sound of Wagner and the latest techniques of the Impressionists. It is an addition of literature to the scientific theories constructed through induction and controlled by the experiments of M. Charles Henry. . . . These theories are founded purely on the philosophic basis of idealism which makes us reject completely the reality of matter, and which admits the existence of the world only as representation.[5]

This formulation anticipated by something like a half-century the *fuite à l'intérieur* of the writers of the Théâtre de la Chimère, and the second flowering of Symbolism in the theatre. The net effect of drama based on such theory would be to represent reality as a shadow-play, a projection of the inner life of the individual. To this extent it anticipated Expressionism. "Let us push the analysis of self to the extreme," Kahn had written some months earlier in *La Vogue*. "Let us constitute the fairyland of literature by annulling the mode of a forced and intellectual modernism; let us compose a personal vocabulary on all levels of the work, and strive to escape from the banality of the traditional molds."[6] It was along these lines that Maeterlinck proceeded.

The renaissance of the French theatre took place slowly on the periphery of the thriving commercial enterprise that supplied the popular audience with nightly entertainment on an impressive scale. In the 1880's Scribe was considered old-fashioned, but French drama was dominated by his spiritual descendants. Great stars—Bernhardt, Réjane, the two Coquelins, Mounet-Sully, Gôt, Worms—determined the fortunes of the theatre. Such gifted writers as Brieux, Octave Mirbeau, Porto-Riche, Curel, Lavedan, Lemaitre, Hervieu, and Donnay supplied estimable plays which demonstrated fine workmanship and also the influence of new and progressive ideas. From the viewpoint of the avant garde the theatre was dead.

In fact, a style of playwriting was evolving that reconciled the Scribean mode with the more austere manner which the school of Zola was propounding. In general, clarity and movement were of the essence of the commercial theatre. The boulevard writers applied themselves to more or less serious questions which could be developed in carefully contrived situations involving some element of the *mirabile* without putting an undue strain on the mentality of an audience which came to the theatre mainly for distraction. The result was a dramatic genre with a socially meaningful subject, a relatively complex plot, extensive type-characterization, and a style of dialogue which did not unduly exaggerate the forms of cultivated speech.

Antoine had established the Théâtre-libre in the sincere hope of bringing to the stage some measure of artistic integrity. He was, to begin with, an amateur actor. Edmond de Goncourt described him as a "slight, frail, nervous fellow with a rather debauched looking nose, and soft, velvety, altogether seductive eyes. . . . It is a real pleasure to listen to this young Antoine who admits with a certain modesty that women are mad about him. You feel from his brilliant, hallucinated eyes that he believes in his work. There is something of the evangelist in this actor."[7]

His first bill of one-act plays, presented on 31 March 1887, found, as might be expected, small favor in Symbolist circles. The following year, however, he produced Tolstoy's *The Power of Darkness*, and the Symbolists began to pay him some attention. In its issue of 27 August 1888, *La Revue indépendante* printed a translation of *A Doll's House*, and in October of that year a translation of *Ghosts*. Antoine presented *Ghosts* in 1890. The following year he produced *The Wild Duck*. The line that divided Realism from Symbolism was rapidly becoming indistinct. Evidently there was need for a purely Symbolist theatre.

In 1890 Louis Germain founded Le Théâtre idéaliste, a venture specifically intended to provide the Symbolist writers with an audience. The same year, Paul Fort, at the age of eighteen, joined with Germain in establishing Le Théâtre mixte. It was conceived as a reaction against the naturalistic tendency which Antoine was supporting in his rapidly expanding Théâtre-libre. In 1891 Fort instituted Le Théâtre d'art, dedicated to "the revelation of the miracle of daily life and the sense of mystery in it." This provided a stage for poetic readings, and also mounted a few productions, among them Shelley's *The Cenci* and Maeterlinck's *L'Intruse* and *Les Aveugles*. Fort was now joined by one of Antoine's principal associates, Aurélien Lugné, at this time a youth of twenty-one, who claimed some family relationship to Edgar Allan Poe, and therefore hyphenated his name as Lugné-Poë. With the aid of Camille Mauclair and the painter Vuillard, Lugné-Poë proceeded to organize Le Théâtre de l'oeuvre. Its purpose was "to make of the theatre in whatever way possible a Work of Art, or at least to stir up some ideas."[8]

Le Théâtre de l'oeuvre lasted thirty-seven years, from 1893 to 1930, always under Lugné's management. After the closing of Le Théâtre-libre in 1893 it was, for a time, the only art-theatre in Paris. Professedly, it was anti-Naturalist and anti-Realist; but the choice of Symbolist plays was embarrassingly small, and it became necessary for Lugné to broaden the scope of his productions, and even the nature of his mise en scène. Lugné presented plays by Maeterlinck, Régnier, Rachilde, Verhaeren, and Claudel; in addition he brought to Paris—as Antoine had done—a number of eminent plays which could not gain access to the state theatres, much less to the commercial stage, plays by Ibsen, Oscar Wilde, Jarry, Gide, Crommelynck, and Salacrou. His initial contribution, however, was the introduction of the plays of Maurice Maeterlinck, at that time the chief proponent of the Symbolist drama. The opening performance of Le Théâtre de l'oeuvre, 17 May 1893, was Maeterlinck's *Pelléas et Mélisande*.

Maurice Maeterlinck came to Paris in 1886. He was introduced into Mallarmé's circle by Villiers, whom he had met by chance at a café. Like

Villiers he was an admirer of Poe and of Baudelaire, and the mystical aspects of Symbolism, as he came to know it, were very congenial to his temper. He was of a religious turn of mind, much inclined to the type of pantheism that was then in vogue—the idea that a single mysterious force pervades the universe, of which the soul of man is a manifestation. Moreover, like Carlyle, he felt that the mystical communion of man with man, and of man with the universe, takes place in silence. The moment something is expressed, Maeterlinck wrote, it is strangely diminished. "The true life, and the only life that leaves any trace, is made only of silence." [9]

When Maeterlinck returned from Paris to his native Ghent in 1889 he was thoroughly imbued with Symbolist ideas. He now published his first volume of poetry, *Serres chaudes*, a collection of pieces which clearly reflected the influence of Baudelaire. *La Princesse Maleine*, his first play, was also published that year. It was 1890. The following year he published *Les Aveugles* and *L'Intruse*, and, the year after, *Les Sept princesses*. *Pelléas et Mélisande* appeared in 1892.

Four years later he brought out the collection of essays entitled *Le Trésor des humbles* (1896) in which he made clear the theoretical basis of his work for the theatre. It was a position which, in fact, he later abandoned as impractical; but the views he expressed at this time were destined to play an important role in the development of the drama. In 1896 it was his idea that the tragic mood is essentially contemplative, a meditation best induced by a quiet and static situation rather than by a bustle of plot and movement. The fundamental theme of drama was, as Mallarmé had intimated, the confrontation of man and the universe, a relation that was inevitably tragic for the individual. This fact was observable everywhere and at every turn. It was unnecessary to look for tragedy in great events and unusual personages. Tragedy could be found in ordinary happenings, among ordinary people.

These views were exemplified in *L'Intruse* and *Intérieur;* but *La Princesse Maleine*, the first example of Symbolist drama to excite attention, was not at all of this character. It was a nightmare, the horror of which went far beyond anything the Naturalistic theatre had so far ventured to depict. *La Princesse Maleine* is set in the landscape of early romanticism, the world of "old, unhappy far-off things." It tells a story of innocent children and wicked parents, a fairy tale. The lovely little princess Maleine escapes from the ruined tower where she is held captive, and goes to join her beloved Hjalmar. He has been told she is dead, and is now betrothed to the princess Uglyane. This lady's mother, Anne of Jutland, is an extremely wicked woman. She has designs on young Hjalmar and is at the same time involved with the old king, his father. When she learns that Maleine is hidden among the attendants of Uglyane, she attempts to have the girl poisoned. This fails. Then, with the help of the king, her lover, she strangles Maleine in her bed. In revenge, Hjalmar stabs the wicked queen to death, and afterwards kills himself. The old king survives them all, in a state of imbecility.

In this Gothic cocktail, elements of Elizabethan blood-tragedy are blended with folk-motifs in an obvious attempt to recreate the atmosphere of primitive myth. The dialogue has none of the richness of the Elizabethan genre, nor yet the straightforward artlessness of the brothers Grimm. On the contrary, it has a peculiarly child-like quality, allusive and mysterious, apparently calculated to operate on a level well below the intellectual plane. It is possible that this childish prattle was intended to approximate what Mallarmé had called "the language of humanity brought back to its essential rhythm." But Maeterlinck was in fact a poet, and his language, while disconcertingly simple and naive, is also strangely resonant and musical.

Émile Chasles's *Note sur la philologie appliquée*, published in 1865, had by this time gained considerable ground in Symbolist circles. It included a discussion of the special properties of elementary sounds, phonemes which had in the course of time lost their purity. The linguistic reforms which Mallarmé had advocated entailed, it is clear, not only a thorough laundering of the vocabulary, but also the rediscovery of the verbal magic of primitive speech. Maeterlinck did not imitate Mallarmé. In the dialogue of his Symbolist plays he concentrated on language calculated to work on the emotions in accordance with the principles of sound-coloring which Poe had set forth so convincingly in *The Philosophy of Composition*, and which Chasles had more recently elaborated in his study. He was singularly successful. In reducing the speech of his characters to the point where it made the effect of song rather than sense, Maeterlinck managed to suggest something of the eternal silence that the human voice barely serves to accentuate. Thus, in spite of the manifest puerility of its narrative and its characters, *La Princesse Maleine* brought to the theatre an authentic strain of poetry which it long had lacked. It is not tragedy, obviously, in the sense that *Agamemnon* and *Hamlet* are tragedies. It was, in some sense a new genre, and perhaps not entirely respectable. Some years later, when Strindberg wrote *Swanwhite* in rather obvious imitation, he felt it necessary to give his fairy tale a naturalistic turn.

Octave Mirbeau, in his celebrated review of the play in the *Figaro* of

24 August 1890, wrote that *La Princesse Maleine* was "the most highly inspired work of the time and also the most extraordinary and naive, comparable and—I dare say it—superior in beauty to whatever is most beautiful in Shakespeare." Mirbeau was a Symbolist. But it is possible to understand his enthusiasm. *La Princesse Maleine* is in no sense great drama; but it succeeds in conveying something of the play of inexplicable forces in an inexplicable universe. From a rational viewpoint it is, undeniably, an absurdity, something with which to frighten children. But it is to the child in us that it was addressed, an entity that is fastidious in a very special way.

In 1891 Maeterlinck told Huret, "When I wrote *La Princesse Maleine* I said to myself, I will try to write a play in Shakespeare's manner for a theatre of marionettes."[10] The implication is that in playing tragedy with puppets the author is not only visibly reducing its scale, but also stressing the point that his characters are pulled about by invisible strings. There is no hint of supernatural forces in *La Princesse Maleine*. The motives that bring about the catastrophe are the normal motives of Renaissance tragedy—love, lust, jealousy, ambition—all working with their customary precision toward a denouement that makes no sense. Apart from the disparity in style, the difference between this play and its seventeenth-century counterparts is in the framework of reality that supports the action. Plays like *The Maid's Tragedy* or *Philaster* take place in a moral universe under the scrutiny of a just God. In such plays all transgressors are guaranteed divine retribution. Thus the dramatist is able to give the most improbable situation some measure of credibility in terms of its moral structure, and the action becomes believable at least as an exemplum. Maeterlinck, however, assumes nothing of this sort. In his play there is neither God nor Providence. The action takes place in a moral void, which is also a metaphysical void, a world that anticipates the hopelessness of the world of Ionesco. All the characters are helpless in the hands of an inexplicable destiny, and whatever is done is the result of primitive motives of desire and passion that no one understands or ventures to question. In this sense the play is set on a cultural plane well below the level of plays like *Thérèse Raquin* and, insofar as it is believable at all, *La Princesse Maleine* represents a mood of more cruel pessimism than the Naturalists permitted themselves to display.

The play, however, is believable chiefly on the level of myth. The myth is, to be sure, artificial and clearly imitative, but it operates on the unconscious with the powerful simples of myth, the bad mother, the dangerous father, the innocent children, the menacing unknown, and the rest of the phantasms that people the underworld of dreams and are dimly reflected in the terrors of waking life.

It is perhaps no longer possible to take *La Princesse Maleine* with a sufficient degree of seriousness, but it is altogether possible to see what Maeterlinck had in mind to do. His play was meant to do in the theatre what the Symbolist poem was meant to do on the printed page. It was a fantasy intended to evoke emotion through symbols which have special meaning for those mental faculties which do not become adult. It was, in short, an attempt at primitivism—Mirbeau called it naive—that paralleled on the stage what was being attempted also in contemporary painting.

Pelléas et Mélisande was published in 1892. After Mirbeau's extravagant praise of *La Princesse Maleine* both Antoine and Lugné hastened to offer Maeterlinck a production in Paris. Maeterlinck chose Antoine. It was a mistake; for however eclectic Antoine might be in his tastes, as a director he was committed to a naturalistic mise en scène, and Maeterlinck fared badly at the Théâtre-libre. In 1891 Lugné's repertory had already included *L'Intruse* and *Les Aveugles;* but *Pelléas et Mélisande* was too big a production for his tiny Théâtre d'art.

On 17 May 1893 Le Théâtre de l'oeuvre opened triumphantly with a production of *Pelléas et Mélisande* at the Bouffes-Parisiens. The Symbolists acclaimed it; but it was not an unqualified success. The influential critic Sarcey favored it with a sneering review. Other critics were frankly puzzled. It was by this time possible to accept the obscurity of Symbolist poetry as the inevitable price of mystery and novelty, but on the stage obscurity was synonymous with ineptitude. In *Pelléas et Mélisande* one looked in vain for a decipherable allegory, and for the first time the drama critics were faced with a play that seemed to mean something, but in fact communicated no message. What could be heard in it was simply, *le chant mystérieux de l'infini*, a song distinctly without words.

Something of the sort might be said, of course, both of *Hamlet* and *Phèdre;* but by this time *Hamlet* and *Phèdre* had been pretty much rationalized out of existence. If Symbolism were to be taken seriously in the theatre, it appeared, the question raised by the great masterpieces would have to be reopened, and they might have to be seen in a new light. The possibilities were frightening. It was with great reluctance that the discussion was opened. By the time it had ended, both Shakespeare and Racine had taken on an unaccustomed look that was by no means com-

forting in the classroom, and the classic drama of the Greeks also assumed a look of disquieting mystery. *Pelléas et Mélisande* was certainly a
better play than *La Princesse Maleine*. It was no great masterpiece. It
was only that after it Western drama was never the same.

So long as realism was in vogue, clarity was the supreme goal of the
dramatic author. His function was to clarify existence, to reduce its elements to some semblance of order, and to reveal on the stage, as on a
canvas, the just and elegant line of God's creation. The beauty of a play,
accordingly, was in proportion to the cogency of its message. The Symbolist artist, however, had nothing in hand that he could render intelligible. At the core of Symbolism was the sense of mystery. Its drama,
like its poetry, was an exploration of the unknown. The Symbolist playwright, like the Symbolist poet, set his stage on the borders of the infinite, an untracked wilderness that presented serious problems for the
scene-designer as well as for the spectator.

Joséphin Péladan, the Sâr of the Rose-Croix, himself a dramatist,
expressed the Symbolist viewpoint quite explicitly in a passage of *L'Art
idéaliste et mystique:* "The essence of art is to figure forth the mystery, and
not to explain it; to render it present and conceivable, to produce it and
to unveil it. . . ." And elsewhere he added: "Mystery is the bread and
wine of man, and genius is the ability to feel it profoundly, and to reveal
it, that is to say, to make men aware of it."[11]

Péladan in his role of seer professed special insights into the supernatural, and special reasons for keeping his knowledge from the eyes of the
profane. Not all the Symbolists were Rosicrucians; and few shared the
certainties of the Sâr. For many, as for Mallarmé, the mystery of being
was both fascinating and impenetrable. But in all cases the occult remained opaque to the eye of reason, making it necessary for the poet to
turn from the logic of Aristotle to the logic of dreams and the processes
of the primitive mind, which associates images without recourse to causality and, having nothing definite to say, makes a fetish of ambiguity.

The desire to make explicit statements depends, obviously, on the assumption that there is something that can be stated explicitly, an assumption that implies some degree of human pride. By the time of Maeterlinck nothing was certain. Under such conditions ambiguity is the
only truth. Among the Symbolists, those who, like Claudel, were able to
find their way to a source of faith, regained the capacity to make clear
statements. For the rest there remained only the possibility of truth, a
vague territory, the direction of which might perhaps be indicated by a

gesture, or a silence, but certainly not by words. In general, Maeterlinck's plays were not based on a solid foundation of common sense,
but represented honestly a reality of which he was specially aware. He
saw neither very far, nor very clearly, into what he felt was the Beyond,
a landscape so dimly visible that no action could truthfully depict its details. But at least he could indicate the nature of his vision, and he could
handle its texture; and in this respect he foreshadowed Giraudoux, Ionesco, Pinter, and Beckett, that is to say, the major dramatists of our
time. Inevitably, he encountered resistance. It was to be expected. In
1937 Giraudoux had no difficulty in expressing his impatience with those
who insisted on understanding drama. In 1893 such a position was still
premature.

Three years after the opening of *Pélleas et Mélisande* Chekhov produced
The Sea Gull in Moscow (1896). It included not only a parody of the
Symbolist style in drama, but also a compassionate depiction of the
reception of Trofimov's little Symbolist play by the haughty profes-
sionals to whom it was shown. Apart from this, *The Sea Gull* teems with
symbols, and Chekhov's plays often recall Maeterlinck's *Le Trésor des
humbles*, but Chekhov did not consider himself a symbolist. He thought
of himself as a realist, if anything, but by 1896 Symbolism had developed so far that his audience might be expected to understand the sympathetic allusion to Maeterlinck and the new drama for which he stood.

For a time Maeterlinck was the mainstay of the Symbolist theatre in
Europe. Under his guidance the new genre developed in two directions,
seemingly divergent. One was a dramatic genre of legendary character
which was plainly related to the Gothic novels of the early part of the
century. The other was a quiet, melancholy *tableau vivant*, of the order
of *L'Intruse*. In both cases Maeterlinck seemed to aim at making the
strange familiar, and the familiar strange, in the manner of Wordsworth
and Coleridge in the time of the *Lyrical Ballads*.

The Gothic plays are set in an indefinite place and time, and are
steeped in the mysterious atmosphere that is indispensable to the Symbolist effect. The characters have names that recall the *Morte d'Arthur*. In
our day, unhappily, they have less glamorous connotations, they suggest
the brand names of proprietary medicines—Ygraine, Yssaline, Méli-
grane, Sélysette. The action takes place in moldering castles with ravens
and damp cellars where of old much blood was shed and the cobwebbed
darkness is full of menace. In the earlier plays the language is sparse and
musical; the silences are significant; words are used instrumentally.

Later, Maeterlinck's technique changed. The characters became increasingly loquacious, and lectured one another unmercifully. Evidently in time Maeterlinck lost faith in the rhetoric of silence and stopped trying to recover the magical rhythms of the primitive language. In *La Princesse Maleine*, for example, the characters speak mainly in monosyllables:

MALEINE: I'm frightened.
HJALMAR: Let's go on.
MALEINE: Listen. Someone is crying.
HJALMAR: Someone is crying?
MALEINE: I'm frightened.

But in *Aglavaine et Sélysette*, instead of affording his beloved some opportunity for the silent communion of kindred souls, Aglavaine finds it necessary to give Sélysette a lesson in the art of communication:

> Let us talk like human beings, like the poor human beings that we are, who speak as they can, with their hands, with their eyes, with their soul, when they wish to say things that are more real than those that words can reach.[12]

His exhortation is in vain. There does not seem to be anything that these lovers have to say to one another that could not be said in normal speech; but the implication is that if there were, the way at least would be open.

What is true of the communion of lovers on the stage is equally true of the communion of author and audience in the theatre. There too the wall of words stands firm. In addition there is the necessary presence of the living actor, an alien intermediary who obtrudes himself between the author and the spectator and thus makes intimacy impossible. In *Le Trésor des humbles* Maeterlinck notes with evident bitterness that when a play works properly on the stage it does so in spite of the actors. In *Macbeth*, for example, where "the mysterious song of the infinite" should be central, "the destiny or fatality which is inwardly perceived without our being able to say by what signs it is recognized, could not these be brought closer to us if by some introversion of the roles the actors were further removed?"

Actors, in Maeterlinck's view, obtrude their personalities between the Idea, and the play which symbolizes it, so effectively as "to destroy the mystic density of the work of art." They insist on understanding everything, and therefore tend to make everything unduly explicit. Marionettes are preferable. They have no personalities to exhibit at the ex-

pense of the play, no need to understand, no ideas of their own, and no
need to draw attention to themselves. All that is necessary on the stage is
a symbol of the Idea:

> A symbol never accepts the active presence of the man who moves in it.
> The symbol of the poem is a burning center the rays of which diverge
> into the infinite, and these rays, if they spring from an absolute master-
> piece of the sort we have in mind, have a trajectory that is limited only
> by the power of the eye that follows them. But now in the midst of the
> symbol the actor advances. At once there is produced, with relation to
> the passive spectator, an extraordinary phenomenon of polarization. He
> no longer sees the divergence of the rays, but their consequences; the
> particular has destroyed the universal, and the masterpiece, in its es-
> sence, is dead.
>
> We should perhaps remove the living being completely from the
> stage.[13]

Maeterlinck's ideas were widely taken up, particularly in Italy. Pirandello developed them at considerable length in *Six Characters in Search of
an Author*. But it is doubtful that the symbolism of *Pelléas et Mélisande*, for
example, would be greatly clarified in the absence of actors, or that
Alladine et Palomides and *La Mort de Tintagiles* work best with puppets.
The dramatic symbol, presumably, is the stage image which objectifies
the psychic state of the poet, and thus evokes a corresponding state in
the mind of the spectator. It is a psychic bridge, facilitating communication, but ultimately the Idea can be grasped only by an act of intuition on the spectator's part. In *Pelléas* the anecdote is complex and
perhaps too familiar to serve in this manner. What is most readily apprehended is the stereotype it embodies.

Pelléas et Mélisande tells the story of a young girl who marries a rich
man much older than herself and then falls in love with his young
brother. The lovers are discovered. The irate husband kills his brother,
wounds the girl, and almost kills himself. The wife gives birth prematurely. She dies, and the husband is left, tormented by doubts as to the
paternity of the child. It is the sort of story that in France might be
found in the pages of a newspaper, or in any of a dozen popular novels.
It is the story of Paolo and Francesca.

By transferring this well-worn anecdote from the world of the actual
to the world of fantasy Maeterlinck evidently thought to abstract from it
la notion pure which it symbolizes, the universal anecdote. "To compose
durable works," he told Huret, "is it not necessary precisely to rise

above our times, to separate oneself from the accidents of civilization, the contingencies of the immediately actual?" [14]

In order to give his story tragic magnitude Maeterlinck set it in a gloomy medieval fairyland, a dying land, sick with some ancient doom. But it is questionable if the story in this setting yields up the Idea more readily than the same story set under a bridge in New York, or in the precincts of a roadside diner in California. In *Pelléas*, at any rate, the Idea is elusive. There are many symbols. Mélisande is a lost princess. Her ring is at the bottom of a fountain. She has long, blond hair, and seems unduly innocent, not to say childish. Something awful is happening to King Axël; his trouble is unspecified. Throughout the play we are aware of mystery, and forebodings of disaster, of the aimless action of the Will, and the helplessness of those whose passions kindle. Beyond that, the divergence of the rays that radiate from this center is too great for the normal eye to follow. It is a sad story told in elegiacal tones. The effect is musical. But it is the music of the commonplace, a music quite appropriate to the circumstances of *L'Intruse*. In *Pelléas* the setting rather overwhelms the theme, and not even the music of Debussy is enough to rescue it.

In seeking the eternal in Gothic surroundings Maeterlinck was more or less indebted to Villiers, and perhaps also to Coleridge, Tennyson, and William Morris—it was certainly no new idea. In the 1890's the Gothic was once again in fashion. Its costumes and draperies jostled the imagination out of the common-sense attitudes of the everyday world, so that the high passions inappropriate to the twentieth century acquired glamor through their remoteness. The early German romanticists of the school of Jena, Novalis, in particular, and Schelling, had done much to renew myth as a significant element in contemporary literature, and the Symbolists had before them also the more striking example of Wagner's music-drama. In 1891 Jean Thorel published a scholarly essay on the relations of German romanticism to the Symbolist movement in France, but it was apparently Wyzéwa who first popularized the idea in France that myth is a symbolic representation of reality, "the expression of life" on a level of purity that civilization has obscured. It was an idea which, through the influence of the new psychology, was to have interesting consequences in literature, as well as in anthropology. Meanwhile it served to bring legend, in Wagner's use of the term, dangerously close to allegory, so that Mallarmé, for one, resisted the introduction of legendary material into the poetry of Symbolism, more particularly as he considered it a foreign intrusion.[15]

Maeterlinck did not resist it. Consequently the temptation to read his plays as allegories is well-nigh irresistible. The result is in every case disappointing. But as a Symbolist Maeterlinck had other resources. Along with the Gothic plays, he developed in *L'Intruse* (1891), *Les Aveugles* (1891), and *Intérieur* (1894) a second line of Symbolist drama which was destined to have consequences of equal, and perhaps greater, importance than the Gothic plays.

The theory that underlies these plays was amply set forth in the essay, *Le Tragique quotidien*, one of the essays in *Le Trésor des humbles*. There we read:

> There is a tragic element of the life of every day that is far more real, far more penetrating, far more akin to the true self that is in us than the tragedy that lies in great adventure. . . . This essential tragic element comprises more than mere psychology. . . . Its province is to reveal to us how truly wonderful is the mere act of living, and to cast light on the existence of the soul, self-contained in the midst of ever-restless immensities. . . .[16]

In this essay Maeterlinck looked well beyond the ideas of Diderot and Beaumarchais with regard to the tragic in everyday life. Evidently he had in mind a purely lyrical approach to the drama, a type of play foreshadowed in the poetry of Mallarmé, but of much simpler texture:

> I have come to believe that an old man, seated in his armchair, waiting patiently beside his lamp, attending unconsciously to the eternal laws that reign about his house, interpreting, without comprehending, the silence of door and windows . . . an old man who does not know that all the powers of the world, like so many heedful servants, are mingling and keeping vigil in his room, who does not suspect that the sun itself is supporting in space the little table he leans upon, and that every star in the sky and every fibre of the soul are directly concerned in the flicker of an eyelid or a thought that springs into consciousness—I have come to believe that he, motionless, yet lives in reality a deeper, more human and more universal life than the lover who strangles his mistress, the captain who conquers in battle, or the husband who avenges his honor.[17]

Very likely in this rhetoric there is some element of romantic extravagance, but it has also the ring of truth. In the theatre the pulse of life is more readily apparent in stillness than in movement. Chekhov was soon to prove that it is possible to convey through stasis and silence a poignancy of emotion that is quite beyond the play of violent action. "The moment we have something to say to one another," Maeterlinck wrote, "we are obliged to keep still." It is perhaps true; but, in the theatre, action is carried forward mainly by means of words, and silence is usually an embarrassment for the actor. Maeterlinck therefore stresses the silent language that is in counterpoint with the spoken word:

> Only those words that seem useless are of consequence in a work of art. It is in these that its soul resides. Side by side with the indispensable dialogue, there is almost always another dialogue which seems superfluous. Look carefully and you will see that it is this alone that the soul truly hears, because it is in this way only that the soul is spoken to. You will recognize also that it is the quality and extent of this seemingly useless dialogue that determines the quality and the ultimate reach of the work.[18]

The assumption that souls communicate through channels other than those available to the conscious intellect was a fundamental tenet of Symbolism, which customarily inclined to suggestion and intimation rather than to direct statement. In the theatre this technique results in an odd sort of dialogue of inconsequential character, which Maeterlinck often described, but seldom illustrated. Such dialogue is occasionally met with in Ibsen's later plays, and Jean-Jacques Bernard made a specialty of scenes written in this fashion; but the best examples of the language of the unexpressed are to be found in *The Three Sisters* and *The Cherry Orchard*.

In *L'Intruse* the central character is offstage, and is never seen. The scene is a family gathering. The half-blind grandfather sits in his armchair beside the lamp, waiting for the nun who is attending his son's laboring wife in another part of the house. There is the fear of death, and a sense of death hovers over the play. Death is heralded by ambiguous symbols—the sound of scything in the dark garden, the flutter of swans in the lake, the inexplicable dimming of the lamp, a door which will not close. In each case the portent is negated; but the old man knows. Blind as he is, he can see "les grandes clartés" which the others miss. At last the clock strikes twelve. The newborn child, until now unnaturally still, suddenly begins to cry. The black nun appears. The woman is dead.

It is an effective *tour de force*. The situation is by no means unusual—a family waiting quietly for the birth of a child. It is not stressed that we are witnessing the miracle of life and death. The dialogue barely rises above the hushed tones of suspense. The action plays on the emotions of the audience in musical fashion, building and relaxing minor climaxes which are at last resolved in certainty. There is the cry of the newborn and the announcement of death; these are juxtaposed. There is hardly any other action. Death is intangible, yet his presence is felt. He wields a scythe. He dims the light. He passes through closed doors. The suggestions are made and then withdrawn. It is all equivocal until at last, at its highest point, the suspense is ended and we are faced with the fact. As a demonstration of the technique of Symbolism, *L'Intruse* is rudimentary. What it amounts to is a translation to the stage of a short-story in the style of Poe, that is to say, symbolism on its lowest level. Yet, without doubt, it is a masterpiece in this genre.

Les Aveugles (1890) is even more artificially contrived than *L'Intruse*, and is equally effective. Twelve blind people go for an afternoon walk in the sun, led by their priest. They are characterized by type, so that, taken together, they make a cross-section of humanity. The priest leaves them for a moment. He never returns. They cast about for him blindly, in fear. At last a child leads them to their leader. He is dead. If we cannot resist drawing from this action the analogy it implies, we have a simple allegory, an exemplum. But there is no need to limit the play in this manner. *Les Aveugles* suggests more than it states. Its rays diverge as far as the eye can reach. The interest of the play lies not in its obvious statement, but in the wealth of possibilities that it suggests.

Les Aveugles is not static in the sense that *L'Intruse* is static, but it resembles it in the way that the suspense is built. There is only one blind person in the earlier play, and it is he who sees clearly. In *Les Aveugles* they are all blind, and only the child can see. What he sees is death. It is an interesting variation on the theme of *L'Intruse*, and evidently Maeterlinck did not feel that he had exhausted its possibilities. In *Intérieur* he rang another change on this situation. In this case the suspense depends upon the staging rather than on the action. The stage is divided. The speaking characters are grouped on one side of a window. On the other side a family group is seen, sitting quietly in their drawing-room in the lamplight. The question is, what will happen when they learn that the daughter has been drowned. In fact, when they hear of the disaster, they all rush out of the picture, leaving the Stranger who feared to tell them of their misfortune alone on the silent side of the window.

Intérieur is clearly a later version of *L'Intruse*. The symbol is of much the same order—the family group seemingly secure in the warmth of the living-room and, just outside, the vague menace that suddenly becomes explicit. The idea that death is always at the door seems to have haunted Maeterlinck. It was, in any case, an idea indispensable to the sense of the mystery of life which the Symbolists cherished.

Static plays of the order of *L'Intruse* and *Intérieur* are essentially lyric rather than dramatic compositions, tableaux that recall poems like *The Cotter's Saturday Night* or, more directly, the type of genre painting that was still much in vogue at the end of the nineteenth century. The subjects of such paintings were usually domestic—the family dinner, the death-bed, the return of the prodigal son, the wedding. Paintings of this sort were seldom of a high order of art, but undoubtedly they found a ready sale, for they were produced in quantity for the trade, and often served as models for the stage. In giving such scenes symbolic overtones, as in *Intérieur*, Maeterlinck raised the quality of domestic melodrama to heights of which Kotzebue had never dreamed; nevertheless after the publication of *Le Trésor des humbles*, Maeterlinck wrote no more in this style. After 1896 he turned once again to Gothic themes, this time with marionettes very much in mind.

The underlying concept in these plays is quite clearly defined. The characters are puppets, completely at the mercy of the passions that move them together and drive them apart. The Will that moves them seems dispassionate and impersonal. It cares nothing for the suffering of the individuals who are its creatures, so that, on the plane of being which it commands, existence is necessarily a tragic experience. The ideal world, however, is beyond the power of the Will. On the plane of the ideal, love triumphs over the shoddy intrigues of the flesh, and here it may find fulfillment and permanence. But on the physical plane there is no hope of happiness. At the end of the nineteenth century this was hardly a novel idea. It was in some sense a restatement of the Greek idea of tragedy. But it seemed novel; and these plays appear to have puzzled some of Maeterlinck's critics very much.

In 1891 Maeterlinck published *Ruysbroeck and the Mystics*. It included selections from Jan van Ruysbroeck's *The Adornment of the Spiritual Marriage*, a fourteenth-century mystical treatise in which Maeterlinck saw clear analogies to the Symbolist ideas he was developing in the theatre. These ideas were further elaborated in his essay, "La Sagesse et la destinée," a commentary on his plays which he published in 1898. In the

light of these commentaries his plays might well seem impenetrably abstruse.

In Villiers's *Axël* the hero and heroine choose to die at the very moment they find love, since life can give them nothing to equal the perfection of this ideal instant. The idea, however impractical for common
mortals, has a certain sublimity: in *Axël* the situation is memorable. Not
so much can be said for the situation in *Aglavaine et Sélysette*. The idea is
the same as in Villiers's play, but here a practical problem arises—in
choosing the ideal one is left with the problem of disposing of the real. It
is a difficulty which furnished Giraudoux with the theme of several
beautiful plays—among them, *Ondine, Intermezzo,* and *La Folle de
Chaillot*—but it is an insoluble problem. In *Alladine et Palomides*, Palomides makes what might seem to be a sensible choice. He renounces the
spiritual love of Astolaine, to whom he is affianced, in order to enjoy the
more tangible Alladine. But he still loves Astolaine, even more, as he
says, than his new love. The beautiful Astolaine, for her part, lets him
go; indeed, she even tries to rescue him and Alladine from the dungeon
to which Ablamore has consigned them in his mad jealousy. But it is too
late. They lie dying in adjoining rooms, and only their voices mingle as
their souls pass into the infinite. The implication is not entirely clear. It
would seem that Palomides would have done better to have continued
with his spiritual love instead of yielding to the blandishments of the
flesh; but, in the circumstances, the desire to survive might appear to be
too practical a reason for preferring the ideal.

Maeterlinck was awarded the Nobel prize for literature in 1911. By
that time he had changed his style and his views, and was perhaps no
longer a Symbolist. He was, no doubt, a major force in the theatre, now
chiefly important as a precursor. His Gothic plays are all versions of
domestic drama in medieval costume. In each there is clear evidence of
an attempt to sound the universal aspects of human relations. But while
he was the first of the Symbolist playwrights to reach a wide audience,
he was unable to extend the technique of Symbolism beyond the limits
of a fairy tale. It remained for Giraudoux to develop Symbolism properly in the theatre; and it is much to his credit that he was able to see the
strength of Maeterlinck where most critics of his time saw chiefly his
weakness.

These critics were excusable. The transposition of themes that by this
time had become the property of the boulevard theatre to a legendary
Beyond could not in itself clear Maeterlinck's plays of their contin-

gencies, nor could he in this manner hope to reveal the eternal truths that melodrama embodies. Myth creates its own ambience, but the unconscious substructure on which it is based is not altered by the symbols it employs. It seems unnecessary to look beyond life for what is mysterious in human behavior. What we know of the Beyond we find within the psyche: beyond that we can predicate nothing. When the Symbolists understood that, they became Surrealists. It was no great advance, but it made a difference in the theatre.

Maeterlinck was in no sense a psychologist. The Unconscious that rules his puppets is neither the Freudian nor the Jungian unconscious. It is von Hartmann's Unconscious, the primordial spirit of which both man and nature are manifestations—a metaphysical conception. Since this is an irresponsible force which is heedless of the pain it occasions, it is, from the human viewpoint, both evil and senseless, and, as it is irrational, it is inexplicable. The tragic element that all of Maeterlinck's plays exemplify is the conflict of the individual, conscious and helpless, with the implacable power, external to his concerns, which creates and destroys without pity and without malice, and with utter indifference to his individuality. In these circumstances, the only hope of the individual is to transcend into the sphere of the ideal, that is to say, into the world of fantasy, which perhaps does not exist. Maeterlinck's idea of drama was thus in complete accord with the ideas of Mallarmé.

In Maeterlinck's eight Gothic plays the philosophy that is implied is completely deterministic. The characters are passive. Things happen to them, and they react like automata; they resist nothing, and barely protest. There is only the sense of doom, the scream of anguish, and the question, Why?—which is the point of the play. The question, Why? is of the essence of tragedy; but Maeterlinck was no more successful with his answer than was Sophocles. Unfortunately, these plays fall short of the tragic effect. They are all in their fashion romantically sentimental and solicit pity in ways inappropriate to tragedy. The result is that in Maeterlinck's plays the familiar features of melodrama grin self-consciously through the mystical draperies in which the action is enveloped, and too frequently one is tempted to grin back.

In their day, doubtless these plays aroused admiration; but their day was brief. They appealed to a wider audience than the Symbolists had so far reached, and by generalizing their subject-matter, provided an interesting change from the endless discussions of middle-class morality which encumbered the stage in this period. When, after the turn of the century, their vogue passed, Maeterlinck turned to other things. The French theatre relapsed gently into its former idiom, from which, in truth, it had hardly departed. The romantic tradition did not die. There was, among others, Edmond Rostand to keep it alive. But he could not be accounted a Symbolist. By the time of the World War it seemed that the Symbolism of the 1880's had run its course. In France, at least, the Realists were once again in undisputed possession of the stage.

There were, however, other forces at work in the theatre outside France. Long before the war of 1914 unsettled the equanimity of the middle-class, a new generation of writers was occupied in sapping the foundations of reality. These were not Symbolists. They were Realists of a new sort. In the theatre the powerful figure in this movement was one who had no connection with Mallarmé, and very little direct relation to the school of Zola. Luigi Pirandello was a Realist. He began his artistic career under the influence of Giovanni Verga and the Italian *veristi*. By the end of this career in 1936 he had done more than Einstein to shake man's faith in reality.

PIRANDELLO

Pirandello's fame rests principally on two plays. He published forty-three. Outside of Italy he is seldom accounted a poet. Yet he published eight volumes of poetry. His canon includes, besides, seven novels; two long essays on literary topics; innumerable articles and reviews; and a great many short stories, so many and so beautifully told that he must be ranked, beyond question, with the greatest masters of the genre. Whatever else may be said of Pirandello, it must be conceded that as a man of letters he covered the ground.

He wrote, he tells us, as men breathe, in order to live. His first published work was a collection of youthful poems entitled *Mal giocondo*. It was issued in Palermo in 1889, when he was twenty-two. The night before he died, 10 December 1936, he was working on the third act of his new play, *I giganti della montagna*. He was a contemporary of Zola and also of the Futurist, Marinetti, and came, in some sense, under the influence of both. When he was awarded the Nobel prize in 1934, nine years after it was awarded to Shaw, and thirteen years after Maeterlinck received it, Valéry and Chesterton were passed over in his favor. It might well be expected, therefore, that his writings would reflect the moving currents of European taste in the course of a half-century of very rapid social change. They do.

Pirandello, indeed, showed himself to be as sensitive to the current literary mode as Strindberg or Shaw, and quite as avid of novelty. He was, like them, a very widely read writer, a man of letters. He was not a scholar; he had not Shaw's enormous sophistication, nor his wit; little of Chekhov's tragic insight; and nothing of Strindberg's spiritual intensity, nor his madness. But he had qualities that made his special talents more readily accessible than those of any of his great contemporaries, and he was therefore able to exert a very powerful influence on the thought of his time.

Even after he was famous nobody beyond his immediate circle knew anything about Pirandello's personal life. In 1932, four years before Pirandello's death, Nardelli published a biography, *Pirandello: L'uomo segreto*, the first book to provide any insight into the life and character of a man whose face was familiar to millions. Two years later, Pirandello was a Nobel laureate; after that it was inevitable that subsequent studies should fall into the mood of romantic sensibility that Nardelli had effectively evoked around the figure of the great man. Pirandello's humor, his irony, and his bitterness now all appeared to be the distillation of his tragic life, and this life took on the character of a legend. But Nardelli's romantic study, with its idealization of the author's stoicism, and his spiritual *forza*, hardly did justice to a man of Pirandello's dimension and complexity of character.

Twelve years before, Adriano Tilgher, in his study of Pirandello's plays, had so successfully systematized his work that Pirandello emerged from this essay as a philosophical writer somewhere between Kant and Pyrrho. Nardelli pictured him as a tragic Titan, a Promethean hero chained to his agony by a heroic sense of obligation to an insane wife. More modern interpretations, more amply documented, more thorough, and less imaginative, have since been proposed. But the more we learn about Pirandello, the less distinct the man becomes. What can be said with certainty is that whoever wishes to sort out the man from the trappings of his lifelong disguise would do best to look for him in his works. It was chiefly there that he showed himself, and it is there, if anywhere, that he is to be found.

Until he was well in his thirties Pirandello affected the tight clothes and varnished shoes of the provincial dandy. Then his life changed, and his appearance with it. He took up the sober academic garb of a university professor in Rome. His early photos show a young man with a sensitive mouth and wistful eyes. But when he managed at last to catch the public eye, his expression changed radically. He now adopted the quizzical look of one who has questioned everything, and come to his own conclusions. Henceforth he showed himself in public with the raised eyebrow and the saturnine smile of the *raisonneur* of *Così è (se vi pare)*. It was a pose that had served Shaw magnificently in England. In Italy, it served Pirandello even better; for Shaw's Mephistophelian look was intended to befuddle chiefly the bourgeois, but Pirandello had it in mind to bewilder every-body. It is true that the Satanism of the eighties was rather out of date in the 1920's, but Pirandello's diabolism was of some account in a land where people still made gestures to ward off the evil eye.

On the whole it is apparent that for one who was painfully aware of the vanity of human wishes, Pirandello advertised himself with extraor-dinary vigor, as widely and as assiduously as any of the other famous showmen of his time. They were, after all, gifted mountebanks, all of them, and therefore motivated by a degree of exhibitionism well above the capacity or the needs of ordinary people. In Pirandello's day it was still necessary for a man of talent to play the charlatan occasionally in order to make his mark on the world. Pirandello did what was needful in this regard, and perhaps in the end rather reluctantly. But all that was part of his professional apparatus. The air of mystery with which he sur-rounded himself was protective, and it was genuine. It has never been dispelled.

Luigi Pirandello was born in Agrigento, 28 June 1867. His father was a well-to-do man of business, a powerful and violent man who ruled his family, Sicilian fashion, with a hand of iron. In 1882 an unfortunate speculation in sulfur landed him in bankruptcy, and he moved his family to Palermo. Luigi was sent to good schools. In the *liceo* he received an ex-cellent classical education, came early under the influence of the roman-tic poets, particularly Carducci, Foscolo, and Arturo Graf, and lost his faith. He began his legal studies at the University of Palermo; but when his father sent him to Rome to finish his studies, he enrolled instead in the faculty of letters, became interested in Romance Philology, and even-tually went to Bonn to study with Foerster. He earned his doctorate with a dissertation on the development of the vowel system in the Agrigentean dialect. At twenty-four he was back in Rome, with a di-ploma, a portfolio of poems and plays, a burning ambition, and a gener-ous allowance from home.

At this time Rome was the literary center of Italy. The cafés of the Via Veneto teemed with artists and writers, mostly of Southern extrac-tion, and mostly poor. The great men of letters had by this time retired to the provinces. Their followers were organized in contentious cliques, the realists ranged against the romantics, with a host of little reviews and journals in which to air their views, very much in the manner of their contemporaries in Paris. Pirandello threw in his lot with the realists, and amused himself by publishing attacks on D'Annunzio.

The Sicilian literary coterie in Rome was small, but remarkably active. Pirandello was a man of warm friendships, and a stout partisan. With the help of his compatriots Luigi Capuana and Ugo Fleres he soon acquired a foothold in literary circles, so that by the time he was thirty he was contributing regularly to various periodicals and gaining considerable esteem, without remuneration. The life of a free-lance writer, however glamorous, was nevertheless lacking in status. In 1897 Pirandello accepted a post at the Istituto Superiore di Magistero, a teachers college for women, as substitute for the incumbent professor of literature, his friend Giuseppe Mantica. This position kept him busy two hours a day three days a week. The rest of the time he was free to pursue his literary work.

He was by this time a man with responsibilities. At twenty-seven he had married Antonietta Portulano, a girl chosen for him by his father. She was the daughter of his father's business partner, a handsome girl of modest attainments, strictly brought up in the Sicilian manner. She brought him a fine dowry and, in the course of six years of happy marriage, bore him two sons and a daughter.

The disaster, when it struck, was completely unexpected. The paternal sulfur mines were suddenly flooded, and both families were ruined. The remittances stopped. The dowry vanished. Antonietta was so severely shaken that she suffered a temporary paralysis, and it was not long before she began to exhibit signs of madness. At thirty-three Pirandello's case was desperate. The meager stipend he received from the Magistero barely sufficed to pay the rent of his apartment. He pawned his wife's jewels, contemplated suicide, began giving language lessons at five lire an hour, and settled down to the life of a hack journalist.

Under these conditions Antonietta's madness became agonizing for her husband. She could not bear him to touch her; at the same time she gave way to mad fits of jealousy, which culminated in accusations of incest with his daughter. But Pirandello could not do without his wife, and it was not until 1918 that he could be persuaded to settle her in a clinic. His writings during this period were motivated by intense financial necessity. They were also a refuge from a life which had grown intolerable. Consequently his output was enormous. Stories, articles, and reviews poured forth in a torrent, uneven in quality, but of prodigious volume, and he peddled them earnestly to the journals and reviews of all the major cities of Italy.[1]

Pirandello lived much of his life in Rome, where it was well to be Roman. But he was a Sicilian. In Rome he moved mainly in Sicilian circles, and he made his debut in the theatre with plays on Sicilian themes written in dialect for Sicilian actors. A great many of his *novelle* are set in the Sicilian landscape, and describe characters native to the vicinity of Agrigento and Palermo. Pirandello knew these people intimately, their fierceness, their jealousies, their cruel jokes and rages, their loyalties, and the smell of their kitchens. In time his locale shifted, but not his ideas. He came to know the Italian middle class on the mainland as well as a stranger might come to know it. The Italian upper classes he knew less intimately, so that the plays that are set in aristocratic circles seldom have a solid ring. From first to last his tastes were those of a Sicilian gentleman, and as an artist he was at his best in a provincial setting.

Chekhov, with whom Pirandello invites comparison, composed by preference in a low key. In stories like "The Duel" and "Ward No. 6" the climaxes are muted. The climactic scene in *Uncle Vanya* is deliberately minimized, and in *Three Sisters* the location of the climax is a matter of opinion. Pirandello, however, had not much taste for the drama of understatement. His plays, like many of his stories, are emphatic. His characters are excitable people, and when they are not excited it is because they have chosen, as they repeatedly assure us, to withdraw from life in order to subsist in the emotional shallows of a contemplative existence. Their quiet, accordingly, is volcanic.

The striking difference between Chekhov's art and the art of Pirandello cannot be explained simply in terms of a difference in temperament. It has to do with the traditions within which each artist worked. Both were essentially story-tellers with a keen eye for character and situation; but while Chekhov developed the Russian *rasskaz* into a supremely touching tale of ordinary things, Pirandello took his departure from the Italian *novella*.

The *novella* is a form of ancient lineage. Its ancestry is traceable far beyond the *Decameron*, to the *Cento novelle antiche* of the thirteenth century, a collection of tales involving an element of the *mirabile*, tales intended to arouse wonder as well as to provide amusement. These anecdotes center on sexual intrigues, the wiles of women, ingenious tricks and deceits, disguises, mistaken identities, practical jokes—*beffe* and *contrabeffe*—and crimes of passion and revenge. The emphasis in such tales is normally on plot, not character, though certain type-characters provided useful armatures on which stories might be mounted. Boccaccio was however, a master of characterization, and in this respect Pirandello rivaled him. His *novelle*, like those of Boccaccio, create a magnificent gallery of Italian types.

As a story-teller Pirandello was amazingly versatile. Stories such as "Un cavallo nella luna" are masterpieces of naturalistic writing, genre tales of great originality and sensitivity, written in a style that no master has surpassed. But many of his stories, like his plays, reflect the classic modes. Much history separates Pirandello from Terence and Plautus. In his plays, the Roman masks have become characterological constructions; mistaken identities are given unusual social significance; and recognitions become revelations of character that occasionally surprise the subject as much as those around him. But in spite of these innovations, which belong very much to our time and have contributed substantially to our modern manner of thought, his plays appear quite often to be cast in the traditional molds of Latin comedy.

The metaphysical superstructure which Pirandello imposed on his thought served to obscure its classic foundation, just as the profound skepticism he so emphatically professed served to conceal the living springs of his faith. It is nonetheless clear that his world-view was at bottom deeply Christian, and his work everywhere reflects the ideals of a culture that constantly disappointed him. His was a world, like the world of the *Decameron*, very far removed from the gates of Eden. Nevertheless this world was pervaded by nostalgia for a lost innocence which faith and good works might perhaps restore. In Pirandello's world all values were relative save the basic human values—love, courage, and the nobility of the spirit; and while the soul might be said not to exist, there was no doubt of the power of suffering to cleanse it and purify it. His was a world in which everything was dubious, except the ultimate triumph of right and justice. It was, in short, the world of romance—formulated in terms of the most pitiless realism.

Pirandello doubtless considered himself a realist, an atheist, and a skeptic, and in this guise he masqueraded the greater part of his life. There is no objection to one's thinking of him in this light, particularly since it was in this manner that he presented himself to the world, save that this description does not describe him. His works are too various,

and his attitudes too many, for anything in the way of a rigorous clas-
sification. He was very conscious, especially in his later life, of the relation of life and form—*vita e forma*—and after 1922 he took every opportunity to demonstrate their incompatibility. Perhaps this was a way of
justifying his inconsistencies. In his view the essence of life is change;
consequently to define is to kill, and the need for consistency imposes intolerable limitations on the vital spirit. In "La carriola"—"The Wheel-
barrow"—the hero tells us:

> He who lives, while he is living, does not see himself live. . . . If one
> can see his own life, it is a sign that he is no longer living it: he endures
> it, he drags it along. He drags it along like a dead thing. Because every
> form is a dead thing. Very few know that. Most, almost all, struggle,
> strive to find themselves, as they say, a position, to attain a form: when
> it is attained they think they have conquered life, and instead they have
> begun to die. . . . Only he who succeeds in seeing the form he has
> given himself . . . sees himself as he is. But if we are able to see this, it
> is a sign that our life is no longer in it: because if it were, we would not
> see it, we would live in it without seeing it. . . . We can therefore
> know and see what in ourselves is already dead. To know is to die.[2]

Pirandello very likely never knew himself, and perhaps this was the
secret of his extraordinary vitality. It would be fair perhaps to consider
him in terms of a series of paradoxes, but this is hardly a characterization. What can be said of him with confidence is that he belonged to
the school of thought that extols nature at the expense of custom and
convention. He wrote in the tradition of the great romantics. In the eternal conflict of mind and heart, he took up arms stoutly in support of the
natural impulse. He was too good a logician to put any trust in logic.
Most of his life he was a prisoner of one obligation or another, and
clearly he suffered from claustrophobia. Only his imagination was free.
That was his life, a complex of contradictions, and he made the most of
it. He was, one might say, six authors in search of a character.

The new drama came but slowly to Italy. In the pre-war period, before
1914, the Italian stage was dominated by star-actors and actresses who
toured the Italian cities with their own companies each season with a
new repertory of plays. There were few resident companies. The great
luminaries—Tommaso Salvini, Eleanora Duse, Irma and Emma Grammatica, Ruggero Ruggeri—were accustomed to think of plays mainly as
vehicles for the display of their talents, and everything written for the

stage was subject to summary revision to that end. In the pre-war years D'Annunzio was the reigning Italian dramatist, and the theatre was under strong romantic influence. The first productions of Ibsen's plays aroused wrath, and then wonder. Shaw's plays were discussed by the learned, but they aroused little popular interest. Chekhov was found puzzling. Henri Becque excited attention: *La Parisienne* shocked its audiences into some awareness of French realism, and the Italian managers soon saw the commercial possibilities of Donnay, Porto-Riche, Curel, and Vildrac, the heirs and next of kin of the Théâtre-libre.

Pirandello had come to Rome in the hope of making a career as a dramatist. In 1896 he finished a play in three acts called *Il nibbio—The Hawk*—but after an unpleasant experience with Flavio Andò, the actor to whom he submitted it, he developed a studied contempt for the stage, and henceforth professed to know nothing about Italian drama from the time of Goldoni. Nevertheless, in 1899 he wrote a piece for the *Marzocco* of Florence in which he expressed very decided views regarding the composition of plays:

> In our day most dramatic works are essentially narrative, drawing for their subject-matter upon novels or *novelle*. This can only be a mistake: first, because in general a narrative is not easily reducible to the proportions of the stage; second, because these proportions are further narrowed and shrunken by the excessive and (in my opinion) misapplied rigidity of modern stage technique.

Pirandello was at this time thirty-two, and he was beginning to be known in journalistic circles as a writer of some originality, but chiefly as a writer of short stories. His compatriot Luigi Capuana had long ago persuaded him to turn from poetry to fiction, and in 1894 he had published a novel, *L'esclusa*, in realistic style. It excited little interest. That same year he began to submit *novelle* to the newspapers. His first volume of collected stories, *Amori senza amore* (1894), clearly demonstrated his talent, and in the following years he devoted his efforts almost exclusively to the production of short narrative pieces.

As a writer of *novelle* he was amazingly prolific. From 1903 to 1920, volume succeeded volume in a seemingly inexhaustible stream of narrative. His best stories are leisurely monologues spoken by a narrator in the company of an imaginary listener whose reactions are casually noted by the speaker so that both narrator and listener are characterized dramatically in the course of the tale. The narrator is invariably a man of

tact, warm, excitable, informed, and at the same time curiously diffident, a gentleman who is careful not to presume on the fleeting intimacy of an occasion which brings two strangers together long enough
to exchange a confidence. The listener is never impatient. He is a sensitive and sympathetic character who never obtrudes a remark, but whose
occasional smile or nod of understanding is immediately reflected in the
narrator's speech. In this manner each short story becomes a little play
within which the anecdote is developed between a pair of actors, one of
whom is the author and the other the audience.

Such stories as "Acqua amara" and "Ciàula scopre la luna"—poignant
tales told with a smile—are in the highest sense dramatic; but the type of
story which Pirandello tells better than anyone is intimate in a way that
cannot be reproduced under the conditions of the theatre. In the theatre
there are too many people for this sort of intimacy. Indeed when Pirandello visualized his stories in terms of the living actor he lost, inevitably,
much of his grace as a raconteur. In his day the Italian dramatist was by
temper and training never so far removed from the operatic tradition as
to transcend wholly the melodramatic tendencies of the profession; and
if, by some miracle, he managed this feat, the actor did not. Doubtless in
his early article in the *Marzocco* Pirandello had such difficulties in mind,
and his observations with regard to the adaptation of stories for the stage
were both wise and just. Unfortunately when he came to write for the
theatre thirteen years later he did not heed them. His first ventures in
the drama at that time were straightforward adaptations of his own
novelle, and of the forty-three plays he wrote during his long career in the
theatre, by far the greater part were drawn from stories he had written
long before. His two masterpieces, however, were written directly for
the stage, and in both cases he broke new ground in the theatre.

In 1893 he had written of Ibsen:

> It is enough for someone to be momentarily incomprehensible for him
> to be immediately surrounded by a swarm of admiring individuals as
> insistent and oppressive, if I may be allowed a vulgar image, as flies
> buzzing about a gob of spit.[3]

At this time, also, he appeared to have no affinity with the Symbolists in
France. He was a Realist. He did not understand Mallarmé. He disliked
Verlaine; and in 1896 he expressed a strong distaste for the irrationalism
of Maurice Barrès and those of his circle. But, as with most writers of his
time, his views were liable to change without notice. Twenty-five years

later he himself was making a virtue of incomprehensibility; the same swarm of admiring individuals who had earned his contempt in the early days was now buzzing merrily about him, and his work was so far advanced along Symbolist lines that Marinetti claimed him as a Futurist.

"With the help of God," he wrote in December 1909, "I will never write plays . . . to me a play is an illustration in a book, or a translation beside the original; it either spoils or diminishes what it represents."[4] His immediate circle of friends, however, included a number of playwrights, theatre directors, and drama critics, among them Giustino Ferri, Ugo Fleres, Lucio d'Ambra, and Nino Martoglio. For a long time Pirandello refused to participate in their discussions of the theatre. It is said that when their talk turned in that direction he at once withdrew into a game of solitaire. But in 1912 Martoglio persuaded him to adapt one of his *novelle*, "La Morsa"—"The Vise"—for the Sicilian stage in Rome. The play did well. Other adaptations followed. They were all written in dialect for the Sicilian theatre, and all dealt with Sicilian subjects.

The Italian theatre meanwhile was undergoing a striking transformation. A new school of playwrights was making its mark, and a new type of realism was being very rapidly developed. Luigi Chiarelli's *La maschera e il volto—The Mask and the Face*—was presented for the first time on 31 May 1916 at the Teatro Argentina in Rome. It created a sensation. The author called his play a *grottesco*. The "grotesque" was a term Victor Hugo had used to describe a dramatic genre that would combine tragedy with comedy in the manner of Shakespeare. *The Mask and the Face* was neither Shakespearean nor romantic; but the term was apt, so much so that in the following years everything that was new in the Italian drama was likely to be called grotesque.

The Mask and the Face is a funny comedy with tragic overtones. The protagonist Paolo has solemnly proclaimed that his sense of personal honor is so delicate that if ever he should find his wife Savina unfaithful he would, without a moment's hesitation, kill her. Quite unexpectedly he is put to the test. But, having made his fatal discovery, he also discovers, to his astonishment, that he is not at all the man he thought he was. In spite of everything, he loves his wife, and has no wish whatever to kill her. He does, however, feel the pressure of public opinion so strongly that he pretends to act in accordance with his public image. Savina is spirited away and changes her name. Paolo then declares that she is dead and that he has cleared his name. He is duly arrested, tried, and sentenced, and on his return from prison is borne home in triumph by his fellow townsmen. But these extravagances are more than he can bear. When Savina secretly visits him, he decides to put an end to his pretense and to affirm his autonomy as a free man: "I am not going to render an account of my life to anyone, neither to society, nor my friends, nor to the law, nothing, it's enough!" But in spite of this declaration of independence it is necessary for him to fly the coop with his wife in order to escape the legal consequences of his fraud.

The play, as Tilgher pointed out, makes no comment on the situation. Paolo's psychic somersault is presented with comic gravity, simply as a fact. The fact, of course, speaks for itself, and it found immediate acceptance. Henceforth the way was open on the Italian stage for a full-scale assault on the time-honored traditions of Italian culture. What was under fire in *The Mask and the Face* was, ostensibly, the ideal. The approach to the unquestionable duty of the Italian husband to avenge his honor was in this case realistic, and from this viewpoint the result was comic. Chiarelli did not ridicule the ideal of feminine purity, nor the blood-sacrifice which had so long sustained it. The joke is at the expense of the individual who submits to a social code in which he does not really believe, and which nevertheless operates tyrannically to dictate his behavior. What is serious in the play is the tragic relation of the social group to the individuals who comprise it, and the consequent despotism of customs in which perhaps nobody any longer believes. Thus Chiarelli took up in 1916 the assault on the ideal which Ibsen had initiated with *Ghosts* in 1881. The result was a new wave of realism in the Italian theatre.

The Mask and the Face was Chiarelli's masterpiece. His later plays maintained his ironic mood, but they were not equally cogent. *La scala di seta—The Silken Ladder—*is an interesting study of a demagogue, but the caricature is not wholly convincing. *Chimere* is excessively melodramatic, and *La morte degli amanti* is confusing. All these plays in some way illustrate the essential theme of the grotesque, the contrast between the conventional face which society imposes on the individual and the feelings which are the spontaneous expressions of his personality—in general terms, the contrast of truth and fiction. Underlying this theme was an even more basic issue—the conflict of freedom and order.

The school of the Grotesque included a number of ambitious young dramatists, among them Luigi Antonelli, Carlo Veneziano, Enrico Cavacchioli, Fausto Martini, and Massimo Bontempelli. With the exception of Martini, none of these was highly talented as a playwright. After Chiarelli it was Piermaria Rosso di San Secondo who most ably developed this genre, and it was he who put Pirandello in touch with the new realism in the theatre.

Rosso was more directly in touch with the French theatre than Chiarelli, and he did not follow Chiarelli's line. He was an Idealist. Like Ibsen he found a source of dramatic tension in the contrast between the cold Northern temper and the Southern—"the South all impulse and passion, the North all discipline and will"—an idea traceable to Buckle's *History of Civilization*. The ideal world, Rosso believed, is common to all men in their infancy, but when Northerners grow up they believe that the phenomenal world is real, whereas the Southerner remains in this respect a child. The realities of everyday life do not convince the Southerner, consequently he spends his life wandering aimlessly "between dream and day," an alien and a transient in an unreal world. In this dubious state of mind, life seems to him in the nature of a practical joke, until the magic moment when suddenly a vision of the ideal world of his childhood flashes before his eyes and transforms the shadowy reality around him into something wonderful and true. But the moment of insight is pitifully brief, and when the intuition of eternity fades away what is left is only a cry of anguish. In Rosso's "Elegie a Maryke," in "Amara," and in "Per fare l'alba" the influence of French Symbolism is unmistakable. It requires no effort to see in Rosso's poetry the influence of Mallarmé.

In the theatre Rosso's fame rested chiefly on three plays—*Marionette! che passione!* (1918), *La bella adormentata* (1919), and *La scala* (1926). The first deals in mysterious fashion with three characters whom life destroys. Each feels himself to be a tragic figure, suffering mightily. In reality all three are no more than puppets on strings, without volition of their own. Love is the hand that works their strings. They are the toys of love, and when it is done with them, it casts them aside like toys. Their grandiose postures and their displays of passion, consequently, can only move the spectator to laughter, for what seems tragic to the figures in the guignol is merely comic to the objective observer; their tragedy is a farce. In this play Rosso made the idea of the Grotesque entirely explicit. The idea was far from new, but the style was original, and Rosso's irony made a deep, though distinctly unpleasant, impression on an audience that was attuned mainly to romantic and sentimental displays. The relation of Rosso's play to the work of Maeterlinck and the doctrine of Schopenhauer in his *Metaphysics of the Love of the Sexes* was, of course, unmistakable, but few of the contemporary critics were disposed to discuss it.

The Sleeping Beauty is another sort of play, but it shares in some ways the abstract quality of *Marionettes! What passion!* The play is subtitled—doubtless in deference to the synaesthetic notions of the Symbolists—"una avventura colorata"—a colored adventure. La Bella is the village prostitute. She lives in a dream, entirely acquiescent. She has neither will nor any sense of guilt, and is a pure manifestation of life, so simple that people marvel at its ideal quality. Quite unexpectedly she finds herself with child. At this point she renounces her profession and takes the child to the notary who first seduced her, and who is thus in some sense answerable for it. The play has a *raisonneur* in the person of The Black Man of the Sulfur, a romantic character whom life has made a cynic: perhaps it is the author. Life to him is a colored adventure, and he colors it further by forcing the notary to marry La Bella in accordance with right and justice.

Rosso di San Secondo was some twenty years younger than Pirandello, and one of his closest friends. When Rosso became editor of *Il Messagero della Domenica*, we are told, Pirandello stopped by his office every afternoon. It was through Rosso that he turned from his Sicilian plays to the avant-garde drama that the Grotteschi were trying to develop. In 1918 Pirandello wrote admiringly of *Marionette! che passione!*: "Here every logical preparation, every logical support has been abolished. . . . The apparent lack of logic . . . is in fact the supreme logic." Two years later he was prepared to give a more scholarly interpretation of the Teatro del grottesco. In an article published 27 February 1920 in *L'Idea nazionale* he wrote:

> A good phrase to define the most significant modern works of the Grotesque is "transcendental farce . . ." Hegel has explained that the Subject, the only sure reality, can smile at the vain appearances of the world. It constructs them, but it can also destroy them; it need not take its own creations seriously. Hence we have irony, that force which, according to Tieck, allows the poet to dominate his subject-matter. And, according to Friedrich Schlegel, it is through irony that this same subject-matter is reduced to a perpetual parody, a transcendental farce. . . . The farce of the Grotesque includes in its tragedy its parody and its caricature, not as extraneous superposed elements, but as its own shadow, the awkward shadow of every tragic gesture.

It is doubtful if either Chiarelli or Rosso intended their plays to carry this much weight, but the idea of the grotesque certainly warranted a philosophical interpretation, and its later consequences may be studied to advantage in the plays and the theories of Ionesco and Dürrenmatt, among the other specialists in transcendental farce. Pirandello's sense of reality had by this time been seriously shaken. The mutability of his fortunes and his wife's nagging delusions had done much to undermine his sense of the world's stability, and the senseless destructiveness of the war years greatly aggravated his mental discomfort. In October 1915 he wrote his son Stefano, at that time a prisoner of war in an Austrian camp: "I feel that my whole life has been devoid of meaning; I no longer see any point in the things I do or the words I speak, and it astonishes me that there are others moving about outside this nightmare of mine and that they can act and speak. . . ."[5]

Pirandello's personal doubts as to the nature of reality and the problem of identity—matters that were to occupy him all the rest of his life—were not at all the result of his early studies in German philosophy. His training was in philology. It was not until his late forties that he manifested any special interest in metaphysics or epistemology, and very likely at that time it was his personal problems that motivated his reading in those subjects. In 1915 he wrote Stefano that he was reading philosophy, "and learning very little." His skeptical turn of mind manifested itself long before he came in contact with the writings of Kant or Hegel. *Pensaci, Giacomino!*, his first important play, was adapted from a *novella* he had published in 1910. It was not a work capable of carrying the philosophical superstructure of "transcendental farce," but it was a first-rate example of the Theatre of the Grotesque, and in it are contained in embryo most of the ideas that were to occupy him in his later drama.

The *novella* from which *Pensaci, Giacomino!* was adapted is a story ten pages long which has to do with a tangle in an aged gentlemen's domestic arrangements. Professor Toti is seventy years old. He is waiting until his pension reaches its maximum to retire from the *liceo* where he teaches. Meanwhile he has married a young girl called Maddalena, the daughter of the school beadle. Her little son Ninì is the apple of the old man's eye. Officially Professor Toti is the boy's father. In truth the father is Giacomino, Toti's brightest pupil. He has come to live with Toti and Maddalena. The arrangement is a happy one, and the fact that the whole town is laughing about it does not in the least trouble the professor.

Toti is now a man of means. He has recently inherited a large legacy, and has consequently been able to get Giacomino a job in the local bank, where Toti is the largest depositor. He has also arranged for Maddalena to inherit his fortune when he dies so that she and Giacomino can get married. But now Giacomino's sister intervenes. She shames Giacomino into leaving the professor's house and also arranges to have him marry a poor girl who is her friend. Toti defends himself valiantly. He goes to see Giacomino, threatens him with severe reprisals unless he comes back, and then goes off triumphantly with his little Niní by the hand, leaving behind him the admonition, "Think it over, Giacomino!"[6]

Pirandello adapted this story for the stage in 1916 at the insistence of the director Nino Martoglio. Martoglio needed a play to fill out the repertory of the Sicilian actor Angelo Musco. The first version, in dialect, was presented at the Teatro Nazionale in Rome on 10 July 1916, two months after the opening of Chiarelli's *The Mask and the Face* at the Teatro Argentina. It was inevitable that the two plays should invite comparison. Chiarelli's play was written with true objectivity. *Pensaci, Giacomino!* fairly drips with sentiment. The ironic quality and the theme of the two plays are very similar; but the tragic undertone of the farce in each case is strikingly different. In the case of Chiarelli's Paolo what is tragic is the necessity that forces the individual to submit to the exorbitant demands of society. In *Pensaci, Giacomino!* the source of tragedy is deeper. It is in the cold hatred that society arouses in the individuals who comprise it, and the terrible cynicism with which it is necessary for the individual to defend his happiness against the invasion of the collective.

In Chiarelli's play Paolo makes the most elaborate concessions to public opinion. Professor Toti, however, does nothing special to save face. It is enough for him that he has provided a façade of respectability behind which his *ménage à trois* can operate, and he insists that, however false it is, it be respected. Moreover he is prepared to enforce his demands with economic and social sanctions more cogent than anything the opposition can devise. Toward the end of a dreary life he has arranged a happy ending, with a young woman singing in his kitchen, smiles everywhere, and a little boy, whom he loves as a son, to brighten his last years. In the teeth of public opinion, represented by the upright sister, the priest, and the beadle's wife, all of whom are determined to ruin his happiness, he defends heroically a position which from the standpoint of bourgeois respectability is indefensible.

Toti's official status is that of a happy father, somewhat advanced in years, with a pretty wife and a little son. Everyone sees through this ludicrously artificial construction. But so long as it is maintained, it serves the purpose every bit as well as if it were true. The implication is clear: reality is what passes for reality.

The relation of appearance and reality, which elsewhere is central in Pirandello's drama, is touched upon in this play only by way of implication. The metaphysical problem was obviously not uppermost in the author's mind when the story was written, and the play derives its pathos and its comedy not from any philosophical consideration but from the situation of the individual who strives mightily to convert illusion into reality, and in fact succeeds. At bottom the situation in *Pensaci, Giacomino!* is similar to the situation in *The Wild Duck*. It centers on the maintenance of what, in that play, Dr. Relling calls a *livslögnen*—the lie that makes it possible for people to live. In Ibsen's view the conflict is between the humanity of the individual and the inhumanity of the vague entity called society, expressed in terms of the Ideal. Pirandello formulated the issue in other terms, as the conflict of Life and Form, the contrast between the vital energy and the rigid mold which shuts it in.

The social implications of the *novella* and the ambience of the narrative were greatly extended in the play, which benefited also from ideas that Pirandello had first expressed in his early novel *Il fu Mattia Pascal* (1904). There it was demonstrated that to live in society it is necessary to have civil status. But civil status implies social duties and obligations, not all of which are in the individual interest, and some of which are unendurable. In "La Carriola" the eminent jurist relieves the pressures of his position in society by playing childish games with his little dog. In *Pensaci, Giacomino!* the Professor assumes the role of husband—absurd in the circumstances—in order to arrange a suitable domestic environment, but he has use only for the form, not its substance. It is the same with the role he plays as a schoolteacher. He tells the director of his *liceo:*

> You see the profession and you don't see the man: you hear that I want to take a wife—you imagine a wife—and he married to her—and you burst out laughing; or you are disturbed, as you were a little while ago, thinking that the boys were making fun of me, while all the time it was the professor they were making fun of. The profession is one thing, the man is something else. Outside the school the boys respect me; they kiss my hand. Here they practise their profession of students, and

therefore they have to rag anyone who follows the profession of schoolmaster, and especially someone who does it as I do, as a poor, tired and
bored old man. . . .[7]

The distinction between the two orders of reality is very clear in
Toti's mind. The one is public and it is, in his view, both necessary and
formal, but not of vital importance. The other is private and personal,
and it is his only true concern:

You are now imagining that you will see me (He makes an ample gesture indicating the cuckold's horns) . . . I'm on the list, you know. Signed, sealed and delivered. But not for me: they will go on the head of
my profession as husband, which concerns me only for the appearance.
I, however, will see to it that the husband, as husband, wears them.
Not I.[8]

Since in this play, even more clearly than in the story from which it
was taken, the elements that became the basis of Pirandello's later work
are all in some measure present and active, it is reasonable to suppose
that at this early point in his dramatic career Pirandello's philosophic apparatus was already virtually complete. Here, as elsewhere in his drama,
what is principally effective is not the doctrinal aspect of the situation,
but its pathos. *Pensaci, Giacomino!* is first-rate romantic comedy. In comparison with *L'École des femmes*, which treats a similar subject in far different fashion, it reveals warmth and a depth of understanding entirely
foreign to the rigid assumptions of classic comedy even at its best. Few
plays of the modern theatre make one more keenly aware of the loneliness of life, the loneliness of age. There is much to be said for this play;
but what is chiefly memorable is the picture of the old man walking happily down the tree-lined road with the little boy by the hand—"a charming companion on the way to the grave." It is a picture that would, no
doubt, appropriately grace a bank calendar; but in the theatre a work of
art sometimes has greatness not because it is in itself great, but because
of the unwritten—and perhaps never-to-be-written—masterpiece it
suggests. *Pensaci, Giacomino!* is not a great play. But the play it symbolizes is among the great masterpieces of the drama.

The Theatre of the Grotesque was an aspect of the revival of Naturalism at the end of the nineteenth century; but it had also a romantic tinge.
The French drama of the Second Empire, under the influence of such
masters as Dumas *fils* and Émile Augier, had amply demonstrated the
social inconvenience of non-conformity. In the 1880's Ibsen made the

disadvantages of conformity more clearly evident, and the cause of individualism began once again to take on the heroic aspect of the time of Byron and Shelley. Until Pirandello's day there were few devil's disciples on the Italian stage. But in the period following the *Risorgimento* the social tensions of the earlier period were once again manifested in Italy, and it was natural that the theatre should reflect them. The writers of the Grotesque did not have much in common as a group, but they were all opposed to the stuffiness of social convention and the despotism of traditional ideas. Pirandello himself was deeply rooted in the social traditions of Sicily; but he had been brought up among Garibaldian fighters, and whatever spoke of freedom stirred his blood like a trumpet call. *Pensaci, Giacomino!* was, and is, a play of revolutionary ideas. Its assault on the social order and the hypocrisy of middle-class morality was circumspect, but it was unmistakable. The author could hardly stop at this point. The next step was distinctly subversive. *Pensaci, Giacomino!* was intended to unsettle received ideas of respectability. *Così è (se vi pare)* was intended to unsettle all ideas.

In a review he published in *La Concordia*, 12 July 1916, Adriano Tilgher summarily dismissed *Pensaci, Giacomino!* as an inconsiderable comedy, not worth serious discussion. But he was in error. Pirandello was, from the first, a serious writer. In 1887, when he was twenty, he had written to his sister Rosalina in the tragic tones of a university student who had been reading Foscolo:

> Greatness, fame, glory no longer stimulate my soul. Is there any point in exhausting one's brain and one's spirit in order to be remembered and appreciated by men? Ridiculous! I write and study in order to forget myself!

In 1916 he was forty-nine; and a great deal had happened to him since he was twenty to confirm him in these ideas. His melancholy doubtless retained some vestige of Byronism, but it was by now both systematic and systemic. It had become a world-view. The essence of irony, he wrote now, was the awareness that being is insubstantial, an illusion peopled by shadows. Thus, what is experienced as tragic is actually comic, and our entire life-experience is a pitiful absurdity. From this standpoint all dramatic representation is, in one way or another, grotesque, and all that is necessary to make this evident is for the dramatist to view his characters from a sufficient height. To the gods on Olympus all human passion must seem grotesque. In the preface to *Erma bifronte*, a collection of stories published ten years before, in 1906, he had written:

> I see a sort of labyrinth in which the soul moves through all sorts of diverse, opposed and intricate paths, without finding any way out. And in this labyrinth I see a herm with a laughing face and another face that weeps; it laughs indeed with one face at the tears of the other.

This is the basis of the Theatre of the Grotesque, as Pirandello understood it, and also the theme of the essay entitled "L'umorismo" which he wrote in 1908. But already in his middle years there appeared behind the double mask of his Hermes a face that neither laughed nor wept, but wore an expression of infinite weariness. In the *novella*, "La distruzione dell'uomo," one Nicola Petix, accused of murder, will not speak a word in his own defence. He is poor. He has spent all his life in universities, meditating on the ways of men, and the fruit of his studies is unendurable tedium. He has made nothing of his own life because in trying to find some reason for existence he has arrived at the quintessence of things, the void. For ten years he has contemplated the children running about noisily in the filthy courtyard beneath his window, and also the strenuous efforts of his neighbors to bring more progeny into the world. Among these neighbors is Signora Porella, a lady of forty-six who, after suffering fifteen miscarriages in her nineteen years of marriage, is now on the point of bringing forth a child:

> When he was sure that this sixteenth pregnancy would at last reach fulfillment, Petix decided to destroy mankind. Mankind. Not one man out of many, but all mankind in one, in order through this one to avenge all those little brutes who live merely in order to live, without knowing that they live, except for that bit, always the same, that they are condemned to do each day.

In accordance with this pious resolution, Petix performs the one useful action of his life. He pushes the pregnant Signora Porella into the Tiber.

The success of his Sicilian plays under Musco's management so far encouraged Pirandello that his friends readily induced him to adapt others of his *novelle* for the stage. *Pensaci, Giacomino!* was followed that same year by *Liolà* at the Teatro Argentina. It too was written in dialect, and later normalized in Italian. The following year Pirandello dramatized the *novella*, "La Signora Frola e il Signor Ponza." He called the resulting play *Così è (se vi pare)*—in English, "That's how it is (if that's how it seems to you)"—which was rendered by the English translator as *Right You Are, If You Think So.*

It was presented at the Teatro Olimpico in Milan on 18 June 1917 by the company of Virgilio Talli. The following week, on 27 June 1917, Musco produced *Il berretto a sonagli* in dialect at the Nazionale in Rome, and followed it in October with *La giara,* a rollicking one-act comedy. On 27 November 1917 Ruggero Ruggeri played *Il piacere dell'onestà* in Torino. For Pirandello, evidently, a new day had dawned. He had long ago given up the idea of becoming a playwright. Now he had four plays running concurrently in major Italian cities. Nevertheless none of the critics was as yet disposed to take him seriously. He was considered a gifted and amusing caricaturist of provincial manners. The public came to his plays in order to laugh at rustic antics, and his plays were applauded as a welcome consequence of the rising interest in the regional customs and the folklore of Italy.

Così è (se vi pare), however, was not folklore, and it was not entirely funny. It caricatured provincial types; but it was a disquieting play that inevitably provoked discussion, and was intended to do so. Whatever might be done about the others, this play could not be summarily dismissed. With it Pirandello made his debut in the theatre of ideas.

The play purports to be a demonstration, in comedic terms, of the illusory nature of truth—a theme perhaps more apt for a class in elementary philosophy than for the stage. In the *novella* on which it is based, the epistemological question is marginal. The problem there is a more difficult one—the impossibility of distinguishing madness from sanity.[9]

The *novella* is presented in the form of a *dubbio,* an anecdote that raises a debatable question. It is a genre rooted in the literature of the Trecento: Boccaccio has a series of *dubbii* in the *Filocolo.* Pirandello's anecdote centers on the singular domestic situation of a minor government official in a provincial capital. In accordance with the veristic tendency of his early stories, Pirandello identifies the locale with precision. The action takes place in the town of Valdana, and the story is faithful both to its topography and to the character of the local population. Signor Ponza has been recently assigned to Valdana as secretary to the prefecture. He has brought with him his wife and his mother-in-law, Signora Frola. But it has been discovered that Ponza has settled his wife in a sixth-story flat in a building on the outskirts of town, while his mother-in-law lives in furnished rooms in the center. It is further noted that Signora Frola and her daughter are not permitted to speak to one another, although they communicate every day by means of messages sent up and down in a basket from the daughter's balcony. Signor Ponza, moreover, appears to be on excellent terms with his mother-in-law. His wife is kept locked up in her rooms, and does not go out.

This bizarre situation excites such a buzz of interest that an official investigation is deemed necessary. It is Signora Frola who first dispels the mystery. Her son-in-law, she says is an excitable man, the victim of a delusion which must be maintained to preserve his sanity. Signora Frola's daughter was a delicate girl, and Signor Ponza's sexual ardor was such as to endanger her health. It was therefore deemed advisable to spirit her away secretly and to put her in a sanatorium to rest. Ponza, however, was certain that she was dead. The idea drove him to the verge of madness, so that when his wife was restored to him he could not believe it was really she. There was a second marriage. He is therefore now under the impression that the woman in his house is his second wife, and it is necessary for mother and daughter to stay apart so as not to disturb his illusion.

This explanation satisfies everybody until Signor Ponza appears with further explanations. In reality, he tells them, it is not he who must be humored in his madness, but his mother-in-law. Her daughter in fact died four years ago, and her death sent Signora Frola into so deep a depression that it seemed she would not survive. But means were found to convince her that her daughter had in fact recovered and was living happily with Ponza. His second wife lends herself willingly to this deception, and Signora Frola is once again herself. But it is obviously not possible for them to meet.

The enigma, the narrator says, is insoluble, but "this much is certain, in any case: that both show, the one for the other, a marvellous spirit of sacrifice, most touching, and that each demonstrates the most exquisite consideration and compassion for the presumed madness of the other." As for those who pass Signor Ponza and his mother-in-law walking together happily arm in arm in the town, they "study, stare and spy, and nothing! in no way do they succeed in understanding which of the two is mad, where is the fantasy, and where the reality."

On this note the *novella* ends, and it is here that the play begins. The element of the marvellous that recommended the strange case of Signor Ponza to the author when he first took it up was not uppermost in his mind when he adapted it years later for the stage. By that time Pirandello was apparently thinking of himself in terms of the distinction he was to draw in the preface to *Six Characters in Search of an Author*, the distinction between the historical and the philosophical writer. He was already well aware of the brutal intrusion of society into the life of the individual, and also of the ingenuity of the human psyche in devising the fictions which make life possible. *Pensaci, Giacomino!* had touched on both these points. Pirandello now transformed the social question into a philosophical problem.

Così è (se vi pare) can hardly be considered a triumph of rational analysis. As it is presented, the case of Signor Ponza and his mother-in-law is far too special to warrant a generalization. The *novella* presents an interesting case of domestic relations, a description of the psychological adjustments of two overly sensitive people in a painful situation. But for the purposes of the play Pirandello found it necessary to posit the total annihilation of all the objective evidence. Signor Ponza's village, accordingly, is totally destroyed by an earthquake, and the shock of the disaster in which Ponza lost his entire family, and Signora Frola all her relatives might well be expected to unhinge the minds of even the most phlegmatic survivors. The question of whether or not Signora Frola's daughter is still alive thus ceases to be a matter of fact. It becomes a matter of faith.

The action takes the form of an inquest into what is obviously an insoluble problem; but Pirandello left nothing to chance. He took care to provide the play with a personal representative who explains everything and points the moral, lest the audience miss the point. Lamberto Laudisi is described as a man in his forties, slim and elegant, a skeptic with a saturnine sense of humor. He plays no part in the action, save as the *raisonneur*, and it may be that he is unduly obtrusive even in that role. When the strange situation with regard to Signor Ponza and his mother-in-law is explained to him by the local busybodies he points out at once that all efforts to arrive at the facts will be fruitless since the parties have evidently conjured up opposed realities which cannot, and must not, be reconciled—"and not because these factual data which you are trying to find have been destroyed . . . but because they have destroyed them in themselves, in their souls—will you try to understand? She creates for him, or he for her, a fantasy that has the same subsistence as reality, in which these people live henceforth in perfect accord and tranquillity."[10]

Since the conflicting testimony of the two principals can neither be reconciled nor authenticated, Counsellor Agazzi arranges for a confrontation of the two. The result is a scene in which Ponza, greatly excited, drives Signora Frola from the room in tears. When she is gone he instantly calms down, and explains that his excitement was feigned for her benefit, since he must pretend to be mad in order to ensure her sanity. In the third act, Laudisi, still playing the wise buffoon, causes the ladies to shudder by suggesting that Signor Ponza's wife does not really exist as a woman, but only as a phantom. For Signora Frola she is the phantom of Lina, her daughter; for Signor Ponza she is the phantom of Giulia, his second wife. The Prefect, now thoroughly aroused, orders Ponza to fetch in this phantom, who alone is in a position to define her identity. When she makes her appearance, heavily veiled, both Ponza and Signora Frola rush up to her, the one crying, "Giulia!", the other, "Lina!" But Signora Ponza calmly tells them to leave her and not to be afraid. They go off together, embracing one another, in tears. Then the veiled woman takes command of the situation. They are the witnesses of a misfortune, she tells the assembled company, the details of which must remain forever hidden, since only in this manner can it be remedied. The Prefect insists they must have the truth.

SIGNORA PONZA: The truth is this. For Signora Frola I am her daughter, and for Signor Ponza his second wife. Yes. And for myself, nobody! Nobody!

THE PREFECT: Ah no, for yourself, you, Signora, must be either the one or the other.

SIGNORA PONZA: No sir. For myself I am whatever I am believed to be. (*She leaves the room.*)

LAUDISI: And there you are, ladies and gentlemen. That is how the truth speaks. (*He bursts into laughter.*)

The curtain comes down on what is supposed to be a comic note, but it must be difficult for the actor to force a laugh at this point. The situation is not funny; quite the contrary, it is sad. Perhaps it is grotesque.

In spite of Laudisi's philosophical demonstrations, the play is not so much concerned with the nature of reality as with the difficulty of eliciting a fact through the examination of witnesses. In a court of law there is neither time nor room for metaphysical speculation. There the truth is the opinion of a jury, reality is given a statistical basis, and truth is established by a consensus. In the case of Signor Ponza, Pirandello puts his case in terms that admit of no verdict. The mood of the final curtain is not one of puzzlement, but one of pathos.

The intellectual exercises which amuse the *raisonneur* in this play are not the source of its power as drama. For that we must look to the situation, the way in which these characters, out of their love for one another, are able to sustain a reality which, however fragile, is capable of sheltering them from the pain of existence. What they have arrived at is both ridiculous and infinitely pathetic. The implication is inescapable: the reality we normally construct for ourselves, with its moral structure, its just and omnipotent God, its promise of eternal bliss, and its basis in the love that passeth understanding, is as fragile a construct, and as useful, as the realities of Signor Ponza and his mother-in-law, with which it is best not to meddle. As a demonstration, perhaps, the play leaves something to be desired; but as a parable it has cogency.

Così è (se vi pare) was a bold stroke for one who had come but lately to the theatre, and evidently it caused Pirandello some uneasiness. A few months before its production in Milan, he wrote his son Stefano that the play was "a great piece of deviltry . . . more of a parable than a play: I am satisfied with it. It is certainly of an originality that cries out. But I don't know what its fortunes will be, on account of the extraordinary audacity of the situation. . . . In the judgment of our friends it is the best thing I have done so far. I think so too." He added: "It is not improbable that Ruggero Ruggeri will produce it next May here in Rome . . . it may have a very great success . . . as you can see, the dramatic parenthesis is not yet closed."[11]

Ruggero Ruggeri, however, was not inclined to produce the play. Pirandello had submitted it to him with true Italian enthusiasm. It was, he wrote:

> A parable, truly original, new in its conception, and most daring in its development, and destined—insofar as one can judge in the reading—to a most certain effectiveness by reason of the intense and uncommon interest that it quickly provokes from the very first act, and which it maintains, progressively increasing it, throughout the other two.

He went on to stress especially "the last words of the play, in which are placed all its profound meaning: words put into the mouth of a lady whose face is covered by an impenetrable veil: a most vivid dramatic character and a pure symbol of truth."

In spite of this fervent recommendation *Così è (se vi pare)* was not performed in Rome; but it had, as Pirandello wrote Stefano later, an extraordinary success in Milan. "Talli said that in over 25 years in the theatre he had never seen such a strange and interesting *première*." He added: "I don't know if I've told you that the parable deals with the value of reality . . ."[12]

Il berretto a sonagli was produced in Rome almost concurrently with the run of *Così è (se vi pare)* in Milan. The title might well be translated *Cap and Bells*. The play is set in a Sicilian town, and it is an outstanding example of the sort of comedy at which Pirandello excelled. The action is framed around a singular character, a man of great charm and intelligence. He is the stage counterpart of the peasant Tararà in the *novella*, "La verità," from which the play was taken. In *Cap and Bells* the hero, Ciampa, is not a peasant. He is a bank clerk, with a pen stuck behind his ear, and a young wife whom he keeps ostentatiously locked up in his house. It is rumored, but not certain, that she is the mistress of his employer, the cavaliere Fiorisco. Fiorisco's wife, Beatrice, is pathologically jealous. She desires to teach her husband a lesson by causing a scandal and, to this end, she arranges to have the local constable surprise the lovers *in flagrante delicto*. Her plan almost succeeds, but the proof is not conclusive, and the erring couple, arrested in haste, must now be released for lack of evidence. Nevertheless, in the public eye, everyone is disgraced, but most of all Ciampa, whose head will henceforth be adorned with invisible horns.

Ciampa, it is suggested, was not unaware of his wife's misconduct, and it was in order to cover it that he was so circumspect with regard to her behavior. His code is strict: "I march with a principle: wives, sardines and anchovies: these two under oil and brine, wives under lock and key." He has, he says, an agreement with his wife: "Here is the window. The door I will lock. Lean out of the window. But see to it that no one comes to tell me: Ciampa, your wife at her window is about to break her neck."[13]

They are all of them puppets, he tells Beatrice:

> the divine spirit enters into us and makes us puppets. Each one of us, afterwards, constructs a puppet for himself—now there are two, the puppet he is, and the one he has made. And there the trouble starts! Because each puppet, dear lady, wants to be respected for the character he represents to the world. At bottom nobody is content with his role. Each man, face to face with his puppet, would perhaps spit in its face. But as to the others, no; by the others it must be respected.[14]

Accordingly, when the breath of scandal touches him, Ciampa announces that to save his honor he must kill his wife and also her lover.

From this resolve, he can be turned only on condition that Beatrice, who is said to have acted in a moment of madness, be declared officially insane. She is thereupon condemned to spend some months in a clinic, and the curtain falls on Ciampa's triumphant laughter, "horrible laughter, a mixture of rage, of savage pleasure, and despair."

Il berretto a sonagli followed *La maschera e il volto* on the stage by something less than a year, and obviously the two plays are comparable. Like Paolo in Chiarelli's play, Ciampa is more concerned with appearances than with reality. Whatever the sorry truth may be, he insists on being considered a man of honor in the community. To this end he exacts unquestioning obedience from his wife, and insists also on being obeyed to the letter by the wife of her lover. If it is suspected that he is a conniving cuckold, at least no one can affirm this with confidence, not even his employer; and in any case the truth is of no particular consequence. As in the case of Signor Ponza, what passes for reality is real. There is, insofar as the public is concerned, no other criterion.

There are, however, private criteria. Ciampa knows that his wife betrays him, and the pain he feels is real. The figure he cuts in public—the puppet he has constructed to represent him to the world—has no true existence, and it feels nothing. But the man it represents is sick at heart. Ciampa, like most of Pirandello's eccentric characters, must be played by a gifted comedian; but he is a tragic character, and has very pathetic lines to speak:

> Ah, Signora—I speak now . . . not for myself . . . I speak in general. How can you understand, Signora, what so often a man suffers—let us say, an ugly man, an old man, and poor—for the love of a woman who crushes his heart as in a vise, but who, when she makes him cry, Ah!—at once quenches the scream in his throat with a kiss, so that the poor old fellow melts and is intoxicated—. How can you know, Signora, with what pain, what torment, this old man resigns himself to the point where he can share the love of this woman with another man— rich, perhaps, young, handsome—especially, if afterwards this woman gives him the satisfaction of knowing that he is the master, and that nobody can possibly be the wiser? I speak in general, please note! I don't speak of myself! —It is like a wound, a thing like that, Signora: a hidden wound of which one is terribly ashamed. And you—what do you do? You reach out your hand and lay it bare—so—for everyone to see.[15]

It is out of this blend of comedy and pathos that Pirandello's plays are made—the special comic mood that is described in "L'umorismo." The similarity to Ibsen's idea of comedy—or Chekhov's—seems clear. The difference is a question of climate and temperament. Even in his most pathetic scenes Ibsen is deliberately cold; he preserves his composure with what seems to be an almost morbid fear of betraying some trace of sentimentality. His characters are made to suffer deeply; but in Ibsen's plays nobody screams. In Chekhov's plays, also, one must listen intently to catch the sound of heartbreak. But Pirandello's characters have no shame. Their screams—like those of Ariosto's Isabella—may be heard *a molto miglia*. Their lungs are strong. These characters touch the heart; but they make one smile. Four centuries lie between Ariosto and Pirandello. But it requires no great critical acumen to see the resemblance of the calligraphy.

De Sanctis, in a familiar passage of his *History of Italian Literature*, speaks of the *Decameron* of Boccaccio—a Human Comedy, in contrast with the *Divine Comedy* of Dante—as an exploration of the pit of Malebolge in hell. Pirandello also explored a world that elicits in the minds of the just both horror and pity, as well as laughter. It is the world that Augustine characterized as *massa perditionis*. This was the special domain of classic comedy from the time of Plautus, and Pirandello's realism is notably in the classic tradition. But Pirandello had trouble with realism. He was by temperament a romantic, steeped in the sensibility of a heroic age. What he saw of humanity excited in him both disgust and amusement, but it also stirred depths of anguish that were altogether foreign to the classic tradition, and that had nothing to do with the realism either of the *trecento* or of the nineteenth century. He thought of himself primarily as a humorist, like Chekhov, but his humor was typically Italian and never far from tears, and it is this blending of the absurd and the pathetic that gives his work, from first to last, its characteristic savor.

Five months after Musco's production of *Il berretto a sonagli* Ruggero Ruggeri presented *Il piacere dell'onestà* in Torino. *The Pleasure of Honesty* was adapted from a *novella* which Pirandello had written in 1905. It developed a situation in some ways quite different from that of the earlier play, but however different they may be in detail the two plays are cast in the same mold, and it is evident that the ideas they embody were at this time uppermost in Pirandello's mind.

The situation in *Il piacere dell'onestà* was perhaps suggested by an incident that took place in Pirandello's youth. While the family was living in Palermo, Pirandello's father managed to get his widowed niece with child. To save her from disgrace a man was paid to wed her, and the child was thus legitimized. Subsequently Stefano moved his family back to Porto Empedocle, leaving Luigi to study at the *liceo* in Palermo. In *Il piacere dell'onestà* the Marchese Fabio Colli, now estranged from his wife, has got himself into a similar scrape with Agata Renni, a lady of twenty-seven. Agata's mother, Maddalena, has connived at their affair, and in the present emergency, she and the Marchese commission Fabio's cousin Maurizio to find a suitable match for the pregnant girl. Maurizio finds a man of good family who, after some suspicion of dishonesty, has fallen on evil days. He is called Angelo Baldovino.

Baldovino is one of Pirandello's most engaging characters. He is described as a man in his forties, with red hair and a short beard, and a deep, slow voice. He carries his pince-nez in his hand. Occasionally he perches it on the end of his nose. He is, like Ciampa, a man of method, rigorously logical and far-sighted, and in the course of a misspent life he has acquired philosophical attitudes which curiously color his speech and his actions.

When he is introduced to the Marchese and his mistress, Baldovino takes immediate command of the situation. He announces that he is revolted by the part he has so far played in the world. He realizes also that the part he is now asked to undertake is contemptible. But if he is to play this part properly his performance must be respected. He insists therefore on a completely honest management of the position he is accepting. He has noted in his pocketbook all the relevant data—the situation of the parties, their ages, and respective relationships. The Marchese desires to purchase a form. Baldovino is willing to supply one, but solely on the conditions he prescribes:

> I enter here, and at once I become, so far as you are concerned, what I am expected to be—I *construct* myself—in other words, I present myself to you in a form adapted to the relation I am contracting. And a similar transformation takes place automatically with you who receive me here. But, at bottom, in these constructions of ours, behind the jealousies and pretences, there remain hidden our most secret thoughts, our most intimate feelings, everything, in short, that we are for ourselves alone, outside the relationships that we desire to establish. . . .[16]

The distinction that Baldovino draws between his two selves, th public self and the private, is the source of the dramatic tensions of th situation which now takes shape. What is required of him at this junc ture is to take on a new form. Thus far he has played the scoundrel. He welcomes the chance to play the honest man. But the part implies the play. In order for him to play the husband successfully it is necessary that the others improvise roles in accordance with his. This will involve, necessarily, some inconvenience for the lovers who have engaged him. Now that he is here their former relations must cease.

For Fabio the discomfort of the part that is thus forced on him is such that, ten months later, after Agata's child is born in legitimate wedlock, he longs to rid himself of the superfluous husband. It is not easy. Baldovino is now the manager of Fabio's firm, and has been playing the part of the honest man with such zeal that his honesty has become a nuisance to everyone. He is no longer, he admits, a living person. He has become a pure abstraction, like a saint in a church mural, an embodiment of honesty.

In these circumstances Fabio contrives, with the help of one of his directors, to place Baldovino in a position where he can embezzle a large sum without being detected. Baldovino sees through the trick. He had hoped to enjoy his newfound honesty by springing the trap that has been set for him, and thus showing up the wily director. But now he realizes that if Fabio is willing, out of love for Agata, to brand the father of his child as a thief, the pleasure of honesty must come from something other than the forms of honesty. For the sake of the self which underlies the parts he plays, Baldovino is willing to play the scoundrel once more so as to rid Agata of his presence. But here, once again, he insists on his conditions. He is willing to play the thief, just as he was willing to play the husband. But he accepts only the form, not the substance of evil. He agrees to take the blame for the theft; but it is Fabio who must actually steal the money.

At this point life takes a hand in the game. Baldovino has fallen in love with Agata. He can no longer play his part with the logic and good sense of a conscientious actor. He is no longer an abstraction. He has begun to live again and to feel desire and passion. So far he has been able to see clearly among these people whom life has blinded. Now the situation has become critical. "When one lives," he says, "one lives and does not see oneself. I came here in order not to live, therefore I can see.—Do you wish to make me live by force?—Look to yourselves if life takes me again and blinds me also!"

As Baldovino's life begins to influence his mind he becomes not only emotional, but confused in his aims. He had anticipated the pleasure of forcing Fabio to steal. Now he resolves to embezzle the money himself in order to punish himself for stepping out of character with regard to Agata. While he is turning over these ideas, Agata quite unexpectedly settles his hash. If he goes, she tells him, she will go with him, taking her child. But Baldovino has scruples. He has been wearing so far, he tells her, the mask of the honest man—an unnatural form against which he may be prompted to rebel. Agata does not know him as he really is. But his scruples do not serve. Now that Agata has come to love him, her faith in him prevents him from relapsing into his former role. He has in fact become what he purports to be, an honest man. Thus the play ends happily. She has found a husband, and he a wife, a son, and a way of life.

Il piacere dell'onestà ends happily, but not well. Baldovino's scene in the first act is magnificent. In comparison his final scene seems confused and sentimental. Obviously in the theatre form has its advantages. Life is messy. Pirandello prided himself on his realism, his objectivity. In fact his romantic disposition was irrepressible. For all his vaunted cynicism and skepticism Pirandello nourished secretly ideas of the fundamental nobility of human nature and the power of love to heal and to restore, which would do credit to Rostand. Baldovino is a cynic and an ironist, but he has the gentle heart; and, in the words of Guido Guinizelli, "al cor gentil ripara sempre amore." The result in this play is a happy ending which is not entirely convincing, but which amply suggests Pirandello's compassion for the creatures of his fantasy, creatures which were, after all, himself, and which characterized him more fully and accurately than the forms he assumed, like Baldovino, to represent him to the world.

Il berretto a sonagli and *Il piacere dell'onestà*, early as they are, mark a high point in Pirandello's career in the theatre, a point at which his work centered primarily on a characterization. The two plays have a common theme. *Il berretto a sonagli* develops fully the idea of the mask and the face which is characteristic of the Grotesque plays in general. In *Il piacere dell'onestà* this idea is carried some steps further, and involves the contrast of *vita* and *forma*. This becomes a dominant consideration in a great deal of Pirandello's later drama. Both plays deal with the embarrassing situation of the complaisant husband, and in the case of Baldovino there is

also the perplexing question of spiritual, as opposed to physical, paternity, a problem which Pirandello explored at length in a whole series of
short stories and plays.

Many of his *novelle* are based on extraordinary characters involved in
singular situations. Such characters could hardly be put on the stage
without the cooperation of highly gifted actors. In this respect Pirandello
was fortunate. The Italian theatre had specialized in highly talented
character actors from the time of Goldoni, and the *novelle* which Pirandello selected for dramatization in these years were shaped so as to give
such actors the fullest opportunity to display their skill. The result is
that plays framed in this fashion lean heavily on a single part, and
require very little of anyone else. After the opening of *Il giuoco delle parti*
Pirandello complained to Stefano, his son, "Except for Ruggeri . . .
none of them satisfied me, but we must adapt ourselves to what we find
in a company that rests on the exceptional ability of a single actor." [17]
His complaint, though understandable, was probably unjustified. In that
play, as in *Il berretto a sonagli*, apart from the principal part there is not
much for anyone to do.

In *Il piacere dell'onestà* Pirandello developed the notion of *costruzione* for
the first time in detail. The conception of the world as a stage, and its
men and women as merely players, antedated Shakespeare by some centuries; but in 1918 the idea seemed novel and stimulating. Pirandello put
the metaphor through its paces with the skill of an animal trainer. In his
view the form which the individual "constructs" for himself in order to
survive in the world of forms is analogous to the part in which an actor is
cast in a play. An individual, as Ciampa points out, is a dual entity, and
when the vital self, which is formless, is confronted with the form which
it has for the time constructed a discovery occurs which gives rise to
drama. The analogy with the situation of the actor in the theatre is thus
particularly striking.

In the *novella* called "Il pipistrello" (1920) Pirandello describes the
disruption of the reality principle that results when a bat—a real bat—
flies into a play during a rehearsal, frightens the leading lady out of her
part, and completely shatters the distinction between illusion and reality.
In Pirandello's view this distinction is too fragile to withstand so much as
a breath of doubt, much less the intrusion of a bat. Thus, in the *novella*,
"La realtà del sogno," a lady of exceptional modesty suffers a nervous
breakdown as the result of dreaming that she has had sexual relations

with her husband's friend, a man whom she obviously admires, but whose presence causes her constant uneasiness.

It is a short step from the conclusion that illusion and reality are indistinguishable to the idea that life and form—*vita e forma*—must not be confused. If it is assumed that the self is a Protean entity that is capable of assuming as many forms as an actor, it becomes impossible to say where its reality resides. The next question is whether it can be said to have any reality whatever. From this viewpoint the self of the individual is always provisional; essentially it is something *in posse*, an indefinable self-consciousness; and all identity seems questionable. This was a reflection which Pirandello found, perhaps for personal reasons, particularly congenial. From the time of *Così è (se vi pare)* it became the kernel of his dramatic system.

Pirandello was now working with incredible speed. He had discovered a seemingly inexhaustible vein of dramatic material in his *novelle*, and he labored like a *caruso* of the sulfur mines to bring his stories to the stage. *Il piacere dell'onestà* was followed by *Ma non è una cosa seria* in November 1919, and the following month, *Il giuoco delle parti* was played by Ruggeri in Rome.

Ma non è una cosa seria is an amusing play of no great intellectual pretensions. The title means *But It's Not a Serious Thing.* The plot recalls Molnar's *The Glass Slipper.* The heroine, Gasparina—called Gasparotta, an unflattering inflection—combines the most appealing features of Cinderella and Boccaccio's Griselda. She is a patient slave who runs a boarding house for single men. The hero is Memmo Speranza, an elegant young man of thirty who has just returned from the hospital after a duel. He is a very susceptible young man. His fancy is caught by every girl he meets, but he has trouble reconciling his romantic nature with his native common sense. Everyone, he explains, feels the bliss of love's eternal moment, but women—and more particularly their relatives—insist on protracting the eternal moment eternally. Memmo gives his word each time he falls in love, only to withdraw it immediately after. The consequence is the periodic duel with the father or the brother. In eighteen years he has been engaged twelve times. The last incident almost killed him. But he has hit on a remedy. He has decided to marry his landlady, Gasparotta, in order to avoid future engagements. He is marrying her, so he says, in order not to get married. He will settle an annuity on

Gasparotta, and give her the country villa which he owns. For the rest, she may do as she pleases, and he reserves the same liberty of action for himself: "As a marriage it is strictly a matter of form."

But once he is safely married, Memmo falls in love once again with his former flame, causing his mistress of the moment, Loletta, to suffer because of his sudden coldness. His friend, Magnasco, a logician, gives Loletta a graphic explanation of the need for logic in human relations:

MAGNASCO: Ah, you don't understand, dear Loletta! Logic, you know what that is? Here—imagine a kind of pump with a filter. The pump is here. . . . (*He points to his head.*) The filter is between the pump and the heart. You feel something in your heart, here. The machine called logic pumps it up and filters it. The feeling at once loses its heat, its cloudiness; it is cooled, it is purified, it is i-de-al-ized! Everything works marvellously well here because—naturally, now we are outside of life, in the abstract. Life is there, where the heat is, and the cloudiness, where there is no logic, you understand? But does it seem logical to you, forgive me, to cry? No. It's human.

LOLETTA: I'd like to know then why logic was given to us.

MAGNASCO: Because . . . because nature, which loves us so dearly, does not wish us to suffer only through our feelings and our passions, it wants us to poison ourselves also with the corrosive sublimate of logical deduction. Example: it is not enough now that you should suffer: I demonstrate to you with logic that you must necessarily suffer.[18]

Some months later Memmo has repented of his marriage with Gasparotta. Meanwhile rest and fresh air have restored her to her primal beauty, and now a secret admirer insists on marrying her in earnest. An annulment of the formal marriage is proposed. But when Memmo sees her, after a long absence, her beauty works upon him with such power that his passions are kindled, and he hastens to consummate the union. Thus the jest becomes serious, and the philanderer is caught in his own trap.

Ma non è una cosa seria is in fact not *cosa seria*. The character of Gasparina is charming, and affords an actress a delightful role, but her transformation from ugly duckling to beautiful swan is too much in the style of a fairy tale to carry conviction on a serious plane. The play was a pot-boiler—one of many—and the fact that Pirandello condescended to write pot-boilers at this time of his life testifies not so much to his need for money as to his deep-seated need to keep his name before the public at whatever cost.

Il giuoco delle parti makes a more serious impression. It was dramatized from a *novella* entitled "Quando s'è capito il giuoco"—"When the Game Is Understood"—published in 1913.[19] The title recalls a passage in Pirandello's novel, *I vecchi e i giovani* (1913), in which Don Cosmo Laurentano expresses once again Pirandello's recurrent theme:

> One thing is sad, my friends: to have understood the game! I mean the game of this daemonic joker that each of us has in himself, who amuses himself in representing for us a reality which he himself soon after shows to be an illusion, laughing at the troubles we have given ourselves because of it, and laughing at us also for deluding ourselves with it, since aside from these delusions there is no reality.[20]

In Pirandello's view to understand the game is also to withdraw from the table, and this is a kind of death. Thus in *Il giuoco delle parti—The Game of Parts*—the hero, Leone Gala, having understood the game, condemns himself to an existence which is something less than life. In the tale on which the play is based, a certain Memmo Viola is called upon to fight for his wife's honor. He is, in fact, a man of peace who lives by himself and divides his time between his kitchen and his books. His wife, from whom he has long been separated, is mainly a nuisance to him, and he pretends not to be aware that his close friend Gigi Venanzi is her lover. One evening his wife is insulted by a drunken roisterer. Memmo agrees to challenge the man—the man turns out to be a formidable duellist—and chooses Gigi as his second. But when the time comes to fight, Memmo flatly refuses to take up arms, so that Gigi, forced to act in his place, goes off to certain death.

There is a clear analogy between Memmo Viola's reasoning in this story and Baldovino's logic in *Il piacere dell'onestà*. In that play Baldovino is the form and Fabio the reality. Hence it is just that Fabio should be guilty of the theft for which Baldovino is ready to accept the blame. Similarly, in the case of Memmo Viola, it is only just that the man who actually enjoys the woman should bear the burden of defending her honor.

In the story the action is in the nature of a *beffa*, in this case a practical joke with a grim ending. The play follows very much along the same lines. The title—*The Game of Parts*—is derived from a passage in the *novella*. "I have told you," Memmo tells his friend Gigi, "that I am obliged to play my part, and you are obliged to play yours. My wife has been insulted. I am the husband, therefore I have issued the challenge.

But as for my actual fighting for her, that is something else. It is some time since it was my obligation, dear Gigi, to defend my wife's honor; that belongs now to you. . . . let's be just."

In *Il giuoco delle parti* the protagonists' names are changed. Memmo Viola becomes Leone Gala; Gigi has become Guido; and the wife, now called Silia, is a neurotic woman who delights in attracting attention to herself. Her behavior has been such, indeed, that her husband has erected between herself and him a barrier of indifference so thick that she is powerless to penetrate it.

For Silia, Leone's indifference is a provocation that can be removed only by his destruction. But Leone is not easy to destroy. He has cultivated a true philosophical apathy; he yields to every pressure, agrees to whatever is asked of him, and contrives to exist as little as possible. "It is sad," he remarks, "when one has understood the game of life. The only recourse is despair without bitterness. To have nothing, to feel nothing, so far as possible to cease living."

In order to preserve appearances Leone has agreed to spend a half hour each evening in his wife's apartment. When the play opens he finds Guido is already there. He is in no way disturbed. On the contrary, he seizes the opportunity to explain himself to his friend. To live, he says, is to inflict pain and to suffer pain. Consequently the only escape from the pain of existence is to live as little as possible, to cease to be a participant and to become a spectator of life. Since he has made a hobby of cooking, he paraphrases Schopenhauer in culinary terms:

LEONE: You eat meat at table. Where does it come from? From a chicken or a calf. You don't even think of them. We all hurt one another and, in living, each of us hurts himself . . . it's unavoidable. It is life. We must empty ourselves of life.

GUIDO: Fine. And after that, what is left?

LEONE: The satisfaction of living, no longer in ourselves, but in watching others live; and watching even ourselves live, from the outside, the little that we are forced to live.

GUIDO: No. I beg your pardon. That's not much.

LEONE: No. But in exchange you have the marvellous pleasure of the intellect, of the game that clarifies all the cloudiness of your feelings, that fixes in placid and precise lines everything that moves in tumult within you. . . .

Leone concedes, nevertheless, that this state of emotional abstraction would be dangerous unless one maintained some connection with the world outside himself which would keep him from being carried off into the air like a balloon. In cultivating the art of cooking he has found the necessary attachment to reality. The cook, he says, is able to balance the void with the plenum, and thus to restore his equilibrium each time life upsets him. And besides, he reflects, what better place to face disaster than in the kitchen? To defend oneself from the feelings that assault one it is only necessary to grasp the cause and to abstract its essence:

> It's as if someone suddenly threw you a raw egg. If you're not quick to catch it, you're taken unawares; you let it fall. But if you're quick, you catch it, you puncture it, you suck out its contents. What is left in your hand is an empty shell. You play with it a moment, then pof! you crush it and toss it away.[21]

As Leone leaves the apartment his wife hands him an empty eggshell. He gives it to Guido, remarking that it was not he who sucked it. Silia rushes to the window to throw the shell at his head. But he has already gone, and the eggshell lands among a group of young men who are milling about in the courtyard. A moment later they burst into the apartment, quite drunk and, taking her for Pepita, who lives on the floor below, they push her about merrily. Among them is one Miglioriti, accounted the best swordsman in the city, and a dead shot. When he realizes his mistake, he tries to apologize for the intrusion, but Silia deliberately makes a scene, calls in the neighbors to witness and, declaring that her husband will require satisfaction, takes Miglioriti's card. When her visitors have gone, she feels sexually excited and retires to her bedroom with Guido, who has meanwhile been hiding.

In the morning Silia orders Leone to challenge Miglioriti. Leone has never handled arms, but he agrees at once. Guido, acting as his second, arranges the meeting for the next morning. It is to be a duel to the death. While these arrangements are being made, Silia's mind whirls about like a weathercock. Now that she has condemned Leone to certain death, she feels regret, remorse, compassion, wonders if she is mad, and so on. Leone dismisses her summarily, and sits down quietly to his breakfast.

It is dawn when the third act opens. Leone is still asleep. There is a comic scene between his grumpy servant and the doctor who is to attend the duel. The doctor, in frock coat and top hat, is laying out a huge assortment of surgical cutlery. The two seconds come in. Leone is awakened. He announces he has no intention of fighting anybody. It is his second who is to fight. The seconds point out that in such case Leone will be disqualified as a man of honor. He laughs in their faces. Guido, however, takes the matter seriously. He says, "Addio," and goes out to fulfill his obligations. Silia comes in, and a moment later the doctor, trembling, rushes in for his instruments. Guido is dying. Leone sits down to his breakfast.

The day after the play opened in Rome, Pirandello wrote his son that it had been badly received, owing to the incomprehension of the audience. Some days later, 12 January 1919, he wrote again, complaining of "a batch of newspapers, all but one, which are fiercely opposed not so much to my play, but to me, my drama, the so-called 'new drama.' " *Il giuoco delle parti* is not, in truth, at all difficult to understand, but in 1919 it must have been difficult to stomach. It was one thing for Chiarelli's Paolo to prize his wife above his social obligations, or for poor Ciampa to content himself with a share of his wife's love. In these plays the attack was aimed at social values that time had already eroded, and the Italian audience was sophisticated enough to feel sorry for the victims of a cruelly restrictive code of sexual behavior. But in 1919 it was not prepared to trifle with the chivalric principles that had so long shaped its thought and its drama. The audience liked men of heart. In the opinion of the critics, Leone Gala, for all his philosophy, was despicable. The time had not yet come when anyone of that sort, no matter how interesting, could be applauded in the Italian theatre.

In devising Silia, Pirandello evidently had it in mind to depict a vampire woman in the style of Strindberg's heroines; but Silia was no better off as a character than Leone. In order to justify Leone it was necessary to exaggerate Silia to the point where one loses touch with her. In the play, the young men who invade Silia's apartment have just come from a performance of Bizet's *Carmen*. The implication seems to be that it is some such role that Silia chooses to play in life. The marriage of Silia and Leone is, accordingly, a dance of death from which, on this occasion, Leone is able to escape at Guido's expense; but there is no indication that the dance is over when the play ends. At the end of the second act, Silia is terrified at what she has done. Leone reassures her:

LEONE: Don't be afraid. I am here.
SILIA: But what will you do?
LEONE: What I have always done from the time when you made me see the necessity.
SILIA: I?
LEONE: You.

SILIA: What necessity?
LEONE: (*A pause, then in a low tone*) Of killing you.

He is speaking metaphorically. It is Guido he intends to kill, not Silia. He continues:

LEONE: Don't you think that more than once you have given me a motive
    for killing you? Of course, often; but it was a motive that was armed
    with a feeling, at first of love, then of anger. It was necessary to
    disarm these two feelings, to empty oneself of them. And I emptied
    myself of them so far as to let the motive go and to permit you to go
    on living, not as you wish, because you yourself don't know what you
    wish, but as you can, as you must, since you are unable to do as I do.
SILIA: And what is it that you do?
LEONE: (*With a vague, sad gesture*) I abstract myself.[22]

Silia, of course, does not understand him. He is talking, presumably, in
Schopenhauerian terms, mysterious to the uninitiated. What he seems to
have in mind is the drive of the Will, irrational and inexorable, from
which it is possible to escape only into the world of abstraction.

With Ciampa, Baldovino, and Leone Gala Pirandello offered an impressive trio of portraits. All three are men who succeed, at least for a time,
in rising above their humanity. They are witty men who are able to see
clearly and to act logically because they have emptied their hearts of
emotion, and all three have a heavy price to pay for their victory. Insofar
as they are able to free the mind from the promptings of the heart, they
are Machiavellian characters who are able to manipulate the actions of
others less gifted intellectually than they. In Strindberg's *The Father* the
Captain is infinitely more intelligent than his wife Laura, but she divines
his weakness and is able to trap him and kill him. Leone Gala is less vulnerable. His emotions are under control and he is more than a match for
Silia, who is all passion. Those who abstract themselves to this degree, it
is implied, do so at the cost of life itself. If they cease to feel it is because
they have ceased to live. Leone has not actually reached this state of be-
atitude. His stoicism is a pretense. It is the part that he plays in order to
survive; but the role is sustained by a living man, and it is only occasionally that he permits us some insight into his reality.

But while Leone can play his game coolly and skilfully, Guido cannot
play it at all. For him life is not a game, but a reality in which he is completely involved. For Leone the social code is laughable. For Guido it is

sacred. What is real for the one is not real for the other. The result is
that the one goes to his death while the other sits down to his breakfast.
From the author's standpoint both parts are equally senseless, equally
comic, and equally sad. The game of parts is a foolish game in which the
stakes are worthless, and it makes no difference who wins or who loses.
Il berretto a sonagli ends on a saturnine note, *Il piacere dell'onestà* has a sentimental ending; but *Il giuoco delle parti* ends on a note of utter hopelessness. It is a very bitter joke.

L'innesto—The Graft—was produced in Milan in 1919, and shortly after it
came *L'uomo, la bestia e la virtù—Man, Beast and Virtue*. Both plays are
variations, and by no means the last, on the theme which Pirandello first
took up in *Pensaci, Giacomino!* and afterwards in *Il piacere dell'onestà*—the
eternal story of the wife, the husband, and the lover. In *L'innesto* the
problem is posed in terms of the relation of physical and spiritual love.
Laura and Giorgio have been married seven years and are childless. One
day Laura is raped by a hoodlum. A month later she is with child.
Giorgio is furious. He insists on an abortion. Laura insists she will bear
her child. Following the rape she has given herself to her husband with
unusual ardor, so that while there is reason to doubt that the child is his,
there is no certainty that it may not be his. In these circumstances
Laura's old gardener provides a saving thought. He explains that when a
bud is grafted, the root stock will not accept the graft unless it is *in
succhio*, rich with sap and bursting with the will to reproduce. At such
times it will welcome the graft regardless of the cruelty of the incision
and the provenience of the alien material. Laura's love for Giorgio and
her desire for his child thus makes the child she is bearing virtually his,
in spite of the stranger's brutal intervention. This reflection, and the fact
that he cannot bear to part with Laura, decide Giorgio to accept the situation and his vicarious paternity.

    L'innesto is not one of Pirandello's masterpieces, but it indicates the
progressive nature of his outlook in this period. Its philosophy is familiar: reality is what we make of it. As in *Così è (se vi pare)* the anecdote is
framed so as to give rise to a *dubbio*. In this case the issue is one of paternity—whether the child's father is the man who actually engendered it,
or the man who was in her mind at the moment of conception, in other
terms, whether reproduction is the result of the union of souls or of bodies. Pressed far enough, the biological question becomes metaphysical;
but in *L'innesto* there is no question of irony, or of a facile rationalization.
The issue is resolved on a sentimental basis, and this seems quite satis-

factory in the circumstances. *L'uomo, la bestia e la virtù* deals with a similar situation, but here the whole intention is ironical.

L'uomo, la bestia e la virtù illustrates another aspect of the Grotesque. It is a light-hearted farce in the tradition of Boccaccio, and the view it takes of humanity is both comic and extraordinarily sordid. It has to do once again with the question of the mask and the face, but this time the joke is at the expense of the *Grotteschi*. In this case, the face under the mask is also a mask on a face, and it is evident that a personality has as many husks as an onion. The characterizations are very broad. The moral implications are shocking. The play has no need of interpretation. What it needs is fine character acting, and a director with a light hand. The Beast in the play is Captain Perella, a seafaring man of uncertain temper. He is seldom at home and, in the long intervals between his visits, his wife has taken up with Professor Paolino, who tutors her little son, Nono. Now, quite inappropriately, she finds that she is pregnant. The situation is terrifying. In addition to his legitimate ménage Captain Perella maintains a mistress and a large family in a seaport further down the coast, and for financial reasons he is firmly resolved to have no more children. Consequently, in his periodic visits to his wife he invariably provokes a quarrel after dinner which ends by his slamming the bedroom door in her face. This time, however, it is imperative that he be induced to perform his marital function without delay. The question is how is the romantic lover to induce the beastly husband to sleep with the angel of virtue, his wife.

Paolino does what he can. He procures a reliable aphrodisiac and spikes the Captain's favorite cake with it. Signora Perella is induced to make herself look seductive. It is in vain that the poor woman protests at the violence of the transformation. The professor is persuasive:

> Oh, my soul, my soul, forgive me! Believe me, I suffer more than you this agony of yours which must be atrocious! I would die myself, believe me, I would die sooner than see this spectacle of virtue forced to prostitute itself like this! Come, come. . . . It is your moment of martyrdom, my dearest! You must face it with courage! And it is I who must provide you with this courage!

And in order to raise her spirits he capers about like a monkey. She refuses to laugh:

SIGNORA PERELLA: But it's a horrible mask!
PAOLINO: That's what you need for a man like that.
SIGNORA PERELLA: And Nono? Nono? I am a mother, Paolino!

PAOLINO: (*Embracing her, with tears in his eyes*) Yes. Yes. You are right, poor
dear soul, yes! You are right! But what can we do? This is the way he
wants you, like this. He doesn't want you as a mother! And you will
offer this up to him, this mask, to his bestiality! Under the mask you
are, after all, yourself, suffering with it: you as you are for yourself,
and for me, dearest. And all our love!

Their efforts, unhappily, are in vain. Captain Perella is not aroused by
his wife's whorish appearance. On the contrary, it revolts him, and directly after dinner he provokes the customary quarrel. But he has eaten
the doctored cake, and the medicine does its job. Paolino has arranged to
keep track of the Captain's amorous assaults by means of the flowerpots
Signora Perella sets out on the balcony overlooking the square. In the
morning there are five. When the Captain leaves for the port, Paolino is
at his door to congratulate him. The Captain is modest:

PERELLA: Eh, my dear Professor, we must be men.
PAOLINO: For you, it's easy, Captain. — With a wife like yours. The per-
sonification of virtue![23]

L'uomo, la bestia e la virtù amply deserved its success. The plot recalled
Labiche and Becque; even more clearly it recalled Boccaccio and Machia-
velli—it was a type of risqué farce by no means uncommon in the Italian
theatre. It was, indeed, typically Italian naughty comedy of the sort that
in time became the gainpenny of the Italian film maker. It did little to
enhance the author's reputation as a serious writer. Very likely, at this
point, Pirandello did not much care. He was now very much a man of
the theatre. In 1919 he was actively associated with Nino Martoglio in
the direction of a small repertory company called Il Teatro mediterra-
neo. In 1920 Ruggero Ruggeri presented *Tutto per bene* in Rome, and almost simultaneously *Come prima, meglio di prima* was performed in Venice, *Cecè* was played in San Pellegrino, and *La Signora Morli una e due* was
performed by the company of Emma Grammatica. These were all plays
of mainly commercial interest, evidently intended for performance by a
star with a popular following.

Tutto per bene—All's Well That Ends Well—is a dramatized *novella*, and the
play suffers from the rigors of adaptation. The plot is extremely complex, and necessitates a long and tedious exposition. Pirandello managed
this through a pair of protatic characters who are needlessly characterized in detail. We are thus informed that, many years before, one Ber-

nard Agliani, a gifted physicist, died in an explosion that wrecked his laboratory. One of his students, Manfroni, managed to get hold of his notes and, with their aid, published a scientific treatise that has since brought him honor and fame. After Agliani's death his daughter Silvia came to Rome seeking a post in the Department of Education. There she met Manfroni, now an important official, and there she also met Lori, a subordinate, whom she later married. She has long since died. Palma is her daughter.

Manfroni is now a senator, and accounted a great man. Lori is retired. He is pitiful. Manfroni has always befriended him, and he reveres the senator as his benefactor and his friend. But he has somehow lost his daughter to him. From the first, it appears, Manfroni has been a father to her. He has undertaken her education, and has now gone so far as to arrange her marriage to a *marchese*. It is at this point that the play begins.

As Palma's wedding party returns from the church it is evident that Manfroni is the real head of the household. Lori is not only *de trop* in his own house, he is treated with barely disguised contempt. He is by nature a modest and submissive man, and he bears his slights patiently; moreover, he is neurotically attached to his dead wife, with whom he has communed, at her graveside, every day for the past sixteen years. He now expects no more of life than an early opportunity to join her in the other world.

But, quite unexpectedly, Lori discovers why it is that he is considered an object of scorn. Silvia, he learns, was once Manfroni's mistress. She was pregnant when she married Lori. Palma is really Manfroni's daughter, and has long been aware of it. Meanwhile Manfroni has given her, and everyone else to understand that Lori has always known the truth, and has pretended ignorance only in order to benefit from Manfroni's patronage.

When he discovers how shabbily he has been treated, Lori is furious, and decides to exact a terrible revenge. In the presence of Palma he confronts Manfroni with the proof of his misdeeds and threatens to unmask him before all the world as a fraud and a scoundrel. But when Manfroni is completely crushed, Lori relents. He has savored his revenge, and does not require its consummation. He has reason now to believe that Silvia's brief affair with Manfroni ended in disgust when she realized what sort of man he was, and that in the three years of her marriage she really loved only her husband. Palma is now restored to him and, in the end, Manfroni is banished from the house where he had planned to install himself as paterfamilias for the rest of his days. Henceforth all that he had plotted to gain for himself will belong to Lori—his home, his armchair, and his daughter. It has all turned out well—at least, well enough.

The situation in *Tutto per bene* is evidently a variant of the relation of Baldovino and Fabio in *Il piacere dell'onestà*, and the outcome is of the same order. The difference is, of course, that Baldovino is fully cognizant of the part he is playing, while Lori becomes aware only at the end of the part he was forced to play. *Tutto per bene* has some strong scenes, and an interesting character part, but Pirandello did not do his *novella* justice in adapting it for the stage. In the *novella* one Verona, now a senator, having foisted his mistress Silvia on his friend Lori, frequents his house daily, brings up the daughter Ginetta as his own, and ultimately marries her to a rich *marchese*. At this point, Lori, who is no longer necessary, is politely sent about his business. But when, after twenty years, he discovers the trick that has been played upon him, he is completely at a loss:

> What should he do now, after so many years? Now that all that had been done was done? So. . . . silently. . . . courteously, as elegant people do things, people who know how to do things properly? Had they not let him see, with politeness, of course, that henceforth he had no longer any part to play? He had played the part of the husband and afterwards of the father. . . . now it was over: there was no longer any need of him, now that these three were so well accorded among themselves. . . .[24]

And so, in the *novella*, Lori goes sadly once again to sit beside his wife at her grave, but this time, perhaps to explain and to forgive.

The *novella* ends sadly. The play has a happy ending, perhaps as a concession to popular taste. It is perhaps possible to discern in the ultimate vindication of a man whose whole life has been ruined by a misunderstanding some element of irony. Aside from this there is, of course, the theme of the mask and the face to provide the Pirandellian touch in what might well be considered a sentimental melodrama involving a detestable villain and an overly pathetic victim of injustice. The unfortunate Lori unwittingly wears the mask of the conniving cuckold that Manfroni has constructed for him, while Manfroni flaunts the mask of the beneficent patron that he has constructed for himself. When the unmasking takes place, there is a classic recognition scene and the con-

sequent peripeteia is conventional. All this works quite well in the theatre, but the mold in which the play is cast was too rigid to permit an
original departure, and perhaps there was no need to make one. As it
was, the play was a popular success, and was widely applauded in the
press.

In *Signora Morli una e due* Pirandello took up once again the question of
personal identity. The plot is simple. Signor Morli returns from America
to visit his wife Evelina whom he had abandoned fourteen years before,
together with their young son, in an effort to escape his creditors. His
wife meanwhile has been living in Florence with the lawyer who saved
her estate, a man called Lello, of whom she is fond. They are thought to
be married, and have a young daughter called Titti, whom Evelina
adores. Morli's sudden appearance in Florence upsets everything. He is a
gay dog, a spendthrift and full of joy. The lawyer Lello is a sober and
serious person of the utmost probity. Morli's son Aldo has his father's
temperament, and he takes to his father at once. Father and son go off
together merrily to Rome.

Although Morli has promised not to upset his wife's domestic arrangements, he entices her to Rome on the pretext that Aldo is ill, and she
spends a week with them. Inevitably she falls into the pattern of her
former joyous life, and for a time she seems a different woman from the
dignified lady that Lello knows. But when she learns that her little
daughter is really ill, she leaves abruptly for Florence. A stormy reception awaits her. Lello naturally suspects her of infidelity with her former
husband. He complains of the hopelessness of his position, and there is
an interminable discussion of their relationship. In the end she assures
Lello that she will not see Morli again, and that she is willing to accept
the position of dignity that is appropriate to her life in Florence. She admits, nevertheless, that the decision has cost her something. She has, she
says, two personalities, each of which mirrors the temper of the man she
lives with. Now she is forced to give up one side of her nature:

> I have experienced it in myself, with all the horror of seeing in myself
> *another*—that other—different from the woman I am here for you and
> for myself—*two* in a single person! One body that would belong to
> "this one" or "that one," if it did not seem monstrous and absurd that
> then, for itself, this body would be nothing aside from the feeling that
> makes it belong now to "this one" and now to "that one," and all the
> time with the memory of the one and the other—you see? that is the

terrible part of it—terrible because it destroys the illusion that each one
of us has of being "one," always, always oneself. It's not true. I have
seen it. I have felt it.[25]

Evelina is a good deal more articulate than the mysterious Signora Ponza
in *Così è (se vi pare)*, but she describes herself in somewhat the same
terms. There is, of course, a difference. With Signor Ponza it is a question of identity; with Signora Morli her duality is a matter of character.
Pirandello was evidently not thinking of Signora Morli as a pathological
personality. There is no hint of schizophrenia in her behavior. It is only
that Morli is able to awaken in her the gaiety of her youth, and at thirty-
seven she prefers the gravity of her life with Lello. But without doubt
she is a versatile woman, and in depicting her as such Pirandello means
us to consider that personality, like identity, is a variable entity, and that
the soul, the vital principle, is flexible enough to assume whatever form
is suitable to its environment.

In *La Signora Morli una e due* Pirandello did not succeed in doing justice
to the theme of multiple personality. But he returned to it many times.
Evidently the notion that an individual is irrevocably committed to a
single form gave him some discomfort, and in mutability he saw some
possibility of escape. But even in fantasy freedom from the self was difficult to attain. In the novel *Il fu Mattia Pascal* the hero, in changing from
one form to another, finds himself helplessly lost between the two; while
in *Quando si è qualcuno* the successful poet finds that the form he has constructed for himself is no longer detachable. The problem of identity
provided Pirandello with material for many plays. He reworked it in
Come prima, meglio di prima, in *Trovarsi*, and in *Come tu mi vuoi;* and in
Enrico IV he made it the basis of a masterpiece.

*Come prima, meglio di prima—As Before, Better Than Before—*was performed
in 1920. It was adapted from a *novella* called "La Veglia"—"The Vigil."
In the *novella* the famous surgeon Silvio Gelli is summoned to the bed-
side of his wife Fulvia, who is dying in a *pensione* in a small Tuscan town.
Gelli has not seen his wife in thirteen years, ever since the day he caused
her to abandon him and his little daughter, and to run off with another
man. In the course of these years Fulvia, a passionate woman, has had a
long succession of lovers. She has walked the streets as a prostitute, and
has recently come to the attention of the police in Perugia. The examin-
ing magistrate, Mauri, is her latest lover. It was after a visit from Mauri's

wife that Fulvia attempted to put an end to her life. Mauri has followed her. He refuses to leave the *pensione* without her, and he and Gelli sit up together all the night talking. While they talk, the woman dies.

In the play the woman does not die. Fulvia is saved by a timely operation, and, when the play opens, is barely convalescent. The scene description, when first she appears on the stage, takes up a full page of text. The style is noteworthy:

> The door opens, Right, and Fulvia Gelli appears, uncertain, very pale, like one who has recently been snatched from the hands of death. She has still a hint of darkness in her eyes; and her face has hardened, as if petrified, in an expression of sombre despair. Having come here to die, deprived of everything, rising now from her bed, she has put on — for lack of anything else — the gay dress of a professional prostitute, which shrieks in contrast to the unhappiness which is written on her face. Even more shocking is her magnificent thick hair, disordered and shamelessly dyed a flaming red, which surrounds her pale face with tongues of flame. She has not taken the trouble to fasten her blouse over her breasts, almost bare and coldly provocative, since she has an evident disdain and truly intimate hatred of her beautiful body, as if it had not belonged to her in some time, and she no longer knew even how it was, not even having shared, except with fierce revulsion, the joy that others have taken in it.[26]

Fulvia expects to see the surgeon, her husband, but the man who appears is not Gelli, but the police magistrate Mauri, with whom she lived in Perugia for twenty days before coming to the *pensione* to kill herself. Mauri is a character out of comic opera:

> He speaks and gesticulates with that special theatricality which belongs to excitable people: a warm and sincere theatricality which from time to time becomes self-conscious and blazes up, as if in revulsion, in angry gestures.

He is, indeed, an amusing and pathetic character, typically Italian. He is aware of his own absurdity, and ashamed of the violence of his outbursts, but, as he says, it is his passions, not he, that shout and posture. He explains his situation for the benefit of the innkeeper, who wonders at his presence. Before his marriage, he says, he had served ten years as magistrate in a small town. The woman he married was nine years his senior. He married her because she was rich enough to own a piano, the only one in the neighborhood, for he is at heart a musician, and the woman seemed beautiful to him because of the piano. One day in the course of his professional duties he met Fulvia. She had been picked up as a witness to a vulgar crime. He fell in love with her at once, lied to her about his marriage, abandoned his post and his wife for her sake, and now that he is free, he intends to support her, if she is willing, by giving piano concerts. If she refuses, he will kill himself.

Fulvia looks upon him with complete indifference.

In this play Pirandello once again demonstrated his mastery of the Grotesque, his special domain as an artist. The situation is tragic. The characters—with the exception of Fulvia—are caricatures; and the action oscillates between the comic and the pathetic with disconcerting agility. In his preface to *Cromwell* Hugo had described something of the sort with reference to Shakespeare. In the distance that separates Pirandello from Hugo it is possible to appraise the rapidity with which this idea had developed in the course of the century.

Pirandello observed his characters with the eye of a Naturalist, and drew them, even when it was unnecessary, in merciless detail. In this play the minor characters—Zonchi, the innkeeper, La Naccheri, and her hapless daughter Giuditta—none of whom survives the first act—are meticulously delineated types, rewarding roles, vivid and memorable, and also superfluous. It is the sort of luxury, obviously, that an author can afford himself only when he is writing for a repertory company. Pirandello's dialogue bristles with exclamation points and dashes. His phrases are broken, suspended, full of emphatic repetitions. His scenes are often noisy and needlessly turbulent, but Pirandello was keenly aware of the absurdity of his characters and, in exaggerating their postures, he caricatured the operatic behavior of a passionate race that feels deeply, talks loudly, and is not afraid of hyperbole. The result is a special strain of irony which is quite extraneous to the plot, and is yet essential to the texture of the narrative.

Fulvia Gelli is a whore. At thirty-one she has known every degradation, and through martyrdom has achieved something like sainthood. Silvio Gelli insists that she come home with him to care for their daughter Livia who is now sixteen. But as Livia has been told that her mother is dead, Fulvia is to come back as a second wife. She agrees.

In the second act Fulvia is living with Silvio and Livia in a country villa where no one knows her. There is trouble. Livia venerates her saintly mother, and she detests this woman who has come to take her place. Legends have grown up like mushrooms around the dead Fulvia.

It is the anniversary of her "death." The old nurse remembers vividly how she died in her arms. Everyone is in mourning. Masses are to be said for her soul. As for Fulvia, she is in the curious position of having to join with the others in veneration of herself in heaven.

The rehabilitation of the fallen woman was a favorite theme of nineteenth-century drama; and the situation in *Come prima, meglio di prima* is strongly reminiscent of *The Second Mrs. Tanqueray*. In that play, it will be recalled, Paula is rescued from the demi-monde by Aubrey Tanqueray who takes her to a country house where nobody knows her. His pious daughter Ellean comes unexpectedly to live with them. She is devoted to her sainted mother and burns with resentment at the fancy woman who has usurped her mother's place. The situation is detonated by the appearance of Paula's former flame to whom Ellean has somehow managed to become engaged, and the play ends with Paula's suicide.

Under very similar conditions, Pirandello is more merciful than Pinero could have been twenty-seven years earlier. In Pinero's time and country a fallen woman was beyond redemption, save by death. Pirandello's prostitutes, on the other hand, are almost always sympathetic characters, whose sins are readily forgivable. In *La nuova colonia*, for example, La Spera, formerly a shameless slut, becomes the symbol of pure womanhood and survives the shipwreck of her world with her child in her arms, in a pose that recalls the iconography of the Blessed Virgin.

The cosmic transformation that Pirandello was helping to bring about naturally brought with it a relaxation of the strict moral structure of the preceding age. In Italy, as a practical matter, the priesthood had come long ago to a reasonable understanding with sin, and there was the reassuring example of Mary Magdalen to serve as a guide to salvation. In *Come prima, meglio di prima* the fallen woman rises from the abyss with redoubled strength and purity, and becomes in all respects the most admirable character in the play.

To continue the narrative: in the third act, Livia having discovered that there is no record of a second marriage, concludes that her stepmother is a common whore, and refuses to stay in the same house with her. Meanwhile Fulvia—now called Francesca—has borne her husband a second daughter. To save this child from the reproach of illegitimacy she tells Livia at last that she herself is the sainted Fulvia. Then she prepares to go away with Mauri, taking her little daughter with her. The child is also called Livia, and now Fulvia feels that once again she is beginning life, and better than before.

Come prima, meglio di prima has many longueurs, and the end seems forced, but the dialogue and the characterizations are among Pirandello's best, and the situation is exceptionally ingenious. The action centers mainly on the question of Fulvia's identity. In the course of her life she has been forced to undergo several modulations. As Silvio Gelli's young wife she was the pure and innocent Fulvia who has since been sanctified by her daughter. During her bad years she became Flora, a woman who abandoned her body to her trade without making any spiritual concessions to its practice. After that she became Francesca, a respectable married woman with a recalcitrant stepdaughter. None of these metamorphoses has essentially changed her. In the end she is conscious of herself in all three aspects—the ideal Fulvia who never existed, the prostitute who no longer exists, and the new Fulvia, purified by death and reborn, who now alone exists. There is also the living substrate, the self which has persisted unchanged throughout these modulations.

In contrast to this richly conceived character, the daughter Livia is a pallid caricature, a neurotic child. The sacred mother-image which she has constructed serves a useful purpose in justifying her egotism. The lengths to which her father goes to preserve her illusions doubtless measures the extent of his own guilt-feelings and, in this sense the characterization is psychologically sound, but in Pirandello's plays parents generally feel it necessary to preserve the illusions of their children at any cost. The inference is that each generation carries with it a burden of guilt which it vainly attempts to conceal from the generation which follows, and these extravagant efforts to idealize human behavior have a comic aspect of which Pirandello was evidently as well aware as Ibsen.

By the time of *Come prima, meglio di prima* the revolt of the children had been in progress for a good many years, but in spite of Ibsen's well-publicized efforts to secure justice for parents, the parent's revolt against the tyranny of their offspring was still some way off. In *Ghosts* (1881) Mrs. Alving's obligation to idealize her dissolute husband for her son's benefit is the subject of tragedy, but a dozen years later Pinero made everyone conspire in his play to maintain Mr. Tanqueray's priggish daughter in her primal innocence. It may well be that, a quarter-century later, Pirandello meant to treat these extravagances with appropriate irony. In the *novella* "Vexilla Regis" the father virtually turns handsprings to prevent his adolescent daughter from seeing the mother who shamelessly abandoned her in her infancy, and it is unlikely that Pirandello was unaware of the absurdity as well as the pathos of these excesses. The situation in that story is in some respects similar to that of *Come prima, meglio di prima*, and in both cases, Pirandello's treatment of the situation leaves room for doubt; but it is impossible to exclude the suspicion that these scenes are touched with some trace of Pirandellian *umorismo*.

It would be a mistake, at any rate, to take with complete seriousness those scenes in Pirandello's plays that in our day seem embarrassingly melodramatic. Pirandello was certainly no stranger to melodrama; but he was not above spoofing its idioms. In the *novella* "Le tre carissime" Irene despairs of finding a husband and decides instead to become an actress. To this end she rehearses scenes of passion with her mother holding the book:

> The poor old lady patiently assisted her, sitting and reading placidly with her glasses on the end of her nose:
>
> ODETTE: So you intend to force me to leave?
>
> THE COUNT: (*The mother read*) My house. Yes. And at once.
>
> ODETTE: And my daughter?
>
> THE COUNT: My daughter. . . . I shall keep with me.
>
> ODETTE: Here? Without me?
>
> THE COUNT: Without you.
>
> ODETTE: Come, sir—you're mad. . . . My daughter is mine, and you cannot hope to succeed in separating me from her.[27]

The scene makes one smile; but it is possible to find very similar scenes set forth in Pirandello's plays with apparent earnestness. In certain passages he expresses very conventional idealistic views with regard to the purity of women and the sanctity of marriage. In others he waves aside traditional moral concepts with the smile of the enlightened realist. In "Le tre carissime," for example, the three lovely daughters of Signora Marúcolli, having got nowhere in the strict path of virtue, find husbands quite readily once they begin to tread the primrose path. The narrator comments:

> There come to us effectively from society a goodly number of laws and regulations which should keep in check this wicked animal called man . . . but every so often the wicked beast plays us one of his tricks. Then we start blaming society as if the damage were all her fault, whereas the fact is that we insist on making society impose obligations on nature which nature declines either to recognize or to respect. So that a woman, for instance, cannot make love, even by mistake, with a man who is not exactly her husband because society has duly informed her that she must not. Society, poor society, orders it and commands it; now how is it her fault if nature laughs in her face?[28]

It is thus not altogether unreasonable to suspect that underlying the pathetic aspects of *Come prima, meglio di prima* there are comic currents that go beyond caricature and are perhaps at the very core of the play. Aside from the comic rivalry of the real and the ideal Fulvia, there is something vaguely comic in the abject subjection of Silvia Gelli to his daughter, and the consequent idealization of the absent mother. It is unlikely, however, that, given the conditions of the theatre, the play could ever be produced so as to bring out all its values, and the likelihood is that, excellent as it is, this play will never seem more than ingenious domestic melodrama.

As it happened, the part of Fulvia proved to be remarkably rewarding, and in its first production Maria Letizia Celli was vigorously applauded in this role. Signora Morli was not nearly as good a part and, in spite of the fine acting of Emma Grammatica, *Signora Morli una e due* failed. The following year *Sei personaggi in cerca d'autore* opened in Rome.

Before the production of *Six Characters in Search of an Author* Pirandello's position as a dramatist was both uncertain and ambiguous. The international success of *Six Characters* changed everything. Bit by bit his work was reexamined and reappraised, and, after he received the Nobel prize in 1934, even those plays which had once seemed inconsiderable were seen to be endowed with hitherto unsuspected poetic beauty. When *Il piacere dell'onestà* was revived by Ruggeri at the Teatro Quirino in Rome in 1949, it was received with the reverence appropriate to a work of genius, and Silvio d'Amico noted that the critics marvelled at the indifference of its reception thirty years before in the same theatre with the same actor in the same part. The highly charged language which in 1919 had seemed merely emphatic sounded a little theatrical in the 1940's, but the "philosophical sophistries" of which the critics had once complained now seemed vibrant with meaning. The critic Pierre Gobetti wrote admiringly, "in Pirandello dialectic becomes poetry."[29]

The idea of *Six Characters in Search of an Author* appears to have had a slow organic development. Ten years before, in 1911, Pirandello had published in *Il Corriere della Sera* a *novella* entitled "La tragedia di un personaggio." In this story the author notes that it is his custom to give audience to prospective characters on Sunday mornings from eight to one. The applicants are generally querulous: "I can't imagine why it is, but usually there come to my audiences the most discontented people on earth, people afflicted either with strange troubles or entangled in the most remarkable situations, with which it is truly painful to deal."[30] Normally he questions the seriousness of their predicaments, for one can sympathize with their misfortunes only on condition of smiling at them. One, who came back from America in his eighties, was permitted to die gracefully in a story called "Musica vecchia."[31] But a character called Dr. Fileno, whom he had once run across in a novel, came to complain that he had been so badly mistreated by his author that he deserved assistance. "Nobody knows better than you," said Fileno,

> that we are living beings, more alive than those who breathe and wear clothes, perhaps less real, but more true! One is born into the world in so many ways, my dear sir—you know as well as I how nature makes use of human fantasy in order to carry on the work of creation. And whoever is born through this creative activity that resides in man is destined by nature to a life that is far superior to that which is born through the mortal womb of a woman. A born character, one who has the luck to be born a living character, may thumb his nose at death. He will not die. The man will die, the author, the creative instrument of nature, will die. But his creation will not die. And in order to live forever he has no need of extraordinary gifts or feats or prowess. Tell me, please, who was Sancho Panza! Tell me, who was Don Abbondio! And yet they live forever because—once alive—they had the good fortune to find a fecund matrix, a mind that was able to nourish them and send them forth properly into the world.

Dr. Fileno, we are told, had the good fortune to be born a character destined for immortality. Unhappily, he fell into unworthy hands and is now condemned to perish in an artificial world, a world of ink and paper in which everything is a pretence. A real person can sometimes escape from a desperate situation, but a poor character cannot; he is the prisoner of the author's imagination. Fileno begs Pirandello to set him free so he too can live in the great world. But Pirandello declines. He cannot bring himself to rescue the creature of another man's mind.

This conceit evidently captured Pirandello's fancy. In a *novella* called "Colloqui coi personaggi," published in two installments in *Il Giornale di Sicilia* and reprinted in *Berreche e la guerra* in 1919, he informs his readers that a placard is now posted on the door of his study:

Notice
Suspended, as of this day, all audiences for characters of either sex, of every class, age and profession, who have previously made requests or

presented claims for admission to novels or short stories. *N.B.*—All applications and claims are being held at the disposition of such characters as, unashamed to exhibit their personal miseries in the present circumstances, may wish to turn for relief to other authors if such are available.[32]

In spite of this patriotic gesture, the story continues, the author was forced into a long discussion with a most obstreperous character who had been trying all year to induce Pirandello to put him into a novel which, he insists, is sure to be a masterpiece. This character was found one morning standing on tiptoe at the door of the study, with his spectacles perched on his nose, peering at the posted notice which he was trying in vain to decipher: "In his quality as a character, that is, a creature enclosed in his ideal reality, and outside the transitory conditions of time, he had no obligation, I know, to be aware of the horrible, miserable mess in which Europe found itself in those days. Thus he had stopped at the words, 'in the present circumstances,' and now requested an explanation. . . ."

Pirandello's excuse for not attending to this suppliant was the impossibility of devising stories on the eve of the impending war, particularly at a time when his son was about to depart for the front. But the character was importunate, Pirandello caught sight of him later seated in an armchair overlooking the rose garden in the May sunshine, listening to the song of a bird. When questioned, the creature held forth at some length:

> We know nothing of war, my dear sir. . . . because these are things that pass. . . . great as they are, they are only facts. They pass. . . . Life remains, with the same needs, the same passions as before. . . . What counts is something infinitely smaller and infinitely greater: a tear, a smile, to which you—or if not you, then someone else—will be able to give life outside of time, thus transcending the transitory reality of these passions you feel today; a tear, a smile, no matter whether of this or some other war, for all wars, one with the other, are the same, but this tear will be unique, this smile will be unique.

After, when his guest had departed, the author was aware that for some time he had not been quite alone in his study. There were shadows moving in a corner of the room, personages coming into being:

> They watched me, they spied. They stared at me so long that at last, without meaning to, I turned to them.
> With whom, really, could I communicate at a time like this if not

with them? And I moved toward that corner and forced myself to look from one to the other at these shadows born of my passion, and I began to talk to them, softly, softly.[33]

This was, in effect, Pirandello's excuse for writing fiction during these years when all energies were being directed toward the war effort. But the anecdote had also a *sovrasenso;* it was a restatement of the doctrine of *vita e forma* which in these troubled times Pirandello found particularly comforting. What is called reality—he never tired of repeating, evidently—has no reality. In life we see only the transitory forms in which is manifested the vital energy, life, permanent only in mutability, utterly remote and unknowable, and completely indifferent to the concerns of the individual. In the life of man, accordingly, the only certainty is in his own creations, in the ideal creatures of the world of art. His only refuge is there, and his only hope of permanence.

By this time, apparently, Pirandello the Realist was indistinguishable from Pirandello the Idealist. His views, at any rate, were precisely those on which the Symbolist movement had been grounded in France; and it was in France, not in Italy, that Pirandello's genius first came to light. The discovery of Pirandello's greatness in the Paris of the 1920's was actually the rediscovery of the genius of French Symbolism. For two decades it had been in abeyance. Mallarmé had died in 1898. Maeterlinck had hardly survived the resurgence of realism in the theatre. Now realism had run its course. The war was over; but the battlefields still stank. There had been a surfeit of realism. It was once again the turn of the Ideal.

In the lengthy essay he prefaced to the 1925 edition of *Six Characters in Search of an Author* Pirandello recalled in detail the conceit of his shadowy visitants of the war years. A group of characters, he wrote, appeared to him one day demanding that he realize them in a story. But these characters had not the universality which he, as a philosophical writer, required of the creatures of his fancy. Therefore he rejected them. These characters, however, insisted so strenuously on being realized that at last he relented so far as to give them such reality as might enable them to find an author who might be persuaded to undertake their story. The play is therefore subtitled *commedia da fare*—"a play to be written"— presumably by someone other than Pirandello. Until someone is found to take up the project, it is suggested, these characters, rejected by their creator, are condemned to wander about miserably with their story *in*

petto. They have no way of penetrating the ideal sphere where fully con-
summated characters have their being. Their rejection is so far all the
story they have—it is their sole reason for being, and their only claim on
life. They exist; but as yet they exist nowhere, and to no purpose. They
are, so to speak, in limbo.

The assumption in *Six Characters* is that the life of a character is not
qualitatively different from the life of a real person, save that characters
exist on a different plane. Characters, like people, are figments of the
imagination, constructions to which we give as much reality as we think
they should have. Thus our impressions of real people live comfortably
side by side with the impressions we have of the characters of fiction;
often these impressions are indistinguishable. The six characters of
Pirandello's play, having been born of his mind, have existence, though
at the moment they have no future. In this respect they share the normal
human predicament.

Pirandello's preface draws the customary distinction between allegory
and symbolism: "I hate that symbolic art in which the representative
loses all spontaneous movement in order to become a machine, allegory.
. . . This is rooted in a concept, is, indeed, a concept which makes itself, or tries to make itself, into an image; the other, instead, seeks in the
image, which must remain alive and free in all of its expression, a meaning that will give it value." His six characters, unfortunately, did not, he
says, sufficiently lend themselves to metaphor: ". . . no matter how I
tried, I did not succeed in discovering such meaning in these six characters. And for this reason I considered that it was useless to give them
life." [34]

This passage is odd, since what gives the play its universality and its
mysterious allusiveness is precisely the symbolism that Pirandello declines to attribute to his characters. The metaphor is transparent. Those
who live in the real world and are called persons, it is implied, are also
characters in search of realization. Mankind has always been a character
in search of its Author. Moreover, since this Author has at all times
proved singularly elusive, it may well seem to the creatures of His fancy
that they are rejected, and condemned to wander about disconsolately in
the environs of being. The analogy is, indeed, so obvious that it seems
unlikely that Pirandello was entirely ingenuous in denying its possibility;
and it may well be that he considered such a metaphor too close to allegory to be artistically acceptable.

In any case, the author did not succeed in excluding these characters from his mind or his studio.

> Creatures of my spirit, these six already lived with a life that was theirs alone and no longer mine, of a life I had no longer the power to deny them. So much so that these characters kept coming back at certain times to propose this or that scene for representation or description, urging the stage-effects one might draw from them, the new interest that a certain unusual situation might evoke, and so on.

At last the author decided, he tells us, to free himself from the importunity of these obsessive fancies by representing their case to the world, the remarkable situation of a group of autonomous characters who insist on living out their lives in despite of their creator. The conceit thus prefigures a purely literary embarrassment, the case of an author who is willing neither to develop nor to abandon a dramatic idea.

The idea, nevertheless, is quite thoroughly developed. Although *Six Characters* is subtitled *Play To Be Written*, the plot is in fact sketched out in considerable detail; the exposition is complete; only the conclusion needs to be composed, and that, in the nature of the case, is best left unwritten. The technique is retrospective. There are fully three acts of exposition managed ingeniously by having the protagonists relate and, in part, enact their story for the benefit of a character who has no part in the plot, the *capocomico* of the theatre which they visit in search of fulfillment. The exposition is exceptionally vivid—particularly as there is some disagreement among the characters as to what really happened—and the situation is brought directly before the eyes of the audience by means of flashbacks. All this, however, is by way of prologue. What remains to be written is, presumably, the play. This is never written. At the end, when the lights are out and the actors have left, the original family group—father, mother, and son—is reunited. What is to follow is not yet imagined, nor is it readily imaginable.

Ostensibly *Six Characters* describes an episode in the fantastic itinerary of the unrealized characters. In fact the author has found an interesting way of telling a story without telling it. The technique is far from straightforward. It is, indeed, a first-rate example of Symbolist indirection. Had the narrative been formulated along the lines of a well-made play the climax would have hinged on an unbelievable coincidence and, save for a few vivid scenes, the action must have consisted of a series of

tedious confrontations, full of reproaches and excuses. As it is, all this is
merely suggested and need not be represented. In the form which the action takes, only the interesting scenes are played, the *scènes à faire*. For
the rest, the spectacle of a group of imaginary beings, whose fate it is to
re-enact their tragedy forever, takes place in the eerie atmosphere of a
ghost story.

Pirandello gives his six characters a more vivid reality than that of the
other characters of the play, but there is nothing spectral about them.
They look and act like creatures of flesh and blood, and so they would
seem in a prose narrative. On the stage the difference between real and
imaginary characters can be accentuated by cosmetic effects, costume,
make-up, and lighting. Nevertheless the play makes unusual demands on
the audience. From a logical viewpoint dramatic characters, before they
are realized by actors, exist only in the mind of those who think about
them. In the present case one is expected to assume that they exist, visibly and audibly, even before they are realized. Once the author has
thought them up, it is assumed, they have an independent existence, an
unreality which is complete down to the color of their eyes and the laces
in their shoes. But even if the assumption is accepted that these images
have somehow detached themselves from the author's fancy like soap
bubbles from a pipe, it is difficult to rationalize their presence.

The difficulty springs from the juxtaposition of the ideal world and
the real, two spheres which normally are associated only in the imagination. Normally the ideal is not visible; when it becomes so the effect is
necessarily uncanny. Under ordinary stage conditions the character and
the actor are presumed to be identical; what existed *in posse* now exists *in
actu*, more or less; and we have no difficulty in accepting the identification. But in *Six Characters* the ideal beings and the actors who are to represent them are specifically dissociated. They confront one another as
strangers, and the result—if one attempts to reason it out—is confusing.
But it is not necessary to reason it out: one can manage with a bit of intellectual discomfort. Here, as in much Symbolist art, the effort to comprehend serves only to dispirit. As it is, the fantastic characters are
present, enveloped in Surrealistic lighting, ready and eager to enact a
human tragedy and, in defiance of all logic, they do so. The consequence, inevitably, is to arouse reflections disparaging the nature of reality both in the theatre and in the world outside it, and this, doubtless,
was Pirandello's intention.

The play opens on a group of actors rehearsing *Il giuoco delle parti*—which they dislike—in an empty theatre. The rehearsal is interrupted by the intrusion of six strange people who walk into the theatre unannounced. They declare that they are the characters of an unwritten play which they would like to have performed then and there. After much discussion the *capocomico* agrees to serve as author, or at least as a sort of amanuensis. The play is then explained to him in detail, and parts of it are enacted by the characters themselves in order to give the actors an idea of what is expected of them.

When they first appear, the characters form a tableau. The Father and the Stepdaughter are evidently at loggerheads; they bicker incessantly. It is they, chiefly, who are in search of somebody who will give them an opportunity to exhibit their situation, to explain, reproach, and justify. The other four characters are dragged in more or less reluctantly as witnesses. The Legitimate Son feels superior to them all and speaks only when he must. The Mother does nothing but weep. The Young Boy hangs his head in shame and wants to die. Only the Little Girl is innocent and happy.

The plot, as it is pieced together, recalls the last *novella* of the *Decameron*, the story of Gualtieri of Saluzzo and Griselda, his wife. It is a plot, doubtless, that engaged Pirandello's fancy, for he had already rung several changes on it, among them the story of *Ma non è una cosa seria* and *Come prima, meglio di prima*. In this case it involves the actions of a rich man of perverse temper who marries a poor woman of simple tastes. She bears him a son. He takes the child away from her and has it brought up by peasants in the country, ostensibly to give it the benefit of the country air. The wife, in her loneliness, is innocently drawn to her husband's secretary, a man of her own class and tastes. The husband dismisses the secretary; but the wife gets on his nerves, and in the end he packs her off to live with her lover. But now that he is left alone, the husband feels irresistibly drawn to his wife's new family, and he tries to win the affection of the little daughter whom his wife has borne in his absence. His intrusion causes the secretary to move his family to another town, and the contact for a time is broken. Years pass. The secretary dies. The wife, along with her grown daughter, her young son and a baby girl, moves back to her husband's city, and finds work as a seamstress in the establishment of Madama Pace, a modiste.

Madama Pace's shop is a secret house of assignation. The Father, now in middle age, but still sexually agile, is one of her regular clients. The Stepdaughter, now eighteen, is one of the Madame's girls. Thus it happens that the Father and Stepdaughter are surprised in embarrassing circumstances by the Mother. This is the scene which, in the opinion of the characters, is sure to make the author's fortune when it is done on the stage. But the actors, when they attempt it, do it so theatrically that the characters themselves undertake to demonstrate the scene, brutally and realistically, as they think it should be played.

After this unexpected reunion in Madama Pace's back room, the Father, filled with remorse, takes the whole family under his roof, and his domestic situation becomes impossible. The climax is precipitated by an accident: the Little Girl falls into the garden pond and is drowned, and the Young Boy, unable to save her, shoots himself. The actors who have witnessed this scene, played for their benefit, rush in to find that the Boy is not acting. Apparently he is dead. He is carried off; and there is a heated dispute as to whether a character is dead when he dies. At this point the *capocomico* has had enough. He consigns them all to the devil, and puts an end to the rehearsal. The actors leave. The lights are put out, save for a ghostly green light which projects the enormous shadows of the Characters. This is extinguished. The stage is almost dark:

> Slowly, from the Right, the Son comes out; then comes the Mother stretching her arms out to him. Then, from the Left, the Father comes. The three stop center stage, standing there as if bewildered. At last, from the Left, the Stepdaughter appears. She runs to the stage ladder, pauses a moment on the top step, looks at the other three, and bursts into strident laughter. Then she runs down the steps and up the aisle, stops once more and, looking up at the three on the stage, laughs once again. Then she vanishes; but from the theatre lobby comes still once more the sound of laughter. Shortly after this the curtain falls.[35]

The final curtain thus suggests several planes of reality. The Six Characters have come into the theatre supposedly from the street; but in the end they remain on the stage, all but the Stepdaughter, who is last heard from in the lobby—one might rub elbows with her in the bar. On the other hand, the Young Boy and the Little Girl no longer seem to exist. Their bodies have been carried off, and it is not clear in what manner they are dead, whether in fact or in fancy. One may conjecture that, insofar as they are real, they are dead, and certainly it must appear so to the other characters. But since their reality is purely ideal, they may be expected to revive in time for the next performance. In any case nobody troubles further about them. The death of imaginary beings is of no interest to the police.

In this play the question of illusion and reality is squarely posed. In the theatre characters acquire reality only at the expense of the actors. The more real the character, the less real the actor. On the stage, ideally, the actor does not exist, and the character lives only in the absence of the actor. Maeterlinck had enunciated this principle repeatedly. It was an idea to which Pirandello also several times returned—in *Trovarsi*, for example, and in *Questa sera si recita a soggetto*. The suggestion in *Six Characters* is broader than this. Insofar as the play stresses the reality of the unreal, it forces an inference as to the unreality of the real.

It is doubtful that Pirandello had this idea in mind when first he wrote the play. At that time he was evidently fascinated by the vividness of the characters he dreamed up in his study, and very likely he exaggerated the vividness of his impressions for literary reasons. But whether or not his fantasy amounted to hallucination, as he said, the effect of the play on the audience was in fact hallucinatory. The result was to further the erosion of the reality principle which had been going on slowly among the Symbolists ever since they had first discovered Schopenhauer. Whatever merits it may have had as a metaphysical demonstration, *Six Characters* came at a time when it could exert extraordinary influence in certain quarters. At any rate, after its appearance the stranglehold of realism on the drama perceptibly relaxed.

Six Characters in Search of an Author, however, also embodies a protest against the lack of realism in the theatre. The action depicts the process through which the author's fantasy is worked through a series of obtrusive stereotypes toward a specious reality with which his fantasy cannot accord. The director—the *capocomico*—does not dare to play the scene in Madama Pace's back room as it actually occurred:

THE DIRECTOR: But what truth, if you please! We're in the theatre here! Truth, of course, but up to a certain point!

THE STEPDAUGHTER: And what, may I ask, is your idea?

THE DIRECTOR: You will see. You will see. Leave it all to me. I'll take care of everything.

THE STEPDAUGHTER: No, sir. Out of my nausea, out of all the things, one more cruel and more vile than the other, through which I have become what I am, you will surely manage to cook up a little romantic sentimental scene with this man who will ask me the reason for my black dress, and then I will tell him tearfully that two months ago my father died? No, no, my dear sir, no! He must say to me what he really said to me, "Let's take it off then, right away, this little dress!" And I, with my grief, hardly two months old, heavy in my heart, I went behind there, see—behind that screen, and with these fingers that tremble with shame and horror, I unbuttoned my bodice, I unbuttoned my dress. . . .

THE DIRECTOR: For God's sake, what are you saying?

THE STEPDAUGHTER: (*Crying wildly*) The truth! The truth, sir!

THE DIRECTOR: Yes, well, I don't deny it, it may be the truth . . . and I fully understand, I understand all your horror, Miss—but please understand, you too, it is not possible in the theatre!

THE STEPDAUGHTER: No? Not possible? Well then, thanks very much. I'll have nothing to do with it.[36]

The notion that characters, once conceived, have lives independent of their creator had occurred, of course, to many writers, from Balzac to Shaw; but Pirandello gave it currency. In *Six Characters* the imaginary personages speak and act with the authority of self-sufficient entities. We are told in the preface: "They have learned to defend themselves from me; they will be able now to defend themselves from the others." But, of course, what is true of the Six Characters must also be true of the other less fortunate characters of the play. The actors are also characters and have autonomy, so that in making the ones defend their ideal reality against the professional realism of the others, Pirandello is simply confronting Naturalism with the conventional realism of the stage. From this standpoint the play is merely an episode in a literary polemic, and an argument for a more honest style of representation in the theatre.

Supposedly, in their search for a concrete existence, the Six Characters have been reduced to the point where they are willing to settle for the dubious services of a *capocomico* to realize their story. But the subterfuge is transparent. As they are depicted, the characters are themselves the authors of their play, and their insistence on representing their case independent of the director's repertory of clichés indicates the difference between the realism of reality and the realism of the stage. The play deals therefore, in comic fashion, not only with the dramatist's troubles in getting a play properly produced, but also with the difficulty of composing a play outside of the traditional forms. It deals, that is to say, with the tension between truth and literature.

In Italy Pirandello was accounted a Realist, and his play was naturally interpreted as a demonstration of the need for honesty in the theatre. But in spite of Pirandello's expressed intention, *Six Characters* by the very nature of the demonstration was hardly cogent in support of the Realist position. In the Realist drama there was no room for phantoms and planes of reality. The Symbolist tendencies of the play were, on the other hand, quite clear, and even more so in France than in Italy. It is not surprising, accordingly, that when *Six Characters* was shown in Paris it took its place at once in the forefront of the Symbolist drama. Apparently, when this happened, only Pirandello was surprised.

Pirandello's preface to *Six Characters* was written three years after the play's disastrous production in Rome. By that time the play already promised to become a modern classic, and the preface reflects not only the author's satisfaction but also something of his astonishment at its success. *Six Characters* was not, we are told, preconceived. It came into being as a spontaneous illumination of the author's imagination in which, by a miracle, all the spiritual elements worked together in a divine accord.[37] Such phrases approximate the language of Symbolism; but Pirandello was apparently not speaking of the sudden flash of intuition that affords the mystic a glimpse of the ultimate. What he had in mind was the sudden convergence in this play of the various ideas which had long been occupying his mind. It was through the confrontation of his imaginary characters that this took place:

> Without intending it, without knowing it, in the turbulence of the exalted soul, each one of these, to defend himself from the accusations of the others, expresses in terms of his own living passion and his own torment, the thoughts which for many years have been troubling my spirit: the impossibility of mutual comprehension, the irremediable consequence of the empty abstractions of words; the multiple personality of the individual conformable with all the possibilities of being that are found in each of us; and finally the immanent tragic conflict of life—which continually moves and changes—and form, which fixes it in immobility.[38]

It may be that in this preface Pirandello extended the intellectual range of his play somewhat beyond its original outlines. On its face, *Six Characters* seems to deal principally with an aesthetic problem; but it does, in fact, admit of wider interpretations. The inadequacy of language as a means of communication, the kaleidoscopic nature of personality, and the antithesis of *vita* and *forma* were themes which Pirandello had already developed in a variety of contexts. *Six Characters* centers on none of these; but in one way or another it touches upon them all. There are no words by which the Father can communicate with his Stepdaughter. Each is isolated, incommunicado, in his particular niche of hell. There are no words with which to touch the Mother's grief, or the shame of the Little Boy, or the pride of the Son. Their situation, moreover, is hopeless, for the characters, once they are defined, cannot change. We are told—but not in the play—that once born they are free; but in fact they are not free. They were fixed in their forms when they were first conceived, and since their reality is ideal, nothing can be done to change them. Like the figures in Dante's Hell, they are forever fixed in the postures of their agony. The immortality of which Dr. Fileno boasts in "Colloquio con un personaggio" is by no means a blessing. In life there is always the possibility of change, and for mortals there is, in any case, the certainty of death and cessation. In life one can hope for liberty. Imaginary characters have no liberty. They are the captives of the script.

In the *novella* "La trappola"—"The Trap"—first published in 1912 in *Il Corriere della Sera* and reprinted by Treves in 1915, Pirandello had amply explored this ground, though from a somewhat different standpoint:

> You set a value on everything, and never tire of boasting of the constancy of your feelings and the consistency of your character. And why? Why, always for the same reason. Because you are cowards; because you are afraid of yourselves, that is to say, of losing—of changing—the reality that was given to you, of recognizing that this is nothing other than one of your illusions, that there is in fact, no reality save that which we give ourselves.
>
> And what does it mean, I ask, to give oneself a reality, if not to fix oneself in a sentiment, to curdle, stiffen and incrust oneself in it? And thus to arrest in oneself the perpetual movement of life, to make ourselves into so many little wretched stagnant pools, awaiting putrefaction, while life is a constant flowing, incandescent and indeterminate . . . ?
>
> Life is the wind, life is the sea, life is fire: not the earth that hardens and takes on form.
>
> All form is death. . . .
>
> We are all of us beings caught in a trap, detached from the eternal flow and fixed for death.[39]

The conflict of life and form which is developed in "La trappola" was of interest to Pirandello relatively early in his career, but it became obsessive only after Tilgher identified it as the central tenet of Pirandello's system. In *Six Characters* the imaginary personages are still vibrant with the vitality of those who are not yet completely defined—their drama is, like themselves, still *in posse*, though their general outlines are irrevocably fixed. It may seem that logically there is no way in which characters in this condition can make themselves perceptible to anyone but their author. But since these characters presented themselves to the imagination of Pirandello, it is conceivable that they might present themselves to the imagination of someone else; in any case Pirandello was not seriously troubled by logical considerations. In his view characters are not invented by authors; they turn up unexpectedly out of nowhere and clamor for attention. They live, they have names, they ring doorbells and stay to lunch. If the conceit is acceptable, the rest follows without difficulty.

The action in this play is, indeed, based on a paradox. The audience is required to contemplate the actions of non-existent beings acting with complete realism in a situation that is utterly unrealistic. It is entirely capable of accomplishing this feat, for these are the normal conditions of fantasy, and the imagination of the audience accommodates itself to them with the effortlessness of dreams. In *Six Characters* only the logical faculty experiences confusion. The implication is that in the theatre the logical faculty is mainly an embarrassment and should be checked, like an umbrella, in the lobby. But, as we can see in *Il giuoco delle parti*, Pirandello, while caring nothing for logic, prided himself on being a logician. It troubled him, for example, to have Madama Pace appear spontaneously in the crucial scene in her shop. There is obviously no way to justify her presence logically, since she is neither one of the Six Characters, nor at all in search of an author. But she is a necessary part of the anecdote, and in order to accommodate her, the unity of the conceit must be sacrificed. The author tells us in his preface:

> The birth of a creature of human fantasy, a birth that is the crossing of the threshold between the void and the eternal, can also take place unexpectedly, if there is some need for the gestation.
>
> The birth is real, the new character is alive, not because it was already alive, but because it was happily born precisely in accordance with its nature, so to speak, of an "obligatory" character. For this

reason there has taken place by a sleight of hand a spontaneous shift of the plane of reality, since a character can be born in this way only in the fantasy of the poet and certainly not on the boards of a stage. Without anyone noticing it, I have suddenly changed the scene; in this moment I have taken it back into my mind without withdrawing it from the gaze of the spectators: thus I have shown them, instead of the stage, my mind in the very act of creation. . . . The stage, as it takes on the fantastic reality of the Six Characters, does not exist for itself alone as a fixed and immutable thing, just as nothing in this play exists as fixed and preconceived: here everything is done, everything changes, everything is tried and improvised.

This is a somewhat involved way of saying that Madama Pace is necessary to the action, therefore she is there—but it furnishes a recipe for the drama of Surrealism. The Symbolists had contributed greatly to the cult of the irrational, but so far no major dramatist had ventured to declare his independence of the logical faculty. Nor did Pirandello. What was irrational in his play, he rationalized as well as he could. Doubtless *Six Characters*, like *Così è (se vi pare)*, was intended to provoke a scandal, but Pirandello was not willing to leave himself open to the charge that his play lacked logic. In 1925 it was still necessary, in the theatre, to be logical, at least up to a certain point.

Six Characters in Search of an Author was first produced on 10 May 1921 by the company of Dario Niccodemi at the Teatro Valle in Rome. The opening performance was a stormy session which labored to a close through a hubbub of whistles and catcalls, and ended in a brawl in the street. When Pirandello pushed his way through the milling crowd with his daughter Lietta to hail a passing taxicab, his passage was accompanied by hoots and shouts, and his departure was punctuated by the rattle of coins flung after him as the cab drove off. Four months later *Six Characters* was performed again by the same company at the Teatro Manzoni in Milan. By this time the text had been published by Bemporad, the critics had had time to study it, the promotion was skilful, and the audience properly receptive. The performance took place in awed silence, and when the curtain came down there was an ovation. But insofar as Pirandello was concerned, the damage done by its first reception was irreparable. Rome had rejected him. He never forgave it.

Six Characters was, in truth, a remarkable feat of the imagination, and it marked a wholly new approach to the drama. From a philosophic standpoint the play is not, perhaps, so impressive as subsequent critics have made out. But it was not intended as a contribution to philosophy. In 1921 the nature of reality had been the subject of literary exploitation for some years; but it had not been treated seriously in the theatre since the time of Calderón, and never before in so striking a manner as this. *Six Characters*, indeed, had to do primarily with realism, not with reality. But though the question of reality was not central in it, it was inescapable for anyone who thought about the play. The time was ripe in the theatre for a discussion of metaphysics on a popular level. It was in fact this aspect of the play that stirred the imagination of its audience.[40]

In the course of the six years following its initial showing *Six Characters* was performed in little theatres all over the world; but it was a long time before it reached a wide audience. In England the censor forbade a public showing on the ground that it might be spiritually disturbing; but Shaw used his influence with the Stage Society so that a private performance was arranged in February 1922. The following November it was seen at the Fulton Theatre in New York, and in April 1923 it opened at the Studio des Champs Elysées in Paris. It was in Paris that it achieved its great success.

The Paris avant garde, by this time well marshalled and fully documented, if not well subsidized, had made no great fuss over Ibsen, when Antoine produced *Ghosts* in the season of 1889–90, or over Strindberg, when Antoine produced *Miss Julie*. Twenty years had passed since then; but Paris was still not ready for Pirandello. In December 1922 Charles Dullin played Baldovino at Le Théâtre de l'Atelier with indifferent success. That same year Benjamin Crémieux took his translation of *Six Characters* to Copeau. Copeau rejected it as unplayable. Crémieux then applied in turn, and in vain, to the other members of the Cartel. At last Georges Pitoëff saw the light. What attracted him mainly in the play was the possibility of bringing down the characters from the flies in an elevator, an idea that filled Pirandello with horror when it was proposed to him. Evidently he had not so far thought of his characters as supernatural beings, and he thought they should walk in off the street like ordinary people. In the end, however, he was persuaded to come to Paris to attend a rehearsal. He sat in the audience incognito. The elevator worked perfectly. He was overcome with admiration and told Pitoëff this was exactly how he had imagined it.[41]

On 5 April 1923 Pirandello wrote his daughter Lietta from Paris that his play would open April 10th and that it had already aroused the greatest interest. It opened, in fact, on schedule. The elevator came down slowly, bringing to the stage Ludmilla and Georges Pitoëff, Maria Kalff, and several other actors, all bathed in a sepulchral light. The machine stalled a yard above the stage deck. The Six Characters had to climb down one by one. The audience thought the effect was planned. The next day Lugné-Poë wrote that a new era had dawned in the theatre.

The new era in the theatre had been dawning persistently for some years. The little theatres in Paris were busy with all sorts of new and unheard-of projects. Radical manifestoes were appearing every other week. *Six Characters in Search of an Author* made a sensation at the Studio des Champs Elysées, but it did not play consistently to capacity audiences. His success was great, but the sun did not yet shine brightly on Pirandello. It would be some time before it did. His plays were interesting, but they were confusing, and before the critics committed themselves, they awaited clarification.

Strindberg had justified the strange modulations of *The Dream Play* on the ground that the action simulated the events of a dream. Pirandello spoke instead of planes of reality, a more impressive conception which, unfortunately, did not convey much meaning even to the intitiated. In fact, in *Six Characters* the illusion depends on the willingness of the audience to accept as equally real the several unrealities with which the play deals. From a common-sense point of view the only reality of the play is in the actors moving about the stage. These actors, however, represent other actors—imaginary actors rehearsing a play on an imaginary stage—who are interrupted by the arrival of another group of actors who symbolize beings who are not yet in being. The juxtaposition of the real and the unreal on the same picture plane is for the moment dazzling, and the audience's sense of reality is momentarily unsettled; but it soon reasserts its control, and puts all the characters on the stage on an equal footing. So long as the play works, there is thus no difference between the real and the unreal, and the claims of the unreal to a superior reality can only be substantiated by some exaggeration in the representation. In his preface of 1925 Pirandello accordingly recommended that the Six Characters be masked, with their faces immutably fixed in the ideal expression that typifies their basic feelings—in the case of the Father, a mask of remorse; a mask of scorn for the Son; revenge for the Stepdaughter; for the Mother, sorrow—her face should recall the Mater Dolorosa depicted in churches. For obvious reasons this suggestion did not recommend itself. Pitoëff did not mask his characters. He contented himself with making them look like *revenants*. Thereafter *Six Characters* was played in the mystic aura of the supernatural, and the Six Characters from the ideal world took on a spooky look. Thus what had been conceived originally as ironically realistic was transformed into a ghost-story, and Pirandello gracefully accepted the mantle of a seer.

Six Characters was hardly a popular favorite at any time, but for the avant garde it became a landmark. The Symbolists, the Cubists, the Futurists, and the Surrealists all claimed it for their own. The efforts of the Cubist painters to disintegrate reality and to reconstitute it in ideal terms dated back at least to 1907; by 1923 the movement as such was no longer alive. But its influence was felt very widely in artistic circles, and Pirandello's position accorded well enough with this type of modernism so that *Six Characters* was hailed as the spearhead of Cubism in the theatre. It soon acquired Surrealistic status as well. A dozen years before its opening, in connection with his Paris exhibition of 1911–12, Chirico had written: "Everything has two aspects: the current aspect, which we see nearly always and which ordinary people always see, and the ghostly and metaphysical aspect which only rare individuals may see in moments of clairvoyance and metaphysical abstraction." This was the language of Symbolism. Chirico anticipated Breton's Surrealist Manifesto of 1924 by a dozen years—in 1924 it required great critical acumen to distinguish Cubist attitudes from those of the Surrealists, but the Symbolist basis of these schools was perfectly obvious. In *Thesée* (1946), a work written toward the end of his life, Gide recalled the Symbolist position in terms that virtually restate the thesis of *Six Characters* as it was understood twenty years before. "In time," the wise Daedalus informs young Theseus,

> as we mortals measure time, we grow up, fulfill our destiny, and die. But there is another, truer, eternal plane which is timeless; on this plane the representative gestures of our race are inscribed, each according to its special significance. Before he was born Icarus was the image of man's disquiet, of the impulse to discovery, of the soaring flight of poetry—all the things which he incarnated during his short life. He exists as that image after his death.

Accordingly, in *Thesée*, Icarus appears as a living being, delivering a long and labyrinthine monologue, though he has been dead for some time.[42]

In the year following Pitoëff's production of *Six Characters* André Breton announced that Surrealism was based on "pure psychic automatism by means of which one sets out to express verbally, in writing, or in any other manner, the actual functioning of the mind without the authority of reason, or any other aesthetic preoccupation." To the Surrealists Pirandello's characters appeared as images moving in accordance with psychic laws beyond the control of the rational faculty. This view of the play found ample support in Pirandello's preface, if not in the play itself. It was not a coincidence. Pirandello was no stranger to the modernistic theories of the day; and in 1925 he was entirely willing to throw in his lot with the avant garde. He was well acquainted with Chirico, Marinetti, Boccioni, and Romagnoli. He frequented the Futurist gatherings in the art gallery which Bragaglia had opened in Rome in 1918, so that in time Marinetti also staked a claim in *Six Characters* for his movement. But it is doubtful that Pirandello shared with the Futurists much more than their revolutionary posture and their pleasure in shocking the bourgeois, and it is unlikely that he was ever in direct contact with the Surrealists. Nevertheless, insofar as it stressed the fragility of the concept of reality, *Six Characters* accorded very well with the newest currents of artistic thought, while its unsettling ideas regarding form and life had useful political connotations. Most of all it helped to open the way for the development of the anti-realist drama along lines less radical than those of *The Dream Play*, and more sensible than those of *Pelléas et Mélisande*. In sum, few plays had comparable influence on the course of the drama in our time. Whatever its value as drama, *Six Characters*, like *Ghosts*, marked a turning-point in the theatre.[43]

In the arts, in general, the nineteenth century may be said to end with the death of Victor Hugo in 1885; thereafter, in poetry, painting, and music, the new era was ushered in with considerable fanfare. In the theatre the rupture with tradition was less abrupt, and the changing state of affairs became fully apparent only after the end of the First World War. Then quite suddenly, as it seemed, the decline of realism was accelerated, and the logical principle relaxed its age-long hold on the drama. In Paris, by 1925, a play such as Cocteau's *Les Mariés de la Tour Eiffel* could find an audience, and the way was open for every sort of dramatic experiment provided the necessary management could be found. Pirandello experimented a little with Futurism. He wrote the scenario for a Futurist pantomime called *Salamandra*, performed in 1928 under Prampolini. Two years before that Pirandello's company produced Marinetti's *Vulcani* in Florence. But *Six Characters* had carried him as far into the irrational as he cared to go. His next play dealt with madness, but Pirandello's approach was eminently sane.

Enrico IV is without doubt the most poignant of Pirandello's plays, and in some respects the most personal. *Quando si è qualcuno* affords an unhappy glimpse of the author trapped by success; but success is easier to bear than failure, and in *Enrico IV* there is surely some aftertaste of the disastrous reception of *Six Characters* in Rome. In 1921 Pirandello was fifty-four. He had had little joy in his life. *Six Characters* was the best he had done in the theatre, his most original effort, and it had been rejected in Rome with jeers and insults. He had long cherished the conviction that the Italian press was arrayed against him and the "new drama" he represented. Now he was certain of it. Success came to him soon thereafter, unexpectedly and in full measure. It rescued him from despair and from poverty, and provided him with impregnable defences; but it came too late to restore his genial spirits. After the initial rejection of *Six Characters* there were no more light-hearted stories, and it was irony rather than humor that colored his plays.

Enrico IV was in some sense the fruit of despair. He began writing it immediately after the first performance of *Six Characters*, and went at it furiously. In four months it was finished. He distilled into it all the bitterness with which a lifetime of misfortune had inspired him, and all the scorn and indignation of an unforgiving nature. It was a magnificent act of revenge, and it was the high point of his genius. He never wrote better, or as well.

In all probability, had *Six Characters* been gratefully received he would not have been capable of writing *Enrico IV*. And afterwards, when his talent was recognized and applauded, he had no need to reach so high. *Enrico IV* marks both the pinnacle of his effort and the beginning of his decline as an artist. He was to write twenty plays after it. But after it there was no more madness, and there were no more masterpieces.

All art tends to self-portraiture. The temptation to see in the hero of *Enrico IV* a likeness of the author is well-nigh irresistible, but it is best to resist it. There are no doubt some analogies. As for a likeness—if there is a likeness, it is exaggerated and romanticized out of all semblance to its subject. Pirandello had an example of madness vividly before his eyes from the early years of his marriage to Antonietta until two years before the composition of this play; he himself, however, was sorely afflicted with sanity. As an acute and sensitive observer of the lunacies of others, it is true, he could hardly escape some breath of contagion. Such are the psychic hazards of the profession. Doubtless when he wrote he had himself in mind; but the degree in which he identified himself with his characters must remain a matter of conjecture. Between himself and his characters he invariably interposed an intermediary. In his stories the narrator does not lose sight of himself for a moment, nor we of him.

In his youth, we are told, the man who in the play becomes Enrico IV was often carried away emotionally, yet always, so to speak, in cold blood:

BELCREDI: I don't mean to say that he was only pretending to be carried
away like that. No, on the contrary, he was often really excited. But I
am ready to swear, doctor, that no sooner did he feel himself carried
away like that, than he would catch sight of himself in the very act,
so. And I think this happened to him more and more often. What's
more, I'm sure it annoyed him. Every so often he'd get into a perfect
fury with himself. It was comical.

DONNA MATILDE: That's true.

BELCREDI: (To Donna Matilde) And Why? (To the doctor) I think because that
sudden clarity of perception made him feel, suddenly, a stranger to
his own feelings, so that they seemed to him—not feigned—he was in
fact sincere—but like something to which he had to give, then and
there, the value of—what shall I say—an intellectual act—something
artificial he did in order to compensate for the warmth of heart which
he lacked. And then he would improvise, exaggerate, he would let
himself go, you understand, in order to lose sight of himself again.
That made him seem unstable, fatuous, and even sometimes—why
not admit it—sometimes even ridiculous.[44]

In *Enrico IV* the protagonist is nameless. At twenty-seven he was a studious young man of uncertain temper, hopelessly enamored of the beautiful Matilde Spina, at that time a girl of nineteen. Matilde made him suffer. One day he took part in a ceremonial pageant in which the young people of the town costumed themselves as historical figures. He chose to represent the Emperor Henry IV, the penitent of Canossa, whose history he had diligently studied in preparation for the pageant. Matilde was costumed as the Countess Matilda of Tuscany, his enemy, in whose castle Pope Gregory was installed at the time of the Emperor's humiliation. In the course of the cavalcade, someone prodded the Emperor's horse from behind. The horse reared. The rider suffered a fall and hurt his head. When he recovered consciousness, he had regressed mentally in time 800 years. He believed now that he was really Henry IV, and for twenty years he remained suspended in time between January 1076—the date of Henry's excommunication—and the time of his pilgrimage to Canossa in January of the following year.

When the play opens he is still playing the madman, but he is no longer mad. It is fully eight years since he recovered his wits, and he has taken mischievous pleasure in continuing the role to which his accident consigned him twenty years before. At that time a wealthy sister contrived to surround him with the trappings of his delusion—the ancient castle, which he took to be Goslar, the costumes, and the imperial retinue. Thus he has lived out an elaborate masquerade, forcing all those who approach him to act out their assigned parts as characters in his fantasy, an artificial reality he constructed for himself within the less satisfactory reality that was the work of others. But now, after eight years, he is weary of the game. He would like to conclude his performance and to rejoin the rest of the world.

There are difficulties. The reality of the outerworld has a formal rigidity which does not yield readily to the wishes of the individual. In fantasy Enrico IV was permitted to take interesting liberties with time. He has in fact taken twenty years to live through some days or weeks of history. Thus, in fantasy, he is still a young man of twenty-seven. But while his mind was obedient to his wish, his body was synchronized with other rhythms. In twenty years his body has aged twenty years. He is forty-seven.

There are those who, at forty-seven, refuse to accept middle age; but Enrico IV is not mad. He is entirely aware of his temporal situation and is disposed to poke fun at his pretence. His make-up is deliberately clownish. He has made up his face in a caricature of youth, just as he has made his sanity into a caricature of madness.

Unexpectedly an opportunity is presented for him to escape from his dream. His sister is now dead; but before her death she had suspected that her brother was coming to his senses. His nephew, Di Nolli, has brought a group of friends to visit the madman, among them a psychiatrist. There is Enrico's former flame, Donna Matilde, now a widow; and her daughter Frida, who is engaged to Di Nolli; and Belcredi, an old friend, who is now Matilde's lover. The doctor has devised a plan. He proposes to shock Enrico out of his delusion by forcing his mind back to the moment of his trauma, and then plunging it suddenly into the present time-current, thus forcing a readjustment of his sense of time. The means are at hand. There is a life-size portrait of Matilde in her masquerade costume hanging in the throne room of the castle alongside the portrait of the Emperor. The doctor proposes to bring these portraits to life by having Frida impersonate the Countess Matilda in the costume her mother wore on the day of the pageant, while Di Nolli impersonates Enrico IV. At a suitable moment, both these figures will step out of their frames, and, confronted with two Countess Matildas, one at nineteen and the other at forty-five, Enrico will have to reset his inner clock-mechanism back twenty years to the time of his fall, and forward 800 years to the present.

The plan works perfectly. The pretended madman is shocked into an admission of sanity. But it is not clear to him, as matters stand, whether sanity is preferable to madness. In the end he chooses madness, and in a momentary fit of excitement—which may well have been simulated, an act of the intellect, as Belcredi put it at the outset—he runs a sword through Belcredi, whom he holds responsible for his misfortune, and thus condemns himself to play out his part for the rest of his days.

Unlike *Six Characters in Search of an Author*, *Enrico IV* is a well-made play, logically conceived and provided with all the traditional apparatus of the genre—a proper exposition, a sequential complication, climax, and denouement, and a full complement of surprises. But while the form is conventional, the idea is strikingly original, and the texture extraordinarily rich and dense. *Six Characters* is full of ambiguities. In comparison *Enrico IV* is straightforward and unequivocal. What is said of the relations of madness and sanity, life and form, reality and unreality, constitutes a precise and compendious statement of Pirandello's attitude toward life at the high point of his career. The play is, in this sense, definitive.

Like *Il giuoco delle parti*, which in some ways it resembles, *Enrico IV* is a play of jokes, a *scena delle beffe*. The practical joke that Belcredi played upon his friend and rival, by goading his horse into throwing him, cost Enrico twenty years of his life. He repays the jest twenty years later with a trick that costs Belcredi his life. But while this action provides the framework of the play, it is not the source of its dramatic energy. That depends on other motifs. Among them is the theme of alienation, the theme which gives tragic color to the novel, *Il fu Mattia Pascal*. Mattia Pascal escapes from his world by pretending to commit suicide. When he tries to return to his former life he finds the way barred by time and change. Enrico, similarly, escapes—in this case into the past—and he too finds it impossible to readjust his life:

> I open my eyes, little by little, and at first I don't know if I am awake
> or asleep; but yes, I am awake; I touch this thing and that: I can see
> things clearly once again. . . . Ah, as he says (*He points to Belcredi*) off
> with it, off with it now, this mask! this prison! Let's open the windows:
> let's breathe the air! Let's go, let's run out! (*Then, stopping suddenly*)
> Where? to do what? to have people pointing me out, secretly, as Henry
> IV, not as I am here, but walking arm in arm with you, among my old
> friends? [45]

For the sane, reality is a house of detention as closely guarded as an
asylum for lunatics. The penalty for escape is alienation; but there is no
other way to achieve wisdom. In *Enrico IV* the hero has gained, through
madness, insights which sane people lack and do well to avoid. He has
discovered the fragility of the structure upon which the everyday world
is based, and tested for himself the gossamer which holds it together.
From his own experience he knows that madness offers an alternative reality, no more irrational or inconsequential than the reality of normal
people and, for all but practical purposes, of equal validity. It is for this
reason, Enrico says, that madness inspires terror in those who are not
normally accounted mad:

> Because to find yourself before a madman, do you know what that
> means? To find yourself before one who can topple from its founda-
> tions everything that you have built up in yourself and around yourself,
> your logic, the logic of all your constructions! Well, what do you ex-
> pect? They construct without logic, these blessed creatures, the mad-
> men. Or with a logic of their own that flies in the air like a feather.
> . . . You say, this is not possible, but for them everything is possi-
> ble.—But, you say, it's not true. And why? Because it doesn't seem
> true to you, to you, to you, and to a hundred thousand others. Ah,
> friends! You should see what seems true instead to those hundred thou-
> sand others who are not called madmen, and what a spectacle they
> make of themselves with their agreements, their flowers of logic! [46]

There is reason, certainly, to believe that *Enrico IV* affords a closer
look at the author than any of his other plays; but, it may be repeated, it
would be a mistake to insist on its autobiographical character. Those
who might enjoy seeing in Enrico IV a self-portrait of the author, will
find there, obviously, a Pirandello magnified to imperial proportions; and
the likeness will reflect chiefly those aspects of the author's personality
that clamored for exhibition at this time. It could not represent the
whole man, for the reason, as Pirandello so often pointed out, that the

whole man cannot be represented. If, in any case, the singular character of his hero does in some way represent the character of the author, then what we are invited to see is the case of the unfortunate man who, by a sudden stroke of fortune, had been condemned, eighteen years before, to spend his life in the company of a madwoman and a throng of imaginary beings in a world of his own devising, and who was now afforded a chance to escape into a more normal reality.

But, in truth, it was not the fall of his father's fortunes that condemned Pirandello to a world of fantasy. He had freely chosen this world for himself from the time when his brother Innocenzo agreed to substitute for him in his military service so as to leave him free to pursue a literary career in Rome. The tragedy of *Enrico IV* may well have a more general implication than one is usually inclined to see in it. It might reasonably be said to exemplify the predicament of those who abstract themselves—like Leone Gala—from the world of men in order to live in the world of art, the ideal world where the Will To Live is not operative, and where nothing changes and nothing dies. This world has the permanence of history. It is fully lived out and formed, and is therefore dead and relatively harmless. But it has also its terrors. Enrico IV tells the Abbot of Cluny, that is to say, the doctor,

> I believe, Monsignore, that phantasms, in general, are at bottom none other than little fragments of spirit: images that one does not succeed in containing within the kingdom of dreams: they reveal themselves also during waking hours, by day; and they are frightening. I am always so frightened when by night I see them before me—so many disordered images, laughing, dismounted from their horses.[47]

For Pirandello, also, there was something frightening about the writer's profession. More than once he feared that he would go mad. But *Enrico IV* is not a study of madness. Enrico is not mad. It is a study of sanity. In this play the madman belongs to the type of the Wise Fool, a familiar character who, under cover of his cap and bells, is permitted to utter truths which are normally not spoken. Enrico is a superb *raisonneur*. He also has the advantage—like Ibsen's Dr. Relling in *The Wild Duck* and Dr. Stockman in *An Enemy of the People*—of being a bit unbalanced, just enough to add salt to his utterance. He is exceptionally convincing precisely because his credibility is in question and he is, as a character, entirely ambiguous. He tells Bertoldo, his retainer,

> It suits everyone, you understand? It suits everyone to make the world believe that certain people are mad in order to have an excuse for shut-

ting them up. You know why? Because you cannot bear to listen to them. What did I say about those people who have just left? That the one is a whore, the other a dirty libertine, the other a quack. . . . But it's not true! No one can believe that! Yet they all stand there listening, terrified. Well, now—I'd like to know why they are afraid if it's not true.—You can never take anything seriously that a madman says! All the same they stand there, listening like that, with their eyes glazed with fear—. Why? Tell me, you tell me—why? [48]

Before *Enrico IV* was finished Pirandello must have realized that he was engaged on his masterpiece. But he had not yet fully recovered from the shock of the opening of *Six Characters* in May, and he badly needed reassurance. In the summer of 1921 he sent a summary of his plot to Ruggeri with a covering letter: ". . . without false modesty I may say that the subject is worthy of you and of the power of your art. But before setting to work, I should like you to tell me what you think, whether you like it and approve of it." Ruggeri liked it very much, and Pirandello went on to finish it. Meanwhile, in September, Niccodemi presented *Six Characters* in Milan. Pirandello was much encouraged.

Enrico IV opened at the Teatro Manzoni in Milan on 24 February 1922 before an appreciative audience which hardly knew what to make of the play, but heartily applauded Ruggeri's performance. Pirandello was elated. He wrote to his daughter Lietta, now newly married and living in Chile, "*Enrico IV* is a triumph, a real triumph. Ruggeri gave a magnificent performance, and the play was repeated every evening during the company's stay in Milan, with superabundant marks of public enthusiasm. It has been the greatest success I have had so far; the daily papers of Turin, Rome, Venice, Genoa, Florence, Naples and Sicily have all devoted two columns to the event." [49] Six months later Palmarini presented the play in Rome, with equal success.

The press was, in fact, extremely respectful; but the critics had reservations. There had been a good deal of applause. Ruggeri's performance was, by all accounts, spectacular. The critics, however, were unable to distinguish the play from the performance, and they preferred to withhold a final judgment. Silvio d'Amico declared it a masterpiece. For the rest, the Italian press was unanimous in praise of *Enrico IV* only after the success of *Six Characters in Search of an Author* in Paris the following year.

In the fall of 1923 *Enrico IV* was produced in New York, together with *Six Characters* and *Come prima, meglio di prima*. The following year it was performed in Warsaw and in Athens and, in 1925, Pirandello's own company presented it in repertory in London. Two years later *Enrico IV* had been played in most of the great cities of Europe, bringing confusion and controversy wherever it was seen. In 1934 Pirandello was awarded the Nobel prize. Then it became a classic and was chewed over extensively in seminars.

By 1923 Pirandello was a famous man. His publisher Bemporad undertook to bring out his collected *novelle* in an edition of twenty-four volumes. Fifteen volumes actually appeared, between 1922 and 1937. The general title of the collection was *Novelle per un anno—Stories for a Year*—a title which recalled Boccaccio's "Stories for Ten Days," the *Decameron.* His plays were now being performed in a variety of translations, often with Symbolist and Expressionist trappings calculated to enhance their mystery and to heighten their chic. But in France his popularity was short-lived. In the Paris production of *Enrico IV*, in 1925, Georges Pitoëff, made up in the guise of a marionette, caused the walls of the castle of Goslar to tremble each time a visit disturbed the madman's dream. The Paris press dutifully applauded Pitoëff's performance, but the critics, on the whole, were unfavorably disposed to the play. It was said to be incoherent, confused, and, in general, a bore. The author was maligned because he was an Italian, and the translator because he was a Jew. The manifest doctrine of the play was labelled "intellectual Bolshevism." André Antoine deplored the fact that the mise en scène and the costumes were alien to the French theatre. It was obvious that, with regard to Pirandello, a reaction had set in.

Nevertheless *Enrico IV* continued to do good business in Paris. The production was spectacular, the play was controversial—in the theatre little more is necessary for success. The receipts, we are told, were sufficiently gratifying to enable the Pitoëffs to think seriously of producing *Saint Joan* the following season. But the Paris press, which had lionized Pirandello two years before, continued to find him an unwelcome intruder, and the public soon proved equally fickle. After the opening of *Ciascuno a suo modo—Comme ci, comme ça*—in May 1926, Lucien Descaves wrote in *L'Intransigeant:* "Monsieur Pirandello, called to the stage with great ironic shouts, lent himself to the game and came out at last to salute his audience again and again. The fact that Monsieur Pirandello has come from Italy to amuse himself at our expense gives us no good reason to repay him in the same coin. Let us not forget that he is a stranger and a guest. Let us not insist: it is certainly the last of him. . . ."[50]

In America, Pirandello fared better. The United States had only recently made the world safe for democracy: in New York everything
foreign was welcome. Henry Ford offered to finance a Pirandellian tour.
But Pirandello was not impressed by the Americans. After his first visit
to New York in 1923 he told his interviewers in Italy that life in America
was generally lacking in spiritual essence, a fact that might well have
been true, but could not have been immediately perceptible to a visiting
playwright.[51] Five years later his views apparently had changed. In an
article in *Il Corriere della Sera* he wrote that what interested him most of
all in the United States was the birth of new forms of life. In Europe, he
continued, life was rooted in the dead. In America life belonged to the
living. The publication of these clichés was pardonable: a successful
writer is obliged to keep up his public relations, and the supply of useful
stereotypes is, after all, limited. The article in question was printed on
16 June 1929, five months before the Wall Street crash unexpectedly unsettled the eternal verities.

In Italy the world-wide interest in *Six Characters in Search of an Author*
brought about a revaluation of Pirandello's work, and soon the groundwork was laid down for a serious study of his *oeuvre*. In his review of
Pensaci, Giacomino! Adriano Tilgher had written, five years before the
first production of *Six Characters:* "Pirandello's art is the art of leisure and
amusement, without any profound content, without moral seriousness,
without any vital interest in the mind and its problems. Fools may mistake for profundity the ironic smile with which Pirandello presents his
characters, but men of good taste will not let themselves be deceived."[52]

Pirandello's later plays caused Tilgher to alter his position. After the
furor attending the production of *Six Characters* he began to see in Pirandello's works a clear reflection of his own ideas, and consequently a
prime expression of the problems of the age. In the *Studi sul teatro contemporaneo* which he published in 1922, Tilgher devoted some sixty pages of
text to an analysis of Pirandello's ideas. In this essay he identified, under
twenty-eight sub-headings, all the themes which, in his opinion, Pirandello had so far developed as a dramatic author. Among these were the
questions of life and form, appearance and reality, logic and the irrational, the inadequacy of language, the question of identity, the question of
truth, and the opposition of the individual and society. The result of this
detailed exegesis was to give Pirandello a foremost place among those
who were currently involved with the intellectual life of Italy.[53]

Adriano Tilgher was at this time at the height of his influence. He was
a Neapolitan of very decided views and of a distinctly militant disposition. He was widely read, had come successively under the influence of
Schopenhauer, Dilthey, Bergson, and Georg Simmel, and was sharply
opposed to the historical school of criticism associated with Croce and
Gentile. In Tilgher's opinion Pirandello had a distinct affinity with Simmel, particularly with respect to the duality of life and form. Tilgher
wrote:

> All modern philosophy since Kant is founded on the deep intuition of
> the dualism that exists between Life, which is absolute spontaneity,
> creative activity, continual creation of the new and diverse, and the
> Forms, constructions, schemes, which tend to enclose it within itself,
> schemes which Life constantly destroys in order to go beyond them in
> its unwearied activity.[54]

For Pirandello, in Tilgher's estimation, life was basically dramatic,
and the essence of this drama was the struggle between the primal nudity of life and the clothes and masks with which "men pretend, and
necessarily pretend, to clothe it." He continued:

> The philosophy implicit in Pirandello's art all centers on the fundamen-
> tal duality of Life and Form: Life perpetually mobile and fluid, which
> sinks and cannot help sinking into a form; yet profoundly opposes any
> form; and Form which, determining Life, while giving rigid and precise
> limits to Life, freezes and kills its restless heat.[55]

Pirandello's titles—"Naked Life," "Naked Masks"—according to
Tilgher, make the underlying thought apparent. The nucleus of this
thought is the intuition that every form is a definition and a limitation,
and therefore a negation, of life. To think is to construct, to give form;
consequently, as Bergson had indicated, to think is to limit and to suf-
focate life.

In this manner Tilgher propelled Pirandello directly into the forefront
of the avant garde, and identified him with those Bergsonians who, con-
sidering logic to be an aberration of the mental faculties, looked to the intuition as the only access to truth. It was by no means Pirandello's idea.
Pirandello was perhaps not too clear as to the validity of intuition, but he
considered himself a logician. In *Il giuoco delle parti* he had Leone Gala
beating an egg while he took Bergson severely to task for his assault on
the power of reason:

LEONE: I'm beating, I'm beating. . . . but just listen to me a moment! All that in our reality is fluid, living, mobile, dark, yes, I admit it, it escapes reason. . . . How it escapes reason, however, I cannot quite see, from the very fact that Signor Bergson can say it! How does he manage to say it? What makes him say it, if not reason? And so, it seems to me, it does not escape reason. Am I right? . . . Listen to me, Venanzi: it is a lovely jest, this that reason plays on Signor Bergson, making him believe that it is dethroned and humiliated by him, to the infinite delight of all the irrational ladies of Paris! Listen to me. According to him, reason. . . .

And Leone launches into a discourse in dispraise of Bergson that is mercifully curtailed by his culinary activities.[56]

But while he did not go along with Tilgher in the matter of the logical faculty, Pirandello found the theme of the duality of life and form entirely congenial. The idea that the individual has two contrary drives, the one dynamic and therefore resistant to fixation, the other static and opposed to change, was inherent in Pirandello's idea of drama from the beginning of his career. The vital flux and the forms it assumes were, in his view, in perpetual conflict, and in the individual psyche this conflict was a prime source of dramatic tension. This idea was developed in detail in a number of *novelle* long before the date of *Enrico IV*, and very fully in "La trappola" in 1912. In July 1922, soon after Tilgher's book came out, Pirandello told an interviewer for *L'epoca*: ". . . these ideas were mine alone; they had come spontaneously out of my spirit, they imposed themselves naturally on my thoughts. It was only afterwards, when my first dramatic works appeared, that I was told that these were the problems of the age, that others in this same period were troubled by them as I was."[57]

Pirandello gratefully accepted Tilgher's formulation of his principles, but he was by no means ready to agree that he wrote from a formula. He wrote, he insisted, as an artist:

My works are born of living images, the perennial source of art, but these images pass through the screen of concepts which have taken form in my mind. My works of art are never concepts trying to express themselves through images. Quite the contrary, they are images, often very vivid images of life, which through the operation of my mind assume universal significance by themselves, through the formal unity of art.[58]

In his evaluation of Pirandello, Tilgher however defined him in accordance with more precise preconceptions. He saw him neither as a realist nor as an idealist in the Platonic sense. "Pirandello," he wrote,

> contemporary with the great spiritual and idealistic revolution in Italy and Europe at the beginning of the century, transports into art that anti-intellectualism and anti-rationalism which pervades all contemporary philosophy and which culminates in Relativism. Pirandello's art is anti-intellectual because it denies that any order of truth pre-exists, or that there are facts already determined of which thought has only to take account. It is, however, an art that affirms intellect insofar as it is full of the drama of the thinking thought which breasts the waves of the ocean of life and struggles to dominate it. Thought enters the paste of life and puts it in ferment. Therefore reality, which for other writers is monolithic, is for Pirandello broken and folded into planes which generate one another.[59]

This was the rhetoric of Symbolism; and very likely these ideas pushed Pirandello somewhat further into the current of contemporary thought than he wished to go. The phrase *il pensiero pensante*—the thinking thought—was directly borrowed from Mallarmé's *ma pensée se pense*. The self-generating planes of reality recalled Jarry's "iridescent mental kaleidoscope." Pirandello did not normally use such language. His attitudes were certainly radical for the time, but his radicalism was closer to the Parnasse than to the Symbolists. As a philosophically minded writer he was very willing to negate reality, but as an artist he was rather inclined to observe nature than to destroy it. He had somehow blundered into Symbolism. Yet, like the painter Nane Papa in the *novella*, "Candelora," he was at bottom a Realist. Of Nane Papa he had written:

> All his life everything that was alive in him he had put, he had given, he had spent, for the pleasure of making a leaf seem fleshy, making himself into the fleshy paste, the fibre and vein of the leaf; or a stone, rigid and naked, so that it should feel and live as a stone on the canvas, and only this mattered to him.[60]

There is no doubt that as an artist Pirandello was very much of Nane Papa's persuasion. It was indeed as a Realist that he had come to doubt reality, and in this respect he made common cause with the later Impressionists, the post-Impressionists. For him, as for them, the appearance of things was the ever-changing mask with which life was veiled; but life itself was unknown and indefinable, and Pirandello was more concerned with the mask than with what lay behind it. He himself had assumed the mask of a philosopher. It suited him badly. He was an artist and, at bottom, a Verist still. He was entirely willing to accept Pirandellism, now that it was coming into fashion. But he was never really a Pirandellian.

Nevertheless in accepting the system that Tilgher fathered on him, Pirandello found himself associated, willy-nilly, with all the various disruptive movements that were currently gnawing away at the bases of Western culture. He was no doubt in some degree a part of these himself. From the time of *Cosi è* (*se vi pare*) he might be considered a minister of disruption; but he was a minister without portfolio. He was so far not aligned with any movement. In an early essay entitled "Arte e coscienza d'oggi," published in 1893 when he was twenty-six, Pirandello had written:

> As the ancient norms have crumbled and the new are not yet sorted out or established, it is natural that the concept of the relativity of all things has so far extended itself in use as to make us lose our judgment of practically everything. . . . Never before, I think, has our life been ethically and aesthetically more broken up. Disconnected, without any principle of doctrine or faith, our thoughts whirl within the active drives that hang like clouds around a ruin. From this, it seems to me, derives the major part of our intellectual uneasiness.

Enrico IV, however, displayed something more than intellectual uneasiness. It was aggressively iconoclastic. But Pirandello's aggressiveness was not politically dangerous. What aroused his indignation was not the world-order, but the absence of order in the world; not faith, but the impossibility of faith. It is easy to understand the appeal of Mussolini's fascism to a man of Pirandello's temper. He deplored its excesses, but fascism served to bind together a world that was visibly falling to pieces and, much as he disliked its methods, he preferred it to the political and moral chaos which preceded it. His attacks upon the conventional acceptances of his time, its specious truths and evanescent realities, were not those of a genuine nihilist, but those of an outraged moralist. His nihilism, such as it was, was born of the contrast between the ideals he had inherited and the reality into which he was thrust. It was the hypocrisy of those who tried to pass off the one for the other that angered him. His fury was the fury of the 1860's, the high fury of Garibaldi, not the cold madness of the 1920's.

Tilgher wrote of him, in a later article:

Pirandello is a relativist. He denies the existence of objective reality and truth, and maintains that for each of us Being and Appearance are identical, that there is no such thing as knowledge, but only opinion (*Cosi è (se vi pare)*), and that one opinion is as good as another (*Ciascuno a suo modo*), precisely because for him all theories, affirmations, laws and norms are nothing but ephemeral forms within which life is momentarily trapped, in themselves ultimately devoid of truth and consistency.

This might well serve as a definition of *pirandellismo*, and from a superficial reading of Pirandello such an inference might perhaps be drawn. But essentially his work does not support such a view. On the contrary, what is evident in his *novelle* and in his drama, from *Pensaci, Giacomino!* to *Enrico IV*, is a clear affirmation of his faith in traditional principles—in justice, truth, honesty, honor, and love—the solid virtues of middle-class culture, without any trace of cynicism or doubt. It is, obviously, difficult to square these beliefs with the skeptical and relativistic attitude he so often assumed; but Pirandello made no special claim to consistency. In 1929 he wrote that though life and form were fundamentally opposed, certain forms were indispensable to life:

So long as forms remain alive, that is, so long as the vital force remains in them, they constitute a victory of the spirit. To destroy them simply in order to replace them with others is criminal. . . . Some forms are a natural expression of life itself. It is therefore impossible for them to become obsolete or to be replaced by others without destroying life in one of its true and natural manifestations.[61]

Ultimately the position at which Pirandello arrived was not far removed from the position of Ibsen. The Pirandellians were bent on destroying the world, but Pirandello had no idea of abetting their efforts. He wished, on the contrary, to substitute the order of nature for the disorder of man's world. Reality, in his view, was the product of the human mind, not a system arbitrarily imposed on chaos by an omnipotent deity. It was therefore incumbent on mankind to devise a reality that would be appropriate to the human condition, and this reality would be subject to change as humanity improved its circumstances, morally and intellectually. His assault upon the cosmic order was, accordingly, intended to free humanity from the tyranny of the unreal. His doctrine was, so he believed, in the truest sense liberal and constructive. He was aware that it was generally misunderstood. In the interview published in *L'epoca* in July 1922, in which he discussed Tilgher's analysis of his philosophy, Pirandello told the journalist: "What most people see in me is only the negative side of my thought. I seem to be a destructive devil who cuts the ground from under their feet. But surely the fact is the other way round. Before I pull the ground away, do I not show them where to put their feet?"[62]

The truth is that all Pirandello's plays have a moral intention. But in the 1920's there was not much profit in being a moralist in the theatre. The pose of the destructive devil, the Satanist, the skeptic, had far greater glamor. Until he wrote *Six Characters in Search of an Author* Pirandello was pretty much in the mainstream of European drama. He had not advanced much beyond Ibsen's Dr. Stockman, and hardly as far as Shaw's Dick Dudgeon or Don Juan. In 1922 he was a radical writer in need of an intellectual affiliation, and when Tilgher offered him a post in the radical avant garde, he hastened to accept it. The result was that he was drawn into relativism without really being a relativist, just as, some years later, he was drawn into fascism without being a fascist. At any rate, it is clear that, whether he agreed with it completely or not, he accepted Tilgher's formulation of his principles with gratitude, and in his future work went to some trouble to demonstrate its validity. After 1922 his articles and his lectures are resonant with phrases taken verbatim from Tilgher's book, and such plays as *Diana e la Tuda* are obviously composed in strict accord with Tilgher's recipe.

But Tilgher was not entirely laudatory in his evaluation of Pirandello. After elevating his plays to an intellectual level commensurate with his own, Tilgher went on to deplore Pirandello's excessive cerebrality. The dangers of drama conceived in the manner of Pirandello, he wrote, was its tendency toward an arid and intellectual excogitation. In his opinion, Pirandello's characters, and his situations, lacked variety: "It is undeniable that the Pirandellian characters resemble one another like drops of water: rather than different characters they seem to be one and the same character in situations that are always different and always the same." Moreover, he deplored the lack of balance between the grandiose metaphysical conception that the characters embodied and the meanness of their station. But, he added, Pirandello had not yet said his last word. In *Six Characters* and *Enrico IV* the metaphysical idea had more ample scope, and the familiar themes developed in a higher and rarer atmosphere. This was all preliminary work. There was, he concluded, bound to be a future masterpiece.[63]

Immediately after the publication of Tilgher's book, Pirandello wrote him, expressing his gratitude for the service he had done him in clarifying his views. For a time he acted the part of the faithful disciple. But before long the affiliation became annoying, the more so as Tilgher insisted on posing publicly as his muse and mentor. Nevertheless their personal relations remained cordial until political considerations drove them apart. After Pirandello's association with the Fascist party, Tilgher, who was affiliated with an opposition paper, launched an attack against him, and their relations ended in bitter hostility.

It has been said that in furnishing Pirandello with a blueprint for his future work Tilgher did him a distinct disservice. In some measure this is true. But Tilgher came into his life at a time when Pirandello was in urgent need of a blueprint. In 1922 he was fifty-five, and he had worked at top speed for some thirty years without having time to take stock of his ideas. Tilgher furnished him with a precise inventory and assigned him a place in current thought. The idea that in accepting this form Pirandello lost his vitality has both glamor for the scholar and irony, but the facts do not bear it out. Tilgher provided a mirror in which Pirandello could see himself, and Pirandello was keenly aware that to see oneself is dangerous; for at this point, as he often wrote, life stops and thought begins. But Pirandello did not by any means stop living in his fifties, either as a man or as an artist. On the contrary, in these years his activity was immeasurably enhanced. It was as if he had gained a second hold on youth, and he developed impressively in every direction. He became a power in the theatre, a manager, a stage director; and nationally a man of consequence, a senator and a Nobel laureate. But he wrote nothing finer than the two great works of 1920's. His future masterpiece was in the past. It needed only to be revalued. This happened.

The aging poet in *Quando si è qualcuno* resigns himself to the tragedy of success, stifling, for the benefit of his family and his friends, the vital impulse that stirs once again in his veins. But while it is tempting to identify this monumental figure with Pirandello, there is no close relation between them. With time—it has often been noted—human genius tends to crystallize in intelligible forms. After 1922 Pirandello became *"qualcuno"*—a Somebody. It was perhaps not an altogether enviable fate; but Pirandello could hardly complain. It was the goal to which he had aspired all his life. He had attained it, and it was sad for him; but not as sad, perhaps, as if he had not attained it.

Until quite recently almost everything that has been said of Pirandello by way of interpretation has echoed Tilgher's analysis, so that Pirandello's work has been thought of principally in terms of the duality of life and form, and his style has been decried for its cerebral quality. In truth, most of Pirandello's plays hardly involve the contrast of life and form, and his style is rather melodramatic and passionate than cerebral. Many of his plays require, it is true, the services of a *raisonneur*, sometimes an intrusive character such as Laudisi in *Così è (se vi pare)*, sometimes one who is an active protagonist such as Baldovino in *Il piacere dell'onestà*, Ciampa in *Il berretto a sonagli*, the Father in *Sei personaggi in cerca d'autore*, or the madman in *Enrico IV*. These characters talk a great deal, and unquestionably they served the author as useful intellectual vehicles. But only in an age when the drama was expected to provide grandiose displays of passion could Pirandello's plays be called "arid intellectual excogitations." By 1922 Shaw had amply demonstrated the dramatic possibilities of intellectual discussion, and in England his plays were respected as entertaining doctrinal demonstrations. But in Italy in this period the theatre was not expected to serve such purposes. It would be thirty years before an audience would be carried away so far as to consider dialectic a form of poetry.

There is, as a matter of fact, not much that can be called poetry in Pirandello's dialectic. What is poetic in his plays is not their logic, but the absence of logic. In Pirandello's plays reason is a purely defensive device. It is the armored shell which shelters the naked creature that lives in it, the refuge the character constructs to protect itself from the world outside. The dialectic is, moreover, seldom convincing. But it is invariably touching. Compared with Shaw's magisterial debaters, Pirandello's logicians are poor things, by turns comic and pathetic, and the philosophical mask that they affect, even in its most rigid forms, never quite serves to conceal the contorted face behind it. Leone Gala is a stoic with a good stomach, but for all the ingenuity of his rationalization, he cannot manage to digest his bitterness.

Pirandello's crowning masterpiece, which Tilgher so confidently predicted, did not in fact materialize. But, taken together, the twenty-one plays that followed *Enrico IV* almost compensated for its absence. Some were of prime importance; none was altogether negligible; all in all, it was a masterly achievement. In these later plays the dominant theme, expressed in a wide variety of situations, is the illusory nature of what passes for reality, so that, by the time he had done with it, Pirandello's world was in shreds. When he began work on his last play, *I giganti della montagna* (1936), the chief wonder of the modern world was that it was still intact.

Soon after finishing *Enrico IV* Pirandello wrote one of his most successful plays, *Vestire gli ignudi* (1923)—*To Clothe the Naked*. It is of classic design, and unfolds retrospectively an action that extends back some months before the play begins and resolves it in the space of a day. In the construction of this play there is some hint of *Six Characters;* but in this case it is an author who goes in search of a character, and the action concerns the efforts of the protagonist to give the world, through the author, a becoming account of her life.

At the beginning of the play Ersilia Drei has drawn attention to herself in Rome by attempting suicide in a public park. She lands in a hospital, and a journalist who comes to interview her publishes the story of her life in his paper. The novelist Lodovico Nota is so deeply impressed with this story that he takes Ersilia to his home, intending to work her life story into a novel. Her story, in fact, reads like the libretto of a sentimental opera. She was employed as governess in the house of the Italian consul in Smyrna. A naval lieutenant won her heart and, after he promised to marry her, she gave herself to him. But Lieutenant Franco, in the way of naval officers, never came back. The girl was disgraced. Then the consul's child had an accident and was killed. The blame fell on Ersilia. She was dismissed. In despair, she came to Rome in search of her lover, only to find that he was about to marry another. Now quite hopeless, she gave herself to the first man she met and, in her revulsion, took poison.

This story, when it is published, makes a deep impression in Rome. The naval officer, now a civilian, renounces his engagement and hastens to make good his promise to Ersilia. She rejects him. Then the consul appears. He is furious. Bit by bit the facts of the case come out. The consul is actually a kindly man married to a sickly wife who has had much reason for jealousy. Ersilia, after having been seduced by Franco, became the consul's mistress. At the time of the child's fatal accident, the two lovers were surprised together by the jealous wife. There was a scene, and Ersilia was dismissed at the wife's insistence. Later, in Rome, alone and with no means of support, she tried to earn a living on the streets. Failing that, she took poison. Afterwards, in the hospital, sure that she was on her deathbed, she told the reporter the romantic tale that was published in the press.

In her present circumstances Ersilia refuses to have anything further to do with any of the men around her—neither with the novelist who desires to romanticize her tale, nor with the naval gentleman who offers to marry her, nor with the consul who now wishes to have her back with him. She wishes only to finish dying. In the end she manages that by taking another dose of poison. This time it is effective.

A play couched in these terms might easily lapse into sentimentality, but Pirandello saved it from mawkishness by giving Ersilia Drei a singularly strong and resolute character. She is nothing, she tells them, a lump of clay modeled by chance, without any personality of her own. In fact, she displays such nobility of character that she dwarfs the men who, more or less unwittingly, have collaborated to destroy her. The men are, indeed, pitiful creatures, and the scene in which they wrangle among themselves over the dying girl is sufficiently comic to give a grotesque tinge to what is essentially a tragic situation. Franco, jealous of his honor, offers to fight the consul because he suspects him of having seduced Ersilia before he did. The consul is worried about his reputation and denies having had any relations whatever with the girl. The father of Franco's bride insists that his daughter's marriage must take place at any cost. The novelist and the journalist try desperately to extricate themselves from a situation which promises to be professionally embarrassing. In the midst of these noises Ersilia appears, pale, dying, and completely dignified. Her curtain speech is in the nature of an aria. In all her life, she tells them, she had never been able to put on a decent dress without some dog tearing it away from her. Now the dogs are at her again. Her pathetic attempt to find a dress to cover her nakedness even now has been denied:

> I wished to make myself a nice one to die in—the nicest—the one I had always dreamed of—and which was also torn away—a bride's dress— but only to die in, to die in, to die in, and no more—So—with a few tears of sympathy—and no more. Well, no! No! No! I wasn't allowed even this. Torn off my back, stripped off, even this! No! To die naked! Uncovered, humiliated, despised! Well, there we are—are you satisfied? And now go away, go! Let me die quietly, naked—.[64]

The portrait of the aging writer Lodovico Nota is interesting. He is by no means a sympathetic character. Like the naval officer Franco, the consul, and the journalist, he is a self-centered man who sees in Ersilia mainly a subject for exploitation. He is made to say that Pirandello's work fills him with loathing. It is amusing, therefore, that the manner in which he is described suggests that he is a caricature of the author himself,

> a handsome man of commanding appearance, although he has passed his fiftieth year. Piercing eyes, sparkling, and on his still fresh lips an almost youthful smile. Cold, reflective, entirely deprived of those natural gifts which win sympathy and confidence, unsuccessful in stimulating any warmth of emotion, he tries to appear at least affable, but this affability which is intended to seem spontaneous and is not, instead of reassuring, disturbs, and is sometimes disconcerting.[65]

Lodovico Nota is an honest craftsman, a realist and an ironist. Ersilia's true story is, in his opinion, incomparably more beautiful than the romantic tale he had at first intended to compose, and it is more deeply comic. It is inevitable also that in these circumstances Lodovico should play the Pirandellian *raisonneur:*

> The facts! The facts! My dear sir, the facts are what you assume them to be and, therefore, in the mind there are no facts, there is only life that appears sometimes this way and sometimes that. The facts are the past. When the soul recedes—you said it yourself—and life abandons it. I have no faith in facts.[66]

Lodovico Nota goes a step further than Lamberto Laudisi in his scepticism, but the situation in *Vestire gli ignudi* does not center on the question of truth. The question here is one of psychology. In Ersilia's case the facts are not long in doubt. She has been telling lies, evidently, and she admits it readily—lies not for profit, but for cosmetic reasons. She has adorned herself with pretty lies in order to die decently. When her pathetic subterfuge is discovered, the issue, insofar as the facts are concerned, is settled. From a philosophic viewpoint the problem on which the play concentrates is the relation of life and form, the problem of the Theatre of the Grotesque. The assumption is that, in general, life inclines to beauty and strives to create harmonious forms. The form to which Ersilia aspires, her ideal, is that of a *fidanzata*, a bride-to-be. It is supremely ironical that for a woman in her position life can offer nothing more beautiful than the prospect of marriage. But the fact is that the wedding day is, for her, the summit of earthly happiness, the culmination of her dreams, the one enviable moment of existence, and in the moment of death she longs to clothe herself in this beauty.

Ersilia is denied this happiness. It is pathetic that in the end she is not permitted to embellish herself suitably. It is even more pathetic that she should wish to do so. In death, as in life, what is important is not the reality, but the appearance of things; and one can sympathize readily with the girl's wish to look nice even for a moment before her life is forever extinguished, at the same time that the irony of the situation puts her death in a grimly comic light. In Pirandello's canon there is no better example of the Grotesque.

For the rest, Ersilia is the victim of her environment. She has been exploited not by villains, but by ordinary, well-meaning people in the ordinary course of business. There is no one to blame for her misfortunes, least of all herself, and there is nothing said in this play of a social system which sees women chiefly as a means of reproducing the race. This play doubtless involves some measure of social criticism, but Pirandello was not energetic as a social reformer: the play speaks for itself. Ersilia Drei makes one ashamed of humanity; but her play offers no remedies. It is, at best, a gesture of despair.

Vestire gli ignudi is certainly one of Pirandello's finest plays. It made a profound impression. In Rome the part of Ersilia Drei was played by Maria Melato, and by Emma Grammatica in Milan. Ruggero Ruggeri produced the play in Torino. The following year Pirandello produced *La vita che ti diedi* (1924)—*The Life I Gave You*. He had written it with Eleanora Duse in mind for the role of the devoted mother who keeps her dead son alive in fantasy, and Duse in fact agreed to do it. But Duse was closely identified with D'Annunzio. She postponed the rehearsals on various pretexts and at last withdrew from the venture. She was wise.

The theme of *La vita che ti diedi* was one of Pirandello's favorites. He had used it in several *novelle*, in "La camera in attesa," in "I pensionati della memoria," and quite recently in "Notizia del mondo," which was published in 1922. The play is said to have been Pirandello's favorite play. It has to do, at least in theory, with the power of the imagination to create a reality. It is in fact a celebration of mother love, very touching, but somewhat too sentimental to be revived, and it was no great success even in its original production. It was followed, the following year, in May 1924, by *Ciascuno a suo modo*, a most ambitious experiment.

By this time Pirandello was in every sense a professional showman. He had never been averse to publicity. Now he threw himself into the role of the intellectual mountebank with all the fervor of one who had been forced to bottle up his natural exhibitionism the better part of his life. *Ciascuno a suo modo—Each in His Way*—made a new departure in the theatre, and Pirandello was resolved to make the most of it. The text, published by Bemporad, was made available some days before the opening. It served the influential critic of *La Gazzetta del Popolo* of Turin, Domenico Lanza, as the basis of a spirited attack on Pirandello and everything that Pirandello stood for in the theatre. Pirandello countered with an equally vigorous article in the Milanese *Corriere della Sera*. There were other explosions in the Italian press and, amid all the hubbub, the play opened in Milan before a capacity audience at an advanced scale of prices. Pirandello had gone so far as to plant actors in the house with instructions to create a commotion in classic style. But the thing had been overdone. To the author's extreme disappointment the play was received with respect. There was applause at the end, but neither catcalls nor brawls. When the play was over the audience left the theatre, evidently chastened, but not excited.

Pirandello subtitled this play *Commedia a chiave, A Play with a Key*. The key is supplied by the play itself. The action involves an imaginary situation which is based, supposedly, on an exactly analogous situation which is supposed to be real, and is documented by news reports distributed to the audience as it enters the theatre. Pirandello's play thus represents on the stage with fictitious names the consequences of a sensational affair which—we are urged to imagine—actually took place and was widely reported in the press. The people who were "actually" involved in the suicide of the young sculptor Giacomo la Vela—the actress Amelia Moreno and Baron Nuti—have come to see the play that has been written about them, and are seated in the audience with their friends. The action thus takes place on two planes of being which mirror one another. In fact, of course, neither is real; so that the audience is required to distinguish reality on three levels—its own, the presumed reality of Moreno and Nuti, and the drama of their counterparts on the stage. Difficult as this seems, it presents no difficulty at all in the theatre.

The plot of *Ciascuno a suo modo* is extremely complex. The curtain rises on an upper-class salon. It transpires that Doro Palegari and his friend Francesco have had a violent disagreement regarding an actress called Delia Morello, whom neither has met. Delia is notorious for her many lovers. On the eve of her marriage to the gifted young sculptor Giorgio Salvi, she was found by her fiancé in the arms of his friend Michele

Rocca, who was engaged to his sister. As a result Giorgio shot himself. The scandal has since stirred discussion throughout Italy.

In arguing the pros and cons of this affair Doro and Francesco have almost come to blows. But Doro, who had originally defended the lady, now sees the matter in a different light. The same thing has happened to Francesco. Since each has reversed his opinion, the two are once again at loggerheads, and this time Doro insults his friend so thoroughly that he provokes him to a challenge. At this point the actress Delia Morello appears. She has come to thank Doro for defending her so warmly and, since he has taken her part so confidently, while she herself is confused, she asks him to help her clarify her motives in acting as she did.

Evidently Doro understands her better than she understands herself. In the ensuing scene, by means of a series of curiously linked speeches, Doro and Delia evolve a theory that thoroughly satisfies them. Delia, they decide, is a female Don Juan, a *femme fatale* engaged in a vendetta against all men. Men have so far considered only her body. She has found this humiliating and has reacted by systematically arousing them and then frustrating their desires. The sculptor Salvi, however, was not attracted to her physically. He was concerned only with her form, from which he was modeling a figure. But Delia found his objectivity irritating: "An angel is always more irritating to a woman than a beast." She did her best, therefore, to excite his passions. When she succeeded in this, as was her custom, she denied herself to him. The result was a proposal of marriage. She had no intention of marrying him; but she asserted her power by forcing him to present her—a notorious woman—to his mother and his sister. The sister's fiancé, Michele Rocca, was violently opposed to Salvi's marriage. It was, however, only to rid herself of Salvi that she contrived to have him surprise her in his studio with Rocca.

Doro understands that Delia has no malice. She merely manifests the vital spirit, flowing from one form into another, playing as many parts in life as she does in the theatre, in the vain hope always of finding out one day what she is in reality. Francesco has a quite different idea. In his opinion Delia is a vulgar adventuress, using her charms in order to advance herself in society. Thus when she discovered in Rocca the chief obstacle to her marriage to Salvi, she proceeded to seduce him in order to expose his hypocrisy and so to discredit him. To Doro's extreme surprise Delia concedes that this interpretation may also be true. He is now completely confused. He has provoked a duel with his best friend:

"For what? For something that nobody understands—what it is, how it is—neither I, nor he, and not even she herself!"[67] The curtain falls on this effect.

It rises at once on "The First Choral Interlude." The scene now represents the corridor at the rear of the auditorium. People are leaving their seats for the entr'acte. The stage direction goes so far as to indicate the behavior of the audience:

> It is nowadays known to all that at each act curtain in the irritating plays of Pirandello there will necessarily be discussions and disagreements. Let those who defend him assume before their intractable adversaries that smiling humility which always has the marvellous effect of irritating them beyond endurance.

Following this suggestion, the interlude consists of a heated critical discussion carried on by actors costumed as spectators, so that the audience is invited to view itself on the stage in the act of arguing heatedly over the situation it has just witnessed.

In the second act, while a fencing master is preparing Francesco for his forthcoming encounter with Doro, Diego Cinci takes the opportunity to deliver a lecture on the difficulty of knowing oneself. For social purposes, he says, we construct some sort of personality, a form that will represent us to the world, and this fiction regulates our behavior. But in a critical moment we may see the whole façade we have erected crumble before the vital current that flows through us without our being aware of it:

> Put aside the little puppet you construct, with the feigned interpretation of your acts and feelings, and you will soon see that it has nothing to do with what you really are, or can be, with what is in you of which you are not aware. You will see that this is a terrible god, and woe to you if you oppose him; but this god becomes a compassionate being ready to forgive your every fault if you simply abandon yourself to him, and stop trying to justify yourself.

His homily is interrupted by the entrance of Michele Rocca. He comes with still another explanation of Delia's behavior, and also with another challenge. The reason he betrayed his beloved friend, he says, was to discredit the shameless woman his friend intended to marry. Therefore he must fight the man who dares to justify Delia, and who thus impugns his honor. It turns out that this man is now Francesco. In these circumstances Francesco refuses to fight Doro, and offers to fight Rocca instead.

The seconds are outraged, and begin to quarrel. Then Delia comes in and rushes into Rocca's arms. As the two go off lovingly together, the truth at last becomes manifest to all. Delia and Rocca were in love from the beginning. They falsified their true motives for themselves and for the world in order to give some rational basis to their passion. The play makes its point: we mask the natural impulse—which is insuperable—by inventing fictions in conformity with the social forms to which we are subject.

The point is doubtless valid; but as drama the play leaves much to be desired. The recognition scene, with its peripeteia, is needlessly exaggerated. In order that we may see Life, in all its madness, bursting through the cultural veil that normally conceals it, Rocca and Delia are made to act like wild beasts mating in the jungle. The scene is embarrassing; but for all its clumsiness, it makes its point. As these lovers embrace and run off, presumably to copulate, Francesco makes an appropriate comment:

FRANCESCO: But they are two lunatics.
DIEGO: Take a look at yourself.[68]

This speech brings down the curtain. It goes up immediately on the "Second Choral Interlude," which is intended to represent the effect of the second act on the audience. The effect is, in theory, electric. The real-life protagonist, Amelia Moreno, breaks away from her friends and rushes up to the stage, which is now depicted in reverse. Applause, boos, and sounds of tumult come from the auditorium backstage. La Moreno appears to have slapped someone in her fury—who it was, exactly, is not clear. Then, amid wild excitement, she and Baron Nuti—Rocca's real-life prototype—repeat the scene they have just witnessed, this time in "reality," and run out of the theatre together. There was to have been a third act. But the actors are by now thoroughly disturbed. They refuse to go on. The curtain is lowered. The *capocomico* appears before it and announces to the audience—this time the real audience—that the play cannot continue.

For all its seeming novelty the situation in *Ciascuno a suo modo* is a variation of the *dubbio* of *Così è (se vi pare)*. The technique is an extension of the technique of *Sei personaggi in cerca d'autore*. In *Così è (se vi pare)* Laudisi drives home the idea that truth is a matter of opinion, a conclusion which has much in its favor, but is not the point of the play. In *Ciascuno a suo modo* the *raisonneur* is Diego Cinci, a character who demonstrates logically that it is impossible to discover the true motives of people's actions. His argument, also, has not much to do with the play, for in the end the true motive for the behavior of the characters is made clear. The play is thus mainly a drama of mask and face, and only incidentally a demonstration of the relativity of truth.

The dramatic framework that encloses the action of *Ciascuno a suo modo* is in many respects similar to that of *Sei personaggi in cerca d'autore*. The difference is that in the present case the characters are presumed to be real people seated in the audience, while the actors who depict them move about on the stage. Moreover the action on the stage does not falsify the "real" action. On the contrary, it is by seeing themselves objectified on the stage in the roles they played in real life that Amelia Moreno and Baron Nuti come to realize why they behaved as they did, and it is this realization that brings about their reconciliation in real life. Thus *Ciascuno a suo modo* is in effect an exercise in psychotherapy, a revelation of repressed wishes through dramatic projection.

The technical innovation, however, through which Pirandello undertook to motivate and control the behavior of the audience as well as the business of the actors, was largely ineffective. The device was perhaps suggested by the technique of *Fanny's First Play* (1911), in which Shaw caricatured his critics by putting them in the audience of the play-within-play, where he made himself the subject of discussion. Pirandello, in similar fashion, put his principal adversary, the critic Lanza, on the stage. But Pirandello's touch was heavy, and the effort at self-advertisement is painfully evident. His attempts to stir up the audience, also, were misdirected. Evidently the audience did not enjoy seeing itself caricatured on the stage. At the first performance of *Six Characters* in Rome, the scandal was, by all accounts, spontaneous; and, in spite of its effect on his nerves, it did much to establish Pirandello's reputation as a provocative author. It was probably naive to engineer a repetition three years later, and, predictably, it did not work. There was obviously no need for the paying guests to stir themselves up about a play when there were actors present who were paid to do it for them. As it turned out, the actors were excited. The audience was calm.

The principle, nevertheless, was interesting, and was destined to have interesting consequences. There was, of course, nothing new in putting a fictitious audience on the stage. It was a device familiar to Shakespeare. Actors had been put in the audience from the time of Beaumont and Fletcher's *The Knight of the Burning Pestle* (1613); but no one could have predicted the effect of *Ciascuno a suo modo* on the development of the drama in the following years. As it happened, the moment was critical and, in putting this play on the stage at this time, Pirandello indicated the direction of a whole new movement in the theatre.

The Milanese production of *Ciascuno a suo modo* was accounted a success, but the play was not produced again in Italy in Pirandello's lifetime. When Pitoëff produced it in Paris two years later, the more conservative critics considered it a piece of effrontery in questionable taste, but it soon became evident that, whatever its merits as drama, this play implied a wholly new conception of theatre. Among other things, it rejected the idea of the stage as a reality apart from the reality of everyday life, together with the realistic tradition that the Théâtre-libre had so carefully nurtured. In this play the fourth wall, seemingly impenetrable, which had so long divided the play from the audience, was suddenly whisked away, and the reality of the stage was merged with the reality of the people who sat before it. Henceforth the auditorium no longer offered a safe refuge from the author's fantasy. It was enclosed in it. The play could therefore take on the seriousness of a real experience, and the audience sat in the playhouse at its peril.

It was difficult, obviously, to go much further in this direction without endangering the very idea of theatre, which accords the events depicted on the stage an enhanced reality in virtue of their fictional character. There were those, nevertheless—among them Artaud and Brecht—who were eager to take the risk. Thus the techniques of *Ciascuno a suo modo* contributed a good deal to the theory of The Theatre of Cruelty—the First Manifesto was published in 1932—and to the Brechtian experiments with *Verfremdung* about 1936.[69]

Diana e la Tuda (1926) belongs to a more conventional type of drama. The title, *Diana and Tuda*, refers to the contrast between the beauty of the ideal and living beauty: this is the subject of the play. It is a play about sculptors, a variation on the myth of Pygmalion and the beloved figure which Aphrodite, in answer to his prayer, brought to life. In Pirandello's version, the legendary situation is reversed. In his desire to infuse into the clay the soul of his living model, the sculptor Sirio all but kills her, and is himself killed. In this situation Pirandello evidently saw an opportunity to demonstrate once again the conflict of life and form which Tilgher had identified as the nucleus of his thought. So closely, indeed, does this play follow Tilgher's analysis that one might conclude that it was written under the critic's direction. But, in fact, this theme had already been handled several times by others in a manner that approximated Pirandello's plot quite closely; and in *Ciascuno a suo modo* Pirandello himself had anticipated, in the affair of the sculptor Salvi and the actress Delia, the strange relation of the sculptor Sirio and La Tuda, his model.

Émile Zola's novel, *L'Oeuvre*, stirred a controversy in artistic circles when it first appeared in 1886. It is possible that Pirandello read it. At any rate, the similarity between Zola's plot and Pirandello's play is striking. In *L'Oeuvre* the painter Charles Lantier makes his wife Christine pose for him in the nude to the point of exhaustion. She expects, naturally, some sign of gratitude. Instead he loses his heart to the painted figure into which he has conveyed her beauty of body and her spirit. Christine is jealous of the painting. She does what she can to woo the artist back to a more normal love; indeed, she succeeds. But the rivalry between the real and the ideal for the soul of the painter ends in tragedy. Torn between the one love and the other, Lantier hangs himself.

The implication seems to be that one who concentrates on the ideal to the exclusion of the real is in danger of losing his mind. The Symbolists took Zola's novel to be a direct attack on their brand of idealism, and the book appears to have cost Zola the friendship of Cézanne. Doubtless Zola had a broader theme in mind. In this book he appeared to be concerned less with the question of Naturalism and Symbolism than with the conflict of life and art. It was with this question that Ibsen also was concerned in his last play.

In *When We Dead Awaken* Ibsen extended the theme which he had long ago taken up in *Brand*, and later developed in *The Master Builder* and in *John Gabriel Borkman*—the predicament of the artist. The hero, in these plays, inevitably comes to see that, in sacrificing his humanity to his vocation, he loses both his happiness and his talent. It was a theme that had, more recently, greatly occupied Shaw. It is treated from one standpoint in *Man and Superman*, and from another in *The Doctor's Dilemma*. It was certainly no new problem when Pirandello took it in hand.

In *Diana e la Tuda* the problem of the artist is posed in terms of life and form, rather than the real and the ideal; but the difference is no more than verbal. The two principles are embodied in the character of the two sculptors who are involved with the beautiful young model called La Tuda. She loves them both. Giuncano is sixty. After a lifetime of work he has given up his art. Now statues inspire him with horror, so that he sees them as so many corpses in a charnel house. Consequently he has broken up all the figures in his studio and has ceased to model anything. The young sculptor Sirio is perhaps his son. He is rich and jaded. The figure of Diana on which he is presently engaged engrosses all his interest. This figure is to be perfect. When it is finished, he plans to kill himself.

Neither Sirio nor Giuncano appears to be entirely sane. In Sirio's view the function of art is to fix life in ideal forms, which are its only permanence. But where Sirio sees permanence, Giuncano sees only death. Consequently the life-task that Sirio has undertaken of fixing in imperishable marble the transitory beauty of La Tuda seems to Giuncano a sacrilege.

Sirio has no interest in Tuda as a person. He sees in her only the form which he desires to abstract for his figure of the virgin goddess. But he is jealous of Tuda's beauty, and when he learns that a rival artist, the painter Caravani, has engaged her also, Sirio proposes to secure a monopoly of her services by marrying her.

Evidently Pirandello fancied the idea of a purely formal marriage as a dramatic device. Marriage was one of the formal "constructions" available to the individual, a useful resource in the social masquerade. In *Ma non è una cosa seria* and in *Pensaci, Giacomino!* the formal marriage has a happy outcome. In *Diana e la Tuda* it turns out badly. Tuda serves Sirio's purpose very well, but she cannot abide his indifference to her person, and the situation is complicated by the presence of Sirio's mistress, a lady called Sara Mendel, who belongs to the chic society of Rome. Tuda is jealous, and at last she is moved to spite Sirio by running off to Caravani.

When she returns, after a long interval, she is ill. Her body is emaciated, and she is no longer fit to pose for the Diana. Meanwhile Sirio has been unable to carry on his work. It now develops that Sirio has deliberately used Sara Mendel in order to torture Tuda into the expression he desires his Diana to have, with the eyes of a cat and a hand clenched in fury. Since it is this growing wickedness in his model which he has transmitted to his statue, his Diana is now a beautiful and evil thing, and almost finished. But it is never entirely finished, for when Tuda learns what he has done, she rushes to destroy the statue. Sirio comes after her with a carving tool. And now Giuncano intervenes. He knocks Sirio down and strangles him.

Of all Pirandello's plays *Diana e la Tuda* is most vulnerable to the reproach of being overly cerebral, and the abstract nature of the plot is hardly redeemed by the realism of the characterization. The portrait of Giuncano is chiefly interesting. In his portrayal the contrast of life and form is dramatized in terms of the youthful spirit and the aging body of a man of sixty. When Tuda offers herself to him, Giuncano refuses bitterly. His body, he tells her, disgusts him. His joints are stiffening. He no longer recognizes himself. He loves La Tuda. But he is too old now for love, and he is unwilling to unleash his emotions: "Life was finished for me long ago. I no longer care for anything: Empty. Spent. I wasted it all—what madness—in making statues." [70]

Pirandello was sixty when he wrote these lines.

The suggestion that soon after he wrote *Enrico IV* Pirandello's inspiration failed and that thereafter he wrote according to formula has nothing to recommend it. It is true that the plays of his later life have not the geniality of character and situation that heighten the plays of his youth. But the faults of his later plays are less attributable to a lack of imagination than to some lapse of critical judgment. Pirandello wrote a great deal; perhaps he wrote too much. His output was necessarily uneven. But as long as he lived he struck out vigorously in new directions. He was not always fortunate, obviously; and as the world, which had formerly disprized him, now relentlessly confirmed him in his self-esteem, he grew cynical. He had nothing but contempt for the press. Nothing in his correspondence indicates that he was in the least aware of any failure of his creative powers as an artist. His letters signalize chiefly his hopes and his triumphs. His plays, perhaps, tell another story. In *Diana e la Tuda* the aging sculptor, and in *Quando si è qualcuno* the aging poet speak unmistakably of the author's uneasiness. Nevertheless, in *Come tu mi vuoi*, which he produced in 1929, Pirandello gave himself a distinct proof of artistic vigor. This play, written at the age of sixty-five, was certainly worthy to stand with his best work.

Come tu mi vuoi—As You Desire Me—is centered on the problem of personal identity. It belongs, therefore, to the group of plays which stem from the story of Mattia Pascal: *Così è (se vi pare)*; *Come prima, meglio di prima*; *La Signora Morli una e due*; *Enrico IV*; and *Vestire gli ignudi*. It has some affinity with each of these. Both in theme and in detail, however, this play comes closest to *Come prima, meglio di prima*, of which it may be considered a variant.

The plot involves the fortunes of a night-club dancer in Berlin. She is young, beautiful, nameless, and dissolute, a Venetian woman swept northward by the tide of war after a terrible experience which she cannot describe. She has lost all recollection of her past. She calls herself Elma. In Arabic it means water.

When the play opens she is living with a degenerate novelist called Carlo Salter and his daughter Mop, a lesbian girl. Both are in love with her. Both inspire her with loathing; and she welcomes the thought of death. She is rescued unexpectedly by a photographer called Boffi. He has recognized her as the long lost wife of his friend Bruno Pieri, and he persuades her to come away with him to meet the husband she has not seen in a decade.

Ten years before, while Bruno Pieri was with the Italian army, the Veneto was overrun by Austrian troops. His villa was burnt to the ground. His wife Lucia was raped. An Austrian officer took her away with him to Vienna and, after a time, abandoned her there. She drifted to Berlin, supporting herself as best she could. Boffi is convinced that Elma is the lost Lucia. For her part, she has no memory of Bruno or of his villa in the Veneto; but, as matters stand, she is willing to accept the identity which she is so suddenly offered. At the moment she is no one:

> All I know is that I live—a body, a nameless body waiting for someone to claim it! Well, yes: if he will re-create me, if he will give this body the soul of his Cia—let him take it. . . . and let him fill it with memories—his memories—a beautiful life, a beautiful life—a new life—I am desperate!

Four months later she is installed in the beautiful villa. Bruno has restored the property at great expense. She too has renewed herself in the likeness of the young bride whose portrait hangs in the living room. She has been received lovingly by the aged aunt and uncle, the only relatives who have so far been permitted to see her. And now that her period of rehabilitation is over, a family gathering has been planned at which the declaration of her death will be annulled, and she will be formally accepted as Bruno's wife.

Unfortunately it has come to her attention that Bruno's love for her, and his faith in her identity, are not entirely disinterested. The estate has come to him through his wife Lucia, and if Lucia is dead, it will go to her sister. It is therefore important to Bruno that Elma be accepted as Lucia. The family meeting takes place. Elma has no trouble in convincing the sister that she is really the lost Lucia, even though the identifying birthmark on her flank cannot be found, and the family declares itself ready to accept her formally. Now, in the nick of time, Carlo Salter drives up with a Viennese doctor and a nurse. They bring with them a poor demented creature who in several particulars answers the description of the lost Lucia, even to something that approximates the birthmark. And now, suddenly, no one is certain who Lucia is. Elma soon settles the problem. She cannot forgive Bruno for concealing the true motive for his love, and she punishes him by going back to Berlin with Carlo Salter, leaving Bruno with his villa and the idiot girl who is henceforth to pass for his wife.

This play, which provided the young actress Marta Abba with a magnificent role, has several interesting facets. There is the question of revenge, the vendetta that Elma has with humanity. After a life in which she has suffered untold humiliation because of the bestiality of mankind, Elma has been led to believe that she can at last take refuge in the pure love of a man for the bride of his youth. She is willing to play the part of the lost Lucia for his sake; but for love, not for money. When she learns that she is once again being tricked into something like prostitution, she avenges herself by saddling Bruno with the fragment of humanity which is the price of his estate. Her action is thus in the nature of a *beffa*, a dramatic device which Pirandello found especially congenial. Bruno has played a cruel joke on her. She retaliates with one even more cruel.

There is also the question of identity.

Pirandello several times disclaimed any tendency toward Idealism; but in this play, as elsewhere, a somewhat confusing distinction is drawn between the self and the soul, a distinction which is neither entirely Christian nor Aristotelian. For Pirandello the self is infinitely mutable. Like water, it can adapt itself to any form; it exemplifies Life, and is in a constant state of reconstruction. In Pirandello's novel *Uno, nessuno e centomila* (1925–26) Vitangelo Moscarda is made to say: "Ah, you think that only houses are constructed? I construct myself continually, and I construct you, and you do the same. And the construction lasts as long as the material of our feelings holds together, and the cement of our will endures." In consequence Moscarda understands that for his wife and his friends he is not the man he believes himself to be. Indeed, he has no idea of what he is. In order to see himself as others see him he requires a mirror. When he at last sees himself he loses all spontaneity of action: "To live is to be reborn constantly in new forms. To know oneself is to die." The result of his self-contemplation is the realization that for others he is a hundred thousand people, while for himself he is nobody. It is a declaration which was enunciated long before by Signora Ponza in *Così è (se vi pare)*, and it defines the doctrine which is traceable throughout so much of Pirandello's work that it may be considered his hallmark.

The plays which deal with the problem of identity involve a contradiction which necessarily diminishes the cogency of the argument and renders it, in general, irrelevant to the action, an extraneous element with which one grows impatient. While each of these plays purports to demonstrate that the individual is essentially nobody, each culminates in a triumphant affirmation of the somebody that is essentially he. The individual ego is said to be formless, like water; in fact, as Pirandello depicts it, the ego is rather like bamboo, a flexible stalk with a mind of its own, which asserts its individuality whenever it can. In these plays the ego is Protean. It is capable of taking on different forms and various appearances, but these forms and appearances are by no means equally valid. Behind the forms of Proteus there is Proteus. In order for modes to be assumed it is necessary to posit a substrate that modulates. In Pirandello's plays this cannot be said to be simply vital energy in the abstract, for his characters—Elma, Fulvia, Signora Ponza, Ersilia Drei, Baldovino, and the rest—are not nobody. Each has his essential nature which at the critical moment asserts itself, and this assertion is, in general, the turning point of the play. Nearly all Pirandello's plays turn upon a recognition; but there could be no recognition were there not something to recognize. In these plays, behind the mask there is, invariably, a face. At the climactic point the mask is removed and the face appears. The dramatic design—an *anagnorisis* and peripeteia—is from the antique. It is classic.

In the second chapter of *Les Données immédiates de la conscience* (1889), an early work which in many ways anticipates Pirandello's doctrine, Bergson distinguished two elements of the ego—the public and the private self. Our external life, he wrote, our social life, has a more practical importance for us than our internal and individual life. For this reason there is formed a second self which covers the first. This second self is a superficial personality superposed on the other as if it were a skin, callused against the inclement hostility of the outerworld. We live in the continual alteration of our secret intimate self. It is constantly "making itself." But with reference to the world outside itself this self assumes a cold rigidity. Consequently, Bergson concluded, it is impossible in our daily life to understand the spiritual states of others: the defence is impenetrable.[71]

For Pirandello, however, the defence is not impenetrable, and it is the business of the playwright to contrive situations in which the defence is penetrated and the inner self is revealed. All Pirandello's plays which deal with the question of identity—and, one might interject, all of Shaw's plays on similar subjects—are revelatory of a truth, not of the absence of truth. Pirandello wrote in "L'umorismo": "We feel with feelings and reason with thoughts, which, after long forgetfulness are obscured, extinguished, cancelled in our actual consciousness, but which a shock or a sudden agitation of the spirit can reanimate, showing in ourselves another unexpected being." In every case this being, when it is revealed, is seen to be a fundamental self, unchanging in the midst of change.[72]

In *Come tu mi vuoi* Elma amply demonstrates the flexibility of human character; but that is not the point of the play. Elma is driven into an unenviable situation by circumstances beyond her control. She exemplifies the helplessness of a woman in a brutal world, and she lets herself drift joylessly on a current she cannot stem. Nevertheless she is in a sense beyond the reach of those who have conspired to degrade her. She is a pure being, and at the first opportunity she affirms her essential purity. The outcome is not happy as in the analogous case of Fulvia and her assiduous musical lover, but it is noble.

Between this view of things and Pirandello's idea of Life as *kinesis*, and Form as *stasis*, there is not much relation; but they do not absolutely exclude one another. They represent two levels of sensibility, the one essentially idealistic and romantic, the other realistic and skeptical. One is surprised to find them coexisting in a single context, but consistency was not Pirandello's main concern as a writer. Elma plays the role of *raisonneur* in this play, but her remarks do not go beyond the problem of truth and opinion. She points out with entire propriety that people believe what their hearts tell them, and as evidence she cites the Judgment of Solomon—which also served Brecht in *The Caucasian Chalk Circle*.[73] For the rest, she remains mysterious. It is hinted that she knows more about her past than she admits but, as in the case of Signora Ponza, she commits herself no further than she wishes. It is possible that she knows she is Lucia, equally possible that she knows she is not, and it is entirely possible that she does not know whether she is or is not Lucia, and therefore has the choice of assuming or not assuming the identity which is offered her. Each possibility involves a different characterization. In the situation as it is set up, what is certain is the unequivocal nature of her ambiguity, and this is the basis of the *dubbio* with which the play leaves us.

It is noteworthy in this play that while the heroine is eminently sympathetic, none of the men makes a favorable impression. As in *Vestire gli ignudi*, the woman is surrounded by a pack of greedy dogs each intent on tearing away something for himself. Certainly Pirandello had no high opinion of the human race in general, but as between men and women he appears to have preferred women. In *Come tu mi vuoi* the men are treated with stark realism, but Elma is treated idealistically. The portrait is romantic, not to say melodramatic, and her generosity is calculated to show up, by contrast, the meanness of the respectable middle-class environment into which she is momentarily thrust. In these circumstances, of course, her behavior is not entirely convincing; it is, one might say, quixotic, and the play suffers in consequence. It is the price one pays for the pleasure of melodrama; but in this case it is not exorbitant.

Shaw also had made systematic use of melodrama as a basis for a theatre of ideas, but with a difference. For Shaw melodrama was in every case a means to an end. With Pirandello it was an end in itself: it furnished the staple of his drama. The difference between Shaw's *Pygmalion* and Pirandello's *As You Desire Me* fairly leaps to the eye. Both are plays of *déclassement*. In each the heroine voluntarily makes herself over into a preconceived form, and in both plays she deliberately relinquishes the position to which her new form entitles her. At this point the resemblance ends. Shaw used these symbols to demonstrate the illusory nature of social class-barriers. Pirandello's play ostensibly demonstrates the relativity of truth. Actually in *As You Desire Me* the result is a character sketch of a fallen woman in unusually rewarding circumstances. Elma's idealism is such that she prefers the hell from which she has come to the kind of heaven which is offered in its place. The one is true; the other is false. There is no question of relativity here. Her action is based on an absolute; and, like Ibsen's Brand, Elma is not disposed to compromise. She must have All or Nothing. And—like Brand—she is pitiless in her demands.

The situation in this play, obviously, could have been approached from another angle; but Pirandello wasted neither pity nor understanding on Bruno. He is at best a shadowy figure, a puppet, really, which the author manipulates for his purpose, which is rigorously moral. The unsavory realities of the world of nice people revolted Elma as they did Pirandello, and when she leaves Bruno at the end of the play she consigns him to a level of hell some stories below her own.

A moment's reflection makes it apparent that Bruno does not entirely deserve this fate, but the play does not pause long enough for that, and Bruno is swept along quickly on the current of melodrama which brings the play to its end. There is in all this, of course, some element of absurdity. It is impossible to exclude the possibility that Pirandello meant to touch Elma's heroism with a tinge of irony. In his view humor involves the consciousness of the contrary. Unquestionably in Elma's sublimity of character there lurks some suspicion of the aggressiveness of Delia Morello. But it is never easy to say, in the case of Pirandello, where sensibility ends and irony begins. Perhaps the two were so inextricably intertwined in his mind that he himself did not distinguish the promptings of his reason from the impulse of his heart. In the *novella* "Notizia del mondo" he envies the freedom from thought that a rabbit enjoys: "otherwise it would have reason to believe that there is not much difference between heroism and imbecility."[74] It is not impossible that in *Come tu mi vuoi* Pirandello went so far in his depiction of the ridiculous as to imply that Elma was, in her way, as mad as a hatter. Yet, as the play is written, it is difficult to see how this aspect of her character could be displayed without detriment to the plot. Here again her motives, like her character, form part of the *dubbio* in terms of which the play is formulated, and this uncertainty is by no means out of line with the general drift of Pirandello's thought.

Come tu mi vuoi was first presented by Marta Abba and her company at the Filodrammatici in Milan on 18 February 1930. It was a success; it was, indeed, one of the few great successes of Pirandello's later life, for although his last years were full of honor, they added little to his artistic reputation. In the five-year interval between the writing of *Ciascuno a suo modo* and the production of *Come tu mi vuoi* Pirandello's life changed radically. His ideas did not change at all. The result was a series of plays that, however interesting they may be in themselves, all seem to be variations on the same theme.

Until 1917 the Teatro Argentina in Rome and the Teatro Manzoni in Milan had housed repertory companies; but in the years following the war there were no true repertory theatres in Italy. Toward the end of 1924 Pirandello's son Stefano, together with a group of friends, thought to remedy this lack by establishing an art theatre in Rome. Eleven associates, most of them writers, contributed 5000 lire apiece to fund this venture. The group, known as Gli Undici—The Eleven—was actually organized under the management of Luigi Pirandello. The hall under the Palazzo Odescalchi, which Zio Podrecca had constructed some years earlier for his puppet theater, was leased, thoroughly modernized, and furnished with 300 seats. After much study and soul-searching it was decided to offer a repertory which would include plays by Pirandello, Dunsany, Vildrac, Evreinov, and also Ramuz's *Histoire du soldat* with Stravinsky's music.—Mussolini contributed a state subvention. On 4 April 1924 the new theatre opened with an elaborate production of Pirandello's *La sagra del signore della nave*. Pirandello described the production as "a violent mural in which I wished to represent all that is tragic in human bestiality." This pageant—it was, in effect a pageant—employed a cast of 130. It had music and a color-symphony. The performance was an occasion of state, attended by the Duce and the royal family in the Royal Box. After this auspicious beginning Pirandello's company offered Dunsany's *The Gods of the Mountain*, De Stefani's *Il calzolaio di Messina*, Vildrac's *Le Pelegrin*, and Bontempelli's *Nostra dea*. Bontempelli's play required the services of a gifted actress. Pirandello thought of engaging Emma Grammatica. Meanwhile the critic Marco Praga had written a glowing review of a young actress, new to the theatre, who had saved Talli's production of *The Seagull* in Milan. Pirandello offered her a contract, sight unseen, as leading lady in his new company. It was Marta Abba. She played the lead in *Nostra dea* with great success. Thereafter she became a central figure in Pirandello's life and in his works.[75]

The new theatre succeeded beyond expectation. It played a three-month season in Rome, and afterwards toured England and Europe. It was widely acclaimed; but in spite of several government subsidies it consistently lost money. Pirandello soon discovered what it means to be the manager of an art theatre. In a very short time he found himself in financial straits. In 1927 the Art Theatre brought Ibsen's *The Lady from the Sea* to Naples. The tour ended in Viareggio playing to an empty house. Pirandello dissolved the company. It was the end of his adventure as a theatre manager.

It had no doubt been a valuable experience. For three years he had served his company as *capocomico*, a post which combined the functions of producer, manager, and stage-director. During this time, with very little theatre experience, he had borne all its burdens, artistic and financial. The Italian theatre at this time was in the main an actor's theatre.

The traditional style, the style of Salvini, Zacconi, and Duse, depended heavily on the spontaneity of the actor, and his ability to improvise a performance. Pirandello's theatre was primarily a writer's theatre which required a highly disciplined type of acting and the faithful service of the written text. It was thus at variance with current stage practice all over Italy. By all accounts Pirandello was a hard taskmaster. As a director he was profoundly influenced by Stanislavsky. As a theoretician he much admired Evreinov, whose "pantheatrical" conception of life as drama and the world as a stage accorded closely with Pirandello's ideas of art and reality. In his function as stage director he found himself greatly hampered by the presence of the prompter, that indispensable fixture of the Italian stage. Regardless of what the director did or said in the course of his rehearsals, it was the prompter who actually guided the actors during the performance. Sitting in his box on the forestage with the manuscript before him, hidden from the audience but plainly visible to the actors, the prompter controlled everything. In his memoirs Dario Niccodemi quotes Pirandello:

> The prompter does not merely say the words: he has inflections of his own: he makes faces, and his grimaces can influence the actor who lacks confidence. The prompter acts in his box. You should see him in action. He is like an imprisoned lunatic, twisting, turning, clenching his fist for emphasis, cupping his hands around his mouth so as to throw his voice. In a word, he directs the play. . . .[76]

Pirandello felt that until the prompter was banished from the stage no director could work effectively. Eventually he was able to rid his company of this troublesome appendage. It was perhaps his principal contribution to Italian stagecraft, but it was not the only one. In his theatre the text became the nucleus of the production, and for the first time in Italy the interest of the audience was made to center on the play instead of on the actors who performed it.

Pirandello's plays, like his *novelle*, are full of exclamation points and dashes. His dialogue most often reproduces the speech of excitable people whose syntax can hardly keep pace with their emotions. The effect is vital, incoherent, nervous, and repetitious. It is far from restful. It is a special sort of rhetoric, jagged, lively, and savorous, a series of phrases emitted in gasps in a torrent of speech which seems uncontrolled, but is in fact very carefully composed in distinct and varied rhythms, an intricately woven texture of sound and sense. Contrasted with this tumultuous utterance is the closely reasoned argument of the *raisonneur*, setting forth—often with excessive rigor—an ordered analysis which functions effectively to reveal the underlying currents of life and thought.

In this manner Pirandello's dialogue serves the purpose of characterization almost to the point of caricature, and it is significant that as a *capocomico* he is said to have begun his rehearsals with a reading of the text in which he himself acted out all the parts with enormous virtuosity, so that his actors were invited to be, in some sense, extensions of himself. The same may no doubt be said of his characters. His constant admonition to his actors was to sink themselves into the part they played, an idea he had from Stanislavsky which on its face hardly seems remarkable until one reflects that the custom in the contemporary theatre was to sink the character in the actor rather than the actor in the character. The consequence of his method of direction, we are told, was to give his plays in performance the same nervous rhythm which is apparent on the printed page. Pirandello began by distrusting his actors, and he never entirely came to terms with them. He was, after all, an actor who did not act, with a very precise idea of how he wished his lines to be read. For actors this type of direction is seldom a blessing, but it has at least the merit of conveying to the audience what it was the author had in mind. [77]

In the Italian theatre great attention was being directed at this time to the radical innovations in the mise en scène which resulted from the theories of Appia, Copeau, and Gordon Craig. There was much talk of the autonomy of the theatre, the autonomy of the actor, and the autonomy of the drama. The role of the *régisseur*, first magnified in military fashion by the Meininger, was in these years expanding to the point where the director became virtually a dictator. The *régisseur* was neither an actor nor a writer. He was a newcomer to the theatre who assumed a dominant role analogous to that of the conductor of an orchestra. It was a position that followed naturally from the Wagnerian idea of drama as a synthetic art. Pirandello, however, was primarily a writer, and, in the face of the rising tide of modernism in the theatre, he continued to stress the supremacy of the text. Here, as elsewhere, he demonstrated his essential conservatism; and while the experimental theatre ventured further and further into Expressionistic staging, he maintained a position that was in most respects traditional. After *Ciascuno a suo modo* only one of his plays—*Questa sera si recita a soggetto*—was innovative as a theatre piece, and that play involved a spoof of avant-garde methods on the stage.

In 1928 Pirandello left Italy in self-imposed exile. His popularity had passed. The Italian managers were no longer avid for his plays; the press was generally hostile; and he was angry with the Italians. *Questa sera si recita a soggetto—Tonight We Improvise*—was written in Germany. Pirandello finished it in March 1929 in Berlin. It opened in Koenigsberg in January of the following year, and was pleasantly received. But when it was shown at the Lessing Theatre in Berlin at the end of May its reception was disastrous. The audience interrupted the play repeatedly. There were boos and catcalls. The leading actress, Elizabeth Lennartz, played her part in tears, and the performance ended in a hubbub of angry shouts that recalled the disturbance in Rome at the first performance of *Six Characters*. The critic Oscar Büdel wrote that the performance was the most scandalous ever seen in Berlin.[78]

This was not at all what Pirandello was looking for at this time, and he took it badly. The next day he wrote a pathetic letter to Marta Abba, intimating that his German translator, with whom he had quarrelled, had sent a gang of hoodlums to disrupt the performance, so that while most of the audience applauded, there were those who booed. It is possible to discern in his letter some hint of the kind of paranoia one associates with Strindberg:

> I remembered my ex-translator and how we had parted on bad terms. I had even been warned that something was afoot against me and the play. Everywhere I am pursued by hatred. Perhaps it is only right that this should be so, that I should die in this manner, annihilated by the hatred of triumphant cowards, by the incomprehension of idiots. After all, they are in the majority. The catcalls of these imbeciles and of my enemies would not hurt me if my spirit were still what once it was. But I have lost even the pride of my isolation, the love of my disconsolate solitude. . . . My two staring eyes remain invariably fixed, despairing, proud, tired, heavy-lidded with a pain that none will ever understand or know.[79]

Questa sera si recita a soggetto was adapted from a *novella* written in 1910 entitled *"Leonora, addio!"*[80] It has a touching plot. In a dour and dusty Sicilian town there is a single joyous household. The head of the house is a shiftless mining engineer nicknamed Sampognetta—"Whistler"— because it is his habit to whistle in the face of misfortune. There are also his Neapolitan wife and his four pretty daughters, all of them musical. The officers of the neighboring garrison are made welcome in this house and, to the scandal of the community, they amuse themselves "in the continental manner" by singing and dancing until late at night.

Among the officers who frequent the house is Ricco Verri, a Sicilian reserve officer. Verri falls in love with the eldest daughter, Mommina, and, after fighting a duel because of her, he marries her. He feels, however, that she owes the community some compensation for her former lightness. Consequently he keeps her locked up in a shuttered house with only a single attic window open on the sea. There she spends her life, growing enormously fat for lack of exercise, with a bad heart, and only her two little children for company.

One evening she comes by accident upon an advertisement announcing the opening of *La forza del destino* at the local theatre. It recalls to mind her former carefree life, and she surprises the children by singing the opera for them from beginning to end. The following day she entertains them with *The Huguenots;* but the effort exhausts her. On the third night, as her husband comes home, he hears her singing the last lines of the Miserere from *Il trovatore*, ending with "Leonora, addio!" When he enters the room he finds her made up grotesquely as a man, with her children waiting expectantly for her to continue. She does not continue. She is dead. The *novella* ends there.

The performance of *Questa sera si recita a soggetto* is advertised to the public with posters announcing a play to be improvised by a company under the direction of Dr. Hinkfuss, from a scenario by an unidentified author. The stage directions of the play specify not only the manner of the performance, but also the behavior of the audience. The curtain is to be delayed a long time so that the audience will become restive before the opening gong. There are to be actors in the audience, impersonating the puzzled and impatient spectators, shouting protests. When at last the gong sounds, the play does not begin. Instead, Dr. Hinkfuss walks angrily through the house and mounts the stage. The play is not to begin, he says, until he gives the order. It is to be an improvisation based on an inconsiderable *novella* by Pirandello. He has the scenario in his hand. The production is his alone, and he assumes full responsibility for the play. As for the *novella*,

> I have preferred one by him because of all the playwrights he is perhaps the only one who has demonstrated his understanding of the fact that the work of the writer is finished the moment he has written his last word. . . . Because in the theatre the writer's work no longer exists.

. . . What exists is the scenic creation which I shall have made, and which is mine alone.[81]

Dr. Hinkfuss then proceeds to lecture the audience at length on the artistic relations of himself and the author. The stage directions make it difficult to take him seriously. He is, we are told, a little man, hardly more than a yard tall, with a very large head and a shock of unruly hair, and little hairy fingers which inspire even him with disgust as he waves them in the air like the tentacles of a squid. One wonders whence such a man may have issued. He is, in fact, not indigenous to the theatre. Pirandello appears to have translated him to the stage from the village of Milocca where nothing is ever done because of the possibility that science may bring something better to light. In the *novella*, "Acqua è lì," there is a quack doctor named Piccaglione who treats the sick of Milocca with the aid of a box of pills and a fortune teller. The description of Dr. Piccaglione is identical with that of Dr. Hinkfuss:

> Piccaglione, who is a little man a yard tall with a large head of disordered hair, watches his little hands which perhaps inspire him too with disgust with their delicacy, and with their little pale and hairy fingers like maggots.[82]

But, strange as he looks, Dr. Hinkfuss speaks with conviction:

> The writer's work, here it is. (*He shows the roll of paper.*) What do I do with it? I use it for my scenic creation just as I use the skill of the actors I have chosen to represent the parts according to the interpretation I give them, and of the scene-designer whom I order to paint or build the settings, and of the crew that sets them up, and of the electricians who light them, all according to my instructions, suggestions and indications.

In some other theatre, he continues, the scenic creation would be different. This proves that what is seen on the stage is never the work of the author, since his text is always the same though its various productions are always different. The only way one can judge the work of an author as such is to have the text represent itself, not by actors, but by the characters themselves who, through some miracle, should assume body and voice. In such a case the play could be judged directly. But, Dr. Hinkfuss asks, with becoming archness, is such a marvel possible? To this day nothing of the sort has ever been seen.

His lecture then takes on a familiar turn:

A work of art is forever fixed in an immutable form that represents the poet's liberation from his creative labor. . . . Do you suppose, ladies and gentlemen, that there can be life where no longer anything moves? . . . If life moved always, it would never be; if it were one thing always, it would never move. And life needs both to be and to move. . . . If a work of art survives, it is only because we are able to release it from the fixity of its form; to loose this form by ourselves in vital movement; and then it is we who give it life. . . . Art in a certain sense vindicates life; because its own life, insofar as it is a true creation, is liberated from time, accident and obstacle, without any other end than itself alone.

Dr. Hinkfuss is outrageously caricatured, but as a *raisonneur* he is obviously serving as Pirandello's mouthpiece. This makes for some confusion. It is usually assumed that Dr. Hinkfuss—Pirandello's landlord in Berlin was named Hinckefuss—was intended to be a caricature of Max Reinhardt. The identification is tempting. Pirandello had a bone to pick with Reinhardt. Four years before, Reinhardt's version of *Six Characters*, produced 6 October 1925 at the Komödie in Berlin, had been the most successful production the play had ever had. Max Pallenberg played the *capocomico* in that production 131 times, setting a record for the theatre. The critics, unanimous in praise of Reinhardt's Expressionistic mise en scène, had suggested that Reinhardt, not Pirandello, was the true dramatic poet. This impression was strengthened when Pirandello brought his own company to Berlin, and his simple staging was compared, to his disfavor, with the magic atmosphere of the Reinhardt production.

The idea that the text is simply another element in the director's apparatus along with the acting, the setting and the lighting, and by no means the most important element, was hardly agreeable to Pirandello. It was, moreover, directly opposed to the ideas of the directors with whom Pirandello had come in contact in Paris. Whatever their actual practice may have been, Copeau, Pitoëff, Dullin, and Baty all stressed the primacy of the text in a dramatic production. On the other hand Pirandello himself had worked as a *régisseur* of other writer's plays. He had been deeply impressed with Reinhardt's theories, and his close associate Guido Salvini was one of Reinhardt's most devout disciples. The characterization of Dr. Hinkfuss thus presents some difficulty. As a person Dr. Hinkfuss is ridiculous, and doubtless insufferable. But the play which is improvised under his direction is in large part his work, vastly amplified from the suggestions in Pirandello's *novella*. In spite of the fact that the actors find his constant intrusion intolerable, and at last drive him out of the theatre, he is the true genius of the play. The conclusion is inescapable. Dr. Hinkfuss was intended as a caricature, not of Reinhardt, but of the domineering sprite that usurped the mind of the novelist when he turned playwright, and forced him to adapt his fantasy to the conditions of the stage. Dr. Hinkfuss, in short, seems to be none other than Pirandello, the showman; and the play he improvises is in the nature not so much of a contest between the author and the director, as of a collaboration of the author and the playwright.

In the practical conduct of the play Dr. Hinkfuss turns out to be an uncompromising spirit, and his trials are great. The leading man, who is to play Ricco Verri, insists on being given complete freedom in his improvisation. The leading lady will suffer no restraints; and the character-actor who plays the engineer Sampognetta is furious because in the course of her passionate performance the leading lady slapped his face so hard that it hurt. Dr. Hinkfuss's analysis of life and art is fully borne out by the facts. The actors are accustomed to the tyranny of the written text. Once they are released from this servitude they become the characters they portray and, like the personages of *Six Characters*, they can no longer be controlled by any external discipline. Dr. Hinkfuss, seated in the front row of the auditorium, the visible incarnation of the formal principle, jumps up periodically, cracking an imaginary whip like an animal trainer in a circus act. The actors step out of their parts unexpectedly, interrupting the performance with demands and protests, so that the illusion is alternately shattered and reconstituted, and the audience is seldom permitted to forget that it is witnessing a theatrical performance. In this manner the play maintains two actions in counterpoint—the story of Ricco Verri and the wretched Mommina, and the story of a group of unruly actors who are attempting to realize it on the stage.

The juxtaposition of these mutually incompatible realities creates a strangely disturbing effect. In this seeming improvisation the story appears to develop spontaneously under the eyes of the audience as if it were really happening, and since it is created out of the life of living actors closely identified with, and at times actually possessed by, the characters they represent, it results in a more vital expression than is usual in the theatre. The story, with many hitches and stutterings, seems to tell itself in a magnificent confusion of *vita* and *forma*.

In truth, of course, the whole affair is a deception. There is no improvisation. Every speech is written, and every move prescribed in the text. In spite of their pretensions, the actors are no more than marionettes manipulated by the author. The action is thus conveyed through a series of images that reflect one another as in a play of mirrors, and the result is an uncanny and uncomfortable realization that this experience in its unreality is deliberately aimed at unsettling the normal operation of the reality principle upon which the dramatic experience depends.

There is a clear distinction between a play conceived after this fashion and the alienation effect of the Brechtian theatre. Brecht desired to dissipate the dramatic illusion in order to isolate the situation on the stage for the audience's dispassionate contemplation. Thus, in a production of *King Lear* Brecht thought of stressing the breakdown of the feudal patriarchy rather than the tragic plight of an outraged patriarch, and in his epic theatre Brecht took care to remind his audience periodically that the play was a fiction designed to demonstrate a truth, and not a truth in itself. In effect this transformed the stage into a lecture platform and the theatre into a classroom. Pirandello did not tamper with the dramatic illusion for any such purpose. There was no need to estrange Mommina from the audience in order to elicit reflections on the need for the liberation of women, or the modernization of the tribal mores of the Sicilian hinterland. In Pirandello's play the lesson is implicit in the narrative, but the play was not primarily intended to teach the audience a lesson in human relations. Its purpose was to arouse its sensibility. The "estrangement" that is achieved by having an actor step out of his part in order to complain that he is being upstaged has for its purpose not a scientific analysis of the art of the actor, but a more intimate relation of actor and spectator in the realization of a living character. This is at the other pole from the Brechtian *Verfremdung*. In *Questa sera si recita a soggetto,* when the actor steps out of his part the spectator is invited to step into it.

Brecht's use of alienation effects in his epic theatre is usually attributed to Russian influences, and he is said to have owed something also to the Chinese theatre of Mei lan-fang which he saw in Moscow during his exile. It may be that these were indeed the operative influences, but the phrase associated with his technique of alienation was not used by him prior to 1936, and there is no reason to believe that this technique occurred to him as a useful dramatic device much before 1933. Since *Questa sera si recita a soggetto* provoked a considerable scandal in Berlin in 1929 just a year before Brecht's successful production of *Die Dreigroschenoper* at the Theater am Schiffbauerdamm in Berlin, it may be conjectured that there was some relation between Pirandello's innovative technique and the devices that later characterized the epic theatre.

In an early scene of the play Dr. Hinkfuss projects, in epic-theatre style, a sound film of *La forza del destino* for the benefit of the theatre party that is seated on the stage. In the entr'acte he sends the actors into the lobby of the auditorium to order refreshments and to continue their improvisation among the spectators. These devices failed in performance. Very likely such effects required more of an audience than an audience could at that time manage. In real life it is frequently possible to obliterate the line that divides fact from fiction; but in the theatre, seldom. Apparently the dramatic effect depends on the audience's awareness that what is happening on the stage is true without being true, a complex psychic state with which it is ordinarily wise not to tamper. Nevertheless in *Questa sera si recita a soggetto* there is a scene in which the consciousness of make-believe actually strengthens the dramatic effect in a most unusual way.

In the scene in which Ricco Verri interrupts the impromptu performance of *Il trovatore* in Signora Ignazia's house the principal actors suddenly step out of character and begin to wrangle about the conduct of the scene. In the midst of the fuss, Sampognetta comes in bleeding, with a knife thrust in the belly. It is his death scene. But instead of dying as expected, he complains bitterly that his entrance has been ruined for lack of preparation. Accordingly he goes out and makes another entrance. This time he is properly supported, but he still refuses to die since, as he says, he has not had a chance to improvise a proper death. He then describes in detail what he would have done had he been given the necessary cooperation, paraphrases the lines he would have spoken, and shows how he would have died, whistling valiantly with his last breath. The leading lady is so deeply affected with this performance that she begins to weep in earnest. The other actors are equally moved—suddenly the actors have become an audience, so that the audience, joining them, becomes, in some sense, an actor. Dr. Hinkfuss mercifully puts an end to the confusion by ordering a blackout.

The scene is completely successful. Had Sampognetta died on the stage in the usual course of business, the scene would have been embarrassingly melodramatic. As it is, it is at the same time very funny and deeply touching—a first-rate example of the Grotesque—and the desired effect is achieved without even the need to act it out. The character dies; but the author has not yet finished with his joke. Dr. Hinkfuss takes full credit for the scene. Pirandello, he remarks, would never have written a scene that might give the impression that the use of the knife is common in Sicily. Left to himself, says Hinkfuss, Pirandello would have had Sampognetta die of heart failure.

Since the next scene takes up the story four years later, Hinkfuss's speech at this point is meant to cover the actors' costume change. But in fact the actors do not change costume. Instead they stage a rebellion, and Hinkfuss, along with his crew, is expelled from the theatre. The actors now take charge of the production, and the final scene is improvised without benefit of *régisseur*. The effect is frankly theatrical, but the emotional response it elicits—in some measure enhanced by the honest admission of its contrivance—is remarkably strong. The theatre is seen to have its own reality. It is, as Dr. Hinkfuss explains, a machine for the production of emotional effects and, while the means are illusory, the emotions are real.

In the end it develops that Hinkfuss has not really left the theatre at all. He has directed everything, from beginning to end, and when Mommina dies, singing "Leonora, addio!," he appears and praises her performance. It was all his idea, he says; it is not in Pirandello's *novella*. The leading lady, however, does not immediately revive to take her bows. She has had real trouble with her heart. When one sinks deeply into a character, one tends to become that character—one's life acquires that form. The result in this case is that when Mommina dies, the actress who impersonates her comes very close to death. To ensure the safety of actors, Hinkfuss agrees, it is necessary to preserve a certain distance between actor and character. That is the function of the script.

Questa sera si recita a soggetto is an extremely interesting play that has never been successful. The reasons are many. It is confusing and difficult. Dr. Hinkfuss's speeches are interminable; there is a great deal of wrangling on the stage while the audience wants to get on with the story; the result is annoying. As a play in process of creation, it exposes the bare bones of dramatic production and affords fascinating glimpses into the author's mind. But the kernel of the play, the *novella*, "*Leonora, addio!*," can hardly be considered a happy choice for this type of adaptation. The story of Verri and Mommina was undoubtedly chosen for its operatic values; unhappily, the sentimentality of the final scene, toward which everything converges, can be made endurable only with the aid of a magnificent voice with full orchestral accompaniment.

This was the last of the plays with which Pirandello broke new ground in the theatre. Of the half-dozen plays he wrote after this time none fulfilled the promise of his middle period.

Non si sà come was first presented in Paris in December 1934, immediately after Pirandello was awarded the Nobel prize. It was received with appropriate respect; but it was generally misunderstood and, in any case, it aroused little interest. It deals with an involuntary moral lapse on the part of a man and woman who are swept up in a sudden inopportune surge of passion for which they cannot account, and which is seemingly completely impersonal. The lady is deeply in love with her husband, whom she is awaiting with impatience. The gentleman is the husband's dearest friend. Their guilt-feelings are such that they are impelled to confess their transgression. At the first intimation of the fact, without waiting for any explanation, the outraged husband, a naval officer, pulls out his pistol and shoots down his worthy friend.

On the whole, this is not very sensible. The play is, at the most, a naive demonstration of the irrationality of Life, and the absurdity of the forms that seek to limit its drives. Life, it is intimated, is impulsive and knows no law. There is no way to account logically for the drive of the vital impulse, and not much sense in assuming responsibility for the lapses in social behavior which occasionally manifest its power. The social forms that are rigidly imposed on the vital energy are consequently disastrous to the individual who is taken unawares by the life force. Romeo and Ginevra feel as if they were thrust together sexually in a dream. Accordingly, Romeo disclaims all moral responsibility for his act. But Ginevra's husband Giorgio is too much the realist to take into consideration the fine line that divides dream from reality. He shoots his friend as if by a reflex, without thinking, impelled to destroy by the same mindless energy that impelled Romeo to go through the act of creation. Romeo is also, in some sense, a realist. He does not blame his friend for killing him. "This too," he says as he dies, "is human."

The situation in this play is not very different from the affair of the *novella*, "Il sogno," in which the high-strung wife suffers torments of guilt because she dreamt of having sexual relations with her husband's friend. But while impure thoughts of that category are reprehensible in the casuistry of the Church, it is only when they are translated into action that they are likely to have social consequences; therefore it is important that there be a clear distinction between dream and day. *Non si sà come* dwells ironically on the absurdity of insisting on social codes which have no relevance to the demands of life. The implication is clear that in a world of marionettes worked by invisible strings of passion it is ridiculous to speak of moral responsibility. The naval lieutenant Giorgio can no more help killing his friend than his friend could help betraying him with his wife. Both are puppets managed by an invisible hand. In life, as it is presently constituted, nothing can be justified and nothing requires justification. From a logical viewpoint the entire operation is senseless, and it is even more senseless to try to rationalize its consequences.

In the *novella* "La verità," on which *Il berretto a sonagli* was based, the peasant Tararà, who is on trial for killing his erring wife, shows considerably more insight into the human condition than his upper-class counterpart in *Non si sà come;* but the result is the same. Tararà tells the judge:

> Man is man, Your Excellency, and women are women. Certainly a man must have consideration for women, who have it in their blood to be unfaithful even without the excuse of being left alone. I mean, with the husband away at work almost all the week; but the woman, for her part, must show consideration for the man and understand that a man cannot have his face stung by the neighbors, Your Excellency! Certain insults—yes, Your Excellency,—I appeal to the gentlemen of the jury—certain insults, gentlemen of the jury, go beyond stinging, they cut up a man's face beyond endurance. . . . A man cannot let the neighbor sting his face. What then is a man to do? [83]

As a result of this obviously incontrovertible defence, Tararà, we are told, was condemned to thirteen years of hard labor. This too was human.

Quando si è qualcuno is memorable chiefly as autobiography. It was written in 1932 and doubtless commemorates Pirandello's love for Marta Abba, the inspiration of his later years, and also his despair at the impossibility of achieving at his age the spiritual and physical rejuvenation which this love demanded. By 1932 Pirandello was a very famous man, a "Somebody." He had striven mightily to attain a form which would represent him monumentally to the world. But now that he had it, he felt imprisoned in it. Some years before, in 1929, he had written in the *novella*, "La carriola," a passage that seems to come very close to self-appraisal. There the old jurist says:

> I do not see what is dead in me; I see that I never was alive; I see the form that others, not I, have given me and I feel that in this form my

life, my true life, never existed. . . . And I cry, my soul cries within
this dead form that never was mine—But, how?—I, that?—I like this?
But how could that be? And I feel disgust, horror, hatred for this thing
that I am not, that I never was, at this dead form in which I am
imprisoned and from which I cannot escape.[84]

In *Quando si è qualcuno—When One Is Somebody*—the eminent poet, long
married and with grown up children, falls in love with a charming young
girl, a very modern young girl, who adores him. Under her influence he
publishes a book of poems in a revolutionary new style. For this purpose
he uses an assumed name, thus creating a new poet, so far unknown. But
when the literary youth of Italy rallies noisily around this newcomer to
the literary scene, the old poet finds himself in dangerous competition
with the rival he has created. He is on the point of announcing that the
new poet is himself when he discovers that this is impossible. He is
Somebody and he stands for something. His family, his publisher, and
the conservative press which backs him are all grimly opposed to any
defection on his part: they would consider it an act of treason. In the end
he resigns himself to his fate. He must remain forever in the form that
has been given him. He sorrowfully renounces his young love and his
new-found youth, and relapses into the monumental figure he has become and is destined to be. He is a great man; and the great, petrified in
the semblance of themselves, are not subject to change. To become
Somebody is to die.

No manager in Italy was willing to undertake the production of this
play.

It was first performed in Buenos Aires on 20 September 1933. In
November of that year Marta Abba produced it in San Remo without
success, and it was hissed in Rome and in Naples, amply confirming
Pirandello's idea of the growing hostility of the Italian audience toward
his work and himself.[85] The hostility he incurred was understandable.
Pirandello was an iconoclast, and in Italy at this time the icons were
sacred. Moreover, his radical tendencies, as he himself insisted, had little
to do with any ordered system of philosophy. Ostensibly a Fascist, he
really belonged to no party and had no partisans. The rationalistic basis
of his aggressive fantasies was something which, in all likelihood, he
himself took less seriously than did his critics. He had chosen to quarrel
with the world. It had done him harm, so he thought, and he did what
he could to vent his spite. In these terms his writings are entirely consistent and comprehensible.

Taken together, his work—his poems, his 254 *novelle*, his 40 plays, his novels, his essays, "L'umorismo," "Arte e scienza," and the rest—is the outcome of his vendetta with reality, one of the most complete and painstaking enterprises of this sort since the time of Dante. There is, un-questionably, something pathetic in this destructive effort for, beyond a certain point, his heart was not in it. His best work shows how dearly he loved the world he was trying so hard to destroy. Toward the end of his life he wrote his biographer Vittorini thanking him for depicting a Piran-dello in whom Pirandello could at last recognize himself, in a biography so conceived "that he who has never known himself now finds someone who at last sees that if so many dislike him, it is only because he is him-self, and not like others." He added:

> A man, I wished to say something to men, without any ambition ex-cept, perhaps, that of avenging myself for having been born. But never-theless life, in spite of all it has made me suffer, is so beautiful![86]

Much had happened to Pirandello since the year when he was sud-denly catapulted into the limelight; but by 1932 essentially nothing had changed for him. Now that he was Somebody, thoroughly bemedaled, thoroughly disliked, and greatly respected, he enjoyed most of all the idea that he was nobody, an internationally famous non-person. It was a pose he evidently cherished, and he maintained it bravely all his days.

It is impossible in the face of so complex a performance to sum up Pirandello's work with any confidence; impossible also to distinguish the mask from the face, the artist from the mountebank, the thinker from the showman. Nor is it necessary. Pirandello was a puzzle to himself, still more of a puzzle to those who knew him intimately. What we know of him is mainly what he intended us to know, and that seems just. He was an artist. The self-portrait that he left may not be a likeness, but it is un-likely that we shall come any closer to his mystery than he meant us to come.

In the *novella* entitled "Niente," which he published in 1922, we come upon Dr. Mangoni, a medical practitioner of the humblest sort, on duty in an all-night pharmacy in Rome. He is roused from his doze by a boy to attend a young poet who has asphyxiated himself with the fumes of a charcoal-burner. The doctor is in no hurry to go, and he calls the boy an imbecile for coming to hinder a man from dying who has no wish to live. He himself, he remarks, is a *dimissionario*—so far as society is con-cerned he has resigned his membership. Nevertheless he visits the squalid apartment on the dirty street where the young man was rooming with a retired schoolteacher, his grotesque wife, and three children. Going up the dark stairs, he twists his ankle. The young man, as it turns out, is dead. The schoolteacher's two daughters were both in love with him. He was expected to marry one of them. As the girl passes him in the dim hallway, the doctor has a glimpse of her young breasts bobbing seductively under her blouse, and the sight fills him with such fury that he can hardly contain himself. He proceeds to deliver a lecture on the subject of the poor country boy who came to seek fame in the capital with a few lire in his pocket and a sheaf of poems in his bag, and who ended by suffocating himself in the fumes of his brazier. "You will admit," he says,

> "that this poor boy was perhaps dreaming of glory, since he took the trouble to write poetry. Now think a little of what his glory would have amounted to even if his poems had been printed. A poor, useless little book of verses. And his love? Love, that is the most vital and most sacred thing that is given us to experience in this life? What would this love have become? A woman. Rather—worse still—a wife: your daughter. . . . I imagine her to be most beautiful and adorned with all the virtues. But still a woman, my dear lady, who after a little time, we know very well, what with her poverty, dear God, and her children, to what a state she would be reduced. And then, the world! The world in which I am going now to lose myself with this foot that hurts me so, what would it have become for him? A house. This house, you understand?"
>
> And, raising his hands in strange gestures of disgust and scorn, he made off, limping and muttering: "Books! Women! Houses! Nothing. . . . Nothing. . . . Nothing. . . ."[87]

Thirty years before, Pirandello himself had come to Rome with a handful of poems and a dream of glory, and although by the time he wrote of Dr. Mangoni he had savored much success, it is clear that he was able to share fully in the bitterness of one who had long ago resigned his share in the human enterprise. The mask he chose to wear in life had seen much use by the time he put it on. It had been worn by every disgruntled sage from Lao-tze to Strindberg. Pirandello wore it with a difference. He did not withdraw from life like the others. He wandered about in the world, homeless, an honored pariah living in deluxe hotels, scornful of the public, but mindful of its applause and its hostility, accumulating honors with the avidity of a collector, while all the time aware of the emptiness of everything.

For the greater part of his life he did what he could to advance his vendetta with the world, firing off salvo after salvo in his effort to demolish its reality, and in this respect he paralleled the work of the Italian Futurists, and anticipated the work of Dada. But he was neither a Futurist nor an anarchist. His roots were in the past, and for all his skepticism he believed firmly in the eternal verities which, he labored to prove, were neither eternal nor true. In the end, he made his peace with everyone, with the Church and the state; but he forgave nobody. When he died, in December 1936, his friends found his last wishes jotted down on a scrap of notepaper twenty-five years old:

> Let my death be passed over in silence. I beg my friends and my enemies not only not to discuss it, but not even to mention it in the press. Neither notices nor announcements. . . .
>
> A hearse of the lowest class, the cart of the poor. Bare. And let no one accompany me, neither relatives nor friends. The cart, the horse, the driver and that's all.

The government delegate whose duty it was to arrange the great man's funeral made a face when he read the will. "He went out," he said, "slamming the door."

A half-century before, Victor Hugo had asked to be driven to his grave in a pauper's cart. His wishes had been disregarded, and Hugo's funeral cortege was the most magnificent that had ever been seen in Paris. Pirandello's instructions were scrupulously followed. Few were present at his house to see him off, and no one accompanied him to the mortuary. That morning in Rome it was snowing. The streets were slippery. The cheap wooden coffin was loaded in silence, and the cart pulled slowly away from the curb. When it came to the street corner, Via Antonio Bosia, the old horse broke into a trot.[88]

It was a piece of showmanship that Hugo might well have envied.

GIRAUDOUX

By the time of Mallarmé's death in 1898 Symbolism had lost whatever distinctive character it might have had, and its doctrines were dispersed in a wide spectrum of aesthetic attitudes which had in common mainly their opposition to Realism. *La Revue indépendante* had by this time gone under. Its place was taken by *La Revue blanche* and by the long-lived *Mercure de France* under the editorship of Alfred Vallette and his wife Rachilde. At the regular Tuesday receptions of the *Mercure de France* two generations of Symbolists met to exchange views—on the one hand Fénéon, Kahn, Gourmont, Régnier, and Pierre Louÿs, and on the other Valéry, Gide, Ravel, and Jarry. In this manner the views of Mallarmé and his immediate entourage were transmitted to still another generation of writers, among whom could be numbered Guillaume Apollinaire, André Salmon, Max Jacob, Jean Cocteau, Jean Giraudoux, André Breton, and Antonin Artaud.

In 1894 Lugné-Poë emphasized the progressive character of his theatrical venture by engaging Alfred Jarry as *secrétaire-régisseur* of his company at the Théâtre de l'oeuvre. Jarry was perhaps not the most gifted of the young radicals attached to the *Mercure de France*, but he was certainly the most picturesque. He was a young Breton who had come to Paris to prepare for the École supérieure normale. Alfred Vallette had taken him under his wing and in 1893, when Jarry was twenty, published his first book, a collection of poems and prose in the Symbolist manner entitled *Les Minutes de sable Mémorial*, illustrated with Jarry's own woodcuts. The young poet soon attracted attention. He wore his hair long and dressed in women's blouses and a long cape with a hood. In later years he affected the costume of a bicycle racer, and went about the streets of Paris armed to the teeth as a precaution against a possible attack by anarchists.

Ubu roi was the fruit of his adolescence. The professor of physics at the lycée Jarry attended at Rennes was a well-intentioned fat gentleman called Hébert whose bumbling habits made him a favorite butt of the students. Jarry, in collaboration with his classmates the Morin brothers, improvised a farce called *Les Polonais*, inspired possibly, by Chabrier's comic opera *Le Roi malgré lui*, which had had a huge success in 1887. This play, in which Hébert was amply caricatured as the usurper of the Polish throne, was acted in the attic of Morin's house in Rennes in 1888 with Jarry in the leading role of Père Ebé. This production by no means exhausted the subject. By 1896 Jarry had published a half-dozen fragments based on the original text and, in June of that year, Charles Fort published a full length version of *Ubu roi* in *Le Livre d'art*. This was subtitled "Drama in Five Acts, restored in its entirety as performed in the Théâtre de Phynances in 1888." It was favorably reviewed in the Symbolist press, and Jarry urged Lugné to stage it.

That year Lugné produced *Peer Gynt* without success. The Théâtre de l'oeuvre was in the doldrums, and in November the idea of staging *Ubu roi* did not seem altogether preposterous. Jarry had thought of doing it as a puppet show, but in the end Firmin Gémier was induced to play the part of the fat revolutionist, and on 11 December 1896 *Ubu roi* opened on the stage of the Théâtre nouveau in the rue Blanche. The setting was fantastic, a montage of disparate elements which brought together all the elements of the play in a single composition. Jarry, Bonnard, Vuillard, Lautrec, and Sérusier all had a hand in the painting. Before the curtain went up Jarry treated the audience to a long harangue. Then the curtain rose, and Gémier delivered the first word of the play. The audience gasped.

The moment was historic. The forbidden word had never before been spoken on the French stage in any form. It is said that it took a full quarter-hour to hush the audience, doubtless an exaggeration. The play itself was no great thing; but the impression it made was unforgettable. The plot had by now developed into a comic-strip version of *Macbeth*. Père Ubu, a trusted colonel of the royal guards, urged on by his wife, conspires to murder the king and most of the royal family, usurps the Polish throne, fleeces the country to within an inch of its life, and is at last thrown out by the king's thirteen-year-old son. He then sets sail for France. It was a spectacle well adapted to the guignol; but on the stage the effect was hilarious. *Ubu roi* might well have been hailed as a masterpiece in its genre. But as yet there was no such genre. It was unique.

Very likely Jarry was mad, and his play was certainly childish; but in the 1890's madness was much in fashion, and childishness was already a respected form of primitivism. The naiveté of *Ubu* was not at all the naiveté of the douanier Rousseau, yet it had something in common with it—it was in its way equally innocent and equally appealing. For all his miserable nature, Ubu radiated an undeniable air of health. He was basic man, cowardly, treacherous, gluttonous, dirty, and greedy, a Rabelaisian character, completely transparent, a caricature of all that is unpleasantly human. One might say the characterization was essentially realistic. But Jarry was a Symbolist. His play, done in a Symbolist theatre, under Symbolist management, with a Symbolist decor, was naturally claimed as a Symbolist work of art. Mallarmé sat quietly throughout the opening performance, and afterwards praised the work enthusiastically.

It was performed only twice, and precipitated a month-long polemic in the Paris press, in the course of which the question of the language proper to the theatre was debated, and also the relative merits of the Symbolist and Realist aesthetic. Jarry died in November 1907 at the age of thirty-four, wasted by tuberculosis. He had literally drunk himself to death. The year after Jarry's death, Gémier gave *Ubu roi* a brief revival. Then it was forgotten.

In 1919 the vogue of Dada brought Jarry once again into fashion. Then came the turn of the Surrealists. Apollinaire had been, in his youth, one of Jarry's most fervent adherents. He lit upon him as the father of Surrealism. Antonin Artaud had also been a devoted member of his circle. When, in 1927, with the help of Roger Vitrac, Artaud established a new theatre dedicated to "the ruin of the theatre as it exists today in France," he called it Le Théâtre Alfred Jarry. But there was to be a long parenthesis between the Théâtre Alfred Jarry and the theatre of Ionesco, Genet, Arrabal, and Beckett. The parenthesis was largely occupied by Giraudoux, and with him the drama of Symbolism at last approached greatness.

It is not far, as the crow flies, from Jarry to Giraudoux, but the gulf between them seems immense. The quarter-century that separated them included a cataclysm. The Great War began in 1914. When the dust had settled, the hospitals were full, the woods were blackened, the fields were scarred with trenches and reeked of death. Apart from these alterations of the landscape there was no apparent change. In Paris in the time of Jarry the mood had been one of mild hysteria, with recurring depressions that marked the anxieties of a world in transition. It was much the same in the time of Giraudoux.

The Great War changed the face of Europe, but not its expression. All the ferments that had been at work in the decaying culture of the nineteenth century were active after the great guns were parked, and the fevers of war gave new vigor to the forces of disintegration. Anarchism had been in vogue a good while before the turn of the century. In the time of Jarry a number of French terrorists had been arrested, tried, and executed under conditions that approximated grand opera. In the course of his trial the anarchist Vaillant had quoted Darwin, Ibsen, and Octave Mirbeau to justify his tossing a bomb into the chamber of Deputies. He was duly guillotined, and became a martyr. In the summer of 1894 thirty anarchists were tried *en masse*. Among them was the Symbolist writer Félix Fénéon, who entertained the court by making witty remarks at the expense of the public prosecutor. All thirty were acquitted; but the trial did much to confirm the dangerous temper of the artistic *bohème*.

In Paris the early years of the new century were turbulent. Novelists outdid one another in inflaming the popular imagination with visions of secret agents, revolts of angels, worlds in collision, and mysterious forces busily arranging the end of everything. In Paris the terraces of the literary cafés teemed with dangerous characters who slowly piled up saucers while they calmly discussed the future of art and the best way to overturn the government. The radicalism of the 1920's was perhaps less good humored than that of the 1890's, but it was not essentially different in its aims. The Naturalists were by this time quoting Marx and Lenin. The Symbolists were trying to define Cubism, Simultanism, Dada, Surrealism, Futurism, Vorticism, and Expressionism. There seemed to be at this time as many cults as there were artists, and their differences were seldom clear. But in one respect these dissidents were all in accord—the world they knew must come to an end.

The only question in this regard was as to how far the past must be destroyed in order to make room for the future. In the preface to *Ubu enchaîné*, which Jarry wrote in 1900, Père Ubu exclaims: "Ventrebleu! We should never have knocked everything down if we had not meant also to destroy the ruins! But the only way we see to do this is to put up some handsome new buildings." By 1912, indeed, the outlines of new construction were becoming visible. That year Diaghilev staged Debussy's *L'Après-midi d'un faune* and also Stravinsky's *Le Sacre du printemps*. The following year Apollinaire published *Les Peintres cubistes*, Proust brought out *Du Côté de chez Swann*, D. H. Lawrence published *Sons and Lovers*, Gide prepared *Les Caves du Vatican* for the press, and Copeau founded the Théâtre du vieux colombier. The following year the world was at war.[1]

The Great War did nothing to encourage idealism. On the contrary the mood of the post-war years was preponderantly materialistic and positivist. For a time the theatres in Paris were occupied with plays about returning soldiers, unfaithful wives punished or forgiven, collaborators and resisters, and the repair of the social dislocations of the wartime years. As the wave of patriotism that had engulfed the nations of Europe slowly receded, the consequent disenchantment found expression in the theatre mainly in sexual displays and ribald comedy, along with some plays of grimly realistic nature. Inevitably the old tensions were reasserted. To the new materialism, presumably American—in 1931 Benjamin Crémieux called it "Le Taylorisme et le Fordisme"—was opposed a new idealism—presumably French.

The works of Baudelaire, Verlaine, Rimbaud, and Mallarmé were now re-edited and reprinted, and Symbolism became once again the subject of serious study and imitation. There ensued a corresponding spiritual revival with mystical overtones, philosophically associated with Bergson's emphasis on the intuitive faculty. The little theatres reopened. Pierre Veber revived the Théâtre-libre; Lugné-Poë reopened the Théâtre de l'oeuvre; Jean Copeau reassembled Le Vieux Colombier. The innovations associated with the new theatres were largely concerned with stage techniques and the mise en scène.

Antoine had attempted to coordinate the elements of naturalistic production in a unified statement that would make the effect of reality. The new directors tended to reject these effects as illusionistic and unduly restrictive of the imagination. Under the influence of Adolphe Appia and Gordon Craig the new theatre inclined sharply toward Symbolism. Appia had worked with Wagner in Bayreuth, and was thoroughly imbued with Wagnerian notions. It was his idea that the stage decor and the mise en scène should have the fluidity and the suggestive power of music, so that the spoken word, the moving actor, and the illuminated space in which the actor moved should merge in a perfectly synthesized artistic effect. Since the element that would fuse all these various elements into a transcendent unity would be light, the illumination of the play must be managed so as to move the emotions in the same way as the sounds of a symphony. These ideas, first published in 1895, were

vigorously publicized and elaborated by Gordon Craig, and in a remarkably short time the Symbolist decor became the high style of even the
commercial theatres of Europe.[2]

Craig had been much impressed by Maeterlinck's theory of the drama,
and particularly by the essays of *Le Trésor des humbles*. He himself
thoroughly shared the Belgian's distrust of the living actor and his preference for marionettes. In his periodical *The Mask*, and his other writings, Craig very ably developed a theory of drama as a non-represen-
tional art that worked mainly through suggestion and allusion, and was
in no way an imitation of nature.

In 1910 Jacques Rouché summarized these innovations in a study
called *L'Art théâtrale moderne* which had wide currency and did much to
bring French theatre up to date. In Paris theatre production soon acquired status as a fine art. Lugné-Poë had for some time been employing
fine artists to design settings which would evoke an *état d'âme* appropriate
to the spirit of his productions. The Ballets-Russes, first seen in Paris in
1909, had from the first outdone the opera in visual splendor; now
Diaghilev moved smoothly with the times from the magnificence of
Bakst to the provocative austerity of the Cubists. By this time Picasso,
Braque, Derain, Matisse, Léger, and Chagall were all actively involved
with the theatre, and great strides were made in the staging of plays. But
the great wave of dramatic writing which Ibsen had propagated did not
crest in Paris. Scores of skilled craftsmen supplied the commercial stage
with plays. The Société des auteurs flourished as never before, but, aside
from the classics, the true masterpieces of the theatre in Paris were all
translations. So far as the French drama as such was concerned, the
aspiring director grappled chiefly with Molière and Musset.

In 1909 Jacques Copeau, together with Gide and Jean Schlumberger,
had founded *La Nouvelle Revue française*. As the latest offshoot of the
Symbolist press this periodical had a more eclectic view than the *Mercure
de France*, and also a more decidely classical orientation. Copeau was its
literary director. At the age of thirty-five he resigned his post at the
N.R.F. in order to organize a new art theatre. This was Le Théâtre du
vieux colombier. It was destined to have enormous influence on the
drama of the following period.

Copeau's views were first aired in an article in the September issue of
the *Nouvelle Revue française*, in 1913. The article, entitled, "Un Essai de
rénovation dramatique," proposed a very radical departure from established theatre practice, an attempt to bring about in the theatre what

the young men of 1885 had tried to do in poetry and in painting, a reduction of art to its first principles. The theatre of his time, he felt, was being stifled by commercialism and machinery. At the Vieux Colombier all the apparatus of the professional stage would be eliminated. He would begin with a *tabula rasa*—a bare stage, a text, and some human beings to serve it.

The purpose of play production, in his view, was the realization of the dramatic text. Whatever might work to distract the audience from the author's words—the setting, the spectacle, or the acting—he considered detrimental to the production. His staging was intended to be meticulous and utterly simple. To accommodate the sort of production he had in mind he devised, with the help of Louis Jouvet, his stage-manager, a construction which would serve to mount any play. He called it a *dispositif fixe*—a permanent facility. This structure, patterned after the stage in the time of Shakespeare, was to be entirely functional, a platform with several practical levels reached by steps, an alcove upstage, and a forestage apron.

These ideas obviously contrasted sharply with the Wagnerian concept of the "artwork of the future," but Copeau's Symbolist orientation was evident in his reverence for the spoken word; and, in his insistence on the ritualistic element in the drama, he came close to the ideas of Mallarmé. For the rest, he was a craftsman who demanded the utmost of his actors, and the school which he established in 1921 in connection with his theatre became a model for the acting schools of the next generation. In the following years his pupils and his associates exerted great influence on the development of the art of drama, and without doubt the establishment of his playhouse was an event of the first importance in the history of the theatre. His theatre was lacking only in two respects. It had no dependable audience and it developed no writers.

The Vieux Colombier enjoyed four years of prosperity, from 1920 to 1924, then closed its doors. Copeau retired from active life, defeated and ill. His pupils were dispersed. But in one way or another they carried on his tradition. Charles Dullin, one of his best actors, had left him in 1919. Two years later, with Copeau's help, he founded Le Théâtre de l'Atelier. In 1922 Louis Jouvet left to assume the direction of the Comédie des Champs Elysées. That same year Georges Pitoëff and his wife Ludmilla took up permanent residence in Paris and entered upon a brilliant career marked by constant financial difficulties. Meanwhile, in 1921, Gaston Baty organized the Théâtre de la chimère, taking this compendious beast as the symbol of "an art which aimed at the reconciliation of mind and matter, nature and the supernatural, men and things."[3] By the year 1925 the age of the little art theatres was well under way in Paris. They had much in common. They were all small and indigent. They were all ambitious. And they were all managed by actors.

Gaston Baty was a cultivated man. Like Copeau he was a Symbolist; but there the resemblance ended. He was a Wagnerian. He saw the drama as a harmonious fusion of all the arts. The classic theatre, which above all emphasized the text, seemed to him to be suffering from "a hypertrophy of the verbal element." "The universe," he wrote,

> is not merely men and social groups. Around these is all that lives, all that grows, all that has being. And all that has being is the subject of drama: animals, plants, things. All of everyday life and its mystery. . . . There are inanimate personalities: the factory, the ship, the city, the forest, the mountain: there is the marvel of mechanical things, the man-made machine which afterwards goes by itself. There are the great forces of nature. . . . more powerful than man, which oppress him, overwhelm him, transform his body, exhaust his will, dry up his soul.[4]

Drama, in Baty's opinion, should reflect not merely the individual in the universe, but also the universe in the individual. It should suggest the cosmic significance of the human conflict. So profound an intimation would ordinarily transcend the possibilities of verbal expression and would lead the intuition into realms beyond the sphere of language. Communication on this plane would depend, accordingly, on gesture, atmosphere, light and movement, in short, on the means peculiar to the theatre. It would be the function of the director, in staging such plays, to render explicit by such means what would otherwise remain implicit in the text.

In order to re-theatricalize the theatre—"rethéâtriser le théâtre"—Baty developed a theory of play production that anticipated the doctrines of Dr. Hinkfuss by nearly a decade, and it is entirely possible that Pirandello was mindful of Baty in his caricature of the dictatorial *metteur en scène*. The result of Baty's theories was the development in France of rival schemes of play production which, without precluding the possibility of collaboration in the ideal situation, tended in practice to pit author and director against one another in the management of a performance.

Baty's theories found expression in a group of plays, written more or less under his immediate influence, in which the author relied a good deal on the virtuosity of the actor and the ingenuity of the director. These plays, sometimes grouped under the rubric *le théâtre intimiste*, were mainly realistic in detail; but all were tinged more or less deeply with Symbolism, and in all of them an effort was made to convey significance through non-verbal means, often through silence. Jean-Jacques Bernard's *Martine* (1922), and his later comedy, *L'Invitation au voyage* (1924), Gantillon's *Maya* (1924), Vildrac's *Le Paquebot Tenacity* (1919), and Lenormand's *Simoun* (1920) all made their points by indirection.

The use of significant silence as a means of communication was certainly no new thing in the theatre. Sophocles had practiced this technique expertly, and also Racine; and more recently Chekhov had shown what could be done with the artful manipulation of pause and silence. But in French drama the systematic use of silence as a means of communication was directly attributable to Maeterlinck. In 1922 Jean-Jacques Bernard wrote, in a program note to *Martine:* "The drama is above all the art of the unexpressed. It is less through speech than through the effect of speech that our deepest feelings are revealed. Under the audible dialogue there is an underlying dialogue that the dramatist must make manifest." Thus far, Bernard did no more than to paraphrase a passage in "Le Tragique quotidien." But he went on to make the current issue explicit: "Thus drama has no worse enemy than literature. Literature expresses and dilutes what should only be suggested. Once feelings are communicated they lose their power. The logic of the theatre rules out feelings that the situation does not impose. And if the situation imposes them there is no need to express them in words."

In 1922 the dependence of "the Theatre of the Unexpressed" upon Maeterlinck's famous essay could hardly escape notice. But Bernard was not wholly of Maeterlinck's persuasion. "Means," he wrote, "work-tools, that is what silence and indirect language should be, along with attitude and mime. To follow the path indicated by Maeterlinck and some others would be as grave an error as that which many other authors commit, those who do not use the word as the tool it must be, but who employ it for itself and become intoxicated with language."[5]

Like Mallarmé, Maeterlinck had aspired to represent on the stage: "The mysterious song of the infinite, the menacing silence of spirits or gods, the eternity which growls at us from the horizon, the fatality of which we are inwardly aware."[6] Jean-Jacques Bernard had read Freud. He was more interested in the workings of the individual soul than in the cosmic rivers which flow through its depths. Since he was convinced that the dramatist's function is to represent, in the words of Mallarmé, "not the thing, but the effect it produces," in his most striking plays he deliberately omitted the *scène à faire*. In *L'Invitation au voyage* the romantic Philippe, who has occupied the imagination of Marie-Louise all the years he has been away, is never seen on the stage, and her disillusionment when at last he returns is suggested only by her behavior after their meeting. When Marie-Louise sits at her piano after the long awaited meeting with the man of her dreams, she puts aside her favorite piece—it is Duparc's setting of Baudelaire's *Invitation au voyage*—and plays instead the Chopin nocturne that her husband loves. There is no need of words.

Bernard specialized, like Maeterlinck, in representing characters who live somewhere between dream and day, but for all their reticence his characters have solidity. They are not mysterious beings. Their silence is the silence of those who have nothing to say. A skilful writer can convey a fully formulated thought quite successfully in words, but, as Mallarmé long ago pointed out, by the time a thought is fully formulated it has lost its truth. Among the commonplaces of Symbolism perhaps the most common had to do with the inadequacy of language. The *théâtre intimiste* was in the main a product of the search for effective symbols. The result was a number of marvellously delicate characterizations, but their success inevitably provoked a critical reaction. André Beaunier insisted that drama should consist of words, not of silences; and Pierre Brisson criticized *L'Invitation au voyage* for its lack of clarity. In Italy Silvio d'Amico wrote that this play departed from the tradition of the *pièce bien faite* only through the instrumental use of the mute.[7]

The conflict of Realism and Symbolism was thus renewed in terms of the use of language in the theatre, but the issue went deeper. For the Symbolists the essence of drama was mystery. For the Realists it was clarity. Their viewpoints and their goals were diametrically opposed. The filiation of attitudes from Mallarmé to Artaud on the one hand, and from Zola to Brecht on the other, is not simple to trace, but it is traceable. More obvious, but much more complex, is the line that leads from Mallarmé to Giraudoux.

"The function of the drama," Jean-Jacques Bernard wrote, "is to awaken echoes in the soul of the spectator. And in this it will succeed in proportion as it leaves room for the need to dream that is either clear or latent in every human being. . . ."[8] It is impossible to quarrel with such an assertion, but its implications lead as far as the art of the blank canvas and the silent orchestra and, in the theatre, to such incomprehensible spectacles as Beckett's *Theatre I* and *Theatre II*. The Symbolists found the language of everyday commerce both ambiguous and inexpressive, but Mallarmé had sought to renew the efficacy of language, not to abolish it. The style of Claudel, Valéry, and Giraudoux in French, like the style of Yeats and Synge in English, reflects this concern, and similar concerns are evident in the early plays of Maeterlinck and the plays of Jean-Jacques Bernard. But while Maeterlinck thought to recover the primitive transparency of language by reducing speech to nursery levels, and Bernard and Vildrac went so far as to eschew the use of words altogether in the high moments of their plays, Claudel and Giraudoux aspired to enhance the expressive power of words, and in this manner succeeded in raising the language of the theatre to a level it had not reached since the time of Racine.

In 1927 Pitoëff organized the Cartel des quatre, a league of art-theatre managers which included Jouvet, Dullin, and Baty. These four now banded together for mutual aid against the competition of the commercial theatre and the attacks of the commercial press. Under the auspices of the Cartel the best of the foreign drama was brought to Paris, and some new French playwrights—Vildrac, Cocteau, and Jules Romains among them—were given an opportunity to show their work. In 1936, during the ministry of Léon Blum, Jouvet was offered the directorship of the Comédie-Française. He declined. The post was given to Édouard Bourdet, but the four Cartel managers accepted appointments as special directors attached to the Comédie-Française. The new movement in the theatre initiated twenty-two years earlier by Copeau at the Vieux Co-lombier was thus given official recognition, and the Symbolists were ab-sorbed into the establishment.

Meanwhile in France the literary mode had experienced significan changes. Bergson was widely influential; Proust and Gide were well t the fore; there was renewed interest in Rimbaud, Mallarmé, and Valéry Claudel had not yet fully emerged as a force in the theatre, but *Le Par tage du midi* and *Le Soulier de satin* were attracting attention to his talent By the 1930's the trend of French thought and French taste was agai decidedly anti-realist.

The year after Jouvet's unprecedented success with Giraudoux's *Sieg fried* (1928) the Great Depression closed in, and the stage was being s for the coming war. In the theatre new voices began to be heard. The spoke in terms that were increasingly troublesome.[9]

Jean Giraudoux became a playwright at the age of forty-five.

In 1927 Jouvet was more or less firmly established at the Comédie des Champs Elysées. He had been there five years. His first year, 1923, was blessed with the success of Jules Romains's *Troubadec* and *Knock*. In 1925 he put on Crommelynck's *Tripes d'or* with disastrous results, and Vildrac's *Madame Béliard* did not help him to recoup his losses. By 1927 Jouvet was in dire need of something new. He turned in desperation to Gogol's *Revizor*. That year Dullin was featuring Aristophanes' *Birds* and Achard's *Le Joueur d'echecs;* Baty was involved with *The Adding Machine* and *The Dybbuk;* Pitoëff had just ended a run of Cocteau's *Orphée* (1926), and the periodical *Commedia* was preparing a series of articles on the crisis in the theatre and the decline of public taste.

Giraudoux's novel, *Siegfried et le limousin,* had been published in 1922, three years after the First World War. For some unaccountable reason it had been awarded the Prix Balzac. Four years later Giraudoux dramatized a passage of his novel as his contribution to a Festschrift entitled *Mélanges offerts à M. Charles Andler.* The title of Giraudoux's piece was "Première scène d'une adaptation théâtrale de *Siegfried et le limousin.*" It was five pages long and poked mild fun at university life. The little play came to the attention of Crémieux, who advised Giraudoux to expand it into a full-length play. This was done.

Giraudoux and Jouvet had met in the spring of 1926. The Siegfried adaptation came into Jouvet's hands the following year. In this version the play was long and, like the novel, far from coherent. It was not Giraudoux's habit to revise anything; he re-wrote instead. Under Jouvet's influence, *Siegfried* was re-written no less than seven times. The result was the version which Jouvet presented at the Comédie des Champs Elysées on 3 May 1928.

Siegfried opened in an atmosphere of fear and trembling, and was given an ovation. Madame Arletty, an actress of vast experience, had predicted that it would have, at the most, a week's run. It played 302 performances, a run surpassed in Jouvet's theatre only by *Ondine.* The critics wrote enthusiastically of a return of letters to the theatre, marvelled at the attention with which the public listened to the long tirades, and thanked the author for administering a blood transfusion to the dying theatre of France.[10]

Fifty years after the fact it is difficult to account for the immense success of this play. It is certain that the audience of 1928 was tired of the theatrical contraptions of Bernstein, Bataille, Verneuil, and Guitry, and the elevated tone of *Siegfried* must have come as a surprise to those who associated high style in the theatre with Racine or Rostand. It is true, also, that after some decades of Naturalism the well-made play was no longer respectable in intellectual circles. *Siegfried* is a most untidy play, full of ambiguities and inexplicable turns, and its plot, such as it is, makes enormous demands on the credibility of the audience. On the other hand, *Siegfried* deals with a subject which in 1928 was of crucial importance to a generation which had its uniforms still hanging in the closet. *Mein Kampf* was first published in 1925. The following year Germany was admitted to the League of Nations. On the program of *Siegfried* was published a quotation from the last scene of the play, a scene omitted from Jouvet's production: "You know what I think of our two countries. The question of their concord is the only important question of the universe."[11]

By the time *Siegfried* was performed Giraudoux had published nine volumes of prose writings, most of them novels, and was generally considered *précieux*. It was an epithet of no precise application, one of those adhesive descriptions which, once applied, is seldom detachable. His preciosity was manifested in a mannered style, syntactically loose and somewhat difficult, distinguished by the use of unrelated clauses, ambiguous allusions, paradox, and an extended vocabulary. It was, in short, the style of an admirer of Mallarmé, the affected prose of a Symbolist, and it was completely unsuited to the theatre. Giraudoux used it in none of his plays; but they were invariably called precious.

Giraudoux came honestly by his style. He was by birth a Limousin, the son of a provincial functionary. He was born in 1882 in Bellac, Haute Vienne, population 5,000, a little town astride the *route nationale* from Poitiers to Limoges, which differs in no way from any of the other 35,000 little towns of France. For Giraudoux it was "*la plus belle ville du monde.*"

In 1893 he was sent, along with his brother, to the lycée at Chateauroux. He studied diligently, won a scholarship to the École normale at Lakanal, and in due course was admitted to the École normale supérieure, rue d'Ulm, in Paris. There he studied for the *licence* in German under Charles Andler, with a major in the German romantic period. There followed a year of study in Munich.[12]

Germany fascinated him. He disliked the industrial Germany of his day; but the Germany of romance, its castles and its folklore, filled him with happiness. When he returned to Paris, the following year, to prepare for the *agrégation*, he took this Germany back with him. He failed the examination. That year he was offered an exchange fellowship to Harvard, and was able to spend a memorable year in Cambridge. In 1908 he was back in Paris perceptibly changed, a thin, red-haired, gray-eyed young man, short-sighted, very elegant, sporting a Cambridge hair-cut and American shoes. He had also a crimson pennant which he proudly displayed on his bedroom wall.

At twenty-seven, with no desire to pursue a teaching career, and no other prospects in view, Giraudoux took a secretarial job at *Le Matin*, and wrote some sketches for it. Meanwhile he maintained contacts with the *Mercure de France* and the *Grande Revue*, and frequented the literary cafés on the boulevard St. Michel. There he rubbed elbows with such celebrities as Jean Moréas and Guillaume Apollinaire, and there, quite by accident, he met Bernard Grasset. Grasset had some money and was eager to become a publisher. Giraudoux gave him some sketches he had written of the life of a small town as seen through the eyes of a little boy. Grasset published them under the title, *Provinciales*. Gide gave the book a pleasant review in the *Nouvelle Revue française*. In four years it sold thirty copies.

In these circumstances it occurred to Giraudoux to try for a post in the foreign service. He failed the *grand concours* which screened applicants for embassy positions but, some months later, he passed the *petit concours* at the top of the list and, in 1910, was assigned to the political and commercial bureau at the Quai d'Orsay. The following year, by reason of his connection with *Le Matin*, he was attached to the foreign press service. He served in the diplomatic corps the rest of his life.

His work at the Quai d'Orsay evidently gave him plenty of leisure in which to write. Shortly after issuing *Provinciales* Grasset published *L'École des indifférents*. It consisted of three narrative sketches—"Jacques l'égoiste," "Dom Manuel le paresseux," and "Le Faible Bernard"—set respectively in Cambridge, in Paris, and in a small town in Central France. It requires no great insight to understand that in the egotism of Jacques, Manuel's laziness, and Bernard's lack of spine the author meant to make some public display of his own characterological shortcomings. It may be wondered why in his early thirties Giraudoux found it necessary to compose a self-portrait that was less than flattering, but it is evident that in exorcising his personal devils in this manner he was fulfilling a personal need of some importance. What the three characters of *L'École des indifférents* have in common is a certain romantic detachment from life and its contingencies. In this they affect neither an Epicurean ataraxy nor the apathy of the Stoics, and least of all the analgesic isolation of Camus's *L'Étranger*. It is rather a defensive withdrawal into the world of the imagination which recalls the Schopenhauerian escape from the drive of the Will into the calm regions of the ideal. In their case it is not, however, a complete withdrawal. Jacques does not approach anything closely, for fear of seeing it fade before his eyes; and since whatever he touches turns to ashes, and every contact is a disillusionment, he finds it possible to enjoy life chiefly as a spectator. The same is true of the other two characters. Essentially diffident and sensitive people, they inhabit a world that borders the ideal without being ideal, and is real without having much reality—a kind of painless limbo.[13] It is possible that Giraudoux found an environment of this sort congenial; but he was also a man of considerable ambition, and this caused him some difficulty.

The Great War hardly interrupted Giraudoux's literary career. He joined his regiment in August 1914 as a sergeant in the infantry, took part in the invasion of Alsace, was wounded in the battle of the Marne, and, after a long furlough in Paris, was sent to the Dardanelles as a second lieutenant. Thereafter, through the able support of Berthelot, his chief at the Quai d'Orsay, he was posted first to Portugal, then, with a group of military instructors, to Harvard. By 1915 he had finished *Simon le pathétique*. It was published three years later. He followed it with three short war-novels—*Lecture pour une ombre*, *Adorable Clio*, and *Amica America*.

In January 1919 Giraudoux was demobilized as a reserve lieutenant. In spite of his wounds and some lengthy bouts of dysentery, he had thoroughly enjoyed his war, and he emerged relatively unscathed, ambitious, and also settled in life. In 1918 he had married Suzanne Boland, an elegant divorcée of his own age. She already had two children, a daughter who died young, and a young boy, Christian Pineau.

In the following years he published a series of novels in quick succession—*Elpénor*, *Suzanne et le Pacifique*, *Siegfried et le limousin*, and *Juliette au pays des hommes*. None of these was a masterpiece and none had a wide sale. His style had not changed essentially since the time of *Provinciales;* if anything it was even more mannered. Though he could write clearly and even concisely when he chose, Giraudoux still preferred the opaque style of the early Symbolists and aimed at mysterious effects as far removed as possible from the ordinary patterns of speech. In this, of course, he was following the newest vogue. In the 1920's obscurity was in fashion. It was above all necessary to distinguish oneself from the obtuse bourgeois. The *Mercure de France* and the *Nouvelle Revue française* were assiduously carrying on the Symbolist tradition in the teeth of the middle class, and the pre-war eccentricities of the age of Nerval, Jarry, Satie, and Henri Rousseau took on renewed glamor as the perspective lengthened.

Aside from his literary tastes there was nothing eccentric about Giraudoux. Both in manner and appearance he was a model of aristocratic conservatism. It was only as an artist that he felt committed to the radicalism of the previous generation. In 1930, when he had already made his mark in the theatre, he told Simone Ratel in an interview that in his youth he had been among those who wished to do for French prose what Verlaine, Rimbaud, and the Symbolists had done for French poetry: "We proposed to react, to break the molds, to open the way for invention."[14]

Some years later he wrote: "What this world, in fact, is seeking at this juncture is not so much its balance as its language. The secret of the future is a sylistic secret."[15] Expressions of this sort were hardly news in intellectual circles. It was a period of intense preoccupation with language. In the absence of God, the idea that the Word was God took on new and terrifying meaning, and there were many who spoke in tongues. The belief in the creative power of words, at first an esoteric notion peculiar to mages and mystics, was by this time firmly established, and to many it made sense that words were the building blocks of reality. In this period philology—an important by-product of German romanticism—had dominated literary studies practically to the exclusion of literature. The study of words, their etymology and phonology, involved scientific attitudes, positivistic in nature, and those who took it up felt that they were realists, and professed contempt for what was called aestheticism. But from the time of Blake and Coleridge, poets also had been fascinated by the magic of words, and after Mallarmé artists in every field were assiduous in their efforts to find symbols of power with which to open the gates of the unknown.

There was also the question of individuality. "Le style c'est l'homme même," Buffon had written. It was an idea that made sense even from a biologic standpoint, if one considered that the vital impulse differentiates its forms stylistically. From the time of the Renaissance, and doubtless even before that, artists had tried to distinguish themselves from the herd through special ways of interpreting experience. In most cases mannerism did not go much beyond a superficial eccentricity; but once it was assumed that reality is in itself a way of seeing—that is to say, a work of art—style became more than an aesthetic idiosyncrasy. "Seule vit l'âme": by 1885 the phrase had become a Symbolist commonplace—"only the soul lives." A generation later Giraudoux wrote: "Rien ne vit que le style, et rien ne survit—tout est dans le style." Pirandello did not use this language; but the idea was the underlying assumption of his doctrine of Life and Form.

Until the publication of *Bella* there was no conflict between Giraudoux's literary work and his career in the diplomatic service. The Foreign Ministry did not at all resent the presence of a man of letters at the Quai d'Orsay. On the contrary it is said that it was Claudel who first brought Giraudoux to the attention of his bureau chief, and Philippe Berthelot took every opportunity to advance the young writer's position in the ministry. But in 1922 Giraudoux made an ill-advised move. Berthelot— at that time general secretary of the Ministry of Foreign Affairs—was at loggerheads with the new Foreign Minister, Raymond Poincaré, who had formerly been president of the Republic. There was a power struggle, with the usual unpleasantness and, as a result of a family scandal, Berthelot was disgraced. Giraudoux rallied to his support. In the end the affair recommended itself to Giraudoux as material for a novel. In *Bella* Berthelot and Poincaré were recognizable in the characters of Dubardeau and Rebendart, and other colleagues in the Ministry furnished interesting models for caricature.

Bella was a mistake. The internal affairs of the Ministry were sacred, and Giraudoux's exposé, when it appeared most inopportunely in 1925, embarrassed everyone. In consequence, Giraudoux was banished from the Quai d'Orsay to an inconspicuous post as head of a commission to assess war damages in Turkey. He served in this capacity eight years, more or less isolated from the center of diplomatic activity. The story of *Bella*, however, did not end with *Bella*. It was further elaborated in *Églantine*, in *Le Mirage de Bessines*, and *La Menteuse* (1936), the final text of which appeared in 1969. Very likely Giraudoux had it in mind to develop these tales in a series of linked novels along the lines of the Rougon-Macquart of Zola. But the success of *Siegfried* on the stage turned his thoughts in quite another direction. After 1928 he thought of himself chiefly as a playwright.

In the course of an interview Giraudoux told Frédéric Lefèvre that the novel, *Siegfried et le limousin*, was written in twenty-seven days without any preconceived plan.[16] It is, in fact, a loosely woven web of anecdotes and commentaries which might as readily be called an essay as a novel. The story, told by a French narrator named Jean, concerns the fortunes of an unknown soldier found in a railway depot at Cologne in a mass of German wounded. The man was shot in the head, has nothing to identify him, and has lost his memory. A compassionate nurse, Eva von Schwanhofer, christens him Siegfried von Kleist, and undertakes his rehabilitation as a German. The unknown soldier proves to be a man of extraordinary aptitude. In six years time he becomes an influential jurist and a power in the government. Meanwhile, in France, a series of articles in the *Frankforter Zeitung,* signed S.v.K., is brought to the attention of the narrator. Their style is such that he is convinced that they must have come from the pen of the journalist Jacques Forestier, his friend, who was long ago reported missing in action.

At the Café de la Rotonde in Montparnasse, Jean happens to meet a German friend, Count von Zelten, who is passing through Paris on the way to Germany where he is preparing a leftist putsch. Through Zelten, Jean contrives to meet Siegfried and, in the hope of helping him to recover his memory, offers to give him lessons in French conversation. In Munich, also, Jean meets Zelten's divorced wife, a sculptress named Geneviève Prat, who is attracted to Siegfried.

In due course Siegfried ruins Zelten's projected revolution and, in retaliation, Zelten reveals the secret of Siegfried's French origin. Siegfried, now in an impossible position, is spirited away to Oberammergau. The sculptress Geneviève dies suddenly. Siegfried then takes the train back to France with Jean, leaving Germany, presumably, forever.

It must be admitted that, as a novel, *Siegfried et le limousin* is no great thing. But Giraudoux was aiming neither at coherence nor at verisimilitude. What he had in mind, evidently, was to establish through a fanciful tale the relation of two distinctly different ways of reconstructing an identity, and the psychological effect on the individual who, through an extraordinary accident, is made to superpose one reality on another. By education and tradition Siegfried and Forestier are totally strange to one another, just as the two nations they represent are strangers. But they are in fact one person. The problem of reconciliation is therefore not insuperable. It is a matter of spiritual adjustment. The two cultures reflected in this dual personality cannot be reconciled in a common world-view without the mediation of someone who is equally cognizant of both. As it happens, Siegfried is just such an individual. The implica-

tion is that if world peace is ever to be achieved it will be through the efforts of someone like him.

This novel is obviously autobiography in the same sense as *L'École des
indifférents* and *Simon le pathétique*. It suggests through a series of imaginary situations the inner conflicts of a mind troubled by opposing viewpoints and impulses, which on the social and national plane are seen to
correspond with world-views and national concepts that culminate periodically in violence. These correspondences naturally involve some element of allegory; but the rambling nature of the anecdote makes it unnecessary to treat the detail with the solemnity of a realistic portrayal.
The events of the narrative, and the characters involved in them, are intended to serve mainly as symbols, and have therefore no more solidity
than is required to prefigure a fantasy. The attention in this tale is concentrated on the psychic predicament of the hero, and on its reflection in
the mind of Jean, the narrator—that is to say, in the mind of Jean
Giraudoux, the author. What happens there is the essence of the story,
and that is best developed lyrically, as a kind of revery, a poem. It was
in this manner that *Siegfried et le limousin* was conceived.

In 1928 a play, however, was thought to require a more substantial
outline.

In the first version of his dramatic adaptation, entitled *Siegfried von
Kleist*, Giraudoux replaced Jean with Robineau, a genial professor of
philology. Robineau, like all good philologists of the period, had studied
at Bonn with Diez and Foerster, and was therefore in a better position
than most to explain the Germans to the French. Zelten became a romantic, an energetic frequenter of the Montparnasse cafés. In the play he
is a professed revolutionist, and Siegfried is a thorn in his flesh. He has
therefore brought Robineau and Geneviève to Germany to unmask Siegfried as the former French journalist Jacques Forestier.

In this manner Giraudoux tightened the plot by introducing a villain.
There was still lacking the indispensable love-interest. This was provided by Geneviève Prat. Her equivocal, and largely aimless, role in the
novel was normalized in the play. Here she is no longer Zelten's divorced and disconsolate wife. She is now Forestier's bereaved fiancée,
the girl he was going to marry, who has piously preserved his image in
her heart, and is therefore able to reconstruct him as the man he once
was. In this manner the normal triangular design of French domestic
drama was superposed on the novel, so that in a climactic scene French
Geneviève and German Eva are able to struggle, both as women and as

national representatives, for the soul of the ambiguous hero whom they both love.

In this form the symbolism of *Siegfried* comes even closer to allegory than it did in the novel. Zelten desires to restore to Germany the medieval romantic character which the modern republic has lost. Siegfried is trying to impose on the German state a tight and workable constitution modeled on the constitution of France. Thus, on the political plane, the spirit of romance is opposed to the classic spirit of law, clarity, common sense, and a sound fiscal structure. Ludendorff and Hindenburg support Siegfried. He has also the support of several generals, including the Prussian Fontgeloy, the military descendent of a Huguenot exile. It is difficult to understand who supports Zelten; but it is suggested that he is backed by a group of romantic radicals, cocaine addicts, and Cubists.

The uprising is soon put down but, after Zelten reveals Siegfried's true identity, the Germans cannot permit Siegfried to leave. In the garden of the palace of the Prince of Saxe-Altdorf where Siegfried has retired, masked conspirators in extravaganza style lay an ambush for the defecting leader. After the Prince has charged him with the mission of explaining Germany to the French, Siegfried takes a turn in the garden. A shot rings out. He is brought back on a litter, wounded in the head precisely where he was wounded seven years before and, miraculously, his memory is restored. At first he believes himself to be still in the trenches. Then he recognizes his beloved Geneviève and, in spite of a wound which would doubtless reduce a lesser man to silence, he tells her: "It seems to me that I recover an infinitely different memory, of an existence far anterior to that which ours has been, of the life which was erased by my life on this earth, the life I lived before becoming a human being and your friend. Memories flow to me of silences, of moveless gestures. I find all my habits once again in an infinite void. You see, Geneviève, you see?"

GENEVIÈVE: What?

SIEGFRIED: If you don't see it is because your real memory has not yet come
    back to you.—You hear?

GENEVIÈVE: Do I hear what, Jacques?

SIEGFRIED: What one hears, here below. I know now what life is, Gene-
    viève.

GENEVIÈVE: A terrible weight.

SIEGFRIED: Wrong. A breath.

GENEVIÈVE: A helmet of lead.

SIEGFRIED: A winged circle.
GENEVIÈVE: An iniquity.
SIEGFRIED: The dawn.[17]

This Wagnerian scene does not appear in the final version of the play. It was published later in *La Fin de Siegfried*. The version that Jouvet finally brought to the stage has a beginning, a middle, and no end, and it is a poor example of well-made playmaking. The narrative sequence is more or less that of the novel; apart from that, the relation to the novel is vague. Aside from indicating the danger of a political neighbor of uncertain temper, *Siegfried* has no special political orientation. Its concerns are primarily psychological and literary. It lights with the innocence of a butterfly upon some interesting irrelevancies, and leaves inexplicable gaps in the action for the spectator's imagination to bridge as it will. The subject is intensely serious; but the play is mischievous—often—as in the scene of the masked conspirators—it is deliberately and inappropriately comic. The result is puzzling. Evidently Giraudoux meant the action to make something of a Surrealist effect, reflecting the spontaneous flow of images and associations in his mind. But this lyric technique was not well suited to the exposition of a serious idea. The matter is more or less lost in the manner. After the production Giraudoux complained that the critics had concerned themselves mainly with his technique, and overlooked his message. It is easy to see why.

Siegfried is a good example of the application of Symbolist principles in a period when successful drama was still primarily realistic. In plays like *Pelléas et Mélisande*, Maeterlinck had attempted to give universality to a realistic situation by withdrawing his characters as far as possible from actuality. But Siegfried is not in any sense a fairy tale. It is set in the city of Gotha in Thuringia, in an architectural milieu which is in part medieval, in part baroque, and in part modern, and its date is precisely specified. It takes place in the week of January 12, 1921, and makes use of historical characters with impressive names—Ludendorff, Rathenau, and Hindenburg. But apart from these realistic touches everything is fanciful. The narrative depends on cinematic effects difficult to manage on a stage—a revolution, shooting in the streets, parliamentary oratory, brass bands, and parades. The principal action is an attempted coup d'état in a Graustarkian atmosphere which recalls sometimes Wagner and sometimes Offenbach. In 1928, in a theatrical environment which had not yet experienced Symbolism on this plane of reality, under Jouvet's artful direction, it created a sensation.

In the appendices to *Siegfried*, which Giraudoux continued to write after the production of the play, we are told that "the author, who has never understood dramatic architecture save as the articulate sister of musical architecture, could not forego the opportunity to write a funeral march."[18] The musical structure he had in mind was less that of a symphony than of a suite, for, in addition to his *marche funèbre*, he added two "fugues," a divertissement, and a *lamento*. These are, in fact, scenes that were cut in the stage version and that he was reluctant to relinquish. Thus, even in its final version, *Siegfried* remains unfinished and chaotic. It represents a compromise between the freedom of prose narrative and the exigencies of the stage; but in spite of all the restriction to which the novel was subjected, the play preserves the effect of revery and at least to some degree evades the control of the ordering principle. Thus what was at one time considered bad craftsmanship was by 1928 elevated to the dignity of an artistic principle. Giraudoux was not ready at this time, or in fact at any time, to define artistic probity as "a minimum of rational interference." That was Beckett's phrase. But *Siegfried*, without being an especially radical departure, indicated the direction in which the drama of the future might be expected to develop. Its success was, in a sense, prophetic.

Giraudoux's technique crystallized into traditional forms as he became more and more the dramatist of his age, so that *Siegfried* exhibits more clearly than his later plays the process of spontaneous association that attends poetic composition. The result in this case is the spontaneity of invention that even after much reworking enlivens this play and is also the source of its disorder. On the stage, happily, the chaotic impression was mitigated by the acting and the direction. *Siegfried* had a memorable cast. Pierre Renoir played Siegfried; Valentine Tessier was Geneviève; Eva was played by Lucienne Bogaert; and Jouvet took the part of Fontgeloy. The final scene, which is not only badly chopped up, but entirely ambiguous, could hardly be expected to succeed with mediocre actors. On the railway station that straddles the frontier of the two countries Siegfried tells his generals that he has decided to leave the 60 million Germans who love him in order to return to France where only his dog awaits him. In this resolve he is strengthened by Geneviève. She takes the opportunity to brief him thoroughly on his former existence as Jacques Forestier. But as he is about to board the train she stops him, just short of the gate:

GENEVIÈVE: You hear me, Jacques?
SIEGFRIED: Jacques hears you.
GENEVIÈVE: Siegfried!
SIEGFRIED: Why Siegfried?
GENEVIÈVE: Siegfried, I love you.[19]

The curtain falls on this line. Presumably as the lovers embrace on the German platform, the train chugs off to France, leaving the couple to make the best of their way back to Germany; or else the station master holds the train so that they can board it together. The author neglects to resolve the situation, and Geneviève's last minute declaration only serves to stress the dual nature of the hero. *Siegfried* does not end. For those who prefer plays with endings, Giraudoux generously provided the comic assassins of the *Fin de Siegfried*, and the Platonic aria which concludes it. But for Jouvet's audience he left the lovers on the station at the frontier.

Amphitryon 38 was staged the following year, on 8 November 1929, at the Comédie des Champs Elysées. It was written quickly and with gusto, and Jouvet staged it imaginatively. The plot was familiar, but at this time relatively fresh, and the theme provided a useful point of departure for the type of poetic divagation to which Giraudoux was professedly addicted. The allusion in the title to thirty-seven previous versions of the comedy was a pleasant exaggeration. Nobody thus far had troubled to count the Amphitryon plays. Giraudoux certainly knew three—the versions of Plautus, Molière, and Kleist. He may have known others also, but what he borrowed from tradition was negligible compared with what he brought to it.

Classic comedy was traditionally bawdy, and the Amphitryon legend, with its divine seducer and its tangle of identities, was particularly well suited for ribald treatment. But while Roman comedy was mainly concerned with low types, the seduction of Alcmena involved heroic characters whose passions were normally treated in the high style of tragedy; so that for seriously minded people this type of comedy bordered on the blasphemous. The cuckolding of Amphitryon, accordingly, was considered to have serious connotations, and like the other escapades of Zeus it was subject to allegorical interpretation.

The renewal of interest in myth as the subject matter of drama in this period was largely due to the influence of Wagner; but in the case of *Amphitryon 38* it is easier to see the influence of less serious writers. In 1929 *La Belle Hélène* (1865) was sixty-four years old; Cocteau's *Orphée* (1926) no more than two. *La Machine infernale* was yet some years off, but in *Les Mariés de la Tour Eiffel* (1924) Cocteau had offered interesting hints for the comic treatment of the Maeterlinckean Beyond. Much of the groundwork for *Amphitryon 38* had been laid down by the time Giraudoux took up the theme. It remained only to elevate an appropriate superstructure.

Amphitryon 38 is a bedroom farce. But a bedroom farce on a cosmic scale necessarily has serious overtones. It was indeed the first of the plays in which Giraudoux exhibited his life-long preoccupation with the theme of love and marriage. Marriage, as he saw it, had both metaphysical and psychological aspects, and its tensions reflected on the level of the individual the plight of humanity in general, uncomfortably situated between earth and heaven, torn between its need for security and its longing for adventure, its need for order and its craving for freedom.

In *Siegfried* Giraudoux had described the psychic situation of a tragically divided personality, torn between two loves and two loyalties. That this condition of spiritual ambivalence meant much to him as an artist is attested by the persistence with which the problem recurs in his work. In several of his later novels the theme of escape is posed in terms of a metaphoric prison-break from the finite into the uncharted world outside the gates, the infinite Beyond. In these stories the fugue takes place not, as in the case of Jacques Forestier, through an accident that results in death and rebirth, but as the result of a deliberate choice. In *Suzanne et le Pacifique*, indeed, there is a liberating accident. But Suzanne is one of Giraudoux's elect: she is predisposed for adventure. Alcmena, in *Amphitryon 38*, is not at all of her mind.

Suzanne knows only Bellac; but beyond its confines the world beckons to her with imperious gestures. She enters a newspaper contest, writes the winning maxim—the subject is boredom—and wins a trip abroad. Her reward is unexpectedly rich. Her ship is wrecked in a storm, and she spends five years on a desert island in the South Seas. There, quite by herself, she leads an idyllic existence in which her every action refutes the Puritan work-ethic. Then, having effectively reduced *Robinson Crusoe* to absurdity, she is rescued, comes home, and is overcome with emotion at the sight of the local functionary who symbolizes civilization:

"I am the Controller of Weights and Measures, Mademoiselle. Why are you crying?"[20]

The autobiographical implications of this story are open to conjecture, but it is more than likely that they exist, for there are reminiscences in it of *Dom Manuel le paresseux*, and it touches closely on themes that will recur in *Intermezzo* and in *Supplément au Voyage de Cook*. The theme of the fugue and the return is developed at length in *Juliette au pays des hommes*, in *Les Aventures de Jérôme Bardini*, and in a somewhat different way in *Combat avec l'ange*. Obviously this theme meant much to the author. But unlike Mattia Pascal in Pirandello's novel, those who run away from home in these stories are not driven off by an intolerable domestic situation. They are all, it is emphasized, quite comfortably installed and might be happy if they did not suffer from claustrophobia. As it is, they are displaced by an irresistible urge to get away, an agonizing malaise which makes it impossible to continue as they are, an obsessive Wanderlust. Logically these flights are inexplicable. One is forced, in order to understand them, to go some distance beyond logic. In Giraudoux's view, their victims are possessed. They are the chosen, the elect.

This notion is rather vaguely advanced in *Suzanne et le Pacifique*. It is developed more forcefully in the later stories and in *Choix des élues* (1939), the very last of Giraudoux's novels, it is developed fully. It is the story of an errant wife. Edmée is the wife of a French mining engineer in New York. She is happily married and has two small children, but she suffers periodically from inexplicable attacks of anxiety, so great that they amount to pain—"What one might feel after being released from the embrace of a demon, that was it, the opposite of human voluptuousness." She has accompanying feelings of guilt, as if in the course of these attacks she had betrayed her husband. After some time she finds her situation unbearable, abandons her husband and her little son Jacques, and runs off with her daughter Claudie to take up a new life on the West Coast. After twelve years, and a number of unfruitful adventures with men, she is summoned home by her son, who is now grown up and engaged to be married. Her husband, a kindly and unimaginative man, takes her back without question, and Edmée settles down once again in comfortable domesticity. But she is convinced that in the interval she has been possessed by a spirit.

The power which separated her from her husband and her home was, she feels, a spiritual lover—perhaps it was God—who segregated her for his use. She has been neither a saint nor a nun, simply one of the chosen, one of the elect:

> God did not want her for a legitimate spouse, he wanted her for a friend. He wished to feel the secret joys of an unconsecrated union with mankind. She was set to one side, in the background, but she was the friend. . . . It was understandable that God had need of a presence that was not altered by his presence. . . . This peace she had at last attained, this freedom in herself, it was the nameless divinity. That was what Jacques had seen in his mother, a kept woman. The lover was never there . . . the lover was always there. . . .[21]

Her son's intervention is coupled in Edmée's mind with an engraving she had seen in her grandfather's house, in which a Russian Countess, booted, whip in hand, bursts into the room of the inn where her daughter is having tea with the music master with whom she is eloping, the Abalstitiel, according to the caption. The Russian word *Obolstetiel*, in fact, means Seducer. Edmée understands that for twelve years she has been under the spell of the Seducer: she has been his mistress. Now that her son has come, like the Countess with the whip, and put the Abalstitiel in his place, she is free to return to her husband. The Abalstitiel has left her, and with him has gone the sense of calm and grace and the secret voluptuousness for which she sacrificed her home and her family. She feels that she has been deceived. In the absence of the Abalstitiel the world has gone on proliferating: "One could really see now what the universe amounts to, an imposition and a lie. But that the eternal should be fickle, that is incomprehensible!"

Thus Edmée gives herself, out of spite, to the professor of gymnastics who is exercising himself on the beach—"From above, God saw all that, horribly vexed." Then she goes back to her home in New York, and is next seen at a family dinner celebrating her granddaughter's christening. The sacramental turkey is carved; the family group is composed once again. Edmée is untroubled. The Abalstitiel, she notes, is still hovering in the vicinity; but it is no longer Edmée that interests him. He has his eye now, unmistakably, on her daughter.[22]

It would seem that Giraudoux himself had come more than once under the influence of the Seducer; at any rate, this enterprising power haunts his works. He does what he can to seduce Isabelle in *Intermezzo;* he gives Ritter Hans a bad time in *Ondine.* Possibly he is the Angel in *Sodome et Gomorrhe,* and the indefatigable Count Marcellus in *Pour Lu-*

crèce. In *Amphitryon 38* the Abalstitiel is no less a being than Jupiter, and his success with Alcmena poses a question.

Giraudoux's first play has precise scene descriptions and stage directions. There is little of this in *Amphitryon 38*. With few exceptions the mise en scène is left to the imagination. The curtain rises on "A terrace near a palace." The palace is in Thebes. It is night. The gods Jupiter and Mercury are hiding in the shrubbery watching the shadows cast by Amphitryon and Alcmena on the curtains of their bedroom window. Jupiter has assumed human shape for this occasion. Consequently he cannot see through stone walls. But Mercury is not inconvenienced in this respect. He can see clearly. He describes what he sees very graphically, and his description affords a complete preview of the marital delights which are in store, presumably, for Jupiter in his turn.

The opening scene is comic, learned, erotic, and excessively arch. Taken together, this string of adjectives may well serve to characterize Giraudoux's style in this play. The characterization is marvellously light and deft. Jupiter is properly majestic; but for the moment he is at a loss, for Alcmena's chastity is celebrated throughout the universe. Mercury however knows what is to be done. He advises his master to whip up a little war with the neighbors in order to get Amphitryon out of the way, and then to take on his guise and thereby his wife. The scene that follows is, from a technical viewpoint, outrageous. Amphitryon's servant Sosia is to read a proclamation to the sleeping city. He orders the City Trumpeter to sound a call. The Trumpeter insists that he must first know the tenor of the proclamation. He can blow, we are told, but a single note on his instrument, but among one-note trumpeters he is accounted preeminent. The note he blows will be the concluding note of an entire symphony, inaudible but perfectly imagined; consequently it must be properly inspired. Sosia tells him he is going to proclaim peace. The trumpet sounds. The proclamation follows, and it is long. It is scarcely ended when a huge warrior appears. He orders the Trumpeter to sound another note. He is about to proclaim war.

The scene of the Trumpeter is entirely characteristic of Giraudoux's dramatic style. It is a decorative interlude, barely functional. In the economy of the play, it cannot be justified. But one would not willingly dispense with it. It gives the action the lyrical quality of a poem. Similar things might be said of Giraudoux's dialogue. His speeches are ample, musical, and artfully composed with clausulae and parallelisms that recall the copious style of the Roman orator. Nobody had ventured to write like this for the modern theatre, not even Hugo, and to those who were accustomed to the calculated tirades of Brieux and Henry Bernstein, Giraudoux's style seemed extravagantly affected.

There were those, however, who liked it very much. "I consider everything I have written," Giraudoux told an interviewer, "a sort of poetic divagation."[23] The phrase recalls the title—*Divagations*—of Mallarmé's collection of poems and essays of 1897; but, unlike Mallarmé, Giraudoux was a professional dramatist, and in his later plays the lyrical element is normally subordinated to the progression of the action. *Amphitryon 38*, however, is not essentially dramatic. It is a sequence of tableaux hung on a narrative armature which hardly amounts to a plot, and it depends more on the wit of the presentation than on the ordering of events which, from the time of Aristotle, has been said to be the soul of a dramatic composition.

The scene that follows the scene of the Trumpeter is essentially operatic, a formal duet, but it is more than merely decorative. It serves to characterize the ideal couple whose intimacy Jupiter proposes presently to invade. Alcmena is blonde and beautiful and delicately plump—in Jupiter's phrase, she is *grasse à point*—and, like Edmée, she is one of the elect, singled out by the divine spirit to serve mysterious purposes beyond her ken. But Alcmena is indomitable in her chastity, and absolutely obdurate in her resistance to any intrusion, however divine, on the sanctity of her marriage. There is no room in her life for a lover: "I want no slave and I want no master. Because it is bad manners to deceive a husband even with himself. Because I like the windows open and the linen fresh."

Such obduracy, of course, is dangerous. Her chastity is hubristic. It has attracted the attention of the higher powers and is certain to evoke nemesis. It is not only because she is beautiful that Jupiter has chosen her to be the mother of his immortal son, but because she poses a problem. She is difficult, therefore she is desirable.

Perhaps it is also because she is a coquette, and consequently amusing. When Amphitryon steals back from the camp to spend the night with her, she keeps him waiting interminably at the door while she puts him through an examination. When it is over, she informs him that the door was not locked, he had only to push it open. But she is ill-advised to let him in. It is not Amphitryon who pushes it open. It is Jupiter.

In the morning Jupiter awakens to the fact that he is really in love with this woman who thinks he is her husband, and he feels that he would like to be loved in return, for himself. It is in vain, however, that he tempts Alcmena with hints of his divinity. She has no interest in metaphysics; the secrets of the universe, the reasons of things, the life of the other planets, none of this in the least arouses her curiosity. She is a good bourgeoise: the neighbors do not interest her. Her horizons are cozy. She has no desire to extend them. And when it is suggested that she might enjoy immortality, she puts away the idea scornfully. Death has no terrors for her: "When for sixty years one has been annoyed by badly dyed cloth and badly cooked meals, to be given death at last, silent and constant death, that is a recompense out of all proportion. . . . Why do you look at me with this sudden air of respect?"

JUPITER: It is because you are the first truly human being I have ever met.
ALCMENA: It is my specialty among mankind.[24]

It is a singular conversation, obviously, for a husband and wife in the morning, after an extensive night of love. Alcmena apparently sees no incongruity. She is not imaginative. She cannot imagine, and has no desire to imagine, that she has spent a night with God. But they have not reckoned with Mercury. Now that Hercules has been duly engendered, Mercury feels he can safely proclaim to the world the proximate visit of Jupiter. The Thebans have already got wind of the honor that is to be done them, and are busy organizing processions of welcome. Alcmena is, accordingly, officially apprised that the god will visit her that very evening so that she may bear the future savior of mankind. She answers that she would rather die.

At this point a new element is introduced into the story. Leda providentially turns up in Thebes. As a former recipient of Jupiter's favors, she does not at all mind serving as a substitute for the chaste Alcmena. Accordingly, when Amphitryon appears according to schedule, Alcmena is certain it is Jupiter. She greets him tenderly and spirits him off into the darkened room where she is to join him, and where Leda in fact awaits him. Alcmena has a moment of triumph. No power in the universe, she boasts, can prevail against the will of a constant wife. Echo, her faithful guide, does not on this occasion reflect her sentiments.

When the third act opens, Leda is gone, the war is over, and on the celestial public-address system angelic voices are describing the future exploits of Hercules, whose conception is scheduled to take place that evening. Jupiter now arrives in his godlike semblance. He woos with skill, but Alcmena defends her chastity with the grace of an accomplished duellist. But when she offers herself to the god as a friend instead of as a lover Jupiter accepts with such alacrity that she becomes suspicious; and when he takes her in his arms in token of their friendship she feels that she has been there before in other circumstances. The realization troubles her deeply, and she begs the god to grant her oblivion, for she is not, she says, a woman who can bear a troubled day, not even one, in her life. Jupiter grants her prayer:

JUPITER: Then forget everything, except this kiss. (*He kisses her.*)

ALCMENA: (*Coming to herself*) What kiss?

JUPITER: Oh, as for the kiss, spare me the fairy tale. I took care to place the kiss after the oblivion.[25]

In spite of the humor of the situation and the delightfully erotic atmosphere in which it develops, *Amphitryon 38* may be taken seriously. The parallel between the holy nuptials of the pagan god and those of the God of the New Testament is made with great delicacy, but it can hardly be missed. The ceremonies attendant on the relatively immaculate conception of the Greek messiah are thoroughly looked into, and when Alcmena ventures to give Jupiter some practical hints on how a friendly god would run the cosmic establishment it is to be hoped, evidently, that her advice may be borne in mind by future divinities.

Amphitryon 38 approaches, perhaps for the first time in the contemporary theatre, the special sort of Gallic wit that one associates with La Fontaine. Its humor is not the humor of Molière; still less does it resemble the desperate clowning of Labiche or Feydeau. Molière's laughter touches the heart. It is the distillation of the tears of humanity, the comic spirit at the core of tragedy. The wit of *Candide* involves a less humane approach to the human problem. It has too much of the intellect in it to provoke laughter, though one cannot restrain a smile. Giraudoux's wit is warmer and probes more deeply. Like Voltaire, Giraudoux was an accomplished rhetorician. He spoke with the tongues of men and of angels; but he had charity. And, unlike Voltaire, Giraudoux was a Symbolist, and therefore had intimate dealings with the infinite. Consequently his sense of the comic was at once Olympian and earthy, and while his wit is sharp, his humor is warm. "Thank Jupiter, darling," Alcmena tells her husband at the end of the play. "He insists on restoring me to you, intact, with his own hands." "Only the gods observe such courtesies," says Amphitryon. The scene continues a moment longer:

ALCMENA: He wished only to try us. He asks only that we have a son.
AMPHITRYON: In nine months time we shall have one, my lord. I swear it.
ALCMENA: And we shall promise to call him Hercules, since you like the
    name so much. He will be a sweet and good little boy.
JUPITER: Yes. I can see him from here.[26]

Amphitryon 38 had, like Siegfried, the advantage of perfect casting: Valentine Tessier played Alcmena; Pierre Renoir was Jupiter; Jouvet played
Mercury; and Lucienne Bogaert was Leda. The critics, who had overex-
tended their enthusiasm for Siegfried, had reservations; nevertheless the
play was a success. The portrait of Alcmena was memorable. In Siegfried
the characters are in bas-relief. It is the dialectic mainly that detaches itself. But Amphitryon 38 gave Giraudoux an opportunity to do a subtle
and striking portrait. Alcmena is the most womanly of his heroines, the
most attractive and the most complex.

Compared with Alcmena, Leda is merely chic, a beautiful mondaine.
Alcmena clings tenaciously to an ideal of purity which is profoundly sincere, but not so extensive as to exclude some trace of feminine guile. She
is willing for all the world to believe that she has been Jupiter's mistress,
since that is historically necessary, but she is not willing to believe it herself, even though she knows it to be true, and even enjoys the recollection. Her pretense, nevertheless, is no ordinary hypocrisy. It is the quintessence of pretense, a distillation of hypocrisy which is chemically pure,
and may rightly be called precious. Her marriage is the ideal bourgeois
marriage; consequently her deceit is elevated to the plane of the ideal.
Her seduction is an act of God against which there is no defence, and
which therefore need not be taken seriously. But the implication is that
even in the pure soul of an Alcmena there is a corner where the Abalstitiel may find occasionally a night's lodging.

Judith opened at the Théâtre Pigalle on 4 November 1931.

In 1928 Giraudoux was promoted to the rank of Conseiller d'Ambas-
sade, but it was clear that he had been shelved, and perhaps for good.
His career was certainly at a standstill; on the other hand, in his office on
the rue Malakoff he had plenty of time to write. Églantine came out in
1927; Aventures de Jérôme Bardini in 1930; Combat avec l'ange in 1931. In
these years nausea was already in fashion, and it was considered naive to
evince anything but disgust with the world. But it is also true that in this
period of his life Giraudoux had reason to be despondent and that perhaps he really shared Jérôme Bardini's disgust with the thought of existence. In any case, Judith is not a happy play.

The year before *Judith* opened, Jouvet had been offered the post of artistic director at the newly built Théâtre Pigalle. He had refused it; but it was agreed that he would act as resident director for one season. He opened his season (1930–31) with Jules Romains's *Donogoo-Tonka*. It had a very long run. His next play was *Judith*. It was hurriedly put together in an unfamiliar theatre, with an unfamiliar cast, and it fared badly.

Judith is the only play of Giraudoux that is subtitled a tragedy. It might as well have been called a comedy, for essentially it belongs to the genre of the tragic-absurd; but evidently it was not meant to excite loud laughter. Like *Amphitryon 38* it deals with legendary material that had already been variously exploited. It is unlikely, however, that Giraudoux researched his topic extensively. The day after the première he told an interviewer: "I write a play as ingenuously as I write a novel, with ignorance constantly renewed." This was witty: everything indicates that he had studied Hebbel's *Judith* with some care before he ventured on his own version.

In *Judith*, Giraudoux rang a change on the theme of *Amphitryon 38*. The pattern is essentially the same. Both plays involve a seduction, and in both the heroine has a willing surrogate. In each case the heroine touches the infinite only to return voluntarily to earth. And in both cases God uses his chosen vessel somewhat shabbily. The technique of the Abalstitiel varies considerably in these plays, but Alcmena comes off better than Judith.

The legendary Judith was a young widow of Bethulia. Holofernes was a general commanding a punitive expedition sent by the Assyrian Nebuchadnezzar into Syria with orders to subjugate the territory. Holofernes invested Bethulia, cut off its water supply, and, after forty days, reduced the population to despair. Judith visited him in his camp, gained his confidence, and at the first opportunity cut off his head. The Hebrews then attacked the camp and raised the siege. Judith was canonized. The story is apocryphal.

Giraudoux's Judith is a virgin, a celebrity, rich, proud, modish, and hard—the scriptural counterpart of the modern society girl. The city is starving, but her uncle is a banker. She is not hungry. It has been prophesied that the city will be saved only if the purest and loveliest thing in it is sacrificed to Holofernes. For the Hebrews this describes Judith. But while her beauty is beyond question, her purity is no more than formal. If she is pure, she says, it is because "I have not loved any of the young men around me, because I loved them all and could not choose among them." In the eyes of God, and the chief rabbi Joachim, this satisfies the requirements. She is chosen for the sacrifice, and she accepts.

Meanwhile Jean, who loves her, has arranged for the prostitute Suzanne to go to Holofernes in Judith's place. Suzanne is a perfect replica of Judith. She has made a career of imitating her, and is in great demand among the young men whose desires Judith has systematically aroused and frustrated. Judith will have none of the planned deceit. She sets forth in person, suitably adorned, to save the city.

The procuress Sarah, meanwhile, has busied herself about the enemy camp, so that when Judith enters the tent of Holofernes, she encounters, not Holofernes but the homosexual Egon. He is impersonating Holofernes for her benefit, and he treats her brutally. She draws her dagger to defend herself. Egon, in a rage, orders the negro slave Yami to rape her. The slave refuses and is cut down on the spot. Then Egon himself seizes Judith. She screams for help. Holofernes appears.

Holofernes is magnificent. Judith's head is turned, and that night she gives herself to him, body and soul. In the morning, when she awakens, she kills him in his sleep. Suzanne and Jean are waiting outside the tent in the company of a drunken guard. The news of Holofernes' death disrupts the camp; Jean leads in his troops; and, at this point, the rabbis Paul and Joachim come to bear Judith off to the city in triumph. But Judith demurs. She did not kill Holofernes, she tells them, out of hatred, nor had she any thought of saving the Jews. She killed him because she loved him.

The rabbis are thunderstruck. And now—while the others are suddenly frozen in a trance—the drunken guard reveals himself to Judith as an angel of God. In speaking to her, he says, he is risking rank and seniority in the celestial service, nevertheless he confesses that Judith's every step was guarded by angels, and that in spite of her night's wantonness her virginity has been miraculously preserved. Her deed, he tells her, was predestined. She had no choice in the matter. It was her function merely to go through the necessary gestures in order to realize what already existed in the mind of God. After this revelation there is nothing for Judith to do but to submit to the rabbi's terms, which are cruel. She accepts the official version of the event, accepts sainthood and lifelong sequestration, and at the age of twenty becomes a national monument.

Like the comedy of Alcmena, the tragedy of Judith centers on a deception. In both cases the gods deal in Machiavellian fashion with their elect. In this sort of trickery, of course, the gods have no lack of classic precedent. All the tragic heroes of antiquity were in one way or another betrayed. But while in *Amphitryon 38*, Jupiter goes quite directly about his business with Alcmena, it must be admitted that Jehovah takes a somewhat roundabout way to dispose of Holofernes. Angels lead Judith to the tent of her victim; but once she is there she is left to fend for herself, and is subjected to brutal humiliation. Thus it is because she feels that God has betrayed her that she gives herself wholeheartedly to Holofernes, and is consequently able to kill him while he is completely off guard. It is a subtle bit of trickery on God's part, almost too subtle for comfort—evidently God knows what he is about much better than Judith. She thought she was following her impulses in spite of God; but God was with her when she least felt his presence. In killing Holofernes she had no thought of serving God. Nevertheless she has served him. She had no idea of humbling the Assyrians. But they are humbled. God has had his way in everything. As for Judith, the facts matter, the motives do not; and she is, in any case, expendable. Her case is perhaps tragic, but it involves some element of the absurd.

The implications of this ambiguous situation are more or less clear. Between God's will and the will of Judith there is no apparent accord; but there is an effective analogy. She has no idea that in killing Holofernes she is acting under divine direction. For her the sacrifice of Holofernes is a consecration of his humanity, an act of love that her own death will further sanctify. Her rationalization for his murder is indeed precious to the point of idiocy, but it has authoritative precedent. It is the reasoning that brings about the death of the lovers in Villiers's *Axël*. In their night together Holofernes and Judith have known the acme of human bliss; they have touched the ideal. Life can offer nothing more. She cannot permit time to tarnish this moment for Holofernes, therefore she kills him. It is an act of tenderness. The idea runs through her head as she awakens with her lover lying next to her, breathing gently, and not yet awake to the exigencies of the day:

> What a terrible thing! Everything was already in the past; it was all yesterday. A whole future full of doubt and jealousy was getting ready to assault a marvellous memory. It was going to be necessary to get up, to resume life upright after this eternity of lying down. In me, already enveloped in my eternal death, he inspired a boundless pity, so ill protected, by his fleeting death, from the threats of the coming day![27]

Thus the slaying of Holofernes is the ultimate caress. From the idealistic viewpoint it makes perfect sense, no doubt, but for the chief rabbi

Joachim it is so much dangerous rubbish. For his purposes it is necessary that the story of Judith be assimilated to the sacred history of the Jews. It must be molded into an acceptable cliché. History, after all, is the art of organizing human behavior in convenient patterns. That is not God's affair. It is the function of rabbis. To the killing of Holofernes, accordingly, the rabbi Joachim gives a form appropriate to his calling. In this form it will stand forever as an act of heroism, a bit shady perhaps, but nevertheless dedicated to the greater glory of God and his chosen people. However it may seem in heaven, this is how it must be on earth.

Judith is not a pleasant play. Its philosophy is relativistic, and it does not incline one to piety. Contemplated in the aspect of eternity, reality has a different texture than is revealed to the finite eye, and truth is, as the angel suggests, a matter of lighting. What is true for Judith cannot be true for Joachim; and God's truth is beyond mortal ken. As for mankind in general, the angelic press service appears to operate very much in the manner of the *Services d'information* of the Foreign Office. It molds reality from day to day in accordance with official policy, and humanity believes what it is told to believe. And if it does not, so much the worse for it.

The history of the world, from the standpoint of *Judith*, is the enactment of the divine comedy; and all that is necessary for humanity is for each to play the part that is assigned. It is not exactly Pirandello's idea, but it is not altogether removed from it, and the result is to give reality the provisional quality of a theatrical production. In the case of Judith her personal feelings in the course of her performance are of interest mainly to Judith. She is called upon to play the part of Judith in the legend of Judith. She plays her part, not well, but well enough for an amateur, and what existed *in posse* in the mind of the Creator takes place through her in the mind of man, that is to say *in actu*. For the rest, she is transformed in the end into an idea, and ceases thereafter to have any independent existence. Judith is not entirely unaware of what is going on. After her scene with Egon, she tells Suzanne:

> I know him better than you, God. God concerns himself with the appearance and the whole, not with the detail. God requires that our work wear the mantle of sacrifice, but he leaves us free, under those ample folds, to follow our own inclinations, and even the basest. Since he has used up my devotion and my hatred with these puppets before bringing me to the real Holofernes, it is because he needs my gesture

and not my help. Any laundress would have discovered Holofernes
disguised among his servants. Not I, the saint! God wishes to ruin me!
I will ruin myself![28]

But Judith is not permitted to ruin herself. The whole universe conspires to transform her into a symbol. Thus she plays her part as best
she can amid a throng of invisible actors, whose presence she cannot suspect, on the stage of an eternity she cannot imagine. Thus diminished,
her part seems minuscule. For a moment on God's stage she is in the
spotlight. In a moment the spotlight will shift elsewhere. Under these
conditions it would be extravagant to suppose that God would take the
trouble to spare her feelings.

Holofernes, on the other hand, has a certain magnitude, and Giraudoux treats him with respect. He is, he boasts, "God's worst enemy," a
free man, for in a world where all is determined, a free man is an embarrassment. Therefore Giraudoux makes Holofernes singularly sympathetic. The ground on which his tent is pitched, he says, is from the
human viewpoint, holy ground:

> It is one of the rare human corners that is truly free. The gods infest
> our poor universe, Judith. From Greece to the Indies, from north to
> south, they swarm everywhere, each one with his special vices, his
> odors. . . . But there are still some spots that are forbidden to them. I
> alone know how to find them. They lie on the plain or the mountain
> like traces of the celestial paradise. The insects that inhabit them are
> free of the original sin of insects. On such spots I pitch my tent. By
> chance, just opposite the city of the Jewish god, I found this one. . . .
> I offer you for one night this villa on a pure, wind-swept ocean.[29]

Holofernes is clearly guilty of hubris. He is, he says, what only the
king of kings may permit himself to be in this age of gods—"a man of the
world. The first, if you like." His humanity, indeed, is more magnificent
than divinity; but he has mistaken his ground. His tent is full of angels.
God has laid a trap for him. Judith is the bait:

JUDITH: There is no strength save in God.
HOLOFERNES: Exactly. God delegates himself. He delegates himself to the
    satyrs, the novelists, the commanders in chief. I have already substi-
    tuted for God several times in this office.[30]

To Judith also he seems godlike; but not to God. He might, it is true,
seem more godlike if he were less garrulous. But, unlike God, he has a

passion for words. He is perhaps excusable, for his part in the action is secondary. He is there only to be killed. The great part is Judith's.

In the light of God's cosmic drama her role is, indeed, minor; but the play concerns the tragedy of a minor character. The characterization is intricate. Judith is completely equivocal. She is both pure and passionate, sincere and dishonest. She is the hardest and least sympathetic of Giraudoux's heroines. Suzanne, by contrast, is a soft, compassionate, and lovable girl. Judith sees herself reflected mercilessly in this prostitute who is her double and her rival, and she both loves her and hates her. The theory of correspondences encouraged a mystical belief in doppelgänger. The idea that the individual is duplicated—cloned—so that carbon copies of the same soul exist simultaneously on several planes of being was a natural consequence of the theory that the levels of creation precisely reflect one another in the spiritual hierarchy of the universe. Péladan made much use of doubles in his writings. Strindberg was convinced that the individual expiated in his waking life the wrongs committed by his double in the world of dreams. There is no reason to believe that Giraudoux took these fancies seriously, but there is a mysterious use of doubles in his plays. Sometimes these serve to objectify an ambiguity of character as in the case of Siegfried-Forestier. The doubling of Jupiter and Amphitryon was, of course, traditional. The doubling of the executioner in *Intermezzo* is puzzling—it serves only to emphasize the general spookiness of the situation. But the relation of Judith and Suzanne makes a case for womanhood, the first of several in the plays of Giraudoux.

Suzanne belongs to everyone; Judith to no one. Together they make a whole woman. But the two are not together. They are eternally opposed, and their lack of accord is a sign of the spiritual malaise of womankind in the world of men. In the presence of Holofernes Suzanne seeks at all costs to preserve the purity of Judith. Judith insists on playing the whore. In the case of Siegfried and Forestier there is some hope that the two contrary spirits will somehow be reconciled. But Suzanne and Judith cannot be reconciled. They can only coexist. Suzanne is the infinitely receptive female. Judith gives herself aggressively. She is Giraudoux's version of the *femme fatale* of the romantics. In Carmen the two aspects of femininity are merged. It is her mutability that is dangerous. But Judith is constant to an ideal that precludes human love and, in the affair of Holofernes she recalls the affair of Salomé, of Hérodiade, the love that kills.

The portrait of Judith in this play is fascinating, but it is both complex and confusing, and it presents an actress with an almost impossible task of interpretation. In the original production the part was not played by a member of Jouvet's company at the Comédie des Champs Elysées. It had been intended originally for Elizabeth Bergner; but it was Rachel Berendt who played it. The rest of the cast was almost entirely Jewish, an obvious piece of folly. The rehearsals lasted only a month. The audience did not like the play, and after a run of six weeks it was withdrawn. A dozen years later Jouvet tried it again during his South American tour. It fared no better. In 1961 Barrault revived it at the Théâtre de France. It failed.

Intermezzo opened on 27 February 1933 at the Comédie des Champs Elysées with Valentine Tessier in the role of Isabelle and Jouvet as the Supervisor of Weights and Measures. Félix Oudart played the Inspector. Pierre Renoir was the Ghost. The entrances were underscored in the manner of the old melodrama with harpsichord music written by Francis Poulenc. It was staged with loving care, and was a success.

Some years after the première Giraudoux told an interviewer that *Intermezzo* was suggested by a sixteenth-century painting depicting a troupe of *comici dell'arte*.[31] Save for the traditional name of Isabelle, there is not much in *Intermezzo* that recalls the scenario of a *commedia dell'arte;* but there are several scenes which might by some stretch of the imagination be called *lazzi*—the scene of the Mangebois sisters, the examination of the little girls, the astronomy lesson, the exorcism perhaps. These are interpolated episodes which justify themselves principally as "numbers," and they are delightful; but they are divertissements not strictly germane to the plot. They are, of course, in no sense professional improvisations. They are independent comic routines strung together on the narrative thread in a manner far removed from the strict economy of well-made plays. They are intermezzi. The title of the play bears out this idea. It refers to the interlude in the life of a woman, the passage from girlhood to womanhood, a period of special interest to the author.

Intermezzo is a ghost story. It reflects the intense interest in spiritism and the occult that characterized the Symbolist movement of the 1880's, and was still influential in the first decades of the twentieth century. Giraudoux's works are full of supernatural manifestations. It is true that he treats the spirits with less than complete solemnity. Here, as elsewhere, he forbears to commit himself: he was the least *engagé* of the writers of his time. Nevertheless his world is populated with angels, spooks, dryads, and nymphs, and the nature he show us is sentient and vibrant with life.

Giraudoux's habitual posture as a writer, his *persona*, is invariably comic. It wears the sceptical smile and raised eyebrow of the learned sophisticate, the look that one associates with Jouvet or Pirandello. Like the monocle he affected in his youth, this expression was perhaps *de rigueur* in diplomatic circles, but all his life he cherished the wistful simplicity of a young boy who observes from his window the movement of life in the public square of a little town. It is probable that Giraudoux did not really believe in ghosts. But his characters do.

Most of his characters, that is to say, have a stake in the supernatural, but certainly not all. A great deal of Giraudoux's work centers on the conflict of materialistic and idealistic currents in contemporary society; and in this it echoes the conflict of thought of the previous generation more clearly than the literary concerns of the period *d'entre deux guerres*. In *Intermezzo* the Droguiste is a mystic and a mage. The Inspector is a stout Positivist. Isabelle is one of Giraudoux's *élues*, and most accessible to spiritual influence. The little girls see spirits because they are at the age when little girls see spirits: they are the natural *voyants* of their generation. The others are more or less neutral observers. They see ghosts when there are ghosts, but they do not seek them out in shadowy corners.

In addition to developing the question of the supernatural, *Intermezzo* touches closely upon the *querelle des femmes*, the age-long controversy as to the merits of the feminine half of the western world. By this time this was becoming an important political issue outside of France, but within its borders it could still be treated without seriousness. Dramatists from Ibsen to Sudermann had done much to keep the issue active in the theatre, and it was important to Giraudoux. In *Intermezzo* women are expressly associated with the world of the spirit. The Inspector is not only a materialist, but a staunch anti-feminist. The Supervisor of Weights and Measures is the local champion of women. He is also, in a curious fashion, a realist who transcends somehow into the world of the ideal.

The triangular plot of *Intermezzo* recapitulates the design of *Amphitryon 38*. The heroine, Isabelle, is required to choose, like Alcmena, between two loves, an earthly and a heavenly love. In this case, the heavenly lover is not a god. He is not even a spirit. He becomes a spirit only toward the end of the play. Isabelle is not a queen, like Alcmena. She is a young schoolteacher. The Supervisor of Weights and Measures is no

Amphitryon. Nevertheless he serves very well to exemplify the solid Philistine virtues of a good middle-class husband, and also to display the modest fancy which constitutes the poetry of everyday life. The Supervisor is totally excluded from the world of the elect, the transcendental sphere. Marriage is the chief bulwark of humanity against the encroachments of the spirit.

Intermezzo takes place in a small town in Limousin. The first act is set in a field near a lake. The second, a fortnight later, is set in the woods bordering the lake. The last act takes place in Isabelle's apartment in a house overlooking the public square.

The town is enchanted. In this community, for some time, chance has been given a semblance of order, and life has ceased to be absurd. The situation is uncanny, and a commission has been appointed to look into the matter. It consists of the Mayor, the Druggist, and the Supervisor of Weights and Measures. An Inspector has been dispatched from the Departmental Prefecture to take charge of the investigation.

It is soon discovered that the untoward events are in some way associated with Isabelle, the substitute in charge of the class of little girls at the local school. A ghost is rumored to be haunting the vicinity of the woods around the lake. A diary has been found in which Isabelle notes her intention of enlisting the aid of this ghost in her subversive activities. Since the living, as she believes, are incapable of improving the lot of humanity, she proposes to invoke the aid of the dead. She needs therefore to open communications with the other world. The appearance of the ghost is therefore most opportune for her purposes.

The Ghost, when at last she meets him, turns out to be a handsome young man in black who is in dire need of sustenance. He is entirely amenable to her ideas and, a fortnight later, their conspiracy is well under way. Meanwhile the Inspector has ascertained that the Ghost is really a young man who is sought by the police for a crime of passion. The Inspector is authorized to normalize the situation by liquidating the young man. To this end he has recruited the services of the retired executioner.

The Supervisor is in love with Isabelle. He warns her of the impending ambush. But Isabelle laughs at the idea of executing a ghost. She keeps her rendezvous. The young man is shot. The fraud is discovered. But the moment the pretended ghost is killed his ghost arises. And this time Isabelle makes an assignation with a genuine representative of the other world.

Threatened now with a serious spiritual invasion, the Inspector and the Mayor, with the aid of a choir of little girls, goes through a form of exorcism intended to prevent the intrusion of the spirit who is coming to meet Isabelle in her apartment. The ritual is interesting, but evidently ineffective, for at the appointed hour the Ghost appears. The Supervisor, however, has been beforehand with him. He has come, in his most formal attire, to solicit Isabelle's hand in marriage, and, in support of his proposal, he describes for her the life she may expect to lead as the wife of a civil servant. It is a life full of the suspense, the adventure and the many surprises which attend the snail-like progress of a French *fonctionnaire* from post to post until his career ends in Paris and retirement with pension. She is fascinated by the prospect:

ISABELLE: What a beautiful voyage your life is! One can see its wake in your eyes!

THE SUPERVISOR: In my eyes? That doesn't surprise me. People always speak of the eyes of naval officers, Miss Isabelle. It is because when the taxpayer pays his dues he does not look into the eyes of the collector. Because the motorist, when he declares his baggage, does not look deep into the pupils of the customs agent. It is because the litigant never thinks of taking the head of the presiding judge in his hands in order to turn it gently and tenderly toward himself in the light. For then they would see the reflection and the foam of an ocean deeper than all the others, the sea of life.

ISABELLE: It is true. I see it in yours.

THE SUPERVISOR: And with what does it inspire you?

ISABELLE: With confidence.

THE SUPERVISOR: In that case, do not hesitate.[32]

It is at this moment that the Ghost appears. There is an auction scene, similar to the one in Shaw's *Candida*. Each of the rivals offers her what he has. The Ghost has all eternity to offer; but in the end it is the living man who wins. As between death and transfiguration and life in the civil service, Isabelle chooses life. But the conflict has been too much for her. She faints, and her spirit leaves her. The Druggist comes to the rescue. He organizes a symphony of the sounds of life to entice her soul back to her body. Her spirit cannot resist the thought of a dress lined with red satin. She revives; and at once the town relapses into its normal disorder. Chaos is reestablished. The interlude is over.

Intermezzo marks a high point in Giraudoux's career as a dramatist, perhaps the highest. It was not his most successful play. But it is one of his masterpieces. From the standpoint of construction both *Siegfried* and *Judith* are open to criticism, and one may find fault, of one wishes, with *Amphitryon 38*. *Intermezzo* is beautifully articulated. The main plot concerns the conflict of Isabelle and the government Inspector. The sub-plot develops the rivalry of the Supervisor and the Ghost. The resolution of the sub-plot results in the solution of the primary conflict. The pattern is classic.

Classic also are the discovery and the reversal which precipitate the denouement. At the end of the second act, when the Ghost is unmasked as an impostor, all seems lost for Isabelle. But the death of the man releases his spirit, and for a brief time the fate of the world hangs in the balance. Then Isabelle makes her choice, and the danger passes. From the viewpoint of the *pièce bien faite*, this leaves nothing to be desired. At a time when it was considered stupid to write well *Intermezzo* provided refreshing evidence of the advantage of fine workmanship. Its mechanism is efficient, and completely unobtrusive. It makes a delightful effect of freshness and spontaneity, the result of a work of art that, being carefully thought out, gives the inventive powers full rein. Its spontaneity is at the other pole from what we think of as Surrealist spontaneity. It was not by accident that Poulenc wrote the incidental music of *Intermezzo* for the harpsichord. *Intermezzo* is a piece in the style of Haydn.

But this play does not belong to the eighteenth century. It deals with the prime philosophical preoccupations of its time, and its time is the present. The theme is the eternal conflict of matter and spirit, the very same that inspired *The Dream Play* and also *Man and Superman*. In the struggle between the government Inspector and the young schoolmistress there is figured the conflict between the material and idealistic currents which cross in the individual soul and, in the aggregate, in the soul of humanity. The ideal—ordered, rational, and calm—evokes in the imagination the dream of the earthly paradise. Normally this dream remains a dream, for normally in the course of a lifetime the spiritual adventure is set aside in favor of the adventure of the body. The unfailing victory of the material principle is attested in this play by the maintenance of the realities which the Inspector is authorized at all costs to defend. But, in spite of the Inspector and the agencies he represents, the spirit asserts its power. The ideal is always betrayed; nevertheless it is there always, out of reach, but dynamically effective, the subversive dream of perfection which, if it had its way, would destroy the world we live in, and in any case regularly reduces it to absurdity.

For Giraudoux the ideal is most readily visible in the radiance of young womanhood. Doubtless he was susceptible to the charm of *jeunes filles en fleur* as much as anyone; but his feelings in this respect were supported by a venerable literary tradition. For Dante also the beauty of woman was the earthly counterpart of the Absolute. *Intermezzo*, however, is a human comedy. Beatrice leads Dante to heaven. Isabelle will take her husband to bed. She will not, of course, be forever faithful. The Ghost is her appointed lover, and sooner or later he may be expected to come for her as the Abalstitiel comes for Edmée. Meanwhile her seduction is averted and the world is saved. There is a moment when young girls are dangerous. The moment is brief:

THE GHOST: Like flowers in summer, in winter like thoughts of flowers, they arrange themselves so artfully amid the mass of humanity—the generous hidden in the family of misers, the unconquerable among the feeble—that the masters of the world take them not for humanity in its infancy but for its supreme flowering, the ultimate fruit of this race whose true fruition is senility. But suddenly . . .

THE SUPERVISOR: Very simplistic—.

THE GHOST: But suddenly the man appears. They all contemplate him. He has found recipes for augmenting his earthly dignity in their eyes. He stands upright on his hind legs in order to shed the rain better, and to hang medals on his chest. They tremble before him in hypocritical admiration, and with such fear as not even the tiger inspires, for they are ignorant that among the carnivores this biped alone has perishable teeth. And then all is over. All the walls of reality in which there once glimmered for them a thousand filigrees and heraldries grow opaque, and it is finished.

In the fate of young girls, it is suggested, one may read the fate of humanity, for mankind has no hope of communicating with the Absolute save through beauty, and the acme of beauty on earth is the beauty of woman. Unfortunately we are unwilling, in general, to follow this beauty into the Empyrean as Dante followed it, going first through hell. We insist on marrying it. The results are macabre:

THE GHOST: And then the pleasure of the night begins, and the habit of pleasure. And the pleasure of the table begins. And jealousy.

THE SUPERVISOR: Dear Isabelle!

THE GHOST: And revenge. And indifference begins. On the man's breast his only necklace loses its luster. All is over.

ISABELLE: But why are you so cruel? Save me from happiness, since you think it contemptible!

THE GHOST: Farewell, Isabelle. Your Supervisor is right. What men love, what you love, is not to know, not to understand, but to vibrate forever between two truths or two falsehoods. . . . I will tell you nothing more. Not even the name of the charming little flower that pricks up everywhere through the fields of death, whose odor greeted me at the gates of death and whose name I will whisper fifteen years from now into the ears of your daughter. Take her into your arms, Supervisor! Take her in the wolf-trap of your arms, and may she never again escape.

ISABELLE: Yes. Once more! (*She rushes to the Ghost, who kisses her and vanishes. She grows pale. She swoons.*)[33]

It is clear that the affair of Edmée and the Abalstitiel in *Choix des élues* is an elaboration of this situation in *Intermezzo*, and that the honest engineer Pierre in that novel develops the predicament of the Supervisor at a later stage of his life. When we compare these passages with the analogous passages in Pirandello's "La trappola" or "La distruzione dell'uomo" Giraudoux's special quality becomes evident. The theme in each case is the same. But, unlike Pirandello, Giraudoux remains on terms of civility with the material principle and the beings that embody it. The world, as it is presently constituted, did not please him any more than it pleased Pirandello, but he did not break off diplomatic relations. Pirandello was, at bottom, a realist. For him, as for Strindberg, it is the woman who springs the trap in which mankind is forever caught, and it is her beauty that forges the chain of mortality. For Giraudoux it is the other way round. In his view, woman mediates between spirit and matter. It is she who constitutes man's link with the eternal. The strain of gallantry that is so often evident in Giraudoux's treatment of women is more than merely Gallic. Possibly there is a tinge in it of something like piety.

In *Intermezzo* the Droguiste is a *voyant*, a mystic. He is able to tune nature as a concert master tunes an orchestra, and with the aid of his pitch-pipe he arranges the modulations through which one scene flows smoothly into the next. But the music of *Intermezzo* is in the main the music of words. Confrontations in the plays of Giraudoux are symphonic; the duels are duets. In *Siegfried* it is with words that Eva and Geneviève battle for the soul of Siegfried. In *Amphitryon 38* Alcmena, so she thinks, conquers Jupiter verbally. In *Judith* the heroine arms herself against Holofernes with dagger and poison, but she puts her trust in words. "En fait," she tells Suzanne, "toute la journée je ne me suis guère préparée à une offre de mon corps, mais à une espèce de concours d'éloquence."[34] It is with words also, and with words alone, that the rivals duel for the life of Isabelle, and it is with words that her soul is recalled from the other world.

The magic and the power of words were a central tenet of Symbolist theory. There is, occasionally, some show of violence in Giraudoux's plays. There are dagger thrusts and pistol shots, but they are largely cosmetic effects. "The stage play," Giraudoux wrote, "is a trial, not a deed of violence. The soul is opened, like a safe, by means of a word. There is no need of an acetylene torch." Drama devised after this fashion depends, naturally, on the availability of actors who can speak, and of audiences that are disposed to listen. In the 1920's, as it happened, Paris could provide such actors and such an audience, small enough, no doubt, but choice. The lycées and the Comédie-Française had done much to keep the great rhetorical tradition alive in France, and the disciples of Copeau were sworn to the service of the text. As for Giraudoux, Jouvet suited his needs miraculously well. Jouvet had laid down the golden rule of stage production early in his career: "A text, a style, and a light around them—and that is all." It was, of course, by no means all. But Giraudoux had no objection to the addition.

For Mallarmé stage-action was an unnecessary and unwelcome accessory to the dramatic ode. In the ideal theatre the movement of the word was all that was necessary: "Quant à l'act, il est parfaitement absurde sauf que mouvement (personnel) rendu à l'infini. . . ."[35] The ideal drama would be, accordingly, a monologue. Giraudoux's idea of theatre was very far from this; in many ways he followed Maeterlinck. He did not write like Maeterlinck. His characters dream a good deal, but they are not somnambulists. Their dreams are distinguishable from life for, unlike Maeterlinck, Giraudoux maintained close personal relations with reality. At the same time his central concern as an artist was never the representation of an event, but the evocation of a mood, and to this end all the effects of his drama were subordinated. "When a reader opens my book," he is reported to have said, "I should like him to say: I am going to make contact with a living soul."

The living soul, as Giraudoux depicted it, is an extremely complex organism. The tinge of skepticism which is everywhere apparent in Mallarmé, the reluctance to commit oneself even to one's own doctrine, the affirmation of doubt which, from the time of Montaigne and Pascal, is at the core of faith in France, was entirely characteristic of Giraudoux. In his world all is equivocal, nothing is certain. What seems sure is that appearances are deceitful; but even that solid axiom is open to question. In *Intermezzo* the zigzag voyage through life with which the Supervisor captures Isabelle's fancy is as much of a fantasy as the fields of asphodel which carpet the realms of the dead. The humdrum life of a *fonctionnaire* in the Weights and Measures has as much room for glamor as the life of the spirit in the other world. For Giraudoux the fact depends on the artistry of the representation. Truth is a matter of style.

Giraudoux set his stage habitually on the frontier of the worlds, between the real and the unreal, in the full awareness that no man can say which is which, since in reality the universe is perhaps no more than a verbal structure, a syntactical arrangement. If he set his stage at this point it was, no doubt, because in all honesty he saw no other place for it. From his viewpoint the artist can be sure only of his art: two steps beyond its confines he comes upon the void. But, for Giraudoux, between the artist's fantasy and "the void that is reality," there is an open space where the sun shines, the brooks flow, and birds sing. This space is nature, and, however ambiguous it may seem, there for a time one can breathe. It is possible that Giraudoux was not entirely at home in this reality. But he did what he could to make his characters comfortable in it and, in truth, in his plays it seems delectable.

La Guerre de Troie n'aura pas lieu was produced on 21 November 1935, some months after the publication of *Fin de Siegfried*. The timing was opportune. In 1933 Adolph Hitler had assumed the title of Führer of the Third Reich. On 16 March 1935 he announced his intention of re-arming Germany, and a week later he denounced the Treaty of Locarno. The war that was to have ended war forever was still vivid in the minds of those who survived it. The Maginot fortifications had been building ever since 1919. They were not yet fully manned.

In 1934 Jouvet moved his acting company from the avenue Montaigne to the Théâtre de l'Athénée on the rue Caumartin, behind the Opéra. In this location he was deliberately inviting the competition of the commercial theatres. He opened his season with a revival of *Amphitryon 38*, with Madeleine Ozeray in the role of Alcmena. The next production was *Tessa*, Giraudoux's version of Margaret Kennedy's *The Constant Nymph*. Ozeray had a long and successful run in *Tessa*. Then she took the part of Helen of Troy in *La Guerre de Troie*. The casting was faultless. Jouvet played Hector, and Pierre Renoir, Ulysses. The play made a deep impression and was said to be a modern masterpiece.

La Guerre de Troie n'aura pas lieu is a short play with a plot of classic simplicity. In Hector's absence Paris has brought Helen to Troy, and in reprisal the Greeks have sent Ulysses with a fleet and a declaration of war. The incomparable Helen meanwhile has taken the city by storm. When she takes her walk along the ramparts the old men ogle her shamelessly. The adolescents are ready to die for her. Only the fighting men, recently returned from battle, are indifferent to her beauty.

Hector, in particular, is determined that there shall be no war on her account, and he launches a vigorous campaign to avert conflict. He persuades Paris to give up Helen, and gets Helen to agree to leave. Lastly he wins over Priam to the cause of peace. There remains only the speaker of the senate, the aged poet Demokos. But Demokos is a very militant patriot who is convinced that the return of Helen would forever stain the honor of Troy.

Hector's struggle to avert war thus resolves itself into a struggle with Demokos. But behind Demokos there is the implacable power of destiny, against which it is useless to struggle. Cassandra, the prophetess of Apollo, is in close touch with fate. Helen too is a *voyante*, and in her mind's eye the scenes of future carnage are brightly colored. Both express grave doubts as to the efficacy of Hector's efforts. Nevertheless Hector closes the Gates of War.

By this time the Greek ships are moored in the harbor. A drunken Greek warrior comes raging up to the citadel to kill Paris. Instead he meets Hector, and provokes him almost beyond endurance before he is finally placated. And now Ulysses appears, the perfect diplomat. When Hector solemnly assures him that Paris has not actually touched Helen, Ulysses professes himself very willing to believe it, in spite of the fact that the Trojans insist on describing the amorous voyage across the Aegean in the most minute detail. Ulysses is not interested in the amours of Helen. He tells Hector very frankly that for economic reasons the Trojan war is inevitable. Nevertheless he would like to postpone it, if possible, indefinitely. He agrees to take Helen back to Greece. They bid farewell to Troy, and make their way down to the ships.

The drunken Oiax comes in their wake, and makes lecherous advances to Andromache. Hector bears even this with patience. But just as Oiax is about to leave, Demokos bursts in with the war song he has just composed. Hector stabs him. The dying poet screams that Oiax has killed him. The Trojans rush in. The curtain, which had begun to fall on the words, "There shall be no war," stops, and begins to rise slowly. The Gates of War swing open by themselves.

This play proposes a wholly deterministic view of history. Hector is determined to avoid bloodshed. Demokos is bound to have war. Each does what he can to gain his end. But, as the wise Ulysses says, what great men do, or do not do, matters not at all in the course of time. In spite of all, what is fated to happen will happen.

The operations of *moira* in these circumstances may well be rationalized, and Ulysses tries hard to rationalize them. But he is at bottom a fatalist. "The universe knows that we shall fight," he tells Hector. "This morning I was still not sure. But the moment I set foot on your jetty I was sure." From the way Giraudoux arranges the action one might conclude that the universe is a sentient organism with a will of its own to which men are subject without being privy to its purpose. Essentially this is the view of history that is suggested also in *Judith*. In his scene with Ulysses, Hector is entirely hopeful of a peaceful accommodation. Ulysses does not share his hopes:

> You are young, Hector. . . . On the eve of each war it is customary for the heads of the conflicting nations to come together in some innocent village, on a terrace on the banks of a lake, in a corner of a garden. And they agree that war is the worst scourge in the world, and each of them, following with his eyes the reflections and undulations of the water, seeing the magnolia petals falling lightly on the other's shoulders, is peaceful, modest and true. And they study one another. They gaze at one another. And warmed by the sun, softened by a pale wine, each finds in the face opposite him nothing that justifies hatred, nothing that does not evoke human love, and nothing in the least incompatible in their languages, their ways of scratching the nose, or of drinking. And they are really filled with peace, with the desire for peace. And they part with a handshake, feeling that they are brothers. And each leans out of his carriage window to exchange a smile. . . . And the next day, all the same, war breaks out.[36]

The causes of war, in the opinion of Ulysses, are organic; but destiny is not benevolent. It nourishes nations and trains them, as animal trainers nourish and train animals, only in order to pit them one against the other in battle:

> When destiny, in the course of years, has exalted two peoples, when it has opened for them the same future of invention and omnipotence . . . the universe well knows it does not mean to prepare for men two ways of color and expansion, but to arrange its festival, the unleashing of that human brutality and folly which alone is reassuring to the gods. . . .

Unlike Hector, who seems relatively untried, Ulysses is a thoroughly experienced type of hero. His view of history anticipates the theory of Herodotus by some centuries, evidently; but his mood is equally tragic. In the history of nations, he observes, everything indicates that human prosperity makes the gods uneasy. Thus when a nation develops beyond a certain point, it attracts nemesis and is destroyed. The immediate cause is not important. "Nations," Ulysses says, "die for imperceptible discourtesies. It is by their way of sneezing, or of wearing down their heels, that doomed nations are recognized. . . . It was beyond doubt, a bad thing to have carried off Helen."

"You see some proportion," Hector asks, "between the carrying off of a woman and a war in which one of our peoples will perish?" Ulysses sees a relation. Helen, he says, is one of those rare creatures whom destiny puts in circulation on earth for its own personal use. Paris could have ventured with impunity into all the beds of Sparta or Thebes, but in touching Helen he has affronted destiny. Consequently Troy is lost.

But Ulysses is an empiricist as well as a fatalist. "I am curious by nature," he says, "and I am not afraid. I accept Helen. I will give her back to Menelaus. I possess much more eloquence than is needed to make a husband believe in the virtue of his wife. I will even make Helen believe in it herself. And I shall leave at once in order to avoid surprise. Once aboard ship, perhaps we may venture to baffle the war." His intentions, as he walks off with Helen, are of the best. But it is a long way to the wharf.

The fate that broods over the plays of Giraudoux is a more explicit power than the malevolent doom that pervades the drama of Maeterlinck. In *La Guerre de Troie* destiny is a sleeping tiger which it is well not to disturb. But it has, at least, a discernible purpose. It is a force that keeps humanity within bounds lest it rival the gods. But if Greek *moira* destroys nations only in order to reassure the gods, mankind has cause for complaint, and the tinge of anger that colors Giraudoux's plays plainly echoes the tone of indignant resignation which is evident in the plays of Euripides.

The gods are not silent in *La Guerre de Troie*. They speak plainly, but mainly to contradict one another. Iris appears in the heavens with a message from Aphrodite forbidding the separation of Paris and Helen. She also bears an order from Pallas commanding their immediate division. The penalty for disobedience in each case is war. There is also a message from Zeus. He orders Hector and Ulysses to separate Paris and Helen without bringing about their division: "And let these two arrange matters so that there shall be no war. Or else he swears, and he has never threatened in vain, he swears to you that there shall be war!" With this impressive declaration Iris vanishes, leaving a rainbow in the sky to mark her passing. "It is certainly she," Helen notes. "She has forgotten her girdle along the way."[37]

Helen's remark indicates the mood of the play. It is serious without being serious. To the solemn-minded the treatment will seem frivolous. For Giraudoux, as for Pirandello, the absurdity of life precluded any over-zealous treatment of its problems. But the difference of temperament in these two authors could hardly be more strongly marked. Life seemed outrageous to Pirandello, and it made him angry. It seemed equally outrageous to Giraudoux; but it made him smile. Pirandello set his stage in a corner of hell. Giraudoux preferred the atmosphere of fairyland. For Giraudoux the ambiguity of life was its saving grace, something to be preserved at all costs, and he found its masquerade delightful, a veil behind which all sorts of wonders might be glimpsed. In his plays, as in his life, he dwelt in two worlds, taking refuge from the one in the other. Unlike Pirandello, he was an idealist; but he was an idealist only on condition of being a realist also. In *La Guerre de Troie* the hero is a realist. The idealist is Demokos.

For the aged poet the idea of love is more real than love, and the ideal of beauty is more accessible than its physical counterpart. For Demokos the idea of Helen has quite supplanted Helen. She is a symbol worth dying for.

DEMOKOS: A symbol, what? For all you are a warrior you must surely have
    heard of symbols? You have surely met women who even at a distance
    seemed to you to personify intelligence, harmony, sweetness?
HECTOR: I have seen some.
DEMOKOS: What did you do then?
HECTOR: I came closer, and that was it. . . .[38]

The discussion of Realism and Symbolism in this play goes no further than this; but this is hardly a literary discussion. Hector is no poet. He is a warrior, and he is tired of war. Demokos, who does not bear arms, is extremely warlike. He feels that it is sweet and decorous to die for one's country, for one's ideals, and so on, and is eager to write songs inciting others to glory. It is clear that in 1935 Giraudoux was weary of warmongers, and the caricature of Demokos is merciless, a comic-strip version of the incendiary journalist. The portrait of the incorruptible jurist Busiris is also excessively broad: plays that incline to allegory naturally tend to exaggerate their symbols. In *La Guerre de Troie* the points are made with what, for Giraudoux, is unusual emphasis. The characterizations, as a result, necessarily suffer some impoverishment.

It is not in the major characters, but in Andromache, Hecuba, Troilus, and Polyxena—the members of the family—that the human aspects of the play are concentrated. Their scenes emerge in the round from what is essentially a bas-relief. In the presence of young Troilus, quite unexpectedly, Helen becomes a woman. The little Polyxena, in the same way, transforms the wife of Priam from an abstraction into a person, a mother. But not even Andromache succeeds in animating Hector. He remains throughout the play a monumental figure, admirable and sympathetic, but very much the statesman, and quite remote from life.

In *La Guerre de Troie* Giraudoux deliberately flaunted many of the conventions of the stage and, on the whole, with admirable results; but in his desire to deal realistically with the monolithic characters of antiquity he ran inevitably into stylistic difficulties that no actor could hope to resolve. *La Guerre de Troie*, in spite of the originality of the treatment and the seriousness of the subject, is likely to make the impression of a puppet play, and for this reason those of its characters that are obviously drawn from life seem curiously out of style with the others. Helen of Troy is mysterious, and the occasional attempt to reduce her to human proportions results mainly in confusion. It is impossible to understand Helen, and the role is complicated by the fact that, although the play centers on her, she takes no part in the action. As the plot is designed, Helen matters less to the play than Demokos or Oiax, for it is they, and not she, who provide the immediate pretext for war. She is indispensable, but she is, on the whole, an embarrassment not only to Hector, but to the author. In *La Guerre de Troie* the cream of the jest—and its irony—is that the face that launched a thousand ships and so on is not the face of the incomparable Helen but the sooty muzzle of the drunken Oiax.

La Guerre de Troie deserves to be numbered, certainly, among the great plays of the modern theatre, but it is a difficult play, and it suffers from the contrast between the earnestness of the intention and the levity of its expression. Giraudoux was irrepressibly mischievous. Evidently he could not resist the temptation to poke fun at his characters even in their most solemn moments. The play constantly reflects his changing mood, his sudden smile, his surprising earnestness, his grimace. This effect of intimacy is altogether *sui generis* in the theatre but, delightful as it is, it has its disadvantages. *La Guerre de Troie* has something to say that borders on the tragic. It is also a species of joke. These are two aspects of drama that are more difficult to reconcile on the stage than the Janus masks of Pirandello.

At the Athenée *La Guerre de Troie n'aura pas lieu*, in two acts, was considered too short a play to fill out an evening. *Supplément au Voyage de Cook* was added as a curtain raiser. The choice was felicitous. This one-act comedy is among the funniest and most light-hearted of Giraudoux's plays; but it invites reflection. It was well calculated to leave an audience laughing in a mood appropriate to the play of Hector and Helen.

By 1934 the affair Berthelot was all but forgotten, and Giraudoux was restored to grace. He was not, however, again employed at the Quai d'Orsay. Instead, he was appointed Inspector of Diplomatic and Consular Posts abroad, a position which entailed much travel. Giraudoux took on this assignment with pleasure. In the next four years his work led him to every corner of the globe, from the Antilles to the Far East. It was apparently while he was preparing for a trip to Tahiti in 1935 that he read, or perhaps re-read, Diderot's *Supplément au Voyage de Bougainville*.

Bougainville's account of his voyage around the world was first published in 1771, some twenty years after the publication of Rousseau's *Discours sur les arts et sciences*. Rousseau's famous paradox on the superiority of the noble savage over the corrupt products of civilization had precipitated a long controversy regarding the actual conditions of life among savages. The issue was of particular interest to those who were at this time espousing the cause of romanticism against the entrenched interests of the classicists. These early romantics found strong support in Bougainville's descriptions of the beautiful people of Tahiti, the more so since Bougainville had brought with him a living specimen, a handsome youth called Aoturu, whose natural dignity and native intelligence quite captivated the susceptible ladies of the court of Versailles.

The original suggestion for Rousseau's essay appears to have come not from Montaigne's famous piece on cannibals, but directly from Diderot, when Rousseau visited him in prison at Vincennes. Soon after the publication of Bougainville's *Voyage autour du monde*, Diderot published a dialogue, entitled *Supplément au Voyage de Bougainville*, in which the mariner is taken severely to task by an aged Tahitian for introducing the un-spoiled Tahitians to the degenerate culture of Europe. The aged Tahi-tian is especially offended by the European work-ethic which incites peo-ple to labor where labor is unnecessary, and to strive after luxuries of which they have no need.[39]

Giraudoux had an obvious motive for renewing in the 1930's the eight-eenth-century controversy of the noble savage. The issue of primitivism in art was still very much alive. From the time of Nietzsche all sections of the avant garde had collaborated in an effort to upset the existing cul-tural structures, and to make a fresh start on the basis of nature and the natural impulse. In the 1930's the Benin bronzes, the douanier Rousseau, American jazz, crime, occultism, myth, the Balinese dance-theatre, Dada, Japanese prints, madness, homosexuality, the plays of Pirandello, and the writings of the Marquis de Sade were all more or less equated as expressions of the vital current which the decaying forms of Western cul-ture were trying to stifle. Especially glamorous among these expressions of nature was the life of the South Seas which in recent years Stevenson and Gauguin had vividly publicized.

At the heart of the romantic movement was that nostalgia for a lost Eden that had long ago sent the Barbizon painters into the forest and the Symbolist poets to the banks of the Seine. More recently, coteries such as the circle of Charles Vildrac ventured into the countryside to found phalansteries modeled on the Abbey of Thélème.[40] Almost from the first there had been a perceptible reaction among the Symbolists against the exclusive absorption in the interior landscape which was one of the con-sequences of idealistic subjectivity. After the death of Mallarmé the rift widened between those who trusted only the inner vision and those who could read in nature the signs of the Absolute. The developing cult of nature and the primitive brought Symbolism closer to the pantheism of Wordsworth and Coleridge than it had ever been before, and shafts of bright sunlight began to penetrate the Symbolist void. The consequence was that, without relinquishing its hold on the spiritual world, Symbol-ism began once again to assume a receptive attitude toward the out-erworld upon which it had not long ago contemptuously turned its back.

The period between the wars was characterized in France by a healthy return to the life of the senses, in part stimulated by the thought of its brevity. It was an attitude particularly congenial to Giraudoux. In this period it was more than ever necessary for a man of letters to be a par-tisan, but the issues were not yet entirely colored with Marxism, and the slogans of the 1890's were still meaningful. Giraudoux was by conviction a Symbolist. He was on the side of the *Nouvelle Revue française*, and had grown up in the shadow of Mallarmé. At the same time both his tastes and his way of life implied a realistic turn of mind which was at variance with traditional Symbolist attitudes. The consequence was the paradox which is evident in all his works, the contradiction which in some sense constitutes the dynamic element of his drama, and perhaps of his life.

The working of this psychic dialectic become increasingly clear in the writings of his middle years. In *Intermezzo* the life of the dead seems irresistible to Isabelle; but she chooses the life of the living. In *La Guerre de Troie* Hector's realism seems far more attractive than the fanatic idealism of Demokos, and there the point is made quite succinctly that youth in its vigor is inclined to realism, while idealism expresses the impotence of those who are capable of living only in the imagination. It is a view for which *Intermezzo* does not in any way prepare one; but there is no need to insist on consistency in an age when every statement implies its contrary.

In *Supplément au Voyage de Cook* the contrast between the healthy hedonism of the Tahitians and the crabbed fantasies of the invading missionaries leaves no doubt as to the author's position. The issue here is clear-cut and entirely familiar. It symbolizes the conflict of *Physie* and *Anti-Physie* in the Fourth Book of *Pantagruel*, the conflict of nature and the anti-natural.

Giraudoux's interest in Diderot's Tahitian dialogue long antedated the present play. *Suzanne et le Pacifique* was published fourteen years before. It shows clearly the influence both of Diderot and of Bougainville. The *Supplément au Voyage de Cook*, however, makes no allusion to Bougainville's visit to Tahiti and says nothing about French ideas of industry, morality, or property. The satire is directed exclusively at the English. But, obviously, the assault on middle-class culture is not limited in its scope. It has its basis not only in Rabelais and Montaigne, but also in Rousseau, Saint-Simon, and Proudhon, and from a critical standpoint it pretty well covers the ground.

The *notable* Outouru in Giraudoux's play is borrowed directly from Diderot. For the redoubtable Mr. Banks, Giraudoux levied on Sir Joseph Banks of Captain Cook's expedition. Some of the other characters come from Bougainville's *Voyage*, but most originated in Giraudoux's fancy. The play is delightful. It describes the preparations ordered by Cook for the reception of the crew of the *Endeavor* on the island of Otahiti after a two-years voyage from England. The landing party consists of three Britishers: the King's Lieutenant; Quartermaster Solander; and Mr. Samuel Banks, the ship's taxidermist. Mr. Banks is a churchwarden of the Presbyterian Church of Birmingham, and is therefore uniquely qualified to indoctrinate the natives in the elements of British civilization. Quartermaster Solander is a magician. He attempts to give the local population some idea of British magnificence by extracting eggs from his nose.

Mr. Banks proceeds without delay to instruct the *notable* Outouru in the fundamentals of the Presbyterian ethos. His task is difficult, for there is no ground on which Mr. Banks and the Tahitian chief can arrive at an understanding. Mr. Banks's mentality is ironclad. It is, he knows, his God-given duty to rescue these savages from the abysmal ignorance in which they are plunged, and it is inconceivable to him that there is anything he can learn from them. Outouru, for his part, is eager to learn the ways of the civilized. But to Outouru it seems that Mr. Banks is mad.

He seems mad also to Giraudoux. Outouru has no trouble in demonstrating the absurdity of Mr. Banks and his teachings; and the confrontation of savage wisdom and the folly of civilized man results in the sort of comedy which Giraudoux manages better than anyone since the time of Voltaire. The fundamentals of civilization, according to Mr. Banks, are three: Work, Property, and Morality. He takes them up one by one, with illuminating examples. But Work, Outouru points out, is folly in an environment where no labor is necessary. Mr. Banks has an answer: "The greatness of man is precisely that he finds a reason to labor where an ant would rest." Moreover, it is work that makes men beautiful. Mr. Banks says:

> Outouru, there is a moving spectacle that comes to my mind when I see your lazy bodies asleep among the flowers or afloat on the waters. . . . It is a picture of our miners emerging from the mine. They are not dressed in your brilliant colors. A drugget covers their bodies, smelly and dirty. They have no chaplets of beads on their arms, but a cheap wrist watch which is the reward of every minute and second of their day in hell. They do not know the sun. When they come out of the earth it is always raining. Their sweat is washed only by the rain, and it streams from them all black; and black also is the blood that oozes from their scratches. They have no glistening insects in their hair. They put out the mine candle only to light the supper candle. They walk in a semi-stupor, propping themselves up against the fog. They

have a bitter taste in their mouths, and not only because they had to
drag out some asphyxiated brother, or push the car when the horse
broke its leg, but because they have eaten too much coal. They do not
realize that English coal is of unequalled quality and that in all the
world there is no finer coal to eat. They seem overcome with nausea.
But for all those who cross their path, shopowners and bankers, poets
and water colorists, they personify labor to such a degree that these go
more joyously to the great fires of clear and pure carbon that in every
club pays homage to the mineral resources and the sweat of England,
and there they take their dinner of roast beef and port with hearts that
burst with pride. That is what labor is, Outouru; it is magnificent![41]

It is interesting to compare these passages with the corresponding passages in "Ciàula scopre la luna." Pirandello's story goes deeper; it does
not incline one to laughter; and it is more limited in its scope: Giraudoux
had evidently read Proudhon. The idea of work in Mr. Banks's allocu-
tion leads him naturally into the question of property, a conception unknown in Otahiti, where all share equally in the bounty of nature. Mr.
Banks graphically indicates the nature of property by trading a cork-
screw in exchange for Outouru's pearl necklace, his diamond bracelets,
and his ruby earrings. But the idea of property is quite beyond the
savage's simple mind. Mr. Banks explains that while England as a whole
belongs to all the English, only a few are entitled to possess its parts, so
that the only way for the poor to acquire what the rich possess is to steal
it. The idea of theft seems very practical to Outouru; but he is utterly
confused by Mr. Banks's idea of morality until it is explained that morality consists in approaching a woman sexually only with the idea of giving
her a child. At that, Outouru joyfully presents Mr. Banks with his
daughter, who would very much like to have a child.

The demonstration of Puritan morality in the face of the temptations
so innocently offered by the Tahitians entails some personal sacrifice on
the part of Mr. Banks. And Mrs. Banks, who comes to join her husband
at this critical juncture, also meets with difficulties. In both cases Presbyterian virtue is triumphant; but virtue of this sort is a costly commod-
ity on a South Sea island. Mrs. Banks is fifty, dry, thin, plain, and childless; but she seems desirable to young Vaiturou and he is ready and
eager to provide her with a son. But she is a confirmed idealist, not to
say a Symbolist. She informs her would-be lover:

At my age I have taken on habits, my dear Vaiturou, or manias: I no
longer love any but invisible men. My only joys come from them. To

the presence of Mr. Banks, wonderful though he is, I even prefer the absence of Mr. Banks, and I would very much like, precisely because you attract me, to place you for the rest of my life, in the ranks of my unseen friends. If I spent this night with you, that would be impossible. You would no longer be anything for me but a body. . . . And you would not come with me to England because your body would remain here.

Vaiturou answers: "In sum, if I understand you correctly, this is the choice that destiny offers white women: one night with real bodies or a lifetime with invisible ones?" And Mrs. Banks: "Exactly. And that sums up the course in morals which we teach this evening to the island."[42]

In the end Mr. Banks and Mrs. Banks lie down to sleep, fully clothed, side by side in their two camp beds, while Solander and Sullivan mount guard over their hut:

MR. BANKS: . . . Look, Evelyn. What a symbolic picture of England: two
  magnificent sailors guarding the dreams of a pair of churchwardens.[43]

There is no great passion in even the most passionate of Giraudoux's characters. Nobody dies for love in any of his plays, save perhaps Ritter Hans in *Ondine;* and there are no great romantic scenes. But Giraudoux is a master of erotic writing. There is a wealth of sexual allusion and sexual description in his plays, ranging from the very broad discourse of the *gabier* in *La Guerre de Troie* to the delicate, but quite tropical, sensuality of *Supplément au Voyage de Cook.* In the last decades of the nineteenth century, pornography as a literary genre had an outstanding development in France, and the writing of highly colored erotic works became associated with the question of freedom and the rights of the individual. In 1885 Edmond de Goncourt found Sade's *Justine* revolting: "The originality of this abominable work lies not in its filth, nor in its vileness, but in the celestial punishment of virtue, that is to say, in the complete inversion of the denouement of all other novels and plays."[44] A generation later Guillaume Apollinaire wrote of Sade: "This man who appeared to be of no importance during all the nineteenth century may well dominate the twentieth."

There is no perversity in Giraudoux's plays, nor sign of any but a normally healthy interest in sexual matters. His works are colored by a genial eroticism which seldom exceeds the permissible bounds of sexual innuendo in polite circles. It is nevertheless a highly sexed literature in which the actively amorous couple is considered the basis of a stable social structure, and sexual prowess is a sign of health. The old men in Giraudoux's plays are rarely admirable. His world is the world of the young and vigorous, in which time is an unwelcome intruder. His idea of manhood is classic, the *kalokagathos* of the ancients, represented by such men as Amphitryon and Hector, well-made, virile types, attractive to women and handy with the javelin.

When he gave Jouvet the manuscript of *Electre*, Giraudoux was fifty-five. He was, by all accounts, still active and strong, but he was no longer young, and he was not happy. The little that is known of his domestic life indicates that his once idyllic marriage had become increasingly unpleasant, and in 1936, we are told, he was seriously contemplating divorce. It was thus with some relief, apparently, that after the production of *Electre* he embarked on a trip around the world in the course of his diplomatic duties.[45]

Judith was subtitled, "A Tragedy"; *Electre*, simply, "A Play," but the story of *Electre* is more deeply tragic than that of the earlier play. Giraudoux took up the story of the Argive princess more or less in the form given it by Euripides. Euripides had made some innovations in the plot of the *Choephoroi*. He had Aegisthus marry off Electra to a Mycenean peasant so that her offspring would have neither a claim to the throne of Agamnenon nor a motive for avenging his death. The action in Euripides' *Electra* takes place not, as was usual in tragedy, before the façade of a palace, but outside the hut of a poor farmer, and Electra is first seen dressed in rags, bearing a water pot on her shaven head. The action in this *Electra* is brutal and swift. It takes place in an atmosphere of mutual fear and hatred. It is only at the end, when the two children wonder why all this butchery was necessary, that we step outside the frame of the myth to speculate for a moment on the absurdity of Orestes' predicament, and the savagery of the forces that brought it about.

In his play, Euripides concentrated attention on the physical conflict. The psychological and metaphysical problems associated with the action evidently were of secondary interest to him. With Giraudoux, on the other hand, the conflict is mainly verbal, a *concours d'éloquence*, and the plot serves chiefly to motivate a series of thematic considerations, problems of truth, justice, happiness, marriage.

Electre is constructed along the lines of a well-made play. The main action is a detective story in the style of *Hamlet*, and Electra plays a leading role in it, first as sleuth and then as avenger. The sub-plot involves the domestic predicament of Agatha Theocathocles. In classic fashion, when the sub-plot reaches its climax it precipitates the denouement of the main plot, while at the same time the correspondence between the crime of Clytemnestra and the revolt of Agatha Theocathocles serves to underscore the universality of their situation. One might imagine that this tidy construction would result in a tightly knit play. In this case the contrary is true. *Electre* is extremely loose in texture. Much of the action is reported, not represented, and the alternation of passages of stage-action and passages of recital vaguely recalls the technique of tragedy, particularly of Roman tragedy. But the antique design is deceptive. The play is distinctly modern in conception, and in it Giraudoux systematically violated all the rules of Sarcey's *système du théâtre*.

Symbolism was essentially the result of an extraordinary effort of communication. The result was to strain language to the breaking point. Among Symbolists, however, Giraudoux was exceptionally articulate. *Electre* is mainly a series of monologues through which every shade of feeling is given expression, every motive analyzed, and every action interpreted. It is a celebration of language as the ultimate symbolic device. But Giraudoux did not depend wholly upon words for signification and, while his words are precise, his other symbols are not. The bird that hovers over the head of Aegisthus is a sign, evidently, of doom, but the *mendiant* who dominates the action is a doubtful figure.

The drunken Beggar and Aegisthus the king are very closely associated, but it is by no means clear what their relation is. The Beggar is announced some time before he appears. When Aegisthus takes his seat on the throne the Beggar takes his place on the scaffold that has been erected for his use. From this point of vantage he oversees the entire action, even the scenes of utmost intimacy, and he comments on everything in a manner that only remotely suggests a chorus. He is said to be either a beggar or a god, and is somehow accepted as both—a supernatural presence that pervades the play without taking any part in the action. He is a mysterious figure; but his presence in the play, and his ambiguity, are understandable. He is, no doubt, the author.

The author is a very useful person to have on the stage, even in disguise; but the use of such characters involves some inconvenience. It entails, among other things, a double perspective, for the author on the stage implies still another author who is not on the stage. Again, once the author is in sight of the audience he is likely to address it at some length, particularly if he has something to say, and this makes for a very chatty play.

Giraudoux's Beggar comes on the stage, Pirandellian fashion, as an author in search of characters. He is said to be drunk, and is therefore licensed to talk seemingly at random; but he is everywhere accorded the respect with which characters customarily treat their authors. He is gifted with prescience, and also with hindsight. Moreover he displays uncanny insights which astonish nobody. In a *pièce à thèse* the *raisonneur* is usually a well-informed person full of good advice. Giraudoux's Beggar is of a different stripe. He knows everything, and no one knows him. There is no attempt to treat him realistically. He is a supernatural manifestation that reeks of garlic and wine and is both there and not there. From his position on the stage he is able to enter the scene or leave it without moving from the spot. When he speaks, others listen. When he is quiet, he attracts no more attention than an article of furniture. Unfortunately, he is seldom quiet.

The Surrealist dimension which the Beggar adds to the action is further enhanced by the treatment of the Gardener. Orestes brushes this personage quite summarily from the stage in the first act, and he plays no further part in the action. It is by an act of exceptional courtesy that this superfluous character is permitted to address the audience in the entr'acte. The result is not only to establish another level of reality, but also to give the play an effect of depth that stage plays normally lack. In *Electre* the Gardener exists independent of the play, and his presence gives shape to the unreality which surrounds the action, to the fields and the forests we do not see, and normally would not need to imagine. Like the Beggar, but in another way, he transcends the plot, and one can think of him cultivating his lettuces long after the curtain goes down on the flaming city.

The effect of extending the character beyond the uses of the play is, obviously, not the same as the objectification of the personages in *Six Characters in Search of an Author;* but it is in some sense analogous to it. Characters in plays are not assumed to have feelings aside from those assigned to them by the author. But the Gardener, like the Father in Pirandello's play, has a life of his own which is quite irrelevant to the action, and through this irrelevance *Electre* gains a dimension which extends the play beyond the ordinary confines of drama. The basis of the conception, of course, is that there is no difference between the figures who people the world of the imagination and those who inhabit what is called reality. When the Gardener steps out of the play he goes about his business as a gardener, while the actor who impersonates him goes about his business as an actor. They are, it is implied, equally real, but they belong to different worlds.

To inflict the Gardener's monologue on an audience that is impatient to get on with the killings might be considered a deliberate act of sadism on the part of the author. But Giraudoux evidently meant it quite otherwise. The Gardener's soliloquy is a way of reaching out of the play, a gesture of friendship. For Giraudoux, if we can credit Jouvet, a play was "an act of love, an enterprise of tenderness, all of it born of a need for communication and communion, a universal sharing of emotion." In taking the audience into his confidence the Gardener establishes a bond of intimacy which draws the audience in a very special way into a situation which, after all, does not especially concern it. Irma's soliloquy at the end of the first act of *La Folle de Chaillot* makes a similar effect. Jouvet found it enchanting:

> Even an unimaginative spectator can hardly avoid feeling the great sublimity, the elevation to which the poet rises through solitude, a solitude which the actress feels with fear as she speaks this monologue which surprises the audience that hears it by this abrupt delivery, this lyric confession, personal, absolute, which is like a song, which is the solo of love in solitude. It is a unique moment. There is not one of us who has not experienced it, felt it, felt the impulse and the desire to give himself. He has not perhaps found the words that were needed to translate it. The poet gives them to him.
>
> This physical state weds the physical state of the poet to the physical state of the actress. It is a resharing of universal emotion. Truly, it is an hour of eternity, the hour of the theatre.[46]

The Eumenides play no part in the *Electra* of Euripides. In Giraudoux's play they live in accelerated tempo. They are mischievous little girls when they first appear, escorting the stranger who is Orestes to the palace grounds. Next morning they are adolescents. And now they try to preserve Orestes from Electra's influence by speaking to him of the joys of love. At the end they are Electra's age, and they resemble her, for it is in the guise of Electra that they will persecute Orestes all the rest of his life.

But the tragedy—insofar as there is tragedy—is not the tragedy of

Orestes. It is Aegisthus who is the tragic hero. He is, to begin with, a contemptible figure. He has been a traitor, a murderer, a usurper, and a philanderer. Clytemnestra, the queen, has been his mistress these seven years. He can become king by marrying her; but Electra poses a threat, and he plans to dispose of her by marrying her to the Gardener. The arrival of Orestes spoils everything for him. In the last act Argos is attacked suddenly by the Corinthians. The troops mutiny. The Argive guard will fight only on condition that Aegisthus will lead them as their king. He rises splendidly to the occasion, confesses his crimes, and offers himself up for punishment if only Electra will permit him to save the city. She refuses. Nevertheless he marries Clytemnestra, assumes the kingship, and puts himself at the head of the troops. It is at this point that Orestes cuts him down. In the end Clytemnestra too is killed, Orestes is driven mad, and the city is destroyed. But Electra has had justice.

As a character, Giraudoux's Electra is obviously a symbol, rather literary than human, and probably impossible to play convincingly. As Giraudoux depicts her, she is a beautiful girl, pure and gentle; but she is inordinately contentious, and she is obsessed with a moral purpose that transcends earthly considerations. The husband of Agatha Theocathocles, the Presiding Judge of Argos, calls her "une femme à histoires," the sort of woman who can let nothing rest.

The Presiding Judge, however, takes too practical a view of the situation. Electra is more than an uncomfortable woman. She is a kind of saint. She is dedicated to her father, not because he gave her life, but because he provides her with a reason for living. In her singlemindedness she brings misfortune to everyone and unhappiness to herself; but it is not happiness that she seeks. It is blessedness. Electra is of the stuff of martyrs, a fanatic, and therefore incapable of mercy or forgiveness. It is her goal to redress the moral balance of the universe, and to this end she is prepared to sacrifice whatever lies in her path, including herself. The Presiding Judge says:

> Over our faults, our shortcomings, our crimes, our truth, there settles each day a triple layer of earth which tempers their virulence: forgetfulness, death and human justice. It is madness not to depend upon these. . . . When the sleep of the guilty continues to be more troubled, after the period prescribed by law, than the sleep of the innocent, a society is seriously compromised. When I see Electra I feel stirring in myself the faults I committed in the cradle.[47]

Giraudoux's Electra is a far more engaging character than Gregers Werle in *The Wild Duck*, but like Gregers she is an All-or-Nothing character; and like Ibsen's Brand she is sadly short in her *conto caritatis*, and is in great danger of being engulfed by the god she worships. "See where your pride has brought you, Electra!" the first of the Eumenides tells her as she contemplates the city Electra has destroyed. "Now you are nothing! Now you have nothing!"

ELECTRA: I have my conscience. I have Orestes. I have justice, I have everything.

SECOND FURY: Your conscience! You are going to hear from it, your conscience, in the little mornings to come. Seven years you could not sleep on account of a crime committed by others. Now you are the criminal.

ELECTRA: I have Orestes. I have justice. I have everything.

THIRD FURY: Orestes! Never again will you see Orestes. We leave you only to surround him. We take your age and your shape to pursue him. Farewell. We shall never again leave him, until he goes mad or kills himself, cursing his sister.

ELECTRA: I have justice. I have everything.[48]

Giraudoux, it would appear, could not follow Ibsen all the way in his attack on the ideal. For Giraudoux was a realist only on condition of being at the same time an idealist. The ideal, he intimates, is inhuman: by the same token it is divine. It is cruel, cold, and merciless; but it is pure. It blinds the eye with the light of a world that is not ours. Electra is terrifying; but she has splendor. Here, as elsewhere, Giraudoux develops the paradox which is the psychic root of his drama: in his mind every idea implies its contrary. In *Electre* the assault on idealism is mounted by an idealist. The destruction of humanity is a purification. "What is it called," Wife Narses asks, "when the day breaks, like today, and everything is ruined, everything is sacked, and yet the air is fresh, and all is lost, the city burns, the innocent kill one another, but the guilty perish in a corner of the day that is breaking?"

ELECTRA: Ask the Beggar. He knows that.

THE BEGGAR: It has a very beautiful name, Wife Narses. It is called the dawn.[49]

There is also the question of Clytemnestra, that is to say, the question of marriage. Clytemnestra declares herself, as the Beggar puts it, only at the very end of the play, but her declaration is anticipated at the beginning of the second act by Agatha Theocathocles' sudden bitter outburst. Caught with a lover, Agatha turns upon her husband like a tigress:

> "I am pretty and he is ugly. I am young and he is old. I am bright and he is stupid. I have a soul and he has none. And it is he who has everything. At all events he has me. And it is I who have nothing. At all events I have him. And until this morning it was I who gave everything, who had to say thank you. Why?—I clean his boots. Why?—I brush away his dandruff. Why? I make his coffee. Why? When, in truth, I should poison him. When I should smear his collar with pitch and ashes. His shoes, at least. I understand that. I spit on them. I spit on him . . ."

The Beggar notes: "They sing very well, these wives."

Agatha Theocathocles, indeed, sings to some purpose, and also at some length:

> ". . . twenty-four hours a day we kill ourselves, we destroy ourselves for the satisfaction of a creature whose dissatisfaction is our only joy, for the presence of a husband whose absence is our only delight, for the vanity of the only man who every day shows us what most humiliates us in the world, the flap of his drawers and the soles of his feet. And then he dares reproach us for stealing one hour out of all this week of hell, one single hour! . . . They think we betray them only with lovers. . . . We betray you with everything . . . I betray you with my fingers, with my eyes, with the soles of my feet. When I look at you, I betray you. . . . Kill the olive trees, kill the pigeons, the little children, girls and boys, and the water, and the earth and the fire. Kill this beggar. I betray you with all of them."

The Beggar answers: "Much obliged."[50]

Clytemnestra's turn comes later. When the Corinthians are at the gates, she speaks at last of Agamemnon:

> Yes, I hated him . . . yes, after twenty years I am going to give myself the joy that Agatha has had! . . . A woman belongs to all the world. There is only one man in all the world to whom she does not belong. . . . The only man who was not for me was the king of kings, the father of fathers. . . . From the day he came to tear me away from my house, with his curly beard and with that little finger always raised, I hated him. He raised it to drink, he raised it to ride, the horse used to rear; and when he held the sceptre . . . and when he held me, I felt on my back only the pressure of four fingers. . . . The king of kings, what

> a joke! He was pompous, hesitant, silly. He was the fop of fops, the
> dupe of dupes. The king of kings had never been more than that little
> finger and that beard that nothing could smoothe.[51]

The question of the joys of marriage and the subjection of women is
by no means central in *Electre*, but in the case of Clytemnestra it was unavoidable. Agatha in some sense doubles the queen as Suzanne doubles
Judith. She betrays her husband, as a matter of principle, at every opportunity: but she does not go so far as Clytemnestra in her hostility.
The justice of these acts of vengeance is lost on Electra. She sees only
the justice that is due her as her father's daughter. In the 1930's this
Electra might have been considered amusing as well as perturbing. In
her way she reduced the ideal to an absurdity; but her behavior served to
highlight some of the conflicts that attended a period of transition when
the values of the past were fast dwindling into nothing.

Electre opened on 13 May 1937 at the Athenée as part of a special
season to accompany the Paris Exposition. Renée Devillers was cast as
Electra. Jouvet played the Beggar. Pierre Renoir was Aegisthus. Madeleine Ozeray played Agatha Theocathocles. The play was applauded;
but, judging by the reviews, it was not understood, and the critics, on
the whole, found it tedious. Seven years later the world had changed.
When Anouilh brought his *Antigone* to the stage during the German occupation in 1944, his play was interpreted in the light of the collaborators and the Résistance, and nobody took the trouble to look into the
question of idealism and realism. It was an issue that had survived two
wars. It was perhaps too much to expect it to survive three.

Much of the unfavorable criticism that was directed against *Electre* came
from those who felt that a play was an action and not a revery, and that
plot and character were the primary concern of the theâtre. Colette, for
example, in her review of the play, wondered whether drama could ever
be justified by displays of rhetoric and *jeux d'esprit*. Others objected to
the incoherence of the episodes and the lack of unity. In spite of the
critics, *Electre* had a run of 178 performances and was accounted a success. Nevertheless Giraudoux felt that its critics deserved a reply. When
it came, it was in the form of an *ars poetica* for the contemporary theatre.

L'Impromptu de Paris was presented as a curtain raiser in the revival of
La Guerre de Troie n'aura pas lieu on 4 December 1937, seven months after
the opening of *Electre*. In *Supplément au Voyage de Cook*, which had pre-

viously accompanied *La Guerre de Troie*, Giraudoux had borrowed a theme from Diderot. The new play followed Molière.

The plot of this little play serves mainly as a pretext for a discussion of Giraudoux's idea of the theatre; but one would be hard put to rationalize Giraudoux's practice in terms of what is said in this *divertissement*. The scene opens on the stage of the Athenée, which is bare. Pierre Renoir and Auguste Boverio are waiting to rehearse Molière's *L'Impromptu de Versailles*. The rest of the company is late. The actors are heard arguing loudly offstage. The stage-manager, Marthe, has rung the bell three times to summon the company when at last its members troop in. They are discussing realism and the Théâtre-libre. The discussion is interrupted by Jules Robineau. He walks in unannounced, falling over the clutter in the wings. Jouvet thinks he is the landlord's agent, and they are about to eject him from the theatre when it develops that he is the Commissioner of the Chamber of Deputies charged with the administration of the Theatre Budget, and that he has a hundred million francs to distribute. He has fifteen minutes at his disposal and wants Jouvet to explain the theatre to him so that he can fulfill his duties properly. The first question that comes up concerns the "literary" theatre.

Renoir complains that the adjective "literary" is a term of dispraise in the theatre, and that the distinction so often made between plays that are meant to be read and plays that are intended to be seen is unjust. For Jouvet also there is no such distinction; and both he and Boverio affirm their faith in the spoken word as a dramatic medium. The point is made that drama is not addressed to the intellect, but to the intuitive faculty. Robineau, however, insists that the public has a right to understand.

JOUVET: To understand? The word understand does not exist in the theatre. Do you understand the word understand, you, Renoir? . . .

RENOIR: It is with this word understand, Monsieur Robineau, that the semi-literate have spoiled the public. Go and see only what you understand—for a whole half-century that is what they keep telling them. Go and see *La Tosca:* when twelve carabineers fire their rifles at her lover, you have a good chance of understanding that they have shot him . . . The good thing is that the real public does not understand. It feels. It can therefore be shown everything without compromise and without reticence. Those who insist on understanding in the theatre are those who do not understand the theatre.[52]

For this reason, Bogar adds, literary talent is indispensable to the drama, for it is through his style that the author is able to scatter over the soul of the spectator the thousand reflections and iridescences which he has no more need to understand than he does a ray of sunshine. The function of the theatre, Jouvet concludes, is to take the place of the decadent press, the corrupt courts. The whole of society may be falling to pieces, but so long as the theatre is there, all is not lost. The Commissioner meanwhile has been seated in the *gloire*, a contraption which is meant to lower a character from the flies. In the course of the discussion it begins to move. It is in vain that they try to stop its ascent, and in spite of all that can be done, it bears Robineau up out of sight, until he is lost, presumably, in the Empyrean.

L'Impromptu de Paris affords a charming glimpse of Jouvet and his acting company; but it can hardly serve as a manual for playmaking. It does, however, help to clarify in some measure the Symbolist viewpoint in the thirties with regard to the drama, and it strikes a blow in defence of the kind of play that Giraudoux liked to write. Jouvet later amplified these views in an essay called *De Molière à Giraudoux*, in which he discussed the relation of the director to the author. The essay affirms the primacy of the text. Dramatic creation, he wrote, is a genuine revelation. It is born of an inner state, an inspiration. "It is not responsive to the explanations of logic or psychology: it is not a fabrication nor a reproduction . . . The author's invention is primal, total, sovereign and impossible to equal. Each of us tries innocently, ingenuously, to bring about a "reinvention" of the work by listening to it. To listen to it, it is necessary to silence in ourselves all feelings of superiority and all sense of criticism, and to abandon ourselves, to lose ourselves in the pleasure it brings and the happiness it contains."[53]

Giraudoux's idea of theatre, as it is developed in *L'Impromptu de Paris*, had something in common with the ideas which Antonin Artaud had published five years before in the *Mercure de France* as the "First Manifesto of the Theatre of Cruelty." Both Artaud and Giraudoux thought of the theatre as a place of communion in which the audience would be united mystically in a common experience, and both conceived of the drama along Symbolist lines. The difference was in the means through which the miracle of the theatre was to be accomplished. Artaud found it, as he said, impossible to express himself adequately in words. In his theatre, consequently, he proposed to destroy the primacy of the text. In his view words should be used in the theatre mainly as dramatic resources which the director would dispose expressively in the same way as gesture, movement, light, and sound. Giraudoux, on the other hand, had no trouble whatever with language, and he was willing to entrust his drama completely to the ministry of words.

There was also the difference of temperament. For Artaud it was necessary to smash one's way brutally through the veneer of civilization to the central core of humanity in order to set free the instinctual life, the vital current from which the drama draws its power. Giraudoux felt it was possible to move the soul through an incantation. The play, in his view, is a rendezvous, and the communion of author and audience is an act of love. For Artaud this relation is sadistic. In his theatre the bonds of humanity must be forged through pain. The goal in each case was the same, but the experience through which it would be reached had not much in common.

On 12 October 1938 Jouvet staged *La Cantique des cantiques* at the Comédie-Française with Madeleine Renaud in the role of the young girl Florence, Debucourt as the President, and Ledoux as Victor. Édouard Vuillard designed the set. It was the only play of Giraudoux to be presented at the Comédie-Francaise, and it was not a success. It was revived after the author's death, and fared no better. It is now seldom seen. It is nevertheless a very beautiful play. Together with *Supplément au Voyage de Cook* and *L'Apollon de Bellac* it makes a trio of one-act plays that have no peer in the modern theatre.

The plot was suggested by a passage in *Églantine*, a novel which Giraudoux had published eleven years before, in 1927, and the play reproduces some of the dialogue; but there is much that is new. The President is a man of importance, healthy and vigorous, an elegant man and handsome. He comes to a café to meet Florence, his young mistress, for whom he has brought an anniversary gift. At the café he is ushered to a good table, where women are invariably pleasant. But Florence does not appear. Instead it is Jérôme who comes. He informs the President respectfully that he is engaged to marry Florence. Beyond this he knows little about her. Now Florence appears, and the young man discreetly leaves her alone with the President so that they may discuss him at their ease. They discuss him. Florence's love-song is a long and detailed complaint. Jérôme has every possible disadvantage: "He burns himself everywhere. He bumps into everything. Every door pinches his fingers. Every umbrella pokes his eye. In the course of a month I have come to know every kind of lotion, suture and ointment. In the middle of the night suddenly he awakes with a boil on his finger. I spend my time annointing him, caulking him. What with the pinpricks and nail scratches he collects, I have to suck his blood ten times a day. I couldn't be more busy if a viper were commissioned to sting him once a minute. He is the god of minor disasters."[54]

In comparison the President is truly godlike. But Florence has fallen in love with Jérôme and there is nothing to be done about it. She has in her handbag the jewels the President has given her. One by one she returns them. They are costly presents, rubies and diamonds. He receives them, and one by one he returns them to her, recalling in each case the occasion of the gift. Florence is touched. For a moment her fate hangs in the balance. Then the young man appears. Having learned from the President that it is her birthday, he has bought Florence a very small false zircon as a gift. It is enough. Florence hands back the President's diamonds, and goes off happily with her young man. After a moment an official car drives up. The President is urgently needed at the Ministry.

The Song of Songs recapitulates the theme of *Intermezzo* and also, in some sense, its plot. In *Intermezzo* Isabelle must choose between the Supervisor of Weights and Measures and the Ghost, between the earthly life and the life of the spirit. The decision is difficult and it brings her to the verge of death. Florence has less difficulty. The President cannot marry her, but he can give her all the fine things of life—art, elegance, jewels, distinction. The young man can give her nothing but trouble; but he is inescapable. In the sadness of her choice there is a hint of the sadness of *L'École des femmes*, in which Jouvet often played Arnolphe, his greatest role. The President has brought up Florence as Arnolphe brought up Agnès. He has taught her all she knows, hoping one day to enjoy fully the fruits of her upbringing. He loses her to the first youth she bumps into on the street. But *The Song of Songs* is not a play of youth and age. The President is far from Molière's comic *senex*. What the two plays have in common is the tinge of bitterness, the heartbreak that gives poignancy to great comedy. At bottom the pathos of the situation, insofar as it is pathetic, is not so much in the fate of the President who loses the girl as in the fate of the girl who is lost, and in the plight of the young man whom she is no doubt destined to torture, without meaning to, all the rest of his life. It is the pathos of humanity, a complex of incompatible parts, which perpetuates itself efficiently in spite of the fact that nothing in it works. To this theme, first announced in *Intermezzo*, Giraudoux returned in *Ondine*, and later still, in definitive fashion, in *Sodome et Gomorrhe*.

Ondine was presented at the Athenée on 27 April 1939, after six months of rehearsal, with Madeleine Ozeray as Ondine, Jouvet as Ritter Hans, and Auguste Boverio as King of the Ondines. Pavel Tchelitchev designed an abstract setting, and there was incidental music by Henry Sauget. Giraudoux wrote a program note:

> In 1909 Charles Andler, who was in charge of literary studies at the Sorbonne, directed his student Jean Giraudoux to bring him, in a week's time, a commentary on Ondine. An excursion to Robinson, and then a particularly busy century, having forced the postponement of this assignment until now, the commentary has taken, thanks to Louis Jouvet, the form of a play, which is now dedicated, as was *Siegfried*, to the memory of the master.

This program note is amusing, but it need not be taken for gospel. Giraudoux's biographer, Professor Le Sage, has turned up the draft of a paper in which Giraudoux apparently fulfilled his scholarly assignment by criticizing La Motte-Fouqué's *Undine* for its lack of unity.[55] The program note was a pleasant piece of showmanship, evidently; and perhaps by the time it was written Giraudoux had forgotten the circumstances of his first encounter with the legend.

The ultimate source of his play was in fact an old poem called *Der Ritter von Staufenberg* which La Motte-Fouqué had used as the basis of the fairy tale he called *Undine*. Fouqué's story concerns the efforts of a water sprite to gain a human soul and, along with it, that eternal life which is reserved for humanity in the other world. In his version, a fisherman's daughter is mysteriously drowned in a lake, and a beautiful water sprite called Undine takes her place. When Undine is eighteen, her uncle, Fraistorrent, guides the knight Huldebrand von Ringstetten to the fisherman's hut. The knight falls in love with the girl, and a priest marries them. The moment she is married, Undine receives a soul, and the wild creature that she was is transformed into a loving and devoted wife. But her husband is seduced by the deceitful Bertalda. In consequence, Undine is forced by the law of her kind to leave him, and afterwards to kill him for his treachery. His end is sad: she drowns him in her tears. At his burial, a beautiful blonde woman appears among the mourners, and is miraculously transformed into a clear spring which forever after embraces the tomb of her unfaithful spouse.

Giraudoux followed Fouqué's version of the myth in somewhat the same spirit as he had followed Hebbel's version of the story of Judith. In

Fouqué's story the metamorphosis of the water sprite is the result of her desire for a soul, an organ which apparently water sprites can acquire only by marrying humans. Giraudoux's version goes far beyond this simple tale. His Ondine is immortal and forever fifteen. She has no need of a human soul since she is herself a soul. She is the soul of water, and participates in the soul of the world. All the elemental forces are in her service. One might imagine that this would be enough for any normal water sprite, but this ondine is one of the elect. The Abalstitiel comes for her in the guise of a young knight, the first she has ever seen, and she is swept away into another world, into an adventure from which, after ten years, she returns to her former life. It is, more or less, the story of Edmée in *Choix des élues* with some elaboration, for something of the sort happens also to Ritter Hans with what are, for him, dire results. It is also—more or less—the story of Kleist's *Das Käthchen von Heilbronn*.

The story of the knight Hans is the story of Ondine in reverse. In his case it is Ondine who is the Seducer, and it is Hans who is whirled away from his world into the unknown. But, unlike Ondine, Hans has no alternative. Once he is embarked on his trajectory it is impossible for him to return to his normal habitat. In juxtaposing these two beings from different spheres through a fateful union, Giraudoux poses the problem of *déclassement* on a cosmic scale, and is thus able to symbolize poetically the impossibility of reconciling the worlds between which the human spirit uncomfortably dwells.

The first act develops, in a delightful scene, the meeting of Hans and Ondine, and the mystic pact through which Ondine is enabled to exchange her world for his. The second act show how it is with them in the world of men. The demonstration is brought about by an Illusionist who produces a sequence of scenes which magically enacts the essential incidents of their lives before they actually take place, and thus compresses the events of a decade in a half-hour's time.

Ondine belongs to the great world, the universe. It is in vain that she tries to conform to the customs of the German court, a little world with which she has nothing in common. At court she plays the part of the noble savage with grace and dignity. Inevitably Hans is humiliated by her behavior; but she easily wins over the king and the queen, and the poet Bertram. When Bertha, the king's adopted daughter tries to shame her, Ondine retaliates with elemental vigor. It is thus revealed that the haughty Bertha is really a fisherman's daughter, the changeling who was spirited away to make a place for Ondine.

In the third act, ten years later, Bertha and Hans are about to be married. It is six months since Ondine vanished, presumably in the company of Bertram. Hans has sickened. There are omens of impending disaster. Then two fishermen bring in Ondine. She has let herself be caught in the Rhine, and she is brought to trial at once. Since she knows that Hans must die for betraying her, she tries pathetically to justify him, pretending that it was she who first betrayed him. The judges easily see through her devices. Nevertheless she is condemned to die as an alien creature, of demoniacal origin. The king of the ondines intervenes. Ondine is saved. It is Hans who dies. Then Ondine loses all memory of him and her life among men, and returns to her proper element, the water.

Giraudoux brought to this fairy tale all the poetic virtuosity he had developed in his earlier plays and also all his dramatic experience. In some sense it sums up his former work. There is no difficulty in identifying *Ondine* thematically with *Siegfried*, *Amphitryon 38*, *Judith*, and *Intermezzo*, all of them variations on a favorite theme. Essentially this involves the contrast of two worlds—the world of matter and the world of the spirit, the real and the ideal—and the predicament of the soul that is torn between its need for the one and its love of the other. In *Ondine* this conflict is given its clearest and most poignant development. The story of Hans and Ondine is no ordinary love story. It transcends its characters. What is described is the tragic love of the two worlds, eternally yearning to be united and eternally frustrated by their very nature.

To Bertram and to Queen Yseult the symbols are clear; but though these *voyants* are on speaking terms with Ondine, they are powerless to reach Hans, and so are incapable of bringing together what ultimately nothing can reconcile. Ondine likes Bertram. He understands her. But she loves Hans, who understands nothing. Hans is the sort of man she requires: ". . . the only man worthy of love is one who is like other men, who has the words and features of other men, who is indistinguishable from the others only by some further defect or clumsiness. . . ."[56] Obviously Ondine is a character similar to Florence in *La Cantique des cantiques:* she is Florence raised to the transcendental plane. Hans is a high romantic version of Jérôme; but his adventure with Ondine gives him, in the end, a degree of insight which Jérôme, in all likelihood, will never need or attain. Through suffering Hans comes to understand in some measure what has happened to him. He has cause to complain: "But why do they all make this error, whether they are called

Artemisia, or Cleopatra, or Ondine? . . . They fall upon some poor General Antony, or a poor knight Hans, on an average human wretch . . . and then it is all up with him. As for me, I had not a spare moment in all my life, what with the wars and the wounds, and the hunt and the chase. No—they had to add the fire in the veins, the poison in the eyes, the spice and the gall in the mouth. From heaven to hell they shook me, thwacked me, flayed me! Not counting that I am not gifted to see the picturesque in adventure. It was not very just!"[57]

Hans is, indeed, the victim of injustice. Neither Ondine nor Yseult gives him much credit for intelligence:

YSEULT: But don't you see that Hans loves all that is great in you only because he thinks it small? You are the light: he loves a blonde. You are grace itself: he loves a cutie. You are adventure: he loves a lark. . . . The moment he sees his mistake you will lose him.

ONDINE: He will not see it. If it were Bertram, Bertram would see it. But I foresaw this danger. Of all the knights I chose the simplest.

YSEULT: Even the simplest of men sees well enough to know he is blind.

ONDINE: Then I will tell him I am an ondine.

YSEULT: That would be the worst thing you could do. Perhaps to him, at the moment, you seem like an ondine, but only because he does not believe you are one. The real ondine, for Hans, would not be you, but Bertha in some costume ball, wearing a suit of scales.[58]

In spite of the Queen's opinion of him, however, Hans has enough imagination to put himself in a tragic dilemma. When he has Ondine, he longs for Bertha; when he has Bertha, he thinks only of Ondine. Giraudoux had in himself too much of the knight not to see the poet in Hans. Hans is depicted as *l'homme moyen sensuel;* but even the average man is a spiritual battleground, and Hans is, in his modest way, one of the elect. In Bertha he sees very clearly what is lacking in Ondine. In Ondine he sees everything that is missing in Bertha. Together the two would constitute the perfect wife, the ideal. Unhappily the law of marriage in the world of Hans allows him but one wife, and the law of the ondines makes no provision for a mistress. What is wrong in the social organism is not, as Rousseau pointed out, the fault of the individual so much as the result of the restrictions society places upon him. The ondines are constant by nature. Men are not. It is because the ondines are not obsessed, seemingly, by a longing for the ideal. Men are. It is a distressing trait which is perhaps in some relation to the principle of evolution.

In any case, Hans is blissfully ignorant of the obligation that Ondine, in her primal innocence, has imposed upon him. It is a condition of his marriage that he must, on pain of death, be faithful to his wife. The condition is, obviously, inhuman. In this case, however, the question of justice is academic. It is unnecessary for the water to kill Hans. He dies by himself, of a broken heart:

ONDINE: He is so young. So strong.

THE KING OF THE ONDINS: He is at the end of life. It is you who have killed him. Ondine, you who use only metaphors of dogfish, you may remember the pair that one day died while swimming together. They had crossed the ocean in a storm without any trouble, and one day in a beautiful gulf they ran into a little wave, and something deep inside was smashed. All the steel of the sea was in the curl of that wave! Day by day for a week, their eyes grew pale, their chaps fell. . . . But there was nothing wrong with them, they said . . . it was only that they were dying. . . . And so with men. It is not the oaks, the crimes, the monsters, that break the heart of the woodsman, the judge, the knight, but a slender reed, an innocence, a loving child. . . . He has an hour to live.[59]

The love of Ondine, her king implies, is too great for a human being to bear. But it is not the love of Ondine that has exhausted Hans. It is the inconvenience of love in general. The symbolism of *Ondine* is not abstruse. It leads directly to the heart of the problem, which is the problem of marriage. Ondine belongs to the infinite; but Bertha is skilful with the needle; she can discuss the financial situation; she remembers appointments. Hans's problem is the problem of husbands. Sworn to monogamy, men invariably marry two women, neither of whom exists. They marry Ondine with Bertha in mind. They marry Bertha, thinking of Ondine. The women are in a similar case, lost between Hans and Bertram. In these circumstances constancy is not possible. Where there is love, there is heartbreak. And when there is love no longer, for Giraudoux it is the end of the world.

Obviously Ondine is a special case, for it is seldom that man, even medieval man, marries a mermaid. Ondine is nature, spirit, that is to say, the noble savage in a particularly attractive form. Brought to a royal court, like Aoturou to Versailles, she charms everyone with her beauty and her distinction; everyone, that is, save those who are blind to such things. Compared with the cultivated Bertha, the uncultivated Ondine is the true aristocrat, naturally noble, and therefore noble to the core. She is generous, pure, and honest because she is herself, and her self is at one with nature, which is generous, pure, and honest. Ondine has the clarity of water. Bertha is false, calculating, and haughty, not because she is a villain, but because she is human and because humanity everlastingly aspires to be what it is not.

Thus, in *Ondine*, Giraudoux takes sides on the issue of primitivism, the return to nature and the naive, to the instinctual life which underlies the veneer of culture. The issue antedates the primitivism of the one Rousseau and the other, together with the artificial primitivism of Picasso, Jarry, and Artaud. Ondine is pre-romantic. She belongs to the elemental beings of the middle ages, to the world of Morgan le Fay. She has a human counterpart in Alceste in *Le Misanthrope*, though she shares only his sadness, not his indignation. She is by nature incapable of the hypocrisy which makes social life possible; but, unlike Alceste, she is willing to conform as best she can if that is the price of joining the human race. And she has a great desire to join it.

Ondine exemplifies, indeed, the desire of nature to become human, which the theory of evolution so convincingly demonstrates, the desire of the water to become soup, of the fish to walk the earth, and the monkey to govern nations. On the other hand it is not feasible to transform an elemental spirit overnight into a member of the Junior League. Politeness and tact are ingenious devices for making life comfortable for those who fear death. Ondine has no need of such things. She is forever young and forever beautiful. Her courtesy, therefore, is cosmic in its scope and takes no heed of niceties. Like Giraudoux's Electra she embodies the therapeutic power of truth and also its destructiveness. Consequently her desire to share the lot of humanity is not only absurd and pathetic, but also dangerous. What is tragic in *Ondine* is not Ondine's experience which, in the light of eternity, is ephemeral, but Hans's dilemma, which only death can resolve.

The Beggar in *Electre* is an enigmatic figure who dominates the play without taking an active part in the action. In *Ondine* a similar role is played by the Protean Water-King, *le roi des Ondins*. He is an elemental power, a god. He is also the Illusionist of the second act, that is to say, the author. It is he who shows the play of Hans, Ondine, and Bertha to the court, and he presents the play of Auguste, Eugénie, and the ondines which forms the interlude of act two. It is not clear whether he is intended to present the third act also, in which he appears first in the guise of a fisherman, and then, at the end, in his own proper character as an elemental power. Nor does it matter, specially. Like *Electre* and *Inter-*

mezzo, Ondine is a revery, a further example of the sort of *divagation poétique* which Giraudoux considered all his plays to be. It would be inept to apply realistic standards to a play of this sort, and in fact it defies logic. *Ondine* is a poem, not a thesis play; and very likely any attempt to extract a thesis from it would be a discourtesy to the author. The problem it suggests is a first-rate subject for meditation. There is no effort on the author's part to suggest a solution. Among the ondines, we are told, marriage presents no problems. It is otherwise in the world of men: there the problem of marriage is, seemingly, insoluble; and Hans very wisely dispels it by dying while he can.

Ondine ran through the spring of 1939. Then the Athenée closed for the summer. In September war was declared, and none of the Paris theatres opened on schedule. *Ondine* was resumed when the Athenée re-opened in March 1940. It closed again on May 15th. It was not given again in Paris until after the war was over.

In July 1939 Giraudoux was asked to take over the Commissariat d'Information. General mobilization was ordered on 26 August, and when war was declared in September, Giraudoux's division was attached to the War Office. His position was now far from enviable. He had no hand in policy making. His headquarters at the Hotel Continental presented a scene of the utmost confusion. His personal radio broadcasts were a failure. After six months, when Reynaud succeeded Daladier as head of state, Giraudoux left Paris and went with the Foreign Ministry to Bordeaux.[60] At Vichy, he was offered the post of ambassador to Greece. He declined, and thereafter accepted an insignificant appointment as Director of Historical Monuments. His diplomatic career was over. He was fifty-seven.

He spent the next two years at his mother's house in Cusset, in the Bourbonnais, not far from Vichy. There, at the end of December 1940, he finished the volume of essays entitled *Littérature*. The following year he went to Lausanne to deliver a series of lectures, later published as *Visitations*. He returned then to Paris, and took up his residence at the Hôtel de Castille in the rue Cambon, near the Athenée.

At sixty his life was in some disorder. He was virtually separated from his wife. His son was in London with de Gaulle. His plays were considered anti-cultural by the German censor. Jouvet was abroad. Unable to work in Paris, Jouvet had taken his company on a tour of South America. It lasted almost four years, from June 1941 to February 1945.

Giraudoux kept in touch with him. In 1942 he telephoned Jouvet from Lausanne that he was sending him a one-act play about Apollo. Jouvet received it in Rio de Janeiro in May, together with a note that read: "Dear Jouvet, dear Louis: Find a name for Apollo yourself. We shall soon meet again."

Jouvet called the play *L'Apollon de Marsac* after a small town in Limousin. It was presented in Rio on 16 June 1942 with Madeleine Ozeray in the part of Agnès, and Jouvet in the role of Le Monsieur de Marsac. By the time it was shown in Paris, in 1947—this time with Dominique Blanchar—a manuscript had been found which Giraudoux himself had entitled *L'Apollon de Bellac*. The title was accordingly changed to conform with this manuscript.

Far from being a poetic divagation in the manner of *Electre* or *Ondine*, *The Apollo of Bellac* is a perfectly constructed one-act play, a marvel of dramatic workmanship. In form it resembles a fable, and is thus somewhat closer to allegory than to symbolism; but thematically it might serve as a manual for Symbolist playwrights. It is a first-rate example of Giraudoux's mature style, an enchanting blend of fancy and wisdom.

Giraudoux must have been sixty when he wrote it, very possibly in Lausanne. The *Visitations* lectures were arranged around a sequence of short scenes, intended to serve as demonstrations of literary theory. In the first of these scenes Madeleine Ozeray comes looking for a job, and Louis Jouvet advises her that the best way to get men to do as she wishes is to tell them they are beautiful. She practices her newly acquired technique on several objects, and at last on a chandelier which, hearing its beauty praised, lights up by itself. It was on the basis of this scene that Giraudoux composed *L'Apollon de. . . .*

In the play, the firm to which Agnès applies is called "L'Office des Grands et Petits Inventions." She asks to see the President. The way to the President is barred by a particularly repulsive Receptionist, and the girl's position seems hopeless, when a stranger who happens to be in the waiting room comes to her aid with the secret which opens all doors. Under his supervision Agnès experiments with the office furniture, on a fly which has lit on her hand, and on various other things, till at last she tries her magic on the Receptionist. It works miraculously. She then practices her art on the officers of the firm, seriatim, up the chain of command as far as the President himself. He offers her a position as his private secretary. In addition, he presents her with the diamond he has bought for his wife's anniversary, and in the end offers her his hand in marriage.

But now that she has reached her goal by telling pious lies, Agnès feels the need to tell the truth. She longs to tell someone who is truly beautiful that he is beautiful. The Stranger, who calls himself simply a Man of Bellac, makes her close her eyes and evokes for her a vision of the supreme beauty of Apollo. But Agnès cannot bear the sight of the Ideal. She feels at ease only with such beauty as her hand can touch. The Man of Bellac who, for an instant, has embodied Apollo, kisses her. When she opens her eyes he has vanished. It is the President who is waiting for her, together with his directors, and they have a great desire to invite Apollo to lunch. They rush to the window and call him. But there is no longer any trace of the God. As Agnès says, he just passed by.

Giraudoux was as skilful as Greuze in portraying young girls. Agnès is a most successful creation. The Stranger is a poet, that is to say, an inventor. He gives an impressive demonstration of the creative power of the imagination and under his influence Agnès goes far. Unhappily she cannot go all the way. Beauty for her, as with most people, is a tangible thing. She has no conception of the beauty that eludes the hand's caress, the beauty of the abstract, and she clings to the things of this earth as resolutely as Alcmena in *Amphitryon 38*. Yet Agnès is not without some degree of insight. She understands that the beauty of the Absolute is not for mortal eyes, and that he who experiences this beauty is lost forever after to the things of this world. The things of this world are precious to her. She is needy, and she understands better than Isabelle that in order to live it is necessary to compromise. She does not dare to look upon Apollo:

> Do not count on me, Supreme Beauty. You know, my life is small. My day is ordinary, and each time I go up to my room I have five flights of stairs to climb in the darkness and in the odor of burnt cooking. Before my work or my rest there is always this preface of five flights and, oh, I am so lonely. Sometimes, happily, a cat is waiting in a doorway. I pet it. A bottle of milk is upset. I set it right. If there is a smell of gas I alert the concierge. Between the second floor and the third there is a turning where the steps sag because the stairs are old and have settled. At this turning I lose my balance and I gasp with the anguish that more fortunate souls feel on the afterdecks of ships. That is my life. It is a thing of

shadows and cramped flesh, a little bruised. That is what fills my mind,
the well of a staircase. So if I hesitate to imagine you as you really are,
it is because I must defend myself. Do not hold it against me. . . .[61]

The Man of Bellac is no stranger to the Absolute. He understands that
the Supreme Beauty is the ideal toward which all living things aspire,
and even the inanimate world, and he knows that by affirming the individual's participation in the ideal one can touch the inner core of being
with a ray of hope. In making Agnès tell men that they are beautiful the
Man of Bellac brings into play the irresistible power of the Heavenly
Aphrodite, for to have one's beauty noted is to be accepted and loved.
Thus in the course of her ministry Agnès restores the individuals with
whom she comes in contact to their place in the cosmic harmony and it is
only natural that she should reap the benefits of their gratitude. Her
role, of course, is equivocal. She believes that she is lying, that she is
flattering. In fact, she is telling the truth, more profoundly than she
knows. The Man of Bellac explains this to the President's wife:

THE MAN OF BELLAC: Agnès did not lie to the President. And Cleopatra told
    Caesar the truth, and Delilah told the truth to Samson. And the truth
    is that men are beautiful, all of them, and always, and the woman
    who tells them so is no liar.
THÉRÈSE: In short, it is I, the liar.
THE MAN OF BELLAC: It is you who are blind. For all one really has to do to
    see their beauty is to look at men at their work and their play. Each
    has his beauty, his beauties. His bodily beauty: the stocky ones hold
    the earth well. The gangly ones hang well from the sky. His beauty of
    place: the hunchback on the ridge of Notre Dame is a masterpiece of
    Gothic beauty. All that is necessary is to get him there. His beauty of
    profession, finally: The movingman has the beauty of movingmen.
    The President, of presidents. The only difficulty comes when they
    change places, when the movingman takes on the beauty of the Presi-
    dent, the President, of the movingman.[62]

It is not through flattery, therefore, that Agnès brings joy into the
lives of men but through insight. This insight, it is true, is not her own.
It is the poet's insight; but that does not matter. In Giraudoux's view it is
chiefly through woman that man sees himself and the world in its splendor. In woman he finds his lost paradise. In *Sodome et Gomorrhe* Lia tells
her husband:

As for me, my body has never been anything but my voice to you; my
breast, my hair, my legs have never been anything but the words of the

language that was banished from our lips by our primal sin. Across the ages, across death, across the thickness of folly and wisdom, across the changing faces of the earth, my hands, my hips, my eyes have told you of the love and the hope of before the Fall. All you know of what were once the real rivers, the real trees, the real life, it is through them that you know it. . . .[63]

Lia is a Symbolist, obviously, and learned. Agnès is a simple girl. The message is the same. For Giraudoux the function of woman is to tell man that he is beautiful. In the 1970's the idea seems quaint. But no one questions the fact, even now, that man's chief function from the beginning has been to tell woman that she is beautiful. Doubtless that too has to do with the evolutionary process.

In *The Apollo of Bellac* Giraudoux proposes a simple solution to the problem of the sexes which seems so complex in *Ondine* and *Intermezzo*. It is essentially a matter of mutual admiration. "This young woman," the President tells his wife, "tells me I am beautiful. It is because she is beautiful. You keep telling me I am ugly. I have always suspected it: you are hideous."[64] Apart from the question of utility, these ideas raise the question of reality and representation in the Schopenhauerian sense. To Agnès the President seems beautiful: he responds by becoming beautiful. In his wife's eyes he is ugly. He obliges her in similar fashion: the uglier she thinks he is, the uglier he becomes. In this world, it is implied, truth is a matter of opinion; but The Man of Bellac is aware of the Absolute. There exists somewhere the ideal beauty by which all earthly beauties are measured, and from which all human ideas of beauty are derived: there is Apollo, whose features The Man of Bellac can evoke, but whom Agnès cannot bring herself to contemplate. There is also the practical question of marriage. Thérèse tells her husband, the President:

I have given you, without reserve, my life and my talent. I share a bed whose quilt I have stuffed and embroidered. Do you slide around in your bed? Your roast is never overdone, your coffee is never too weak. You are, thanks to me, one of these rare men who can be sure that their handkerchief is fresh, that their feet are never bare in their shoes—are they bare in your shoes, your feet?—and the mites, when winter comes, search in vain in your suits the spot of oil or grease that will permit them to settle. . . .[65]

Finally, there is the question of the author. In *The Apollo of Bellac* he supervises everything. In scenes in which he does not speak, he hides behind the statue of Archimedes, and pokes his head out periodically, with grimaces of encouragement or disapproval. Toward the end he assumes the mantle of the *raisonneur*, and at the last, like the Ghost in *Intermezzo*, he kisses the heroine before she is launched into the world of weights and measures. The author is completely identified with The Man of Bellac, and, like the puppeteer of the Japanese Bunraku, he is at the same time visible and invisible, so that without being in the least intrusive, he makes us conscious at every moment of his presence.

Giraudoux never saw *The Apollo of Bellac*. By the time Jouvet brought it to Paris, Giraudoux was dead.

On 13 May 1942 Jouvet received a manuscript in Rio with a letter that read: "I am working well for you. *Sodome et Gomorrhe* is finished. *La Folle de Chaillot* will be ready when you return." There was also *Pour Lucrèce*, of which at this time Giraudoux said nothing. Of these plays of his last years, he was able to see only *Sodome et Gomorrhe*.

The second scene of *Visitations* was the result of a visit to the home of Alfred Lunt and Lynn Fontanne, who had played brilliantly in S. N. Behrman's English version of *Amphitryon 38*, the only play of Giraudoux's which was seen in New York before the production of *The Madwoman of Chaillot* in 1949. Lunt and Fontanne, we are told, had asked Giraudoux to write a play for them. He thought of casting them in a play involving the battle of the sexes and, with them in mind, he wrote the scene of Samson and Delilah which appears in *Visitations*, and was later transcribed into *Sodome et Gomorrhe*. The play was apparently finished in May 1942. It was produced in Paris on 11 October 1943 by Jacques Hébertot, with Edwige Feuillère in the part of Lia and Gérard Philippe in the role of the Angel.

Sodome et Gomorrhe is the most imaginative of Giraudoux's plays, and the least playable. It is inconceivable that it should have served as a vehicle for the comedic talents of Lunt and Fontanne; in any case, they never played it. Its mood is sombre. It reflects the hopelessness of a period of extreme depression, with the Germans in Paris and Pétain in Vichy, when all the things that Giraudoux lived for seemed to be lost, perhaps forever. *Sodome et Gomorrhe* describes the end of the world.

The play had no trouble passing the censor, in spite of Giraudoux's anti-cultural status. The Germans were in Paris, but the theatrical season that year was brilliant. Among the openings in 1943 were Barrault's production of Claudel's *Le Soulier de satin* at the Comédie-Française, Dullin's production of Sartre's *Les Mouches*, and Cocteau's *Renaud et Armide*. An opera based on *Amphitryon 38* was running at the Opéra-Comique. At the Théâtre Hébertot, *Sodome et Gomorrhe* had a run of 214 performances.

It excited much discussion. The press, on the whole, was unfavorable. The consensus was that the play concerned the trend toward homosexuality associated with the current vogue of Proust and Gide. It was a natural inference. The destruction of Sodom and Gomorrah in the Bible is said to be the result of unnatural vice, and at the end of *Sodome* the sexes are completely separated when the world comes to an end.[66] There is, however, no mention of homosexuality in Giraudoux's play, and the separation of the sexes in the final scene extends to the animals and plants, and thus seems to be the consequence of the breakdown of the spiritual relationship involved in sexual reproduction rather than the result of a perverse attraction within the sexes.

In spite of its success, obviously, *Sodome et Gomorrhe* was not understood in 1943; indeed, there is much in it that remains puzzling. Those who are allegorically minded may find it amusing to read its symbols in terms of the political situation of the period. If it is assumed that the twin cities of Sodom and Gomorrah represent the neighboring countries of France and Germany, and that the marital discord of Jean and Lia symbolizes the periodic squabbles of German Hans and French Marianne, the play may be translated into a metaphor appropriate to a period when France was prostrate and Germany lay in ruins. But such an interpretation, while sufficiently banal to be apposite, hardly does the play justice.

Sodome et Gomorrhe is not a good play. It is, in truth, among the most tedious of Giraudoux's writings. It is also among the most profound and meaningful of his works. There is not much in it that can be called dramatic action. It is a duel of words. In Giraudoux's eyes, as we have seen, drama was primarily verbal. In his essay on "The Director" in *Littérature*, he repeated a favorite comparison: "For the Frenchman the soul can be opened in the most logical manner, like a safe, with a word: with the *Word*, and he rejects the use of the blow torch and the jimmy. He refuses not to consider dialogue as the supreme form of duel for creatures having the gift of words."

Sodome et Gomorrhe magnifies a domestic rift to cosmic proportions. It describes the end of a marriage in terms that go to the very foundations of human society. In the author's imagination the fate of the world hangs upon the marriage of Jean and Lia. These two are the flower of the human race, the ideal couple. They have loved one another deeply, and are incapable of any other love. They cannot live without one another, consequently their rift is mortal. And it is final. After five years of happiness Lia complains to her friend Ruth that Jean is no longer the man she married. He is dispersed among their friends, one bit here, another there:

> What is left to me now of Jean? I am speaking of his body, not his spirit. I am speaking of the very features which identified him and adorned him in my eyes. His voice resides now in the mouth of Pierre. His look is in the eyes of André. His hand has gone to attach itself to my uncle's wrist. If I wish to kiss it, or caress it, I must go and find my uncle! Yesterday, after many months, I heard once again the sound of his laughter, that sound that was the true tone of liberty; I ran; I saw a slave laughing. . . .[67]

The man who is left to her, she tells Ruth, is a stranger. Now each of them has his own reality, his own vision, and she feels cheated. With Ruth the case is different. Ruth is a passive creature. She married Jacques in the hope of living through him a life of constant change and movement, like a spectator in a theatre. She tells Lia:

> . . . . It was in him and through him that I was going to taste the delights and excitements of a life that by myself I found dull. I held in my arms the man who was going to live for me, suffer for me . . . I was going to see anxiety succeed confidence, fever overcome health, rage take the place of calm. All the clouds and suns on his face, and I at the bottom of him feeding on the food of women, on his entrails and his heart. Until death.[68]

But, unfortunately, Jacques is immutable. And now Ruth says, "I eat, I think, I suffer, I love, only myself." And she too feels cheated.

What is unusual in this situation is that it has come to the attention of God that there are no longer any happy couples in the world, consequently he is thinking of scrapping the entire enterprise as a failure. The heavenly host has descended on the earth. The land is swarming with angels, all busily trying to find a happy couple for whose sake the world may be saved from destruction. There are said to be only two happy couples in existence. There are Samson and Delilah, and Jean and Lia. The angels know that the marriage of Samson and Delilah is a fraud and a pretense, the union of a false woman and a deceitful man. All depends on Lia and Jean. But now Lia has left her husband.

Lia makes no secret of her unhappiness. But, the Angel explains, she has been chosen. It rests with her, and with her alone, to save the world. For God is disappointed in his creation. In the beginning he had created a single human being. This being was split in two the day that God, in a moment of euphoria, created liberty, and man acquired free will. But God expected this dual being to live as one flesh, and thus to increase and multiply forever in love and harmony. His only joy in his creation is to contemplate the conjugal hearth fires which from heaven can be seen glimmering on earth as from the earth the stars can be seen twinkling in God's firmament. Now he sees but one star on earth. If this goes out, he will put an end to everything.

All the powers of heaven are therefore concentrated on Lia in the effort to reconcile her to her husband. But Lia is of the stuff of Electra. She refuses to save the world by living a lie. She tells her Angel: "I am quite willing that you should choose me. Besides, only God could have singled me out on this day when I see myself vanishing. I am the snow in the fountain, the log in the flame. But that I should be marked out by God, elected by his emissaries as the heroine of the home, that all the tongues of heaven should lick my body and my heart to make me go back to the husband who does not love me and whom I detest, whom I have abandoned and who has abandoned me, that I do not accept."[69]

The Angel, however, cares nothing for truth. Like the God of Judith he is interested not in the motive, but in the outcome. Lia gives him no encouragement. She will accept nothing short of an ideal marriage. In consequence, the only being with whom she can be happy is an angel. If the Angel will accept her, she tells him, she will ask nothing more: ". . . What have I not asked of Jean, what would I not ask of Jacques, that they would not grant me to bring a semblance of activity and love into our union? And what pressures of hands and what gluings of cheeks. And how many useless voyages into the dawn and the twilight! What happiness if all that were finished! I do not have to touch you; with you I no longer have hands or breasts or lips, and I do not need them; I am no longer in these shadows where I have to cling or call. I have the happiness of things that are clear. What do I want? I want only to share your light . . ."[70]

The Angel rejects her offer indignantly. But for Lia no other solution is possible. The situation is the inverse of the affair of Isabelle and the Ghost of *Intermezzo:* here it is the girl who woos the shade. But in this case the angel of God withstands the temptation of the flesh, and in the end Lia is forced to take Jacques instead:

THE ANGEL: The angel or the brute.

LIA: It is heaven that forces me to it. I had chosen the angel.

THE ANGEL: Your name is falsehood, Lia.

LIA: . . . Don't you understand? Are you going to be like God? My voice is not my voice, my love is not my love: they are those of the first woman! Do not call the man in between you and her! Hear me! Listen to me! Angel! Angel!

THE ANGEL: Go away. (*Jacques comes in*)

JACQUES: Were you calling me, Lia?

LIA: With all my might. . . . Come.[71]

The substitution does not serve. The ideal is out of reach, and as for the real, the affair with Jacques, who does not change, does nothing for Lia; nor does Ruth do any better with the changeable Jean. Nothing has been gained by the exchange of partners. In Jacques, Lia sees only a version of Jean; while in Ruth, Jean sees only what he thought was Lia. Marriage without love is a prison; and an exchange of cells is not a liberation. The only possibility of saving the world, the Angel tells Lia, is for her to join the angels in deceiving God by pretending that she is happily united with Jean, whom she no longer loves. She agrees at last:

LIA: If you wish. But I no longer give something for nothing. I want my recompense.

THE ANGEL: You shall have it. God has it ready for you.

LIA: Surely not. He has never known what I needed.

THE ANGEL: You will never again be happy.

LIA: Thank you, Angel.

THE ANGEL: Your beauty will fade. Will pass.

LIA: Thank you, Angel.

THE ANGEL: The earth will swarm with all the men and women you detest.

LIA: Thank you, Angel.

THE ANGEL: And I will forget you. I have already forgotten you.

LIA: Thank you. He understands.

THE ANGEL: And you will forget me.

LIA: I will not forget you. I will forget everything. Not you.

THE ANGEL: From this night, you will forget me.

LIA: Very well. Let Jean come.[72]

What is in store for Lia, evidently, is the life that is in store for those who have had a glimpse of the ideal, the Seducer, and who must afterwards return to their reality. It is the normal situation of marriage, the future which the Ghost predicts for Isabelle when she chooses the Supervisor. But although Lia has agreed to accept Jean under these conditions, Jean also has his conditions. He has learned something during the exchange of partners: "Ruth taught me that one woman is like another. That what we believed to be most secret in devotion and tenderness, what seemed to me to be in Lia an unparalleled example of abandon or of conquest, is at the disposal of every woman, on desire or on demand."

For Lia a reconciliation on these terms is not possible. Jean's disillusionment negates even what no longer exists between them. It destroys her unique character, her identity, and under these conditions she not only refuses the pretense of marriage, she declines even to pose with Jean as a couple about to be destroyed. There is a final exchange of civilities between them. Then they part forever. Jean holds forth on the nature of woman:

JEAN: You have neither vision nor foresight. You are always wrong. We men pretend to believe in your connections with the universe, in your spiritual antennae. It is only to keep you busy, to flatter you, to give your body the curve and pulp that only self-conceit confers, which makes it soft and fruitful. You have none of that. You are not clasped to the flesh of the universe, but only to its skin. . . .

LIA: And man? Is he to keep all the cockades he has pinned on himself? He is good? He is kind? He is faithful?

JEAN: I do not know. But it is he who is inconstant, and responsive to the magnets of the world. It is he who speaks, not only as man, but for every voiceless object in nature, for woman, among other things. It is I who have said through your lips all that you have said today. . . .[73]

This discussion, which is useless, leads them back to the interminable argument about the weather with which the play opens. It was, to begin with, a beautiful day for Jean, and a gloomy day for Lia. Now their opinions are reversed. To him the day seems awful; for her, it is the most beautiful day of her life. It is the day the world will end.

In the final tableau all the women range themselves on one side, the men on the other. The women are joined by the serpents, the birds, the buffaloes. The scene had been envisaged, more or less, a century before, by Alfred de Vigny:

> Et se jetant de loin un regard irrité
> Les deux sexes mourront chacun de son côté.

Lia breathes a sigh of relief:

> It is our gift, the end of the world. Our gift. Those sorrows of men that
> we pretended to feel, those whims of men that we pretended to under-
> stand, those joys of men that we pretended to share, we are now free of
> all that. It is finished, that false coupling of my weakness and their
> strength, of my tender skin and their beards, of our carelessness and
> their zeal. . . .

The men too are relieved. The sexual experiment is over, and forever.
The Angel gives the word. The skies flame. The world is reduced to
ashes. There is nothing left—except the eternal argument:

THE VOICE OF JEAN: Pardon, heavens! What darkness!
THE VOICE OF LIA: Thank you, heavens! What a dawn!
THE ARCHANGEL: Will they never be quiet? Will they never die?
THE ANGEL: They are dead.
THE ARCHANEGL: Who is it then that is speaking?
THE ANGEL: They. It is not enough to die. The scene continues.[74]

It was cold in Paris in the winter, during the Occupation. Fuel was
scarce. In his last years at the Hotel de Castille, Giraudoux did much of
his writing in bed. He wrote a good deal. Among other things, he wrote
an *Hommage à Marivaux* in 1943, which was spoken from the stage of the
Comédie-Française, and *Sans pouvoirs*, published in 1946. By November
1943 *La Folle de Chaillot* was finished. He did not submit it to Hébertot
for production. The cast was large. The setting was ambitious. Evidently he considered that the text required the ministrations of Jouvet.
On the first page of the manuscript he wrote, prophetically, *"La Folle de
Chaillot* was presented for the first time on 17 October 1945 on the stage
of the Théâtre de l'Athenée by Louis Jouvet." The prediction was unduly optimistic. It came two months short of the mark.

Giraudoux's mother died at the end of 1943. Soon after, he himself
was taken ill. In January he suffered an attack of acute uremia, complicated by a meningeal hemorrhage. He was taken from his hotel room to
the family apartment on the Quai d'Orsay. There, after three days of
agony, Giraudoux died, the 31st of January 1944.

He died with his habitual reserve. At the Théâtre Hébertot, where

Sodome et Gomorrhe was still running, the audience was unaware that the author was ill. The evening after his death, Lucien Nat came before the curtain and read the announcement. It closed with the request that there be no applause at the end of the play. That evening the audience departed in silence.

Jouvet was in Mexico. He played a second season there after the death of Giraudoux, then toured the French Antilles. In February 1945 he was back in Paris, and that spring he reassembled what was left of his company—Auguste Boverio, Lucienne Bogaert, Oudart, and some others, and set about reopening the Athenée. He planned to open his season with *La Folle de Chaillot*. The manuscript was in some disorder. It was Giraudoux's habit to rewrite his plays assiduously, and a final text was seldom established before the end of the rehearsals. In this case there were three versions of the final scene of act one. Jouvet wisely chose the shortest. The concluding scenes of the play, similarly, offered some difficulty. Jouvet made no cuts in the text. "He is not here," he remarked, "to defend himself." [75]

In Paris there were shortages of everything. Jouvet appealed to the public to contribute costumes. The public responded with enthusiasm. Attics were ransacked. There was a deluge of old clothes. Bérard designed the settings. The Division of Beaux Arts awarded the production a substantial subsidy. Marguerite Moréno, now in her seventies and long retired, was prevailed on to undertake the leading part. Jouvet played the Ragpicker. The première took place on 19 December 1945, and was treated as an event of national importance. The play was a spectacular success. It had a run of almost 300 performances.

The timing, of course, gave this production unusual interest. At a time when France had scarcely recovered from the German presence, *La Folle de Chaillot* spoke significantly of profiteers, black markets, and war-speculators, and for many it marked the transition from a gracious world that was lost forever to a future that was not only uncertain but profoundly disquieting. It was a play on a level of innocence that approximated the fancies of childhood, and was thus particularly agreeable to the avant garde, to which the wisdom of madness also was normally a most congenial idea. In the less sophisticated it aroused nostalgia for a *belle époque* that doubtless had never existed, and was for that reason especially precious. For all those who had survived the humiliation of defeat and surrender it sounded a strain of optimism which was all the more poignant for being completely and avowedly unrealistic, a madwoman's dream.

Insofar as it had a message, *La Folle de Chaillot* was puzzling. It was obviously a Symbolist play; but precisely what its symbols signified was a question no one could answer with confidence. Its symbolism was, indeed, extremely accommodating. It invited interpretation as an indictment of capitalism, and accordingly delighted the Marxists. At the same time it extolled the virtues of a bygone aristocracy, and thus gratified the Conservatives. The Environmentalists found much in it that was commendable. It extolled the beauty of nature, of liberty, of Paris, of history, of love. It was a very funny play, and profoundly sad. And it was at the same time zany and wise. Such plays deserve success. This one proved to be one of the most durable plays of the modern theatre.

La Folle de Chaillot is an up-to-date version of a miracle play, of the type of the Miracles de Notre Dame, a medieval genre, in which through the intervention of the Blessed Virgin, the faithful are miraculously saved from impending disaster. It was not unusual for such plays to be set in taverns or other resorts where thieves convened, for in the middle ages God's messengers frequented all levels of society. *La Folle de Chaillot* begins in a tavern and ends in a cellar adjoining a sewer.

The Madwoman's world is a nineteenth-century stronghold in the middle of twentieth-century Paris, manned by vagabonds and harboring congenial dogs and cats. In the world outside, the evil powers already have the upper hand. It is a lamentable fact that has not yet been brought to the Madwoman's notice, for she inhabits a world that came to an end a half-century ago, and now exists only in her mind. She has perpetuated this by-gone reality for herself through the power of her fancy, but she is quite prepared to revitalize it once again for everyone if it is necessary.

It is in fact necessary; for in her absence things have come to a critical pass. There has been an invasion of soulless beings who have succeeded in infiltrating the social structure from top to bottom. One by one the good people who have been displaced by these creatures have vanished, and those who survive are neither happy nor safe. When these facts are brought to the attention of the Madwoman, she reacts with extraordinary vigor. It is the Ragpicker who brings her up to date:

THE MADWOMAN: What are they like?

THE RAGPICKER: In the street they go bareheaded, and indoors they wear hats. They talk out of the corner of their mouths. They do not run.

They do not hurry. You will never see one perspire. They tap their
cigarette on their cigarette case when they wish to smoke. A sound of
thunder. They have wrinkles, and bags under their eyes that we don't
have. . . . They have women like ours, but richer and more fashionable. They purchase store-window manikins, furs included, and pay
extra to have them animated. Then they marry them.

THE MADWOMAN: What do they do?

THE RAGPICKER: They don't do anything. When they meet they whisper
together and pass one another 5000-franc notes. . . . They have their
fingers in everything, but they touch nothing and make nothing, except money . . . They manage everything, they spoil everything.
Look at the shopkeepers. They no longer smile at one. They pay attention only to them. The butcher depends on the veal pimp, the service station on the petrol pimp, the fruit-vendor on the produce pimp.
. . . That way, Countess, everything costs more. . . .[76]

La Folle de Chaillot makes a novel effect, but it is constructed along
quite conventional lines. There are two plots. The main plot concerns
the efforts of a group of unscrupulous promoters to convert Paris into an
oil field. The subplot involves the love of a young man called Pierre for a
lovable girl called Irma, who is the dishwasher at the Café Chez Francis,
avenue Montaigne. This love-story, itself quite rudimentary, is doubled
by the tragic love of the Madwoman, the Countess Aurélie, for one
Adolphe Bertaut, a gentleman who never summoned up the courage to
propose marriage to her, and instead married a lady called Georgette.
Pierre has been blackmailed into planting a bomb in the house of the city
architect who has refused permission to drill an oil well on the place de
l'Alma. He tries to kill himself instead by jumping off the Alma bridge,
but he is saved before he can jump. The Countess gives him a new lease
on life. Then he sees Irma and at once falls in love. The Countess now
sets in motion a plot which ends in the liquidation of all the human ver-
min that infest Paris. When these are disposed of, the earth is transfig-
ured, and Paris once again becomes the city of our dreams.

In *La Folle de Chaillot* Giraudoux rang still another change on the
theme of the *élues*. The Madwoman is one of the elect, and she is singled
out for a heroic mission: she is to save the world. In the case of Judith,
similarly chosen, the outcome is bitterly ironical, though it is successful.
Isabelle's mission is forever frustrated. Electra restores justice at the expense of everything else. *La Folle de Chaillot* seems more optimistic. The
Madwoman acts. The world is saved. There are no unpleasant side-ef-

fects. The solution is direct, uncomplicated, and delightfully simple. The evil of the world is flushed down the drain, and at once a new era dawns. There is no irony in this outcome. Only madness.

La Folle de Chaillot is, of course, a kind of joke and, like all good jokes, it has a serious basis. The Madwoman, as the waiter Martial insists, is not mad: "Why mad? I will not permit you to insult her. She is the Madwoman of Chaillot." She is also, presumably, not sane in the way that ordinary people are sane. She belongs, indeed, to the select company of the mad folk of literature, the wise fools, the Touchstones and Chicots, those who are touched with a spark of divinity and are therefore accorded privileges denied to normal people. Her personal life seems to be well known in this corner of Paris which she inhabits and, in a sense, rules. It is known, for example, that time stopped for her the day when she lost Adolphe Bertaut, though when or how that happened is not entirely clear. However it happened, the result was regrettable. Her scene with Pierre touches very delicately on the grotesque without losing an iota of its pathos:

THE MADWOMAN: Why did you leave me, Adolphe Bertaut? Was she so lovely, this Georgette?
PIERRE: A thousand times less lovely than you.
THE MADWOMAN: It was her mind that attracted you?
PIERRE: She was stupid.
THE MADWOMAN: That's just what I thought. That's just what all men do! They love you because you are good, bright and transparent, and at the first opportunity they leave you for a woman who is ugly, dull and opaque. But why, Adolphe Bertaut, why?
PIERRE: Why, Aurélie? [77]

Whether the Madwoman is mad, or only flirting with madness, it is impossible to say, and this ambiguity is essential to the characterization. Poetry and madness had been close relatives for centuries, and for some time, as we have seen, madness had been in the forefront of fashion. In some quarters the view persisted that madness was simply a world-view that differed from the official stereotypes, and perhaps with superior validity. Since this was precisely what the modern artist was after, the question of madness threatened in these years to become perplexing. In Sartre's famous short-story, "La Chambre," published in 1947, the interesting, but dangerous, hallucinations of paranoia are contrasted in equivocal fashion with the stolid certainties of a healthy mind; and the madness of Artaud seemed peculiarly appealing to many who found the sanity of sane people distasteful.

The Madwoman is a product of her time, a genuine character, and therefore inexplicable. The same may be said of the other madwomen of the play, although these are only lightly sketched in. All are glamorous. The villains, however, businessmen all—the President, the Broker, the Baron, the Prospector—are equally mad in their fashion, but not equally glamorous. They are characterized in some detail, but they are not characters; they are symbols and might wear masks. And since they exist only as types, they are at liberty to describe themselves realistically without regard for verisimilitude, and without having any dimension. It is necessary that we should know them before they are consigned to oblivion; but being abstractions, they may be disposed of without arousing sympathy or inducing identification. A breath suffices to blow them away.

Around these shadowy personages others swarm, equally abstract and equally realistic, the Deaf-Mute, the Café Waiter, the Street Singer, the Quack Doctor, the Juggler, and the other street people. Like the angels in *Sodome et Gomorrhe* these characters buzz about, looking, listening, and, when they can, interposing a wholesome presence between the powers of evil and their nefarious designs. Besides these living vestiges of a better world there are, invisibly arrayed against the invaders, the spirits of the past: there is history. The Prospector complains:

> the most potent weapon of our enemies is actually blackmail. On the surface of the earth they arrange, in the guise of sites and cities, ancient beauties which human respect prevents us from exploiting, or sacking, if you like, for where we pass neither grave nor monument ever again is seen. They convince these backward minds that the banal values of memory, history and human intimacy should be held superior to those of the metals and liquids of the infernal regions. . . . Even here they let children play on the sites best suited for excavation! The Rhinegold is less well guarded by its gnomes than the gold of Paris by its park police. . . .[78]

The powers of evil are nevertheless strong and cunning, and they seem invincible. But their fall takes place by itself. Their greed guides them to their doom. They need only a signal to destroy themselves. Their destruction, however, is an act of justice, and justice involves formal procedures and judicial ritual. Like the culprits of *Electre* they are

given a full opportunity to justify themselves, even though they are condemned in advance. The trial in this case is bizarre. The accused are not
summoned and are not present. The tribunal is composed of madwomen. The jury is a group of vagabonds. The millionaires on trial are
represented at the bar of justice by the Ragpicker. The result is rather
reminiscent of Aristophanes than of Kafka.

The Ragpicker's advocacy, indeed, goes somewhat beyond what is
strictly necessary to convict the presidents and the pimps. The trial has
scope. It is a trial of the ideal rich by the ideal poor. It is the Ragpicker's
assumption that, in Proudhon's celebrated phrase, property is theft, and
his defence of wealth gives the proceedings a distinctly socialist coloring.
He speaks, paradoxically, in the guise of a reluctant millionaire: "Money
is theft, a racket; I detest it, I have no stomach for it: but it adores me. I
daresay I have qualities that it finds attractive. It dislikes distinction. I
am vulgar. It doesn't like intelligence. I am a fool. It doesn't like altru-
ism. I am selfish. And that's why it wouldn't let go of me till I made my
40 million. Now it will never let me go. I am the ideal rich. I am not
proud of it, but that's where I am . . ."

The ideal rich defends itself marvellously well, and is duly condemned. The case is declared closed. The court is adjourned. But the
defendant will not admit that the case is closed:

THE RAGPICKER: How closed? I belong to the two hundred families. For a
    member of the two hundred families the case is never closed. . . .
JOSEPHINE: I order you to be quiet. The court is adjourned.
THE RAGPICKER: The two hundred families are not subject to orders. Nor to
    laws. You don't know them! . . . The two hundred families can show
    you its arse, ladies, and people smile and kiss it as if it were its face.
    They kiss it. The two hundred families are not especially fond of that;
    it is the arse-kissers who insist. . . . Touch a hair of my head, if you
    dare. You will see what sealed orders are, what it is like in the galleys,
    and the iron masks. The two hundred families are not wicked. But
    when they are attacked, they defend themselves. That is their motto.
    Lion-tamers take notice! [79]

It is not, however, the two hundred families that go down the drain in
the end. The Ragpicker has confused the issue. It is the Prospectors, the
Presidents, the promoters and exploiters, all the parasites of industry and
commerce. When they have returned to the infernal regions whence they
came, the air of Paris is purified and the sky once again is blue. They are
gone, the Madwoman tells Irma, forever: "Evaporated, Irma. They were

evil. And evil evaporates. They say they are eternal and people believe them. And they do all they can to be eternal. But not at all! Pride, greed, selfishness inflames them to such a degree of heat that if they pass over a point where the earth conceals kindness or pity they evaporate. . . ."[80]

When the evil powers have duly evaporated, the good spirits of the earth emerge from the ground where they have long been hiding—those who have cared for animals, those who have looked after plants. Finally there emerge the Adolphe Bertauts in considerable numbers. They promise to conquer their timidity in future. They ask the Madwoman for her hand in marriage. For her it is too late. But for Irma and Pierre it is not too late. They are united. And now that she has discharged her duty to society, the Madwoman is free to turn to worthier causes. She has her cats to feed.

THE MADWOMAN: Enough time lost. . . . *(She rises.)* You have my bones
    and my gizzard, Irma?
IRMA: They are ready, Countess.
THE MADWOMAN: Let's go up, then. Let's turn to serious business, my
    children! Down here there are only people. Let's concern ourselves
    now a little with beings who are worth the trouble.

There was in fact a madwoman who prowled the streets of the *seizième arrondissement*, more or less unnoticed until Marguerite Moréno brought her to the attention of the world. Then her picture was printed in the newspapers and she became famous. But neither *la tante Bijou* nor her fairy counterpart in the theatre was able in the end to save Paris from the invading hordes. In a little while the Paris that Giraudoux loved was gone forever. It did not become an oil field. It became a parking lot. The Madwoman could not have foreseen that.

Pour Lucrèce was the last of Giraudoux's plays, the most difficult and the most enigmatic. There is reason to believe that it was written as early as 1943. Edwige Feuillère was playing Lia at that time in *Sodome et Gomorrhe*, and apparently *Pour Lucrèce* was written with her in mind. It is said, at least, that one evening Giraudoux read her some scenes of it, and indicated that he would like her to play Lucile. But after Giraudoux's death the manuscript passed into the hands of Madame Giraudoux, and until 1952 she refused to release it for production. Jouvet was by that time no longer among the living. He had suffered a stroke after a rehearsal of Pierre Bost's adaptation of Graham Greene's *The Power and the Glory*. He died on the evening of 16 August 1951. It was Jean-Louis Barrault who undertook the production of *Pour Lucrèce*.

Doubts were expressed from the outset regarding the authenticity of the work. To some only the first act seemed characteristic of Giraudoux's style, and it was suspected that it had been finished by another hand. But Barrault set all doubts at rest with an article in which he called attention to the existence of three variants of the last act written in Giraudoux's own hand, all of them ending with a version of the final monologue of Barbette la Ventousière.

Barrault began staging *Pour Lucrèce* in the fall of 1953. He assembled a brilliant cast. Madeleine Renaud played Lucile, Edwige Feuillère played Paola, Jean Desailly was Armand, and Yvonne de Bray acted the part of Barbette. Barrault cast himself at first as Count Marcellus; but in the course of rehearsals he changed roles with Jean Servais and took the part of the Procureur Lionel Blanchard. The play opened at the Théâtre Marigny on 4 November 1953, and had only a moderate success. Most of the critics had reservations. Generally speaking, they preferred the first act to the others. The rest was found both obscure and precious. There was no evidence that anyone understood the play.

In *Amphitryon 38* Alcmena tells Jupiter: "We sometimes wonder what these young women are thinking whom we see always laughing, gay and delightfully plump, as you put it. They are wondering how to die, without fuss and without drama, if their love is degraded or betrayed."[81]

The speech might serve *Pour Lucrèce* as an epigraph; for this play is in some sense a postscript to the joyous comedy Giraudoux had written fourteen years before, at the beginning of his career in the theatre. But the mood of *Pour Lucrèce* is not joyous. The story of Alcmena takes place in Thebes in the springtime of the world. *Pour Lucrèce* is set in Aix-en-Provence in its decadence, and the mood that is evoked at the end of the play recalls the atmosphere of Picasso's "Les Demoiselles d'Avignon." "Existence," wrote Giraudoux in *Combat avec l'ange*, "is a terrible degradation."[82] *Combat avec l'ange* was published in 1934, nine years before *Pour Lucrèce* was written.

Pour Lucrèce takes up once again the question of the real and the ideal. It was still a live issue; and the exigencies of the war years, the Occupation, and the Résistance, had recently posed it in very concrete terms. After Giraudoux, Anouilh developed its dramatic, and perhaps its political implications in a number of plays, among them *Antigone* (1944),

Colombe (1951), *L'Alouette* (1953), and *Becket* (1959). It is, however, hardly rewarding to seek out political analogies in *Pour Lucrèce*. Its theme is extremely abstract. In spite of the air of realism which vaguely associates it with Second-Empire drama, *Pour Lucrèce* is as fanciful in its way as *La Folle de Chaillot*, and somewhat more puzzling.

The action takes place in the space of two days in the year 1868. Aix-en-Provence is at this time a notorious resort for available ladies and gallant gentlemen, and the arrival in this milieu of the Imperial Prosecutor Lionel Blanchard and his prudish wife is regarded as an unmitigated misfortune. The Imperial Prosecutor is a fanatical puritan. His wife is young and beautiful, and even more strait-laced than her husband. The impact of this weighty couple on the pleasure-loving native population has consequences, accordingly, that recall the descent of Mr. and Mrs. Banks on the hapless natives of Otahiti.

In his vigorous crusade to stamp out immorality in his bailiwick, Lionel Blanchard has publicly denounced Count Marcellus, the local Don Juan, as the living incarnation of vice. Lucile Blanchard works in more subtle fashion. She is normally a chatty and affable person, but the slightest scent of immorality congeals her spirits, so that her cold glance and pointed silence constitute an indictment from which there is no appeal.

The scene opens on the terrace of a fashionable pâtisserie in Aix at the hour of the chocolate. Lucile and her friend Eugénie are seated at a table close to the table occupied by Armand and his wife Paola. Armand greets the ladies cheerfully. Lucile declines to recognize him, thereby making him certain of something he has long suspected: his wife is unfaithful. The realization precipitates a definitive break with Paola.

Paola is a dangerous woman, and she exacts a terrible revenge. She drugs Lucile, then manages to have her conveyed by Barbette, the local bawd, to a house of assignation where she is given the impression that she has been violated, while unconscious, by the dissolute Count Marcellus in reprisal for the slur put upon him by her husband. She is told, moreover, that in her unconscious state she responded voluptuously to the sexual advances of the rapist. Lucile has no doubt that a just God has already struck down the evil man who has outraged her. But when she discovers that God has thus far neglected his duty, she visits Marcellus herself and demands that he expiate his crime at once by killing himself.

Marcellus is on intimate terms with Paola, and has been apprised of the situation. He is advised to take advantage of it by seducing Lucile in

earnest now that her passions have been aroused, thus reducing her to
the normal level of humanity. In his effort to do so, however, he is interrupted by Armand who has come to demand satisfaction for the seduction of Paola. The consequence is that Armand constitutes himself
the champion of Lucile, and he and Marcellus go off together to fight a
duel.

Meanwhile Lionel Blanchard has returned prematurely from his judicial circuit. Lucile is unwilling to face her husband while Marcellus lives;
but in the end she is constrained to inform him of her involuntary transgression. Blanchard, to her amazement, cares nothing for her excuses.
He is concerned only with the stain on his honor, declares that all is now
over between them, and rushes out to do battle with Marcellus. Deeply
shocked by this proof of his egotism, Lucile makes a disturbing discovery. She realizes suddenly that she has always disliked her husband, and
it comes to her quite as suddenly that she is in love with Armand.

The discovery that she is not, as she had imagined, the earthly symbol
of wifely chastity is more than Lucile can bear. She has not the advantage of Alcmena who, in *Amphitryon 38*, is able to beg the gift of oblivion. Lucile cannot forget her dishonor. Paola has by this time told her
that she has been the victim of a practical joke, and that her violation was
no more than a pretense intended to humiliate her pride. But Lucile does
not trouble to disabuse her husband. Instead she takes poison, and thus
gets out of the whole affair by dying in the grand manner. She is, of
course, no longer pure in heart. But by her death she becomes, for all
practical purposes, the symbol of the purity of woman.

It must be admitted that, from a realistic standpoint, all this seems absurd. But *Pour Lucrèce*, obviously, is not to be judged by realistic standards. For all the seeming realism of the detail, it is a fairy tale, and rests
upon assumptions normal to that genre. It assumes, to begin with, the
universal validity of an ideal of feminine purity which was perhaps appropriate to the period in which it is set, but which must seem quaint a
century later. This assumption, while it absolutely governs the thought
and the behavior of the protagonists of the action, does not seem to govern the behavior of the author in composing the play. Thus the main
source of the irony which is everywhere perceptible in *Pour Lucrèce* is in
the disparity between the author's frame of reference and that in which
he placed his characters. For the purposes of what is essentially a hypo-
thetical situation of highly melodramatic character, Count Marcellus is

presented as the embodiment of vice and wickedness, and Paola as a shameless and vindictive woman. Thus the action seems to involve the traditional conflict of good and evil forces under the aspect of eternity and, in what is ostensibly a moral exemplum, these two characters are presented in the guise of villains, while Lucile and Armand play the part of heroes. Such a view hardly does justice to the play. For within this conventional framework the author takes unusual liberties; so many, indeed, that it is not clear which is the frame, and which the landscape it encloses.

This ambiguity is at the heart of the play. The action of *Pour Lucrèce* proceeds on two levels, parallel, but significantly separate. One is the plane of contemporary realism, illumined with the insights of contemporary psychology; the other reflects the conventional morality of the former age. It is from the standpoint of the one that the action of the other is regarded. The result is to take the play out of time into a sphere of abstraction that approximates universality. The viewpoint is Olympian, not romantic.

In his relation to conventional moral standards Count Marcellus looks a good deal like Molière's Dom Juan, even more, perhaps, like the Don Juan of E. T. A. Hoffmann. He is a rebel and, insofar as he represents anything, he seems to symbolize that romantic aversion to authority which results in the train of Satanic characters that follow in the footsteps of Byron. Marcellus is no ordinary reprobate. He is a rake of Restoration cut, a dandy, a Dorimant, who disposes us to take him seriously, for he dies as heroically—and as senselessly—for his faith as Lucile does for hers. On the conventional level he is, of course, a lecherous profligate, whose sole virtue is his courage. He illustrates, therefore, the two aspects of Don Juanism, a malady which had lately aroused much interest in literary circles everywhere. He is a reprobate in search of an ideal.

Paola, similarly, is at the same time a loose and deceitful woman, a later version of Mrs. Fainall, and also a very plausible champion of sexual freedom and feminine emancipation. Lucile's realistic friend Eugénie understands Paola better than Lucile. Lucile is an idealist. She understands nothing but her own special vocabulary, which for her is endowed with magic:

EUGÉNIE: Life is hard for women like Paola, Lucile. They would like nothing better than to offer a virgin to each new lover. But they have twenty lovers and only one body.

LUCILE: They have twenty bodies and no lover.

EUGÉNIE: I hate to see you professing virtue in a café like a Christian martyr affirming her faith in the arena. It is in bad taste and, with a
tigress like that it is dangerous.

LUCILE: Don't mock me with your talk of virtue. Where do you find me involved with virtue?

EUGÉNIE: With purity then, if you prefer.

LUCILE: Isn't that a beautiful word?

EUGÉNIE: Words have nothing to do with this affair.

LUCILE: For me, a great deal. That is what I am involved with, Eugénie,
with the beautiful words, the word fountain, the word spring, the
word April. Do not try to make me pity the fate of a light woman and
a dense husband when there are words like constancy and purity. It is
these that judge them, not I. . . .[83]

Lucile, evidently, is interested in concepts, not in people, consequently she seems inhuman. Her intransigence, however, is specialized. She is rigid because words, in her mind, have no elasticity, and she
sees life in terms of words. In other respects she is human enough, gentle
and compassionate as a woman should be, and she is, we are asked to
imagine, physically a very lovely creature. But with respect to the word
"purity," and the concept it symbolizes, she is implacable; and when she
is touched by the shadow cast by the word "impurity," she feels that she
is irretrievably defiled.

Lucile belongs to the race of Alcmena. She incarnates the ideal of the
bourgeois housewife. In Giraudoux's plays the sensible women are not
martyrs to their ideals. They accept, however reluctantly, the compromise that makes life tolerable. With Lucile, as with Lia, it is All or
Nothing; consequently her situation is impossible. If women are what
Paola says they have always been, Lucile rejects membership in their
clan. Paola has taught her something she would rather die than learn.
She dies, indeed, not to affirm the nobility of the human race, which, as
she discovers, is ignoble; but to affirm the nobility of the ideal, which,
she discovers, does not exist. But she refuses to join the league of liars.
She offers herself as a human sacrifice to the divinity of the Word, and
thus teaches the world a lesson—which, Barbette reminds us, it will
soon forget.

Paola is the antithesis of Lucile. She is wise. In the play most of the
good speeches are hers, and this is fitting. In the garden of Eden the
most interesting creature, the most beautiful and most eloquent, is the

serpent. In comparison with Paola, Lucile seems narrow and ignorant, a convent-bred girl who spends her time playing the piano in the living-room, or in the kitchen, making jam. It is of such stuff that saints are made. Very early in the play we are made aware of her disruptive character. She is a menace to society; at best, a nuisance: it is intolerable, at the hour of the chocolate, to be confronted with the cold eyes of the ideal, a table or so away.

We admire in Lucile neither her primness nor her purity; both seem excessive. But we fear her strength. From this viewpoint the moral question and its implications are secondary. What is central is the question of heroism, the total dedication of the self to a cause that transcends reason and good sense and thus produces martyrs and terrorists. Lucile is un-reasonable and perhaps useless. Her death is the sheerest self-indulgence; but she has the greatness of soul that inspires poets. If Giraudoux had cast Lucile in *Sodome et Gomorrhe* in the place of Lia, they might have seemed interchangeable to the Angel, but God would not have destroyed the city.

Count Marcellus tells Paola:

> I believe you to be jealous of pure women. If you are not aware of it, I will tell you. And I put you on your guard. You become very provin-cial in their presence. You follow them, you stare at them as if purity were a secret to be learned. You make the impression of being some-what behind the mode. In their presence you have the look of one who is trying to copy a hat or spy out the detail of a dress. The secret of this glance which caresses a man without seeing him, which sees him with-out imagining him, the glance of Lucretia, of Madame Lionel Blan-chard.[84]

For Giraudoux, it would seem, the loss of youth was the supreme tragedy of life. It was most clearly visible in the passage from girlhood into womanhood, and this transition seems to have symbolized for him all the degradation that the spirit suffers in the course of a lifetime. Lucile is a child. Paola is a woman. Their antagonism extends beyond the sphere of morality: it is the antagonism of youth and age. It is en-tirely probable, as Marcellus suggests, that, to a woman like Paola, the purity of Lucile seems enviable. But, from another viewpoint, Paola's cynicism—with relation to Lucile—seems coarse and cheap, while—with relation to Paola—Lucile's innocence seems puerile. There might well be found, between the two, some possible middle ground, the sort of posi-tion exemplified by Lucile's friend Eugénie, who fleetingly plays here the role of Philinte in *Le Misanthrope*. But Lucile and Paola cannot be reconciled. They are extremes of nature, antitheses, and their dialectic illustrates once again the psychic tension which furnished, as it seems, the dynamic element in Giraudoux's idea of drama.

Pour Lucrèce is in the nature of an exemplum, and as such it embodies, seemingly, the conflict of good and evil. But in fact there are no villains in this play. Its symbols designate two aspects of life, neither of which seems wholly acceptable. The characters are exemplary insofar as they are loyal to their principles, Lucile to the demands of the spirit, Paola to the requirements of the flesh, and Marcellus to the pursuit of the ideal in its most unlikely excursions. Obviously, these are arbitrary distinctions, made for the author's convenience in arranging the algebra of the play. There is, after all, nothing essentially spiritual—whatever that adjective may mean—about sexual abstinence. The concept sanctifies a social taboo. These, however, are the assumptions on which the drama is based, and the interest of the play is not in any effort to substantiate them, but in following the behavior of those who act in accordance with these principles. Giraudoux allows his characters enough insight into their motives to make them interesting. Marcellus, for example, is by no means a simple character. In justification of his offense, he tells Lucile that through her he has been able to see himself truly: "I have seen one who has avenged himself. Not on a hypocritical judge, but on a facile destiny. It was stuffing me with what is bare, vulgar. But one day I saw something inaccessible, something noble. I wished to have it. The means did not matter. I have had it. If you have come here to find a man steeped in guilt, you will be disappointed."

Count Marcellus's quest for the ideal is, of course, not altogether in the Platonic tradition. It includes the possibility of rape. But while Marcellus is not an admirable character, it is possible to consider him as something of an artist, as a collector, at least, a connoisseur. He is, at any rate, no mere sensualist, and his desire to unite with the supreme beauty in its most tangible form, while pathetic, marks him off from the vulgar, and ranks him with the *philokalos* of the *Symposium*.

Pour Lucrèce sets forth a remarkable series of paradoxes, more perhaps than an audience can be reasonably expected to manage. As between Lucile, who is pure, and Paola, who is not, it is Paola who serves most impressively to symbolize constancy. Paola is constant to the ideal lover. It is her unswerving fidelity to the image in her heart that drives her to seek in each of her lovers the perfection that no man can give. Paola, then, is the eternal Eve in pursuit of the universal Adam. He exists, unhappily, only in the transcendental, and it is not there that she looks for him. But she is eternally faithful to him in his every guise. She says:

> I do not see, I never love, but the one man. He changes. I admit it. I change him, but I love only him. For me he erases all the others from the world. When he is there I do not see the others, they have been rubbed out of their place in this life. I do not see them even in pictures . . . I see other women dance with the void, embrace the void, take it by the hand, chatter to it, swoon over it, but in all the world the only man who has form and flesh and blood is in my arms.[85]

Paola, clasping her ideal image in her arms, has no trouble with love, nor any respite. For her the individual is anonymous, a screen which will for a time accept the image she projects upon it. But Lucile identifies the ideal image with a single individual, to wit, the Imperial Prosecutor Lionel Blanchard whom she has sworn to honor and obey so long as she lives, and this puts her at a disadvantage. When Paola can no longer see the ideal in her lover of the moment, she looks for it in someone else. But when Lucile is disenchanted, she is lost. Paola believes that Lucile has not yet discovered the female principle, the woman in herself, and that her moral squeamishness is based on motives of which she is not aware. Thus she tells her:

> You are one of those women who cannot get over the fact that they are living among millions of male bodies and souls. you spend your days—I say nothing of your nights—in wonder at your state of womanhood. Among our fine ladies of Aix you are the one whose loins press most closely and whose breasts feel heaviest. Your reserve, your modesty, are nothing but your inability to come to grips with your sex. You are curious about, and fearful of, the woman you are, you stare at her in the mirror without quite knowing who she is; your solitudes are assignations with her, you slide anxiously toward her in your bed. . . .[86]

Lucile does not love her husband, Paola tells her, save as a bridge to other men. But whatever her feelings may be, she warns, she must not betray the sisterhood of her sex:

> We consider that the worst crime on the part of one of our members is to defect to the other sex. From the time of the world's creation there has been only one holy alliance, the complicity of women. And evil has raged only among those who do not respect it. Man is simple. In this world in which he plays at horsemanship, work, money, gravity, he

asks of us only one thing—peace. . . . By virtue of his myopia, we can
run naked in the world, we can have our feelings, our emotions, our
delights. But if one of us betrays us, and for five minutes sharpens the
eyes of men, they are all moved, not to anger and vengeance, but to the
mimicry of anger and vengeance, and they are carried away by that so
far as to push it to clamor and scandal.[87]

Lucile betrays her sex. The consequences are disastrous, and in the
end Paola makes her point. But Lucile slips away, leaving them all in the
lurch, including the man she has come to love:

PAOLA: . . . This man, who is here, another woman's husband, you don't
love him?
LUCILE: Yes, I love him. I hate my husband, and this man, who is here,
who only yesterday was still in your arms, I love him.
PAOLA: Then we are in complete accord, Lucile. It is a defeat, my poor
friend, and without recourse.
LUCILE: Without recourse? How wrong you are. It is here in my hand, the
recourse. I was laughing at you just now when you said I was beaten,
for it was already there. I have it from a little girl, who had my name,
my age, and who swore, when she was ten, not to accept evil, who
swore to prove, by her death if necessary, that the world was noble,
and human beings were pure. The earth has become empty for her
and vile, this life is now nothing but a degradation for her; that does
not matter, it is not true, since she keeps her word.
BARBETTE: What are you doing? What is going on? God, she has taken
poison!

This end, it cannot be denied, is embarrassingly operatic. It is also
completely equivocal. Lucile has a final aria:

My last wish, Armand! My husband must never learn the truth. Let
him believe Barbette. If Marcellus chose to die without betraying his
innocence, I am not going to die betraying my guilt, my irremediable
crime, my scorn of life. A flash of judgment has revealed this man to
me to the bone. Henceforth he would have lived with an innocent
woman, each one despising the other. Now he will live with a guilty
woman whom he admires. . . . He will live in a false legend, but
where are the true legends? The poor lamb Truth has its throat cut at
the foot of all the stained glass. Besides, what can I do, Armand? What
can I do but play the heroine? The heroes are those who magnify a life
they can no longer endure. I have come to that. I must do as they
do."[88]

In the long monologue with which Barbette concludes the play, the legend of Lucile has already begun to take shape with its growing complement of false miracles. Purity, says Barbette, is not of this world; but every ten years there is a sudden flash, and by this light all women will see themselves as they are and feel ashamed. It will not last, of course, this revelation, but it will last longer than such things last with men. It will last, perhaps, for some weeks. And the old bawd swears, as she piously strips Lucile's jewels off the dead body of Lucile, to avenge Lucile on the race of men. She engages, she and her sisters, "to give men no respite, neither in the way of business, nor in the way of pleasure . . . neither in their health, nor in their purse, nor in their family, nor in their marrow, in order to avenge you, my little angel, and to lead them straight on to eternal damnation. . . . *Amen*.

These are the last words of Giraudoux's last play, a curse on the race of men pronounced at unconscionable length by a repulsive bawd whose diction leaves room for improvement.

The next step led the theatre in quite another direction.

ARTAUD

In 1948 the post-war theatre was in much the same condition as the post-war world, a bewildering and yet familiar landscape, much of it in ruins. In these years much of the world had been reduced to rubble. The bits that could be salvaged did not fit together very well. In the theatre, as in the world outside, it was a time of sorting out and clearing away before a new departure could be made. There was much confusion.

In the first volume of a three-part anthology of contemporary French drama, Georges Pillemont included excerpts from the work of twenty-three authors whom he considered representative of the avant-garde theatre. The list began with Jarry and ended with Anouilh. Prominent among those who were included were Claudel, Cocteau, Achard, Vildrac, and Giraudoux. There was considerable discussion in the introduction regarding the work of the experimental acting-companies of the preceding period and their *animateurs*—Copeau, Dullin, Lugné-Poë, Jouvet, Pitoëff, and Marcel Herrand. There was some brief mention of Antonin Artaud and of Jean-Louis Barrault. There was no mention of Ionesco—*La Cantatrice chauve* was first played in 1950—or of Beckett: *En attendant Godot* opened in 1953. Pillemont's anthology appeared in 1948.

At the end of his introductory survey, Pillemont wrote: "Let us make clear, finally, that the phrase avant-garde drama, which has always been arbitrary, has at last lost all meaning. At the present hour, there is no longer any avant-garde drama, there is only drama, and it is better so."[1]

Thirty years later, the mists have not yet cleared, though the perspective has lengthened considerably. From the selections in his anthology it is evident that while Pillemont was fully cognizant of revolutionary currents in the theatre of his time, he saw no reason to exaggerate their importance. In his view the drama of the avant garde was virtually indistinguishable from the literary drama, though it was sharply distinguished from the drama of the boulevard theatres. On its fringes there existed, to be sure, a group of eccentrics—Jarry, Apollinaire, Vitrac, Cocteau—who had to be included, and Pillemont dutifully supplied excerpts of their work. But there was little to be said of them. The important names—Giraudoux, Claudel, Neveux, Anouilh, Vildrac, Salacrou—belonged to another category. They wrote plays which lent themselves readily to critical analysis. The anthologist was duly appreciative of whatever in the current drama was novel or droll—the term *cocasse* was then in fashion—but he drew the line at plays that made no sense. The theatre, in his view was infinitely accommodating; but it had no room for madness.

In the course of the next generation the theatre made ample room for madness. The young writers of the 1950's paid lip-service to Giraudoux, Claudel, and Anouilh, but they were inspired by Jarry and Artaud. The new drama increasingly reflected the disorder of a world that made no sense, and the words which Giraudoux put in the mouth of Pierre Renoir in *L'Impromptu de Paris* took on a new shade of meaning: "Those who insist on understanding in the theatre are those who do not understand the theatre." In the following years the avant-garde drama became progressively esoteric, and the ranks of those who did not understand the theatre swelled to alarming proportions. Meanwhile the old issue of realism and idealism was restated in political terms. But insofar as the theatre remained an artistic enterprise it expressed its radicalism by departing as far as possible from the traditional norms of dramatic expression. The irrational became the order of the day.

Alfred Jarry had insisted, in his day, on being taken seriously. It is impossible to say how seriously he took himself, for beyond doubt his eccentricities had their practical aspect. In any case, an air of solemnity was indispensable to his performance. In 1897 he published an article with the title, "Questions du théâtre" in *La Revue blanche*, in which he earnestly advanced the didactic intention of *Ubu roi*. He wrote:

> I intended when the curtain went up that the scene should stand before
> the audience like the magic mirror in the stories of Madame Leprince de
> Beaumont in which the vicious see themselves adorned with the horns
> of bulls and the bodies of dragons in an exaggeration of their vices;
> therefore it is not surprising that the audience was stupefied by the

sight of its ignoble double, which had never yet been completely presented to it, composed, as M. Catulle Mendès has so excellently put it,
"of the eternal imbecility of man, his eternal lust, his eternal gluttony,
his instinctive baseness dignified as royalty, of the respectabilities, the
virtues, the patriotism and the ideals of those who have dined well."
Really, these are hardly the constituents of an amusing play, and the
masks demonstrate that the comedy must be at the most the macabre
comedy of an English clown, or a dance macabre. Before Gémier
agreed to play the part, Lugné-Poë had learned Ubu's lines and intended to rehearse the play as a *tragedy*. And what no one seems to have
understood . . . is that Ubu's speeches were not meant to be funny, as
various little Ubuists have insisted, but as stupid remarks uttered with
all the authority of an ape.[2]

From what is known of its origins it seems clear that *Ubu roi* had, at
least in its inception, a less serious purpose. But the caricature of M.
Hébert, *prophaiseur de pfuisic*, served very well as a caricature of the
human race, and in time Jarry's youthful jape took on monumental character. But however earnest his purpose, and however real the disgust
inspired in him by his fellow humans, Jarry had no intention of stopping
at the bounds of conventional comedy. In his view it was above all necessary to stimulate the mind by eluding comprehension so far as was possible. *Ubu roi* did much to shape the tragic farce of the following period,
but the bizarre opinions of Dr. Faustroll had a wider influence than the
comic picture of the Polish Macbeth. They offered an alternative point
of view that the generation of Ionesco was quick to adopt.

Gestes et opinions du docteur Faustroll 'pataphysicien was published by
Fasquelle in 1911. It occasioned some surprise. The work is trackless, a
jungle of veiled contemporary allusions and erudite terminology of very
abstruse significance. In form it has a distinctly Pantagruelian outline. It
is a mythical journey in a sieve-like bed, the sole article exempt from the
bailiff's distraint, toward a destination that recalls the oracle of Bacbuc.
What emerges from the mists of this disordered fantasy, however, is the
product of a truly amazing mentality. 'Pataphysics, which professedly
goes some steps beyond metaphysics, is intended to explain "the universe supplementary to this one," or, more precisely, "to describe a universe which can be—and perhaps should be—envisaged in place of the
traditional one." This supplementary universe is not the world of dreams
out of which the Surrealists were to concoct a "total reality." It is, on the
contrary, a logical construction formulated, like the Lobachevskian ge-

ometry, on a postulate other than that which governs traditional scientific method. Since in Symbolist circles it was long ago conceded that the world is a work of the human imagination designed in accordance with such assumptions as the existence of time, space, and causality, Dr. Faustroll, in his brief but impressive intervals of lucidity, imagines a world conceived in accordance with other categories. If it is assumed that there is no such thing as causation, and that events are in no way related, the world takes on an interesting appearance, precisely similar to its normal aspect, but essentially different in its significance. Assuming that the so-called laws of the universe are merely correlations of accidental data—"unexceptional exceptions"—Dr. Faustroll proposes through 'pataphysical methods to study the laws that govern exceptions.

The science of 'pataphysics was evidently conceived as a caricature of human thought just as Père Ubu was designed as a caricature of human nature. Obviously a work projected along such lines would be either hopelessly abstruse or very funny. *Dr. Faustroll* is both. Very likely no one has succeeded in following very closely the tortuosities of the author's mind. That work remains for a more leisurely age. But the influence of this work, insofar as it is accessible, in opening up the vista of an alternative universe, has been, if not greater than Einstein's, at least more widespread. It is no great task to trace its influence in the drama from the theories of Artaud to the plays of Ionesco and Genet.[3]

Modernism, as an artistic movement in the theatre, was mainly based in Paris, but with few exceptions those in the forefront of the avant garde were not French. Its proponents did not represent the ordered rationalism which had long been the basis of French education; on the contrary, they reacted against it. The irrational tendencies which had come to the surface with the rise of Symbolism at the close of the previous century had barely made themselves felt in the French theatre during the period between the two wars. For the rest, neither the plays of Strindberg nor those of the German Expressionists succeeded in attracting widespread attention in France during this period. When, in 1923, Pitoëff's production of *Six Characters in Search of an Author* awakened French sensibility to the possibilities of a new dramatic mode, the avant-garde playwrights had not much to go on in French drama aside from *Ubu roi.* Jarry, accordingly, became their leader.

The new drama was certainly a Symbolist offshoot; but it was deeply influenced by Dada and Surrealism, and it owed more to painting than to poetry. It was, to begin with, hardly a literary genre. Its foremost proponent, Antonin Artaud, drew attention to himself principally by proclaiming, in a series of eloquent letters and articles, his inability to express himself properly in words. It was, in consequence, his aim to develop for the stage à purely theatrical language which would not be verbal.

The type of drama that Artaud promoted, the theatre of Adamov, Ionesco, Arrabal, and the rest, was neither lyric nor epic, nor, in the traditional sense of the word, dramatic. The new genre avoided plot, characterization, motivation, and, so far as could be, all the traditional procedures of dramatic writing. It rejected the principle of causality and logical sequence, and abandoned, as false and arbitrary, the narrative patterns which, for some centuries, had given the drama its shape. It could hardly avoid developing an anecdote of some sort, but the radical writers did their best to dispel the effect of ordered narrative. The result was a type of spectacle that was far removed from actuality and had a close connection with the world of dreams. In this connection much attention was paid to *The Dream Play*, which nobody understood, and few would venture to produce.

From the time of Sophocles Western drama was characterized by a more or less realistic appraisal of the external world, governed by superior powers, and rendered comprehensible by the marshalling of events in logical order. Thus the drama affirmed the existence of an orderly universe governed by ineluctable principles of eternal validity which it was disastrous to contravene. The drama, accordingly, was an act of faith and, in this sense at least, the theatre served a religious purpose. But the rational design which was the soul of the classical tradition was precisely the element the avant garde rejected. The new world of the theatre was the world of Dr. Faustroll, subject chiefly to the laws of *'pataphysique*. The new drama was set in chaos. Its action transpired amid the primal confusion that preceded the Creation.

By 1914 the Symbolists appeared to have given over their attempts to decode the universe. In *Les Soirées de Paris* (1911–14) Guillaume Apollinaire officially declared Symbolism bankrupt, and assigned its assets to Cubism and Orphism. Three years later, in connection with Satie's *Parade*, Apollinaire proclaimed the advent of Surrealism, a new aesthetic, which rejected logic, order and rational process, and sought truth in the labyrinths of the unconscious mind. Surrealism appeared, in fact, to be little more than a further aspect of Symbolism. The new poets, like the new painters, were disillusioned idealists, and while they were vociferous in their denunciation of the existing world order, they insisted on the ability of the imagination to re-order the universe in a fashion more conformable to the ideal through the exercise of the primary faculty of the mind.

The new drama rejected the normal categories of time and space, as well as causality, and made capital of incoherence and spontaneity in the association of images. The early successes in this genre, *Les Mamelles de Tirésias*, *Les Mariés de la Tour Eiffel*, and *Victor, ou les enfants au pouvoir*, are interesting plays which take place in an engaging atmosphere of lunacy. Their authors were not mad. Nor did they, like Artaud, proclaim their fanaticism. They were the precursors of a movement that was not wholly mobilized; in effect, scouts. Evidently, with these plays Apollinaire, Cocteau, Vitrac, and the others were consciously exploring a dramatic mode which had not yet taken form in anyone's mind, but which would in some way reflect in the theatre the radical genres that were being developed in other fields of contemporary art, principally in painting.

The irrational in these plays reflected the distrust of logic, and also the attraction of the primitive, that characterized the radical aesthetic of the period. The violence of the attack on convention which they represented confirmed the mounting radicalism of the time. None of these plays was in any way great; some were simply silly. But, taken together, they had importance. They heralded a break with tradition which perhaps would never be healed, a solution of continuity in the history of the drama.

The new drama was, from a historical viewpoint, remarkably opportune. It developed in an atmosphere of cynicism and disillusionment, and was nourished by a public which was distasted with reality and disposed to support any deviation from established norms. Unquestionably, this mood was provisional. The writers who shared it reached a small and unstable audience which was particularly sensitive to external pressures and could hardly be depended on to support any novelty for very long. Under such conditions it was hardly foreseeable that the "modernism" of the period would amount to a decisive force in the theatre. But it did.

Antonin Artaud died in 1948, a relatively happy man. His life had been tragic. Much of it was spent in various mental institutions in circumstances of unbelievable squalor. In his periods of lucidity he had endured a series of crushing frustrations and failures. But in the last years of his life Artaud found some measure of compensation. Before he died he had the satisfaction of knowing that, mad as he was, he was destined to have a profound effect on those who were sane.

In these years, indeed, to many the world seemed a madhouse, and the possibility of alternative realities for the first time seemed attractive even to those who were not mystically inclined. Since those who created such fantasies were usually accounted mad, interesting questions were raised as to the merits of the sanity that periodically brought humanity to the verge of extinction; and the possibility that what is commonly called madness is in fact a sensible aberration from the complacent stupidities of "life-as-it-is" was opened up in a most stimulating way. In the case of such madmen as Artaud and van Gogh the immediate point at issue was one of social injustice, the persecution of the unduly fanciful by those who lacked imagination. Such considerations, later the subject of serious scientific discussion, helped to strengthen the position of those who, in these uncomfortable years, urged a departure from the current norms of art.

The Symbolist aesthetic invited the collaboration of all sorts of interesting charlatans. Its position was supported by the example of highly gifted artists who deliberately chose to derange their wits through the use of drugs and other excitants in their efforts to probe the veil that divides appearance from reality. Since such poets as Poe, Baudelaire, Nerval, and Rimbaud were by this time accorded the reverence due to genius, it was difficult to deny equal honors to such conspicuous eccentrics as Jarry and Artaud.

Modern painting made its debut on the walls of Paris cafés frequented by painters, and in the shops of dealers in art supplies. The new drama grew up in small untidy theatres in the alleys of Montmartre and Montparnesse. This drama was neither literary nor commercial. It owed more to the technique of the guignol, the music hall, the circus, and the comic films than to the Wagnerian *Gesamtkunstwerk* to which the Symbolist dramatists had aspired in the days of Mallarmé. The new drama was, indeed, a popular genre that so far transcended popular taste as to become the exclusive concern of an artistic elite. The type of theatrical presentation that Artaud had in mind in promoting the Théâtre Alfred Jarry had no special resemblance to the genre later developed by Adamov and Ionesco; but without the influence of Artaud the new style, very likely, would not have come into being, and certainly not in the same way.

Antonin Artaud was born in Marseille in 1896 of mixed parentage. He was more Levantine Greek than French. Early in life he began to write poetry. At eighteen he experienced mental difficulties so severe that he had to be sent to a clinic, and before long he was addicted to opium. At the age of twenty-four he was incarcerated in the mental hospital at Villejuif on the outskirts of Paris. There he came to the attention of Dr. Édouard Toulouse, a psychiatrist with literary tastes. Toulouse was at this time involved with a literary periodical called *Demain*. He was convinced that in Artaud he had come upon a writer of genius, and in March 1920 Artaud took over the editorship of *Demain*. In this manner the young poet was introduced at the age of twenty-four to the literary life of Paris. He soon became intimate with the circle of writers and painters presided over by Max Jacob.

Artaud had by this time some little reputation as a poet and essayist, but he was ambitious to work in the theatre. In 1921 Lugné let him play a small part in *Les Scrupules de Sganarelle* at the Théâtre de l'oeuvre. He was then recommended to Charles Dullin who was just organizing his Atelier. Dullin took him in at once, and Artaud served his apprenticeship in Dullin's workshop, designed scenery and costumes and, in 1922, went on tour with his acting company. But by the time Dullin established himself permanently in Montmartre, Artaud's behavior on the stage had become so extravagant and so unpredictable that Dullin found it necessary to part with him. Pitoëff then took him in at the Comédie des Champs Elysées, and gave him minor parts in *He Who Gets Slapped*, *R.U.R.*, and *Six Characters*. Meanwhile Artaud published a book of poems entitled *Tric-trac du ciel*. He now entered into an extensive correspondence with Jacques Rivière, the editor of the *Nouvelle Revue française*, regarding Rivière's grounds for rejecting his poems. Rivière published this correspondence in the *N.R.F.* in September 1924. It aroused much attention.

It was Artaud's contention that the type of poetry that battered, however ineffectually, at the limits of expression was of far greater value than the facile rhetoric of the verbal craftsman. Such poetry, though inarticulate, bore true testimony to the life of the soul. It was likely to bear, as well, the marks of the struggle to bring the unconscious into consciousness, and could hardly be expected, consequently, to have the high finish of the commercial product, nor could it possibly be as readily comprehensible as poetry technically formulated in the conventional molds. True poetry would necessarily be both secret and personal, and it would be difficult. Its images would be of the stuff of dreams, arranged in dream-like sequences. But while poetry composed after this fashion would in some degree elude the comprehension of the reader, it would offer him compensatory insights into the unconscious, the universal life of humanity, which normally eluded expression. The true poet was not a craftsman, merely. He was a seer, a *voyant*. "Where others desire to produce works of art," Artaud wrote, "I aspire only to exhibit my mind."[4]

This correspondence once again brought into focus the linguistic and psychological problems with which Mallarmé had so valiantly wrestled in his day; at any rate, it put Artaud squarely in the Surrealist camp. He was at once made welcome in André Breton's circle and joined Aragon, Eluard, Max Ernst, Robert Desnos, and Raymond Queneau on the editorial staff of *La Révolution surréaliste*. Soon thereafter Artaud was appointed director of the Surrealist "Bureau de Recherches." He now felt that he was in a position of authority. In 1925 he published letters to the Pope and the Chancellors of the Universities announcing the end of the Christian era, and demanding that the world reject the tyranny of reason as an oppressive and stultifying convention.

Artaud posed the problem of the exceptional individual more sharply than any of the eccentric artists of the previous generation. He was highly gifted and, without doubt, he was mad. Like Strindberg he suffered from recurrent headaches, tics, and spasms, and he was often in excruciating pain. His insight into his mental state was intermittent, but astonishingly lucid. He knew that he was a case of unusual interest, took pride in his singularity, and very cannily capitalized on it. He was a fine actor with a very sensitive face, and his portrayal of the young monk in Dreyer's film of the *Passion of Jeanne d'Arc* made a deep impression on all who saw it. But he was not a reliable performer, and could hardly be trusted on the stage. As he grew older, he was increasingly a prey to paranoid fancies, had delusions of grandeur, and assumed Messianic postures which served mainly to confirm his fantasies of persecution.

Early in 1925 Artaud became friendly with Roger Vitrac. Vitrac had recently been declared a traitor to Surrealism, and this association, together with Artaud's refusal to join with the Surrealists in their adherence to the Communist party, brought about the expulsion of Artaud also from this group. Meanwhile Vitrac and he had been planning to organize a Surrealist theatre. Funds were raised, and in November 1926

Jean Paulhan, the new editor of the *N.R.F.*, published Artaud's "Premier manifeste du Théâtre Alfred Jarry."[5]

Le Théâtre Alfred Jarry went into production in June 1927 with a bill of three short plays, one by Artaud, one by Vitrac, and one by their principal backer, Robert Aron. The following January it offered an unauthorized version of the third act of Claudel's *Partage du midi*, vindictively caricatured as an "act of literary terrorism." The third production took place in June 1928. There were two performances of Strindberg's *The Dream Play*, partly subsidized by the Swedish embassy, and acted before an invited audience of prominent people. The first night had been planned as a brilliant gala, but a squadron of Surrealists invaded the theatre and created such a disturbance that the play could hardly be heard. The second performance was attended by the police. There were a number of arrests. The last of the productions of the Théâtre Alfred Jarry was Vitrac's *Victor, ou Les Enfants au pouvoir*.

This play was billed as a metaphysical farce. It celebrated the ninth birthday of Victor, a precocious child one meter, eighty centimeters tall, who in more or less comic fashion brings about, in the course of the day, the death of his father, and then his own death. There was some difficulty in casting the Lady in Black, Ida Mortemart. Ida comes to the birthday party from another world, uninvited, and in some doubt as to whether she has come to the right apartment. She is half woman and half ghost, very beautiful and rich, and sadly afflicted with *pétomanie*, an irrepressible tendency to break wind at inopportune moments.

In the program Artaud printed a letter to Domenica Blazy, the actress who finally played the flatulent beauty, explaining that this character symbolized the human condition. Ida Mortemart was in part pure spirit, and thus embodied the superior intelligence of the transcendental world. But she was also partly a physical being, and the material aspect of her nature was accordingly indicated by her embarrassing infirmity.

In the redolent aura of Ida Mortemart, Victor's father is moved to hang himself from the balcony of his house under the impression that he is the French tricolor, while Victor dies of a colic. "We intend," Artaud wrote, "our subject-matter to be *actual* in every sense of the word. Our means: humor in every form. Our aim: total laughter . . ."[6]

"The First Manifesto of the Théâtre Alfred Jarry," printed four years before this production, gave Artaud an opportunity to discuss the function of the theatre as a social force. By this time the Surrealists had come to the conclusion that their artistic revolution must express itself in political action, and they consequently joined the Communists in advocating the overthrow of the capitalist state. Artaud, however, insisted that the social order would change only when the individual changed. The revolution, he insisted, must take place first of all in the soul of the individual, and in this regard the theatre would serve a paramount purpose. If drama were merely play, there was no place for it in this critical period of the world's history. If it were "a genuine reality" then means must be found to give to each performance the importance of an actual event, not a pretended occurrence. "In the theatre the audience must therefore make contact with life itself, so that the stupidity and brutality of the social order may be brought to its attention with all possible emphasis. The play must be so poignant an experience that the audience will cry out."

After such a performance the spectator might be expected to leave the theatre thoroughly shaken in mind and body. Thereafter he would go to the theatre as he went to the doctor or dentist, not for diversion but for treatment, and in full awareness that the experience might be painful. In this manner the theatre would serve little by little to change the psychic posture of the individual and thus to bring about naturally the changes necessary to improve the social order. Save for the poignancy of the experience, it was substantially the program which, almost a century earlier, Ibsen had advocated in his early letters to Georg Brandes.[7]

Artaud's project was a worthy one, but the disorders attending the production of *The Dream Play* put an end to the Théâtre Alfred Jarry. Robert Aron withdrew his support. The Vicomte de Noailles came to the rescue with a substantial sum; but it was in vain. For the next half-dozen years Artaud was forced to eke out a living as a film actor. He did not, however, altogether renounce his project. In 1931 with the aid of his friends of the *Nouvelle Revue française* Artaud once again organized an experimental theatre. The *N.R.F.* published the "Premier manifeste du Théâtre de la cruauté" on 1 October 1932 and, while efforts were made to finance the enterprise, Artaud began working on the repertory of plays he thought his new theatre should perform. His choices were a version of Seneca's *Thyestes*, and an adaptation of Shelley's *The Cenci*, both of them, as his friend Anaïs Nin noted in her diary, plays "which are like scenes of torture."[8]

Héliogabale, ou L'Anarchiste couronné was published in 1934. It is among the most enigmatic of Artaud's writings. Artaud considered the effeminate emperor who, as high priest of the sun, was the living incarnation of the masculine principle, to be "the image of all human contradiction." There is reason to believe that he identified himself with this ambiguous figure as closely as Jarry had identified himself with Ubu.[9] This work did not prevent him from going on with the Theatre of Cruelty. Early in 1935 he gave a reading of *Les Cenci* at the home of Jean-Marie Conty.

His version was a four-act tragedy in prose. In the projected production he planned to cast himself as Count Francesco. The part of Beatrice Cenci, the special object of her father's attentions, appealed to Lady Ilya Abdy, an amateur actress who had professional ambitions, and the first offering of the Theatre of Cruelty was capitalized largely through her efforts. The production was conceived with great care and originality, but it was housed most unsuitably in a former music hall. Balthus designed the sets and costumes. Desormière composed a very modern score with pre-recorded sounds projected through loud speakers in the auditorium. Roger Blin, Artaud's production assistant, played one of the mute assassins, and Jean-Louis Barrault undertook to play the part of Beatrice's brother Bernardo, but later withdrew from the cast. *Les Cenci* opened on 6 May 1935 before an appreciative audience, but it was not favorably reviewed in the press. Lady Abdy was a fragile blonde of Russian extraction. Her accent was Russian and her voice hardly audible, while Artaud gave a frenzied performance punctuated by screams and shouts. The other actors did not appear to know what they were doing. After seventeen performances *Les Cenci* closed, and with that Artaud's theatrical career came to an end.

The failure of *Les Cenci* marked a critical point in Artaud's life. The production had been a major effort. It was now clear that Artaud's dream of revolutionizing the theatre would never be realized, and at this point he began his withdrawal from the actual into a more rarefied atmosphere. His lifelong addiction to drugs, so far justified as an analgesic measure, was making serious inroads on his health. He was nevertheless convinced that his insights into the other world required something more potent than opium, and he felt that he must try mescaline, the extraordinary effects of which he had read about in accounts of the peyote cult in the Sierra Madre of Mexico.

With the help of Paulhan he persuaded the Ministry of Education to sponsor a semi-official lecture tour in Mexico. Before his departure in

January 1936 he gave Paulhan the manuscript of a book of essays on the theatre, as yet untitled, which the *N.R.F.* was to publish in his absence. It was two years before the book was issued.

Artaud returned to Paris in November 1936 after a disappointing experience in Mexico. The peyote priests had welcomed him, and through their ministrations he had experienced some hallucinations; but he had gained no further insight into the mystery of life. He was now ill and penniless, but he was thoroughly convinced that with the aid of a little sword he had picked up in Havana, and an Irish walking stick that his friend René Thomas had given him, he was destined to bring about a decisive change in the constitution of the universe. In a pamphlet, printed in July 1937, entitled *Les Nouvelles Révélations de l'être*, he predicted the end of the world. The final cataclysm would take place on 7 November 1937. On that day "the tortured man" would be recognized as the Destroyer and the Savior of mankind, "The Revealed One."[10]

In August of that year he set off for Ireland to stage the crack of doom. His mission took him to the Aran Islands, thence to Dublin. Toward the end of September the Dublin police arrested him for creating a disturbance in the street. They kept him some days in jail, then shipped him back to France. He was terribly excited, and by the time the ship docked at Le Havre he had become so violent that the French authorities packed him off to an asylum. He spent the next nine years in mental institutions.

Le Théâtre et son double was published by Gallimard in 1938 while Artaud was confined in an asylum near Rouen in a state of catatonia. The publication of his book served to remind the world of his existence. His friends now managed to have him transferred to an institution in Paris, thence to an asylum in Rodez near Toulouse in the unoccupied zone. There he was looked after sympathetically by Dr. Gaston Ferdière, and after a month, with the help of electric shock-therapy, he was so far recovered as to warrant a provisional release. Two months later, in May 1946, Dr. Ferdière brought him to Paris, and lodged him comfortably in a disused pavilion on the grounds of the asylum at Ivry.

Artaud was now a famous man. His face, once beautiful, had grown hideous, but in the eyes of those who had but recently felt the weight of the Nazi war-machine, he symbolized the plight of the unusual individual in a regimented society, and his ravaged face spoke eloquently of his suffering. He was lionized. An auction of works of art donated by prominent painters, together with a gala benefit organized by Dullin, Jouvet,

Vilar, and Blin raised funds for his support. After years of neglect and misery he found himself suddenly the center of a cult. For Artaud, after nine years of silence, it was as if a dam had burst. Articles, letters, poems, and drawings issued from his pavilion in a torrent of publications. Much of what he wrote was unintelligible, but by this time the public was accustomed to unintelligible writings, and whatever he published was snapped up like the relics of a saint. Gallimard hastily planned an edition of his collected works and when, in 1947, Artaud announced a public reading of his latest poems, the Vieux Colombier was packed with eager listeners. The performance, as usual, turned into a scandal.

Toward the end of 1947, after visiting the retrospective exhibition of the works of van Gogh at the Orangerie, Artaud published one of his most successful books, *Van Gogh, le suicidé de la société*. It was a passionate defence of van Gogh's genius, coupled with a savage attack on psychiatry and psychiatrists, people whose function it was, he argued, to reduce all things to a single level of mediocrity. The book was awarded the Prix Sainte-Beuve. In November 1947 his radio broadcast, "Pour en finir avec le jugement de Dieu," which had been rehearsed and recorded in the studios of *La Radio Diffusion française*, was suddenly cancelled as unduly provocative. Another scandal followed, but Artaud did not live long enough to savor it. On 4 March 1948 he was found sitting up at the foot of his bed in his pavilion at Ivry. He had been dead for some time.

From the available testimony it is reasonable to conclude that Artaud was an uncommonly talented lunatic whose excesses, during his lucid periods, were managed with a shrewd eye for effect and an enviable flair for publicity. His life, beyond doubt, was wretched; but it must not be forgotten that he was, above all, an actor. "Tragedy on the stage," he wrote, "is no longer enough for me. I shall carry it over into my life." His behavior was outrageous; but he was seldom out of fashion. He was, to begin with, a Symbolist, and later a Surrealist, a representative of the most advanced aesthetic of the day. Like Strindberg he was a mystic, deeply involved with magic, alchemy, and divination, and very well versed in the writings of the Gnostics and Cabalists. He was unusually well read, and adept at borrowing and arranging, for his own purposes, ideas from the most disparate sources, from Aristotle, Freud, Augustine, Nietzsche, Ibsen, and Mallarmé. In this manner he concocted a doctrine of great originality in which nothing actually was new. The result was that, in spite of all his failures and frustrations, he succeeded in diverting to the stage, more effectively than anyone else of his time, the vital currents that had their source in the Symbolist revolution of the 1880's, and which now constitute what is distinctively modern in the modern drama.

By the end of 1957 fifteen volumes of Artaud's works were in print, and there were more to come. But the flower of his doctrine was the fourth volume of the series, the collection of essays and letters called *Le Théâtre et son double*. These essays were written over a period of four years, from 1931 to 1935. In January 1936, before leaving for Mexico, Artaud sent Jean Paulhan a letter suggesting the order in which his pieces might be printed. The title of the book occurred to him some time later while he was at sea. In explanation of the title, Artaud wrote, "I think I have found a suitable title for my book. It will be, 'Le Théâtre et son double,' for if the theatre reflects life, life reflects the true theatre. . . . This title will accord all the doubles of the theatre which I believe I have found in these many years: metaphysics, the plague, cruelty . . ." He continued:

> The reservoirs of energy which constitute the Myths, which men no longer embody, are embodied in the theatre. And by this double I understand the great magic power which the drama through its forms prefigures, until the time comes when it is transfigured by it.
>
> It is on the stage that the union of thought, gesture and act is reconstituted. And the Double of the Theatre is the reality which the men of our time do not utilize. . . .[11]

The title was cryptic, but hardly less so than the explanation. Fortunately the essays in some measure clarify both the one and the other. "True theatre," in Artaud's view, is the drama that reflects the hidden life of the spectator, his essential reality. Its "double" is the primal vitality that underlies the false culture of our time. In the manifesto of Le Théâtre Alfred Jarry Artaud had promised to alter the shape of society by showing it its falseness. The Theatre of Cruelty was designed to show mankind its truth.

The essay on Drama and Cruelty begins by recapitulating the ideas of the "First Manifesto of le Théâtre Alfred Jarry":

> An idea of the theatre has been lost. . . .
>
> At this stage of the decay of our sensibility it is clear that what we require above all is a theatre which will awaken us: heart and nerves.
> . . . In these distressing and catastrophic times we urgently feel the

> need of a theatre which events do not dwarf, which will find resonance
> deep within us, and dominate the instability of the times.
>
>   Long accustomed to diverting spectacles, we have forgotten the idea
> of a serious drama which, brushing aside the current shows, will inspire
> us with the burning magnetism of its images and will act therapeu-
> tically on our souls as an experience of unforgettable power.[12]

Plays of this sort would not be diverting. They would be traumatic:
"Whatever acts is cruel. It is with this idea of action pushed to its extreme limit that the theatre must renew itself." The performance would
not be a pretense. It would be an event, entailing real risks and hazards.
In the Theatre of Cruelty the illusion would be complete and of painful
intensity. Its subject matter would necessarily be poignant: "If it is once
again to fulfill its purpose the theatre must give us everything there is in
love, in crime, in war, in madness." Thus the dramatic experience would
approximate the reality of dreams, "and the spectator will believe in the
dreams of the theatre only on condition that he really takes them for
dreams, and not as replicas of reality; on condition that they enable him
to liberate within himself this magical liberty of dreams which he can
recognize only by the stamp of terror and cruelty."[13]

Such procedures, Artaud admitted, might entail some danger, since
the experience of violence in the theatre might perhaps impel the spectator to deeds of violence outside the theatre. "There is a certain element
of risk," he noted, "but I believe that in the present circumstances it is a
risk worth running. I do not think we have succeeded in reanimating the
order of things in the world we inhabit, and I do not think there is any
longer much point in clinging to it, but I propose a way of escaping from
our morbidity instead of continuing to groan about it, and about the
boredom, the inertia and the stupidity of everything."[14]

The principal cause of the decline of the quality of life, in Artaud's
opinion, was not so much man's secret inclination to evil as the torpor
which prevents him from doing anything to improve his situation. Artaud proposed, therefore, to relieve the apathy of mankind by devising a
theatre which would unleash the psychic energy at present locked up
uselessly in its soul. "It will be understood," he wrote, "that the theatre
. . . must break with actuality, and that its object is not to resolve social
or psychological conflicts, but to bring to light by action or gesture that
part of the truth that lies buried under the forms in their conflict with
Becoming."[15]

Artaud evidently proposed to address himself to the antagonism of

Life and Form which had so thoroughly preoccupied Pirandello in his later years. By attacking and dissipating the traditional forms of social behavior, the Theatre of Cruelty would release, presumably, the vital flux which social forms oppress and restrict. The result, for the individual, would be a fuller and a richer life, lived in harmony with his inner truth. For society it would result in a progressive and enlightened future. The alternative was grim. "It is a question of knowing what we want. If we are eager for war, plague, famine and massacre, we do not even need to admit it, we need only go on as we are . . . Our spiritual anarchy and disorder are a function of the anarchy of everything else that we do—or rather, what we do is a function of this spiritual anarchy."

The theatre which Artaud intended to develop would thus have a revelatory and a liberating function. By demonstrating the falsity of the social forms which regulate men's lives, the theatre would open their minds to a more honest recognition of the true nature of man. The program was one which recalled the ideas both of Ibsen and Pirandello; but Artaud went further than either. He had the benefit of Freud's psychology, and therefore could assume that the sort of liberation he had in mind would result in uncontrollable outbursts of aggression and libido.

These ideas had already been expressed fully in the manifesto he had published six years before. They were in the main Surrealist:

> We are not creating a theatre in order to present plays, but to succeed in showing the mind's obscure, secret and hidden aspects by a sort of real, physical projection. . . . What we would like to see sparkling triumphantly on the stage is whatever partakes of the mysterious and magnetic fascination of dreams, the dark depths of consciousness. . . . We consider the theatre a truly magical enterprise. We do not intend to appeal to the eye, nor directly to the faculties that relate to the intellect. What we are attempting to create are certain psychological states through which the heart's most secret movements will be expressed.[16]

In the Theatre of Cruelty the play would work the actor into a frenzy which the actor would transmit to the audience by a kind of contagion. This idea resulted in a strange analogy. In the First Book of *The City of God* Augustine compares the theatre to the plague. In its context the comparison is apt. The Roman comedies were apparently intended to placate the heavenly powers that periodically visited pestilence on the Romans in token of their displeasure. Augustine considered the theatre a worse calamity than the plague: ". . . for the bodily pestilence had hardly ceased when the delicate vanity of stage plays entered into the ears of this people . . . for the wily devils forseeing (by natural reason) that this plague of the body would cease, by this means took occasion to thrust one far worse, not into their bodies but into their minds, in the corruption of which is all their joy. . . ."[17]

In his essay on "The Theatre and the Plague," first published by the *Nouvelle Revue française* in October 1934, Artaud followed Augustine only part of the way. He agreed that the action of the drama on the mind approximates the action of the plague on the body. But Artaud had done some research on the workings of the plague. As he understood it, the plague was a destructive spirit that invades the physical organism, disrupting its internal constitution without leaving any trace on its surface. At the same time it causes irrational images to form in the mind, causing its victims to rush about in delirium, committing strange gratuitous crimes. In precisely this fashion, Artaud wrote, the poetic images of the theatre operate on the mind of the actor, and the actor, in the grip of this madness which the play induces, transmits his delirium to the spectator. In the theatre, consequently, the dramatic experience amounts to a shared hallucination, calculated to release intense psychic energy:

> It would be useless to give precise reasons for this contagious delirium.
> . . . What is above all necessary is to admit that, like the plague, the stage play is delirium and that it is contagious. The mind believes what is presented to it, and it acts in accordance with what it believes: this is the secret of fascination.[18]

In practice it is likely that this theory of stage production would result in an extremely violent mise en scène which might well arouse an equally violent reaction in the audience. This might not be in the best interests of the play; but Artaud did not take account of this possibility. In his opinion, the theatre, like the plague, brings to light whatever is latent and dormant in the psyche, and pushes it up into consciousness. It dredges up long-buried figures and type-symbols and incites dormant conflicts into action, so that "there takes place before our eyes a battle of symbols, the one hurling itself upon the other in an impossible hurly-burly, for the drama exists only at the moment when the impossible actually begins to happen and the poetry of the stage feeds and ignites the symbols that are being realized."

But while, both in actor and audience, the spiritual turmoil stirred up by the drama is profound, it cannot and does not discharge itself in action. The actor, in his frenzy, does not kill, nor does the audience rush out of the theatre to overturn the state. Artaud intended his theatre to be revelatory, but not activist. Brieux's drama—and Brecht's—were calculated to motivate action directly. Artaud desired only to motivate insight: "In contrast to the fury of the murderer, which is dissipated in the act, the emotion of the tragic actor remains in a pure and closed circle . . . it assumes a form which negates itself as it takes shape and thus melts into universality."

This process, accordingly, will not have immediate consequences. The theatre deals in violence, but it does not incite to violence. It brings about changes in the individual psyche which may be expected, in time, to bring about change. To this end the theatre will necessarily resort to drastic methods. The audience must be rescued from its torpor by a species of shock-therapy. "Without an element of cruelty at the root of every play, drama is not possible. At the level of degeneracy to which we have sunk it is only through the skin that metaphysics can be made to penetrate the mind."[19]

Artaud nevertheless took care to define cruelty in a very special way. Cruelty in his theatre would entail the suffering of the artist quite as much as that of the spectator. The play should induce fear: "We are not free. And the sky can still fall on our heads. And the theatre is made first of all to teach us that." The actor must be afraid, literally, in order to induce fear in the audience: if he is to induce suffering, he must suffer. This idea was amplified in a letter to Jean Paulhan commenting on the Manifesto published in the *Nouvelle Revue française:*

> It is wrong to give the word cruelty the meaning of bloody severity, of the aimless and disinterested pursuit of physical suffering. . . . Cruelty is not, in fact, synonymous with bloodshed, martyred flesh or a crucified enemy. This identification of cruelty with torture touches on a very minor side of the question. In the cruelty we inflict there is a kind of superior determinism to which the executioner-torturer is himself subject, and which he must be prepared to endure when the bill comes due. Cruelty is, above all, lucid—it is a kind of rigid direction, a submission to necessity. . . .[20]

The idea that cruelty, and the display of cruelty, are indispensable to the dramatic experience is doubtless attributable to Artaud's special temperament, but for the theoretical basis of his doctrine he was indebted to Aristotle's discussion of the tragic plot in the *Poetics.* According to Aristotle, the plot of tragedy "should be so framed that, even without seeing the things take place, he who simply hears the account of them shall be filled with horror and pity at the incidents. . . . To produce this same effect by means of spectacle is less artistic and requires extraneous aid. Those, however, who make use of the spectacle to put before us that which is merely monstrous and not productive of fear, are wholly out of touch with tragedy; not every kind of pleasure should be required of tragedy, but only its own proper pleasure."

The nature of the pleasure of tragedy is indicated in the same context. In Aristotle's opinion, the sort of incident that evokes fear and pity is one in which the protagonists are so related that the doer suffers along with the victim of the deed of horror, and it is for this reason that domestic tragedy is favorite among dramatists. The passage is well known: "Whenever the tragic deed is done within the family, when murder or the like is done or meditated by brother on brother, by son on father, by mother on son, or son on mother—those are the situations the poet should seek after."[21]

This passage clarifies the choice of *Les Cenci* as the initial offering of The Theatre of Cruelty. The horrors of the Cenci story are without doubt intensely domestic horrors. But in this case Artaud seems to have misconstrued the *Poetics*. In the plays that Aristotle appears to have had in mind, the deed of horror is in every case motivated by a necessity that overrides the reluctance of the doer to injure a member of the family. Count Francesco, however, is motivated chiefly by his sadism, a primal urge, no doubt, but not one calculated to inspire suffering in him or pity in the spectator. The choice of *Thyestes* as a second offering does something to illuminate Artaud's intention. Theoretically his doctrine was based, no doubt, on Aristotle and the practice of the Attic theatre. But practically he admired Seneca, and in this preference he clearly shared Renaissance taste.

In theory, then, Artaud's analysis follows the *Poetics* quite closely. From his viewpoint the tragic situation involves not only a cruel deed, but also a cruel fate which forces the tragic hero to harm someone he loves, or is expected to love. The object of representing such a situation in the theatre would then be, in Artaud's view, to demonstrate the nature of the vital force that makes pain inescapable in this world. Maeterlinck's early plays do much the same thing. In both cases the drama demonstrates the Schopenhauerian notion that the drive of the Will necessarily entails suffering and that consciousness is synonymous with pain. Beyond a certain point Maeterlinck did not persist in this idea; but, in the special circumstances of Artaud's life, the inevitability of pain must have seemed especially clear. At bottom, then, the function of the Theatre of Cruelty was, like that of the Théâtre-libre, simply to show "life as it is," and from this viewpoint Artaud proposed to be even more explicit than Antoine.

In the light of Artaud's discussion, the metaphysics of his "metaphysical theatre" seems to be an innocent blend of ideas derived from Aristotle and Schopenhauer. The Theatre of Cruelty may well be understood as another attempt to revive in contemporary terms the tragic theatre of the Greeks. Artaud intended his theatre to probe not only the workings of the individual psyche but also the nature of the cosmic drive that shaped it, and in his theatre the particular was of importance only insofar as it symbolized the universal. It was not the business of the drama to deal with social or psychological problems, but to reveal the essence of being. In this respect, Artaud thought, Western theatre was far inferior to the theatre of the Orient. "The contemporary theatre," he wrote, "is decadent because it has lost the feeling, on the one hand, of seriousness and, on the other, of laughter. Because it has broken with gravity, with immediate and pernicious effectiveness and so, in a word, with Danger."

It is otherwise with the Oriental theatre, which deals through movement and gesture, not with particulars but with universals: "I know very well, of course, that the language of gestures and postures, dance and music, is less able than verbal language to elucidate character, to reveal human thought, to exhibit clear and precise states of mind, but whoever said that the theatre was created to elucidate character, to resolve conflicts of a human and emotional order, of a physical and psychological order such as those with which our contemporary theatre is stuffed?" He continues:

> Given the theatre as we now have it, one would say that there is nothing more in life than to know if we will love properly, if we will go to war, or be so cowardly as to make peace, how we should cope with our little moral scruples, and whether we shall take conscious note of our "complexes" (to use the language of science), or whether our "complexes" will stifle us. . . .
>
> All these above-enumerated preoccupations stink unbelievably of man, provisional and material man, I will even say, carrion man. So far as I am concerned, these preoccupations disgust me, disgust me in the

highest degree, together with almost all of the contemporary theatre which is as human as it is anti-poetic and which, with the exception of three or four plays, seems to me to stink of decay and pus.[22]

The Theatre of Cruelty was intended once again to tap the vital current, the Dionysian frenzy, that the Greeks once knew, without which the theatre is lifeless. Artaud thought that the release of this energy would at the same time electrify the audience and change the world by altering its ideas of what is real and true in it. "I believe," he wrote, "that the theatre, used in the highest and most difficult possible way, has the power to shape the aspect and the forms of things."

The images displayed in this true theatre would necessarily be bestial, violent, perverse, and obscene in accordance with the true nature of man, as opposed to the polite hypocrisy of a theatre which falsifies his character. They would represent those actions which normally we experience only in revery and dream. Exhibitions of this sort are, of course, when properly tricked out, the showman's gainpenny; but if violence and obscenity are, and have always been, of the essence of the theatre, the reason must lie deeper than the prohibition against them. Evidently these preoccupations represent essential drives. Nothing is gained from suppressing them. By bringing into the open these manifestations of "the great magic agency" which shapes men's lives, the theatre would be, in Artaud's phrase, "a metaphysics in action," a double of that "archetypal and dangerous reality" which underlies our cultural veneer.[23]

Le Théâtre alchimique was first published in a Spanish translation in Buenos Aires in 1932. It indicates the depth of Artaud's commitment to Symbolist theory. Mallarmé had given much thought to the relation of poetry and alchemy. The *Oeuvre* which occupied him the greater part of his life was nothing less, if we can credit him, than the transmutation of matter into idea, a process of refinement designed to extract from the material manifestations of things the essence of their being. The idea that the philosopher's quest of the Absolute might be fruitfully pursued in the theatre was evidently the basis of Lugné-Poë's Théâtre de l'oeuvre. Thus the groundwork for Artaud's conception of the alchemy of the theatre had been fully laid down by the time he took up the question. The idea in his case, however, had purely practical implications since, like Strindberg, he had no doubt that base metal could be transmuted into gold. He wrote:

> The principles of the theatre and of alchemy are in their essence myste-
> riously similar. For, like alchemy, the theatre is in its origin based on a
> certain number of principles which are the same for all the arts, and
> which aim at a capability in the domain of the spirit and the imagina-
> tion analogous to that which in the domain of matter makes it possible
> *in reality* to make gold.[24]

The spiritual connotations of alchemy had been thoroughly explored
by students of the occult long before Jung published his work on alchemy, and the hypothesis had long ago been advanced that before the
Great Work could culminate successfully there must be a concomitant
spiritual purification on the part of the operator. In this regard the material progress of the Work, the decomposition and reconstitution of matter, in the crucible and the alembic served as an apt symbol for the analogous spiritual operations which through the fires of Eros resulted in the
death and resurrection of the individual. All true alchemists, Artaud
wrote, are aware that alchemy is a mirage, just as the theatre is a mirage,
and their writings indicate their knowledge of the correspondence between the plane on which the theatre develops its images and the plane
of illusion on which the symbols of the alchemical process are developed.

> These symbols, which indicate what might be called the philosophical
> states of matter, already put the spirit on the path of that fiery purifica-
> tion . . . of the molecules of nature; on the path of that operation
> which enables, through the power of abstraction, to reconceive and
> reconstitute solids . . . to the point where they at last become once
> again gold. It is not sufficiently understood how the material symbolism
> which serves to designate this mysterious work corresponds to a parallel
> symbolism in the mind, to a manipulation of the ideas and appearances
> through which whatever is theatrical in the theatre is symbolized and
> philosophically distinguished.

Artaud believed that the theatre, as he envisioned the theatre, came
close to the Orphic mysteries through which one envisioned the essential
universe. By making use of whatever is communicative in art, by means
of shapes, sounds, music and volumes, the primitive theatre he hoped to
reconstruct would exteriorize an essential drama. "We must believe," he
wrote, "that the essential drama which formed the groundwork of all the
Great Mysteries relates to the second phase of Creation, the phase of difficulty and the Double, the phase of matter and of the thickening of the
idea."[25]

This language takes one somewhat further into Artaud's metaphysics, no doubt, than it is necessary to go. Practically, his idea, with all its mystical connotations, amounts to a justification of the synthetic dramatic art which he proposed to develop. Philosophically, he appears to have had in mind the familiar neo-Platonic ontology which is common to many mystical systems. The second phase of creation is the union of form and matter. To the resulting duality of being is attributable the difficulty of conscious existence, and the conflicts of the spiritual and material components of human life. The object of the Great Work is to decompose these elements and thereafter to reconstitute the primal oneness from which all else proceeds. In similar fashion, according to Artaud, the Alchemical Theatre would bring together on the stage symbols of power from all the arts, and through the symbolic conflict thus set up, would generate such heat as might be necessary to abstract from the material manifestations on the stage the Idea that informed them. Thus the aim of Artaud's theatre would be, he wrote: "to resolve or even to annihilate all the conflicts produced by the antagonism of matter and spirit, of idea and material shape, of concrete and abstract, and to fuse all these appearances in a unique expression which shall be the counterpart of spiritualized gold." [26]

To such practical men of the theatre as Dullin or Jouvet these ideas must have seemed impossibly extravagant; but they were not new to the editors of the *N.R.F.* It was in much this same fashion that Mallarmé had hoped to arrive at symbols which would yield the key to the ultimate mystery. There was an important difference, however, in method. While Mallarmé hoped to transcend into the Absolute through the alembication of language, Artaud found words useless for this purpose. The Symbolists had expressed interest in the language of movement and the symbolism of the dance, nevertheless for the disciples of Mallarmé poetic power was concentrated in the Word, and poetry was the supreme art. Artaud had studied in another school. He had learned his trade in Dullin's Atelier, and he had served a long stint in the silent films. For him the drama was not a literary art. The theatre spoke its own language, in which he felt fluent. It was a language which the spoken text served often to confuse or to obstruct.

In theory Artaud's efforts were directed toward what he felt was essential in the Greek theatre, the theatre of tragedy and comedy, with its rituals, its mystic connotations, its masks and dances. But from a technical standpoint it was the Oriental theatre that captured his fancy. In the twentieth century one could only imagine the Attic theatre; but the Eastern dance-theatre visibly existed. It could be studied and imitated.

In Dullin's workshop Artaud had been deeply impressed by the idea of total theatre, an artistic synthesis in which dialogue played a subsidiary role, as in the Nō plays of Japan. "The Japanese are our immediate masters and inspiration," he had written, while still a student at the Atelier. "The gods of the school are not Tolstoy, Ibsen and Shakespeare, but Hoffmann and Edgar Poe." And he marvelled, at that time, at his good fortune in stumbling on "an enterprise so closely linked with my own ideas."[27] In fact, aside from their dream-like atmosphere, the Nō plays, with their majestic pace and long-drawn sequences, their stately dances and music, had no possible relation to the sort of drama Artaud had in mind to produce. But in the summer of 1922, at the Colonial Exhibition in Marseille, a company of Cambodian dancers had introduced him to a completely new kind of theatre. Nine years later, at the Paris Colonial Exposition of 1931 he discovered the dance-theatre of Bali.

The Balinese theatre was far from primitive. It was, on the contrary, the last word in sophistication. It made use of an extensive glossary of gesture, sound, and movement that made it possible to dispense entirely with words, and yet conveyed meaning with great economy and precision. For the Western spectator, unfamiliar with its symbols, its effects were richly evocative, the more so as they were rarely comprehensible. The effect thus closely approximated the effect of Surrealist poetry. For Artaud this poetry of movement was a revelation. In the Balinese theatre he saw not only a complete realization of the Wagnerian synthetic work of art, but also a perfect demonstration of the metaphysical and alchemical theatre of his dreams. He wrote:

> The drama does not evolve out of feelings but out of spiritual states, crystallized and reduced to gestures and shapes. In sum, the Balinese realize with the utmost rigor the idea of pure theatre, in which everything, conception as well as realization, has value and being only in the degree of its objectification *on the stage*. They triumphantly demonstrate the absolute preponderance of the stage-director, whose creative power *eliminates words*. Its themes are vague, abstract, extremely general. What gives them life is solely the complex upsurge of all possible artifices of the theatre, which impose themselves on the mind like the idea of a metaphysics drawn from a new use of gesture and sound.[28]

In this theatre the stage business is composed of signs and symbols. The actors are animated hieroglyphs. By such means Artaud felt that he could achieve a Symbolist effect on the stage without any recourse to language. His theatre would make use of sound, not speech. Instead of motivating dialogue, the stage director would fill his three-dimensional space with movement, light, color, and sound, much as a painter fills his canvas with shape and color, and through this "physics of absolute gesture which is itself idea" he would give the impression of things never before seen.

To this end it would be necessary above all to put an end to the subjugation of the play to the text, and to recover the notion of "a kind of unique language midway between thought and gesture." This language would utilize sounds, movements, objects and postures in a kind of alphabet of symbols so that their combinations would convey meaning beyond the capacity of words. In this manner the theatre, rescued from its bondage to purely human things, would concern itself with things of a cosmic order. For all this would be useless unless it served to put the spirit on the track of "a creation of which we possess one face only, but which is completed on another plane."[29]

The "First Manifesto of the Theatre of Cruelty" goes into some detail as to the means of achieving such a result. It would be at the other pole from the kind of theatre conceived by Jouvet and Giraudoux. Here the writer would play a decidedly subsidiary part. The duality of author and director would be dissolved. Its place would be taken by a single creator upon whom would fall the double responsibility of devising sequence and spectacle. The stage director would be the poet of the production, and the language of the drama would be the mise en scène, and not the text, of the play.

The physical aspect of the theatre would also suffer a radical alteration. The new theatre would be all stage. It would consist of a single space within which the action would proceed in such a way that spectator and spectacle, actor and audience would all be in direct communication. The audience, seated on movable chairs in the midst of the acting area would be enveloped and penetrated by the play, and would be, so to speak, an integral part of the production. The auditorium would be enclosed by four white walls to serve as a background for the players. Overhead galleries would run around its periphery, enabling the actors to move from one part of the house to another, so that the action would develop on every level and in every dimension of height and depth. Instead of the fixed stage of conventional theatres a central space would be reserved in which the bulk of the action might be concentrated. There would be no scenery. Instead there would be hieroglyphic characters, ritual costumes, puppets ten meters high, enormous musical instruments, and objects of unknown form and function which would serve better than words to convey concrete images and metaphors.

In this theatre no written plays would be acted. Instead there would be experiments in the direct staging of stated themes or events, or of well-known works. The themes suitable to this type of production would normally be tragic; but in the Theatre of Cruelty there would also be ample room for comedy, since humor has its cruel side and laughter is a force of destruction.

There is no mention of Pirandello in either of Artaud's manifestoes. In *Ciascuno a suo modo* (1924) and in *Questa sera si recita a soggetto* (1930) some of these innovations had been anticipated, discussed, and even, in a measure, ridiculed. *Six Characters in Search of an Author* (1921), in which Artaud himself had acted in Paris, might be said to have inaugurated the "metaphysical theatre" in France. But perhaps at this time Artaud saw no need to bring up the question of Pirandello. The "First Manifesto of the Theatre of Cruelty" was published two years before Pirandello was awarded the Nobel prize, at a time when the master's influence in the French theatre was perceptibly waning. In any case, most of the innovations incorporated in the prospectus of the new theatre had been proposed or attempted somewhere by the time Dr. Hinkfuss took the stage in Berlin, so that Artaud's originality consisted mainly in putting them together in a unified design. The actual application of these ideas, of course, presented difficulties which neither Artaud nor anyone else was quite able to surmount. But many interesting innovations in the art of play production are directly attributable to his influence, and so much that is new and wonderful in the theatre has resulted from his proposals that even his extravagances have served in some quarters as a source of inspiration.

In the "Manifesto of the Theatre of Cruelty" Artaud announced his intention of staging an adaptation of an Elizabethan tragedy, perhaps *Arden of Feversham*, along with a version of the Bluebeard story, "The Fall of Jerusalem," one of the tales of the Marquis de Sade, and also Büchner's *Woyzeck*, all of them productions calculated to make an audience shudder. In his essay, "The Theatre and the Plague," Artaud cited Ford's *'Tis*

Pity She's a Whore as the sort of play that would free the unconscious and reveal its hidden conflicts. From his choice of plays it is difficult to avoid the suspicion that the therapeutic function of the Theatre of Cruelty, though certainly valid from a psychiatric viewpoint, was in some sense associated also with a showmanlike desire to compete with the Théâtre du Grand Guignol in the production of works of horror that had proven their worth at the box-office. There can be no doubt, of course, of Artaud's sincerity as an artist; but he was the heir of a long tradition that included Sophocles, Seneca, Shakespeare, and Webster, all of whom had specialized in gruesome subjects without benefit of Freud, Jung, or Krafft-Ebing. The antique theatre, however, like the Elizabethan, was mainly a theatre of words—even though both had a partiality for gruesome spectacle—while, in his Theatre of Cruelty, Artaud stressed the concrete representation of his subject matter and thus assimilated his theatre more closely to the nightmare itself than to the poetic sublimation of the nightmare.

Thus, with Artaud, the stately ritual of the Symbolist drama of which Mallarmé had dreamed evolved into something that Mallarmé had neither thought of nor intended. The generation that followed the period of the great wars was not inclined to moderation. It looked to the theatre and the screen for excitements more intense than anything reality provided, and reality had but recently provided excitements of unusual intensity. After the annihilation of Hiroshima much of the world lived in an atmosphere of terror which the minor terrors of fiction did something, apparently, to palliate. In the theatre, the films, and on the television screen brutal displays of violence and passion became increasingly familiar. Among the newer dramatists, even those who were primarily men of letters, such as Sartre and Camus, felt drawn to lurid subjects. But many of the writers of what became the avant garde did not think of the drama as a literary art. They preferred the precepts of Artaud and the example of Jarry. With the passing of the vogue of Giraudoux in France, and of Pirandello in Italy, a number of gifted writers with radical leanings made their way to the forefront of the theatre in France. Among these were Adamov, Arrabal, Genet, and Tardieu; and there was Harold Pinter in England, and in Switzerland, Friedrich Dürrenmatt. Of these writers the most successful, and in some ways the most interesting, was Eugène Ionesco, and in his work the mood of the following period found its most characteristic expression.[30]

And there was Beckett.

IONESCO

The Theatre of the Absurd was not a particularly felicitous phrase with which to characterize the avant-garde drama of the post-war generation, but it served a useful purpose. The collocation of such writers as Adamov, Tardieu, Vitrac, Weingarten, Vauthier, Arrabal, Schehadé, and Ionesco—and also Genet, Pinter, Grass, Frisch, and Beckett—under a single rubric did justice to none of them, since their works by no means constitute a homogenous genre. Nevertheless there is among them a certain family resemblance. Somewhere in the ancestry of all of them there are traces of Jarry and Artaud, and possibly of Strindberg, and nearly all their plays show some influence of Dada and Surrealism. They share, moreover, a certain swagger of lawlessness, and an evident desire to strike out in new directions, wherever they may lead. The spectrum that includes them, however, is very broad. It embraces everything that is distinctly modern in the contemporary theatre. Thus the most that can be done with these writers by way of generalization is a sweeping gesture of recognition and respect.

Ionesco is not, perhaps, the most highly gifted of these authors, but he best serves to illustrate the direction that their art has taken. He is the most prolific by far of the avant garde, the most resolute and the most influential. For the rest, there is so little consistency in his work that it is hardly possible to characterize it. Taken as a whole, his *oeuvre* provides no more secure basis for generalization than does the work of his more radical contemporaries. What makes his plays distinctive is not so much what they are as what they are not.

Ionesco made his debut in the theatre in 1950 with the one-act play called *La Cantatrice chauve*—in English, *The Bald Soprano*. It was subtitled aggressively, "An Anti-play." The genre was not altogether new. The groundwork for this type of entertainment had been laid thirty years before by Jean Cocteau and by Raymond Radiguet, and experiments along this line were being made contemporaneously by Arthur Adamov and Jean Tardieu. But *La Cantatrice chauve* had an air of originality that set it apart from other displays of theatrical nonsense. It had, moreover, a curious, but quite indefinable charm and, for reasons which are seldom altogether convincing, it soon acquired a monumental character. It became a landmark, a classic.

It was first performed in Paris on 11 May 1950 by a very young cast in a very small theatre—the Noctambules—before an audience, we are told, of three, all of them Surrealists. Subsequent audiences found the play completely incomprehensible. Heroic efforts were made to keep it running; but after six weeks of empty houses, it closed. Twenty years later it had been played everywhere and in almost every language. By that time Ionesco had produced some thirty plays, and acquired so much reputation that he was received into the French Academy which, in less enlightened times, had refused Molière.

Ionesco's success is readily understandable. He is not a great dramatist, but his works faithfully reflect the mood of his time, and in some sense he reincarnated the image of Jarry. The special blend of humor, irony, satire, and sadness which he brought to the stage accorded marvellously well with the attitude of a generation that felt that it had been deceived by everybody and everything, and was therefore ready to destroy whatever was readily destructible. In the 1960's it was fashionable to treat the established order with contempt while at the same time one expressed nostalgia for a vanished Eden. This mood was the basis of Ionesco's drama. It is unlikely that at any other time in recent history *La Cantatrice chauve* would have found a wide audience even among the very young. But its timing was precise. It found an audience everywhere, and for this audience its nonsense made more sense than anything that was taught in school.

Eugène Ionesco was born in Slatina, in Rumania, in 1912, on the eve of the First World War. His father was a Rumanian lawyer. His mother was French. When war broke out the family moved to Paris. Two years later his father returned to Rumania to join the army and the boy was left in his mother's care in France. His parents were later divorced. His father remarried, and Eugène went back to Rumania to live with him. In due course he took a degree in French literature at the University of Bucharest in preparation for a teaching career. As a writer he came first

under the influence of the French Symbolists; later he inclined to Surrealism. He was married in 1936, and the next year he began teaching at
the lycée in Bucharest. The following year, 1938, he was awarded a
French government grant and came to Paris to write his dissertation.
The title was "Sin and Death in French Poetry Since Baudelaire."

In 1939, when war once again broke out, Ionesco and his wife went
south to Marseille. At the end of hostilities he went back to Paris with
his wife and an infant daughter and found work as a proofreader in a
publishing house. In 1948 he wrote *La Cantatrice chauve*. He was then
thirty-six.

"In 1948," he wrote, "before my first play, *La Cantatrice chauve*, I had
no wish to become a playwright. It was my ambition simply to learn English. The study of English does not necessarily lead to dramaturgy. On
the contrary, it is because I did not succeed in learning English that I became a dramatic author." Ionesco's account of how he came to write this
play is in some ways more amusing than the play. He had bought, he
writes, an English-French conversation manual for beginners, and in
copying out the phrases he became aware of a number of astonishing
facts—that there are seven days in the week, that the floor is below and
the ceiling above, and of other truths of that nature. In the third lesson,
Mr. and Mrs. Smith appeared and informed one another that they lived
in the suburbs of London, that they had several children, that their name
was Mr. and Mrs. Smith, and so on. Their friends the Martins turned
up in the fifth lesson and brought even more complex facts to light.
These conversations inspired Ionesco to write a theatre piece around the
dramatic dialogue he was studying. The result was *La Cantatrice chauve*.[1]

Ionesco's account of this occurrence is engagingly arch, but it does afford a glimpse into the author's mind. As in most language manuals, the
dialogue in *La Méthode assimil* was practical rather than brilliant, and obviously it consisted largely of commonplaces calculated to inspire the
student to progress to higher ground. The analogy to the dreariness of
French conversation in less edifying circumstances was inescapable. In a
mood that is without doubt familiar to every foreign-language student
who has suffered a similar ordeal, Ionesco set about to parody the social
relations of the Smiths and the Martins. "A whole section of my play,"
we are told, "consists of phrases taken from my English manual. . . .
Nevertheless, the text of *La Cantatrice chauve* was a lesson (and a plagia-
rism) only in the beginning. A bizarre phenomenon took place, I don't
know how: the text transformed itself under my eyes, insensibly, against
my will. . . . Mr. Smith, my hero, taught that the week consisted of

three days, Tuesday, Thursday and Tuesday. . . . My characters, my fine bourgeois, the Martins, husband and wife, were stricken with amnesia . . . they no longer recognized one another. . . ."

La Cantatrice chauve does not wholly dispense with action, but the action is minimal. What the play has by way of plot is amusingly mischievous, a *reductio ad absurdum* of what was in the first place absurd. The play is set in the Smith's living-room, which is furnished in what is said to be English style. It is nine o'clock in the evening. Mr. Smith is reading his after-dinner newspaper. Mrs. Smith babbles comfortably, developing the exposition in traditional fashion by telling Mr. Smith a great deal that he already knows. The clock is a free spirit. It strikes seven, then three, and afterwards strikes as the mood takes it, making nothing of the passage of time. When the Smiths have retired, the Martins arrive, expecting dinner. They do not appear to be acquainted with one another, and it is only after a protracted conversation that they come to the conclusion that they are husband and wife. When the recognition at last takes place the clock strikes 29. The Smiths reappear. The ensuing conversation is embarrassingly tedious. It is interrupted by the sound of the doorbell, but there is nobody at the door. This business is several times repeated and gives rise to much discussion, after which the Fire Captain presents himself at the door. He is looking for fires, is welcomed enthusiastically, and proceeds to entertain the company with pointless anecdotes. These are capped by a senseless poem recited by Mary, the maid, who turns out to be the Fireman's former flame. The Fireman then goes off so as not to miss a fire which is scheduled, in his diary, to break out at the other end of town. The talk is then resumed, but the scene breaks down in alarming fashion. The author describes his experience in composing the play. He notes that at this point

> the characters had decomposed, the talk, now absurd, had emptied itself of content, and it had all ended in a quarrel the causes of which it was impossible to determine, for what my characters hurled at one another were not replies . . . but syllables, consonants and vowels! . . . It was a question, for me, of reality giving way. The words had become husks of sound, devoid of meaning; the characters, also, of course, had emptied themselves of their psychology, and the world appeared to me in an unusual light, perhaps in its true light, beyond interpretation and with purely arbitrary sequence.[2]

What Ionesco describes in this passage of his commentary is the gradual unravelling of sense into senselessness, of speech into noise, a Surrealistic effect which hints at a revelation of the ultimate, and the implication is that the gradual disintegration of his fantasy was an automatic process over which the author had no control, and of which he was simply a witness. There is no sign of this in the play. *La Cantatrice chauve* is senseless from beginning to end. Everything that leads to the Fire Captain and his recitations is idiotic, and the transition to the scene of the quarrel seems quite natural, the transformation of one type of madness into another, a progression from imbecility to manic fury. This can be read, if one wishes, as a satire of bourgeois life; but the exaggeration goes beyond satire and the point, if there is a point, is submerged in the violence of the caricature.

La Cantatrice chauve is, in fact, a good example of the Theatre of Cruelty, the first play to reach the stage in which Artaud's blueprint is fully worked out. It is an act of aggression directed not so much at its characters and their environment as at the audience which witnesses their antics. In this play the spectator is subjected, more or less sadistically, to a series of bewildering and uncomfortable experiences, the horror of which is administered in homeopathic doses which at last culminate in a decidedly unpleasant paroxysm. Artaud had indicated that there was room in the Theatre of Cruelty for comedy; but the comic, in his view, is virtually indistinguishable from the tragic. This is, indeed, the feeling communicated by Ionesco's play.

As a satiric parody of the solemn forms of salon comedy *La Cantatrice chauve* was doubtless motivated by the same sort of mischievous spirit that inspired the youthful Jarry to parody *Macbeth* in *Ubu roi*. In this play Ionesco, like Jarry, makes the impression of an intelligent child making fun of the solemn rituals of the grown-ups. But the influence of Artaud takes this play some distance beyond the joyous brutality of *Ubu*. Ultimately *La Cantatrice chauve* is not funny. It evokes laughter, of course, but even more certainly it arouses pity and terror. In the course of time Ionesco has characterized his play in ways to suit every taste, but he has never lost sight of its tragic undertone. In 1958 he wrote: "When it was played I was almost surprised to hear the laughter of the spectators who took (and still take) all this quite happily, convinced that it is a real comedy, that I am pulling their legs." But he himself was evidently disposed to take his play quite seriously, and in time he saw the Smiths and the Martins as potential Nazis, Fascists, and Communists, a comic tribe that was not entirely funny:

> The Smiths, the Martins, can no longer talk because they can no longer think; they no longer think because they can no longer feel, they no

longer have passions, they no longer are, they can "become" anyone, anything, for, having no special being, they are the same as others, the impersonal crowd, they are interchangeables. . . . The tragic character does not change, he breaks, he is himself, he is *real*. Comic characters are people who do not exist.[3]

If not everyone is disposed to take *La Cantatrice chauve* with the requisite seriousness it is probably because its characters are barely human, and the caricature is too broad to be convincing. The Smiths and the Martins are puppets. Puppets are not expected to think or to feel. It is the spectator who is required to fulfill these functions. There is, however, not enough humanity in Ionesco's characters to force an identification. One is at liberty, therefore, not to give them life, in which case the whole affair is likely to seem an exercise in stupidity. The fact is, the play is extremely abstract. It symbolizes a reality which one need not credit, and which depends for its dramatic efficacy on the masochism— or the sadism—of the audience. Its power to amuse or to horrify is consequently a function of the evocative capability of its symbols. From this standpoint the title was well chosen. It is an incantation, a piece of gruesome magic which sets these puppets dancing with the dreadful energy of skeletons in a *danse macabre*.

Originally the author does not appear to have attached any unusual importance to this composition. Its significance became apparent only as a result of its success, which surprised him. In 1959 he wrote:

> I did not think of this comedy as a real comedy. In fact it was only a parody of a play, a comedy of comedy. I used to read it to friends when they came to my house in order to make them laugh. . . . Later when I read Raymond Queneau's *Exercices de style* I realized that my experiment with writing bore a certain resemblance to his. Monique Sainte-Côme then confirmed that I had really written a kind of comic play, so I plucked up enough courage to give her my manuscript and, as she was helping Nicolas Bataille and his players with their staging, she submitted the play to him. Nicolas Bataille and his players . . . decided to put it in rehearsal at once.[4]

According to Bataille's account of the matter, by the time he saw the play Ionesco had already submitted it to Barrault, who rejected it, and to the Comédie-Française. Bataille himself was at this time twenty-three years of age. His company was operating the tiny Théâtre de Poche. There was virtually no money available for the production, but there were plenty of high spirits. Various ideas were discussed for the mise en scène. In the end it was decided to act the play with complete solemnity.

There was some uncertainty as to the title. Ionesco had suggested several possibilities, none of which found favor—*L'Heure anglaise*, *Big-Ben Follies*, *L'Anglais sans peine*, and so on. According to Ionesco the actual title was the result of a slip of the tongue. Where the Fire Captain in the course of his monologue was required to say "l'institutrice blonde," he somehow said "la cantatrice chauve," and Ionesco seized on this happy accident at once for his title.[5]

There was also some uncertainty as to how the play should end. The author commented: "In the beginning I had in mind a more burlesque, more violent production for *La Cantatrice chauve;* a bit more in the style of the Marx brothers, which would have permitted a kind of explosion . . ." In the end, however, it was decided to black out the scene of the quarrel and to begin again quietly *da capo.* The play thus acquired a circular shape, and as this ending was judged to be properly metaphysical, it was retained in the final script.

It is evident that no extensive calculation went into this production, neither in the writing nor in the playing; the ultimate work of art was the result of a series of happy accidents; thus the spontaneity of the composition was strictly in accordance with Surrealist principles. Ionesco wrote later of the alarm he had felt originally at the course his fantasy was taking: ". . . While I was writing this play . . . I was taken with a real malaise, vertigo, nausea. From time to time I was obliged to stop and, wondering what the devil was forcing me to go on writing, I would go and stretch out on the couch, fearful that I would see it sink into the void, and I with it. When I had finished this work I was, all the same, very proud of it. I imagined I had written something like the tragedy of language!"[6]

In this, and other passages of his commentary, Ionesco reflects the mystical tendency that colors so much of his writing. He is quite explicit as to the manner in which this play was composed. It began as a parody, but the form it took eventually was inspired, it would seem, by a power that transcends consciousness, so that the writer was not only astonished by what emerged from his mind, but was also at a loss to explain its significance. In exhibiting the images that take form spontaneously in his imagination, the Surrealist author simply represents as accurately as possible a process of thought over which, in theory, he exerts no conscious control, so that he is, in a sense, like a dreamer, the passive witness of his fantasy. Thus, in Ionesco's phrase, the artist does no more than to furnish testimony.

In describing the method of Gérard Schneider, a painter whose work he admired, Ionesco wrote: "To proceed like Schneider is very, very simple: it is enough to look into yourselves, never outward; and to externalize, to let what is within you speak, develop, whatever you have seen there and heard. In this way it is the world itself, just as it is, that you will succeed in revealing, authentically, whereas if you looked only outside yourself, you would mix everything up, you would alienate the two aspects of reality and make it incomprehensible to others, to yourselves . . ."[7]

From this viewpoint the work of composition is one of free association, and in this respect the process Ionesco describes is close to the practice of poets in every age. In a celebrated passage in the *Purgatorio* Dante gives the poet Bonagiunta a lesson in poetic composition that has served as a basis for all subsequent symbolist theory:

> I mi son un, che quando
> Amor mi spira, noto, e a quel modo
> Ch'e' detta dentro vo significando.[8]

The *Comedy* of Dante is ostensibly a tissue of symbols by means of which the poet bears testimony to what is inspired in him by a higher power. But Dante can hardly be called a Surrealist. The difference between his method and that of the followers of André Breton is a function of the degree of rational control to which the poet's fantasy is subjected. For Dante the intellect was the supreme arbiter of poetic creation. The love that inspired him was an intellectual longing, and the beauty at which he aimed was that absolute beauty in token of which all other beauties exist. Mallarmé also exerted a high degree of control in the selection and arrangement of the images that welled up into consciousness. In the case of Ionesco, at least in the composition of his early plays, the intellectual factor is professedly minimal. He describes his work in terms that might well apply to the poetry of Rimbaud, to *Le Bateau ivre*, for example. "For me," Ionesco wrote,

> the drama—my plays—most often is a confession; all I do is to make admissions (incomprehensible to the deaf, that is inevitable), for what else can I do? I try to project on the stage an interior drama (incomprehensible to myself), telling myself, nevertheless, that since the microcosm is the image of the macrocosm, it may happen that this interior world, tattered and disjointed, can be in some sort the mirror or the symbol of the contradictions of the universe. No plot, therefore, no

architecture, no puzzle to solve, but only the insoluble unknown. No characters, personages without identity (they become at every moment their own contraries, they change places with others and vice versa), simply an inconsequent sequence, a fortuitous chain, without relation of cause and effect, inexplicable adventures or emotional states, a tangle, indescribable but alive; intentions, movements, passions without unity, plunging into contradiction; this can seem tragic, seem comic, or both at once, for I am incapable of distinguishing the one from the other: I wish only to translate the improbable, the unusual, my universe.[9]

These lines, written in 1953, when *La Cantatrice chauve* was beginning to attract attention, obviously overstates the case. Ionesco's early plays are puzzling, but rarely incomprehensible. The sequence of events in *La Cantatrice chauve* can hardly be called logical, but its doctrine and direction are capable of clarification, and have been clarified in various ways, often by the author himself. The same may be said of all his plays, with the possible exception of the skits published as *Sept petits sketches*, and these are simply *rigolades*. Nevertheless Ionesco's plays make a very different effect from what is usual in conventional drama. His symbols sometimes have direct reference; more often communication takes place by a kind of sympathetic magic, a telepathic connection achieved through something like resonance.

The difficulty of finding words with which to communicate the images which present themselves to the poet's consciousness is the basis of the age-long quarrel of poets with poetry. In the communication of ideas logic simplifies everything; this is also its chief disadvantage. The logical faculty is not commensurate with the imaginative mentality; it is capable of dealing with it only in a partial and provisional fashion. It screens out of the area of communication whatever cannot be expressed in terms of its own technical requirements, which are limited. The result is the glossary of stereotypes in which poetry is normally formulated. For the poet who feels tongue-tied by the normal apparatus of communication at his disposal the problem, of course, goes beyond the question of vocabulary, but the linguistic difficulty is both obvious and primary.

Artaud proposed to solve the poet's problem in the theatre by devising a dramatic language independent of speech. Ionesco, however, followed Mallarmé and Breton in his wish to revitalize the spoken word. For Ionesco the chief obstacle to the communication of ideas through discursive language is the use of words that have died and decayed, the ready-made clichés of everyday speech which serve to convey the thoughts of those who do not trouble to think. The living word is a powerful instrument. It can create and it can kill. The poet's function is to restore its power. For that it is necessary to renew the relation of the outward symbol to the world within, for in the absence of the inner component the outward reality has, at best, only a partial existence. The artist's mission, therefore, in Ionesco's view, is to unite the two worlds and thus to create a true reality. *La Cantatrice chauve* is, if anything, a negative demonstration of this hypothesis. It represents a dead world, a morass of stereotypes peopled by robots.[10]

It is a play without plot, and can hardly be said to have characters; and Ionesco was the first to admit that it had no special ideological significance. It is, in Huizinga's sense of the *ludus*, purely a game of the imagination, a *jeu d'esprit*. For this reason it has proved to be a singularly accommodating work of art, receptive to a variety of interpretations, with some of which Ionesco has occasionally found himself in accord. But, along with his fellow Symbolists, Ionesco has never claimed any special authority in the interpretation of his images. It is the function of the poet, in his opinion, to receive and to transmit the symbols that come to his mind. The task of decoding them, he leaves to the cryptographer.

As a result of its thorough ambiguity, *La Cantatrice chauve*, like much contemporary art, has a strangely prismatic quality. Its mystery, however, is far removed from that of such conscious mystifications as Pinter's *The Birthday Party* or Beckett's *Theatre II*. Works of that sort are riddles, and have the charm of riddles; while they lack definite significance, they cannot be said to be meaningless. They are, on the contrary, agencies which are intended to stimulate revery in a special way. They leave the mind in doubt. The assumption is that, for artistic purposes, doubt is quite as valid a mental state as certainty; perhaps it is more valid. The analogy is music that ends on a suspension: it ends without ending. "The particular meaning of a dramatic plot," Ionesco wrote, "obscures its essential significance."[11]

The essential significance of *La Cantatrice chauve* is, however, precisely what is in doubt. The feeling it conveys is akin to embarrassment, a kind of malaise. The Smiths and the Martins are ridiculous; but the caricature is disquieting. The scene—as in *Ubu roi*—is a mirror in which the audience may, if it so wishes, see itself reflected in the manner of the distorting mirrors of amusement parks, mirrors in which we contemplate ourselves, laughing, with mingled feelings of disbelief and horror. Ionesco has not rejected the suggestion that this play satirizes the petite bourgeoisie; he has, on the contrary, both accepted and amplified this idea. *La Cantatrice chauve*, we are told, "concerns above all a kind of universal petite bourgeoisie, the petit bourgeois being the man of received ideas, slogans, the universal conformist. . . ."[12] It would appear, then, that in caricaturing the middle class Ionesco is not indulging in the more obvious sort of class-satire. His satire is leveled not at any particular class of society but at society itself, at humanity; and if, as human beings, we are indeed in such straits as the Smiths and the Martins—and it is difficult to deny the possibility—then the play reveals us in a most disagreeable situation. Thus on a superficial level the play is a ridiculous farce, a parody, and it makes us laugh. But it derives power from depths that cannot be sounded without discomfort and danger, perhaps from the hopelessness of a world that has lived out its term.

Ionesco's fear of ideology amounts to an obsession. In common with many of his contemporaries he tries not to make statements. Nevertheless his plays, from first to last, make statements, many statements, by no means consistent with one another. In this respect he is, happily, beyond reproach. Ionesco is a specialist in paradox. Underlying his plays and his critical and polemical writings is the useful assumption that every statement implies its contrary. Since thought is a dialectic process, to commit oneself to any one statement is to falsify it and, along with it, the mental state which is its source. For Ionesco, therefore, as for many Symbolists of his generation, doubt is more comfortable than certainty, and commitment inevitably invites some degree of claustrophobia.

Jarry long ago remarked that comprehensible things limit the mind and burden the memory. From Ionesco's standpoint also, every belief is a bar in the soul's prison. Consequently, communication on the plane of discursive language, no matter how highly developed the expression, will ultimately be a deception. The symbolism of gesture is preferable, since gesture is less restrictive than language, yet even here the truth will resist formulation. For the Symbolist it is impossible in the present state of things to go beyond intimation. Artistic creation is, at bottom, an exploration of the psyche. It is sometimes possible in this manner to discover what one thinks. Ionesco wrote of *La Cantatrice chauve*:

> I have often been asked to state my aims and intentions in writing
> this or that play. When, for example, I was asked to explain *La Canta-*
> *trice chauve*, my first play, I said it was a parody of "boulevard theatre,"
> or simply of the theatre, a criticism of the verbal clichés and mechanical

behavior of people; I also said it was the expression of a feeling of the strangeness of everyday things, a strangeness that appears at the very heart of the most outworn commonplace. It was thought to be a criticism of the petite bourgeoisie, even, in particular, of the English middle-class, with which, moreover, I had no acquaintance at all: it was thought to be an attempt to break down language or destroy the theatre; it was also thought to be abstract drama. . . .

If I myself say that it was a completely purposeless game, I neither affirm nor confirm the proceding explanations, for even the purposeless game, perhaps above all the purposeless game, is charged with all sorts of meanings which emerge from the game itself. In reality, in writing this play, then in writing those that followed, I had in the beginning no "intention," but a multiplicity of intentions, half conscious, half unconscious. In fact, for me, it is in the course of, and thanks to, the artistic creation that the intention or intentions are defined. The construction is merely the rising of the internal edifice which thus lets itself be discovered.[13]

Some years before making this statement, Ionesco called *La Cantatrice chauve* "an experiment in abstract or non-representational drama, or, on the contrary, concrete drama, if you like . . . a concretization of symbols." This rhetoric seems apt, for the play is in fact both abstract and concrete, and represents without representing. It represents in considerable detail the domestic situation of a middle-class family in England; whether the representation is accurate or not is of no special importance. The point, according to the author, is to discharge the pent up contents of the psyche, hence the process closely approximates the sort of therapy that Artaud had in mind in devising the Theatre of Cruelty. "The point," Ionesco wrote,

is to liberate dramatic tension without the help of any real plot or any special object. One will arrive all the same at the revelation of something monstrous: this is necessary, moreover, for drama is ultimately the revelation of monstrous things or monstrous states without forms, or of monstrous forms that we carry within ourselves. To arrive at this exaltation, or these revelations, without the justification of a theme or a subject that motivates them ideologically, hence falsely, hypocritically. . . .[14]

What is monstrous in this comedy is the vein of tragedy that unexpectedly comes to light. Artaud considered the tragic shock indispensable to the dramatic experience. Ionesco evidently concurred. "The trick," he wrote, "is to push burlesque to its extreme limit. Then with a flick of the thumb, an imperceptible glide, there you are back again in the tragic. It is sleight of hand."[15]

La Cantatrice chauve is, indeed, as funny as the tragic can be. It is impossible to follow its logic, it has no discernible structural scheme, nor any hint of suspense or of calculated climax. The text barely supports the effort of reading. Nonetheless it is a surprisingly effective theatre piece. There had been some attempts at this type of composition, as we have noted. Some were even successful. But with this farce Ionesco firmly established the theatre of non-sense. Its beginnings were humble. It success was spectacular. But in the end Ionesco found this a relatively unfruitful genre. The year after his disappointing experience with *La Cantatrice chauve* at the Noctambules, Nicolas Bataille produced *La Leçon* in his Théâtre de Poche (1951). It aroused some interest; but not enough to warrant further experiment with this genre. With the exception of the *Sept petits sketches* of 1953, this was all Ionesco did in the way of nonsense drama. With *Amédée* (1954) and *Jacques* (1955), he moved further away from Surrealism into a more intelligible sphere of Symbolism, the drama of metaphor and charade. The development of the theatre of nonsense —the Theatre of the Absurd, properly so called—was left to others, and indeed it had no great future, save in the hands of Pinter, who, by making melodrama incomprehensible, brought this genre back effectively into the realm of the Symbolist.

La Leçon is a sadistic fantasy. The action involves an aged professor and a young pupil, a girl of eighteen who is perhaps preparing for an examination. The action takes place in a provincial town, in the professor's living room. The professor is a little old man with a white goatee, a weak voice, and occasionally a lewd gleam in his eye. In the beginning he is extremely diffident and unusually solicitous of his student's comfort. In the end he turns into a vicious monster, a Bluebeard. The young girl is bright and fresh. She has evidently had a most uneven education. She can do amazing feats of mental multiplication, but she is unable to subtract three successfully from four. The arithmetic lesson soon becomes impossibly abstruse. It is followed by a lecture on comparative linguistics which succeeds mainly in giving the girl a toothache, and may well give an audience a headache. In the course of his lecture the professor works himself up into a maniacal frenzy, while the girl wilts. At a climactic moment the professor plunges an imaginary knife into the body of his student. He then symbolically rapes her with the same instrument, and is shaken by an orgasm which leaves him exhausted. The housekeeper comes to his aid. Together they drag the girl's cadaver out of the room into some inner recess where thirty-nine other corpses are awaiting disposition. The doorbell rings. The forty-first victim appears.

La Leçon, like *La Cantatrice chauve*, seems to have its root in childhood experiences associated with the discomforts of the educational process. Both plays are, in a sense, acts of vengeance directed against the image of the stupid and sadistic schoolmaster. The same, of course, may be said of *Ubu roi*. The student-teacher relationship is, at best, an uncanny entanglement susceptible to all the horrors of the Oedipus complex in its various aspects, for the ambivalence of the filial relationship is necessarily in some measure transferred to the image of the schoolteacher. In *Présent passé passé présent* Ionesco specifically assigned his fear and hatred of authority to the baleful influence of his Rumanian father: "Everything that I have done, I have done, so to speak, against him." The little old professor of *La Leçon* who in the course of his lesson is somehow changed into an overwhelming maniac can hardly be identified, of course, with the author's father, but it is easy to identify him with the infantile father-image. He symbolizes, in any case, the tyranny of the schoolmaster as this despot might seem to a sensitive child now grown into a man capable of seeing both the humor and the horror of his childish fantasies.

La Leçon goes well beyond caricature in its extravagance. Beginning on a plane of matter-of-fact realism it proceeds through absurdity into lunacy, and ultimately reaches a sexual climax that includes murder. The characters and the situation take their departure from normal waking life and almost imperceptibly are transformed into the stuff of dreams so that it is difficult to say at what point the nonsense of sanity becomes the nonsense of madness. What is clear is that at a certain point in the play the action somehow passes from the stage of the conventional theatre to the stage of the guignol, and the characters, by a kind of magic, become puppets. The dialogue becomes gibberish. And the spectator—if the production is successful—becomes a frightened child.

Ionesco has several times referred to the influence of the puppet shows in the Luxembourg on his early life, and it is evident that his plays in some measure reproduce the excitements of this youthful experience of the theatre. "The guignol held me there," he writes, "stupefied by the spectacle of these dolls speaking, moving about and cudgelling one another. It was the very image of the world, extraordinary, incredible, but truer than the true world, that was presented to me in an infinitely simplified and caricatured form, as if to underline its grotesque and brutal reality."[16]

In attempting in his work for the theatre to approximate the directness, the simplicity, and the emotional intensity of the guignol, Ionesco came readily under the influence of Artaud. *La Leçon*, in an even more obvious way than *La Cantatrice*, seems to be an experiment in the Theatre of Cruelty, and in several passages of his *Expérience du théâtre*, Ionesco appears to echo Artaud's manifesto:

> The naiveté necessary to a work of art is lacking in the theatre. I do not say that a dramatic poet may not one day appear, a great *naïf*, but for the moment I do not see anyone of that sort dawning on the horizon. I mean a lucid naiveté, arising from the inmost depths of being, revealing them, revealing them in ourselves, restoring to us our own naiveté, our secret being.[17]

Ionesco's dissatisfaction with the contemporary theatre was, indeed, based on grounds very similar to those set forth by Artaud. The theatre of his day, Ionesco wrote, was too literary, over-intelligent, overly discursive. What is magnified was not sufficiently magnified. What was subtle in it was not subtle enough. To restore the drama to its former dignity it would be necessary, he considered, to accentuate its effects to the possible maximum. The former dignity he had in mind, apparently, was the dignity which all the Symbolist theoreticians, from Mallarmé to Artaud, attributed to the Attic theatre, the ritual of Dionysos. To recover that dignity, he felt, one had to make radical departures:

> To push the drama beyond that intermediate zone which is neither drama nor literature is to restore it to its former frame, its natural limits. It was necessary not to hide the puppet's strings, but to make them even more visible, deliberately evident, to descend to the depths of the grotesque, of caricature, beyond the pale irony of witty salon comedy. No more drawing-room comedy, but farce, the extreme thrust of parody. Humor, yes, but humor by means of the burlesque. Hard comedy, without refinement, excessive. No dramatic comedy, either. But back again to the outrageous. To push everything into frenzy, where we find the springs of tragedy. To create a theatre of violence: violently comic, violently dramatic.
>
> Avoid psychology, or rather give it a metaphysical dimension. Drama is the extreme exaggeration of feelings, an exaggeration that dislocates the flat reality of every day. Also the dislocation, the disarticulation of language.[18]

La Leçon is an everyday occurrence studied under a microscope. Under extreme magnification a situation which normally necessitates some show of authority and some degree of submission reveals itself as tyrannical, sadistic, and dangerous, a process in which the helpless pupil is overwhelmed by an authoritarian presence which is intoxicated by its own power to the point where it loses control of itself and becomes bestial. In these circumstances the power of the play derives from the resonance aroused in the mind of the spectator. Education, no matter how carefully it is administered, is likely to be in some respects a disagreeable experience which arouses resistance and aggression. These effects, normally suppressed in adult life, are certainly residual in the psyche, and are therefore capable of being dredged up under appropriate stimulation. The social advantages of bringing about such a reaction are questionable, but there is no doubt that the suppressed material is a source of dramatic power. From a realistic viewpoint *La Leçon* is absurdly excessive; but it is directed to a part of the mind that knows no excess, and in the theatre it elicits a very positive response.

What is actually communicated in the course of the professor's lecture is mainly pretentious nonsense, including what looks very much like a parody of transformational grammar. The result is to reduce both teacher and student to a state of imbecility which terminates in an obscene business which invites the intervention of the police. Thus the demonstration is more than parodic; *La Leçon* is actually a dramatic metaphor, a lewd symbol intended to represent a social situation which, though normally less obnoxious, is nevertheless calculated to make one shudder.

The Professor is, in this case, safe from prosecution. He has a swastika brassard which enables the wearer to indulge his passions with impunity. But this allusion to the educational methods of the Third Reich is of merely passing interest. The intimation is that all education is privileged in a similar manner; that what happens to children in the name of education is a shameful violation of mind and body; indeed, that Nazism was a consequence of normal pedagogical practices; and that professors have always been members of a conspiracy sanctioned and protected by the state. Ionesco spares his Professor nothing. In the end we are given to understand that the old man is not only a dangerous lunatic, but that this monster is at bottom a frieghtened child, wielding an imaginary knife, who is promptly put in his place by the servant—the mother-image—who turns up opportunely to box the ears of the father-image.

This play is a first-rate example of the sort of grotesque comedy that Artaud considered suitable for the Theatre of Cruelty. It is calculated to uncover, and thus to release, the primitive energy normally imprisoned in the unconscious, and normally manifested mainly in the petty acts of wickedness and meanness that characterize human behavior. Artaud stressed the advantage of bringing to the level of consciousness the savage impulses that underlie polite social relations and give them their characteristic quality. It is not clear that Ionesco shared this view; but it seems likely. His theatre is designed to touch a nerve. He nowhere warrants its medical efficacy, but unless his drama is purely vengeful, it can have no other justification than a prophylactic intention. *La Leçon* is a farce that makes one shudder. It serves, in its way, to make one aware of what is monstrous in a cultural system that insists on forcefully transmitting from one generation to the other the accumulated stupidities of the race. But its didactic purpose, if it has one, is surely a secondary consideration. What is primary in these plays is the vendetta which Ionesco, like Pirandello, has carried on against the world into which he was born. *La Leçon*, like *La Cantatrice chauve*, is an aggressive act against society, an act sufficiently destructive to arouse enthusiasm, but much too innocuous to be dangerous.

The following year Ionesco produced *Les Chaises, farce tragique*. It was first played on 22 April 1952 at the Théâtre du Nouveau Lancry. Four years later it was produced at the Studio des Champs Elysées. It was performed again in Paris in 1961 By that time it had made its author famous.

Of all Ionesco's plays *Les Chaises* is the most ingenious, the most successful, and the most enigmatic. The action takes place in a tower on an island in the sea. The set depicts a circular room sparsely furnished with a few chairs, two windows looking out on the water, and a dais with a blackboard. It is six o'clock in the evening. Two old people are seated downstage The man is said to be ninety-five years old. He is sitting in his wife's lap.

In this play, unlike the previous two, the characterizations are detailed. Ionesco is a master of dialogue, and the exposition is thorough, as if the author had people specifically in mind in drawing this portrait of the Old Man and Semiramis, his wife. The Old Man is an old-time radical, an aged Utopian who has failed at everything and antagonized everyone who might possibly be of use to him, so that now he is reduced to earning a meager livelihood as the caretaker of an isolated island tower. His wife is as old as he, and as faithful as a dog. She comforts him, supports him, and echoes his every word. She is his double. Apart from that she is nothing.

The play appears to take place at some point in the future. The Old Man remembers a city called Paris which sank into the water many years before. The situation is now desperate, but the Old Man has devised a system that is guaranteed to save the world, provided people will listen. A great meeting has been organized. People of every class have been invited. All is in readiness. He is awaiting his guests.

They come, one by one at first; afterwards, in throngs. To the audience, they are invisible. But the old couple sees them and hears them. They are greeted warmly and ushered to the chairs which the old people drag in and set out in rows, so that in a little while the room is thronged with invisible people. The Old Man and his wife are jammed against the windows, widely separated by the press. At last, the Emperor arrives. He is greeted with impressive ceremony and seated in a chair facing the dais. From his place by the window the Old Man makes an obsequious speech. He himself, he declares, is incapable of delivering his world-shaking message. But a great orator has been engaged and is momentarily expected. It is he who will speak.

The Orator appears.

Since there is in fact nobody on the stage except the Old Man and his wife, and nothing visible save rows of empty chairs, one might imagine that the Orator also will be imaginary. But the Orator turns out to be a creature of flesh and blood. The Old Man appears to be in some doubt as to his reality: he touches the Orator as if to verify that he really exists. The Orator is, in fact, a figure from the past. He is dressed in the costume of a poet of the Paris bohème of the 1880's, and there is something ghost-like in his presence as he moves through the chairs to take his place on the dais. There he sits silently, writing autographs, entirely oblivious to what is going on.

The Old Man introduces him, and thanks all those present profusely, from the Emperor down to the carpenters who have made the chairs. He then announces that his destiny is fulfilled, and his time has come. After showering the Emperor with confetti, he and his wife jump out of their respective windows into the sea. There is an audible splash.

The Orator rises. He struggles to speak. But he is a deaf-mute, and can make only inarticulate sounds. At last, in his despair, he has a happy idea. With a piece of chalk he writes on the blackboard in large letters the word, ANGEPAIN. He points to this significantly, awaiting a reaction. There is none. He erases the word, and tries again. This time he succeeds in writing something like "Adieu," twice. Certain now that he has conveyed his message, he stands solemnly, smiling, waiting. There is no response. He gives it up now as hopeless, bows ceremonially to the Emperor, and with ghost-like steps, withdraws. For a moment the stage is entirely empty, save for the chairs. Then there is heard a sudden buzz of talk and laughter as if all the chairs were occupied by people. The curtain falls on this effect.

Ionesco wrote a program note for the first performance:

> At certain moments the world seems to be devoid of meaning, and reality unreal. It is this feeling of the unreal, the search for an essential reality, forgotten and nameless—apart from which I do not feel that I exist—that I have tried to express through these characters of mine who wander about inarticulately, having nothing of their own aside from their anguish, their remorse, their frustration, the emptiness of their lives. Beings submerged in the meaningless cannot be other than grotesque, their tragedy can only excite laughter.
>
> Since I find the world incomprehensible, I am waiting for someone to explain it to me. . . .[19]

A program note couched in these terms would seem to serve *La Cantatrice chauve* quite as well as *Les Chaises*. But in fact *Les Chaises* marked a new departure in Ionesco's work, and it had a new seriousness. Artaud had described the type of drama which he considered appropriate to the Theatre of Cruelty in terms of its absorption in cosmic questions of metaphysical character. In *Les Chaises* Ionesco tried to deal seriously with the question of reality. The world which he depicts in this play is both ambiguous and mysterious, both real and unreal. In an entry dated 23 June 1951, almost a year before the date of this production, he described in his journal the problem he had set himself in the play which at that time he called *The Orator:*

> By means of language, gesture, acting, properties, to represent the void.
> To represent absence.
> To represent regret, remorse.
> The unreality of the real. Original chaos.
> The voices at the end, the sound of the world, noises, ruins, the

world goes up in smoke, in sounds and colors that die out, the last
foundations crumble . . .
At the end the voices: the sounds of the world, us, the audience.
Things can be said of this play which are contradictory, and yet
equally true.[20]

The point that seems to have interested the author in this play particularly seems to have been the enigma of being. The old people see and
hear the imaginary guests. These evidently answer them. The reality of
the assemblage is attested also by the Orator. But for the audience the
guests are invisible and inaudible; and the chairs are, so far as one can
see, empty. The normal conclusion would be that the occupants of the
chairs are figments of a shared hallucination from which the audience is
excluded. This idea is specifically negated. When the visible characters
vanish, the invisible throng suddenly makes its presence felt, and is for
the first time clearly audible. This is mischievous, obviously; and it
makes a marvellously uncanny effect. In discussing the impression that
was thus created, Ionesco noted, apparently with wonder: "A friend
said, 'It's quite simple; you are saying that the world is the subjective
and arbitrary creation of our minds?' Of our minds, yes, not of my
mind. I think I am inventing a language; I see it is already known to
all."[21]

As a demonstration of the maxim, "Die Welt ist meine Vorstellung,"
nevertheless, *Les Chaises*, though a magnificent piece of showmanship, is
lacking in cogency. It has something of the spooky character of *Six Characters in Search of an Author*, and in somewhat similar fashion it works on
two levels of illusion. As between the characters who are visible to us
and those whom we do not see it is impossible to say which has the more
authentic reality, for in fact neither seems to have true existence. Indeed,
as the play is framed, the unseen characters appear to have more reality
than those we see, for the visible characters are too bizarre to believed,
while the unseen characters are readily imaginable. From a metaphysical
viewpoint *Les Chaises* will hardly reward close study; but as a piece of
showmanship it is a wonderfully skilful piece of work and, insofar as it
suggests the mystery of reality, a useful one.

In January 1952 Ionesco wrote his director Sylvain Dhomme, "Assuming that the theme of *Les Chaises* is the ontological void, or *absence*, it is, I
think, the representation of that absence that should constitute the last

definitive moment of the play." Accordingly, he indicated that after the Orator has bowed to the Emperor and made his exit, the audience should be left to contemplate for a moment, "in a ghostly light, the empty room, the vacant chairs, the streamers and confetti. Then suddenly the invisible crowd on the stage comes to life, and there is a crescendo of sound—murmurs, laughter, coughs, as if the chairs were really occupied. In this manner the void will come to life inexplicably (this is the effect, beyond reason, true in its inverisimilitude, that we are seeking and must achieve) mixing up the cards completely, and all logic."[22]

This piece of mystification seems gratuitous, for there can be no reason why the invisible characters who make a hubbub at the end of the play should have been inaudible before. But the author evidently set great store by the illogical effect of this bit of business. The implication is clear. In this world everything is possible. Contradictions co-exist. Confusion is the mental state appropriate to the human condition, and the author has no intention of giving a semblance of order to what is really chaos. In the fantasy that passes for reality, absence and presence are indistinguishable.

Among Symbolists the exploration of the void was a favorite preoccupation. Mallarmé, in particular, had been fascinated by the idea of emptiness. His sonnet, "Ses purs ongles," conjures up an incomparable image of absence in terms calculated to confuse the most perceptive reader:

> . . . au salon vide: nul ptyx,
> Aboli bibelot d'inanité sonore,
> (Car le Maître est allé puiser des pleurs au Styx
> Avec ce seul objet dont le Néant s'honore).

It was precisely this sense of sonorous non-being that Ionesco brought to the stage in *Les Chaises*. The result is a masterpiece of Symbolist art. It does not detract from the magnitude of the achievement to add that *Les Chaises* is, nevertheless, a conjurer's trick. For the Symbolist, the creation of the world, and all its consequence, was perhaps no more than that.

The actual technique of conjuring up on the stage the image of the non-existent was, of course, a stage illusion of long-standing, the specialty of the mime. In 1930 Jean Cocteau had managed something of the sort with his monodrama, *La Voix humaine*, and a number of talented *diseuses*—for example, Helen Draper—had developed it on the popular stage. But no one, so far, had exploited this technique for "metaphysical" purposes, nor had it ever before occurred to anyone to conjure up the void on the stage by visible means. In comparison with this feat, the question of communication that is raised in *Les Chaises* seems secondary, though it is upon this problem that the action centers. The sentiment, "Nothing is; and if anything is, it cannot be known; and if it can be known the knowledge cannot be communicated," has long been credited to the Sophist Gorgias. The Old Man and his Orator exemplify this saw quite cogently by way of caricature, and this is perhaps funny. The ironic portrait of the aged might-have-been and his faithful spouse sums up an age of pathetic radicalism, during which so many Utopian proposals were advanced and discarded and so many enthusiasts were discredited and consigned to oblivion. The inarticulate Orator speaks to us quite clearly of the turbulent bohème of the 1880's and of the grandiose projects of the turn of the century, most of which came to nothing. None of this is funny. On the contrary, the term "tragic farce" hardly does justice to what is, ultimately, neither tragic nor farcical, but a prime example of the Grotesque, a nightmare in which is expressed, with appropriate anguish, the distressing reality of the unreal.

Les Chaises is Ionesco's masterpiece and, without doubt, one of the great plays of the contemporary theatre. Ionesco wrote a good many pieces after it, but nothing that can be said to equal it as a work of art. *Victimes du devoir, Pseudo-drame* followed it. It was first produced at the Théâtre du Quartier Latin in February 1953 under the direction of Jacques Mauclair. It was performed again in 1954 and again in 1959; but it had not the success of the former plays.

In an essay entitled "My Critics and I," Ionesco complains that the critics have habitually misrepresented his plays. *La Cantatrice chauve*, which he thought was "the tragedy of language," merely excited laughter. *Les Chaises*, which he intended as a farce, was thought to be macabre. He decided, he continues, to avoid misunderstanding by writing neither a comedy nor a tragedy, but a lyrical text, something "lived through," and deeply personal: "I projected on the stage my doubts, my deepest anguish, and turned them into dialogue; embodied my antipathies; wrote with the greatest possible sincerity, tore out my entrails: I entitled this *Victimes du devoir*. The critics considered I was pulling their legs. I was a cute little wag." [23]

Ionesco's critics might well be excused if indeed they considered this play a spoof, for in it Ionesco quite ostentatiously thumbs his nose at various forms of drama—the detective story, the psychoanalytic thriller, and the Gestapo play—as well as the works of Brecht and Beckett; and perhaps there are other topical references in it which patient scholarship will in time discover. The play is far from funny: it is entirely possible that Ionesco was serious in speaking of it as something deeply personal.

Victimes du devoir was adapted for the stage from a short story by Ionesco in which Choubert, the first of the victims of duty, relates rapidly and in the first person what amounts to a detective story. In this story a young detective is on the track of someone called Mallot or Mallod, someone whose name is also perhaps Montbéliard. Apparently Choubert once knew this man and, in order to dig up his memories the detective rummages extensively in Choubert's mind. His methods, which include hypnosis, arouse the ire of the poet Nicolas D'Eu, and in the end Nicolas stabs the detective to death.

The quest of Mallot, the nature of whose transgression is not revealed, recalls Moran's search for Molloy in the first of Beckett's Molloy trilogy. This had been published in French two years before, in 1951. In Beckett's story, Molloy is not sure of his name. Moran, who is ordered by an enigmatic organization to find him, knows five Molloys. In *Malone meurt* (1951) Molloy seems to have turned into Malone, and in *L'Innommable* (1953) he appears to have lost his name altogether and cannot be identified. In analogous fashion Choubert's quest for Mallot turns out to be an exploration of himself, a psychic journey that leads nowhere.

The formal structure of the play is, for Ionesco, unusually concise. Choubert and his wife Madeleine are discussing current events in their apartment after dinner when the play opens. They are concerned, in particular, with the advantages of a recent government declaration advising city dwellers to cultivate "detachment," the only remedy for the troubles of life in these times. This naturally leads to a discussion of the theatre. Choubert believes that from the time of the ancients all drama is essentially a detective story, and every plot an investigation which culminates in the solution of a mystery. At this point there is a knock on the door. A very young and very timid detective comes to inquire as to the whereabouts of a former tenant called Mallot, or perhaps Mallod. The detective is invited in. His character changes abruptly. There follows a Gestapo-like interrogation in the course of which Choubert is prodded into a descent into the depths of his mind in order to recover some reminiscence of Mallot. Meanwhile, Madeleine assumes various guises.

She becomes a seductive mistress, an aged wife, an adultress, a spectator in the theatre in which Choubert is a performer.

Choubert also goes through successive transformations. He becomes a child. The detective becomes the father with whom Choubert was never able to communicate. After sinking over his head in the mud of the unconscious, Choubert is forced to climb to dizzy heights, into the sky. He is about to fly away in earnest, when he tumbles down into a waste basket. A strange lady in black appears, and sits on the stage silently, eating peanuts. She may well be Ida Mortemart, on temporary leave from Vitrac's *Victor*. Then the poet Nicolas D'Eu appears, a truculent man with very positive ideas on all subjects. The detective produces a great crust of bread. He forces Choubert to chew and swallow so as to plug up the holes in his memory. The sight of his friend in torment infuriates Nicolas. He threatens the detective with his knife. The Inspector begs for mercy, arguing that he is merely a servant of the state, an innocent victim of duty. Nicolas D'Eu is not put off. He stabs him three times. When the detective is dead, however, the others consider it their paramount duty to find Mallot, and Nicolas takes over the detective's job. Madeleine intervenes. It is now Nicolas's turn to chew and to swallow. Finally the Lady in Black takes command and, as the curtain falls, they are all ordering one another to chew and to swallow. They have all, it seems, become victims of duty.

Victimes du devoir is a tangled skein, obviously; a revery into which was woven whatever seemed to be of interest to the author at this time—his passivity, his aggressions, his relation to his father and his wife, his childish terrors, his visions of bliss, his hatred of tyranny, his idea of theatre. The last occupies a good deal of text, and constitutes a sort of manifesto which, in some sense justifies the technique, if not the content of the play.

According to Nicolas D'Eu—Nicolas II—the current drama does not correspond to the cultural style of the time. It should take account of the new logic and the new psychology, which is a psychology of conflict. In the new drama Nicolas D'Eu proposes to show that contradictions are not contradictory. The principle of the identity and unity of character must give way to the concept that there is no such thing as personality, and that characters are what they become. In this connection he refers to Lupasco's *Logique et contradiction*. As for action and causality, the new drama will ignore these completely, at least in the obvious forms of the past, for anything that is clear is false. There will no longer be any serious drama, and no tragedy: "The tragic becomes comic, the comic is tragic, and life is gay."[24]

Ionesco takes the curse off this discourse by punctuating it with the Inspector's orders to Choubert to chew and to swallow, but one wonders whether it is Choubert or the audience that is being subjected to this ordeal. In *L'Impromptu de l'Alma* Ionesco's maid makes fun of him when he presumes to lecture *ex cathedra* along lines similar to these; in the present instance Nicolas D'Eu, being armed with a knife, is less vulnerable. The Inspector, nevertheless, will have none of this nonsense. In theatrical matters, as in all others, he is a staunch conservative: "As for myself, I remain, Aristotically logical, true to my duty, respectful of my superiors . . . I do not believe in the absurd; all is coherent, everything becomes comprehensible . . . (To Choubert) Swallow! (To Nicolas) . . . thanks to the efforts of human thought and science."

There is only one way, clearly, to dispose of this sort of person. But when the Inspector is dead, the others bitterly regret his death; for now, very likely, they will never find Mallot. But they too know their duty, and presumably they will continue chewing and swallowing to the end of time.

Amédée, ou Comment s'en débarrasser was first staged in 1954. It is subtitled, "Comedy in Three Acts," and was in fact Ionesco's first full-length play. Amédée was adapted from a short story called "Oriflamme," first published in the *Nouvelle Revue française* in February 1954. Apparently there was some difficulty in working out the idea in dramatic form. Ionesco insists, as did Pirandello, that as a writer he is completely at the service of his characters, and that in the course of composition he simply observes their behavior and describes it with complete detachment. He is a reporter: "They do what they like, they direct me, for it would be a mistake for me to direct them. I am convinced that I must give them complete liberty, and that I can do nothing but obey their wishes. . . . The author has only one duty, not to interfere, to live and let live, to liberate his obsessions, his fantasies, his characters, his universe, to let them be born, take form and live."[25]

But in renouncing all intellectual control over his fantasy, the author cannot avoid taking certain risks. In *Amédée*, he told Claude Bonnefoy in an interview, his imagination stalled at a certain point. He had trouble, he said, ". . . from the moment that the corpse pushes out on the stage. The two characters stand there, staring at it. I had no idea of how to get rid of this corpse. What was to be done with it? As the characters are there, no longer knowing what to do, they talk; they say whatever comes into their heads. For the second half of the second act you can see that I am more or less treading water. . . ."[26]

The second act includes a long and rather tedious flashback to the time when Amédée and his wife were young and already sexually incompatible. The rest of the act is devoted to the spectacle of the enormous corpse that is manhandled out of the window into the street below. By contrast the third act is short and bright and full of new characters, so that at the final curtain the play, along with its principal character, seems to have slipped happily and completely out of the author's grasp.

Amédée is the story of an unhappy marriage. The hero is a would-be playwright. His wife, Madeleine, is a telephone operator, by nature, or habit, a shrew. They are both in their middle forties, and evidently very poor. There is no love between them, only the dreary domesticity of those whom life has shut in together. Theirs, however, is a *ménage à trois*, for the nuptial bedroom is occupied by the corpse whom they have cherished for fifteen years. On this cadaver their lives are centered. They brush its clothes and shine its shoes. It is a guilty secret that they share and it fascinates them, but they are not sure of what it is or how it got into their bedroom. However it happened, the corpse has by this time grown a long white beard, and every day its body gets bigger until now it threatens to take up the whole apartment with its enormous bulk. Moreover, because of it, great poisonous mushrooms are growing on the floor and the carpets around it.

When its huge feet at last push into the dining room where Amédée works, he is forced to forego his habitual lethargy in order to rid himself of this intruder who is ruining his life. He waits until midnight, then, with great difficulty, Amédée drags the corpse through the window up the street to the little square at its end. There is a bar on the square frequented by American soldiers. When Amédée finds it impossible to drag the corpse further, a drunken M.P. suggests that he wind it around himself like a long macaroni. When this is done, the corpse, to everyone's delight, turns into a balloon and kites Amédée up into the sky beyond the reach of the police and of everyone else. Madeleine runs up anxiously—he has forgotten his raincoat. But he flies, amid bursts of fireworks, up into the stars while the assembled onlookers troop merrily

back into the bar. "It is a pity," says Madeleine. "After all, he had genius, you know." The barkeeper agrees: "A lost talent. So much the
worse for literature!" But the local whore adds, consolingly: "No one is
irreplaceable."

Amédée is obviously a conceit, a dramatic metaphor, but what precisely
it symbolizes is left in some doubt. In some ways it is reminiscent of
Kafka's *The Metamorphosis,* and perhaps it has some relation also to
Vauthier's *Le Capitaine Bada.* But, unlike either of these works, Amédée
has a joyous ending. So long as the corpse resides in Amédée's household
it is an incubus that ruins everything. Once it is dragged out into the
open, it becomes the means of Amédée's escape. From a psychoanalytic
standpoint the inference seems clear. Ionesco, however, said in explanation: "All I can tell is that this play is a simple, childish work, and almost
primitive in its simplicity. You will find in it no trace of symbolism. In
this play there is related a current event which might have been drawn
from any newspaper, a commonplace story which might have happened
to any one of us, and which must have happened to many of us. It is a
slice of life, a realistic play."[27]

Ionesco's explanations are normally more witty than informative, but
there is some basis of seriousness in his description of *Amédée* as a slice of
life. The realism here is obviously not the realism of the Théâtre-libre.
"Naturally, it will be said," Ionesco notes, "that not everyone sees reality
in the same way I do. There will certainly be those who will think that
my vision of reality is in fact unreal or surrealist. I must say that, personally, I reject the sort of realism that is only a sub-realism that has
only two dimensions out of three, four or n-dimensions. Such realism
alienates man from his depth, which is the third indispensable dimension
in terms of which he begins to be true. . . ."

From this and similar expressions of his, it seems clear that Ionesco
thinks of realism as the representation of the forms of the inner life,
rather than the social life, of the individual. If we assume that these
forms come into consciousness as symbols of still another reality, it is
reasonable to conclude that by realism Ionesco means what Symbolists
call symbolism. But we cannot exclude the possibility that Ionesco
seriously regards the creatures of the imagination as realities in and of
themselves, realities that represent nothing aside from themselves, and
exist on an equal footing with all other existent things. In such case, a
growing corpse need not be thought to symbolize a traumatic experience,
a feeling of guilt, a ruinous misunderstanding, a lost love, or a progres-

sive psychic disturbance of the sort that sometimes comes between husband and wife, but simply as a type of corpse that invades bedrooms,
propagates mushrooms, and can also, in a pinch, serve the purpose of a
balloon.

In fact, eight years after writing *Amédée*, Ionesco told Claude Bonnefoy that he saw the corpse as "transgression, original sin." "The growing corpse," he said, "is time." He added, on this occasion, that the
couple in the play was the world itself, man and woman, Adam and Eve.
"The couple here are not simply a man and a woman; they might also be
the whole of mankind, divided and trying to come together, to become
one."[28] Such an interpretation, which recalls the situation in *Sodome et
Gomorrhe*, makes *Amédée* into something like an allegory. It is, quite
likely, an afterthought, and not particularly felicitous. "Oriflamme,"
suggests that the growing corpse is the cadaver of a love that died on the
wedding night because, as Madeleine complains, Amédée killed it by a
brutal assertion of his marital rights. The play is vague on this subject,
but the location of the corpse in the nuptial bedroom, the continual contemplation its presence entails, and so on, support the idea that the dead
body symbolizes a dead love whose ghostly presence is a constant re-
minder of marital infelicity. In another dimension it is apparent that the
dead thing that must be got rid of, along with its sexy odor of
mushrooms, has phallic connotations which it would be naive to over-
look; and it is hardly necessary to dwell on the nature of the fireworks
that attend Amédée's final liberation and his ascent into the heavens. If
Amédée demonstrates, as the title suggests, "how to get rid of it," the way
indicated would seem to pass by the brothel on the place Torco at the
end of the street. Above that, it is intimated, there is a way open—
provided one winds the thing around oneself—a way open to *l'azur*, the
infinite.

Jacques, ou La Soumission was written in 1949, directly after *La Cantatrice
chauve*. Its sequel, *L'Avenir est dans les oeufs*, was written in 1951. Both are
in one act, and neither was staged for some years; *Jacques* not until 1955,
and *L'Avenir* not until 1957. In comparison with *Amédée* these plays seem
remarkably transparent. The technique is extravagant; the effect, somewhere between Dada and Surrealism; the conceits and the *lazzi* recall the
joyous method of Cocteau in *Les Mariés de la Tour Eiffel*. But the mood is
by no means joyous.

Jacques is subtitled, "Comédie naturaliste," a description that would have astonished Zola. It is an unusual sort of prodigal-son play, which depicts in very broad caricature a socio-biological process, the reproduction of the human race. More particularly, it represents in quasi-scientific fashion the capture of a recalcitrant unit by the parent cell, its absorption and assimilation and, in the sequel, its utilization in the process of replication.

Jacques is a very funny play, but the laughter it invites is unwholesome, and the action is calculated to evoke disgust rather than pleasure. In effect it belongs to the Theatre of Cruelty. In an article dated October 1955, written at the time of its first production, Ionesco said: "Like *La Cantatrice chauve*, *Jacques* is a kind of parody or caricature of boulevard drama, a boulevard play which decomposes itself and goes mad. . . . *Jacques* is, first of all, a domestic drama. It might be called a moral play."[29] *Jacques* is, indeed, domestic drama. It marks, in its way, an important transition in the life of a young man, the rites of passage from rebellious youth to manhood and full admission to the tribe.

The scene is laid in the squalid living-room of a middle-class family. Young Jacques sits in a broken armchair, his hat on his head, surrounded by his relatives—his parents, his sister Jacqueline, and his senile grandparents—all of whom reproach him bitterly. Their language is strange, but it is clear that he is being subjected to enormous family pressure to do what is expected of him, and to this end all the clichés of domestic melodrama are trotted out. Jacques resists valiantly; but when his sister tells him that he is subject to time—*chronométrable*—he surrenders. Amid general rejoicing he admits—what is evidently not true—that he adores potatoes *au lard*.

The Roberts, in the adjoining room, have been waiting only for this admission. They troop in at once with their daughter Roberte, who is already in her wedding dress. She is their only daughter, and they show her off proudly and in detail. She has estimable thighs, "the better to eat you, my dear," and also "green pimples on her beige skin; red breasts on a mauve ground; an illuminated navel; a tongue with tomato sauce; breaded shoulders, and steaks enough to warrant the highest consideration."[30] She is obviously a toothsome morsel and, when her white veil is lifted, it is revealed, moreover, that she has two noses. Jacques's family is in raptures. But Jacques is unwilling to marry her. He must have, he insists, a bride with at least three noses. The set-back is serious; but it has been anticipated. Robert, Sr., has another only daughter who is more amply provided in the matter of noses. Roberte I is now withdrawn, and Roberte II is introduced. She is similarly garbed and equally marriageable. But while she has a full complement of noses, Jacques is still dissatisfied. He finds her insufficiently ugly. Her face, he says, will not even turn milk. There follows an uproar of recrimination. Jacques is accused of having lied about adoring *les pommes de terre au lard,* and now he admits he cannot abide them. He cannot help it, he says. He is what he is. They all retire in horror, leaving Roberte II to carry on the battle. "You," says the father. "Mount guard and do your duty."

She does her duty very well. Bit by bit she draws the young man out. Life, he tells her, is a trap from which he must escape at any cost:

> When I was born I was almost fourteen. That is why I was able to see what it is all about more easily than most of the others. . . . I said flatly, I will not stand for this. . . . They assured me that everything would be all right. . . .
>
> . . . They deceived me. But how to escape? They have blocked up the doors, the windows, with nothing; removed the stairs. There is no way out through the attic, no way out up there any more. . . . All the same, they said, they had left trap doors everywhere . . . if only I could find them. I must absolutely get away. If not through the attic, then by way of the cellar . . . yes . . . the cellar. . . .

Roberte II assures him she knows all about the cellar and the traps. The cellar, she says, is her special domain. She proceeds to inflame Jacques with the tale of a burning horse, and then offers to cool his thirst with her own boundless wetness:

> My crevices are full of water. . . . In my belly there are ponds, marshes. I have a house of clay. It is always cool. It has mosses, mouses, roaches, frogs. We make love under drenched sheets—we swell with pleasure. I wind my arms around you like serpents, my soft thighs. You plunge in and dissolve—in my hair which streams with rain. My mouth flows, my legs are flowing, my bare shoulders, my hair, all of it, flows, oozes, pours, all of it flows, the sky, the stars, gushes, bubbles, gurgles. . . .[31]

Jacques finds this description irresistible. He is persuaded at last to take off his hat. His hair is green. In the cellar of her chateau, Roberte II tells him, everything is called *chat*—pussy—no other words are needed; it is so easy to talk there. Jacques is entranced by this linguistic simplification. The family marches in at this point to find the amorous couple wallowing together on the floor, locked in an obscene embrace, murmuring, "Pussy, pussy, pussy." The family does a tribal dance around them.

The stage directions are explicit: "All this must arouse a disagreeable feeling in the audience, a feeling of discomfort and shame. As the curtain comes down, only Roberte is visible, crouched over, with the nine fingers of her hand moving sinuously, like snakes."

The seduction of Jacques is only the first step in the social process. He has now incurred an obligation to society. The duty to produce, that is to say, to reproduce, is the theme of *L'Avenir est dans les oeufs*—"The Future is in Eggs." In this play, the curtain comes up three years later on the very scene on which the curtain fell in *Jacques, ou La Soumission*. Jacques and Roberte are still entwined on the floor, squirming and purring. But the assembled relatives no longer approve. There has been no production. The sister Jacqueline is commissioned to stop the love-making and to turn their thoughts to more practical things. When the two lovers stop making love, they discover that they are hungry. The grandmother brings them the traditional potatoes and bacon. When they are sufficiently stuffed, Jacques is solemnly informed that his grandfather is dead and that it is necessary to weep. In fact the dead grandfather is standing in the frame of his portrait, making faces. Jacques dutifully weeps. The families exchange heartfelt "cordolences." It is then explained to Jacques that it rests with him to furnish society with replacements for those who have passed away. He demurs. It is in vain. Roberte is led away by her mother to receive instruction. In a little while she is heard clucking vigorously like a laying hen. A basket of eggs is brought in, admired by everyone, and piled on the hatching-machine on which Jacques is invited to mount. The cry goes up in choric fashion: "Production! Production!" Jacques, puffing like a steam engine, begins to produce. Roberte clucks away assidously in the adjoining room, producing eggs by the basketful which are piled and poured over the laboring body of Jacques. The curtain comes down on the rhythmic workings of the production machine which is to ensure the continuity of mankind and its attendant wonders.

L'Impromptu de l'Alma is a very different sort of play. It is a spoof in which Ionesco put himself on the stage along with a group of critics in order to give the public at firsthand his views on the theatre, and the criticism of the theatre. It is, in brief, a kind of staged polemic in the tradition of Molière's *L'Impromptu de Versailles* and Giraudoux's *L'Im-*

promptu de Paris. It was first acted in February 1956 at the Studio des Champs Elysées under the direction of Maurice Jacquemont, who also acted the part of Ionesco in it.

This play owes nothing but its title to its predecessors in this genre. It is set in Ionesco's study. When the curtain rises it discovers Ionesco snoring at his writing table amid piles of manuscripts and books. He is awakened by the appearance of Bartholoméus I, a character evidently intended to represent the critic Roland Barthes. This pundit is dressed in an academic gown, and is shortly followed by two of his colleagues, similarly garbed. The dialogue, composed largely of extracts from the writings of Barthes, Bernard Dort, and Jacques Gauthier, is an insufferable display of pedantic nonsense. The play Ionesco is supposed to be writing is not yet written, but Bartholoméus I insists on having the beginning read to him, since he wants it for a new scientific theatre which is being organized, a theatre with seats for twenty-five, and room for four standees. The play in question is entitled *Le Caméléon du berger* because, we are told, Ionesco once noticed a shepherd kissing a chameleon, and was inspired to write a tragic farce on the subject. This play is to provide an opportunity for Ionesco to appear on the stage and lecture the audience on his idea of the theatre. In fact, when he begins reading the text to Bartholoméus I, it turns out to be the very text of the scene we are witnessing. The reading is interrupted by the entrance of Bartholoméus II; later by Bartholoméus III. They each lecture Ionesco on the theory of the drama, then begin squabbling among themselves until the dialogue unravels into gibberish. At this point the cleaning woman knocks at the door. The critics will not admit her until they have set the stage properly for the public, and they keep her banging at the door for a considerable time while they decorate the set, in epic-theatre fashion, with placards. The first is inscribed "Education of an Author," the others identify the furniture, and there are placards that read "Time of Bernstein," and "Time of Brecht." Ionesco is then properly costumed as a poet and a savant. His trousers are taken down. Other trousers are added. He is asked to alienate himself, given a dunce cap, and made to bray like an ass. The others also put on dunce caps. Then the cleaning woman is admitted. She begins by sweeping up all the rubbish, including the critics, and takes the opportunity to slap Ionesco in the face twice, presumably to arouse him from his stupor. Thus stimulated, Ionesco proceeds to take stage and embarks on an interminable harangue. It culminates in a statement of his artistic credo, which mainly involves the idea that as a poet he embodies the soul of humanity: ". . . As I am not alone in the world, as each of us, in the inmost depths of his being, is at the same time all the others, my dreams, my desires, my sorrows, my obsessions do not belong to me alone, all this is part of our ancestral heritage. . . ."[32] It is this heritage which provides the basis of his drama, and gives it its universality, even though what he writes about is himself. While he is engaged in this lecture, the cleaning woman, Marie, proceeds to invest him with one of the academic gowns. He perceives that he has fallen into the trap he prepared for the others, apologizes, and promises it will not happen again.

L'Impromptu de l'Alma adds nothing to Ionesco's dramatic achievement. It is no more than a romp, not particularly successful, written at the expense of some contemporary critics whom he considered overly opinionated, and also at his own expense, for, as a critic, he does not fail to ridicule himself along with the others. His own speech is, of course, meant to be taken seriously; but it simply restates what he had already written in various published lectures and articles. His point here is simply that, since all men are essentially one, if a poet describes his inner life, he will inevitably describe the life of all mankind. It is an idea, traceable to Montaigne, which perhaps, in Ionesco's terms, owes as much to the Jungian *anima mundi* as to Artaud's manifestoes. Unhappily it does not serve sufficiently to reclaim the dreariness of the play, which, for all its clowning, might better have been consigned by the author himself to oblivion.

With *Tueur sans gages* (1959), however, Ionesco took a firm step in the development of dramatic symbolism, and here he parted company, for the time, with the tragic farce. This play is in no sense a farce. The action is based on a short story entitled "La Photo du colonel" which Ionesco published in the *N.R.F.* in 1955.[33] The story is a Surrealist murder mystery, a *roman policier* with a nightmarish coloring. The play is much more than that. It is in three acts, extremely diffuse in structure, a pattern of dream-sequences loosely organized about a central theme which barely serves to bind them together in a unified structure.

Tueur sans gages is not a very practical theatre piece. Unlike Ionesco's earlier plays which were designed for little theatres of limited means, *The Unhired Killer* has a large cast and complicated sound and scenic effects. The hero, Bérenger, is a man of good will and modest attainments, a useful character whom Ionesco employed in three subsequent plays, in

Rhinocéros, Le Piéton de l'air, and in *Le Roi se meurt.* The technique in the first act, at least, is expressionistic or, better still, allusive. The curtain rises on a bare stage. The illusion is sustained mainly by means of the lighting and offstage sound-effects, the sound of wind, the rumble of a street car, and so on. After a moment, Bérenger comes in, together with the Architect who is showing him around the City of Light which he has built on the outskirts of the squalid metropolis where Bérenger lives. In the City of Light, he explains, everything is scientifically controlled— temperature, humidity, sunshine, trees. It is a man-made paradise with apartments to let. Only one thing is beyond control: Death. There is a Killer at large in this Eden, a mysterious figure who bemuses his victims by showing them the photograph of the colonel, and then pushes them into the lake. In consequence the beautiful suburb the Architect has built is being depopulated: fear is driving the residents away. The Architect is also the Chief of Police; but there is nothing he can do, evidently, about the Killer who has invaded his city.

Bérenger is enchanted by everything he sees, and particularly by the Architect's pretty secretary, Dany, to whom he at once proposes marriage. She, however, is quitting her job because of the Killer, and she hardly pays attention to Bérenger, who, for his part, cannot get her out of his mind. But before he leaves the City, word comes that she too has been killed.

The second act is set in Bérenger's ground-floor apartment in the old city. When Bérenger comes in he finds his friend Édouard sitting in the dark, waiting for him. Édouard is ill. Everything he says and does leads one to suspect that he is himself the mysterious Killer, but although his briefcase is stuffed with photos of the colonel, and contains also a list of the dead and a diary in which the names of future victims are noted, Bérenger has no idea that his friend may be the assassin. Nevertheless he hauls him off to testify before the Chief of Police in the City of Light. Édouard quite pointedly manages to leave the briefcase behind.

The third act takes place in a street blocked by a wall beyond which the street continues on a higher level. La mére Pipe stands on top of the wall, her back to the audience, haranguing a crowd. She is soliciting votes for herself and the troop of geese who are under her leadership. Bérenger comes in on his way to the police station, dragging Édouard by the sleeve. When he discovers that the briefcase is missing, he thinks it has been stolen, and begins searching for it among the passersby. The set is strongly reminiscent of a guignol, and this effect is enhanced when the upper half of a gigantic policeman appears on the wall. This officer is armed with a white club with which he pounds the heads of those below him. Suddenly there is a traffic jam caused by two army trucks. Another huge policeman appears, and begins hustling everyone about brutally. Meanwhile Édouard is sent back for the briefcase. He does not appear again. When Bérenger at length gets through the traffic, he is seen walking down the long deserted avenue which leads to the prefecture in the City of Light. And now the Killer appears. It is not Édouard. It is a wretched little man in ragged clothes, with broken shoes on his feet, and a single steely eye. Bérenger launches into a passionate exhortation. This takes up ten full pages of the printed text, and can hardly be spoken on the stage in less than a quarter-hour. It sounds all the stops from indignation to commiseration. The Killer says nothing. From time to time he chuckles. At last Bérenger grows tired of talking. He concludes:

> It is possible that the survival of the human species is of no more importance than its extinction . . . the whole universe is perhaps useless, and if you wish to blow it up, or at least chop it up, creature by creature, bit by bit, you are perhaps right. Perhaps you ought not to do it. I don't know anymore. I don't know anymore. . . .
> You kill without reason; in that case, I beg you, I beg you, without reason, yes, stop. There is no reason in this, it's true, but precisely because there is no reason to kill or not to kill, stop. If it's for nothing that you kill, then, for that same reason, spare. . . .[34]

The Killer chuckles and pulls out a knife. Bérenger grows angry. He produces a pair of pistols, kneels, and takes aim. But his long monologue has evidently exhausted him. He is not able to fire. In the end he bows his head, murmuring, "There is nothing to be done. Nothing to be done." The Killer steps over silently, knife in hand.

Tueur sans gages—the title was doubtless an echo of Anouilh's *Le Voyageur sans bagages* —makes a very strange effect. It is too long, and as incoherent as a dream, but it is not of the stuff that dreams are made on. In it the ills of humanity are demonstrated seriatim in a sequence that leads quite obliquely to the final monologue. As a social document, it must be admitted, it covers the ground. It touches questions of social injustice, human stupidity, bad housing, police brutality, political demagogues, and the predicament of an honest man in a world where everything good is destroyed as a matter of course. The message is clear: it is out of the misery of the world that the Killer arises. He is neither a terrorist nor a sadist. He wants nothing. Consequently he cannot be placated. He desires only to destroy. His action has not even the moral justification of the *acte gratuit* of Gide's hero of *Les Caves du Vatican*. Death at his hands represents the suicide of the human race, a blood sacrifice motivated by its own self-loathing, the workings of a death wish that is as senseless and as terrifying as the will to live.

There is obviously no more justice in the slaying of Bérenger than in the drowning of the lovely Dany, or the illness of Édouard. La Mère Pipe and her goose-stepping followers arouse indignation: we understand only too well what these characters are about. Her refrain is familiar. It is the litany of Orwell's *1984:* "We shall no longer persecute, but we shall punish and we shall impose justice. We shall not subjugate other peoples, but we shall occupy their lands to liberate them. We shall not exploit men, we shall make them produce. Forced labor will be called voluntary work. War will be called peace, and everything will be changed, thanks to me and my geese. . . . The misery of the individual is the happiness of mankind." [35]

The slaying of Bérenger, however, is calculated to arouse not indignation but terror. The end of *Tueur sans gages* is in the high style of tragedy. It is only partially successful. As an individual, Bérenger is not sufficiently concrete to excite sympathy, nor sufficiently abstract to enact the tragic hero. He is little more than a character in a dream, moving amid dream-like images. But the play has too much of the actual in it to work as dreams work, and it has its special logic, which is not the logic of dreams, but the logic of the intellect transposed to a dream-like frame. Bérenger's end does not come about fortuitously. It is because he alone is tracking down the Killer that the Killer tracks him down. The others are indifferent or they are futile. But Bérenger invites nemesis. Thus, in this play, it is not the character, but what the character symbolizes, that evokes the tragic feeling. What dies with Bérenger, it is implied, is that part of humanity that chiefly deserves to live, and it is ironical that here, inevitably, the Killer finds his natural prey.

Le Rhinocéros was produced the following year, in 1960. It was based on a short story that Ionesco had published in *Les Lettres nouvelles* three years before. [36] It is by far the most accessible of his plays and for that reason, no doubt, it has proved to be the most successful with a popular audience.

Ionesco's reputation thus far had been confined to the small, select audiences that frequented the avant-garde playhouses. *Le Rhinocéros* was judged to have a wider appeal. It opened in Paris on 22 January 1960 at the Odéon before an audience of 1200, with Jean-Louis Barrault in the role of Bérenger, and it opened concurrently in Basle. It had already been performed in German at the Schauspielhaus in Düsseldorf. The notices in the Paris press were mixed. "Formerly," Ionesco wrote, "the critics accused me of being incomprehensible. Now they accuse me of being too clear."[37] *Le Rhinocéros* is, in fact, the only one of Ionesco's plays that makes an unequivocal statement. One might judge from the response that a certain opacity becomes Symbolist drama rather better than the transparency of allegory.

The first scene takes place on a square in a provincial town in France. It is a Sunday morning. Bérenger and his friend Jean meet on the terrace of a small café opposite a grocery. Bérenger looks seedy, is nursing a hangover, and is properly humble. Jean, on the contrary, is natty, vain, and superior, and he proceeds to lecture his friend on his unfortunate habits of life. In the midst of the conversation a rhinoceros comes thundering down the street and vanishes in a cloud of dust. There is some confusion among the onlookers, and a spirited discussion as to whether the animal was an Asian rhinoceros with a single horn or an African with two. The argument is interrupted when the animal—or another like it—charges through in the opposite direction. This time there is a casualty. A lady's pet cat is crushed. There follows much talk of logic and syllogisms, and of Asia and Asiatics, and all this ends in a senseless quarrel which sends Jean off in a huff.

The second act takes place the next morning in the offices of the publishing firm where Bérenger is employed as a proofreader. The rhinoceros incident appears to be uppermost in everyone's mind. Botard, a retired schoolteacher of radical sympathies, argues belligerently that the whole thing is a figment of the imagination. Dudard, a more moderate type, takes a more judicial position. It is his belief that since the incident was reported in the press, the animal must exist. It seems to carry no weight with anyone that Bérenger, and also the pretty secretary, Daisy, saw the rhinoceros with their own eyes; the issue is debated purely on a priori grounds. While the debate is raging, Madame Boeuf rushes in, pursued, she says, by a rhinoceros. The others try to calm her. There is a crash. The stairs have given way. Botard continues to insist that all this is an illusion; but after a moment, Madame Boeuf recognizes the rhinoceros as her husband and jumps down the stairs to join him. Meanwhile Daisy telephones the fire department. The firemen set up a ladder, and the office staff escapes through the window.

The scene shifts to Jean's apartment. It appears that Jean is suffering from some mysterious illness. There is a bump on his forehead, and his skin is turning green. Bérenger tries to comfort him, but Jean is soon infuriated, and it is with difficulty that Bérenger avoids being impaled on the horn that has grown on Jean's forehead. At last Jean is locked up safely in his bathroom. But by now there are rhinoceros everywhere. Berénger finds himself trapped. He has to break down a wall to escape.

In act three it is Bérenger who is suffering with a headache, and it is his colleague Dudard who comes to visit him. Bérenger is terrified by the prospect of catching the disease. Most of his colleagues have been infected; and before long Dudard also shows signs of infection. Meanwhile Daisy has brought Bérenger a basket of food. After Dudard leaves, Bérenger declares his love for Daisy, and she vows never to leave him. But in a little while the call of the wild proves too much for Daisy, and she too rushes off to join the joyous herd that is roaming the streets. In the end Bérenger is left alone, hopeless and defiant.

Like *An Enemy of the People*, *Le Rhinocéros* ends on a heroic note, but the implication is that there is not much hope for a human being in a world of beasts. For the rest, certain connotations are clear. Ionesco has confirmed the conjecture that in writing this play he had the Nazis specifically in mind:

> I must say that the purpose of my play was indeed to depict the process of the Nazification of a country as well as the confusion of one who, allergic by nature to the contagion, witnesses the mental metamorphosis of his fellows. Originally rhinoceritis was Nazism. . . .[38]

In *Présent passé passé présent*, Ionesco notes that in 1940 he had described in his Journal the metamorphosis of a friend who had come under Nazi influence:

> I was talking to him. He was still a man. Suddenly I saw his skin harden and thicken. His feet, his shoes, become hoofs; his hands turned into paws. A horn grows on his forehead, he becomes fierce, and charges forward in fury. He can no longer speak. He is turning into a rhinoceros. Suddenly I wish I could do the same. But somehow I cannot.[39]

In 1940 it was normal in France to associate this type of transformation with Nazism. Twenty years later, when the play was produced, the
problem could be stated in more general terms. For Ionesco it appears to
have embraced by this time every variety of totalitarian thinking, whatever in politics smacked of regimentation. In 1961 Ionesco wrote:

> I wonder if I have not put my finger on a burning wound of the con-
> temporary world, on a strange malady which breaks out in different
> forms but which is in principle the same. Ideologies, which become
> idolatries, automatic systems of thought, arise like a screen between the
> mind and reality, pervert the understanding, blind it. . . . They pre-
> vent what is called coexistence, for a rhinoceros cannot get on with any-
> one who is not of his kind. . . .[40]

Le Rhinocéros, indeed, goes well beyond this idea. Bérenger belongs to
no party. He is himself. What he is, of course, is by no means admirable. He drinks too much. He has slovenly habits, and gives no sign of
unusual intelligence. But he has character. The others change with the
times, following the current fashion, each for his own ends. Botard is a
Communist. Dudard is an opportunist, Jean a conformist. Papillon, the
chef de bureau, is a bureaucrat. Daisy is simply a nice girl. They share no
common ideology. What they have in common is the herd instinct. They
are frightening only because Ionesco has seen them in action and knows
they can be dangerous. But they might very well be sheep.

The play, therefore, has more to do with individualism than with
ideology. It is the gregarious tendency of human beings that makes them
glory in regimentation. The fear of being egregious far outweighs the inconvenience of belonging to a group, and the sacrifice of individuality is
seldom costly for those who are, in fact, not individuals, but merely
members of a social organism, symbiotic units.

As Bérenger is depicted, he is nobody in particular, a petit bourgeois,
without ambition and without any special talent. But in one respect he is
inflexible. He is not a slave of the social order. He is by nature singular,
an original, and though he has a great desire to be like other people, he is
incapable of conforming. He drinks because he has *Angst*. To be an individual in the collective is to feel fear:

BÉRENGER: It's not that I like alcohol so much. And yet if I don't drink I
       am miserable. It's as if I were afraid. I drink so as not to be afraid.
JEAN: Afraid of what?
BÉRENGER: I don't quite know. An anguish that is hard to define. I feel ill

at ease in this world, among people. So I take a drink. It calms me. It relaxes me. I forget.[41]

The Bérenger of *Le Rhinocéros* is another aspect of the Bérenger of *Tueur sans gages*. The followers of La mère Pipe are subject to rhinoceritis, along with the police and the others. But not Bérenger. It is his destiny, in that play, to represent sanity among the mad. In *Le Rhinocéros* he represents humanity among the animals. But he has no more hope of saving the world—or himself—than he had in the earlier play. He is defiant; but he is helpless, hopelessly outvoted by the mass of his fellow citizens. He says: "There is no other way but to convince them; but to convince them of what? And are mutations reversible? Hm? Are they reversible? It would be a labor of Hercules, beyond my strength. First of all, to convince them it is necessary to talk to them. In order to talk to them I should have to learn their language. Or would they learn mine? But what language is it that I speak? What is my language?"

The identification of the author with this humble character is touching, though it is in some degree deceptive. When Bérenger first appears in this play he is far from attractive. His clothes are ragged, he yawns a great deal, and he has a headache. It is in some such guise that the author presents himself in the Bérenger plays—the *persona* is far from heroic. It is an unhappy figure in an unfriendly world, terrified of life and afraid to die, and always troubled by the vision of a radiant city, a lovely garden, which is never within reach. In *La Soif et la faim* this Eden, it is suggested, is actually his home and his family. In *Tueur sans gages* the radiant city exists, but it is uninhabitable. In *Le Rhinocéros*, however, the radiant city does not exist. There is only Daisy, and Daisy can afford her lover only a fleeting glimpse of heaven. Her proper habitat is the jungle along with the rest of the beasts. Bérenger is properly envious of those who can live there in joy and comfort:

> Oh, how I wish I were like them. I have no horn, alas! How ugly it is, a flat forehead! I should have one or two to elevate my expression. If only it would happen, then I would not be ashamed anymore. I could go and join the others. . . . How I would like to have a tough skin, a magnificent dark green skin like theirs and be decently naked, without hair, like them. (*He listens to the trumpeting in the street.*) Their songs have charm, a bit rough, but real charm. If only I could be like them!

But Bérenger cannot be like them, and there is nothing for it but to fight for survival: ". . . Well, then, to hell with it! I will defend myself!

Where is my rifle? My rifle! (*He faces the rhinoceros beyond the wall.*) I will defend myself against all the world! I am the last man; I will be a man to the end. I shall never surrender!"[42]

Bérenger's plight, though pitiable, is not unique. He is a twentieth-century version of the romantic outcast of the nineteenth century. He has not, to be sure, the glamor of the Satanic figures of the preceding age. He lacks the poetic halo of a Byron or Shelley, and has not even the messianic posture of a Strindberg. He is, nevertheless, the heir of the romantic hero, and embodies the spirit of negation, which is also an affirmation of man's most precious attribute, his freedom.

The other portraits are less detailed and, since they are stereotypes, are more precise. They are theatrical commonplaces—the pedant, the pantaloon, the braggart, the soubrette. Jean is a shop-window mannequin, very readily mutable in accord with the current mode, and also an ingenious rationalist:

JEAN: Don't talk to me of morality. I've had enough of morality. We have
    to go beyond morality.
BÉRENGER: And what will you put in its place?
JEAN: Nature.
BÉRENGER: Nature?
JEAN: Nature has its laws. Morality is unnatural. . . . I want to breathe!
BÉRENGER: But think. You know very well that we have a philosophy
    that animals don't have, a system of irreplaceable values. Centuries of
    human civilization have gone into their construction!
JEAN: (*Still in the bathroom.*) When all this is destroyed, we shall feel better.
BÉRENGER: I don't take you seriously. You are joking. You are talking
    poetry.
JEAN: Brrrr . . .

The return to nature, to noble savagery, and the instinctual basis of human vitality was, in 1960, still in fashion. But Nazi paganism, and the distortion of the Nietzschean cult for political purposes, had done something to dampen the spirits of the twentieth-century followers of Rousseau. It might be assumed that Ubu was an apt symbol of the nature of man. But Ubu represented man in his lowest form; he was certainly far from the human ideal. The primitive nature of man was the foundation of the Theatre of Cruelty; but Artaud had justified his theatre as a means of purging the Dionysian frenzy that his theatre unleashed. It is therefore not altogether surprising that in *Le Rhinocéros* Ionesco represents Bérenger as opposed to noble savagery and the pagan romanticism which was part of the Nazi ideology, and which also influenced much contemporary art that was not in any sense fascist.

Ionesco's position in *Le Rhinocéros* involves some apparent inconsistency, for, while a good deal of space in the play is devoted to a sophomoric disparagement of formal logic and syllogistic deduction, Bérenger insists on mind and morals as the distinguishing characteristics of humanity. Ionesco evidently set great store by the irrational faculty and, like other Symbolists, went to some lengths to disparage the tyranny of logic. But, as Bérenger indicates, he was unwilling to dispense altogether with reason. Bérenger has no patience with the Logician of the first act; but he is unwilling and unable to return to the primitive state of the beasts. He is willing to defend with his life, if necessary, the traditional cultural values of mankind. Unhappily, humanity does nothing to confirm his faith in their value.

In spite of his anti-Nazi position, Ionesco appears to have avoided any sort of political commitment. If it were necessary to classify his views on the evidence of his plays, one might well call him, like Ibsen, an anarchist. He was certainly influenced by Dada and Surrealism; but he did not follow Dada in its merry course of destruction and, like Artaud, he distrusted the political involvements of the Surrealists. Bérenger has no special love for mankind; but he has no wish to destroy it, and while the carefree social life of the rhinoceros arouses his envy, it does not inspire him with confidence. He prefers man to the animals:

JEAN: Man! Don't use that word anymore.
BÉRENGER: I mean human beings, humanism.
JEAN: Humanism is dated. You are a ridiculous old sentimentalist. (*He goes back into the bathroom.*)
BÉRENGER: Well, all the same, the mind—
JEAN: (*From the bathroom*) Clichés! Stop handing me rubbish! [43]

The scene ends with Jean trying to put a horn through his friend's back.

Daisy, on the other hand, is not belligerent. It is only that she cannot resist the current mode. There are uncouth sounds in the street. She finds them delightful, and she finds infinite grace in the dance of the rhinoceros:

DAISY: They are gods!
BÉRENGER: You exaggerate, Daisy. Look at them closely.
DAISY: Don't be jealous, dear.

Bérenger finds it difficult not to be jealous. In a democracy the majority is normally in an enviable position, and Bérenger is without support in the community. He finds friendship of no avail with Jean, nor logic with Dudard, and the lovable Daisy has a very practical turn of mind. "There is no such thing as absolute reason," she says. "It is the world that is right; it is not you or I." And as for love, she feels that this morbid sentiment cannot be compared with the extraordinary energy that radiates from the magnificent wild things around them. At this, Bérenger is moved to prove his manly vigor by slapping her face, a gesture that does nothing to buy her back. Obviously Bérenger has his troubles, and what is really touching in the play is the depiction of his mental conflict. The animals arouse his envy. They also provoke other feelings. "The very sight of them burns me up," he tells Dudard. "It is a question of nerves. It doesn't make me angry; no, we must not get angry, that can lead far, anger. I try not to show temper, but it does something to me, all the same—there—(*He puts his hand on his heart*)—it makes my heart heavy."[44]

Ionesco's aversion to ideology provoked an attack from an unexpected quarter. In 1958 Kenneth Tynan reviewed for *The Observer* the recent revival of *The Chairs* in London. He concluded his review by taking the author to task for the triviality of his work, which, he wrote, avoided any involvement with actuality. Tynan, who had previously championed Ionesco's plays in England, now cited the work of Brecht, among others, as more indicative of the direction the theatre should take in the future than anything Ionesco had done. A considerable polemic was thus precipitated, into which Arnold Toynbee and Orson Welles were drawn. Ionesco replied in the same periodical with a defence of his viewpoint in which he mainly affirmed the aesthetic doctrine of the Symbolists of the previous generation. "A work of art," he concluded, "is the expression of an incommunicable reality which one tries to communicate, and which occasionally can be communicated. That is its paradox—and its truth."

A number of writers and some actors were drawn into the discussion which followed. It renewed in contemporary terms the debate between the Naturalists and the Idealists of the 1890's: there was, indeed, nothing new to be said. Nevertheless this exchange of views served to define the rift between the Realists—now become Social Realists—and the various sects of Idealists—now dubbed Formalists—and to give it a more strictly partisan character. Thus what had once been in the main an aesthetic issue was rapidly crystallized into a political affray in which communist and anti-communist sympathizers took part and—as is normal in such cases—the aesthetic aspect of the issue was submerged in practical considerations which had little to do with art. As he was now officially ranged on the opposite side from Brecht and Sartre, Ionesco henceforth took every opportunity to express his dissatisfaction with their work, as well as with all plays that actively advocated systems of social reform. For the rest, he admonished his critics: "I beg you, Mr. Tynan, do not try by means of art, or other means, to improve the lot of man. I beg you—we have had enough of civil war up to this time, and of blood, tears and iniquitous trials, and just executioners, and ignoble martyrs, and ruined hopes, and jails." This more or less brought the polemic to an end, but not the rancor that resulted. By 1960 Brecht had become Ionesco's *bête noire*. One of the caged clowns that are tortured in *La Soif et la faim* is appropriately named Brechtoll, and in *Le Rhinocéros* the opening scene is an obvious parody of a street-scene in the manner of the epic theatre.[45]

"The epic theatre," Brecht wrote, "proposes to establish its basic model at the street corner, that is, to return to the very simplest 'natural' theatre, as a social enterprise, the origins, means and ends of which are practical and earthy . . ." And in describing the means by which a common street accident may be rendered "epic," Brecht wrote:

> The following situation might occur. One of the spectators might say, "But if the victim stepped off the curb with the right foot, as you showed him doing . . ." The demonstrator might interrupt, saying, "I showed him stepping off with his left foot." In the course of the argument about which foot the victim actually stepped off with in his demonstration and, even further, how the victim himself acted, the demonstration can be so transformed that the A-effect occurs.[46]

The "street scene" in *Le Rhinocéros* is mischievous. The appearance of the rhinoceros in the street creates consternation, but in the course of the extensive—and quite idiotic—discussion as to whether it had one horn or two, whether it was Asian or African, together with the Logician's lengthy demonstration of the power of syllogistic thought, the alienation effect is very thoroughly achieved, so much so that it is by a heroic effort that the narrative thread is picked up again in the second act. There the pedantic Botard serves admirably to caricature the Brechtian communist, and Botard's prompt transformation into a rhinoceros occasions surprise only in the very innocent Bérenger. *Le Rhinocéros*, aside from its interest as drama, may thus be considered as a sequel to the Tynan-Toynbee-Welles controversy in which Ionesco had been involved the previous year. "M. Ionesco's theatre," Tynan had written," is pungent and exciting, but it remains a diversion. It is not on the main road: and we do him no good, nor the drama at large, to pretend that it is . . ."

Le Rhinocéros was intended to take its place on the main road. It was played everywhere, and aroused more interest than any of Ionesco's earlier plays. It was generally played as comedy; but Ionesco does not seem to have thought it was funny, and he publicly noted his displeasure at the tone of the New York production, in which Zero Mostel took a leading part. He played Jean. "Strictly speaking," Ionesco wrote, "my play is not even a satire: it is a fairly objective description of the process of fanatization, of the birth of a totalitarianism that grows, propagates itself, conquers, transforms a world and, as it is totalitarian, transforms it totally. . . . It cannot be anything other than painful and serious."[47]

But while *Le Rhinocéros* has, doubtless, its serious and even its terrifying side, the truth is, it is written comically, and invites comic treatment. It clowns its way through a tragic experience, and it would be preposterous to expect it to be played in any but a comic style. It is possible that in using humor in this fashion Ionesco was following Artaud's prescription for the Theatre of Cruelty; but *Le Rhinocéros* is not, on the whole, a painful experience. At the most it is grotesque, and while the author's commentary in this, as in other cases, is presumably sincere, it is evident that here again he is thumbing his nose, with all due respect, at his audience.

L'Impromptu de l'Alma ends with the declaration that for Ionesco the drama is the projection on the stage of the world within: "It is these hidden desires, these dreams, these secret conflicts that are at the source of all our actions and of historic reality." Three of Ionesco's later plays—*Le Piéton de l'air, La Soif et la faim,* and *Le Roi se meurt* provide clear insights into the author's inner world, clear especially in the sense that they are preeminently capable of awakening in the psyche of the spectator echoes which persuade him of the existence of that extra-social community to which Ionesco professedly addressed his drama.

Le Piéton de l'air, produced at the Odéon in 1963, is set in Gloucestershire, in England, where Bérenger is spending a holiday with his wife and daughter. Bérenger, who resembles Ionesco like a brother, has stopped writing, for reasons which he explains to a journalist who comes to interview him. The scene is not entirely peaceful. There is a holiday atmosphere. English and French vacationers, among them a little girl who is *la cantatrice chauve*, stroll about aimlessly, waiting for the pubs to open. Meanwhile bombs fall inexplicably from the sky, and the horizon glows ominously red. Offstage there are explosions, fireworks, martial music, and festival sounds. Bérenger, after various vicissitudes, has discovered that he is able to fly, and, leaving his wife and daughter behind, he takes off into the blue. He returns from his flight in considerable dejection, with news of nameless terrors and universal destruction in the vaults of heaven. No one pays attention; only his wife and daughter are uneasy. They beg him to fly off with them to a safe haven beyond the hells he has traversed in the sky. But he has found no safe haven anywhere. The entire universe is in flames, and beyond the fire and the horror of the skies, there is only the void. Still, all this horror is as yet some distance off. For the moment, at least, they are safe, and with fear in his heart, Bérenger comforts them: "There is nothing yet, my darlings. There is nothing yet but the party. You see it's a sort of English Fourteenth of July. . . ." They walk off toward the red lights of the town. "Right now there is nothing; nothing at all right now."[48]

This play is presented as a long dream sequence, but it is a dream only in the sense that *To Damascus* or *The Dream Play* are dreams. Its allegory is transparent. The world is in a festival mood. The signs of the coming holocaust are visible everywhere. No one pays attention. Bérenger is specially privileged. He can see beyond reality to the worlds beyond. The heavenly spheres are in flames. God's paradise is ablaze. The saints are burning. The universe is coming to an end. And beyond the horror of the blazing cosmos there is only the emptiness of the infinite spaces. Meanwhile the pubs have opened.

La Soif et la faim was produced at the Comédie-Française in 1966. It is in nature of an *eventyr*, like *Peer Gynt* or *Lycko-Pers reza*. In this play the little family of *Le Piéton de l'air* is separated, and the hero is no longer called Bérenger. He is called Jean, and he is restless. He leaves the squalor of his basement apartment where he is sheltered—and also imprisoned—by love, and sets off on a quest for the beautiful garden of his dreams. His wanderings are not profitable. In the end he turns up, avid with thirst and hunger, in a monastery which also resembles a prison or a barracks. He is received with courtesy, fed copiously, and entertained with an unendurable demonstration of the relation of food to faith. Then the bill is presented. He cannot pay. As a result he is condemned to work out his debt by serving soup to the hungry fraternity for an indefinite period of time, perhaps forever. As he embarks on his labors he sees, beyond the bars of his prison, a vision of his wife and his daughter, standing in the radiant garden he has been seeking all this time, forever waiting for him.

Le Roi se meurt is more explicit and less sentimental. The theme is death. The mood is elegiacal, mystical. Of all Ionesco's plays, this one comes closest to music. It is not a consistent music. It is a kind of tone-poem; and as drama, it comes closest to the Grotesque.

King Bérenger has reigned 277 years. His kingdom is dilapidated. His domain has shrunk to the size of a back yard. Great cracks have appeared in the walls of the palace. The court consists of a maid of honor, who is also the maid of all work; the royal physician, who is also the royal executioner and court astrologer; and an aged guard with a halberd. There are two queens. Marguerite is old and hard. Marie is young and tender. They try to make the king understand that it is necessary at last to die. But Bérenger refuses to admit the necessity. His life has only just begun, he says. He has no need to die. But he is visibly falling apart. "Plunge into the void," they tell him. "It will free you." He does not believe them. The void terrifies him. He has no idea what it is one does in order to die. The old queen, Marguerite, tries to instruct him:

MARGUERITE: He must stop looking about him. He must not cling to these
    images. He must sink into himself and shut himself off. (*To the King*)
    Speak no more. Keep quiet. Stop seeing. Stay within. It will do you
    good.
THE KING: I don't want that sort of good.[49]

They put him in a wheelchair and cover him with a rug. The maid of honor becomes a nurse. They overwhelm the poor man with a torrent of venerable stereotypes. The old palace guard delivers an encomium on his greatness. It appears that all mankind in its infinite ingenuity is embodied in this king—it is he who has invented everything and devised everything. None of this interests Bérenger. What seems important to him in these last moments of his life is the memory of a pet cat whom he loved. And now, with the help of Marguerite, he begins to slough off his identity. He rises to his feet like a somnambulist. Marie vanishes; then the guard, the maid, the doctor. Marguerite helps Bérenger to shed his burdens, his clothes, his perceptions, and when he is divested of all that life represents, she too vanishes. He sits a moment, quite motionless, on his throne. The walls of the palace dissolve, and at last the king disappears, and there is only a gray light on the stage. In this manner, with the help of his queen, Bérenger uncreates himself as, in Mallarmé's poem, Igitur dreams of uncreating himself in death:

> L'heure a sonné pour moi de partir, la pureté de la glace s'établira, sans ce personnage, vision de moi—mais il emportera la lumière!—la nuit! Sur les meubles vacants, le Rêve a agonisé en cette fiole de verre, pureté, qui renferme la substance du néant.[50]

Le Roi se meurt is the most poetic of Ionesco's plays, the most pathetic, and the most beautiful. It is hardly dramatic. It is a lyric that holds the stage, a poem that acts itself. Unquestionably, it is too long, for whatever virtues Ionesco may have as a dramatist, the terminal principle is not among them. But the feeling of length is not a matter of linear or temporal dimension; the longueurs of a text reside in its soul. The king's dying monologue on the subject of his cat is long. From the viewpoint of dramatic economy it comes at a most inappropriate time; moreover, it marks an abrupt change of style. Yet it does not seem long. It serves to characterize the king better than anything else that is said or done, so that Bérenger is quite unexpectedly rescued from abstraction, and becomes a human being whose death makes us sad. In all this talk of death and dying, one vivid touch of life serves to illuminate the shadows of the drama, so that suddenly it lives. If it happens, however, that the death of the cat moves us more deeply than the death of the king, the fault can hardly be ascribed to the playwright. The cat is someone we know. The king is no one in particular.

For Ionesco it is death that makes men kin: in death is the true community of mankind. In the certainty of death all else is trivial, and life becomes an absurdity. Ionesco wrote, in 1958,

> I have no other images of the world save those that express evanescence and harshness, vanity and anger, the void or hatred, hideous and useless. This is how existence continues to seem to me. Everything has gone to confirm the things I saw and understood in my childhood: vain and sordid rages, sudden cries stifled by silence, shadows swallowed up forever in the night. What else have I to say? . . . It matters little to me if this vision is, or is not, surrealist, naturalist, expressionist, deca-

dent, romantic or socialist. It is enough for me to think that it is as realistic as can be; it is in the unreal that reality is rooted. Is it not true that
we die?[51]

It is certainly true that we die and, if one concentrates on this certitude, the world takes on the aspect of a guignol. It is, indeed, from this
standpoint that Ionesco sees his world. It is a puppet show for children.
Shaw too was troubled by the shortness of life, and for him our periodic
efforts at improving the human lot are thwarted by the brief duration of
individual consciousness. But Shaw considered that while a man's life is
brief, life itself is endless, so that there is a possibility of extending consciousness indefinitely, and in this belief Shaw projected the perspectives
of *Back to Methuselah*. This type of faith, however, depends on one's
opinion of the validity of the human intellect. Shaw founded his church
on the power of the rational faculty. For Ionesco cogitation is a revery
distinguished from other fantasies mainly by its aridity. In *Le Rhinocéros*
the Logician holds the stage at inordinate length with syllogistic stupidities; and Bérenger's faith in an ideal of rational humanity is betrayed at
every turn, both in that play and in *Tueur sans gages*. Without God, the
universe—as Bérenger discovers in *Le Piéton de l'air*—is a stupid dream
full of horror and pain, beyond which there is only the eternal nothing.

Ionesco's theatre, accordingly, is an eerie mummery. On the stage
of his guignol the grotesque gestures of his puppets elicit laughter, and
also pity and terror, childish reactions appropriate to the occasion. But
they seldom carry conviction. None of Ionesco's characters has more
than the provisional reality of the theatre, except perhaps Bérenger's cat
in *Le Roi se meurt*. It is clear that the author had not at any time much
faith in his creation. The result is uncanny. It is the drama of a world
that is not there.

"No event," Ionesco wrote,

> no particular magic surprises me, no train of thought excites me (I have
> no interest in culture), nothing can seem to me more unusual than any-
> thing else, for all is levelled, drowned in the universal improbability
> and strangeness of life. What seems to me inadmissible is the fact of ex-
> istence, of the use of language. Those who do not feel that existence is
> an insanity may find within it that only this or that makes sense, is logi-
> cal, false or just. Since to me existence is unimaginable, within it every-
> thing seems conceivable. For me no personal frontier can separate the
> real from the unreal, the true from the false. I have no criteria, no pref-
> erences. I feel I am here, on the margin of being, outside the historical

process, not at all "with it," bemused, immobilized in this primordial stupefaction. For me the gates are closed, or perhaps they have entirely vanished, together with the walls, the distinctions.[52]

This was written about the time of the first production of *Les Chaises*. It was meant to clarify the mood in which that play was written, and the self-portrait these lines include has served to represent Ionesco ever since. Such a passage might have served Tertullian in the third century, or van Ruysbroeck in the fourteenth; but these mystics had God to give substance to the dream of existence. Ionesco is a mystic without God, an uncomfortable situation for one to be in.

Jarry and Artaud in their day had gone well beyond normal bounds in devising a *persona* that would suitably represent their anguish to the world. Ionesco lags some distance behind Dr. Faustroll, and is well behind Emperor Heliogabalus. He is in no sense a destroyer or a preserver, least of all a Messiah. In the hurly-burly of our time he remains staunchly neutral. His quest was private, and it was fruitless, but it was highly articulate. He was an idealist in search of the real: inevitably he was doomed to disappointment, and it is this disappointment that his works chiefly reflect. He desired to be thought of as a displaced person, homeless in the universe, a *piéton de l'air* bearing evil tidings. Eventually, like Mallarmé, he associated himself with the unknowable, with the spirit that hovers, perhaps, over the face of the void, the *śūnya* of the Mahayana Buddhist. It is at the extreme limit of the romantic flight that we come to the end of the world, a disquieting location, without topography and without future. Bérenger ends there. It is at this point that we encounter Godot.

BECKETT

In 1962 Ionesco wrote in *Notes et contre-notes*, of the art of the future:

> The new world that seems to be opening before us, a perspective either of death or, on the contrary, a total transformation of life and thought, seems bound to lead us into an era in which the very existence of this kind of activity will be called in question. We cannot predict what forms poetic creation and art will take. In any case, already at this very moment, literature is not measuring up to life: artistic expression is too feeble, imagination too impoverished to simulate the horror and the wonder of this life, or of death, too inadequate even to take stock of it. . . . Meanwhile I have done what I could. I have passed the time. But we need to know how to cut ourselves off from ourselves and from others, how to observe and how to laugh, in spite of everything, to laugh.

The desire to laugh in circumstances that approximate the tragic is obviously an alternative to the impulse to scream. The art that caricatures our current reality dignifies the comic as a gesture of despair: the artist thumbs his nose at life. But the gesture, while it is beguiling, is at best provisional. The appropriate psychic posture, when it is found, will have more dignity. It will imply a very high degree of sophistication, one imagines, something godlike, perhaps the realism of one who is content to put up with appearances on condition that it is clear he is not in the least taken in by them. One thinks in this regard of Shakespeare.

Shakespeare summed up an era. But, it must be granted, he had something in hand. The Renaissance world was a marvellous imaginative feat, and along with its mythology it provided a writer with a rich vocabulary and an unrivalled rhetorical apparatus. In the interval the spirit of negation has been busy with these figments, and with the language which bodied them forth. Judging by the work of Beckett, in the theatre there is nothing left to say.

Beckett represents a very advanced stage of nineteenth-century symbolism, perhaps its terminal aspect, the point at which the symbol symbolizes only itself, and poetry ceases to convey anything. Out of his inner darkness Mallarmé had been able to conjure up a vision of dark tragic figures poised on the brink of the abyss, symbolic of man suffering magnificent spiritual agonies. A century later such regal spectres no longer serve to represent the bedraggled race that has survived the latest holocaust, and is looking anxiously to the next. By the time of Beckett the culture heroes of the nineteenth century were making room for less demanding figures. In the theatre of the avant garde, Macbeth was overshadowed by Ubu, Hamlet had dwindled into Bérenger, and the image of God in our time was said to be Godot, or perhaps Godet or Godin.

Samuel Beckett was born in Dublin in 1906 of Protestant parents. He read modern languages at Trinity College, taught French in Dublin, and spent two years as *lecteur d'anglais* at the École normale supérieure in Paris from 1928 to 1930. Simone Weil was a student there at this time. Giraudoux was just making his debut in the theatre. It was the time of the Wall Street crash, and the subsequent economic depression.

Beckett entered the world of letters as a more or less humble member of Joyce's circle in Paris. His first published work was an essay on Joyce's *Work in Progress* entitled, "Dante . . . Bruno. Vico . . . Joyce." This was printed as the first essay in *Our Exagmination Round His Factification for Incamination of Work in Progress*, published in 1929, when Beckett was twenty-three. Twenty-four years later, when *En attendant Godot* was first presented at the Théâtre de Babylone in 1953, Beckett was still virtually unknown as a writer. In the interval, nevertheless, he had published a number of things—poetry, essays, translations, and fiction—the sort of work that might be expected of a gifted young writer of the avant garde who had not yet found the trick of self-promotion.

As an Irish expatriate in Paris, Beckett must have found the life of a man of letters both arduous and dispiriting. He was a handsome man, reserved, taciturn, and neurotic who, it is said, drank a good deal. As a writer he affected the irreverence of the avant garde, and its need to shock the paying guest. He was learned, aggressive, mannered, and difficult—a combination calculated to guarantee a writer's obscurity even in

Paris, and it is understandable that his early works created few ripples. In 1930 an enigmatic poem on the life of Descartes entitled *Whoroscope* won him a prize of ten pounds in a competition presided over by Nancy Cunard and Richard Aldington. It was printed in an edition of 300 copies. His essay on Proust appeared in 1931. A volume of short stories entitled *More Pricks than Kicks*, printed in 1934, was followed in 1935 by a book of poems, *Echo's Bones and Other Precipitates*. *Murphy*, written in 1931, came out in 1938. It is said to have sold thirty-five copies in thirteen years.

The outbreak of war in 1939 found him in Ireland. He returned to France, and although as an Irish citizen he was technically a neutral, he joined a Résistance group in Paris. In 1942, having narrowly escaped arrest by the Gestapo, he was forced to seek refuge in the South of France. He left Paris in the company of a fellow member of the Résistance, Suzanne Deschevaux-Dumesnil, who later became his wife. Together they joined the refugee colony in the village of Roussillon, near Gordes in the Vaucluse. Here he wrote *Watt*. This work waited nine years for publication, and was at last issued by a publisher of pornographic books who, we are told, had no idea what it was about.

Back in Paris after the Liberation, Beckett endeavored to supplement a small annuity by working as a translator, and a teacher of English. About this time, for reasons which he has never entirely clarified, he began writing in French. It was evidently no easy transition for him to make. His French was fluent; but it was not his native tongue, obviously, and at first he required assistance with his style.

"As a rule," wrote Simone Weil in *L'Attente de Dieu* (1950), "it is better for a man to name God in his native tongue than in one that is foreign to him. Except in special cases the soul is not able to abandon itself utterly when it has to make the slight effort of seeking words in a foreign language, even when this language is well known. . . ."[1]

It is impossible to say whether Beckett was hiding in French, or revealing himself in another guise. At any rate it became habitual for him to write first in French and then to translate his work into English, a practice which made his work accessible in two languages, while at the same time it emphasized in a peculiar way the ambiguity of the author. In 1946 he began a short novel in French called *Mercier et Camier*, his first attempt at a novel since *Murphy*. The following year he wrote *Molloy*, also in French. It is a curious tale of a cripple in search of his mother, and a detective named Moran who is crippled while looking for the cripple. The autobiographical thread which runs through this novel was spun further into its sequel, *Malone meurt*, a long monologue spoken by a dying man. When this work was finished, Beckett began work on a play. The play was *En attendant Godot*.

By the fall of 1949 *En attendant Godot* had been rejected by a half-dozen theatre managers, and as many publishers. Meanwhile Beckett had begun another novel, entitled *L'Innommable*, a monologue spoken, it would seem, by a man confined, in a truly pitiable state, in a jar. This nameless personage appears to be the only true begetter of Molloy and Moran, so that the three novels are bound together closely in a trilogy. In the fall of 1950 Jérôme Lindon, who had recently bought Les Éditions de Minuit, agreed to publish the trilogy, and also the play. He was, it is true, at this time on the verge of bankruptcy.

About this time *En attendant Godot*, together with an earlier play called *Éleuthéria*, had been brought to the attention of Roger Blin, one of Artaud's close associates. Blin, a talented actor, agreed to produce both plays.

In those years it was more difficult to produce an unusual play in Paris than it was to publish an unusual novel, but neither was an easy enterprise. Beckett at this time knew nothing of the theatre. *Éleuthéria* had to do—like Ionesco's *Jacques*, which was not yet written—with a young man's resistance to the demands of his middle-class family. It had seventeen characters and required three scene-changes. The hero was called Victor Krap. The other characters rejoiced in such names as Piouk, Skunk, and Meck, names—all but the last—which conveyed more to the English ear than to the French. Blin was apparently much taken with this play; but it was never performed and has not yet been published.

En attendant Godot, however, was written with an eye to economy. It has only five characters. The setting consists of a tree, and nothing more. Even so, the difficulties of production appear to have been immense. Blin had only recently directed *The Ghost Sonata* at the Gaité-Montparnasse. He had no money, no theatre, and no producer. But he had determination. Early in 1952 he managed to secure a small subsidy from the Ministry of Arts and Letters, and toward the end of November 1952 he put *Godot* in rehearsal. There was still no playhouse in which to show it.

On 5 January 1953 *En attendant Godot* opened at the Théâtre de Babylone on the boulevard Raspail. The theatre, formerly a shop, had a tiny stage and 230 folding chairs. Blin directed the play with himself in the part of Pozzo, a role he disliked. The rehearsals had been troubled, confused, and unduly protracted. Beckett had no great opinion of the play. The actors had no idea of what it was about. Nobody had much hope for the production. But on the opening night, to everyone's astonishment, the theatre was filled to capacity, chairs had to be borrowed to accommodate the overflow, and when the curtain came down there was both applause and discussion. The spectators were bewildered. The play was said to be a hoax, an outrage, an impertinence, and there were some also who pronounced it a work of genius. The result was that *Godot* ran comfortably throughout the season, was revived in the fall, and afterwards went on tour. Eventually it was seen everywhere.

Much encouraged by its success—the first success he had ever had—Beckett made an English version entitled *Waiting for Godot*. In 1955 it was played in London and in Dublin and, after an unfortunate production in Miami, it had a successful run in New York in 1956. By the time the surprise it occasioned had subsided, *Godot* had become a modern classic, and Beckett was a celebrated author. He was forty-nine. He had coped manfully with failure all his life. He had now to cope with success.

Like *La Cantatrice chauve* which had been produced in similar circumstances three years before, *En attendant Godot* was written in defiance of all the traditional rules of the drama. It has neither plot, nor complication, climax, nor dénouement. It is not arranged like a play, nor even like a normal narrative, a short story. It is in two parts. The second part more or less replicates the first. There is almost no action, and the dialogue is, on the whole, pointless. For the rest, the design is circular. It leaves off about where it began and, in a literal sense, gets nowhere. One might call it an exercise in futility. This is its point.

Thematically the play developed quite naturally from Beckett's French novels, particularly from *Mercier et Camier* which dealt at some length with the fortunes of two vagabonds in search of a bicycle and an umbrella. *Godot* has to do with two tramps who are waiting at the foot of a barren tree for someone who does not come. They are no ordinary tramps. Estragon and Vladimir are highly stylized hobos of dubious background, well educated, thoroughly battered, and apparently in the last stages of destitution. But they are by no means abject. They have preserved a certain dignity, which is only partly comic, and speak in terms inflated somewhat beyond the pressures of normal speech. Such tramps had been seen in American films—Buster Keaton, Laurel and Hardy, and so on—but Beckett's tramps are idealized beyond any semblance to reality; they are purely literary creations. Vladimir is, of course, a Slavic name, Estragon is the name of a herb: they call one another Didi and Gogo.

The scene description is concise. "A country road. A tree. Evening." It makes the effect of a *haiku*. As the play opens, Estragon is sitting on a mound vainly trying to pry off a tight boot. Vladimir comes in. Their meeting is casual. It is as if they were meeting, without prearrangement and without surprise, at a usual time, at a usual place.

ESTRAGON: (*giving up again.*) Nothing to be done.

VLADIMIR: (*advancing with short, stiff strides, legs wide apart.*) I'm beginning to come round to that opinion. All my life I've tried to put it from me, saying, Vladimir, be reasonable, you haven't tried everything. And I resumed the struggle (*He broods, musing on the struggle. Turning to Estragon.*) So there you are again.

ESTRAGON: Am I?[2]

There is talk of an appointment with someone called Godot. They are not sure of who that is, or whether this is the designated place, the right day or time, or what it is that they expect of him. Vladimir has apparently addressed some sort of request to him,

ESTRAGON: A kind of prayer.

VLADIMIR: Precisely.

ESTRAGON: A vague supplication.

VLADIMIR: Exactly.

ESTRAGON: And what did he reply?

VLADIMIR: That he'd see.[3]

The two men are characterized in detail. They do not resemble one another. Vladimir says he was a poet. He is now a large man with a weak bladder, who has trouble passing water and has pains in his pelvis when he laughs. Perhaps he has a hernia. Estragon's feet hurt. His shoes are too small. He gives signs of effeminacy. Both are high strung and deeply sensitive men, physically uncomfortable and often hungry. Apparently they have been inseparable for many years, constantly pulled apart and drawn together. They are no longer young, and have thought several times of suicide. Now the idea of hanging themselves from the tree excites them, not because it will put an end to their miseries but because hanging is said to produce an erection, at their time of life an unusual and delectable experience.

While Estragon is munching the carrot that Vladimir feeds him, Pozzo appears. He is resplendent in polished riding boots, bears a whip, and is driving Lucky ahead of him at the end of a rope. Lucky is a slave in livery, with white hair and a dejected expression. He bears an immense load of luggage, including two large bags of sand. Pozzo is very grand. He sits ceremonially on a camp chair borne by Lucky, refreshes himself out of a picnic basket under the envious eyes of the tramps, and magnaminously refers Estragon to Lucky for permission to pick up the refuse of his meal. He is, he intimates, a man of wealth, the owner of many slaves. Lucky, being useless, is to be sold at the market. He can be made to dance or to think, at command; but when Lucky begins thinking, the result is an outpouring of gibberish that can be stemmed only when his hat is knocked off his head. When these *lazzi* are over, Pozzo, after many adieus, is hauled off, and the two tramps are left once more alone. At this point, a boy appears. He is looking for Mr. Albert. Vladimir seems to be Mr. Albert. Mr. Godot, the boy says, will not come that evening. He will surely come tomorrow. The message occasions no surprise. Apparently the boy comes with the same message every day. When he is gone, there is some talk of crucifixion. Then the two friends sit down as before:

ESTRAGON: Well, shall we go now?
VLADIMIR: Yes, let's go. (*They do not move.*)

The curtain comes down on this speech. It comes up in the second act on the next day at the same time and place, but on an empty stage. In the interval the tree has put out a few leaves. Vladimir comes in, uncertain of the place. He identifies the tree by the shoes that Estragon has left there, then proceeds to sing a round at the top of his voice. Estragon drags himself in, The dialogue resumes. Estragon remembers nothing of what happened the day before. They talk, he says, in order not to think; but they do think, and there ensues a beautiful elegiacal passage which has no special reference and makes no special sense:

ESTRAGON: All the dead voices.
VLADIMIR: They make a noise like wings.
ESTRAGON: Like leaves.
VLADIMIR: Like sand.
ESTRAGON: Like leaves.[4]

Vladimir seems quite sure of himself. Estragon is disoriented. He lies down to sleep, and Vladimir sings him a lullaby in stentorian tones.

When Estragon awakes there is a moment of panic. They think Godot has come; then that they are surrounded by enemies. They begin to abuse one another systematically. Finally they embrace and break into a sort of dance. Abruptly, it stops:

ESTRAGON: (*stopping, brandishing his fists, at the top of his voice.*) God have pity on me!

VLADIMIR: (*vexed.*) And me?

ESTRAGON: On me! On me! Pity! On me! [5]

There is a sound. Again they think it is Godot. But it is Lucky, burdened as before; now he is dragging Pozzo at the end of his rope. Pozzo is blind. Lucky has been stricken dumb. The two fall down and are unable to get up. Pozzo calls for help. Vladimir continues speaking:

VLADIMIR: . . . and we are blessed in this, that we happen to know the answer. Yes, in this immense confusion one thing alone is clear. We are waiting for Godot to come.

ESTRAGON: Ah!

POZZO: Help!

VLADIMIR: Or for night to fall. (*pause.*) We have kept our appointment, and that's an end to that. We are not saints, but we have kept our appointment. How many people can boast as much?

ESTRAGON: Billions.

It takes them a long time to raise Pozzo to his feet. Pozzo has lost his sense of time, but not his eloquence:

POZZO: (*suddenly furious.*) Have you done tormenting me with your accursed time? It's abominable! When! When! One day, is that not enough for you, one day he went dumb, one day I went blind, one day we'll go deaf, one day we were born, one day we shall die, the same day, the same second, is that not enough for you? (*calmer.*) They give birth astride of a grave, the light gleams an instant then it's night once more! (*He jerks the rope.*) On! [6]

Lucky drags him off; but the two fall down again, this time offstage. Estragon is once more asleep. Vladimir begins to entertain doubts as to the reality of his experience:

VLADIMIR: Was I sleeping while the others suffered? Am I sleeping now? Tomorrow, when I wake, or think I do, what shall I say of today? That with Estragon, my friend, at this place, until the fall of night, I waited for Godot? That Pozzo passed, with his carrier, and that he spoke to us? Probably. But in all that what truth will there be?

Now, once again, the boy turns up with his message. He has met no one, seen no one, and knows nothing.

VLADIMIR: (*softly*) Has he a beard, Mr. Godot?
BOY: Yes sir.
VLADIMIR: Fair or . . . (*He hesitates*) . . . or black?
BOY: I think it's white, sir. (*silence*).
VLADIMIR: Christ have mercy on us! . . .[7]

The boy runs off. They speak of going away. But they are afraid Godot may punish them. They try to hang themselves from the tree with the rope that holds up Estragon's trousers. His trousers fall down. The rope breaks. Estragon pulls up his trousers. They will hang themselves, they say, tomorrow. Unless Godot comes. The curtain comes down as in the first act:

VLADIMIR: Well? Shall we go?
ESTRAGON: Yes, let's go. (*They do not move.*)

The second act of *Godot* may seem redundant, but it is indispensable. In the second act everything that is definite in the first begins to shimmer into uncertainty. Estragon is asleep during much of the action. Vladimir is not sure he is not dreaming. Pozzo seems to have lost track of time. The boy who comes does not seem to be the boy who came before. Somehow the second act dissipates the first as one day dissipates another. The poetry of the dialogue, often quite beautiful, is played against the cheap *lazzi*, the pratfalls, the foolish songs, the dropped trousers, and the rest of the clowning. The incongruity of the action goes beyond what ordinarily is called grotesque. It is as if the play destroyed itself as it developed.

The characters are as ambiguous as the situation. Vladimir and Estragon are in a sense tragic figures, but they could not be less heroic. Their talk borders now upon the sublime, now upon the absurd; actually it is neither, and they do not tell jokes. Vladimir plays the top banana of the burlesque shows, but he plays it with a difference. He does not hail from the burlesque stage, nor does Estragon; nor from the circus. Pozzo and Lucky look like circus figures, but they are not. Nor are there any such characters in the comic films. Beckett's tramps are not clowns. Occasionally they act like clowns, but these actions are deceptive; their foolishness is not the foolishness of clowns; nor is their sadness the sadness of clowns, which Charlie Chaplin sentimentalized in the silent films.

These characters are eloquent. Their rhetoric is vaguely old-fashioned in English, archaic; less so in French. But in both languages—and they are in a sense bilingual—they illustrate, more effectively than the narrator of *L'Innommable*, "the inability to speak, the inability to keep silent, and solitude," which is characteristic of Beckett's personages. It is true that their *lazzi* come, more or less directly from the *commedia dell'arte;* but their cries, when they cry out, express the soul's agony as if they were on the tragic stage playing the tragic hero, and their actions amply justify the subtitle of the play as tragicomedy.

The contrast of the smelly flesh and its untidy demands with the aspiration of the soaring spirit is, of course, a literary stereotype; perhaps it is the most useful of all dramatic commonplaces. Beckett absolves this cliché from its traditional sentimentality. In *Godot* what is Christlike in humanity is represented by a tramp whose pants fall down at the most solemn moment of his life. The joke is cheap and laughter is shamelessly invited. It would be intolerable were the metaphor not so sharp. As it is, this laughter, inescapable, is more poignant than tears.

As early as 1932 Artaud had expressed wonder at the Surrealist antics of the Marx brothers:

> The first film of the Marx brothers that we have seen here, *Animal Crackers* appeared to me, and was considered by everyone, as an *extraordinary thing*, as the freeing through the medium of the screen of a special magic which the ordinary relations of words and images do not usually reveal, and if there is a special condition, a distinct poetic state of mind which can be called *Surrealism, Animal Crackers* shares it entirely.

> In order to understand the power of films like *Animal Crackers*, and *Monkey Business*, one would have to add to their humor the notion of something disturbing and tragic, of a fate (neither happy nor unhappy, but difficult to formulate) which would slip in behind it, like the revelation of a horrible disease on a profile of absolute beauty.[8]

The age of Mallarmé had been much interested in clowns and, long before Mallarmé was moved to write *Le Pitre chatié*, the sadness of clowns had fascinated both poets and painters. Vladimir and Estragon do not in the least recall the joyous irreverence of the Marx brothers, and there is not much about them that invites laughter save the absurdity of their situation, with which it is easy to identify our own. *En attendant Godot* belongs to that stage of symbolism at which the symbol ceases to function as an intermediary and stands forth as a fact in and of itself. The symbol, however, insofar as it remains a symbol, cannot exclude interpretation. On the contrary, all its poetic potency resides in its capacity to accept and to suggest meaning. *Godot* is essentially a metaphor, and if the author declines to assume responsibility for its significance, the reader has some scope for poetic activity in his own right. In *Proust*, Beckett wrote that the world "is apprehended metaphorically by the artist." He wrote also: "Proust does not deal in concepts, he pursues the Idea, the concrete. He admires the frescoes of the Paduan Arena because their symbolism is handled as a reality, special, literal and concrete, and is not merely the pictorial transmission of a notion."[9]

Proust was published in 1931. In a letter dated 29 December 1957 Beckett replied in a similar tone to a request for an interpretation of *Endgame*:

> I feel the only line is to refuse to be involved in exegesis of any kind. And to insist on the extreme simplicity of dramatic situation and issue. . . . My work is a matter of fundamental sounds (no joke intended) made as fully as possible, and I accept responsibility for nothing else. If people want to have headaches among the overtones, let them. And provide their own aspirin. Hamm as stated and Clov as stated, nec tecum nec sine te, in such a place and in such a world, that's all I can manage, more than I could.[10]

Beckett's refusal to lend a hand in the allegorizing of his plays is entirely consonant with nineteenth-century Symbolist practice. Ionesco followed the same course. Six centuries before, Dante had deplored the writing of allegories by those who could not explain them; but from the Symbolist viewpoint to define is to kill. In 1956, we are told, Beckett said that the success of *Godot* was based on a misunderstanding—the public looked for an allegory or a symbol in a play that was striving all the time to avoid definition.[11] But strive as it might, *Godot* could not avoid definition. The metaphor is at its core. Whether the conceit was conscious, or formulated unconsciously, the play defines itself.

Beckett's plays make, in general, an impression of stasis. *En attendant Godot* does not stir from the spot. It has, nevertheless, the kind of animation we sense in the figures of Henry Moore, which seem dynamic in their immobility since they are capable of accepting change in accordance with the subjectivity of the spectator. But, like these enigmatic figures, the play is dynamic only up to a point; beyond that it is limited by its outline, which is unequivocal. Like Moore's figures, Beckett's plays owe much of their power to their mystery. They would be seriously depleted if they were unriddled. Consequently they suggest questions in a more obviously provocative manner than plays like *Hamlet* or *Phèdre;* and perhaps this is a kind of intellectual coquetry. It is, at any rate, entirely characteristic of the Symbolist style, and was so from the beginning.

Beckett has at no time relinquished control of his material. On the contrary, his stage directions are extremely precise, and he is said to be exacting in the supervision of his productions. But while he is insistent on the exact conditions of dramatic suggestion, he appears to be implacable in his reluctance to define its goal. But, of course, to say that "a poem does not mean, but is" does not in any way inhibit its operation on the intellectual plane; on the contrary, the suggestion in itself initiates a train of thought. *Godot*, like *Endgame*, is presented as an artifact, not as a parable; but, however it may be with *Endgame*, the meaning of *Godot*—whatever the intention—is unmistakable, and is conveyed through what seems to be the most transparent allegory. There is not much ambiguity in the picture of two beggars waiting in the wilderness for a savior who does not come. It is a very apt metaphor for the human predicament, and if its success is due to a misunderstanding, the misunderstanding cannot be laid at the door of the audience. It is inherent in the text; and if the image seems unduly melodramatic or over-sentimental, the spectator may well protest that it was not he who thought of it first.

As matters stand, it is hardly possible to assign any definite meaning to *Godot*, and also impossible not to give it meaning. It is of this order of ambiguity. It is possible to say that the absence of God is a sure sign of God's presence. Indeed, it is the surest, Simone Weil assures us in the book of her essays published in 1951, under the English title *Waiting for God*. "The virtue of the dogma of the real presence," she writes, "lies in its very absurdity." She is speaking here of the Eucharist; but Tertullian's *Credo quia absurdum est* is universally applicable, and especially so to plays which deal in the absurd. "The attitude that brings about salvation," we are told in *Waiting for God*, "is not like any form of activity. The Greek word that expresses it is *hypomene*, and *patientia* is rather an inadequate translation of it. It is the waiting or attentive and faithful immobility that lasts indefinitely and cannot be shaken. The slave who waits near the door so as to open immediately the master knocks is the best image of it. He must be ready to die of hunger and exhaustion rather than change his attitude. It must be possible for his companions to call him, talk to him, beat him, without his even turning his head. Even if he is told the master is dead, and even if he believes it, he will not move. If he is told his master is angry with him and will beat him when he returns, and if he believes him, he will not move."[12]

If we are comforted by the thought that Didi and Gogo are blessed among men by the fullness of their faith, and that the inaccessible Godot is looking after them by not looking after them, there is certainly no great objection to our indulging this notion. It does something to enrich the play, while at the same time it impoverishes it, such being the nature of interpretation. Nevertheless the metaphor is sufficiently capacious to accommodate this idea, as well as others that may be advanced, and perhaps this is among its virtues. Beckett may well deal in fundamental sounds, letting the overtones fall where they may, but fundamentals that are not endowed with overtones have no great charm for the ear. In *Godot*, it may be argued, it is the overtones that make the play, and its interest is chiefly in the misunderstandings it provokes.

In his "First Manifesto of the Theatre of Cruelty" Artaud wrote:

> It is a matter, then, in the theatre of creating a metaphysic of the word, the gesture, the expression, for the purpose of rescuing it from its psychological and human exploitation. But all this is useless unless there is behind such an effort a kind of true metaphysical tendency, a reference to certain unusual ideas, the nature of which is precisely that they cannot be defined, or even formally designated. Ideas which touch upon Creation, Becoming, Chaos, and are all of a cosmic order, provide a preliminary notion of a domain from which the theatre has totally removed itself. They can create a sort of exciting equivalence between Man, Society, Nature and things.[13]

It is something of this sort, doubtless, that goes on in *Godot*, even more perceptibly in *Endgame* and *Happy Days*, all of which may fittingly be assigned—for more reasons than one—to the Theatre of Cruelty. As for *Godot*, though professedly it is not symbolic,

> L'homme y passe à travers des forêts de symboles
> Qui l'observent avec des regards familiers.

Beckett has described most succinctly in *L'Innommable* the situation of the poet whose reticence is balanced precariously against his need to exhibit his inmost life; and who is forced therefore to speak so that he cannot be understood. Doubtless all art is in some way self-portraiture; but the result may not be in every case a recognizable likeness. The poet who undertakes to sublimate his inner life in a work of art does so inevitably under some sort of cover. In these circumstances nothing is gained by attempting to penetrate what the artist desires to conceal. On the other hand, a work of art is generally in the nature of a cipher to be decoded. One may well decline to play at this game, and the author of *Godot* may well intend that no one shall. But the nature of his work is such that many have taken up the challenge of the enigma, and not always with the happiest results.

It has been suggested, for example, that Vladimir and Estragon represent Beckett and Mlle. Deschevaux-Dumesnil in the course of their long journey on foot from Paris to the Vaucluse, and also that the endlessly postponed advent of Godot symbolizes the repeated frustration of the author's bid for public recognition.[14] Such conjectures, if they are valid, cast a sad light on the text, but they do not illuminate it as a work of art. Beckett's plays are all plays of loneliness and despair, of people drawn together and thrust apart by incomprehensible forces which make and mar their lives. The task of identifying the people who in reality furnished the bases for Beckett's poetic fantasy is one that concerns the curious biographer. It barely comes within the scope of the literary critic. What is important in the case of *Godot* is the degree of interest that these particular creatures of his fantasy had for the poet. It must have been considerable, for he did not readily relinquish them. He returned to them years later with Bolton and Holloway in *Embers*, with the two inquisitors of *Theatre II*, and also in *Fin de partie*, that is to say, *Endgame*. In *Godot* Pozzo and Lucky in some sense duplicate Gogo and Didi, so that it may well be that the two couples—the one bound together by a rope and the other by the less tangible bond of mutual dependence—are projections of primal images in the author's mind which should properly be associated not with any special individuals, but rather with a psychic situation symbolized by these pairs of wretched men.

On the stage, of course, *En attendant Godot* operates on a more accessible plane of analogy. There the shadow play is interesting as such, and it is unnecessary to wonder what figures cast their shadows on the screen. For the purposes of the theatre it suffices, no doubt, that Didi and Gogo prefigure humanity at a certain stage of its physical and spiritual destitution, and it is certainly in this manner that the play is generally understood. Similarly Pozzo and Lucky readily suggest the complex relations of master and slave, and thus arouse reflections on the ambiguous nature of social injustice, not to speak of cosmic injustice; while Godot serves willy-nilly as a symbol for God.

None of this may have been intended when the play was first composed. But, it is well known, a work of art, once it is out of the author's hands, lives a life of its own and, in spite of anything that may be said about it, it becomes what it is. Thus the tree in *Godot* cannot be dismissed simply as a convenient stage-property, useful for hanging oneself, any more than the ash-bins in *Endgame* can be considered simply as appropriate receptacles for actors. In *Godot* the tree dominates the play from beginning to end. It is a character in the action, mute, but eloquent—it puts out leaves—and even if by an effort of the will it were possible to divest it of significance, the author has deliberately discouraged any such effort by reminding us periodically of its mythology. The tree is the tree of life; it is the tree of the Golden Bough. It is the tree of Eden, and the tree of Calvary, the sacred tree on which was sacrificed the human God, along with the thieves his fellows, Dimas and Gestas, one of whom, being saved, affords us yet another instance of divine injustice. The tree on which these tramps propose one day to hang themselves is also the sign of the eternal *renouveau* of spring and, unlike Godot of the white beard, it is visible, and even in a barren land it gives signs of life and a promise. *Watt* ends with the admonition: "No symbols where none intended." That is all very well for *Watt*, which is in any case indecipherable. But if in *Godot* the symbols were not intended one wonders what the devil they are doing there.

The boy who acts as Godot's messenger is tantalizing in another way. He appears, it is implied, every day, before nightfall, with the assurance that his master will come on the morrow. But it is not the same boy, apparently, who comes each day. It is perhaps his brother; and the one brother, for some reason, we are told, is beaten while the other is not. These messengers, it is specified, sleep in the hayloft of Godot's barn. The hint, like so much else in the play, is mischievous. If we are reminded that Christ was born in a barn and afterwards died on a tree, the association, though useless, can hardly be dismissed as wholly frivolous:

VLADIMIR: Christ! What has Christ to do with it? You're not going to compare yourself to Christ!
ESTRAGON: All my life I've compared myself to him.[15]

The suggestion that the angels rest their limbs in the cosmic hay after a hard day's work herding God's sheep is certainly not obligatory, but it is there. The image is latent in the text and, however trivial or unnecessary it may be, there is no reason to inhibit it. On the contrary, the image is invited. It serves to lend vitality, perhaps a specious vitality, to what might be otherwise an unduly protracted and repetitious narrative. It is out of the constant play of analogy and correspondence that *Godot*— like *Ulysses* or *Finnegans Wake*—derives the rich texture that one admires. But it is not to the interplay of allusion and suggestion that *Godot* owes its power as drama. The texture of the dialogue, however rich, would never in itself suffice to give poignancy to the image of two tramps waiting somewhere for something. What gives efficacy to the image is the symbol it embodies, the metaphor. In the symbol is all the power of the drama. If it did not say *de te fabula*, it would say nothing.

Faber and Faber published the English version of *Godot* in the early part of 1956. By this time Beckett was engaged on another play. By April of 1956 he had finished the first draft of a two-act play in French. It had four characters and much stage-business. After much revision this became a play in one act which Beckett described to his American director as "rather difficult and elliptical, mostly depending on the power of the text to claw, more inhuman than Godot."[16] The title was *Fin de partie*. The text was published in February 1957 by Les Éditions de Minuit in an edition of 3000 copies, along with a mime entitled, *Acte sans paroles I*. But, in spite of the success of *Godot* four years before, Roger Blin was unable to find a manager who was willing to undertake the production.

Beckett had repeatedly expressed his dissatisfaction with *Godot;* but he thought highly of *Fin de partie*. When it became clear that he could not get it produced in Paris, he arranged to have it performed in London, in French, at the Royal Court Theatre. Roger Blin and Jean Martin had been rehearsing the play for some months; nevertheless the London rehearsals were tense and stormy. Beckett had very precise ideas on how he wanted the parts performed. The effect was to be grim and hopeless. There was to be no laughter, and the timing of the movement had to be exact. When the play opened at last, the performance reflected the uncertainties of the actors. The production was unduly pompous. The London critics were puzzled. The reviews were poor.

The enforced première of a French play in London nevertheless caused a flutter in the French press. In consequence the management of the Studio des Champs Elysées was persuaded to stage it in Paris. In this little playhouse *Fin de partie* showed to more advantage than it had in

London. At the Royal Court Roger Blin had played Hamm sitting on a royal throne in regal robes—his performance in some ways anticipated Jacques Mauclair's Bérenger Ier in *Le Roi se meurt* five years later. In the Paris production Hamm was dressed in an old coat and was seated in a wooden armchair that rolled on castors. Clov was in rags. Their faces were painted red because Beckett had read that prisoners in close confinement had red faces. The set was shabby and the staging unpretentious. In this form *Fin de partie* was no more comprehensible than it had been in London, but it proved to be a great deal more acceptable. The English audience had enjoyed neither the cruelty of the play nor its own bewilderment at the plight of the kingly personage who was dying, seemingly, at the end of the world. The French audience was evidently more inured to suffering; moreover, it understood French. It had seen *L'Impromptu de Paris*, and did not insist on understanding anything, so long as it was permitted to feel something. It had read Artaud, and had applauded *Les Chaises*. As a result *Fin de partie* was a success in Paris. It had a run of ninety-seven performances; not a record run, certainly, but respectable. Consequently, when Beckett's English version opened in London in October 1958, over the Lord Chancellor's objections, the press was better disposed to receive it. Nevertheless it failed.

Endgame is in no sense a sequel to *Godot*, but the two plays have some connection. Both deal in oblique fashion with a relation that approximates love, and both make use of much the same characters. Obviously these characters have undergone change. In *Godot* Pozzo goes blind, and keeps falling down. Lucky is stricken dumb. In *Endgame* Hamm is blind, and cannot walk. Clov cannot sit. Hamm is the man of property that Pozzo was. Clov is the burdened slave. But now he is rebellious, and is thinking of leaving his master to die by himself, if he can. It is hinted that Hamm is in some sense his father.

The situation evidently involves the rudiments of domestic drama, the story of the exigent father and the rebellious son; and there are also the two old people, Nagg and Nell, Hamm's parents, consigned to garbage cans, but still wistfully in love. It is impossible to say, without knowing, what father-son images in Beckett's mind engendered Hamm and Clov as dramatic characters but, whatever they may have been, in this play they are caricatured as dream-figures and are thoroughly disguised. If one must, at any cost, find a progenitor for Hamm in historical reality, Joyce may well come to mind. Joyce was going blind when Beckett first came to know him and, in his early days in Paris, Beckett served him as attentively, one gathers, as Clov serves Hamm. By all accounts, Beckett looked upon Joyce as a second father, ran his errands, and imitated him even to the style of his shoes and his manner of writing. The break in this friendship, when it came in 1939, was evidently a painful episode in Beckett's life, and it may be conjectured that something of this colors the situation in *Endgame*, particularly if it is assumed that, with regard to Joyce, Beckett was reenacting in reality the same psychic trauma which he was disposed to enact over and over in fantasy. It is, of course, not at all necessary to find a factual basis for the Hamm-Clov situation. The father figure is Protean and also in the highest degree accommodating: it can be projected as high as the powers of heaven. In this play Hamm goes so far as to call God by an improper name, at least in French.

Endgame takes the drama of Symbolism some steps further toward the edge of the void, perhaps as far as it was destined to go. It is a play that most adroitly eludes comprehension, at the same time that it acts most powerfully on the sensibility of the spectator. In this play whatever is done is done with words. There is virtually nothing to look at aside from the initial tableau, and the fussy choreography that is indicated in the stage directions serves no evident purpose. The phrasing is beautiful, a rhythmic prose, in language that is consciously archaic, that sets the characters off from reality as if they were figures in a museum. The effect is somewhat the same as in *All That Fall*, in which the dialogue seems to translate the action from the Irish countryside into something that approaches surreality. The result recalls the theatre of Artaud, but *Endgame* is in no sense "total theatre." It is literature, spooky and macabre and, so far as it is realistic, unbelievable. But its realism is not of this world; indeed, with this play Beckett came very near to realizing the idea of Symbolist drama of which Mallarmé had dreamed a century before. Its images are not, of course, the images of Mallarmé. They have little to do with the romantic Gothic, for by this time Symbolism had passed through the phase of the grotesque and had come to terms with the smelly realism, and the comic pranks, of the followers of Jarry.

In *Endgame* the action is frankly presented as a play—as an illusion, that is to say, consciously created by actors. Since the actors are identical with the characters they represent, as in *Six Characters*, the effect is designedly confusing. What is presented on the stage is supposedly in the nature of a performance, something which these characters have done before and expect to do again, and its efficacy is periodically questioned and appraised by the characters themselves in asides and aparts, directed to one another, and occasionally to the audience. The effect, however, is far from the Brechtian effect of estrangement, for the asides are all in character and complicate rather than dispel the illusion:

CLOV: (*Imploringly*) Let's stop playing!
HAMM: Never! (*Pause*) Put me in my coffin.
CLOV: There are no more coffins.[17]

Some time later at a low point in the action, Hamm remarks, quite aptly, "This is not much fun." He adds at once: "But that's always the way at the end of the day, isn't it, Clov?" Clov answers, "Always." The passage, obviously, bears different interpretations, and the action thus proceeds on two levels of illusion, passing from one to the other so smoothly that its various dimensions coalesce as in a dream, leaving one vaguely uncomfortable and uncertain. In *Six Characters* the action takes place similarly on several planes, but their disparity is stressed, and a sharp distinction is made between the actors as actors and the characters as actors. Similarly in Anouilh's *Antigone* the effect of distance is achieved through the use of the "Chorus," the narrator, who introduces the characters as actors and comments objectively on their actions in the play. But in *Endgame* the levels of pretense have no definable basis. It is quite clear that Hamm and Clov are giving a performance; the question is for whom, and why, and this is never answered. What they are acting, moreover, does not appear to be a pretense. They are committed, evidently, to "something that is taking its course," in a way that goes beyond play-acting. They appear to be voyeurs of themselves, periodically reenacting a reality which is inescapable and which they themselves are bringing step by step toward a prescribed, but never resolved, conclusion.

The curtain rises on a bare interior lit by two small curtained windows high on the back wall of the room. One opens, it is said, on the earth; the other, on the sea. There is a picture hanging face to the wall. The two ashcans which harbor Nagg and Nell are covered with an old sheet. Hamm sits in his chair, center stage. He too is covered with a sheet, as if he were a stage-property, or perhaps a puppet. Clov comes in, walking with difficulty, and prepares the stage for the performance, like the property man in a Chinese play. He draws the curtains, uncovers the actors, and then goes back to his kitchen to await the whistle which is his cue to enter.

Hamm is an appropriate name for an actor, but nobody calls him Hamm in the play. He is, insofar as the others are concerned, nameless, *innommable*. He is blind; but he wears dark glasses which from time to time he polishes, and his face is covered with a bloodstained handkerchief, though he does not appear to cough.

The opening speech announces the theme of the play. Clov addresses the audience:

CLOV: (*Fixed gaze, tonelessly*) Finished, it's finished, nearly finished, it must be nearly finished. (*Pause*) Grain upon grain, one by one, and suddenly there's a heap, a little heap, the impossible heap. (*Pause*) I can't be punished any more.

His term of servitude, it is implied, is over, and the play will describe the manner of his going. After this suggestion, the play begins. Hamm, uncovered now, and alone on the stage, awakens, yawning, and announces: "Me to play." He launches at once into a brief theatrical tirade. When it is finished he blows his whistle. Clov appears. The dialogue begins.

The dialogue has no special direction, and it leads nowhere. Because of the English title which Beckett gave his play, the action is sometimes considered to symbolize somehow a game of chess. If we think of Hamm as a king—he wears a toque—attended by a pawn, and perhaps supported by two rooks in ashcans, the analogy may engage us for a moment. But it cannot be maintained. There is no adversary; and none of the movement on the stage even vaguely suggests a move on a chessboard. The game, if it is a game, comes closer to Blind Man's Buff than to chess. But it is a game only in the sense that the characters are players. As players, they are apparently tired of the play. Clov makes no bones about it.

CLOV: What's there to keep me here?
HAMM: The dialogue.[18]

The dialogue is apparently an improvisation, and there are misunderstandings, as in Pirandello's *Tonight We Improvise*. Toward the end of the play Hamm says, "Did anyone ever have pity on me?" Clov answers:

CLOV: (*lowering his telescope, turning toward Hamm*) What? (*Pause*) Is it me you're referring to?
HAMM: (*angrily*) An aside, ape! Did you never hear an aside before? (*Pause*) I'm warming up for my last soliloquy.

Clov resumes the action:

CLOV: I warn you. I'm going to look at this filth since it's an order. But it's
    the last time. (*He turns the telescope on the without*) . . .[19]

The filth he is looking at is the world outside the shelter. Presumably
outside the house of Hamm there is only death. Beyond his windows the
light is failing, the sky is gray. In a dying world the survivors are waiting
only to die. There is no hope of a savior. Hamm passes the time between
sleep and talk, telling stories nobody wants to hear, and listening to
stories he has heard before. They have run out of everything—food,
pain-killer, memories, time. A few things are left alive—a flea, a rat.
Outside the house Clov spies a boy—"un procréateur en puissance."
And, apparently, far away, there are animals, plants, somewhere in a far
country, or another world.

There is a story that Hamm, with great difficulty, is composing about
a boy. It seems to have great meaning for him. In speaking of it he acts
the part of a diffident author at a cocktail party. The scene is a sort of
routine, a *lazzo*. It has a punch line, and must be considered a joke:

CLOV: You've got on with it, I hope?
HAMM: (*modestly*) Oh not very far, not very far. (*He sighs.*) There are days
    like that, one isn't inspired. (*Pause*) No forcing, no forcing, it's fatal.
    (*Pause*) I've got on with it a little all the same. (*Pause*) Technique, you
    know. (*Pause. Irritably.*) I say I've got on with it a little all the same.

Clov at last picks up his cue:

CLOV: (*admiringly*) Well I never! In spite of everything you were able to get
    on with it!
HAMM: (*modestly*) Oh not very far, you know, not very far, but neverthe-
    less, better than nothing.
CLOV: Better than nothing! Is it possible?[20]

In *Endgame* the characterizations are precise and detailed. Hamm is
hateful, but he is unfortunate, and he elicits compassion. Clov is patient
and obedient, and also aggressive and hostile. The relation between them
is much less abstract than that of Pozzo and Lucky, much closer to the
relation of Vladimir and Estragon. They are bound together by many
things, evidently, including love, and separated by many more, including hate:

HAMM: Kiss me. (*Pause*) Will you not kiss me?
CLOV: No.
HAMM: On the forehead.

CLOV: I won't kiss you anywhere. (*Pause*)

HAMM: (*holding out his hand*) Give me your hand at least. (*Pause*) Will you
     not give me your hand?

CLOV: I will not touch you.[21]

It is an intricate version of the dance of death, with the symbols virtually
uncommitted; but much is suggested, more than enough. In the end,
Clov tries to clear up the mess that Hamm makes before he leaves him
alone to die:

CLOV: (*straightening up*) I love order. It's my dream. A world where all
     would be silent and still and each thing in its last place, under the last
     dust. (*He starts picking up again.*)

HAMM: (*exasperated*) What in God's name do you think you're doing?

CLOV: (*straightening up*) I'm doing my best to create a little order.

HAMM: Drop it! (*Clov drops the objects he has picked up.*)

Hamm wishes to end, evidently, not in Clov's tidy world, but in the
chaos where, reputedly, the cosmos first began. When Clov has gone, ostensibly, Hamm plays out his last scene by himself—"vieille fin de partie
perdue"—the last Adam at the end of the world. He has foreseen how it
will be:

   . . . There I'll be, in the old shelter, alone against the silence and . . .
   (*He hesitates*) . . . the stillness. If I can hold my peace and sit quiet, it
   will all be over with sound, and motion, all over and done with. (*Pause*)
   I'll have called my father, and I'll have called my . . . (*He hesitates*) . . .
   my son. And even twice, or three times, in case they shouldn't have
   heard me, the first time or the second. (*Pause*) I'll say to myself, He'll
   come back. (*Pause*) And then? (*Pause*) And then?[22]

It is, indeed, in that very way that the game ends. Only, after Hamm
has given up, divested himself of his dog and his whistle, and composed
himself for what is to come, Clov, dressed for a journey, with Panama
hat, raincoat, umbrella, and bag, "halts by the door and stands there,
impassive and motionless, his eyes fixed on Hamm till the end."

   But in the end, as in *Godot*, nobody moves.

Since *Fin de partie* was considered too short to fill out an evening in the
theatre, it was originally played with a mime called *Acte sans paroles*. This
is a sad little pantomime in which the reluctant player is systematically
tantalized by some superior power which dangles a carafe of water just

outside his reach until he is driven into a state of hopeless immobility. There is also a tree from which, as in *Godot*, he is unable to hang himself. As a conceit *Acte sans paroles* seems entirely explicit: apparently it was judged unsatisfactory as a companion piece to *Fin de partie*.

In 1957 Beckett wrote *Krapp's Last Tape* to take its place. He wrote it in English. It was first performed, together with *Endgame*, in London at the Royal Court, with Patrick Magee in the role of Krapp, on 28 October 1958. Neither play was well received. Beckett was depressed and caught cold; nevertheless he translated *Krapp's Last Tape* into French. *La Dernière bande* was given a cool reception in Paris also. It was actually some time before the press in England or in America was disposed to accept *Krapp's Last Tape* as a production of some consequence. Though some critics were impressed, it was treated, on the whole, with diffidence until after Beckett was awarded the Nobel prize. Then it acquired the glamor reserved for literary masterpieces.

Krapp's Last Tape is the most frankly autobiographical of Beckett's plays. It consists of two monologues spoken in counterpoint by an old man and a tape-recorder. It was obviously the author's intention to juxtapose two moments in a man's life at an interval of thirty years. The tape-recorder provides an ingenious method, but the effect of the play depends much more on what is heard than what is seen; the visual component is necessarily minimal. With this play Beckett came even closer to a dramatic technique that depends on the immobility of the actor, or even on his absence, a technique that recalls the monologues of the Molloy trilogy. The result is a form of drama that approximates a poem.

There are nevertheless some visual effects in *Krapp's Last Tape*. Krapp is an untidy old man, costive, near-sighted, and nearly deaf. He is an unsuccessful writer addicted to alcohol and to bananas, in the circumstances an odd choice of fruit. It seems that he is in the habit of recording a spool of tape each year. On this occasion he plays back a spool he recorded thirty years before, in the year his mother died. His own voice speaks to him of that time:

> Spiritually a year of profound gloom and indigence until that memorable night in March, at the end of the jetty, in the howling wind, never to be forgotten, when suddenly I saw the whole thing. The vision: at last. This, I fancy, is what I have chiefly to record this evening, against the day when my work will be done and perhaps no place left in my memory, warm or cold, for the miracle that . . . (*hesitates*) for the fire that set it alight. What I suddenly saw there was this, that the belief I had been going on all my life, namely—

At this point the voice breaks off, for Krapp is no longer disposed to hear about this miracle. Doubtless he has outgrown this experience, for the tape, turned now to "Fast Forward," affords us a fleeting image of a stormy sea and a time in which it became "clear to me at last that the dark I have always struggled to keep under is in reality my most—" Then again the tape is spun forward, this time to a scene of love-making, passionate and apparently hopeless, with a nude girl in a punt. He plays this over twice thoughtfully. Then Krapp begins recording on a fresh spool of tape:

> Just been listening to that stupid bastard I took myself for thirty years ago, hard to believe I was ever as bad as that. Thank God that's all done with anyway . . .

He has nothing much now to record:

> Nothing to say, not a squeak. What's a year now? The sour cud and the iron soul. . . .

There are some memories. There was a vacation in the Baltic, with a girl who was deeply absorbed in *Effie Briest*, a sad novel by Theodor Fontane. The reference has been identified with a holiday that Beckett actually spent with Peggy Sinclair in a Baltic summer resort in 1929:

> Could have been happy with her, up there on the Baltic, and the pines, and the dunes. (*Pause*) Could I? (*Pause*) And she? (*Pause*) Pah!

There are some other recollections of Krapp's youth, and then once again he plays back the scene in the punt with the girl:

> I lay down across her with my face in her breasts and my hand on her. We lay there without moving. But under us all moved and moved us, gently, up and down, and from side to side.

The tape runs on with the voice of thirty years ago:

> Here I end this reel. Box (*pause*) three. Spool (*pause*) five. Perhaps my best years are gone. When there was a chance of happiness. But I wouldn't want them back. Not with the fire in me now. No, I wouldn't want them back.
> (*Krapp motionless staring before him. The tape runs on in silence.*)[23]

The silence permits one to reflect that the voice is thirty years old, speaking at a time when the fire that was kindled in Krapp's soul by the sudden revelation that came to him on the unforgettable night of the storm was still bright and burning. We have already been told the result:

Seventeen copies sold, of which eleven at trade price to free circulating libraries beyond the seas. Getting known . . .

When Beckett wrote *Krapp's Last Tape* he too was getting known, and much more widely than at the time when he had published *Murphy*, nineteen years before. *Godot* and *Endgame* by now were being played often—in little theatres—and his novels were having some sale. He was being asked to write for the radio. But the bitterness of his years of frustration, obviously, was with him still. It was, in some sense, his literary capital, an investment which afforded a rich return all the rest of his life. This bitterness, and the view of life and humanity which it reflects, must have been with him even before he was in a position to court failure seriously. From the very beginning of his literary career, his opinion of mankind is indicated by the scatological names he conferred on his characters, the illnesses and deformities with which he endowed them, and the filth in which he made them wallow. His work, from first to last, amply reflects the nausea with which the bright young men of his day were afflicted. His world was a sick world, waiting to die, and Krapp's brief moment in the sun was pervaded with the hopelessness of his world's infirmity.

Krapp's Last Tape is deeply touching, but while the technique was new, neither the theme nor the mood were new. The theme had been very thoroughly exploited by writers of genius long before Beckett took it up. The sacrifice of happiness to vocation was a theme that had inspired Carlyle, among others, to his best work; but Diogenes Teufelsdroeckh had made his way into The Everlasting Yea at a time when it was still possible to say yes. None of Ibsen's heroes, from Brand to Rubek, could do as much; and each of these, at the end of life, contemplated his ruins in much the same way as Krapp. Shaw also had been much interested in the artist's self-immolation. But Shaw was an optimist. He thought of himself not as cosmic excrement, but as the standard-bearer of the Life Force; and for him, in any case, art was irrelevant to the main issue of life. One might say that by 1958 the artist's romantic self-pity had become a cliché.

Beckett did much with it. He did not, of course, wholly succeed in purging this attitude of its sentimentality. The self-portrait in *Krapp*—if it is a self-portrait—is sardonic and redolent with self-loathing, but not so grotesque as to exclude a glimpse of young Shelley lurking somewhere in the shadows with the mark of Cain or Christ on his ensanguined brow. Unlike Rubek or Brand, Krapp needs no avalanche to do him in, and none is provided: there is only the silent tape running on at the end of his play.

All That Fall was commissioned by the British Broadcasting Corporation. It was first broadcast on radio on 13 January 1957. The script describes Mrs. Rooney's journey from her house to the railway station at Boghill, a village in Ireland, to meet the 12:30 train from the city on which her blind husband is coming home from work. It is a Saturday, and Mr. Rooney's birthday.

Mrs. Rooney is old and very fat, and she journeys afoot, moving with difficulty. She is overtaken on the road first by a dung cart; then by Mr. Tyler on his bicycle, which has a flat tire; then by Mr. Slocum in his motor car. Mrs. Rooney has a sharp tongue. Somehow she manages to offend everyone she meets. Mr. Slocum wedges her buttocks into his car with great trouble, and gives her a lift to the station where, without meaning to, she manages to insult the station master, Mr. Barrell. The train is unaccountably late. A very pious lady named Miss Fitt unwillingly helps her up the platform steps. At last the train pulls in, and Mr. Rooney descends. They walk home together, chatting. She wonders what delayed the train. Mr. Rooney will not tell. Then a boy runs after them with something Mr. Rooney dropped. It is not clear what it is, a kind of ball, something, Mr. Rooney says, violently, that he carries about with him. As they move away, the boy calls after them what it was that held up the train. It was a child that fell off and was killed.

It is June, and halfway home it begins to rain. Mrs. Rooney has great sexual longing, but no use for affection. Her language, like her husband's, is unusually rich and old-fashioned. Evidently these two belong to another era. The text for the Sunday sermon, it is announced, will be, "The Lord upholdeth all that fall and raiseth up all those that be bowed down—" a joke that makes them join in wild laughter. Mr. Rooney has always been ill: "The night you married me, they came for me with an ambulance." He commutes now, a blind man, between a ruined business and a domestic nightmare, haunted by sad memories, and a drear prospect. The two walk home with dragging steps between gusts of wind and rain, and bit by bit it becomes clear that it was Mr. Rooney who pushed the child from the moving train.[24]

All That Fall is an easy riddle intended for a large audience. The relation of Mr. and Mrs. Rooney is not altogether different from that of Hamm and Clov. Dan Rooney is blind and waiting to die. Mrs. Rooney serves him with some reluctance. The world has not yet come to an end, but their special world is ending, and the hoax of which they have been the victims does not altogether amuse them. Like the earlier play, this is a *partie perdue*, a lost game they would prefer to be done with. And just as in *Fin de partie* Hamm sees in the little boy who is prowling about his shelter a potential procreator who may, unless he is prevented, renew the wretched game, so Mr. Rooney does what he can to stop the play by pushing the child from the train, an act of mercy both for the child and for mankind. The idea, here again, is bright and useful, and beautifully developed, but not new. It is the theme of Pirandello's *novella*, "La distruzione dell'uomo."

Happy Days was written in May 1961 in English, and was first produced in New York that year at the Cherry Lane Theatre. It is a play in two acts, staged under blazing lights, in a setting that resembles a scene in the Malebolge of the Inferno. The landscape is a wilderness, an unbroken plain. Winnie, a woman of fifty, is sunk in the earth above her waist. Within reach is a capacious purse with various cosmetic needs, and a revolver, which she does not use. She has a collapsible parasol. There is no alternation of night and day. The sound of a bell puts her to sleep and, after a time, awakens her. Almost within reach is her husband, Willie. He is sixty and dwells in a hole behind her. Occasionally he crawls out.

They might be dead souls in hell, but their situation is, more likely, a metaphor for a certain stage of domestic bliss. Whatever these symbols may portend, the play seems to ring yet another change on the situation in *Godot*, *Fin de partie*, and *All That Fall*—it involves two characters, mutually dependent, exhausted, and waiting for annihilation. Winnie talks a great deal; Willie, very little. She remembers her childhood, some scenes of their marriage, and she remembers Millie, perhaps her daughter. Unlike Mrs. Rooney, she has no complaints. She talks. Willie occasionally reassures her with an answer. The bell rings, and she goes to sleep. Another happy day.

There is apparently a considerable interval before the second act. Meanwhile Winnie has sunk into the earth as far as her neck, and can no longer turn her head to look for Willie. But she has no immediate cause for alarm. He crawls out of his hole, formally dressed this time in a morning suit, and tries in vain to creep up to her face. She sings a song from *The Merry Widow*. There is not much else to be said. She has seen Willie: another happy day.

There is, indeed, not much to be said about *Happy Days*. It makes all sorts of suggestions and does not in the least commit itself. Nevertheless, so far as it goes, it is marvellously effective on the stage, and it tangles the imagination in a way that recalls the best of the Surrealist painters. In spite of poor reviews it had a good run at the Cherry Lane Theatre, a run of some hundred performances, and may be accounted one of Beckett's more successful plays. The author thought well enough of it to translate it into French as *Ah, les beaux jours!*, and in French it loses none of its macabre lustre.

In *Godot* the characters tumble about the stage to some purpose, and in *Fin de partie* there is some vertical and lateral movement. But in general Beckett's plays incline to stasis, and the longer he writes the less he permits his characters to move. It is as if his fantasy were involved in some process of entropy which must culminate eventually in a total absence of motion: his is a universe in process of running down. Beckett is not gracious with his characters. He afflicts them with paralysis, blinds them and mutes them, confines them in jars and ashcans, sinks them into the earth and, in the end, virtually eliminates them from view. It is as if he played the part of a malevolent god whose cruelty matches his compassion. In *Not I* (1974) the visible part of the play is no more than a woman's lips moving in the light while a silent figure raises helpless hands a few times in pity. In *That Time* (1974) there is nothing to be seen but a man's white face. These plays are actually monologues, but it would seem that ultimately Beckett would prefer a play in which nothing is said and nothing is done and there is nothing, the dramatic counterpart of the blank canvas and the silent orchestra.

After *Endgame* those of Beckett's plays that have dialogue more and more resemble conversations in hell. They provide a guided tour of spiritual and physical torments under the tutelage of a kindly spirit with a sharp eye for the absurd. "Nothing is funnier than unhappiness," Nell says in *Endgame: "Le malheur est ridicule,"* wrote Simone Weil.[25] They had not the same thing in mind, apparently, for Nell adds at once, "Yes, it's like the funny story we have heard too often, we still find it funny, but we don't laugh anymore." For Nell what is funny about unhappiness can only be the ridiculous assumption that there can be happiness. This is, in fact, the burden of Beckett's plays. There is not much room in them for the paradox of *Waiting for God*—it would seem that they belong simply to the Theatre of Cruelty. The comic in the tragic provides, however, at best only transitory satisfaction and, when we stop smiling, it is normal to wonder whether there is not in these macabre fantasies something other than the masochistic delight in pain which they seem to express.

At bottom, all of Beckett's plays, and his novels, seem to be in some sense confessions. Almost all the plays are plays of reminiscence, "small chat to the bubbling of Lethe about the good old days when we wished we were dead." Beckett's characters are invariably aged, or rapidly aging, contemplating their lives with dismay from the edge of the abyss. The mood of death and the smell of death pervade all his work, and the fact that it finds favor in our time tells us something of the climate in which we live, more so, indeed, than the plays of Ionesco, who shares his mood. Ionesco is fearful in the way of a frightened child; but Beckett's is an adult depression that suggests some residue of faith.

By all accounts Beckett has been uncomfortable all his life, and it is likely that at some time he read Schopenhauer with some attention, the more so since Schopenhauer writes a very good style. The driving Will, ruthless and aimless, appears in Beckett's plays in various guises, and always as a peremptory and cruel power. In *Godot* it is invisible. It is Godot and what Godot represents. In *Play* one can see it: it is the beam of light that commands the characters to speak. It is the whistle that summons to action in *Act Without Words I;* the goad that prompts to movement in *Act Without Words II;* the bell in *Happy Days;* the invisible spectator of *Endgame.* It is an unquestionable necessity that forces those to speak who might prefer to remain silent, and that drives those to move who would rather be still. In every case it signifies an external power, a necessity which seems needlessly cruel and mischievous unless it has a deeper motive than is immediately apparent.

Beckett's world is in no sense a guignol. The *comédie humaine* that he represents takes place on a plane that transcends the grotesque. Its pessimism is not peculiarly characteristic of the later years of the twentieth century, although there is much in these years that serves to enhance it. What Beckett expresses is the ambiguous mood of the previous century, the anguish of those who, after Darwin, felt deprived of God and continued to seek Him even in the void.

Few have excelled Beckett in the use of the dramatic metaphor. His

plays affirm nothing, and consequently have enormous power of suggestion. Thematically these plays are invariable. Beckett is marvellously inventive, but his theme is almost always the recollection of past sorrow in
present misery, and in developing it Beckett gives a wry twist to Francesca's famous lines in *Inferno* V. Dante, in his gruesome journey among
the damned, was concerned in each case to demonstrate God's justice. It
is the injustice of God that concerns Beckett, or rather—what perhaps
amounts to the same thing—the injustice of the idea of God.

Beckett's interest in Dante has been the subject of considerable scholarly comment. Most of his plays are set in the suburbs of hell, and some
take place well within the confines of the City of Dis. His characters,
confined in jars or pots or pits, or at large in their deserts and beaches,
are racked with pain, and choked with anguish. They grovel in the mud,
wander about miserably, and torture one another in the best infernal
tradition, but while in Dante's hell the damned are at least relieved of
hope, in Beckett's hell it is hope that chains his creatures to their pain.

The *persona* that Beckett constructed for himself as an artist is more
poignant and less theatrical than the professional masks that Pirandello
and Shaw assumed, and it is far more impressive than Ionesco's carefully
drawn self-portrait, but his characters, in general, are among the least
delectable of those hitherto devised for the stage. His art portrays humanity in its most abject form. It is the art of twisted limbs and faces
contorted with agony. Many artists, from the time of Leonardo, have
seen beauty at this end of the spectrum. Some—one thinks of Bosch or
Goya—have justified their taste in didactic terms. One can hardly think
of Beckett as a teacher of moral lessons. Nevertheless his work occasions
wonder. This gallery of graveyard figures reflects the mood of a dying
world with the same ambiguity as the paintings of Botticelli reflected in
his day the mood of a world reborn.

It serves no purpose to locate Beckett's theatre on the shady terrace of
the 4th *Purgatorio* where Belacqua is doomed to wait out a lifetime of
sloth before he is granted access to the torments of the delectable mountain. Beckett's characters are not slothful. Neither are they hopeless. It is
possible that they are already in hell, but theirs is not the hell of Dante.
These are scenes from which the eyes of Beatrice were long ago averted,
studies of pain set in the wilderness of Surrealism, in the vast untrodden
reaches of the unconscious, where even the angels seem fearful and uncertain. They are very modern, these angels, they have schedules to
meet and trains to catch, but whatever paradise it is they hail from, we

may be sure it is not the paradise of Beatrice, or if it is, then it must be "the only Paradise that is not the dream of a madman, the Paradise that has been lost."[26]

After *Happy Days* and *All That Fall* Beckett's plays grow progressively shorter, more enigmatic and more inarticulate, until in the end they approximate gestures. One cannot say that after a time words failed him. Few writers of our age have had words so completely at their command. But the need to speak, so strongly evident in Beckett's early works, seems bit by bit to have diminished once he found a hearing. In his mind, the inability to speak and the inability to be silent appear in time to have reached a state of equilibrium. In his last pieces the verbal apparatus is intact. It is just that there seems to be nothing more to say. His plays make sounds of compassion, gestures of helpless pity such as the dark figure makes in *Not I;* groans perfectly staged. Perhaps they were meant to bring to the ears of the God who is not there tidings of a world that has not quite ceased to exist.

Simone Weil died in 1943 after a brief lifetime in which, for reasons best known to herself, she earnestly sought suffering and found it everywhere. She also found the love that passeth understanding. She wrote:

> there is no contradiction between the love of the beauty of the world and compassion. Such love does not prevent us from suffering on our own account when we are in affliction. Neither does it prevent us from suffering because others are afflicted. It is on another plane from suffering.[27]

Such love is on another plane from anything that can be done in the Theatre of Cruelty, and it may well be that it is to this higher plane of drama that the plays of Beckett must be referred if they are ever to find understanding. There is possibly no connection between these words of a girl who passionately awaited the coming of God and the words of one who wrote of God, "Le salaud! Il n'existe pas!"

But, here again, one cannot be sure.

THE END OF THE WORLD

C'est beau, n'est-ce-pas, la fin du monde?
SODOME ET GOMORRHE, II, 2

It is difficult to avoid the suspicion that those who have from time to time contemplated the end of the world have derived a certain satisfaction from the prospect. Judging from its reflections in the theatre, the world has at no time been a convenient habitation and, while few seem to be in any special haste to leave it, the alternatives have always seemed attractive. Plato long ago observed that the ordered cosmos was reverting to chaos. The author of the Book of Revelation evidently looked forward with anticipation to the terminal ceremonies that were even then at hand. Some dozen centuries later, the compilers of the Nuremberg Chronicle, after devoting 572 pages to the history of the world from the beginning to the date of publication in 1493, thoughtfully provided ten blank pages at the end of the book for the use of those who might wish to note down the few remaining events before the end of everything. The tragic mood that colors the drama of our day is obviously not new. Neither is it old. It is, seemingly, perennial, a consequence perhaps of the nostalgia that assails us soon after we leave the comforts of the maternal womb.

In the twentieth century this mood was significantly accentuated. It was, of course, a time of unexampled scientific progress; but it was not a happy time. "There was an aura about 1914," writes a contemporary historian, "that caused those who sensed it to shiver for mankind. Tears came even to the most bold and resolute. Messimy, opening a Cabinet meeting on August 5 with a speech full of valor and confidence, broke off midway, buried his head in his hands, and sobbed, unable to continue. Winston Churchill, wishing godspeed and victory to the BEF, when taking leave of Henry Wilson, 'broke down and cried so that he could not finish the sentence.' Something of the same emotion could be felt in St. Petersburg."[1] There were many who felt at the outbreak of war that the world would never be the same again. In the theatre, from the time of Maeterlinck, whatever was most notable in some way reflects the sense of impending doom.

The new drama was rooted in an unhappy time when all the values of Western culture were cruelly tested. In the plays of Pirandello and Giraudoux and Ionesco and Beckett may be read the discomfort of those whose faith in humanity did not survive the horrors of the age. The consequence of the return to savagery that enlivens the history of this period was an outbreak of unparalleled vandalism in the world of art. The erosion of the great classical tradition had begun long before. By the time of the great wars, the Renaissance was in ruins, and the new building program which Père Ubu had projected no longer inspired confidence. The new poetry had risen from the old with the sound of peepers in the spring, but it was not yet full-throated. The new art sought intimations of immortality in recollections of childhood, and visions of truth in madness. In the museums and concert-halls room was made for every kind of lunacy lest at some future time our age might be found wanting in foresight.

In the light of the changes that took place in the theatre during this time of transition the revolutionary departures of the past seem singularly timid. The progress of the drama from the time of Jodelle and Giraldi is impressive in its majesty and also in its caution; but in the time of Strindberg, which was also the time of Gauguin and van Gogh, things moved quickly. After seeing Genet's *Les Bonnes* or Beckett's *Play* one wonders at the excitements that attended Guarini's innovations in *Il pastor fido*, or the commotion stirred up by the première of *Hernani*; and even the noises that followed the first productions of *A Doll's House* and *Ghosts* seem out of proportion to the intensity of the provocation. By comparison, the lack of excitement in the contemporary theatre is its most astonishing aspect. Seemingly the modern audience no longer cherishes a sense of tradition. This may be a sign of progress. But the thought is disquieting.

After the turn of the century it was no longer possible to think of drama in terms of the modulations of a fundamental mimetic concept which is in its essence unalterable. From the first decades of this era the avant garde in the theatre attempted to break completely with the classic tradition. The consequence was a rift as sharp as that which developed concurrently in the visual arts and in music. The movements which brought about this rupture were, to begin with, consciously destructive. It was the aim of Dada to laugh reality out of existence. Tzara laid this movement to rest in May 1922 in Weimar, but from its ashes Surrealism sprang full-feathered, with its own special brand of terrorism: "We shall triumph over everything. And first of all we shall destroy the civilization which is so dear to you, in which you are caught like fossils in shale. Western world, you are condemned to death!"[2] In the theatre Surrealism began with an assault on logic. "A poem must be a debacle of the intellect," Breton wrote. "Poetry is the opposite of literature." From Cocteau to Pinter dramatists did what they could to substantiate this doctrine. In the consequent assault on the traditional theatre, meaning has been the major casualty. Whether or not the drama is the better for it is a question that hardly admits of a simple answer.

For the Renaissance artist the universe was charged at every point with significance, and art was intended above all to be meaningful. From this standpoint the artist served the function of mediator between the Creator and the created, and he sought to interpret the one to the other to the best of his ability, making meaningful patterns that defined reality in Christian terms. It was a noble priesthood from which the modern artist still reaps benefits. The great masterpieces of the former age—the *Comedy* of Dante, the cathedral of Chartres, *The Faerie Queen*, the Sistine ceiling, *Paradise Lost*—were frankly encyclopedic works; but every work of art, no matter how modest its intention, was intended to enlighten, and was therefore subject to explication. In the drama the results were more uncertain, since the *Poetics* dwelt on tragedy as a communion rather than a communication; but the Renaissance commentators did not hesitate to find meaning and moral in every play that concerned them. Until the end of the nineteenth century the significative function of drama was strongly emphasized, so that writers such as Dumas *fils*, Sardou, Brieux, and Ibsen, and after them Shaw and Brecht insisted on the stage as a forum for debate.

The primitivism and occultism that distinguishes the work of the later avant garde in the theatre had its roots, as we have seen, in the last decades of the nineteenth century. It was a complex expression of dissatisfaction with the rationalistic bias which the Naturalist writers gave to the

current scene, a bias which led, in one way, to the plays of the Théâtre-
libre and, in another, to the ovens of Dachau. The anti-naturalistic reaction was, of course, by no means limited to the theatre. Its effects are
perceptible in every field of art, and in music, and it is hopeless to attempt any consideration of the new trends in the drama without taking
into account the parallel manifestations in the other arts. It is usual to associate the cult of *l'art pour l'art* with drugs, decadence, and dandyism. It
was, in fact, a serious movement of far-reaching consequence. Doubtless
it represented more than a reaction against the utilitarianism of an un-
holy time. It was, among other things, a sincere attempt to escape from
what was felt to be a pointless and painful reality into what Schopenhauer had indicated was the pure realm of idea, the only refuge from the
driving Will and its attendant discomforts. In this effort, it was bound to
fail. Seemingly, the situation of art *in vacuo* is rarely tolerable for long.
Sooner or later the social aspect of art reasserts itself. Thus Dada ultimately made a common cause with socialism, and the Surrealists joined the
Communist party.

The Symbolists of the decade1885–95 were unwilling to be associated
with decadence. Like Baudelaire, Mallarmé was firmly convinced, so he
said, that in Symbolism was the key to truth, and that it was possible
through association and analogy to arrive intellectually at spiritual realities that elude the grosser methods of science. The semi-mystical tendencies of the Symbolists were certainly not indicative merely of an effort to
escape from the objective facts of life. They represented an effort to
achieve a more significant experience than the material world afforded.
Spiritual insight might be gained in Platonic fashion through the exercise
of the logical faculty, but the mind was not limited by its rational process. It had also the power of imagination and intuition with which to
penetrate the veil of reality.

Like the Parnassians and the Impressionists, the Symbolists began
with nature. They did not end there. Like enthusiastic neo-Platonists
they sought to take the steps of the ideal hierarchy two at a time, with
their eyes firmly fixed on a transcendent reality situated just beyond the
reach of their vision. In the light of this pure reality, the presence of
which they felt in their souls, the material world seemed to them a caricature, a fit subject for comedy. Thus Symbolism, which began as an instrument of discovery and revelation, took on a critical function as well,
developed a sense of the absurd, and vented its disenchantment, when it
came, on nature, subjecting the external world to every sort of exaggera-

tion, distortion, and grimace in the name of the ideal. In consequence, mimesis became caricature; the grotesque was substituted for the beautiful as the object of artistic attention; logic gave way to absurdity; and ultimately art became non-objective and ceased to represent anything but the artist's state of mind, his disillusionment, and his apprehension.

The Symbolists' search for meaning thus ended in despair, and the sum total of their efforts was to drive a wedge between art and meaning. In England, in the time of George Bernard Shaw, it was not at all clear that this was happening. Shaw had no hesitation in maintaining, in the face of all evidence to the contrary, that art—and especially the art of the theatre—is primarily realistic and didactic, and he could cite the examples of Ibsen and Wagner, both of whom he misinterpreted, in defence of his contention. By the time of *Man and Superman* the pendulum had already swung in the other direction. Wagner was recognized as the father of French Symbolism; Ibsen and Strindberg had become Symbolists; and *Man and Superman* itself was a notable experiment in Symbolist drama. Shaw's plays, from first to last, have a stout core of meaning, but in the theatre the search for meaning hardly outlasted Shaw. In the period between the wars the idea became established as a critical principle, questionable only by Philistines, that meaning has no place in the pictorial arts, is wholly irrelevant to music, and quite extraneous to poetry. A poem by Archibald MacLeish, aptly entitled "Ars Poetica," and very widely anthologized, involves the suggestion that

> A poem should be wordless
> As the flight of birds

—an interesting idea, though it is difficult to see in what terms, even in this age of miracles, such poetry might be constituted. The poet, nevertheless, sums up the Symbolist dogma:

> A poem should not mean
> But be[3]

It is probable that this is what Mallarmé had in mind when he described in his letter to Henri Cazalis the "très nouvelle poétique" which his projected drama *Hérodiade* was intended to exemplify: "Le vers ne doit pas, là, se composer de mots, mais d'intentions, et toutes les paroles s'effacer devant les sensations . . ."[4]

From such statements, mysterious as they are, it may certainly be inferred that in the new Symbolist poetic, suggestion and intimation are to play the essential role in the transmission of thoughts and images. The play is to be experienced as a series of sensations. Words are to be used not in their denotative function but as stimuli calculated to awaken a train of associations analogous to those experienced by the poet, whose subjectivity provides the entire substance of the play.

However much these ideas need to be qualified in the light of Mallarmé's other statements on the subject, they do indicate an avenue of approach to such arcane compositions as Mallarmé's *Igitur*, *Hérodiade*, and *L'Après-midi d'un faune*, and even to the enigmatic configurations of "Un Coup de dés." They are obviously in some relation to the theories of Artaud, and may help one also to perceive the connection between the poetry of Mallarmé, the *Calligrames* of Apollinaire, the type of pictorial composition represented by Léger's "Woman in Blue" (1912), and the kind of quasi-literary painting of which Picasso's "Les Demoiselles d'Avignon" (1907) is the monumental example. If they are of less use in interpreting the symbolism of Maeterlinck's *Pelléas et Mélisande*, on the one hand, or of Beckett's *Fin de Partie*, on the other, it is no doubt because these works are based on a more traditional mode of representation, and are essentially mimetic, representing not "the effect that is produced," but the thing itself displaced to a level of fantasy which derives significance through correspondence, that is to say, through metaphor.

Symbolism as such did not long survive the generation of Apollinaire, nor could the faith of its adherents long resist the disruptive influences of the time. After 1914 the theory of signatures fell on evil days; but it did not die. The bankruptcy of Symbolism led to the cheerful iconoclasm of Dada, and these lunacies resulted in the Surrealism of Breton, Aragon, and Eluard, a mode of thought which could be seriously documented and discussed, even if it defied comprehension.

It was in the special world of surreality, between day and dream, that the new art had its most spectacular development. In the light of clinical evidence adduced by Freud and Jung, Breton solemnly declared the total independence of thought, free of the shackles of logic and reason, and the supremacy of the unconscious as the essential mental faculty, the only true source of artistic creativity. From this standpoint the dream-state and the waking-state were seen to merge, the reality principle ceased to exert its censorship, and the area between *Tag* and *Traum* became the "total reality" which was the special province of the artist. In the drama this result had been anticipated by Strindberg as early as 1898, the date of *To Damascus I*, the first truly Surrealist play.

For the dramatist this technique involved the substitution of the logic of dreams for the type of logical sequence on which Western drama had relied from the time of Sophocles. The Surrealist drama was not addressed to the intellect; it was meant to be apprehended but not understood. The Surrealists preserved, however, in spite of the mounting disillusionments of the time, their Symbolist faith in the invisible harmony of creation and the significance of the archetypal correspondences that defined the universal structure. The difference between their faith and that of the earlier Symbolists was measurable chiefly in the translation of their reality from the outer to the inner world. In other respects it remained the same; and their desire to realize in art, and in life as well, the subliminal world of the psyche necessarily included an expression of confidence in the artist's ability to discover these correspondences and to reveal them to the world. The assumption of the reality of the unconscious as the common bond of humanity made it possible also to seek for a universal language, universally comprehensible, which had no need of words. Thus, in addition to the comic and the erotic manifestations of the unconscious life—its aggressive and libidinous aspects—Breton and his associates were able to add an Orphic element which stressed the unity of man and nature, and the oneness of life and death.[5]

It is upon these ideas, in some dilution, that the greater part of the avant-garde drama of our time appears to be based. At the bottom of the Surrealist poetry is the conceit, in its manifestations often more bizarre than the conceptism of Tebaldeo, Marino, or Góngora, nevertheless distinctly a development—whether consciously achieved or not—of the Renaissance "metaphysical" genre. The Surrealist effect was intended to be strong, not elegant. "The simplest Surrealist act," wrote Breton, "consists of dashing down into the street, pistol in hand, and firing blindly into the crowd, as fast as you can pull the trigger . . ."[6] Such activity, however satisfactory from the viewpoint of the unconscious impulse, is normally frowned on by the police, and no Surrealist has been known to indulge his inner life artistically in this manner. Surrealist artists, however, have cherished the right to terrorize the crowd in other ways. For this reason, if no other, they have taken delight in the Marinesque cult of the *mirabile*. About the middle of the sixteenth century Marino enunciated the memorable doctrine with which is associated the art of the *secento*—the goal of the poet is the creation of marvels:

É del poeta il fin la meraviglia:
Chi non fa stupir vada alla striglia.

"Let us not mince matters," André Breton wrote some four centuries later, "the marvellous is always beautiful, anything marvellous is beautiful, in fact only the marvellous is beautiful."[7] What is marvellous in Surrealist art, however, is not the design of the composition, as in the case of Corneille or Caravaggio, but the poetic image. The image is a conceit in the style of Marino or Crashaw. Pierre Reverdy wrote:

The image is a pure creation of the mind.

It cannot be born of a comparison, but from a juxtaposition of two more or less distinct realities.

The more the relationship between the two juxtaposed realities is distant and true, the stronger the image will be—the greater its emotional power and poetic reality.[8]

It is doubtless in this sense that we must rationalize such images as those we encounter in *Le Nouveau Locataire*, *Amédée*, or *Happy Days*.

For the seventeenth-century Conceptist the art of poetry consisted in bringing together dissimilar things in such a way as to reveal their correspondence. For the Surrealist, the image is "a pure creation of the mind," and he assumes no further responsibility. Nevertheless there appears to be no essential difference between the metaphysics of Breton and the assumptions of the metaphysical poets and painters of the seventeenth century. The poet's intuition, unleashed by Surrealism, Breton writes, "alone provides the thread that can put us back on the road of Gnosis as knowledge of suprasensual Reality, 'invisibly visible in an eternal mystery.' "[9] Such statements recall not only the writings of Péladan, but also the more esoteric authors of the Renaissance; but it would be a mistake to conclude that Breton resembles Pico or Bruno in his thinking. Christian metaphysics in the time of Pico rested on a firmer basis of faith than anything the Surrealists could muster in the interval between wars. For the Renaissance artist a valid conceit would be based on the recognition of actually existent correspondences between the several levels of being, so that the poem, the play, or the painting was a demonstration of truth, the result of the play of intellect upon the observable facts of the universe. By the time of the Surrealists, unfortunately, science had moved so far from theology that no one could place much confidence in the type of correspondence in which poetry deals. In the twentieth century the Gnostic explorations of Surrealism were hardly expected to reveal the secrets of nature in terms of the visions of Philo Judaeus or Dionysius Areopagita, or even of Emanuel Swedenborg. It might perhaps uncover the structure of the poet's unconscious mentality and, by extension, the architecture of the Jungian unconscious which humanity perhaps has in common. The consequence, if such be the assumption, is some form of structuralism, and this, however useful to the critic, is of very limited use to the dramatist.

In the drama the more useful manifestations of contemporary symbolism seem to stress, along with the erotic, comic, and ironic elements of Dada, the firm dependence of Surrealism on the metaphor, together with its faith in the value of chance associations, rationalized as divine spontaneity; its aversion to the logical faculty; and its general air of mystery, conscious ambiguity, and enigma. There is room in this sort of art for a good deal of more or less conscious charlatanry. The art of showmanship being what it is, it is obviously easier to succeed with a bad play in the style of Pinter than with one in the manner of Ibsen. Ultimately, what impresses us as poetry in the drama of the present day is not so much a matter of substance as a matter of style.

Symbolist drama of the order of *Axël* or *Pelléas et Mélisande* was formulated primarily in terms of metaphor and correspondence. Such plays were intended to abstract from the individual anecdote which was represented the universal anecdote which was symbolized. Of the later Symbolists it was chiefly Giraudoux who developed this technique. Mallarmé had observed in the article he published in the London *National Observer* that the new writers conceived of the drama as an expression of the inner life and, in their representation of "la scène intérieure," created a theatre of atmosphere and dream, a spiritual action free of the limitations of the actual. To this end they devised plots designed to suggest the eternal plot. The major plays of Giraudoux are, in fact, all based on the dramatic contrast between the two worlds—the ideal and the real—and the tragicomic consequences of the compromise which represents the human condition. The dramatist, in plays of this genre, depends largely on metaphor to indicate the bridge that relates the particular to the universal.

Giraudoux retold in various contexts an anecdote which he called "une légende de l'Opéra." It has to do with two people who suddenly conceive an irresistible attraction for one another. As the moment is inopportune they plan to meet that very night at the masked ball of the Opera under the clock at midnight. At the appointed hour both are there. The clock strikes twelve. They remove their masks. It is two other people. The metaphor is engaging. At least half of Giraudoux's plays exemplify it in some way.

Giraudoux was very conscious of living in a world of incongruences, where nothing comes together according to plan. The world his fantasy conjured up was beautiful and thoroughly untrustworthy. His landscape was a lovely garden, intricately mined. Giraudoux's drama was the fruit of profound disillusionment, but its bitterness has a more subtle savor than Ionesco or Beckett could manage, and even *Sodome et Gomorrhe*, which most clearly reflects his anguish, has a certain gayety of spirit, a rare thing in a joyless age. Very likely, the laughter that pervades his plays was intimately associated with his sense of the absurdity of life, with his sense of paradox. His life, like his plays, involved a series of compromises with which perhaps he was not entirely happy, but there is no trace in his work of the grimness of Pirandello or Ionesco's distress. Perhaps as an artist his conscience occasionally troubled him, but he had the advantage of two useful alibis, those which he attributed to La Fontaine in his apology for La Fontaine:

> Also let us forbear to blame him for this somewhat compromising life, in a world of appearances for which he himself often managed to find two alibis, the two most serious to which a poet can lay claim: mythology and nature.[10]

It is not clear about La Fontaine, but in the case of Giraudoux it is clear that nature and mythology were the foundations of his church. Nature is doubtless the most stable and most durable illusion that humanity has so far conceived, and Giraudoux adorned nature with a mythology that made it enchanting. In this manner Giraudoux became what he called La Fontaine, "an unconscious poet, that is to say, one conscious of all poetry, a free being." His freedom, accordingly, was, like all human freedom, a psychic operation. He escaped life's bondage through the gates of fantasy, like one of his elect, but he was entirely conscious of the contrast between the world of the imagination and the realities of life. For Isabelle, the young schoolmistress of *Intermezzo*, the world is a sunny garden for little girls to play in, and she insists on their right to happiness. The Inspector sees life differently. For him life is

> a lamentable adventure with, for men, wretched beginnings, tortoise-like advancements, non-existent retirements, rebellious collar buttons,

and, for little fools like these, dress-making and lust, casserole and rape.
. . . God has not provided happiness for his creatures: he has provided
only compensations, fishing, love and dotage.[11]

Giraudoux developed to the utmost the contrast between the real and
the ideal both in his plays and in his novels, and in the process evolved
an extremely mannered Gongoristic style, copious, dense, learned, and
frankly eccentric. His prose was not absolutely impenetrable, like Mallarmé's prose, but it was certainly precious. One might imagine a stylist
of this sort would find it impossible to adapt his prose to the thrifty practices of the theatre. The contrary was the case. With Giraudoux a new
literary current flowed into the drama. Dramatic prose had been, at the
most, oratorical. With Giraudoux it became truly poetic. In an age
which was still very much under impressionist influence, and very partial to the ébauche—the sketch—Giraudoux offered examples of exquisite
workmanship. His plays are seldom well-made, but his dialogue is expert, solid, and of high finish. Those for whom art is justified mainly by
its message will find them disappointing. Giraudoux's talent was essentially lyrical. He often described his plays as poetic divagations. They
are more than that. He was not an adherent of the cult of *l'art pour l'art*.
Art, in his conception, is justified by the artist's insight, his special sense
of the rightness of things. It is essentially a moral enterprise. "In my
opinion," he told an interviewer, "the aim of a book, the dominant idea
of an author when he writes a book, ought to be a moral idea."[12]

For Giraudoux morality was a matter of style, and style is the form
that the individual gives to his experience, that is to say, to himself.
What defines the individual is the manner in which he selects, arranges,
and combines out of the confusion of the universe those forms that to
him seem meaningful and significant, the psychological patterns which
motivate his behavior. It is his sense of composition that defines the artist, and the reality he creates for himself, and perhaps for others, is his
work of art.

In a world that has accustomed itself to brutality, Giraudoux may
seem somewhat lacking in alcohol; but the fault is not his. His wine is
subtle and it is old: the grape was planted in the time of Montaigne.
Inevitably it appeals to the connoisseur more readily than to the untu-
tored. It is directed, without apology, to the elite, to the nice palate, to
the discriminating. Obviously these exist, for his plays have had a very
wide hearing, and have it still.

In the 1930's Giraudoux was well aware that he was in the rear eche-
lons of the avant garde. He was by no means out of touch with its out-
posts, but by training and character he was bound to the great literary
tradition of France, and he defended it all his life. In his view drama was
poetry. The poetic principle had been considerably amended in recent
years. Giraudoux was acutely conscious of the literary currents of the
later nineteenth century, of Baudelaire, Nerval, Mallarmé, Laforgue,
Renard, Apollinaire, Rilke. It was inevitable that he should interpret
these influences in his work for the theatre.

In his essay on Théophile Gautier, Baudelaire had written of that
poet's "immense innate understanding of correspondence and universal
symbolism," and of "his repertory of metaphor" which made it possible
for him to define without effort

> the mysterious attitude which the objects of creation assume under the
> gaze of man. There is, in the word, in the Word, something sacred
> which forbids us to make of it a game of chance. To handle a language
> skilfully is to practice a kind of evocatory magic.[13]

Mallarmé too was firm in his faith in the power of the word, but he
knew that even those who are most skilful and circumspect in this
branch of sorcery are engaged ultimately in a game of chance. Giraudoux
tried to minimize the hazardous nature of the poetic enterprise by playing the game of words as deeply as possible. His characters are by no
means laconic; but the impatient must remember that for the Symbolist
words have the efficacy of magic. For Giraudoux the problem was not
semantic but thaumaturgic.

It is necessary, for incantatory purposes, to find the precisely ef-
ficacious expression, the word that opens doors. For the Symbolist *le mot
juste* is not merely the term that exactly identifies an object. It is also the
sound that creates it. The poet—*l'imaginatif*—cannot be certain that the
image his word evokes in the mind of the auditor will instantly materialize as it did for God in the beginning. But it may; and he does what he
can. He weaves his incantation according to the power that is in him.
For Giraudoux, as for Mallarmé, this was not mere fancy. If we consider—as did the Symbolist—that all is mind and idea, and that the
outerworld is a projection of the inner life, then we must accord some
degree of objective authenticity to the poet's creation. As Artaud put it,
the theatre must not deal in pretenses. It must deal in realities.

It is possible to argue that the artist's creation has a more authentic existence than anything else in his experience, since he has the assurance, at least, that he did it himself. This was not the Symbolist position. "Swedenborg has taught us," Baudelaire wrote, "that everything . . . in the spiritual as in the natural order is significant, reciprocal, converse, correspondent . . . thus we arrive at this truth—that all is hieroglyphic. . . ."[14] All the major dramatists of the *fin de siècle* were influenced by this thought—Ibsen, Strindberg, Hauptmann, Chekhov, Yeats, and Shaw—but especially Maeterlinck. Swedenborg's symbolism belonged to the Renaissance, and revealed the moral contours of the universe that was created by the Book of Genesis. Mallarmé's *grimoire*—and Giraudoux's—were of a later date. The Symbolism of the twentieth century did not pretend to reveal the structure of the visible universe, save insofar as it was a projection of the psychic structure; but it was tempting to associate the mental edifice with the divine principle. The revival of mythology as a science was an important adjunct of the Symbolist movement; its ultimate consequence was to equate reality with myth, but Symbolism seldom went so far. It is reasonable to conclude, however, that for Giraudoux myth was an essential aspect of the poetic principle. Giraudoux's world exists on several levels, all of them precarious. It is peopled not only with people, but also with all the spirits of Swedenborg's universe. It is impossible to say how real these presences are, but it is clear that Giraudoux would like to believe that every word we utter vibrates throughout the interstellar spaces. "Have you gone mad?," says the Madwoman,

> Are you so limited as to think that when we are by ourselves, as you put it, we are alone? Do you believe us to be so completely cut off and so silly-minded that of the millions of beings in search of conversation or friendship, illusions or others, not one is happy to be with us? . . . You really lower yourself in my estimation, Constance, if you do not always speak as if the entire universe was listening to you, the universe of real people and of the others. It is a hypocrisy without bounds.[15]

Evidently Giraudoux wrote with the conviction of one whose every word might be expected to echo to the remotest star, a chastening idea for an author; and indeed his audience was vast. It included all those who do not exist, an unimaginable public.

This sense of the cosmic scope of his utterance gives an extraordinary dimension to his plays. It is also the source of the curious frivolity that characterizes his style, a frivolity that borders on Pyrrhonism. Symbo-

lists, in general, speak with the authority of the *voyant*. But Giraudoux
makes no pretenses. At the bottom of his faith there was the doubt that
made it honest. Thus, while his plays, from first to last, embody an idea,
the idea is never insistent. His thesis is proposed in such a way that little
by little it is consumed, like a candle, in the light it sheds, so that in the
end what is left is not a statement, but at the most the echo of a statement, a suggestion, perhaps no more than a mood. To suggest, Mallarmé
had written, is thè goal of the Symbolist, "little by little to evoke an object in order to reveal a psychic state." The technique of the dramatist
would be analogous to the technique of the poet. Giraudoux's effects,
like those of the master, were invariably achieved through indirection. In
his plays the thesis is seldom in the statement, but always in the inference.

It is perhaps for this reason that the literal-minded have found Giraudoux lacking in seriousness, not recognizing that this lightness of touch is
the mark of the most profound sincerity. "To doubt," Montaigne wrote,
"is as good as to know." In the plays of Giraudoux doubt is an artistic
principle. Everything in them is doubtful, unstable, unsure; every prop-
osition implies its contrary. His characters are ambiguous and, in the
main, shrouded in mystery. They are all cultivated, even the lowliest—
the beggars, the gardeners, the angels; they have all been to the university, with the result that they speak, sometimes with delightful incongruity, what René Lalou called "un des plus beaux langages qui se soient
jamais parlés sur une scène française." It is obvious that this language is
unaffectedly rhetorical. Giraudoux did not aim at realism, still less at
what used to be called, technically, decorum. His characters are ready at
any moment to hold forth in high style, like characters in opera; but they
do so at their peril, for the flow of their periods is constantly endangered
by the author's sense of humor, his awareness of the absurdity of all utterance.

Giraudoux denied, as did Baudelaire, that as a poet he had any concern with social problems. But all his plays have to do with problems of
a social or domestic nature. In this regard, he followed the tradition of
the Second-Empire dramatists; but there is little in his plays that reminds us of Augier or Dumas *fils*, and still less of later writers such as
Becque or Brieux. For these authors the problem of déclassement was vital.
So it was also for Giraudoux, but he treated its problems from the standpoint of the Symbolist, never directly. Thematically, *Ondine* has much in
common with *Lè Gendre de M. Poirier*, with *Caste*, *Pygmalion*, or *The Phila-*

delphia Story. It is class-drama, the story of a young man of good family who marries a member of the lower classes and who tries, with lamentable consequences, to introduce her into polite circles. One thinks of Pinero and *The Second Mrs. Tanqueray.* Giraudoux turns this time-honored situation into a myth not only by abstracting it from the actual, like Maeterlinck, but by extending its scope to the extreme limits of the imagination, beyond the realm of natural experience, into the elemental structure of the world.

Intermezzo and *The Song of Songs,* similarly, analyze the question of love and marriage somewhat more profoundly than any playwright had ventured to do in the preceding generations. In 1849 Augier's *Gabrielle* had gone into the question of the husband, the wife, and the handsome secretary at some length. In *Intermezzo,* Isabelle has to choose between the worthy young man in the Weights and Measures and the fascinating spirit with no certain prospects and no certain future. The situation is paralleled in *The Apollo of Bellac.* The problem in *Candida* is almost precisely analogous, though Shaw makes Candida's decision hinge on the relative needs of the husband and the lover. The difference between Giraudoux's treatment of the problem and Shaw's is that Giraudoux explores the matter in its universal aspect, while with Shaw the problem is posed and solved in practical terms. In both cases the solution rests on common sense, and in both the essential conflict involves the ideal, and has a tragic resolution; but we are primarily conscious of the poetry in Giraudoux's play, and of the lesson in Shaw's.

Shaw based his hopes for the future of the race on the experience of life, on age. For Giraudoux youth was the hope of humanity; but there was not much hope in youth. His young girls are far more engaging than Ibsen's, though they are, in their way, quite as frightening. Women like Electre or the Madwoman—or Anouilh's Antigone—were difficult to characterize twenty years ago. They are familiar now as social dropouts who refuse to take part in "life as it is," that is to say, in a world that is less than perfect, and they illustrate the terrible power of unreason in a world based on rational principles. The Madwoman, whose life was arrested at the stage when, normally, young girls marry, demonstrates, like Isabelle, the clarity of youth, its goodness; Electre and Antigone, its harshness, its cruelty, and its purity. Anouilh makes his heroine say:

> You are all like dogs that lick whatever they smell. You with your
> promise of humdrum happiness—provided one doesn't ask too much of

life. I want everything of life, I; and I want it now! I want it total,
complete; otherwise I reject it! I will not be moderate. I will not be content with the bit of cake you offer me if I promise to be a good little
girl. I want to be sure of everything this very day, sure that everything
will be as beautiful as it was when I was little. If not, I want to die![16]

Electre does not want to die. She wants to kill. But in one way or
another these girls wish to bring about the end of the world, just as Lia
does in *Sodome et Gomorrhe*, not because they hate life, but because they
insist it must be perfect in order to be worth living. These girls are in-
transigent, and are the subject of tragedy. Isabelle and Agnès are more
practical souls, and are willing to compromise. But both have had a
glimpse of the ideal and it is unlikely that they will find happiness in the
real. Their plays are comedies; but in both of them we are aware of the
sadness that underlies the happy ending.

In these plays it is not the problem, but the essence of the problem,
that interests the poet. In Giraudoux's mythology the myth that passes
for reality is never very far from the myth that reality symbolizes. In his
view the real and the unreal are on an equal footing. He was entirely in
accord with the tendency to dismantle reality which characterizes the art
of our time, and in this he is comparable with Pirandello; but while
Pirandello was content to demonstrate the mythical nature of reality,
Giraudoux preferred to demonstrate the actuality of myth. Thus he was
able to combine the wildest flights of the romantic imagination with the
objectivity and calm of a classicist. Like Baudelaire, like Gauguin, he
saw signs everywhere, symbols and analogies, and he treated them as the
familiar street-signs of this world viewed under the aspect of eternity. In
his plays the transcendental has not the fevered look of Mallarmé's *île des
iridées*. Its landscape is hardly more exotic than that of the Luxembourg
gardens on a bright morning in June. It is, indeed, barely distinguishable
from the genial prospect in which he set the stage for the end of the
world.

Giraudoux was hardly touched by Dada, but Surrealism was inescapable, and he came early under its influence. But in comparison with
Ionesco and Beckett he seems far too comprehensible a writer to be numbered among the avant garde. The comparison is deceptive. The plays of
Ionesco, Beckett, and Genet present few obstacles to the understanding.
Generally the action centers on the development of a metaphor, and it is
usually sufficient to identify the figure in order to set in motion the train

of associations which clarify the mood and the intention. In *Les Chaises*, for example, the anecdote is ambiguous, the demonstration is mysterious, but the significance of the play is never in doubt. The moment the conceit is clear, the action is instantly intelligible. *Fin de partie* presents a more ambiguous situation. In this play the author forbears to enlighten us as to whether he is describing the end of a man or the end of the world, the end of a life or the end of life. It hardly matters. Dramatically the result is the same, and the figure is sufficiently capacious to receive either interpretation or both. There is, however, a more conscious use of the mysterious in this play than in *Les Chaises*, and the symbols are more abstruse. We cannot tell if Hamm's house is an ark or a skull, a cellar or a tower. The title suggests a game of some sort, possibly chess. From the first words we are led to expect a series of moves and countermoves, attack and defense. There is nothing of the sort; no kings, no knights, no queens, no pawns. It develops little by little that the game is not that sort of game. It is a play. We do not know why it is a play, or how. The characters make their points through periodic flashes of meaning which light up the general opacity of the action only to flicker out at once. It is a piece of dramatic coquetry. Yet there is no doubt that the play is meaningful, a piece of serious poetry which must be treated with the reverence appropriate to a deeply felt and beautifully expressed work of art. In comparison, *Les Mariés de la Tour Eiffel*, *Les Mamelles de Tirésias*, or *Victor* are idle pranks, too deeply infected with Dada to warrant serious discussion.

Rhinocéros is a fable of the simplest sort, the power of which is derived from the clarity, not the mystery of the conceit. *La Cantatrice*, *La Leçon*, and *Le Nouveau Locataire*, on the other hand, are parodies which reduce to absurdity readily identifiable situations, caricatures which make a bizarre effect without actually breaking new ground in the drama. The same may be said of plays of the order of Van Itallie's *America Hurrah!*, the sermonic intention of which can hardly be missed. It is not unreasonable to class plays of this sort as *jeux d'esprit* at the extreme end of the Symbolist spectrum, where Symbolism shades into the irreverent type of parody of which *Ubu roi* and *Jacques, ou La Soumission* were forerunners.

Pinter's plays are not all of a piece, but generally they come closer to the symbolism of the Symbolists than plays like *La Leçon*. *The Homecoming*, *The Birthday Party*, and *Old Times* do not develop a conceit and show only slight traces of Dadaist influence. In these plays, all ostensibly realistic in their setting and handling, the poetic effect is derived from the tantalizing manner in which meaning is suggested or withheld, that is to say, from the manipulation of the mystery. In these plays a good part of the dramatic effect derives from the skill of the writer in suggesting and obscuring motive and meaning. Plays written after this manner make use of a very special sort of showmanship. It depends largely on teasing the audience with intimations that are never substantiated and are probably incapable of substantiation without some risk of banality. Unquestionably this sort of play, when properly written, justifies itself on the stage, if only because it deals openly with the sort of mystery that the greatest drama conceals. *Hamlet* poses a question. *The Homecoming* is a charade. The difference between the two plays is vast, and it is obvious. It is the similarity that is interesting.

"To recount comprehensible things," Jarry wrote, "only serves to oppress the spirit and to warp the memory." Such an observation on the part of a young eccentric might have served as a stimulating instance of bohemian effrontery three-quarters of a century ago. In our day mystery is the normal climate of the poetic experience. It is assumed that whatever in art is understandable is not art. Thus Luìs Buñuel is quoted as saying at the age of sixty-nine, "Mystery is the essential element of every work of art. If a work of art is clear, then my interest ends." Evidently this aesthetic position, essentially romantic, is at the other pole from the attitude of the classicist who values a work in proportion to its clarity. Yet from the earliest days of the Renaissance it was felt that the deepest meaning of a work of art must be veiled from the eyes of the vulgar, and that no poetry of any importance was safe unless it was draped in the vestments of allegory. The difference between this mode of thought and the mystifications of the contemporary artist need hardly be stressed. The Renaissance poet gave himself airs of importance by concealing his meaning from the uninitiate. The modern Symbolist has nothing to conceal. His work is as obscure to him as to anyone else.

This is not to say that *The Homecoming*, for example, is meaningless. On the contrary, with regard to meaning, it presents us with an embarrassment of riches. It means whatever we wish it to mean. Such plays are superbly compliant vessels precisely because they have only the form, not the content, of an idea. They derive from their very imprecision an enormous power of suggestion, and since their reality at any given time depends on the mental state of the spectator, they are dynamic structures which have a vitality denied to works of clearer definition. Of such a work we may say, with Tristan Tzara, ". . . il appartient dans ses innombrables variations au spectateur. Pour son créateur, il est sans cause et sans théorie."[17]

To achieve so salutary an effect in the theatre it is necessary to develop an unusual degree of ambiguity, more even than ordinary human relations suggest, and the degree of control in such compositions is necessarily minimal. Just as Valéry's *La Jeune Parque*, or Kafka's *The Castle*, or Mallarmé's "Un Coup de dés" have infinite possibilities of interpretation, or none at all, so a play like *Old Times* quite defies rational analysis. The dramatic situation it suggests is very similar to that developed in Sartre's *Huis clos* (1944), save that where Sartre took care to indicate what is meaningful in his play, so that his symbols are interpretable and subject to clarification, Pinter has carefully abstracted from his erotic triangle every shred of actuality. The result is, in his case, a degree of ambiguity which reduces the situation to something as nebulous as a mood, peopled with phantoms, an uneasy experience, erotic in character but curiously puzzling, something like the impression made through a carelessly shaded window of nude figures engaged in some embarrassing activity, the nature of which can barely be surmised.

In such circumstances the question of meaning becomes a purely subjective consideration. The play, from this standpoint, must be treated on the same basis as any other natural phenomenon, and the construction that is put on the events presented on the stage will depend on the subjectivity of the individual spectator. The intimation is that in the face of the seemingly inexplicable the spectator's sole recourse is an excursion in self-analysis.[18] Thus the place to look for the significance of plays of the order of *Old Times* or *Happy Days* is within ourselves, and the measure of our insight into the author's mind is the intensity of the resonance which the play arouses in the depths of our own consciousness. This seems meager enough by way of a conclusion, but the result will not differ essentially from the dramatic experience afforded us by such plays as *Hamlet* or *Lear*. If we assume that the function of the Symbolist drama is to reveal to us the reality of our inner world—the outerworld having gone meanwhile by the board—then the theatre has not progressed very far from the time of Shakespeare or Euripides, and from a dramatic viewpoint our reality much resembles the legendary serpent Ouroboros which eternally renews itself by swallowing its tail.

NOTES

REALISM AND SYMBOLISM

MALLARMÉ

1. Paul Bourget, *Essais de la psychologie contemporaine*, 2 vols. (Paris, 1937), Vol. 1, Preface of 1885.
2. *Journal des Goncourt*, 15 vols. (Monaco, 1956), Vol. 8, 14 December 1868.
3. Ibid.
4. Émile Zola, "Les Réalistes," in *E. Zola, Salons, recueillis, annotés et présentés par F. W. J. Hemming et Robert Niess* (Geneva, 1959), pp. 69, 73. Cf. Zola, *Le Roman expérimental, Oeuvres complètes*, 15 vols. (Paris, 1966–70), Vol. 10, p. 1233.
5. *Journal des Goncourt*, Vol. 8, 7 April 1869.
6. Émile Zola, *Le Roman expérimental, Oeuvres complètes*, Vol. 10, p. 1236.
7. *Journal des Goncourt*, Vol. 10, 22 August 1875.
8. George Eliot, *Adam Bede* (London, 1864), Bk. II, chap. XVIII.
9. Gustave Courbet, in *Le Précurseur d'Anvers* (Antwerp), 22 August 1861. See Gerstle Mack, *Gustave Courbet* (New York, 1951), p. 89.
10. Gustave Courbet, quoted in P. Cailler, *Courbet, raconté par lui-même et par ses amis*, 2 vols. (Geneva, 1950), Vol. 2, p. 206.
11. Zola, *Le Roman expérimental, Oeuvres complètes*, Vol. 10, p. 1193.
12. Zola, *Le Naturalisme au théâtre, Oeuvres complètes*, Vol. 11, p. 290.
13. Zola, *Thérèse Raquin*, Preface, *Oeuvres complètes, Théâtre*, Vol. 15.
14. Hippolyte Taine, *Philosophie de l'art*, 2 vols. (Paris, 1872), Vol. 1, p. 63.
15. Charles Baudelaire, *Salon de 1846*, "Du portrait," *Oeuvres complètes* (Paris, (Pléiade), 1954), p. 650.
16. Cf. Baudelaire, *Salon de 1846, Oeuvres complètes*, pp. 692 ff.; *Salon de 1859, Oeuvres*, pp. 773 f.; Taine, *Philosophie de l'art*, Vol. 1, p. 50.
17. G.-A. Aurier, *Oeuvres posthumes* (Paris, 1893), p. 293.
18. G.-A. Aurier, "Le Symbolisme et la peinture: Paul Gauguin," in *Mercure de France*, No. 2 (June 1891), pp. 159 ff.
19. Maurice Denis in *Art et critique* (23 August 1890); reprinted in Maurice Denis, *Théories 1890–1910*, 4th ed. (Paris, 1920), p. 1.
20. *Journal des Goncourt*, Vol. 18, 1 June 1891.
21. Plato, *Symposium*, 212, in *The Dialogues of Plato*, trans. by Benjamin Jowett, 4th ed., 4 vols. (Oxford, 1953), Vol. 3, p. 343.
22. Baudelaire, *Salon de 1859, Oeuvres complètes*, p. 779.
23. Baudelaire, "Theophile Gautier," *Oeuvres complètes*, p. 1035.
24. Arthur Schopenhauer, *The World as Will and Idea* (1883), trans. by R. B. Haldane and J. Kemp, 6th ed., 3 vols. (London, 1907), Vol. 1, p. 136.

25. S. Mallarmé, Letter to Cazalis, 11 May 1867, in Henri Mondor, *Vie de Mallarmé* (Paris, 1950), p. 237.
26. Letter to Mallarmé, June 1868, in Mondor, loc. cit.
27. Rémy de Gourmont, *Le Livre des masques*, 2 vols. (Paris, 1914), Vol. 1, p. 11.
28. Letter to Cazalis, March 1866, in Mondor, *Vie de Mallarmé*, p. 193.
29. Ibid.
30. Schopenhauer, *The World as Will and Idea*, Vol. 1, p. 402.
31. Conrad Fiedler, *Art and Reality, Three Fragments*, trans. by T. Sinclair and V. Hammer (Lexington, Ky., 1951). Cf. H. E. Read, *Icon and Idea: The Function of Art in the Development of Human Consciousness* (Cambridge, Mass., 1955).
32. Mallarmé, "Autobiographie (16 November 1885)," *Oeuvres complètes* (Paris (Pléiade), 1946), pp. 662 f.
33. Baudelaire, *Salon de 1859, Oeuvres complètes*, pp. 773, 776.
34. Letter to Cazalis, 14 May 1867, in Mondor, *Vie . . .* , pp. 237 f.
35. In Mondor, *Vie . . .* , p. 801.
36. Joséphin Péladan, *L'Art idéaliste et mystique*, 2nd ed. (Paris (Sansot), 1909), p. 41; Camille Mauclair (Camille Faust), "L'Esthétique de Stéphane Mallarmé," in *L'Art en silence* (Paris (Ollendorff), 1899), p. 87. Cf., on the general question, Guy Delfel, *L'Esthétique de Stéphane Mallarmé* (Paris, 1951).
37. J. K. Huysmans, *À rebours* (Paris, 1922), p. 103.
38. Édouard Dujardin, *Les Hantises* (Paris, 1886), Preface; Rémy de Gourmont, "L'Idéalisme," in *Le Chemin de velours* (Paris, 1902), p. 198.
39. Mallarmé, "Crise de vers," *Oeuvres complètes*, p. 365.
40. Ibid., p. 368.
41. Mauclair, *L'Art en silence*, p. 190.
42. Baudelaire, "Victor Hugo," in *Oeuvres complètes*, p. 1085.
43. Mauclair, *L'Art en silence*, p. 87; Thomas Carlyle, *Sartor Resartus*, "Symbols," Bk. III, Ch. III, in *Sartor Resartus and Heroes and Hero Worship* (New York, 1909), p. 165.
44. Aurier, ". . . Paul Gauguin," in *Mercure de France*, No. 2 (July 1891), p. 159; Richard Huelsenbeck, *En Avant Dada: eine Geschichte des Dadaismus* (Hanover, 1920), p. 26; transl. in *The Dada Painters and Poets: An anthology*, ed. Robert Motherwell (New York, 1951), p. 24.
45. Piet Mondrian, *Plastic Art and Pure Plastic Art* (New York, 1945), p. 50.
46. Camille Mauclair, *Eleusis, Causeries sur la vie intérieure* (Paris (Perrin), 1893), p. 173.
47. Letter to Cazalis, October 1864, in Mallarmé, *Oeuvres complètes*, p. 1440.
48. Mauclair, *L'Art en silence*, p. 92.
49. Huysmans, *À rebours*, p. 256.
50. See Albert Thibaudet, *La Poésie de Stéphane Mallarmé* (Paris, 1926), p. 110.
51. M. Maeterlinck, *Les Disciples a Saïs*, 2nd ed. (Paris, n.d.), p. viii.
52. Mallarmé, in *La Vogue* (18 April 1886), p. 70; cited in Mondor, *Vie . . .* , p. 438.
53. Villiers de l'Isle Adam, *Axël*, in *Oeuvres complètes*, 9 vols. (Paris, 1922–38), Vol. 4, p. 201.
54. Émile Hennequin in *La Revue indépendante* (19 January 1888).
55. Lewis Thomas, "Information," in *The Lives of a Cell* (New York, 1974), pp. 111 f.
56. Théodor de Wyzéwa, "Notes sur l'oeuvre poétique de Stéphane Mallarmé," in *La Vogue* (July 1886), p. 375.
57. Mallarmé, *Divagations* (Paris, 1897), p. 20.
58. Letter to Cazalis, 12 May 1866; 14 May 1867. Cf. Ibsen, Letters to Georg Brandes, 17 February 1871 and 24 September 1871, in E. Sprinchorn, *Ibsen: Letters and Speeches* (New York, 1964), pp. 107, 114.
59. Mauclair in *Mercure de France*, No. 12 (July 1894), p. 271.
60. See Mallarmé, "Richard Wagner, Rêverie d'un poète français," *Oeuvres complètes*, p. 546; cf. "Le Mystère dans les lettres," *Oeuvres complètes*, p. 385.
61. Mallarmé, "Crise de vers," *Oeuvres complètes*, p. 367.
62. Baudelaire, "Le Spleen de Paris; À Arsène Houssaye," *Oeuvres complètes*, p. 281.
63. Mallarmé, "Planches et feuillets," *Oeuvres complètes*, p. 330.

64. W. B. Yeats, "The Symbolism of Poetry," in *Ideas of Good and Evil* (New York (Macmillan), 1903); *Collected Works*, 8 vols. (London, 1908), Vol. 6, p. 190.

65. Rémy de Gourmont, "L'Idéalisme," in *Le Chemin de velours* (Paris, 1902; Paris (Crès), 1923). Jules Laforgue, "Mélanges posthumes," *Oeuvres complètes*, 6th ed., 3 vols. (Paris (Mercure de France), 1919), Vol. 3, p. 155.

66. Cf. Sven Lövgren, *The Genesis of Modernism* (Bloomington, Ind., 1971), passim.

67. See W. Kandinsky, *Über das Geistige in der Kunst* (Munich, 1912), pp. 37 f.

68. Erneste Raynaud, "Un Point de doctrine," in *Le Décadent* (15 February 1889).

69. Guy Dumur, "Aurier et l'évolution idéaliste," in *Mercure de France*, No. 8 (August 1893), p. 293; Gourmont, "Les Racines de l'idéalisme," in *Promenades philosophiques*, 1ère série (Paris (Mercure de France), 1913), pp. 98, 104. Wyzéwa, *Mercure de France*, No. 14 (April 1895), p. 31.

70. Vladimir Kemenov, "Aspects of Two Cultures," in *Voks Bulletin* (Moscow), *USSR Society for Cultural Relations with Foreign Countries* (Moscow 1947), pp. 20 ff.

71. Émile Zola, *Le Roman expérimental, Oeuvres complètes*, Vol. 10, p. 1200.

72. Letter to Louise Colet, 16 January 1852, *Correspondance*, 9 vols. (Paris, 1926–33), Vol. 2, pp. 345 f.; in *Selected Letters of Gustave Flaubert*, trans. by Francis Steegmuller (New York, 1953), pp. 127 f.

73. Baudelaire, "Théophile Gautier," in *Oeuvres complètes*, p. 1030.

74. Oscar Wilde, *The Picture of Dorian Gray* (1891), Preface, *Works of Oscar Wilde*, ed. G. F. Maine (London, 1948), p. 17.

75. Saint-Pol-Roux, *La Littérature contemporaine* (Paris, n.d.), p. 306. On the complex question of Symbolist aesthetic, see the discussion in A. G. Lehmann, *The Symbolist Aesthetic in France, 1885–1895* (Oxford, 1950; 2nd ed., 1968).

MAETERLINCK

1. Charles Morice, *La Littérature contemporaine* (Paris, 1905), p. 62.

2. S. Mallarmé, Letters to Cazalis, 30 June 1863, and 3 February 1863, in Henri Mondor, *Vie de Mallarmé*, (Paris, 1950), pp. 67, 96.

3. Letter to Cazalis, November 1865, in Mallarmé, *Oeuvres complètes* (Paris (Pléiade), 1946), p. 1442.

4. Mallarmé in *La Revue blanche* (July 1896), p. 96.

5. Gustave Kahn, "Réponse des Symbolistes," in *L'Evénément* (25 September 1886).

6. Gustave Kahn in *La Vogue* (18 April 1886), p. 54.

7. Édouard de Goncourt, *Journal des Goncourt*, 15 vols. (Monaco, 1956), Vol. 15, 6 April 1888.

8. "Dossier du Théâtre de l'Oeuvre," in *La Plume* (1 September 1893).

9. *Sartor Resartus*, Bk. III, ch. III, in *Sartor Resartus and Heroes and Hero Worship* (New York, 1909), p. 165; M. Maeterlinck, *Le Trésor des humbles* (Paris (Mercure de France), 1949), p. 11.

10. Jules Huret, *Enquête sur l'évolution littéraire* (Paris, 1891), p. 129.

11. J. Péladan, *L'Art idéaliste et mystique*, 2nd. ed. (Paris (Sansot), 1909), pp. 65, 67.

12. *La Princesse Maleine*, Act II, sc. 6, in *Théâtre*, 3 vols. (Brussels, 1908–09), Vol. 1; *Aglavaine et Sélysette*, Act II, sc. 2, *Théâtre*, Vol. 3, p. 39.

13. Maeterlinck in *La Jeune Belgique* (1890), Vol. 9, p. 331.

14. Huret, *Enquête*, p. 121.

15. Jean Thorel, "Les Romantiques allemands et les symbolistes français," in *Entretiens politiques et littéraires* (September 1891), pp. 101 ff.

16. Maeterlinck, *Le Tragique quotidien*, in *Le Trésor des humbles* (Paris, 1949), p. 129.

17. Ibid., p. 134.

18. Ibid., p. 138.

PIRANDELLO

1. For details of his biography, see F. V. Nardelli, *L'uomo segreto (Vita e croci di Luigi Pirandello)* (Milan, 1934); Leonardo Sciascia, *Pirandello e la Sicilia* (Caltanisetta, 1961);

and the magnificent study by Gaspare Giudice, *Luigi Pirandello* (Turin, 1963).

2. "La carriola," in *Novelle per un anno*, 2 vols., (Verona (Mondadori), 1962), Vol. 2, p. 718.
3. *Pirandello: Saggi, poesie, scritti vari*, ed. Manlio Lo Vecchio-Musti, in *Pirandello: Opere*, 6 vols. (Milan (Mondadori), 1958–62, Vol. 6, p. 875.
4. See Giudice, *Pirandello*, p. 306 and 306 n.; Lucio D'Ambra (Renato Manganella), *Trent'anni di vita letteraria*, 3 vols. (Milan, 1928), Vol. 2.
5. Letter to Stefano, 24 October 1915, in *Almanacco letterario Bompiani 1938* (Milan, 1938).
6. "Pensaci, Giacomino!," in *Novelle per un anno*, Vol. 2, p. 357.
7. *Pensaci, Giacomino!*, in *Maschere nude*, 2 vols. (Verona (Mondadori), 1958), Vol. 2, p. 276.
8. Ibid.
9. "La signora Frola e il Signor Ponza suo genero," *Novelle per un anno*, Vol. 2, p. 891.
10. *Così è (se vi pare)*, Act II, sc. 1. *Maschere nude*, Vol. 1, p. 1063.
11. Letter to Stefano, 18 April 1917, in *Almanacco letterario Bompiani, 1938*.
12. This letter, dated 6 September 1917, is quoted in Giudice, *Pirandello*, p. 321. See "La verità," in *Novelle per un anno*, Vol. 1, p. 655.
13. *Il berretto a sonagli*, Act I, sc. 4, *Maschere nude*, Vol. 2, p. 369.
14. Ibid., p. 373.
15. Ibid., p. 399.
16. *Il piacere dell'onestà*, Act I, sc. 8, *Maschere nude*, Vol. 1, p. 622.
17. Letter to Stefano, 27 November 1918.
18. *Ma non è una cosa seria*, Act II, sc. 1, *Maschere nude*, Vol. 2, p. 540.
19. "Quando s'è capito il giuoco," *Novelle per un anno*, Vol. 2, p. 839.
20. *I vecchi e i giovani*, 2 vols. (Milan (Treves), 1913), Vol. 2, p. 272.
21. *Il giuoco delle parti*, Act I, sc. 3, *Maschere nude*, Vol. 1, p. 553 f.
22. Ibid., Act II, sc. 9, p. 589.
23. *L'uomo, la bestia e la virtù*, Act III, sc. 4, *Maschere nude*, Vol. 1, p. 768.
24. "Tutto per bene," *Novelle per un anno*, Vol. 1, p. 361.
25. *Signora Morli una e due*, *Maschere nude*, Vol. 2, p. 263.
26. *Come prima, meglio di prima*, *Maschere nude*, Vol. 1, p. 784.
27. "Le tre carissime," *Novelle per un anno*, Vol. 2, p. 204.
28. Ibid., Vol. 2, p. 199.
29. Silvio d'Amico, *Maschere nude*, Preface, Vol. 1, p. 18.
30. "La Tragedia di un personaggio," *Novelle per un anno*, Vol. 1, p. 713.
31. "Musica vecchia," *Novelle per un anno*, Vol. 1, p. 1371.
32. In *Il Giornale di Sicilia*, 17 August 1915 and 11 September 1915. Cf. *Novelle per un anno*, Vol. 2, p. 1126.
33. Ibid., Vol. 2, p. 1131.
34. *Sei personaggi in cerca d'autore*, *Maschere nude*, Preface, Vol. 1, p. 58.
35. Ibid., Act II, *Maschere nude*, Vol. 1, p. 138.
36. Ibid., p. 119.
37. Ibid., p. 61.
38. Ibid., p. 60.
39. "La trappola," *Novelle per un anno*, Vol. 1, pp. 681 f.
40. See Giudice, "L'Ambiguita nei Sei personaggi in cerca d'autore" in *Paragone* (December 1961).
41. George Pitoëff, *Notre théâtre*, ed. Jean de Rigault (Paris, n.d.), quoted in Giudice, *Pirandello*, pp. 368 f.
42. André Gide, *Thesée*, VIII (Paris, 1946).
43. See A. G. Bragaglia, "Pirandello, l'uomo," in *Almanacco letterario Bompiani 1938*, pp. 87 ff.
44. *Enrico IV*, Act I, *Maschere nude*, Vol. 1, p. 335.
45. Ibid., Act III, p. 387.
46. Ibid., Act II, p. 374.
47. Ibid., p. 370.

48. Ibid., p. 373.
49. Letter to Lietta, 24 February 1922. In *Terzo programma*, ed. Sandro D'Amico, No. 3 (Rome, 1961).
50. Cited in Giudice, *Pirandello*, p. 373. See also Aniouta Pitoëff, *Ludmilla ma mère* (Paris, 1955); Nardelli, *L'uomo segreto*, pp. 255 ff.
51. *Il Giornale d'Italia* (8 May 1924).
52. Adriano Tilgher, in *La Concordia* (12 July 1916).
53. Tilgher, *Studi sul teatro contemporaneo* (Rome, 1922; 2nd enlarged edition, Rome, 1923), pp. 159–219. See also Leonardo Sciascia, *Pirandello e il pirandellismo* (Caltanisetta, 1953).
54. Tilgher, *Studi*, 2nd ed., p. 163.
55. Ibid., p. 262 .
56. *Il giuoco delle parti*, Act II, sc. 1, *Maschere nude*, Vol. 1, pp. 570 f.
57. *L'Epoca* (5 July 1922).
58. In *Almanacco letterario Mondadori, 1927*.
59. Tilgher, *Studi*, loc. cit.
60. "Candelora," in *Novelle per un anno*, Vol. 2, p. 601.
61. *Il Corriere della Sera* (16 June 1929).
62. *L'Epoca* (5 July 1922).
63. Tilgher, *Studi*, pp. 213, 215.
64. *Vestire gli ignudi*, *Maschere nude*, Vol. 1, p. 937.
65. Ibid., p. 867.
66. Ibid., p. 931.
67. *Ciascuno a suo modo*, Act I, *Maschere nude*, Vol. 1, p. 173.
68. Ibid., Act II, p. 209.
69. Cf. Frederic Ewen, *Bertolt Brecht* (New York, 1967), pp. 225 ff.
70. *Diana e la Tuda*, Act II, *Maschere nude*, Vol. 1, p. 443.
71. Henri Bergson, *Les Données immédiates de la conscience* (Paris, 1889), chaps. II, III.
72. Cf. José-Maria Monner Sans, *Pirandello, su vida y su teatro* (Buenos Aires, 1947), pp. 68 f.
73. *Come tu mi vuoi*, Act III, *Maschere nude*, Vol. 1, p. 1017.
74. "Notizia del mondo," *Novelle per un anno*, Vol. 1, p. 708.
75. See Giudice, *Pirandello*, pp. 465 ff.
76. Dario Niccodemi, *Tempo passato* (Milan, 1929), p. 81.
77. See Giuseppe Capria in *La Letteratura* (February 1937); Niccodemi, *Tempo passato*, pp. 80 ff.
78. Oscar Büdel, "Pirandello sulla scena tedesca," in *Quaderni del Piccolo Teatro* (Milan, 1961).
79. Letter to Marta Abba, 1 June 1930, cited in Domenico Vittorini, *The Drama of Luigi Pirandello* (Philadelphia, 1935).
80. *"Leonora, Addio!"* in *Novelle per un anno*, Vol. 2, p. 569.
81. *Questa sera si recita a soggetto*, *Maschere nude*, Vol. 1, p. 230.
82. "Acqua è lì," *Novelle per un anno*, Vol. 1, p. 1183.
83. "La verità," *Novelle per un anno*, Vol. 1, pp. 661 f.
84. "La carriola," *Novelle per un anno*, Vol. 2, p. 718.
85. *L'Illustrazione Italiana*, 27 May 1934. Cited in Giudice, *Pirandello*, p. 510.
86. Letter to Vittorini, 30 July 1935. In Vittorini, *The Drama of Luigi Pirandello*.
87. "Niente," *Novelle per un anno*, Vol. 1, pp. 876 f.
88. Alvaro Corrado, *Novelle per un anno* (Milan, 1956), Preface, Vol. 1, p. 6. Cf. R. Cristaldi, in *Retroscena* (15 February 1937); Cf. Giudice, *Pirandello*, pp. 542, 547.

GIRAUDOUX

1. For a delightful survey of this period, see Roger Shattuck, *The Banquet Years* (New York, 1958).

2. See J. R. Bloch, *Destin du théâtre* (Paris, 1930), pp. 53 ff.; Adolphe Appia, *La Mise en scène du drame wagnérienne* (Paris, 1895); Gordon Craig, *On the Art of the Theatre* (London, 1911).

3. See Paul Blanchart, *Gaston Baty* (Paris, 1939), p. 86.

4. Gaston Baty, *"Le Théâtre est sauvé,"* in the program of the Théâtre Montparnasse, cited by Blanchart, *Gaston Baty,* p. 65.

5. J.-J. Bernard, "De la valeur du silence dans les arts du spectacle," in *Les Nouvelles littéraires* (25 April 1931); cf. "Le Silence au théâtre," in *Bulletin de la Chimère,* No. 5 (May 1922); and see Mary Daniels, *The French Drama of the Unspoken* (Edinburgh, 1953), pp. 174 ff.

6. M. Maeterlinck, *Le Trésor des humbles* (Paris, 1896), p. 162; *Le Double Jardin* (Paris, 1911), p. 122.

7. Pierre Brisson, *Le Théâtre des années folles* (Geneva, 1943); Silvio D'Amico, in *L'Idea nazionale* (August 1925).

8. Bernard, "De la valeur . . .", *Les Nouvelles littéraires* (25 April 1931).

9. See Daniel Mornet, *Histoire de la littérature et de la pensée française contemporaine 1870–1927* (Paris, 1927).

10. See Francis Ambrière, "Les Grandes premières" in *Annales-Conferencia* (January 1952), p. 49, and the review of *Siegfried* in *Le Figaro* (4 May 1928).

11. *Fin de Siegfried* (Paris (Grasset), 1934), *Théâtre Complet,* 16 vols. (Neuchâtel et Paris (Ides et Calendes), 1945–53), Vol. 1, p. 184.

12. See Laurent Le Sage, *Jean Giraudoux: His Life and Works* (University Park, Pennsylvania, 1959), Chap. I, and Georges Lemaitre, *Jean Giraudoux* (New York, 1971), pp. 1–52.

13. *L'École des indifférents, Oeuvre romanesque,* 2 vols. (Paris (Grasset), 1955), Vol. 1, pp. 116 ff.

14. Simone Ratel, "Jean Giraudoux et le nouveau romantisme," in *Dialogues d'une seule voix, Le Tambourin* (Paris, 1930), p. 12.

15. J. Giraudoux, "De Siècle à siècle" in *Littérature* (Paris (Grasset), 1941), *Oeuvres littéraires diverses* (Paris, 1958), p. 569.

16. Frédéric Lefèvre, "Jean Giraudoux," in *Une Heure avec . . . ,* Iᵉʳᵉ série (Paris, 1924), p. 149.

17. *Fin de Siegfried, Théâtre complet,* Vol. 1, p. 201.

18. Préface, *Fin de Siegfried,* p. 169.

19. *Siegfried, Théâtre complet,* Vol. 1, p. 133.

20. *Suzanne et le Pacifique,* Chap. X, *Oeuvre romanesque,* Vol. 1, p. 389.

21. *Choix des élues* (Paris (Grasset), 1939), p. 265.

22. Ibid., p. 325.

23. Lefèvre, "Jean Giraudoux," p. 149.

24. *Amphitryon 38,* Act II, sc. 2, *Théâtre complet,* Vol. 3, p. 62.

25. Ibid., Act III, sc. 6, p. 142.

26. Ibid., p. 144.

27. *Judith,* Act III, sc. 4, *Théâtre complet,* Vol. 2, p. 113.

28. Ibid., Act II, sc. 4, p. 92.

29. Ibid., p. 86.

30. Ibid., p. 96.

31. G. Champeaux, "Comment travaillez vous?" in *Annales poétiques et littéraires* (10 September 1935).

32. *Intermezzo,* Act III, sc. 3, *Théâtre complet,* Vol. 4, p. 127 f.

33. Ibid., sc. 4, p. 129 f.

34. *Judith,* Act I, sc. 8, *Théâtre complet,* Vol. 2, pp. 51 f.

35. S. Mallarmé, *Igitur, Oeuvres complètes* (Paris (Pléiade), 1946), p. 442.

36. *La Guerre de Troie n'aura pas lieu,* Act I, sc. 13, *Théâtre complet,* Vol. 6, p. 120.

37. Ibid., Act II, sc. 11, p. 117.

38. Ibid., Act I, sc. 6, p. 35.

39. "Les Adieux du Vieillard," in *Supplément au Voyage de Bougainville, Oeuvres de Diderot* (Paris (Pléiade), 1951), pp. 999 ff.
40. Cf. C. Sénéchal, *L'Abbaye Creteil* (Paris, 1930); R. Lalou, *Histoire de la littérature française contemporaine* (Paris, 1924), Appendix: Bidal, *"Les Écrivains de l'Abbaye."*
41. *Supplément au Voyage de Cook, Théâtre complet*, Vol. 6, p. 159.
42. Ibid., p. 191 f.
43. Ibid., p. 196.
44. Édouard de Goncourt, *Journal*, 15 vols. (Monaco, 1956), Vol. 14, 14 September 1885.
45. See André Bourrin, "Elle et Lui: Chez Madame Jean Giraudoux," in *Les Nouvelles littéraires* (16 November 1950), p. 1; Cf. Jean-Pierre Giraudoux, *Le Fils* (Paris, 1967), p. 84.
46. Louis Jouvet, *Témoignages sur le théâtre* (Paris, 1952), pp. 212 f.
47. *Electre*, Act I, sc. 2, *Théâtre complet*, Vol. 7, p. 24.
48. Ibid., Act II, sc. 10, p. 161.
49. Ibid.
50. Ibid., sc. 6, p. 119.
51. Ibid., sc. 8, p. 150.
52. *L'Impromptu de Paris* (Paris (Grasset), 1937), sc. 3, pp. 43 f.
53. Jouvet, *Témoignages sur le théâtre*, p. 213. Jouvet died 16 August 1951.
54. *La Cantique des cantiques, Théâtre complet*, Vol. 8, p. 91.
55. Le Sage, "Fouqué's *Undine*, An unpublished manuscript by Jean Giraudoux," *Romanic Review* (April 1951), pp. 122 ff.
56. *Ondine*, Act II, sc. 11, *Théâtre complet*, Vol. 9, p. 107.
57. Ibid., Act III, sc. 6, p. 161.
58. Ibid., Act II, sc. 11, p. 107.
59. Ibid., Act III, sc. 5, p. 158.
60. See R. M. Albérès, *Esthétique et moral chez Jean Giraudoux* (Paris (Nizet), 1957), p. 500.
61. *L'Apollon de Bellac, Théâtre complet*, Vol. 16, p. 193.
62. Ibid., p. 183.
63. *Sodome et Gomorrhe*, Act I, sc. 2, *Théâtre complet*, Vol. 10, p. 31.
64. *L'Apollon de Bellac, Théâtre complet*, Vol. 16, p. 182.
65. Ibid., p. 187.
66. See Emanuel Berl, *La Mort de la pensée bourgeoise* (Paris, 1929), p. 82.
67. *Sodome et Gomorrhe*, Act I, sc. 1, *Théâtre complet*, Vol. 10, p. 21.
68. Ibid., p. 25.
69. Ibid., Act III, sc. 7, p. 87.
70. Ibid., Act II, sc. 3, p. 58.
71. Ibid., p. 61.
72. Ibid., sc. 7, p. 94.
73. Ibid., sc. 8, p. 100.
74. Ibid., p. 110.
75. Cf. Jouvet, *Témoignages sur le théâtre*, pp. 205 ff.
76. *La Folle de Chaillot*, Act I, *Théâtre complet*, Vol. 11, p. 62.
77. Ibid., Act II, p. 121.
78. Ibid., Act I, p. 26.
79. Ibid., Act II, p. 116.
80. Ibid., p. 136.
81. *Amphitryon 38*, Act II, sc. 11, *Théâtre complet*, Vol. 3, p. 93.
82. *Combat avec l'ange, Oeuvre romanesque*, Vol. 2, p. 499.
83. *Pour Lucrèce*, Act I, sc. 6, *Théâtre complet*, Vol. 16, p. 37 f.
84. Ibid., Act II, sc. 2, p. 75.
85. Ibid., Act I, sc. 8, p. 50.
86. Ibid., p. 49.
87. Ibid., p. 53.

88. Ibid., Act III, sc. 4, p. 139.
89. Ibid., sc. 8, p. 144.

ARTAUD

1. Georges Pillement, *Anthologie du théâtre français contemporain*, 3 vols. (Paris (Belier), 1948), Vol. 1: *Le Théâtre d'avant garde*, p. 22.
2. Alfred Jarry, "Questions du théâtre," *La Revue blanche* (January 1897), in *Tout Ubu* (Paris (Livre de Poche), 1962); *Oeuvres complètes*, 8 vols. (Monte Carlo, 1948), Vol. 4.
3. *Gestes et opinions du docteur Faustroll, 'pataphysicien*, Bk. II, in *Oeuvres complètes*, Vol. 1; cf. Roger Shattuck and S. W. Taylor, eds., *Selected Works of Alfred Jarry* (New York, 1965), pp. 192 ff.
4. Antonin Artaud, *L'Ombilic des limbes*, *Oeuvres complètes*, 9 vols. (Paris (Gallimard), 1956–71), Vol. 1, p. 61.
5. "Le Théâtre Alfred Jarry, Premier manifeste," in *Oeuvres complètes*, Vol. 2, p. 15.
6. *Le Théâtre Alfred Jarry en 1930*, *Oeuvres*, Vol. 2, p. 38. On the Strindberg episode, see André Breton, *Second Manifesto of Surrealism*, in *Manifestoes of Surrealism*, trans. by Seever and Lane (Ann Arbor, Mich., 1969), pp. 130 f.
7. Artaud, *Oeuvres complètes*, Vol. 2, p. 15. Cf. Ibsen, Letters to Brandes, 20 December 1870 and 4 April 1872, in E. Sprinchorn, *Ibsen: Letters and Speeches* (New York, 1964), pp. 106 f., 120 ff.
8. Anaïs Nin, *Diaries*, 6 vols. (London, 1955–66), Vol. 1, p. 195.
9. Ibid., p. 71. Cf. Artaud, *Oeuvres complètes*, Vol. 8, p. 74.
10. *Les Nouvelles Révélations de l'être*, *Oeuvres complètes*, Vol. 7, p. 174.
11. Letters to Jean Paulhan, 29 December 1935, 6 January 1936, 25 January 1936, in *Oeuvres complètes*, pp. 264–72 f.
12. "Le Théâtre et la cruauté," *Oeuvres complètes*, Vol. 4, p. 101.
13. Ibid., p. 103. Cf. Baudelaire, *Fusées III:* "Moi je dis: la volupté unique et suprême de l'amour gît dans la certitude de faire le mal.—Et l'homme et la femme savent de naissance que dans le mal se trouve toute volupté." In C. Baudelaire, *Oeuvres complètes* (Paris (Pléiade), 1954), p. 1191.
14. Artaud, *Le Théâtre et son double*, *Oèuvres complètes*, Vol. 4, p. 99.
15. Ibid., p 84.
16. *Oeuvres complètes*, Vol. 2, p. 23.
17. Augustine, *City of God*, Bk. I, chap. XVIII.
18. "Le Théâtre et la peste," *Oeuvres complètes*, Vol. 4, p. 33.
19. Ibid., p. 34; "Le Théâtre et la cruauté, Premier manifeste," *Oeuvres*, Vol. 4, p. 118.
20. "En finir avec les chefs-d'oeuvre," *Oeuvres*, Vol. 4, p. 95; Letter to Paulhan, 13 September 1932, *Oeuvres complètes*, Vol. 4, p. 121.
21. Aristotle, *Poetics*, trans. in Ingram Bywater, *Aristotle on the Art of Poetry* (Oxford, 1920), chap. 14, p. 53.
22. "La Mise en scène et la métaphysique," Artaud, *Oeuvres complètes*, Vol. 4, p. 50.
23. Ibid., pp. 54, 95; cf. "Théâtre oriental et théâtre occidental," Ibid., Vol. 4, p. 84.
24. Ibid., p. 58.
25. Ibid., p. 61.
26. Ibid., p. 63. Cf. J. Péladan. *Comment on devient mage* (Paris, 1906).
27. *Oeuvres complètes*, Vol. 3, pp. 118, 121.
28. Ibid., Vol. 4, p. 64.
29. Ibid., pp. 107–9.
30. For a useful conspectus of the works of these writers, see Martin Esslin, *The Theatre of the Absurd* (New York, 1961, 1969), pp. 198 ff.

IONESCO

1. *Notes et contre-notes* (Paris (Gallimard), 1962), pp. 156 ff. Cf. *Notes and Counter Notes*, trans. by Donald Watson (New York (Grove), 1964), pp. 175 ff.

2. *Notes et contre-notes*, p. 159.
3. From a lecture to the French Institute of Italy, 1958, ibid., p. 160.
4. Ibid., p. 162.
5. Nicolas Bataille, "La Bataille de la cantatrice," in *Cahiers des saisons*, No. 15 (1959) cf. *Notes et contre-notes*, p. 163.
6. *Notes et contre-notes*, p. 159.
7. Ibid., p. 241.
8. *Purgatorio* XXIV, 52 ff.
9. *Arts* (1953), *Notes et contre-notes*, p. 136.
10. *Notes et contre-notes*, pp. 75, 108.
11. Ibid., p. 161.
12. Ibid., p. 159.
13. *Arts* (1955), *Notes et contre-notes*, p. 43.
14. Ibid., p. 160. Cf. Ionesco, *Journal* (10 April 1951).
15. *Journal* (10 April 1951), transl. by Donald Watson in *Notes and Counternotes*, p. 182.
16. *Notes et contre-notes*, p. 8.
17. Ibid., p. 10.
18. Ibid., pp. 12 f.
19. Ibid., p. 165.
20. Ibid., p. 170.
21. Ibid.
22. Ibid., p. 169.
23. Ibid., p. 66.
24. *Victimes du devoir*, Eugène Ionesco, *Théâtre*, 5 vols. (Paris (Gallimard), 1954), Vol. 1, pp. 226 f.
25. *Notes et contre-notes*, p. 175.
26. Claude Bonnefoy, *Conversations avec Eugène Ionesco* (Paris, 1966), p. 79; cf. *Conversations with Eugene Ionesco*, trans. by Jan Dawson (New York, 1970), p. 85.
27. *Notes et contre-notes*, p. 174. From a lecture at the French Institute in London, December 1958.
28. In Bonnefoy, *Conversations*, trans. by Jan Dawson, pp. 83 ff.
29. *Notes et contre-notes*, p. 173.
30. *Jacques, ou La Soumission*, *Théâtre*, Vol. 1, pp. 120 f.
31. Ibid., p. 125.
32. *L'Impromptu de l'Alma*, *Théâtre*, Vol. 2, p. 57.
33. *La Nouvelle Revue française*, No. 35 (November 1955), pp. 890 ff.
34. *Tueur sans gages*, Act III, *Théâtre*, Vol. 2, p. 170.
35. Ibid., Act II, *Théâtre*, p. 138.
36. *Les Lettres nouvelles*, No. 52 (September 1957).
37. *New York Times* (31 January 1960).
38. *Arts* (1961), *Notes et contre-notes*, p. 183.
39. *Présent passé passé présent* (Paris (Mercure de France), 1968), p. 114.
40. *Arts* (1961), *Notes et contre-notes*, p. 184.
41. *Le Rhinocéros*, Act I, *Théâtre*, Vol. 3.
42. Ibid., Act III, pp. 116 f.
43. Ibid., Act II, p. 76.
44. Ibid., Act III, p. 114.
45. Kenneth Tynan in *The Observer*, London (22 June 1958), *Notes et contre-notes*, pp. 75 ff.
46. Bertolt Brecht, "Die Strassenszene, Grundmodel eines Epischen Theaters," *Versuche 10*, 1950; cf. "The Street Scene," in *Brecht on Theatre*, trans. by John Willett (New York, 1964); and cf. Frederic Ewen, *Bertolt Brecht* (New York, 1967), pp. 227 ff.
47. *Arts* (1961), *Notes et contre-notes*, p. 186.
48. *Le Piéton de l'air*, *Théâtre*, Vol. 3, p. 198.
49. *Le Roi se meurt*, *Théâtre*, Vol. 3, p. 46.
50. Mallarmé, *Igitur*, *Oeuvres* (Pléiade), p. 439.

51. *Notes et contre-notes*, p. 132; cf. Robert Kanters, "Entretien avec Ionesco," *Express* (28 January 1960), p. 37.

52. *Arts* (1953), *Notes et contre-notes*, p. 136. See also Watson's translation in *Notes and Counter Notes*, p. 157.

BECKETT

1. Simone Weil, *L'Attente de Dieu* (Paris, 1950), trans. by Emma Craufurd as *Waiting for God* (1951; New York, 1959), p. 182.

2. *Waiting for Godot, A Tragicomedy in Two Acts, translated from his original French text by the Author* (New York (Grove), 1954), Act I, p. 7.

3. Ibid., p. 13.

4. Ibid., p. 41.

5. Ibid., p. 50.

6. Ibid., p. 58.

7. Ibid., p. 59.

8. Artaud, *Le Théâtre et son double*, "Deux notes, I: Les Frères Marx," *Oeuvres complètes*, 9 vols. (Paris, 1966–71), Vol. 4, p. 165. First published in *La Nouvelle Revue française*, No. 220 (January 1932).

9. S. Beckett, *Proust* (London, 1931), p. 79.

10. "Beckett's Letters on *Endgame*," in Daniel Wolf, Edwin Fancher, eds., *The Village Voice Reader* (Garden City, New York, 1962), p. 185.

11. J. Fletcher and J. Spurling, *Samuel Beckett: A Study of His Plays* (New York, 1972), p. 39.

12. Simone Weil, "Forms of the Implicit Love of God," in *Waiting for God*, pp. 187, 196.

13. Artaud, *Le Théâtre et son double*, *Oeuvres complètes*, Vol. 4, p. 107.

14. Cf. Deirdre Bair, *Samuel Beckett: A Biography* (New York, 1978), pp. 386 ff.

15. *Waiting for Godot*, p. 38.

16. In "Beckett's Letters on *Endgame*," *The Village Voice Reader*, p. 183. Letter to Alan Schneider, 21 June 1956.

17. *Endgame, Translated from the French by the Author* (New York (Grove), 1958), p. 77.

18. Ibid., p. 58.

19. Ibid., p. 78.

20. Ibid., p. 59.

21. Ibid., p. 67.

22. Ibid., p. 69.

23. *Krapp's Last Tape, A Play in One Act* (New York (Grove), 1960), p. 28.

24. *All That Fall*, in *Krapp's Last Tape and Other Dramatic Pieces* (New York (Grove), 1960), pp. 90 f.

25. *Waiting for God*, p. 125.

26. *Proust*, p. 74. Cf. *Theatre II*, in Beckett, *Ends and Odds* (New York (Grove), 1976).

27. *Waiting for God*, p. 180.

THE END OF THE WORLD

1. Barbara Tuchman, *The Guns of August* (1962; New York, 1976), p. 298.

2. Hans Richter, *Dada: Art and anti-Art* (London, 1965), p. 191. See also Maurice Nadeau, *The History of Surrealism* (New York, 1965), pp. 103, 250; cf. Ihab Hassan, *The Dismemberment of Orpheus* (New York, 1971), pp. 11 f.; and see Anna Balakian, *The Literary Origins of Surrealism* (New York, 1965), p. 18.

3. Archibald MacLeish, "Ars Poetica," in *New and Collected Poems, 1917–76* (Boston, 1976).

4. Mallarmé, *Oeuvres complètes* (Paris (Pléiade), 1946), p. 1440.

5. André Breton, *Situation du Surréalisme entre les deux guerres* (Paris, 1945).

6. Cf. Breton, *Manifestoes of Surrealism*, trans. by Seaver and Lane (Ann Arbor, Mich., 1969), p. 125.

7. Ibid., p. 14.

8. Pierre Reverdy, *Nord-Sud* (March 1918).

9. Breton, *Manifestoes*, p. 304.

10. J. Giraudoux, *Les Cinq Tentations de La Fontaine* (Paris (Grasset), 1963), p. 25.

11. *Intermezzo*, Act I, sc. 6, *Théâtre complet*, Vol. 4, p. 43.

12. Frédéric Lefèvre, "Jean Giraudoux," in *Une Heure avec . . .* , *Quatrième série* (Paris, 1927), p. 118.

13. Charles Baudelaire, "Théophile Gautier," in *Oeuvres* (Paris (Pléiade), 1954), p. 1035.

14. Baudelaire, "Victor Hugo," in *Oeuvres*, p. 1085.

15. *La Folle de Chaillot*, Act II, *Théâtre complet*, Vol. 11, pp. 96 f.

16. Jean Anouilh, *Antigone* (Paris, 1946); trans. by Louis Galantière (New York, 1946). In *Four Contemporary French Plays* (New York, 1967), p. 49. His translation.

17. Tristan Tzara, *Sept Manifestes Dada* (Paris, 1963), p. 25.

18. Cf. Frederic Jameson, "Metacommentary," in *PMLA*, Vol. 86, No. 1 (January 1971), p. 9.

INDEX

451